NARRATIVE THREADS

PALESTINIAN EMBROIDERY IN CONTEMPORARY ART

JOANNA
BARAKAT

SAQI

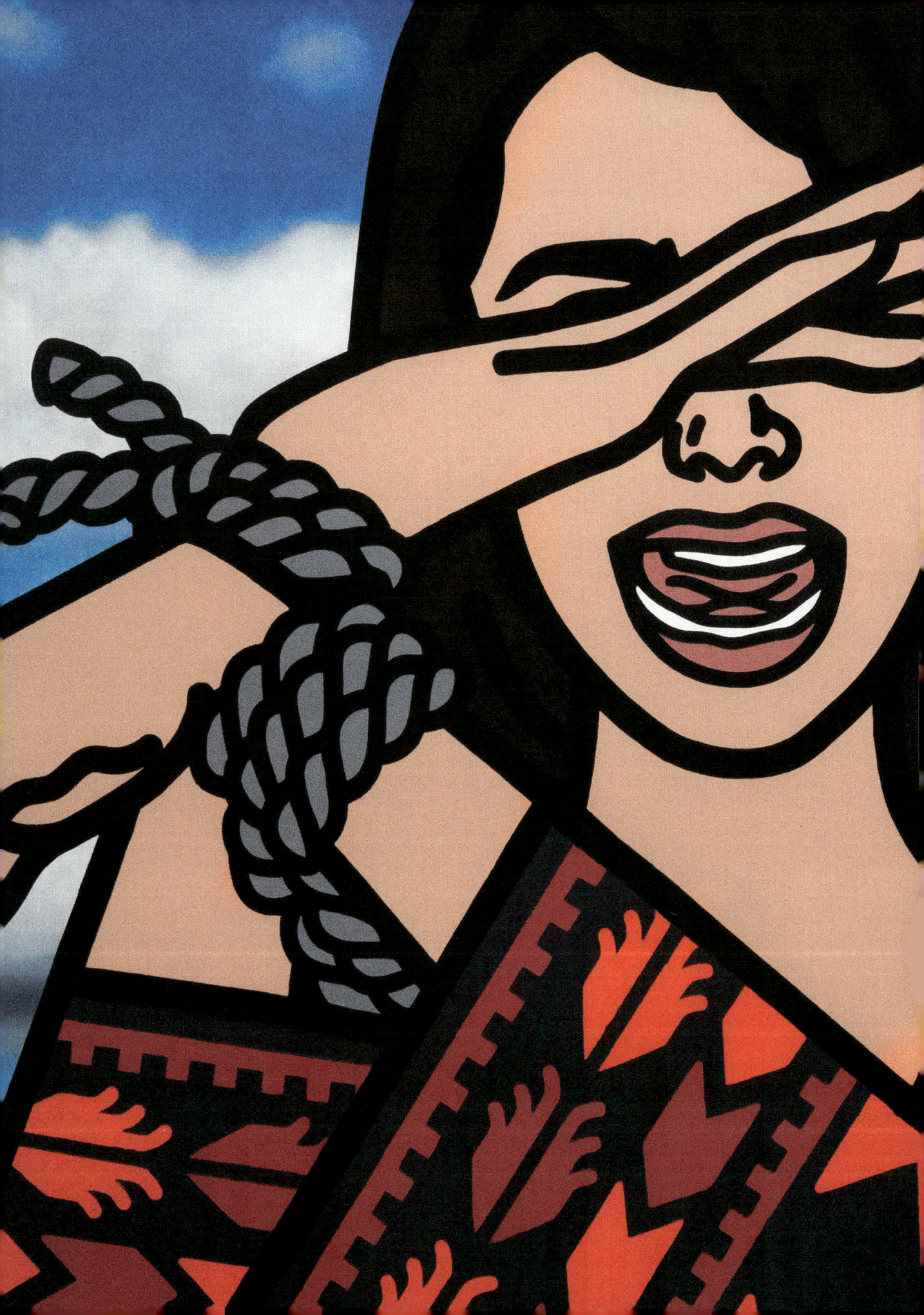

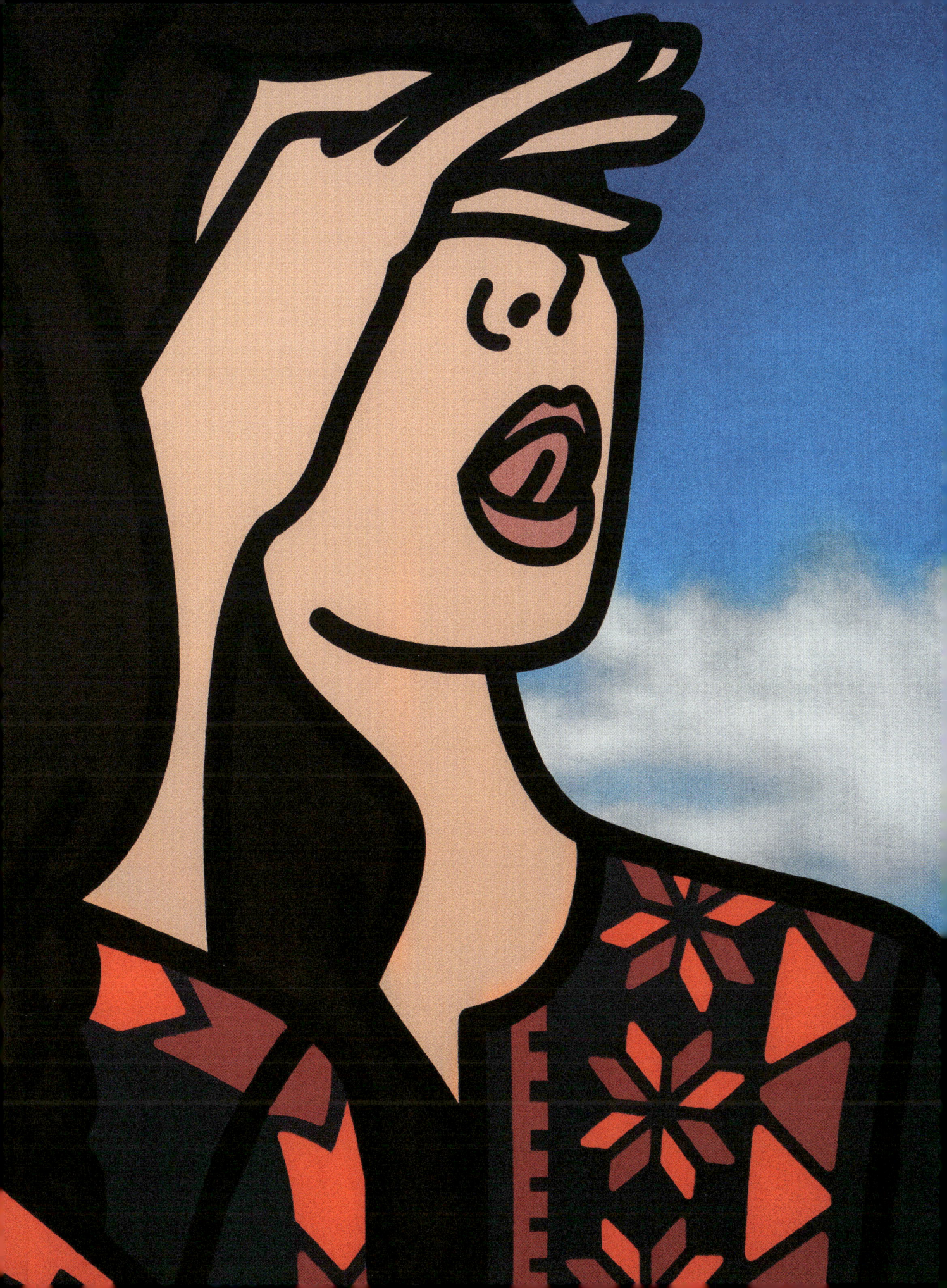

CONTENTS

Previous spread: Rasha Eleyan, *Zaghrouta Solidarity*, 2023. Acrylic on canvas, 115 x 160 cm

INTRODUCTION

JOANNA BARAKAT

A BRIEF HISTORY OF PALESTINIAN EMBROIDERY

Palestinian women speak of life and land through their embroidery. Historically, Palestinian embroidery communicated and embodied the story of Palestinian women living in villages, farms, cities and Bedouin communities. Along with the artistic skill of embroidery and dress construction, a girl learned many life lessons stitching her future wedding dress while sharing stories with the women of her household and neighbourhood. With a needle and thread, she wrote her autobiography in a language of motifs passed down to her.

Her hand-embroidered dress, or *thobe*, is a conversation with the onlooker about her environment, beliefs, marital and socioeconomic status – all fundamental aspects of Palestinian village life. The *thobe* was cherished and passed down generationally, along with ancestral knowledge accompanying its creation. Palestinian embroidery is much more than decorative embellishment. It is an indigenous language which has transmitted Palestinian cultural knowledge for centuries.

When discussing Palestinian embroidery generally, Palestinians use the Arabic word *tatreez*, meaning embroidery, and refer to the wide variety of regional styles, stitches, colours and motifs by their specific names. In Arabic, Palestinian cross-stitch embroidery is *tatreez fellahi falasteeni*, or Palestinian farmer embroidery, designating it to a rural class within Palestinian society that included farmers, villagers and Bedouins. In nineteenth to early twentieth-century Palestine, middle-class urban women preferred Western-style clothes. They considered the traditional embroidered *thobe* appropriate only for the rural class, deeming these dresses as unfashionable and socially unacceptable, clashing with their perceived modern and cosmopolitan preferences. Despite this, upper-class women of that time owned expensive and luxurious Ottoman brocade embroidery to display wealth and political and social status. Many of these women also posed for studio portrait photographs dressed up in an embroidered *thobe* and traditional headdress, reinforcing

their distinct separation from the rural Palestinians while enjoying a glamorised version of their heritage.

The centuries-old, ancestral, indigenous and localised expression of a woman's identity through embroidery abruptly shifted in form and meaning after 1948, with the beginning of the Nakba, the widespread destruction of Palestinian villages, massacres and mass dispossession, expulsion and displacement of Palestinian natives to facilitate the creation of Israel, a Jewish Zionist settler ethnostate. Zionist militia gangs razed to the ground the villages that were Palestine's textile production and weaving centres. Embroidered dresses were left behind in houses forcibly taken by Zionists, and other dresses were sold out of necessity to survive the devastation. The combination of industrialisation and economic need led to commodifying what was once a handmade item for personal use.

By the 1960s, a new *thobe* emerged from the refugee camps. Instead of using motifs specific to a woman's environment and village, women in the refugee camps exchanged motifs and styles, and foreign patterns were also introduced. Organisations working with refugees taught women in camps to embroider and support themselves by selling their work to tourists and international markets. Since the 1970s, synthetic fabrics and machine embroidery have replaced natural fabrics and hand embroidery, owing to their availability and affordability. The embroidered *thobe*, and images of the Palestinian woman wearing it, now symbolised identity, steadfastness and resistance. This change in perception lifted the stigma among urban women around wearing embroidery that was once snubbed as only for rural women. Palestinian women of all backgrounds proudly wore and displayed Palestinian embroidery regardless of their class or position within and outside of Palestine.

The 1980s and 1990s saw the introduction of the Intifada *Thobe*. When Israel outlawed the Palestinian flag and any use of its colours, women secretly began to stitch dresses in red, green, white and black, creating and incorporating motifs of national symbols such as the map of Palestine,

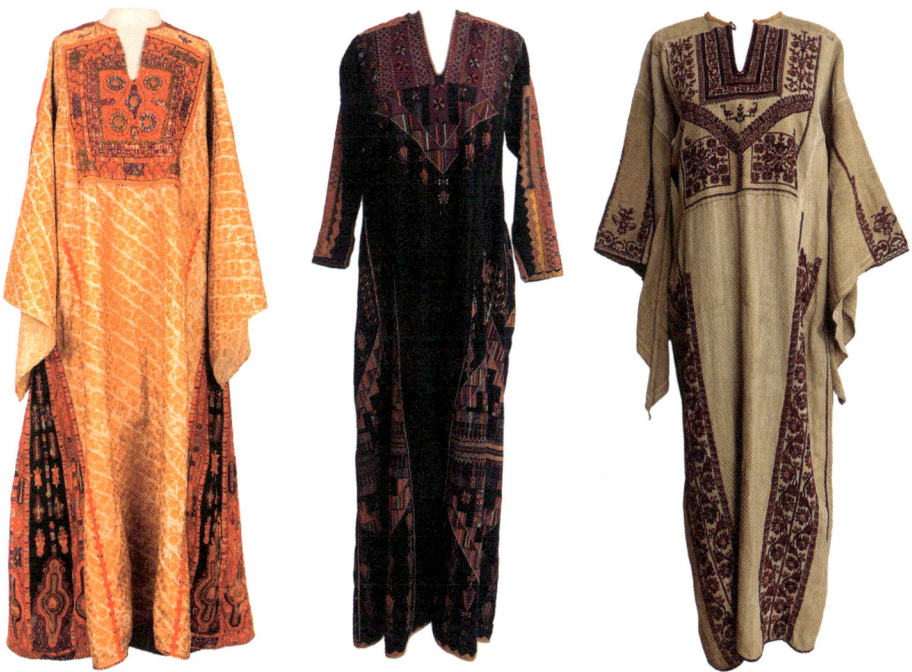

Ghabani thobe from the village of Lifta in Jerusalem, Palestine, circa 1920. Collection of Yasser Barakat. Photo by Ihab Barakat

Thobe from Gaza region, Palestine, circa 1920. Collection of Yasser Barakat. Photo by Ihab Barakat

Thobe from Ramallah, Palestine, circa 1900. Collection of Yasser Barakat. Photo by Ihab Barakat

the key representing the right of return for refugees, the Dome of the Rock, and the Palestinian flag. These dresses and the act of embroidering them continue to represent Palestinian women's agency over their bodies, voices and political participation.

With the growing recognition of embroidery's importance to Palestinian culture and heritage, many efforts are being taken to preserve it. Institutions and individuals in Palestine and the diaspora have collected Palestinian embroidered dresses and textile artefacts for preservation and education; most notably the late Hind al-Husseini, Widad Kawar, Hanan Munayyer, Maha Saca, Yasser Barakat and George Al-Ama. Social enterprises and organisations continue working with Palestinian refugees in Palestine, Jordan and Lebanon to create hand-embroidered items for sale. Palestinian designers recreate traditional

hand-embroidered dresses and machine-embroidered modern interpretations of Palestinian dresses. Others design Western-style clothing decorated with traditional Palestinian embroidery.

Palestinian embroidery has become common to wear for wedding celebrations, henna parties and engagements. In addition, there are modern recreations of traditional belts and headdresses, a decorative nod to Palestinian heritage. Social media and access to more information about Palestinian embroidery has created a revival and greater interest in the practice. As a result, Palestinians in the diaspora and others interested in Palestinian embroidery are learning to cross stitch and sew their own embroidered dresses, bringing back the personalised expression of Palestinian identity and fostering a sense of community.

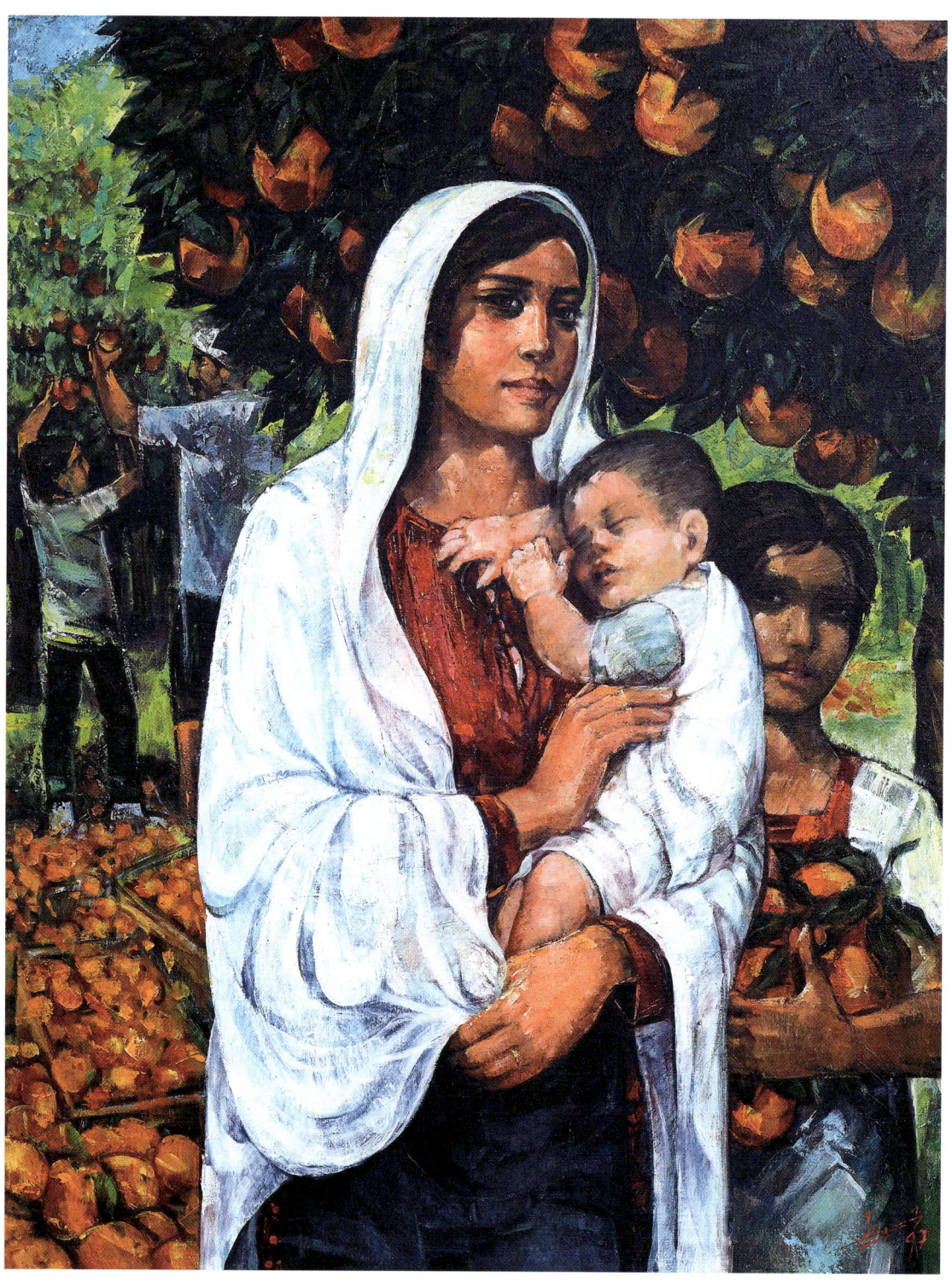

Ismail Shammout, *Madonna of the Oranges*, 1997. Oil on canvas, 100 x 80 cm. Barjeel Art Foundation, Sharjah

EMERGENCE OF PALESTINIAN EMBROIDERY IN CONTEMPORARY ART

Established in 1964, the Palestinian Liberation Organisation (PLO) recognised how art, culture and heritage could shape the Palestinian national consciousness. Israel's theft and cultural appropriation of Palestinian cultural products reinforced the emphasis on creating Palestinian art and preserving Palestinian culture and heritage. Artists Ismail Shammout, founder and director of the Department of Arts and National Culture of the PLO in Beirut, and his wife, Tamam Al Akhal, head of the Art and Heritage section of the Department of Information and Culture, played a prominent role in cultural production and ensuring the preservation of Palestinian heritage. Artists in Palestine and those displaced in other countries worked with the PLO to produce works predominantly about liberation and Palestinian nationalism, introducing a visual vocabulary and iconography still prominent today. Posters of these paintings made the work and imagery accessible and widespread among refugee camps and Palestinian homes worldwide.

These artists transformed embroidery into a collective symbol of Palestinian identity. For example, Abdul Hay Mosallam Zarrara's vivid bas-relief paintings celebrated traditional village life by portraying women wearing embroidered dresses. In scenes of resistance, they became primary characters representing strength and liberation. Posters and paintings by Palestinian artists like Ismail Shammout, Abdelrahman Al Muzayen and Mustafa al-Hallaj featured rural imagery with the Palestinian woman in her embroidered *thobe*, personifying the motherland. This mother figure is a metaphor for the reciprocal deep-rooted connection, longing and unconditional love Palestinians maintained for their native land. Other notable artists whose paintings depict scenes of rural life include Nasr Abdel Aziz Eleyan and Ibrahim Ghannam. Paintings of the utopian Palestinian village shape how many people imagine Palestine.

From the 1970s onwards, Sliman Mansour and Nabil Anani employed the imagery of the Palestinian woman in the embroidered *thobe* and incorporated Palestinian embroidery motifs in their abstract works. Ceramicist and painter Issam Badr also incorporated Palestinian

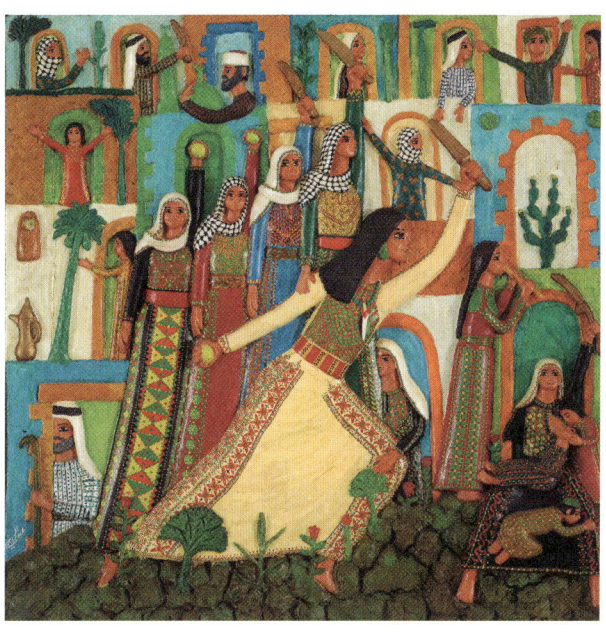

Abdul Hay Mosallam Zarrara, *The Role of Women in the Family and Taking Care of the Uprising*, 1991. Acrylic on sawdust and glue on panel, 71.5 x 72.5 cm. Ramzi and Saeda Dalloul Art Foundation

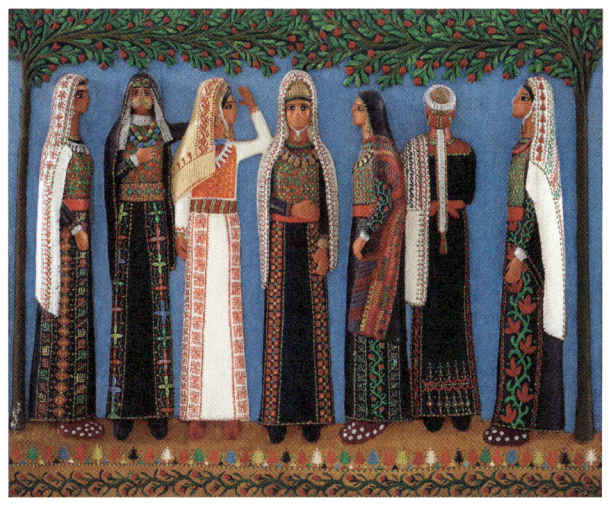

Abdul Hay Mosallam Zarrara, *The Dress of the Five Areas in Palestine*, 1990. Oil and acrylic on panel, 63 x 80 cm. Ramzi and Saeda Dalloul Art Foundation

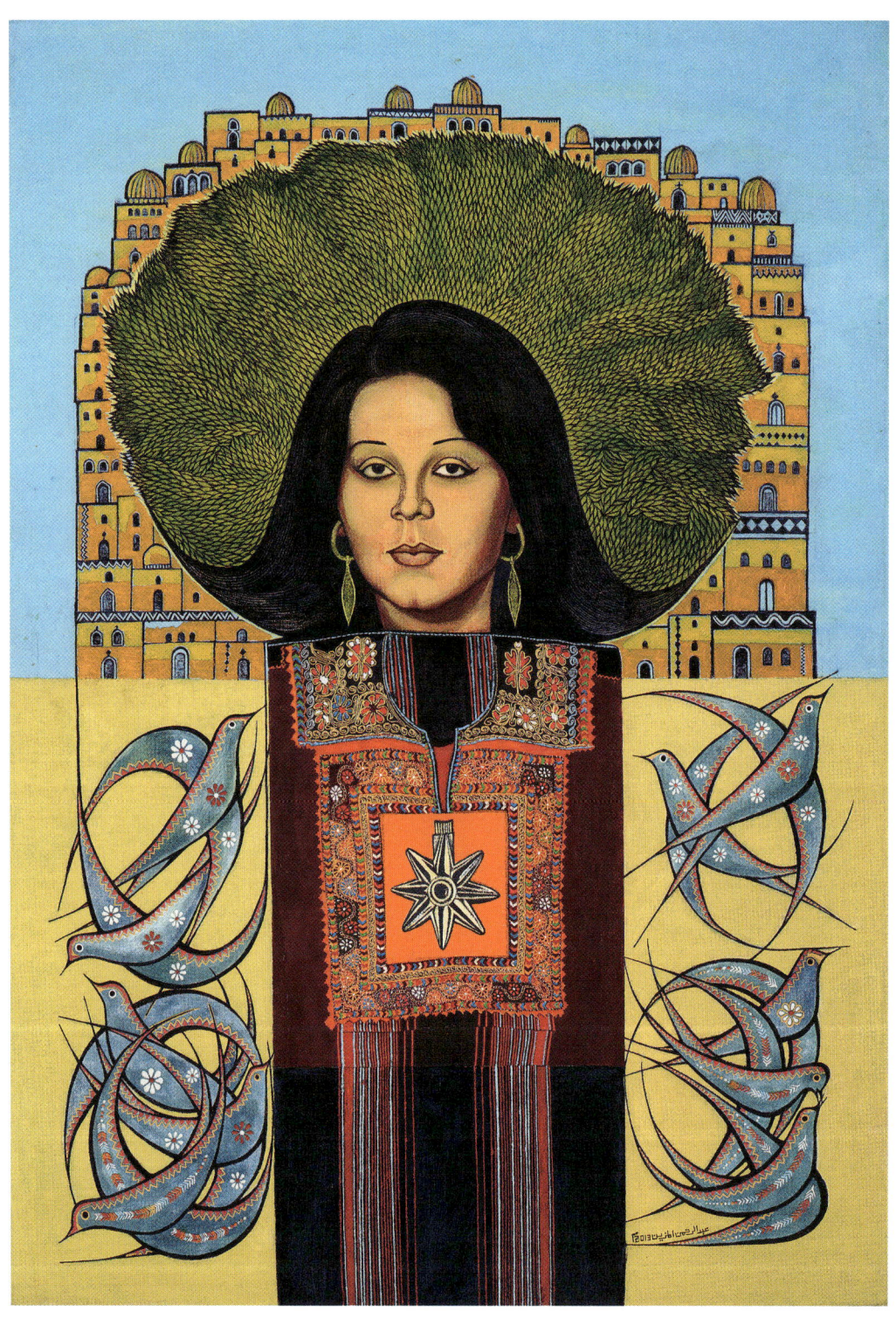

Abdelrahman Al Muzayen, *Untitled*, 2013. Acrylic on canvas, 100 x 71cm. Ramzi and Saeda Dalloul Art Foundation

embroidery motifs into his works. Here, the imagery of the motifs stands alone to represent Palestinian identity and provide a window to a pre-Nakba Palestine. Since the 1970s, multi-discipline artist Samia Zaru used pieces of embroidered fabric in her paintings to express Palestinian identity. The presence of embroidery within Zaru's abstract and landscape paintings makes them undeniably Palestinian. Early in her career as a ceramic artist, Vera Tamari was inspired by field visits with her students to Palestinian villages to study and research Palestinian crafts predominantly performed by women, such as pottery, weaving and basketmaking. She was drawn to the authenticity and rootedness of village culture. Her ceramic relief *Palestinian Women at Work* (1979) depicts Palestinian women seated in the courtyard of their home, dressed in Palestinian embroidered dresses and engaged in pottery making.

In the 1980s, many posters of Gazan artist Fathi Ghaben's paintings celebrated Palestinian folklore and pastoral life. Bashir Sinwar captured similar imagery in his paintings, drawings and portraits, along with scenes of Palestinians suffering under Israeli occupation. Laila Shawa featured the traditional Palestinian *thobe* in her paintings from the 1980s, such as in the *Turkumanyat* series, along with other paintings depicting Palestinian women from Gaza. She also includes geometric embroidery motifs in the backgrounds of her later portrait series from 2017.

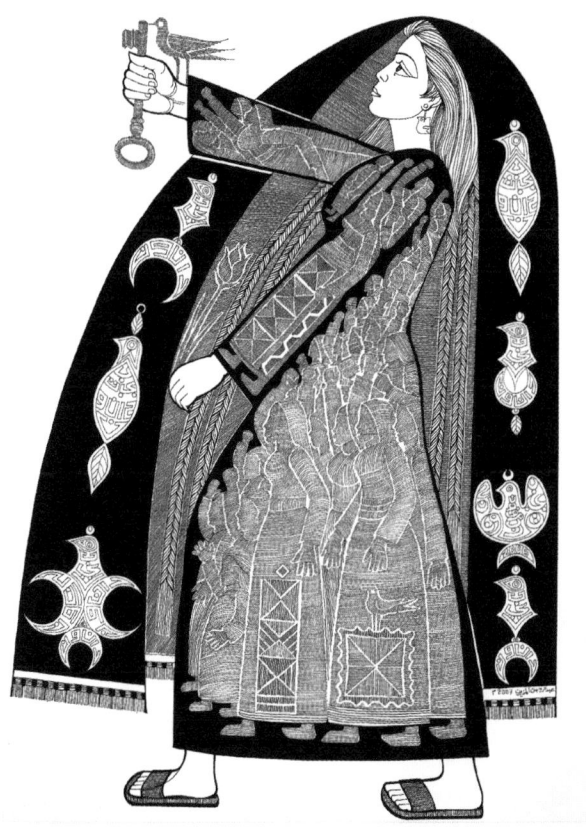

Abdelrahman Al Muzayen, *Palestine* series, 2007. Ink on paper, 65 x 50 cm. Ramzi and Saeda Dalloul Art Foundation

Through their distinct styles using bright colours and colour blocking, Dina Mattar and Rasha Eleyan showcase the strength and beauty of Palestinian women. Gazan artist Dina Mattar celebrates the beauty and joy of Palestinian life through her vibrant paintings with Palestinian women in traditional dress. She draws inspiration from nature, Islamic design and her Palestinian heritage, to abstract and transform the intricate geometric and floral patterns in her work. Rasha Eleyan also uses bold colours and colour blocking, combining realistic painting with her dynamic cartoon-like pop art style. Influenced by the artwork of her father, Nasr Abdel Aziz Eleyan, she presents the Palestinian woman in her embroidered dress, expressing resistance against the Israeli occupation's attempts to steal and appropriate Palestinian culture. Eleyan is dedicated to preserving

Palestinian heritage through her artwork, particularly from the perspective of revolutionary Palestinian women.

Maysaloun Faraj's painting *From Darkness Emerges Light* (2023) expresses her fascination with the beauty and history of Palestinian embroidery while paying homage to Palestinian women. Faraj features this painting in the background of another painting, *In My Home Are Many Homes* (2023). *From Darkness Emerges Light* is seen filling the wall of a room in her home with Palestinian embroidery motifs while also infusing the foreground with the same brightly coloured patterns reflecting off the coffee table. Her stylistic use of outline and striking colours emerge from a black background, creating depth to her lively and captivating scenes. *In My Home Are Many Homes* belongs

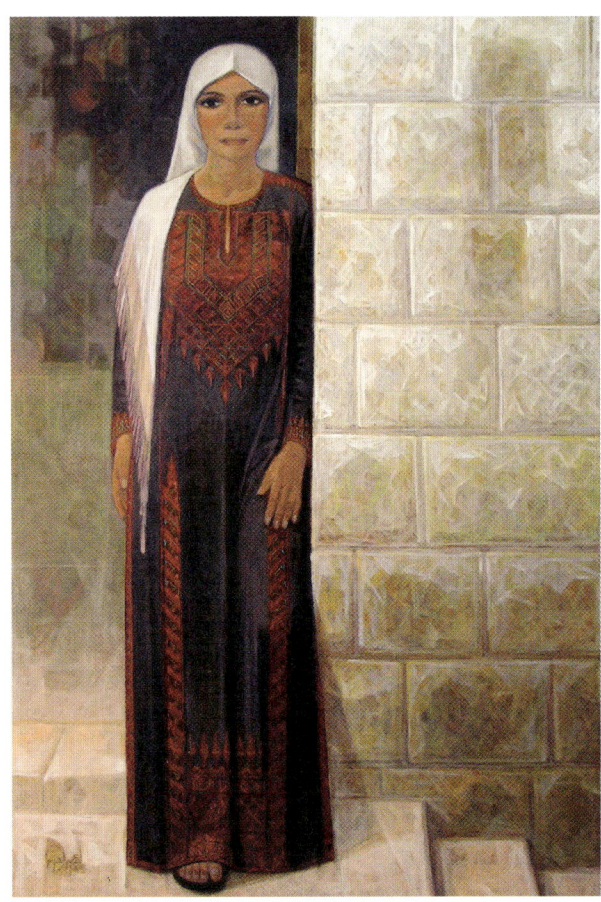

Nasr Abdel Aziz Eleyan, *Waiting*, 2005. Oil on canas, 83 x 122 cm

to a series of paintings in which Faraj explores the idea that a home can harmoniously embody various cultures, traditions and identities. Highlighting the complex and rich tapestry of human experience, she draws attention to the beauty that emerges from embracing the interconnectedness of humanity.

Contemporary artists continue to explore ways of using Palestinian embroidery to question perceptions and narratives about borders, displacement and loss. Mohammed Al Hawajri titled his powerful painting series *Maryam* (2015) after his mother, with each painting portraying the strength and resilience that a Palestinian mother embodies in the face of loss and occupation. In each painting, Al Hawajri places this imagery on her chest panel as a visual representation of what she holds close to her heart, like her martyred son, whose face wrapped in his *keffiyeh* symbolises the resistance against Israeli oppression and occupation. Khaled Hourani's four embroidered works from the *Afrah wa Iftrah* series (2004) focus on how Palestinian women would dye their brightly embroidered dresses when in a state of mourning. The four works move from lightest to darkest, echoing the passage of time during the grieving process.

In his *Protective Edge* series (2015) and *Embroidered Landscape* series (2016), Farid Abu Shakra superimposes delicate needlepoint perforations and colourful Palestinian stitched embroidery motifs over black-and-white imagery of the Israeli military bombing Gaza in 2014. The work visually and conceptually contrasts the beautiful, perforated patterns and embroidery motifs with harsh, violent imagery of fighter jets and explosions. Mona Hatoum's *Twelve Windows* (2012), created in collaboration with the Inaash Association, is an installation showcasing twelve panels of embroidery from different regions of Palestine, hanging from pegs; the viewer must meander through the obstructing configuration to see the work. Khalil Rabah's works *Hide Geographies* (2017) and *Common Geographies* (2019) feature embroidered panels shaped as planimetric maps, hung as if in a tannery. Hatoum's and Rabah's works address the obstacles and restrictions of life and land under occupation.

Shadi Alzaqzouq paints satirical and provocative hyperrealistic paintings that are rich in symbolism,

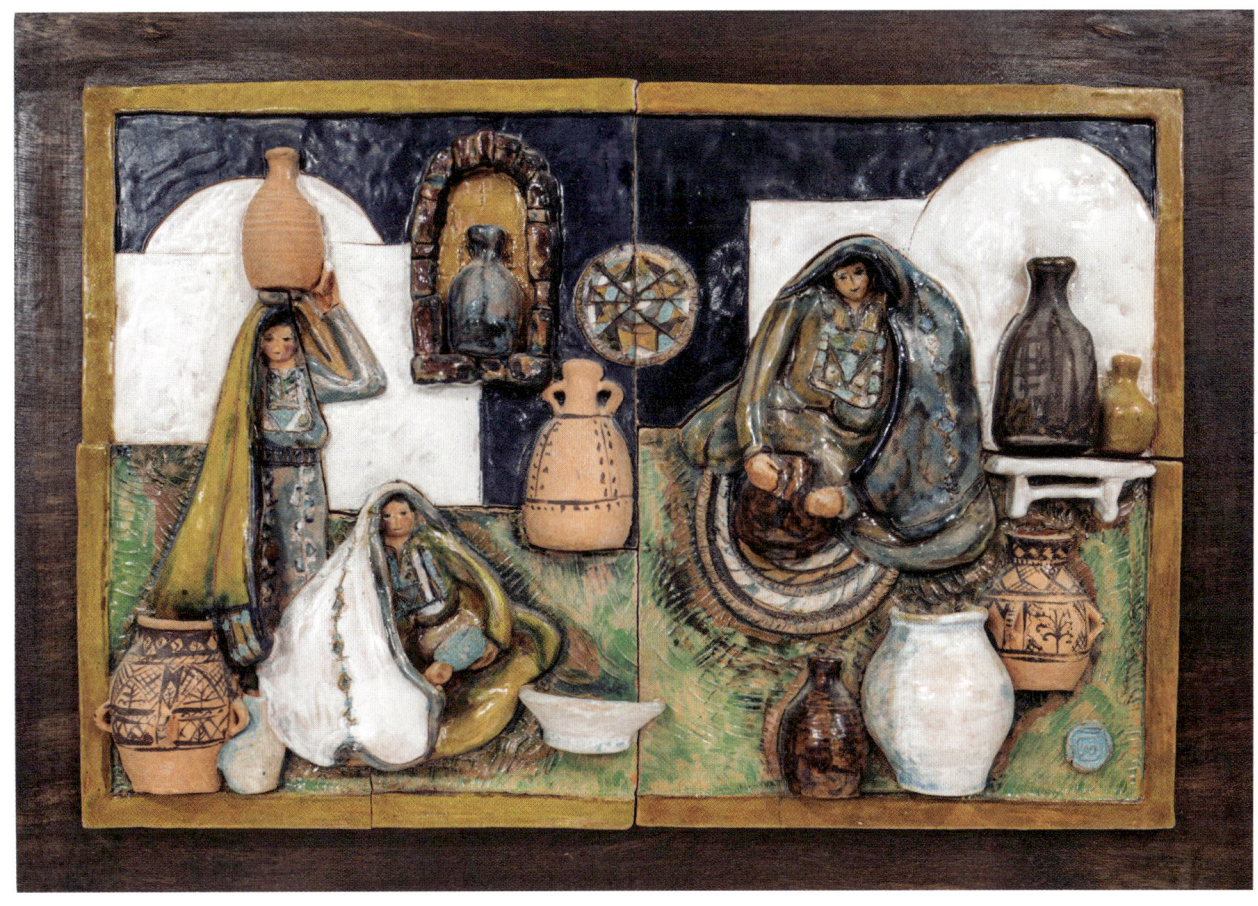

Vera Tamari, *Palestinian Women at Work*, 1979. Ceramic relief, 42 x 60 cm. Barjeel Art Foundation, Sharjah

portraying the cruel absurdity of Israeli occupation and the harsh realities of living under apartheid. In *Le Pardon* (2017), he features a woman wearing an embroidered Palestinian *thobe*, cradling the dead body of a Palestinian man across her lap, reminiscent of Michelangelo's *Pietà*. He critiques the hypocrisy of Western propaganda and how it frames the Holocaust narrative to highlight Jewish European suffering while disregarding Israel's genocide and oppression of Palestinians.

Artists also create digital representations of Palestinian embroidery. In *Dress* (2019), Sulafa Hijazi arranges 372 interactive QR codes that link to various articles, images and videos to form what appear to be embroidery motifs of a dress chest panel using traditional colours. She contrasts the collective female narratives of the digital age with the value of time and sharing of stories within a community through the creation of handiwork like embroidery. Maya Amer, who digitises and animates Palestinian embroidery motifs, created an infographic animation with a chest panel where each cross stitch represents the number of Palestinians Israel killed in Gaza by October 31, 2023, in the first month of the genocide.

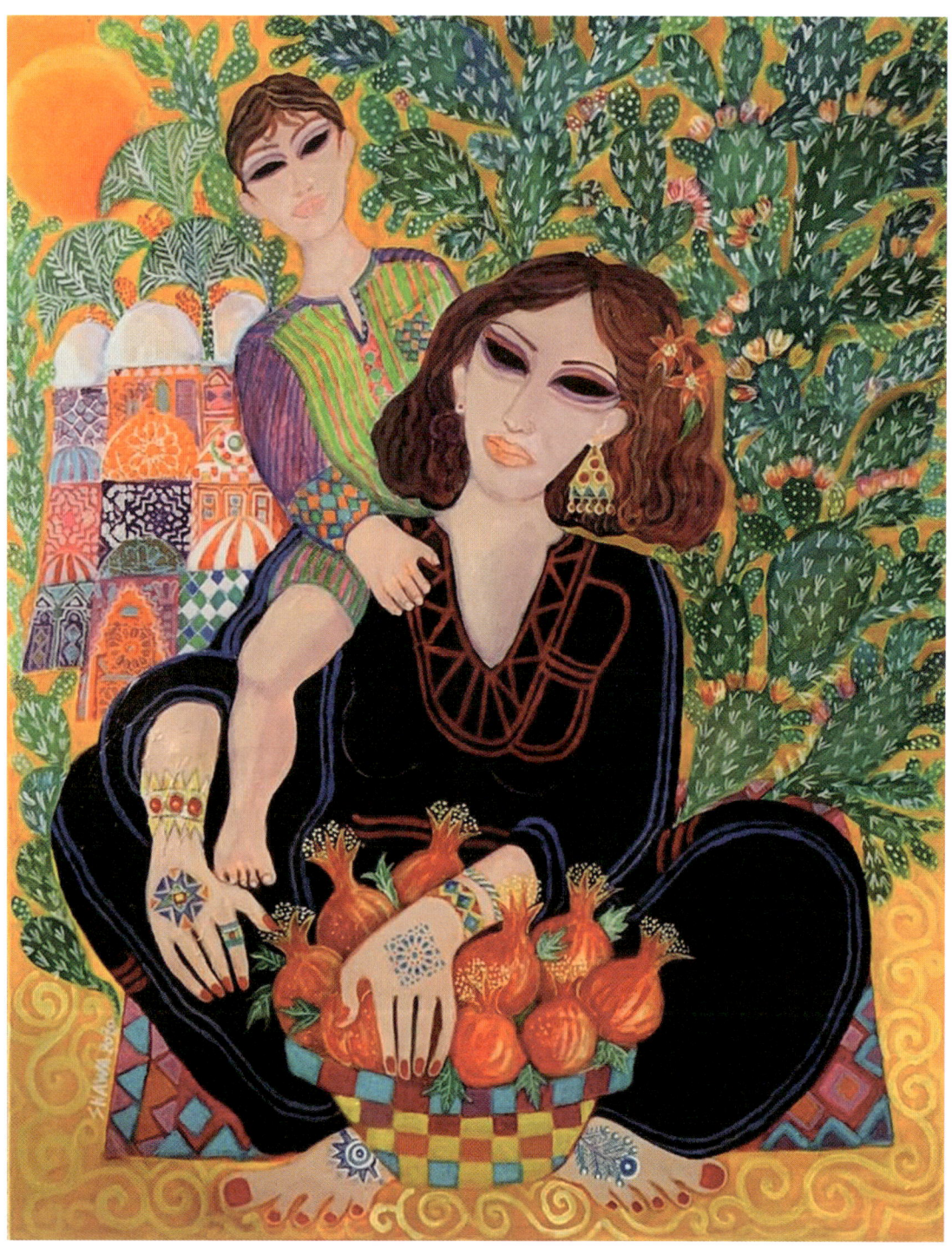

Laila Shawa, *The Turkamanya with Child, The Pomegranate Seller*, 2020. Acrylic on canvas, 80 x 100 cm. Collection of Rula Alami

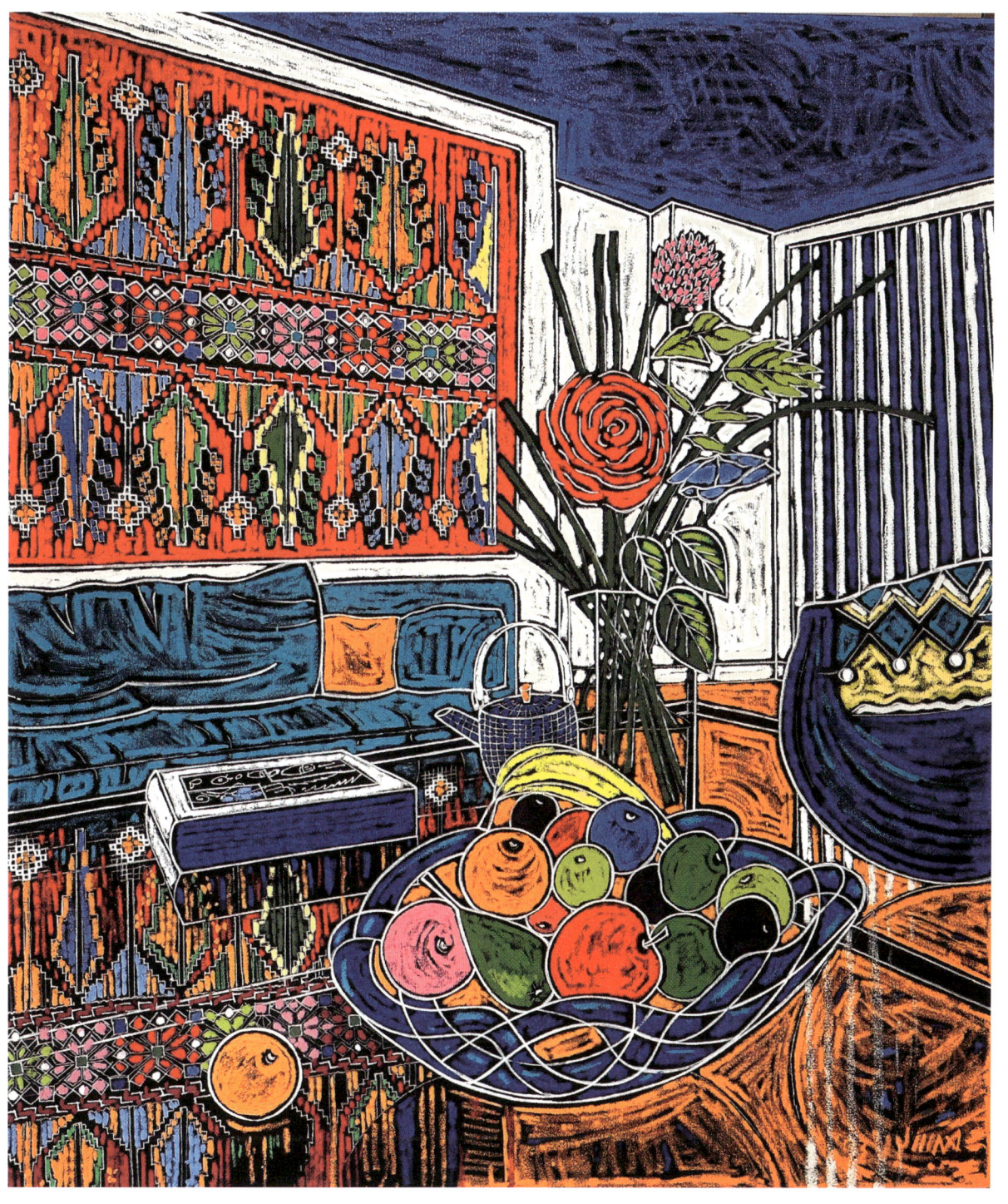

Maysaloun Faraj, *In My Home Are Many Homes*, 2023. Oil pigment on canvas, 160 x 140 cm

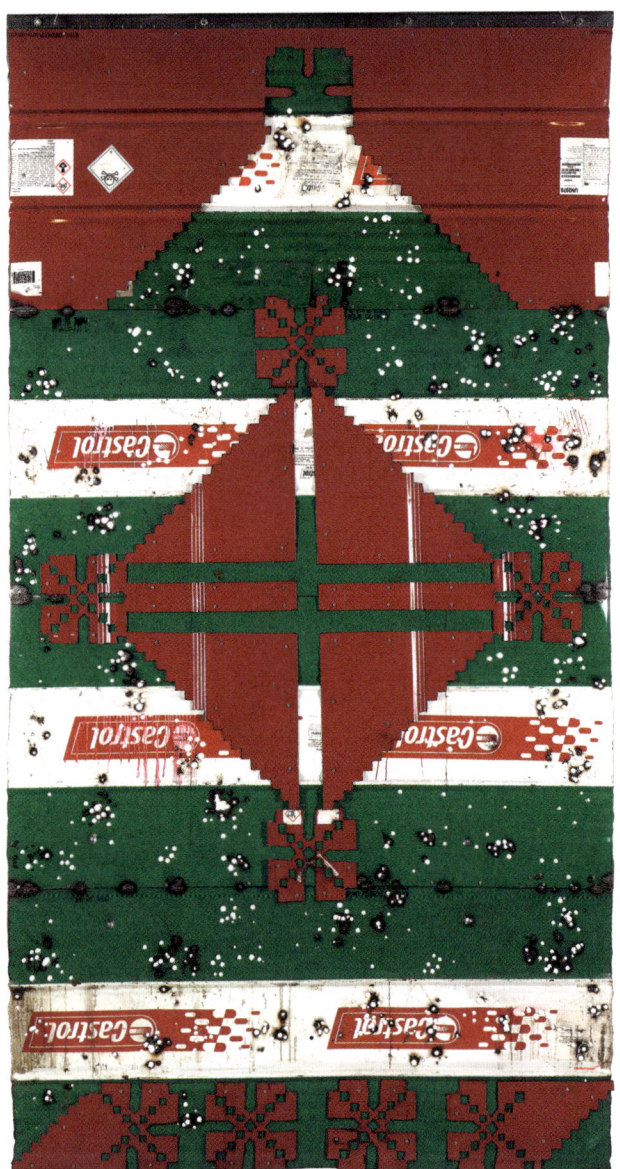

Abdul Rahman Katanani, *Amulet*, 2024. Petroleum barrels, 333 x 179 cm

Palestinian embroidery takes centre stage in Abdul Rahman Katanani's *The Story Portals* series (2023–2024). He drew inspiration for this series from ten embroidered tapestries procured from the Inaash Association by Dr Basel Dalloul for the Ramzi and Saeda Dalloul Art Foundation. Known for his innovative use of barbed wire and scrap metal, Katanani created works for this series featuring large, woven barbed wire embroidery motifs. Other works in the series consist of sheet metal reshaped into compositions of embroidery motifs. By reinventing Palestinian embroidery in metal, Katanani addressed the emotional turmoil he felt from witnessing Israel's extreme violence, destruction and ruthless attacks on Palestine and Lebanon.

In response to Israel's genocide of Palestinians in Gaza, artists, designers and content creators shared their artwork in social media posts reflecting Palestinian and global activism calling for a ceasefire and Palestinian liberation from Israeli occupation and apartheid. Global awareness increased interest in Palestinian embroidery. Palestinian embroidery workshops and meet-ups were held worldwide, while people wore Palestinian embroidery, displayed it in protests, and included it in social media content creation, reinforcing interest in its cultural and political value to the Palestinian narrative. A revival of the imagery of women wearing the embroidered *thobe* appeared across social media platforms and on posters at protests. Examples include *Free Palestine* (2023) by Hassan Manasrah and *We Shall Return* (2014) by Imad Abu Shtayyah, the latter having already circulated after a previous Israeli bombardment of Gaza. Political cartoonists featured Palestinian women in the embroidered *thobe* as characters in their drawings that were shared widely over social media and made into stickers and posters for protests. Again, we see the emotion-provoking imagery of the woman in the embroidered *thobe* as a metaphor for Palestine. This imagery also signifies a resistance movement connected to Palestinian steadfastness and a deep-rooted love for their native land.

Along with recognition of the indefensible and enormous number of lives lost in Israel's horrific genocide of Palestinians in Gaza, there must be an understanding that much of Gaza's cultural and artistic heritage was also targeted and destroyed in Israel's attacks. The devastation caused by Israel's relentless bombing of Gaza reminded Palestinians worldwide of the urgency of preserving their cultural heritage as Israel continues to take extreme measures in the ethnic cleansing of Palestinians. Israel's deliberate and systematic attempt to erase Palestinian culture in Gaza includes but is not limited to the destruction of collections of art, artefacts, embroidered dresses and other heritage items, along with design houses, art studios, art galleries, art institutions, museums, universities, libraries, archives and cultural and heritages sites. Since Palestinian embroidery's existence is evidence of Palestinian indigeneity, the act of preserving it is an act of resistance against Zionist claims and the violent ethnocide of Palestinian culture.

OVERVIEW OF FEATURED ARTISTS IN THIS BOOK

Appreciation for the artistry and skill involved in Palestinian embroidery and its potential to communicate ideas has inspired many contemporary artists to embrace and reinterpret it visually and symbolically. This book examines how contemporary artists continue to find innovative ways to incorporate it conceptually and through various mediums in their artwork. It also highlights the profound impact artists play in shaping, maintaining and evolving the symbolism pertaining to Palestinian embroidery.

In my art practice, I approach Palestinian embroidery as a language and space for connection. I use motifs to relay messages and concepts in my embroidered works and hand-embroidered paintings. Like all languages, Palestinian embroidery is evolving, as is the discourse around it. While many artists still use idealised pastoral imagery of the embroidered *thobe* to celebrate identity and campaign for change, others reimagine this imagery to express ideas about time, space and memory, while confronting colonial and Orientalist misrepresentations. As you read through this book, a conversation emerges among the artworks by the featured artists that concerns preserving and reclaiming indigeneity, dismantling colonial constructs, and celebrating the beauty and impact of Palestinian embroidery.

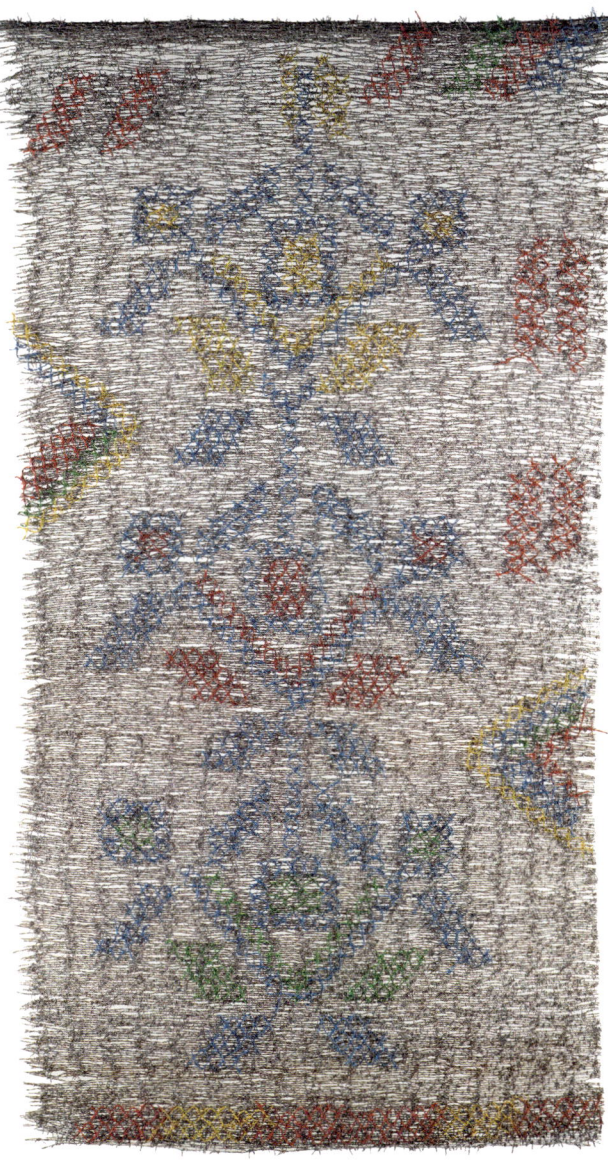

Abdul Rahman Katanani, *Palm Tree*, 2023. Barbed wire, 335 x 175 cm

Next spread: Dina Mattar, *Eid is Not Happy*, 2021. Acrylic on canvas, 200 x 140 cm

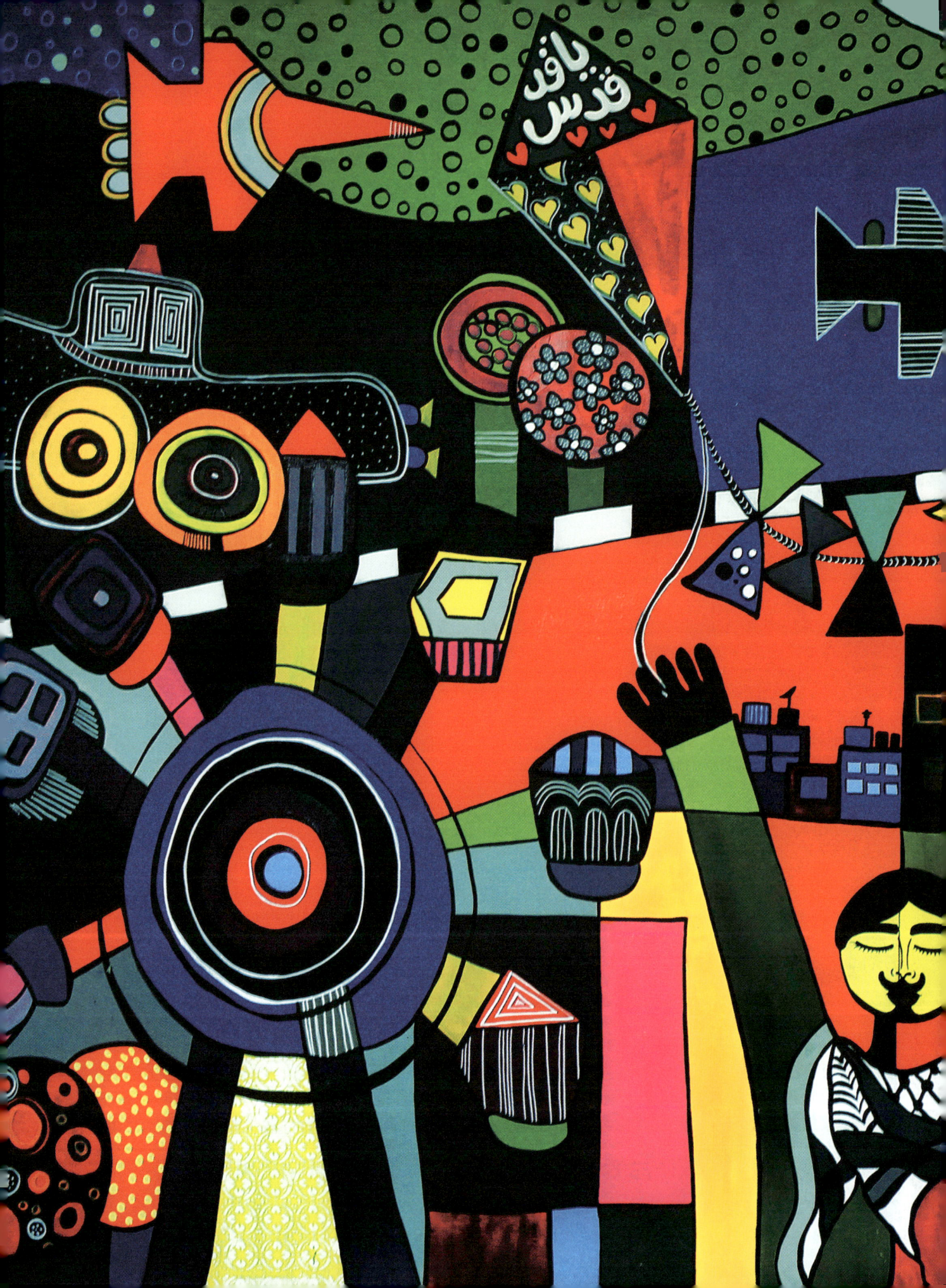

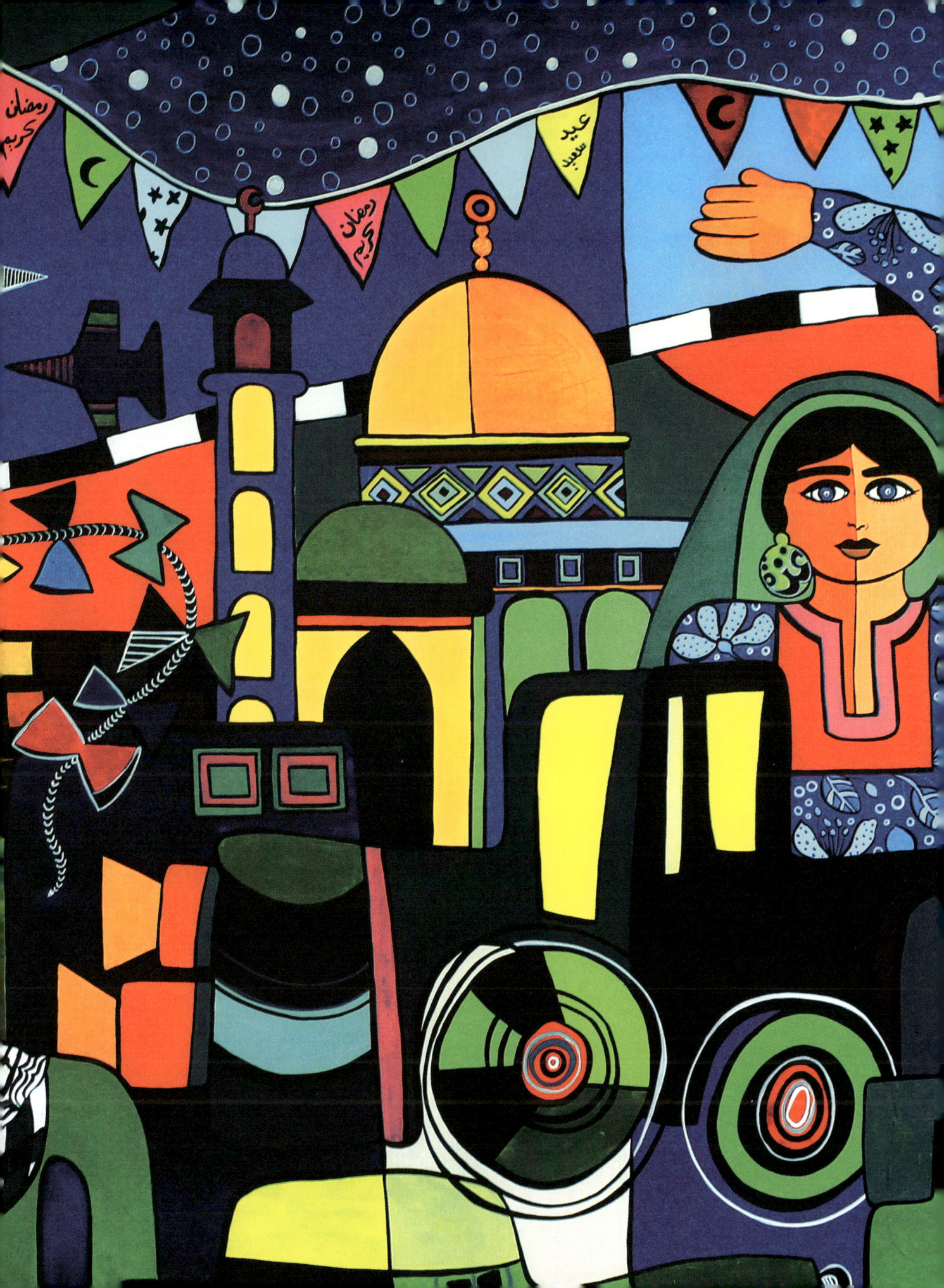

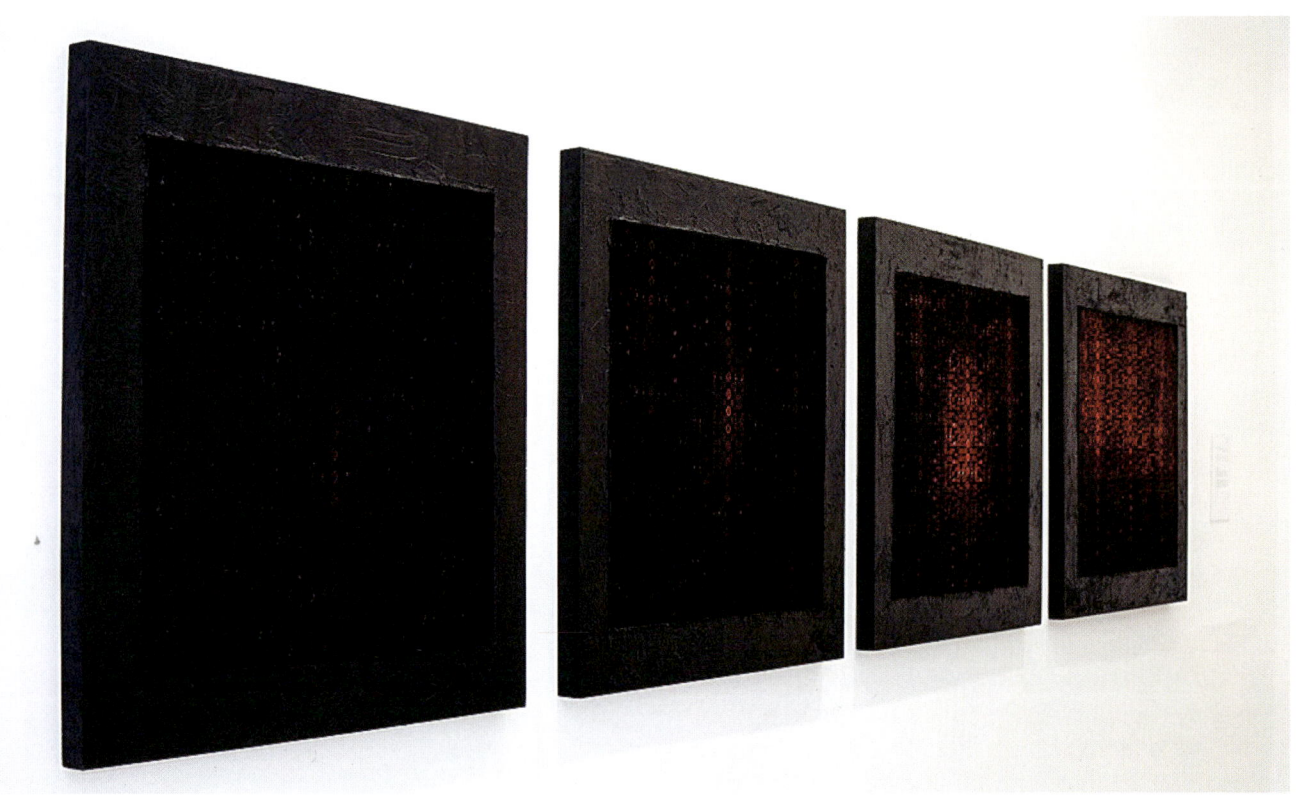

Khaled Hourani, *Afrah wa Iftrah* series, 2004. Thread and dye on fabric, 100 x 100 cm each. Ramzi and Saeda Dalloul Art Foundation

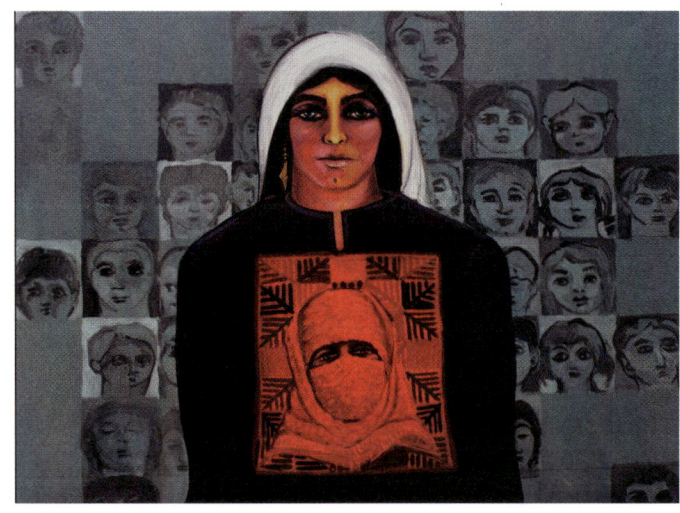

Mohammed Al Hawajri, *Palestine-Gaza*, *Maryam* series, 2015.
Acrylic on canvas, 129 x 180 cm. Dar El-Nimer Collection

Tamam Al Akhal's paintings capture the Palestinian struggle and her experiences of the Nakba, dispossession and displacement. After discovering Palestinian embroidery, she used it as a signifier of Palestinian identity. For Sliman Mansour, the woman in her embroidered *thobe* is pivotal in the visual language expressed in his paintings when referring to Palestine and the Palestinian connection to the land. As he does in his colourful landscapes, Nabil Anani also uses the imagery of the Palestinian woman in her embroidered *thobe* to tell the story of Palestine and love for the land and its people. Mansour and Anani's artwork visually and conceptually paved the way for many artists that followed them, especially in their symbolic depictions of women wearing embroidered dresses and the use of Palestinian embroidery motifs.

Chris Gazaleh has taken the rural representation of the woman in her *thobe* into the realm of street art, painting and illustration to promote social, cultural and political awareness. Mohammed Alhaj incorporates Palestinian embroidery motifs in his paintings, drawings and sculpture to indicate cultural heritage and national identity. Samah Shihadi delves into the complexities of Palestinian identity, experiences and family memories of the 1948 Nakba in her charcoal, hyperrealist depictions of embroidery.

Through photography, photo collage, film and moving image, artists can transform romanticised archival imagery of the woman in the *thobe* into a meaningful dialogue with the viewer. Hazem Harb reframes our notion of history, place and memory using archival photographs to create collages that refashion landscapes and historical imagery. In Larissa Sansour's films, claims to the past are questioned and reformulated in post-apocalyptic settings where signifiers of Palestinian identity, including embroidery, become artefacts of a history written in the future. Sary Zananiri challenges our perspectives on and knowledge of the past by examining class divides, along with colonial and Orientalist narratives, in his altered photographs from the British Mandate period in Palestine. Sama Alshaibi confronts the Orientalist perception of the Arab woman as a motherland. She unpacks the subjects of power, identity, gender and intersectional feminism. In his digital photo collage *Everland*, Steve Sabella pieced together images of embroidery from his photographs

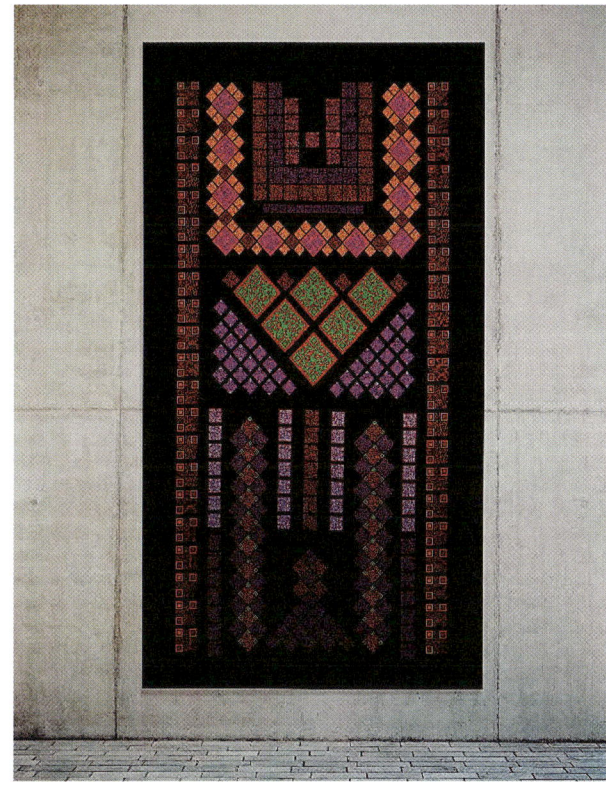

Sulafa Hijazi, *Dress*, ثوب, 2019. Digital print on fabric, 130 x 220 cm

into a boundless garden of floral stitches. He celebrates the beauty of Palestine and opens the imagination to the abundance of possibilities its liberation will bring.

When artists draw attention to embroidery's visual poetry, process and materiality, the medium becomes as essential to the concept as the final piece. The unused balls of embroidery thread in Amer Shomali's *Broken Weddings* series come together to form giant embroidery motifs, reminding us of the disruption of potential dreams and ruptured lives caused by the Nakba. Maha Daya reinvents traditional Palestinian embroidery in her paintings and embroidered works, most recently using embroidery to document the Gaza genocide. Majd Abdel Hamid contrasts violence with the intimate domesticity of embroidery, while also taking an experimental approach when responding and processing his experience with time and locality. Samar Hejazi creates artwork and installations reframing the viewers' understanding of meaning and perception, especially regarding national and cultural narratives.

Jordan Nassar addresses his cross-cultural diasporic identity and cultural participation through embroidered imagined landscapes of an ancestral homeland. After mastering Bethlehem's couching stitch, Deborah Mullins made it a focal point of her textile art practice. Liane Al Ghusain reconstructs the mechanics of the Palestinian cross stitch to send messages through her work and communicate concepts and ideas. With a long familial tradition in embroidery, Kiki Salem pushes the boundaries of embroidery motifs in her murals, textiles and conceptual work. Focusing on materiality and process, Monther Jawabreh draws inspiration from Palestinian embroidery for his embroidered and woven artworks and his community street art initiatives. Samar Hussaini reconciles her diasporic identity through abstract and sculptural art works incorporating embroidery and the embroidered *thobe*.

The permanence of the medium stands out in the work of Najat El-Taji El-Khairy, who developed a highly detailed porcelain painting technique of Palestinian embroidery motifs on tiles. Sisters Nisreen and Nermeen Abudail of Naqsh Collective also emphasise enshrining the embroidery motifs in materials such as marble, brass, stone and wood. They recast scenes and stories from Palestine through their artwork using the language of traditional cross-stitch motifs. Preserving the motifs and the accompanying stories informs the artist's choice of medium to cement indigenous ancestral knowledge and practices in time.

A SENSE OF CONNECTION

In any medium, Palestinian embroidery provokes an emotional response regardless of our background. Every culture has a textile tradition, so the familiarity invoked by the embroidery is like a home-cooked meal. It taps into an essential human need for a connection to home. For Palestinians, that sense of connection and representation is empowering, as it contests Israel's intentional erasure and usurpation of Palestinian culture. Palestinian embroidery has been able to transcend the restrictions on mobility and imposed borders placed on Palestinians living in Occupied Palestine. It also serves as a visual reminder of the meaning and interconnectedness behind these different lived experiences.

Palestinians and those interested in Palestinian culture and heritage embrace Palestinian embroidery with shared enthusiasm and solidarity, whether it has been passed down generationally or learned through books and workshops. The Palestinian experience is as varied and diverse as its stitches. The artists in this book recapture Palestinian embroidery's original purpose, sharing a Palestinian story and communicating internal and external environments. Their artwork is testimony to the power of Palestinian embroidery as a storytelling device – an indigenous language that recounts the past, connects us to the present, and envisages a different future.

HOW THIS BOOK CAME TOGETHER

Collaboration on this book began with my meeting Nabil Anani and Sliman Mansour at Anani's home in Ramallah in the summer of 2019. Over coffee, we discussed the importance of embroidery in Palestinian art and culture. We spoke of its symbolism, how it became part of the visual language, and the urgency around its preservation. I explained my interest in writing a book about Palestinian embroidery in contemporary art. Thankfully, they shared my enthusiasm, and I began to reach out to other artists.

I collected the quotes in this book directly from the artists. I offered them the option to answer questions or write freely about Palestinian embroidery's role in their artwork and art practice. Quotes from primary sources allow the reader to understand the artist's original intention and the concept behind their work.

Right: Hassan Manasrah, *Free Palestine*, 2023

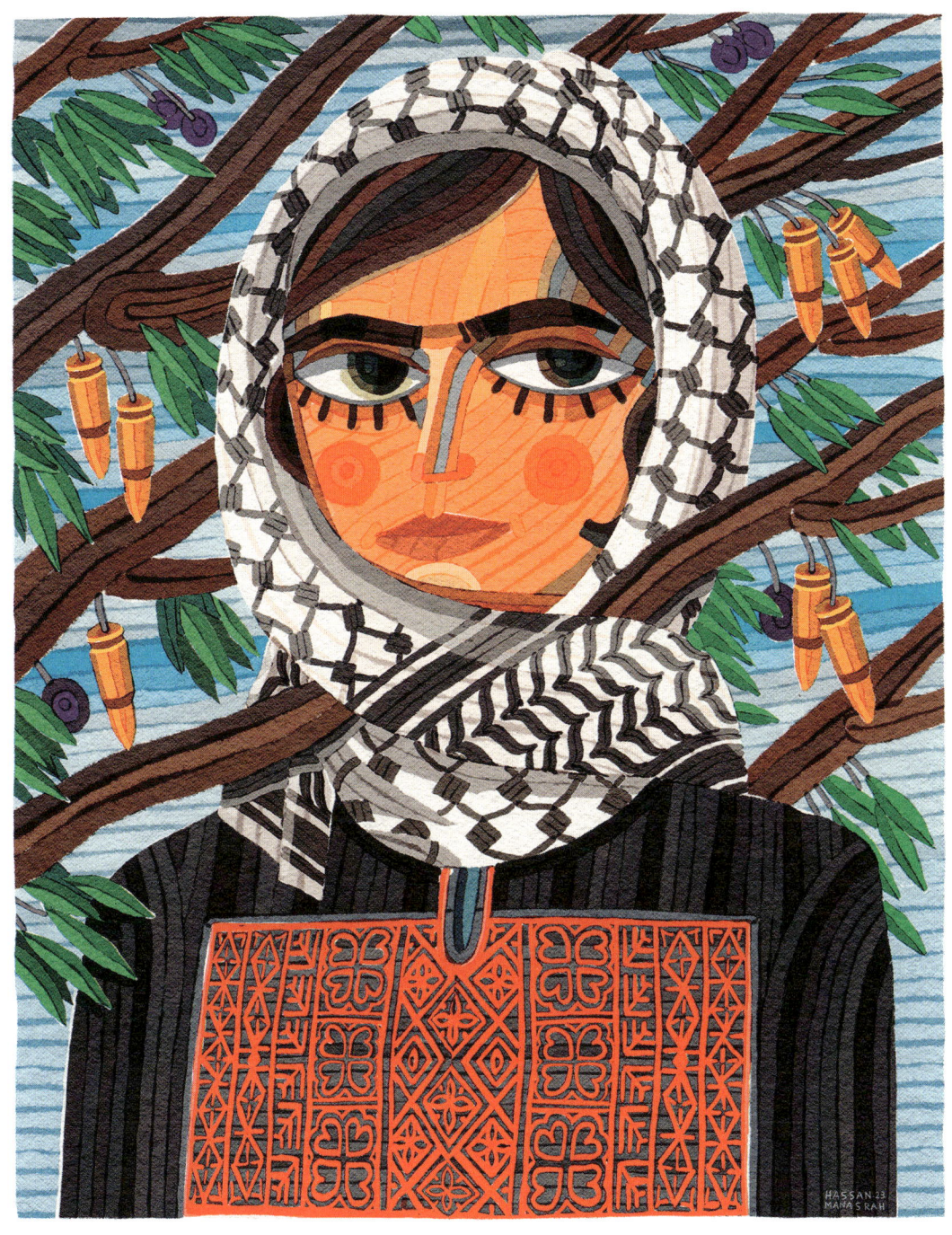

FREE PALESTINE

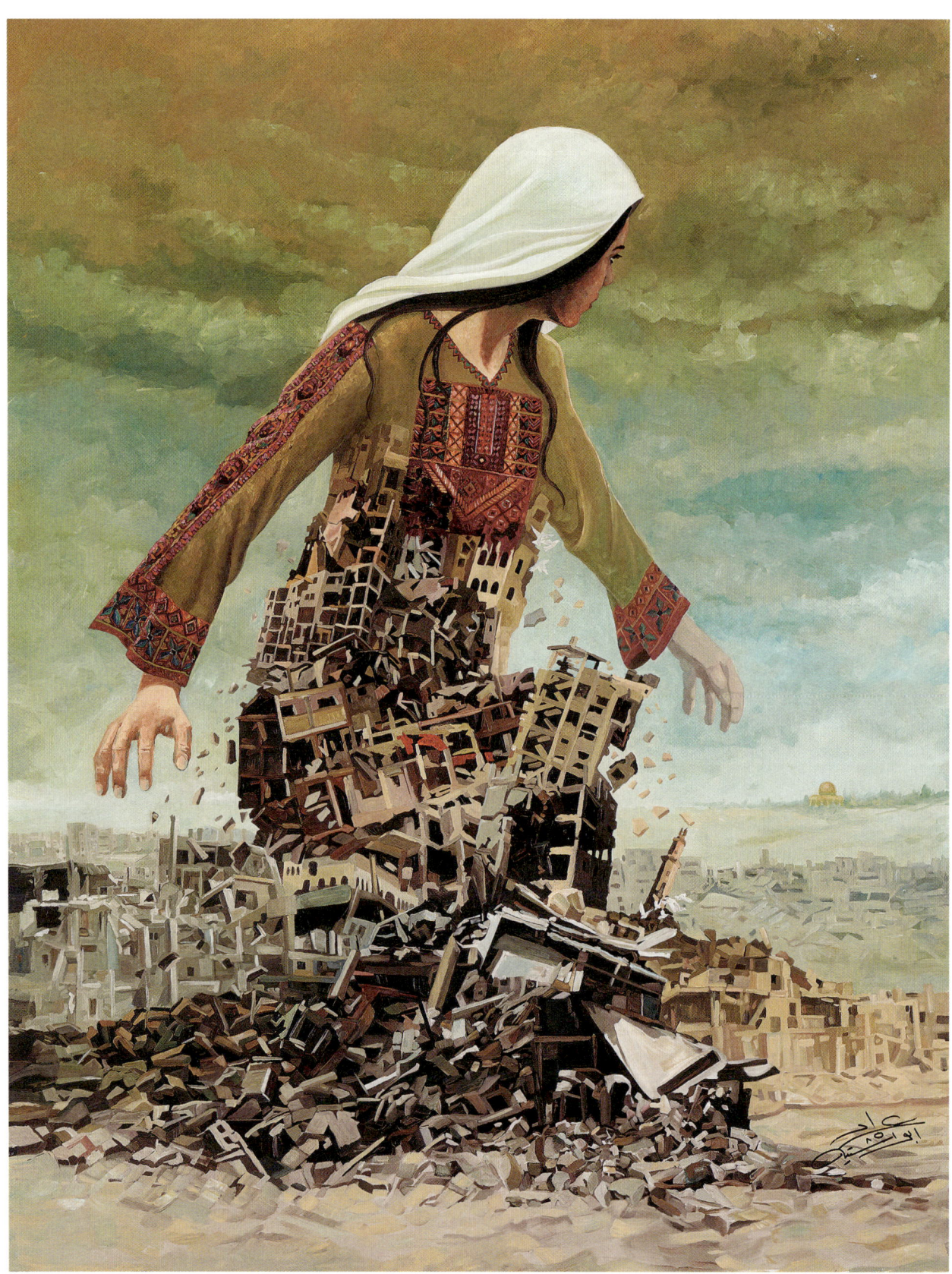

Using primary sources for quotes limited the curation of artists for this book to living artists, namely ones I could contact. Thankfully, I had the pleasure of meeting Deborah Mullins and completing her chapter before she passed away in 2020. It is also important to note that quotes from Sliman Mansour, Nabil Anani, Tamam Al Akhal, Maha Daya, Mohammed Alhaj and Monther Jawabreh were translated from Arabic to English. Sliman Mansour also gave a spoken interview in English, as did Majd Abdel Hamid. I wrote my chapter in the third person to align with the style of the other chapters. Thanks to the contributions of essays by Dr Tina Sherwell, Wafa Ghnaim and Rachel Dedman, and the collaboration with the featured artists, we have a publication that celebrates and documents the integral role of Palestinian embroidery in contemporary art.

BIBLIOGRAPHY

Boullata, Kamal. *Palestinian Art: From 1850 to the Present*, London, Saqi, 2009.

Ghnaim, Wafa. *Thobna*, Washington D.C.: The Tatreez Institute, 2023.

Halaby, Samia A. *Liberation Art of Palestine: Palestinian Painting and Sculpture in the Second Half of the 20th Century*, New York: H.T.T.B. Publications, 2001.

Kawar, Widad Kamel. *Threads of Identity: Preserving Palestinian Costume and Heritage*, Cyprus: Rimal Publications, 2011.

Makhhoul, Bashir and Hon, Gordon. *The Origins of Palestinian Art*, Liverpool: Liverpool University Press, 2013.

Munayyer, Hanan Karaman. *Traditional Palestinian Costume: Origins and Evolution*, Massachusetts: Olive Branch Press, 2011.

Summerer, Karène Sanchez and Zananiri, Sary. *Imaging and Imagining Palestine. Photography, Modernity and the Biblical Lens*, Brill, 2021.

Left: Imad Abu Shtayyah, *We Shall Return*, 2014. Oil on canvas, 182 x 142 cm. Ramzi and Saeda Dalloul Art Foundation

Next spread: Shadi Alzaqzouq, *Le Pardon*, 2017. Oil on canvas, 220 x 327 cm. Ramzi and Saeda Dalloul Art Foundation

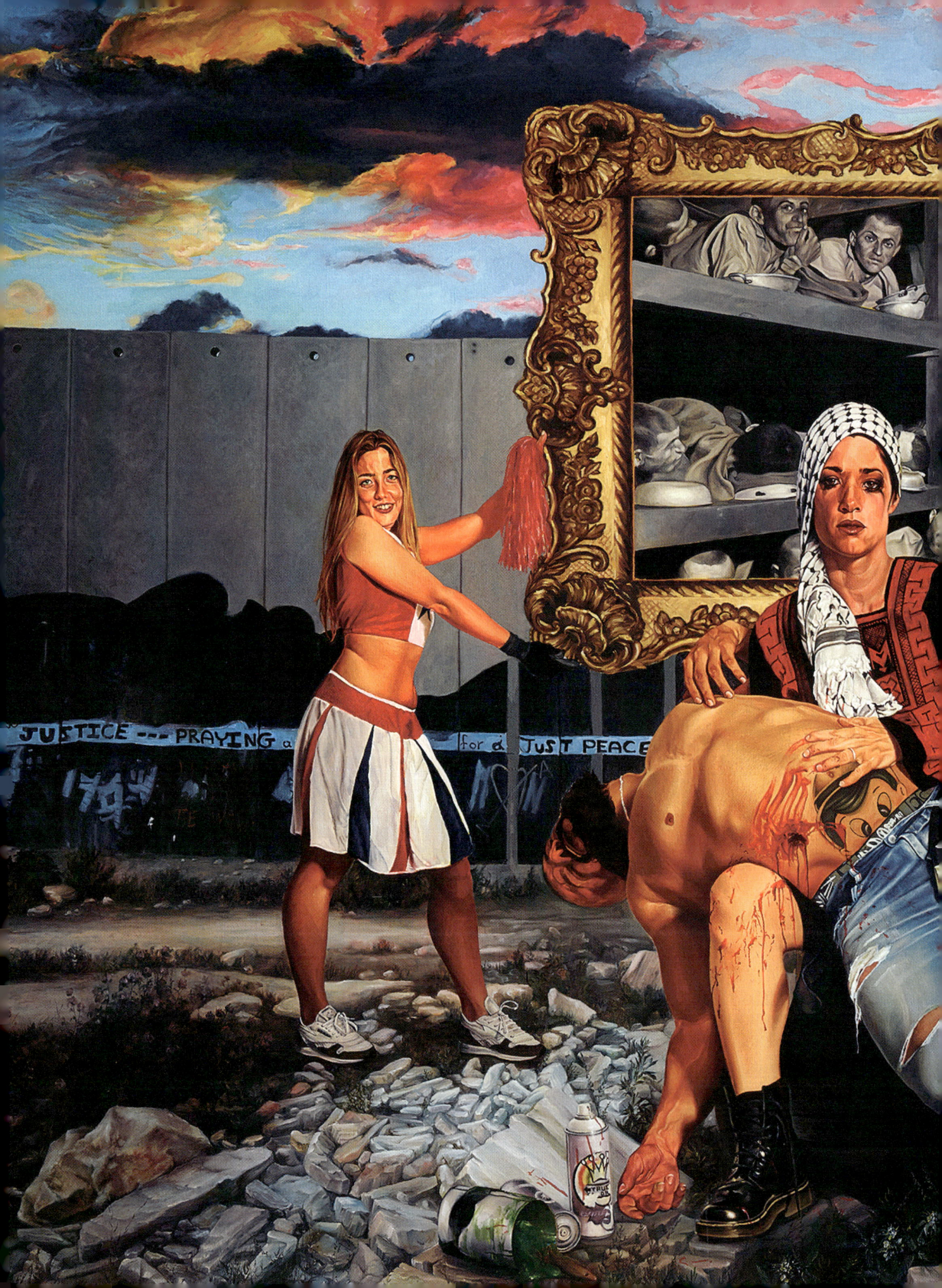

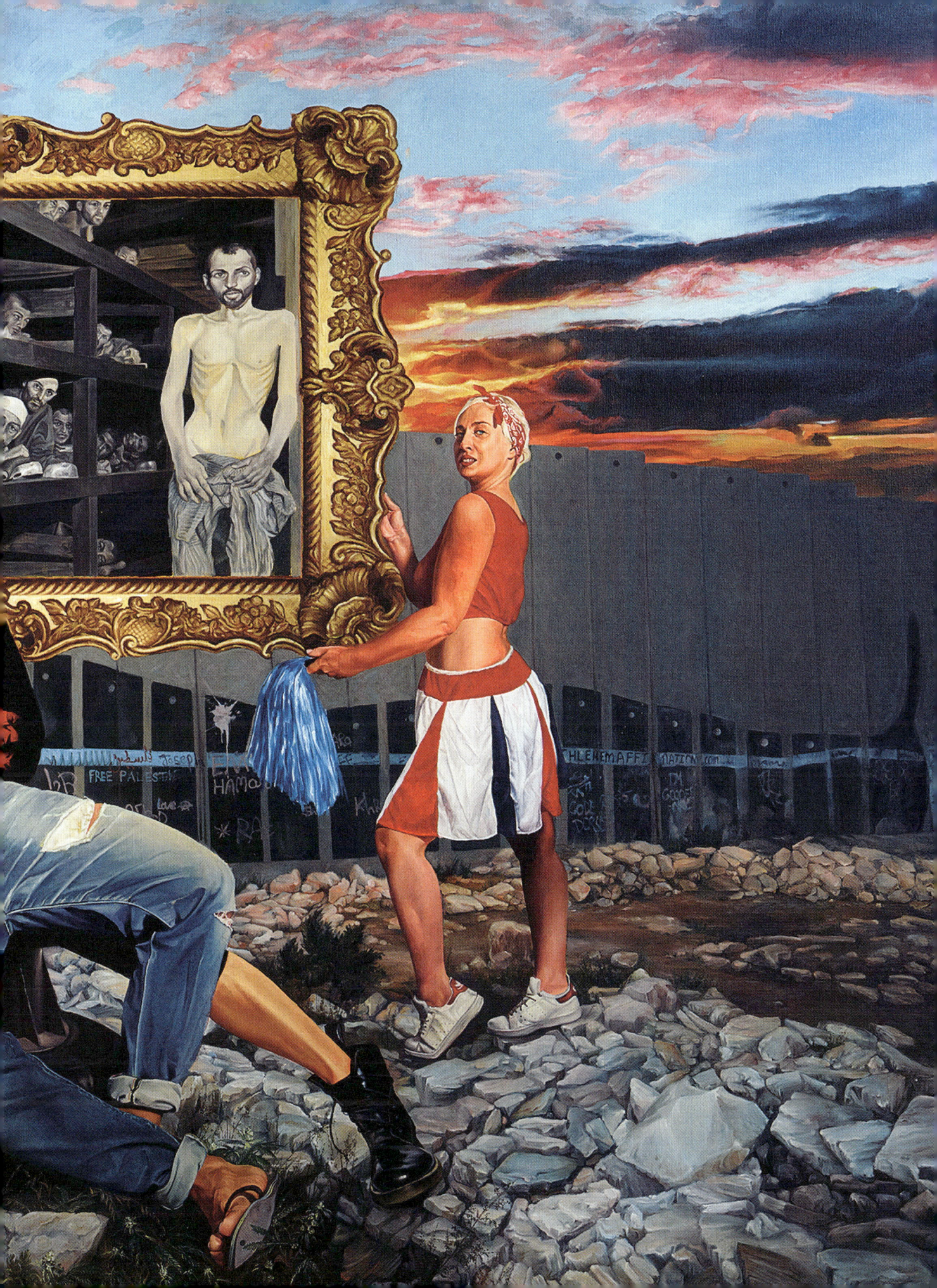

PERENNIAL STITCHES

DR TINA SHERWELL

'Constructed and deconstructed, ephemera are what we negotiate with, since we authorize no part of the world and can only influence increasingly small bits of it. In any case we keep going.'[1] Edward Said

Cushion covers, handbags, hairbands, picture frames, slippers, waistcoats, shawls, jackets, tea coasters, placemats, tablecloths, table runners, stools, mirrors, bags, slippers, keychains, glasses cases, pen sets, earrings and necklaces. A plethora of objects with Palestinian embroidery can be found on the market stalls of street vendors, in souvenir shops, in the Palestinian TV studios' stage sets, on our TV screens, in cultural venues, homes, salons, hotels and restaurants reproduced in paintings and on pottery. Wherever you cast your gaze you are likely to find a pattern, a reference to Palestinian embroidery. Embroidery endlessly floats, attaches itself to objects and circulates all around us. The dress has become disembodied, the embroidery fragmented and objects reinvented in multiple forms in which the women are both present and absent at the same time. What was once a language between women has slowly disappeared, with so many of us not knowing how to read the intricate symbolism of the dresses. The time needed to create embroidery seems no longer compatible with contemporary forms of living.

Many tend to prefer the older costumes to their contemporary forms. It is easy to fall into nostalgia about the Palestinian costume and, in so doing, forget that the costumes were ever-changing forms. Women were inspired by other village women's patterns, new fabrics that arrived in Palestine and patterns on men's uniforms. Circumstances meant women would use different fabrics to enlarge a dress. Therefore, as various writers in the field have suggested, dresses were not static objects but items that reflected their social and economic context, and individual women's flair and creative choices. Today's contemporary forms, with synthetic fabrics, rhinestones and machine embroidery, are part of this

ongoing transformation. The process reflects the ruptures experienced by Palestinian society and communities, and alterations to the trade routes through which fabrics and threads arrive in Palestine today.

Since the late 1970s, landscape representations created by Palestinians living under occupation have been focused on life in the village and work in the rural environment. The artists created a utopia in which a vision of the future Palestinian homeland was cast in the image of an idyllic rural past. In this genre of painting, one cannot necessarily identify a specific time or place, but rather 'dreamscapes'. Salim Tamari suggests that 'The peasantry becomes the idealised cultural hinterland from which nationalist ideology can draw its uncontaminated inspiration and collective self-identity.'[2]

The representation of the landscape was specifically domestic, and the severance and loss of the homeland was imaged as the motherland. The female figure in traditional costume came to embody the land itself, its loss and the community's yearning for return and comfort of the homeland. This articulation was found across literature, poetry, theatre and dance, in which the mother and land became an interchangeable representation, and in which love for the mother articulated love for the homeland and nation.

Rarely does one find large vistas in the paintings. Instead, landscapes centre on the village, the fields or the home and are populated with women and children. Peasant women constitute the central subject of such paintings and are seen gathering olives, wheat, almonds and oranges, or bearing produce. Their presence in the landscape in traditional costumes became the foremost signifier of Palestinian national identity and authenticity.

The peasant woman's embroidered dress has, in the aftermath of the loss of the land, come to function as a way of mapping that land. The style and pattern of each embroidered dress is unique to each region and indicates each wearer's village of origin. The dress, along with artefacts from the peasant's home (and the woman's sphere in particular) such as cooking utensils, baskets and earthenware, have increasingly become fetishised and seen as markers of Palestinian identity. In the process of articulating national identity, women, including their surroundings and belongings, have been represented as the privileged emblems of cultural authenticity. In many paintings we find the monumental figure of a lone woman in a landscape, often deployed to express loss and estrangement.

This motif gendered the homeland in the form of the female figure of the bride and the motherland. It was explored extensively in Palestinian literature, music and theatre, and it significantly influenced the visual arts. Thus, the body of the woman and the land became interchangeable. Ghassan Hage suggests that the use of the mother to signify the nation distinguishes the qualities of the nation as 'caring, protective, and nurturing – a homeland of bodily comfort and security.'[3] Exile, estrangement and loss of the homeland are expressed as separation from the mother figure, a sentiment that was dominant in the visual arts during the 1980s. The image of the motherland permeated Palestinian literature and was a popular motif for articulating the relationship and the longing for the lost homeland, as in this quote from Fadwa Tuqan:

> He recalled the land which had raised him and fed him generously since infancy, he fell passionately on his land smelling the soil, kissing the trees and grasping the pebbles. Like an infant, he pressed his cheek and mouth to the soil, shedding there the pain he had borne for years.[4]

The motherland is primarily a gratifying place, a place for consumption, a place whose subjects perform motherly activities or are children. The motherland is, then, a utopia of bodily comfort, where the subject's emotional and physical needs are met, as is eulogised in the late Mahmoud Darwish's poem, *Give Birth to Me Again that I May Know*:

> Give birth to me again so I can drink the country's milk from you and remain a little boy in your arms, remain a little boy
> For ever […] Give birth to me again, so you can hold me in your hands.[5]

The women in the paintings become generic types; we cannot identify them as the mothers of anyone in particular, rather they are the 'motherland' and identified specifically through their embroidered costume. Embroidery has been severed from the woman's body; fragments of her dress and her personal objects now circulate among us, utilised as markers of cultural and national identity. As Edward Said observes, 'Photographs, dresses, objects severed from their original locale, the rituals of speech and custom: Much reproduced, enlarged, thematized, embroidered, and passed around, they are strands in the web of affiliations we Palestinians use to tie ourselves to our identity and to each other.'[6]

Palestinian embroidery, in its contemporary forms, often takes on portable forms. As Nazmi Al-Jub'eh suggests, this is not a new phenomenon in the context of diaspora:

> Palestinians became known for their keffiyeh and embroidered peasant dresses, their folkloric dabka dance, and various rural symbols that represented their relationship to the land. Immobile cultural heritage (antiquities, architecture and landscape) were to a certain extent absent from such expressions, for such heritage could not be placed in a bag and taken from one refugee camp to another.[7]

As items have become heritage objects, preserved in collections, displayed in museums, and reproduced in paintings, a separation has occurred between them and the contemporary dresses and women who wear them. The consumption of heritage spurs multiplication and reproduction; who wears the embroidered shawl or jacket today? For what function, and for which audience? Who fills their homes with embroidered objects? Who seeks out historic dresses and objects? In our nostalgia, we often eulogise the historic dresses. We are no longer predominantly an agricultural community, as the land shrinks under our feet in daily confiscation, transformation and segregation. The embroidery and the dresses have expanded and transformed into different forms to meet the different symbolic needs of sectors of the community for the articulation of identities and of loss.

Longing, then, takes different forms and reveals the different imaginings we have of the past and our identities. It is interesting to consider that in the above-mentioned objects we carry the embroidery close to our bodies, in our pockets, on our shoulders. We surround our domestic spaces with embroidery, immersing ourselves in environments of embroidery, perhaps as a way to speak of this ongoing loss.

Embroidery is predominantly carried on female bodies or arranged in domestic spaces; but in paintings of the late 1970s onwards, it was predominantly male artists who painted, reproduced and reinvented the stitch in numerous paintings in which the focus was the monumental figure of the motherland adorned in traditional costume.

Palestinian costume and embroidery are constantly being transformed to meet the needs of the communities. Today, when we see the costume and embroidery in demonstrations around the world, it highlights that this enduring symbol is constantly being rearticulated and circulated, revealing the multiplicity of Palestinian identity.

[1] Edward Said, *After the Last Sky: Palestinian Lives*, London: Faber & Faber, 1986, p. 37.
[2] Salim Tamari, 'Soul of the Nation: The Falleh in the Eyes of the Urban Intelligensia'. *Review of Middle East Studies*, 1991, p. 82.
[3] Ghassan Hage, 'The Spatial Imaginary of National Practices: Dwelling–Domesticating/ Being–Exterminating'. *Environment and Planning: Society and Space*, vol. 14, 1996, p. 478.
[4] Fadwa Tuqan, 'A Mountainous Journey', in *Anthology of Modern Palestinian Literature*, New York, Columbia University Press, 1994, p. 720.
[5] Mahmud Darwish, Samih al-Qasim and Adonis, *Victims of a Map: A Bilingual Anthology of Arabic Poetry*, ed. Abdullah al-Udhari, London: Saqi Books, 1984, p. 21.
[6] Edward Said, *After the Last Sky: Palestinian Lives*, London: Faber & Faber, 1986, p. 14.
[7] Nazmi Al-Ju'beh, 'Architecture as a Source for Historical Documentation: The Use of Palestine's Built Heritage as a Research Tool'. *Jerusalem Quarterly* 36, winter 2009, p. 50.

Abdelrahman Al Muzayen, *Dal'ouna (Anat)*, 1977. Acrylic on canvas, 100 x 70 cm. Ramzi and Saeda Dalloul Art Foundation

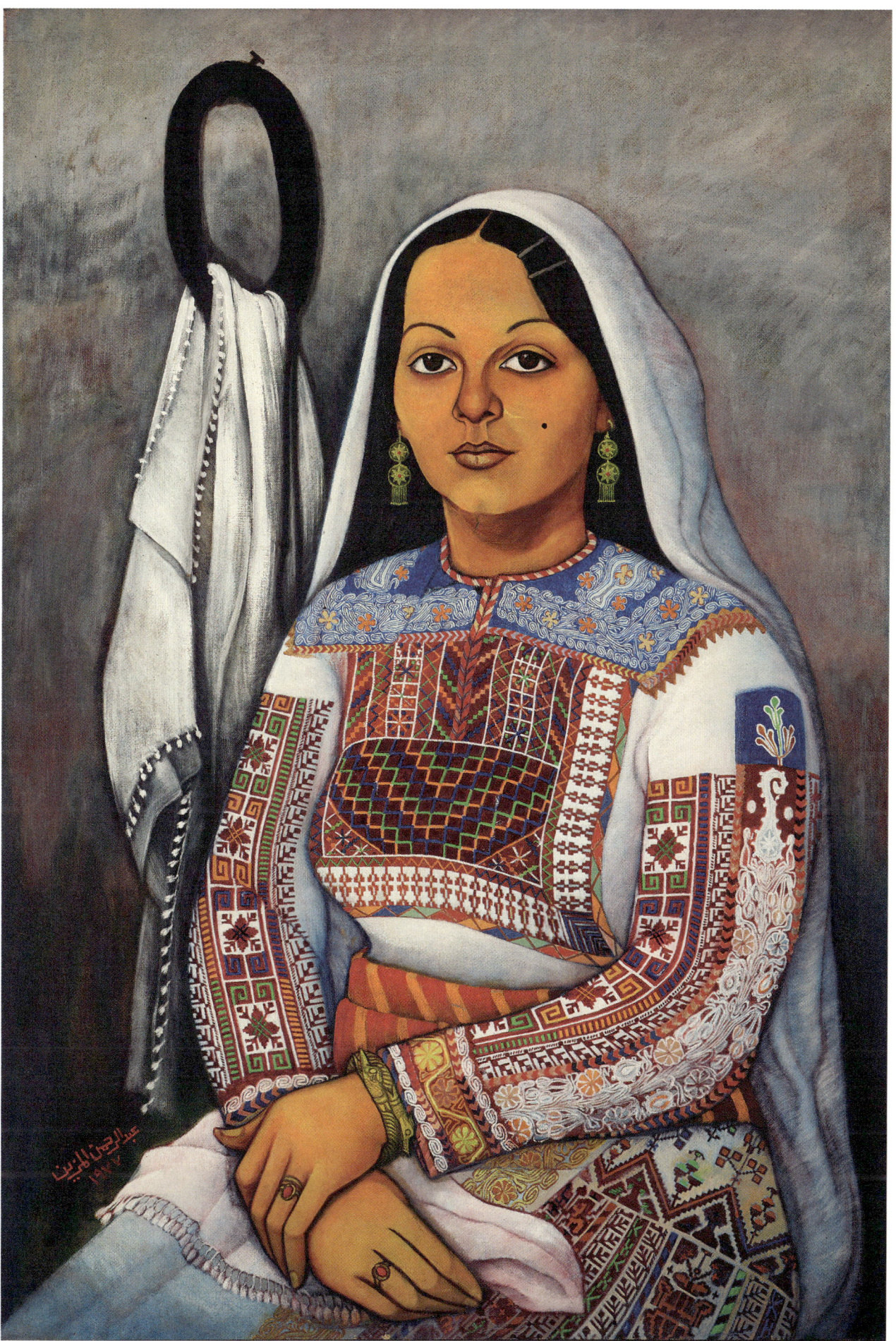

TATREEZ AS CEREMONY: AN ETHOS FOR PRESERVING
WAFA GHNAIM

When we think of Palestine today, visions of destruction pervade our consciousness: boulders in shades of brown atop a cratered earth, desolation and decimation, mountains of rubble. A tall tower of homes that once housed life so warmly is now collapsed over sleeping children and their families. Palestinians become survivors in the avalanche of tragedy, standing on a colossal valley of stone blocks overlooking a land now barren, without fruit or life. Palestine, literally and figuratively, has become a burial place owing to the Israeli occupation's never-ending thirst to destroy. It is a landscape of unmarked graves, interminable.

A man with tears drenching his face, and sweat soaking his shirt, digs for his wife and children in the deafening silence. He searches the dense dirt of rock and rubble beneath him, with only a small hammer and his bare hands. Does he know we can see him through someone's phone camera? The day his home was bombed, I saw him on social media. He could be spotted in the background of all the video footage that day, digging and crying. I wonder what happened to him and if he is still alive...

Once again, amid atrocity, Palestinian life and land, and therefore tatreez,[1] face a threat of erasure. Tatreez was once passed from mother to daughter but, in the wake of al-Nakba,[2] centuries-old intergenerational traditions were severely disrupted owing to the living conditions imposed by ongoing war, displacement and ethnic cleansing. Today, exiled Palestinians around the world have united to restore the ceremony of learning and practising tatreez in the diaspora.[3]

In 2021, UNESCO inscribed the art of embroidery in Palestine, inclusive of practices, skills, knowledge and rituals, on the Representative List of Intangible Cultural Heritage of Humanity. When tatreez is taught from one generation to the next, the teachers are sharing embroidery techniques with the meanings of each motif, transmitting their individual memories and the collective stories passed on to them by their elders. By doing so, the teacher is connecting people, histories, and symbolisms as represented through fashion and dress,

throughout time to the student. Storytelling as an approach to knowledge transfer is a form of indigenous ceremony, that is place-based and 'in relationship with the natural world, which draws together past, present, and future into a space in which personal and collective transformations occur'.[4] Tatreez as ceremony is a ritual and practice that resists cultural erasure, dependent on the teacher's recollection of oral history and proximity to the land of historic Palestine.

The ceremony of tatreez can be understood within a relational context that is enlightened by tea, handwork and storytelling.[5] The indigenous ceremony is '...not just the period at the end of the sentence. It is the required process and preparation that happens long before the event.'[13] As Palestinians in the diaspora trying to preserve tatreez as a practice and as a ceremony, we are also responsible for preserving intangible cultural heritage in preparation for 'the event': liberation. Cultural preservation, which is a part of envisaging the future, requires a meditative practice and ritual that allows for the current generation in exile to spiritually transport themselves to Palestine of the past, present and future.

On this future day of liberation, we will return to our grandparents' villages or towns, and cultivate the weeping land that has been torn apart by endless war and genocide. Where are the cacti now? Where are the cypress trees and poppies? Where are the almond blossoms my mother once told me about? Though the soil will be drenched in the blood of our martyrs and a century of tears from our people, we will be home.

Perhaps we will gather with our neighbours, in the flower fields of Ramallah, the hills of the Galilee and in the orange groves of Jaffa, to tell our stories and memories over tea. We will be able to speak of our Palestinian identity without limits, free from fears of being ostracised or punished. We will gather on the coast of the Mediterranean Sea, or near Lake Tiberias, and feel the wind and earth beneath our feet. Collectively, we will give honour to, and ensure the care and protection of, the surviving families and children of Gaza.

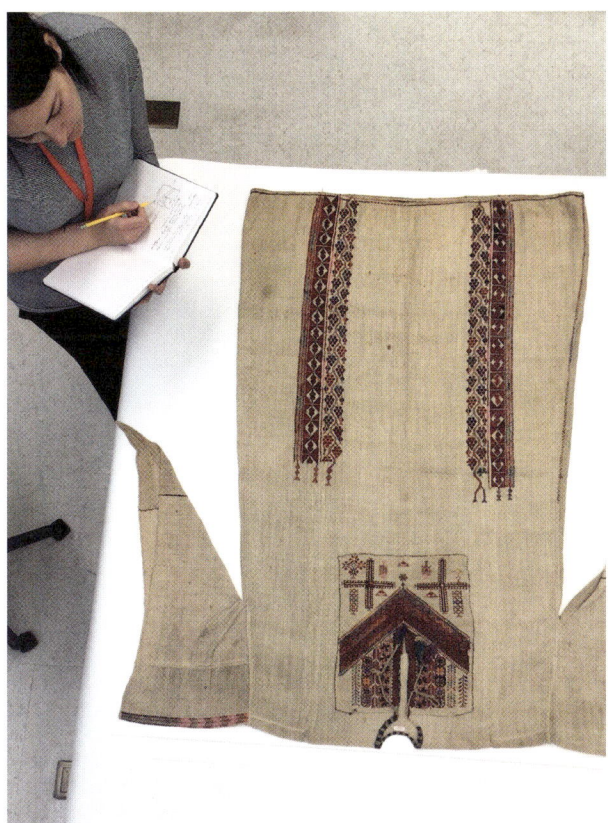

Wafa Ghnaim studying a Ramallah *thobe* in the Met's collection (MMA 45.113) in December 2023. Photograph by Michelle McVicker

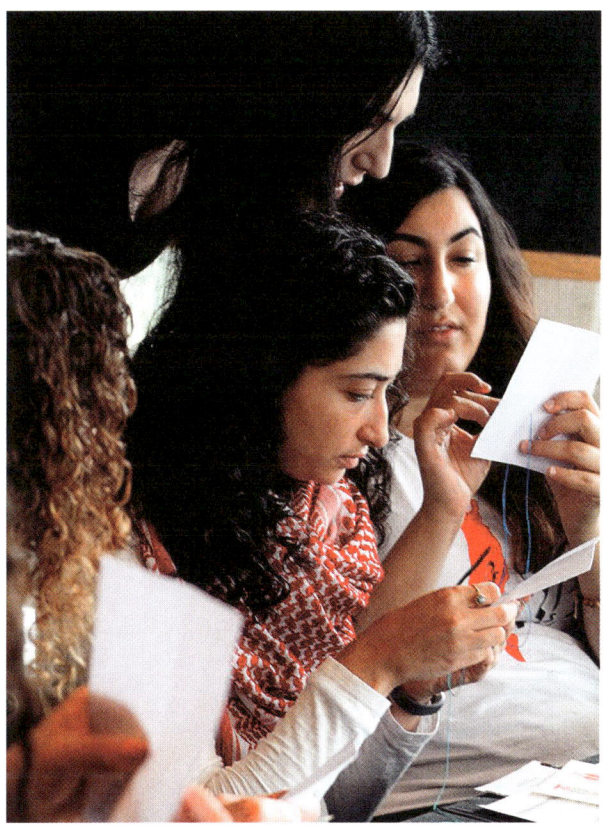

Wafa Ghnaim teaching Palestinian embroidery in Washington, D.C. (2018). Photograph by Bryanda Minix

We will be free to be together. We will be free to care for one another – for our injured children and elderly. We will finally be home. And on this liberated day, when Palestinians around the world return home, what will we have preserved in the diaspora? What rituals, ceremonies and traditions will we return with?

Palestinian rituals, ceremonies and traditions preserved in exile will certainly have changed in response to new ways of life adopted abroad. Every day, through my work in The Tatreez Institute, I carefully consider the research methods, documentation practices and dissemination approaches

I engage with as an indigenous scholar, preserving intangible cultural heritage. After the release of my first book, *Tatreez & Tea: Embroidery and Storytelling in the Palestinian Diaspora* (2016), I began teaching Palestinian embroidery around the world. Since then I have seen a monumental shift in the public's interest in learning Palestinian embroidery.

When I first began teaching *tatreez* in 2016, Palestinian elders would tell me that *tatreez* was extinct and the new generation was too busy to learn. Today, dozens of *tatreez* teachers and cultural preservation initiatives have sprouted

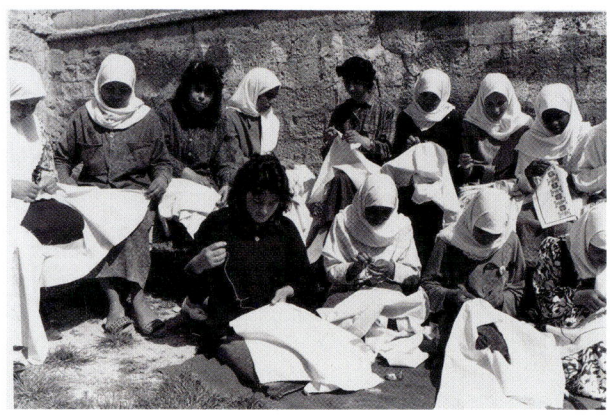

Members of the board of directors of Qalandia Camp Women Handicraft Cooperative Society at an exhibition of Palestinian embroideries (1958). Source: Palestinian Museum Digital Archive, No. 0127.01.0202

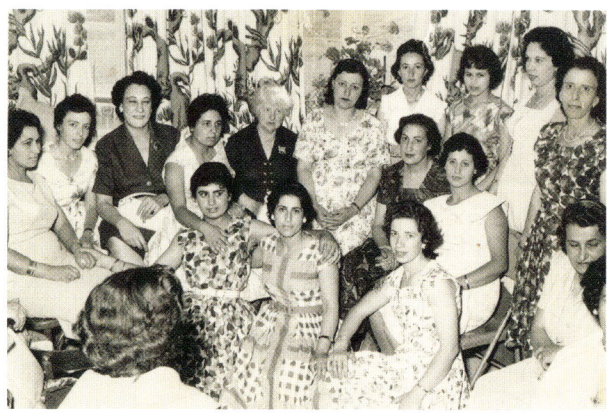

Fatima Othman al-Shalabi (Omar al-Qasim's mother) and a group of women after their graduation from an embroidery course in Jerusalem (1970s). Source: Palestinian Museum Digital Archive, No. 0004.03.0096.

around the world, organising local events and creating online content that promotes preservation of the art form. It has been a tremendous honour to have taught and influenced many of those new *tatreez* teachers, and it has become more important than ever to consider the ways in which the art form is being presented and preserved in the diaspora through these localised initiatives.

What is the most ethical way to teach Palestinian embroidery in exile? Should Palestinians continue to practice, preserve and teach only the traditional techniques? Or do Palestinians in the diaspora have agency to modernise and personalise the traditional art form, and then teach their way to the next generation?

The answer may not be straightforward or fully answered within this essay, but one thing is certain: Palestinian embroidery is not just a hobby. *Tatreez* is a traditional art form that encompasses scholarship, which utilises indigenous research methods to protect the intangibility of its ritual, centring storytelling as ceremony. This *tatreez* ceremony is illuminated by relationships. The embroiderer, artist or maker is the closest relative and storyteller to their work. Whenever possible, they must be given agency to represent their work. When it is not possible to trace the work back to the maker, we must acknowledge the next nearest sources, including oral historians who have attempted to

preserve the maker's voice and have passed it onto the next generation. If the oral historian is separated from the history retold, no matter how many times over, the story and therefore the tatreez ceremony is compromised; it has lost its roots.

When misinformation emerges, as it inevitably does when sources are lost, incorrect retellings and interpretations can have lasting impacts. This is most often the case in publications that attempt to decode the meanings of *tatreez* motifs; due to the subjectivity of a language based in images, the wrong pattern names, village attributions and meanings become associated with motifs. The motifs are represented as a separate unit from the dress in these frameworks, and the reader is unable to discern where the pattern was stitched on the *thobe*, which elder named the pattern and when. These are crucial details inherent to a real-life *tatreez* ceremony, but which are lost through non-traditional preservation formats such as written publications, pattern books and digital databases.

Tatreez storytellers and teachers must take heed to the warning (one that has been repeatedly taught by Palestinian elders) that misinformation and the loss of indigenous sources is impossible for the next generation to put right. For example, ignoring the reality of the undeniable influence of European embroidery traditions in the diaspora could risk total endangerment of *tatreez* for future generations.

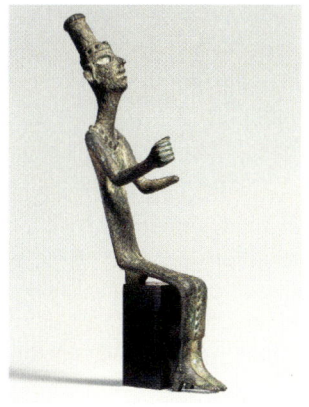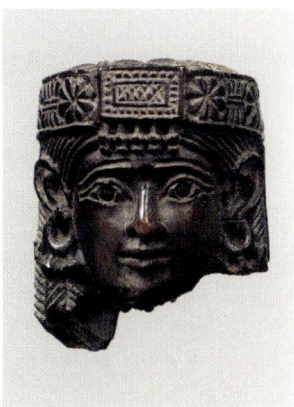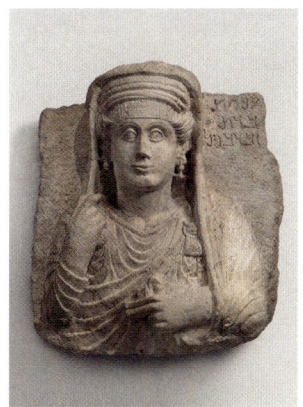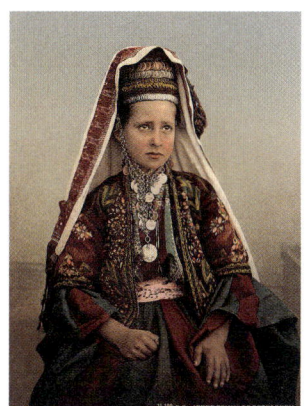

Figure of a seated goddess, Canaanite, 14th–13th Century BCE.
The Metropolitan Museum of Art, MMA 2003
Head of a female figure, Assyrian, 8th century BCE. The Metropolitan
Museum of Art, MMA 54.117.8

Limestone funerary, 150–200 CE.
The Metropolitan Museum of Art, MMA 02.29.5
Young Bethlehem Woman, late 19th century,
Library of Congress

The exclusion of named sources and oral history is part of a greater problem, already entrenched in the dominant systems of colonialism. Palestinian elders and researchers, such as myself, are often omitted from academic publications and excluded from museum spaces altogether. Palestinian dresses in the museum collections of North America and Europe have never been attributed to their maker – anywhere, ever.

However, institutions have recently begun engaging in decolonial practices. They are starting, imperfectly, to include indigenous knowledge that names culture keepers, so that future generations are able to trace who said what and when. As institutions begin to acknowledge the validity of indigenous research methods, Palestinian teachers and culture keepers should lead the charge by example. The passing of traditional knowledge, something that is done through *tatreez* classes and programmes, requires the teacher to become a storyteller and transmitter of oral history. The storyteller holds an important relationship to the story and students; if it is their own story, the story of an elder, artist or former teacher, the storyteller is accountable for preserving all sources of indigenous knowledge along the way – spoken, written or otherwise.

Indigenous research methods are founded on the principles of ethical storytelling that detail names, dates and places

as much as possible, creating accountability between the storyteller, story and listener. 'Ethical storytelling' is making sure that histories and familial accounts are transmitted with accountability at every stage, to prevent cultural appropriation or their distortion, which can lead to false accounts of historical and cultural practices. This allows indigenous knowledge to survive without the distortion of colonialist violence. It is how Palestinian embroidery has survived for centuries. Indigenous research methods reject the notion that subjectivity or personal accounts by named individuals invalidate research outcomes.

As *tatreez* teachers, our stewardship of *tatreez* history is conditional on our ability to preserve indigenous knowledge, name sources that include makers and artists, prevent cultural erasure and disable the appropriation of our arts and culture whenever possible. Without an ethos that respects *tatreez* as a centuries-old ceremony, any efforts to preserve it have failed.

The origins of *tatreez* are often discussed within the context of biblical history. This framing is so prevalent that even Palestinians reference it unknowingly; they characterise the *thobe*, our traditional dress, and elements of the ensemble with the Virgin Mary as its provenance. The connection between modern and ancient world history through dress was strengthened when the art of embroidery in Palestine, inclusive of practices, skills, knowledge and rituals, was inscribed in 2021 by UNESCO, referencing Canaanite civilisation as a traceable source of *tatreez*. Representations of ancient Canaanite figures during the 14th–13th centuries BCE were depicted with high, cylindrical and ornamented headdresses symbolising material wealth and social power – a prevalent regional style and social function that continued into the modern period. For centuries, scholars in dress history often focused only on visually similar depictions of headdresses to prove that these garments have ancient connections. However, a more comprehensive assessment reveals that not only have Palestinian styles evolved throughout the centuries, women have played a crucial role in transmitting *tatreez* through the ceremony of oral histories shared between mothers and daughters.

The *tatreez* ceremony has been so powerful that it has yielded aspects of material culture in remarkably consistent formats throughout the centuries. For instance, the presence of the tall headdress in territories between the Mediterranean Sea and Jordan River provides one way to understand its origins; however, the headdress did not always look the same, did not always incorporate coins and embroidery, and was not always worn by women alone. The main evidence of continuity in dress traditions in Palestine is in the social function of the headdress to symbolise wealth, identity and the family lineage of the wearer. As it relates to the *thobe*, continuity is demonstrated in the process of making and the embroidered patterns.

By the nineteenth century, Palestinian embroidery and dress was descriptive of a woman's regional identity, and this traditional attire captivated the Orientalist imaginations of American and European tourists to the 'Holy Land'. Travellers would return from Palestine and publish their personal observations, perpetuating an untrue depiction of Palestinians and the land, which would in turn bias the next generation of travellers. Palestine, for Europeans and Americans, was conceived as the centre of the known world. They believed that Palestine, its culture and ways of life, reflected that of a distant biblical past. From the mid-nineteenth century, with the liberalisation and decline of the Ottoman Empire, to the British Mandate period (1920–1948), tourism surged, attracting religious pilgrims, missionaries, archaeologists, scholars, historians, politicians, artists and travel enthusiasts. Palestine experienced rapid economic growth, with young Palestinian merchants travelling abroad seeking economic opportunities, as well as investment from European countries. Transportation improvements like rail lines and an airport were implemented, and a more robust tourist infrastructure increased access to places along the 'Holy Land' route. Such changes also altered society, with increased cultural exchange and mobility between foreigners and the indigenous population. In North America, Palestinian dresses collected on the 'Holy Land' path entered museums and private collections.

Visitors were primed by a genre of media depicting Palestine as a portal into the time of Jesus and other stories from the Bible. This 'Holy Land' phenomenon was an indulgence in the religious fantasies of Europeans and Americans: an opportunity to experience the presumably stagnated life and times of the Palestinian people who were erroneously assumed to still be living according to customs, costume and culture present at the time of the New Testament. Tourists were not encouraged to actually engage with local cultures, but rather to ignore the real identities of the indigenous people in favour of a biblical caricature, a type of Orientalism called Biblification. The combined impact of Orientalism, Biblification and the 'Holy Land' phenomenon ultimately altered the world's understanding of Palestine's actual history. Today, I often hear Palestinians themselves discussing this supposed biblical origination of *tatreez*. However, the Palmyrene funerary reliefs in Syria from the first to third centuries CE and the Qartaba Column in Mount Lebanon from the first century CE, for example, depict in great detail the high headdresses – adorned with circular medallions, embroideries and other embellishments, with long scarves draped over them. Thus, Palestinian embroidery and dressmaking traditions pre-date the biblical period and stem from a greater regional practice that was well established before the first century CE, while the earliest evidence of Christian material culture does not begin to appear until the second century CE.

Today, Palestinian women have continued to preserve their lives through each stitch and motif, a colourful, cross-stitched language decoded through dialogue between generations. In this same tradition, my mother, Feryal Abbasi-Ghnaim, passed her stories to my sisters and me, sharing the meanings, history and stories surrounding each *tatreez* pattern. Knowing that my sisters and I would be raised away from our homeland, my mother instilled the lessons of Palestinian embroidery in us from a young age. She would prepare our materials, make a pot of tea, and meet us in her studio every weekend where she laid out our supplies and taught us how to tell stories with our needle and thread. She taught us the ceremony of *tatreez* and the importance of the maker's voice in every stitch.

While the practice of *tatreez* has recently found a revival through workshops and stitching circles around the diaspora, the history itself remains endangered, owing to the omission of makers' and artists' names and elders' oral histories, and because of the violent legacy of colonialism that makes such information difficult to access in the community. In response, a new generation of *tatreez* teachers, storytellers and culture keepers have emerged with the potential to change the course of history, and a thirst to steward the art form ethically. It is my hope that *tatreez* as a ceremony – a greater practice that incorporates traditional techniques, oral history and elder knowledge – takes hold as the ethos for preserving Palestinian embroidery in the diaspora moving forward.

The ceremony of Palestinian embroidery transcends time, space and place. *Tatreez* is a portal that connects me with my ancestors. When I move my hands to the beat and rhythm of my needle and thread, I am performing the same movements as my grandmother and grandchild. Sometimes, I am transported to my mother's childhood home in Safad. Other times, I am transported to my childhood home in Oregon. Our hands have a muscle memory and wisdom that is beyond the current moment, but which includes it. Time is collapsed in *tatreez*; the past, present and future are one.

We trust that our *tatreez* stories will be told someday, when we become elders and ancestors. The *thobe* is a testament to our belonging in this world and to one another. In respect for the land of Palestine, we continue to stitch with *saber* (patience) and *sumud* (resilience) using *tatreez* patterns – old and new – honouring the collective memory of our elders. We continue to *tatreez* stories through time, fight for the day that justice will prevail, and hold close a deep and abiding hope that we will live long enough to see it.

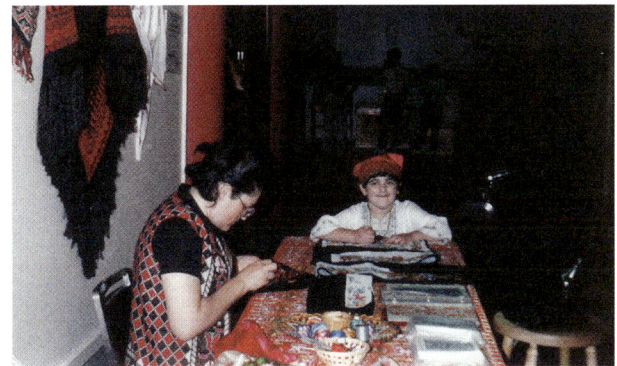

Wafa Ghnaim with her mother, Feryal Abbasi-Ghnaim, at a traditional arts festival in Massachusetts, sharing Palestinian embroidery history and techniques with the public (1989). All the garments worn in the image were embroidered and sewn by Wafa's mother. Photograph courtesy of the author

[1] The Arabic term *tatreez* (تطريز) is generally translated as embroidery, or the ornamentation of cloth. Contemporarily, *tatreez* has become synonymous with Palestinian embroidery and is used as such in this essay.

[2] *Al-Nakba* or *al-Nakba* (النكبة), is a proper noun with a definite article that means 'the catastrophe' in Arabic, and is defined as 'the ruinous establishment of Israel in Palestine, a chronicle of partition, conquest, and ethnic cleansing that forcibly displaced more than 750,000 Palestinians from their ancestral homes and depopulated hundreds of Palestinian villages between late 1947 and early 1949… [It] remains an ongoing and unrelenting ordeal… The 1948 al-Nakba has not only fragmented the territorial integrity of Palestine, constructing a self-identifying Jewish state on top of over seventy-seven percent of its conquered territory, but also ruptured and bifurcated Palestinian memory into "before" and "after". Put simply, the 1948 al-Nakba has produced an ongoing Nakba; the first is an event, the latter is an event, the latter is a structure and a continuous process.' Rabea Eghbariah, 'Toward Nakba as a Legal Concept' *Columbia Law Review*, vol. 124, no. 4, May 2024, pp. 889, 901.

[3] Rana Barakat, 'Writing/righting Palestine Studies: Settler colonialism, indigenous sovereignty and resisting the ghost(s) of history.' *Settler Colonial Studies*, 2017. DOI:10.10 80/2201473X.2017.1300048

[4] W. D. Mignolo and W. Nanibush, 'Thinking and Engaging with the Decolonial: A Conversation between Walter D. Mignolo and Wanda Nanibush', *Afterall: A Journal of Art, Context and Enquiry*, 45, 2018, p. 25. https://www.jstor.org/stable/26558001; polly walker, 'Indigenous Ceremonial Peacemaking', in *Advances in Public Policy and Administration*, 2019, chapter 15, p. 299.

[5] To learn more about the practice and ritual of *tatreez* in the context of storytelling and oral transmission, read Wafa Ghnaim, *Tatreez & Tea: Embroidery and Storytelling in the Palestinian Diaspora*, 2016 and 2018.

[6] Thoughts and contemplations shared on *tatreez* in this essay are inspired by the teachings of Shawn Wilson, *Research Is Ceremony: Indigenous Research Methods*, Halifax and Winnipeg : Fernwood Publishing, 2008. This particular quote is from page 60.

MATERIAL POWER: EMBROIDERY AND CONTEMPORAR
RACHEL DEDMAN

In 2023, I curated an exhibition titled *Material Power: Palestinian Embroidery*, for Kettle's Yard, Cambridge, and the Whitworth, Manchester, both in the UK. The exhibition explored more than a century of Palestinian embroidery, dress and material culture, and grew out of a decade of work and research on this subject.[1]

Material Power celebrated *tatreez* as a rich historical tradition, immersing the visitor in the complexities of the craft in the late nineteenth and early twentieth centuries, and the ways embroidery was shaped by changing social, political, colonial and economic forces in this period. The exhibition went on to explore the impact of the Nakba of 1948, charting the politicisation and commodification of embroidery in the decades following, reflecting on embroidery's powerful role in resistance, and examining the nature of its production today.

Bringing together historical garments, archival material and commissioned film, in conversation with the work of contemporary artists, *Material Power* foregrounded embroidery as a mode for unfolding an intimate, human history of Palestine. Majd Abdel Hamid, Mounira Al Solh, Aya Haidar, Mona Hatoum and Khalil Rabah draw in very different ways upon embroidery as a force for storytelling, a vessel for memory and a conduit for grief, and as a tradition with complex connotations in Palestine. Addressing themes of time, value, labour and land, their work conjures the political, personal and poetic power of fabric.

PEOPLE AND PLACE
Palestinian embroidery is rooted in people and place. Historically, a Palestinian *thobe* was embroidered by hand by a village woman, lovingly made over months and years. In its heyday in the nineteenth century, embroidery in Palestine sang as a shared visual language. A woman's dress – from its motifs and stitches to its textiles and colours – could be 'read' and interpreted by others: her *tatreez* reflected her identity and origins, the traditions of her village, her wealth and status, personality and character. Echoing the fundamental ways in which Palestinian embroidery is intimately connected to women's lives, artists use textiles and embroidery as forms of portraiture and placemaking.

Mounira Al Solh's embroidered hangings in her series titled *She, they, we all had it with the 99 names of the flower*, 2023, honour important feminist women from the Arab world. They include Fatema Mernissi (1940–2015), an influential Moroccan scholar, writer and sociologist whose work explored gender relations, civic society and women in Islam, and Azza Soliman (b.1966), a lawyer and human rights activist devoted to improving women's lives in Egypt. On simple cotton banners, Al Solh hand stitches the women's names and portraits alongside signs and symbols connected to their work and to the etymology of their first names. Azza means 'baby gazelle' in Arabic, so two hand-painted antelopes flank her portrait. The name Fatema is connected to the weaning of children from breast milk, so references to lactation inform the design of her hanging. In creating banners of the kind held aloft in a parade, Al Solh uses embroidery as a form of monument-making, celebrating and memorialising women whose stories deserve to be known beyond small circles.

Khalil Rabah's *Hide Geographies*, 2020, is a series of maps made from patchworks of Palestinian embroidery, taken from old dresses. Two of the maps carry the familiar outlines of the West Bank and Gaza, while another is of 'Area C', a zone which constitutes over 60 per cent of land in the West Bank, contains all illegal Israeli settlements other than those in East Jerusalem, and is more than 99 per cent off limits for Palestinians. The final map is hardest to identify: it's of Vila Nova Palestina, an unrecognised territory/camp just outside São Paulo, Brazil, which has been occupied by activists who built houses and forged a community for those who would otherwise be homeless. The inhabitants voted to name the project for Palestine.

Rabah's work draws attention to the fragmented, occupied, controlled nature of Palestinian land. Yet the series also unites disparate geographies, bringing places

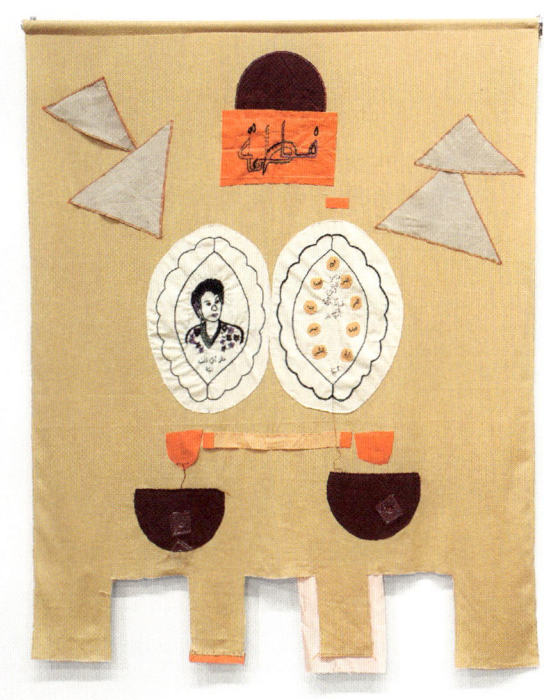 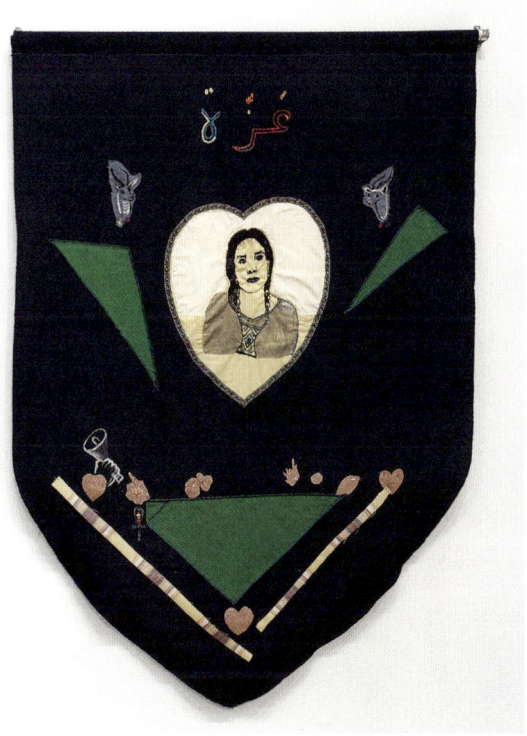

Mounira Al Solh, *Fatema Mernissi* and *Azza Soliman*, from the series *She, they, we all had it with the 99 names of the flower*, 2023. Embroidery on cloth. *Material Power: Palestinian Embroidery* installation at the Whitworth, The University of Manchester (2023). Photo: Michael Pollard

and people from across the world into the Palestinian fold. Embroidery here becomes an instrument of imagination, for the reconciliation of ruptured geography. Slung over a pole, however, the embroideries feel less cartographic and closer to frayed flags or animal skins, some hunting conquest. Associated with the bodies and labour of women, *tatreez* is domestic and individual, yet it has also become a dominant symbol of the nation, shorthand for Palestinian heritage. Rabah's works oscillate between passive hide and active map, an ambiguity that reflects the tension in which embroidery and its meaning exist.

Invoking the power of embroidery as a form of storytelling, Aya Haidar's *Safe Space* series, 2023, documents her mother's memories of growing up in Lebanon during the Civil War (1975–1990). From a distance the circular samplers seem bright and playful but, as one comes closer, the stories are dark – the stitched scenes depict the actions her family took to stay safe from everyday exposure to conflict. We see children sleeping underneath their beds in case the roof caves in at night, and taking shelter in a doorframe during an air raid. In another, the family go to the market wearing pan lids on their torsos, protecting themselves from snipers' shots with makeshift bulletproof vests. In another, the family's furniture is piled up in the living room, after Haidar's grandmother became fed up with repeatedly having to pick shattered glass from their broken windows out of the upholstery.

Although ostensibly about a specific conflict, Haidar's work represents the experiences of all those who live through war, and its deep effect on the fabric of domestic life. Her practice speaks to the ability of embroidery to bear witness, contain memory and tell stories, and to constitute a quiet form of resistance against such horrors.

In contrast to the vivid hues of *Safe Space*, Majd Abdel Hamid's white-on-white embroideries bleach *tatreez* of its colour and motif. The series is titled *Son this is a waste of time*, quoting the professional embroiderer who originally refused the artist's commission. Although a 'blank' embroidery requires the same amount of time and work as one with pattern, for the embroiderer the apparent lack of content and meaning rendered the job pointless. Why stitch it at all? The Nakba of 1948 broke the connection between embroidery and daily patterns of rural life in Palestine and catalysed the slow commodification of the craft. Abdel Hamid's works call attention to the connection between embroidery's symbolic meaning and the financial value of the labour it requires, reflecting on the contexts in which Palestinian women now embroider for pay.

For a long time now, Abdel Hamid has stitched these pieces himself, and embroidery has become a daily ritual whose restorative calm derives from its slowness. As the series has evolved, the works have morphed into things that mark time – maps or diary entries,

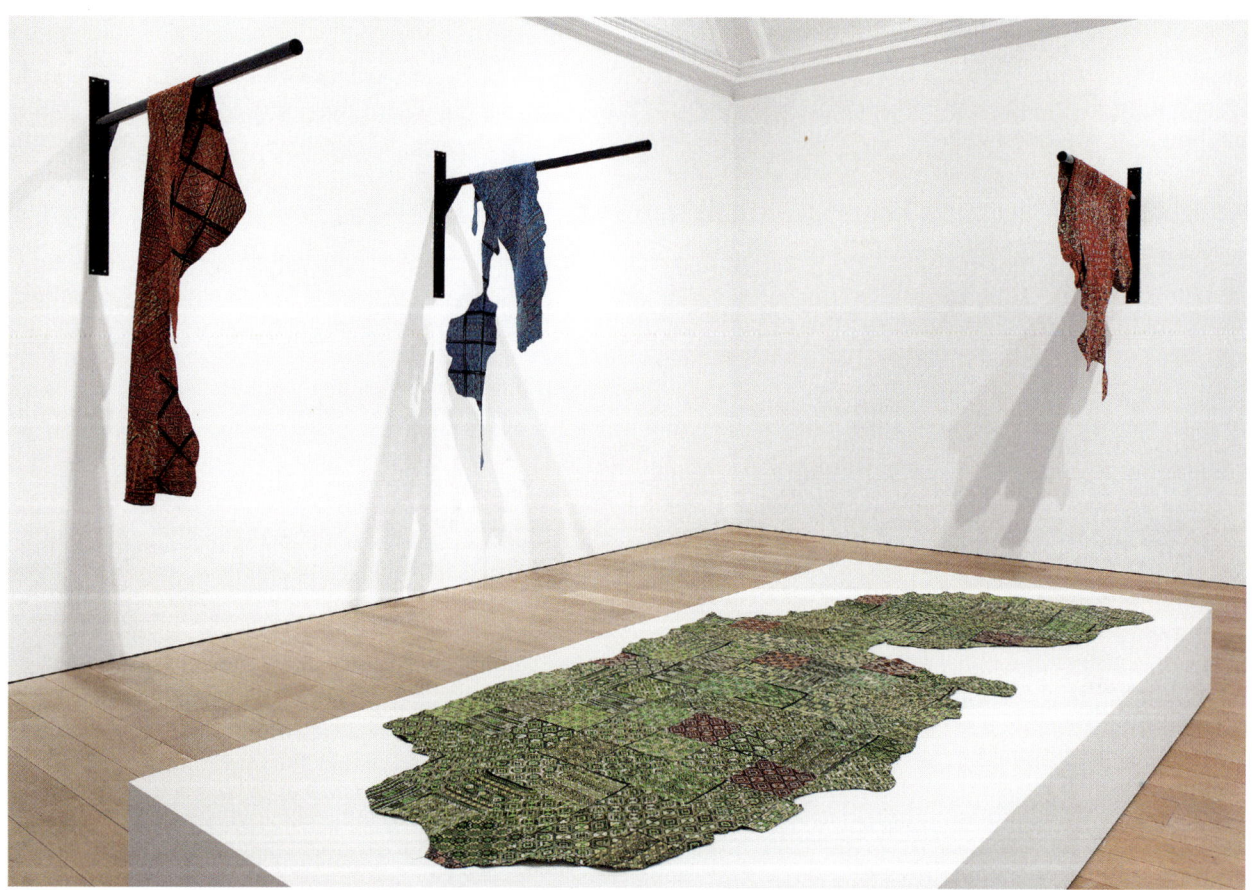

Khalil Rabah, *Hide Geographies*, 2020. Palestinian embroidery, fabric and metal installation. *Material Power: Palestinian Embroidery* installation at the Whitworth, The University of Manchester (2023). Photo: Michael Pollard

perhaps – with each individual panel titled for how long it took to stitch. Leaning into the extended temporality of embroidery, Abdel Hamid sees his practice as reactivating a traditional medium as a mode for engaging with the present. Particularly in its colourless form, embroidery is underscored as a timeless gesture, an accumulation of material, meditative and abstract.

HEARTACHE, RAVELLED AND UNRAVELLED

Another work by Abdel Hamid is inspired by a powerful tradition of mourning in Palestine. Historically, women who were widowed would express their grief by drenching their brightly embroidered dresses in indigo, turning them dark blue. Over time, as the garment was washed and exposed to the sun, the indigo would fade and the colourful thread would reappear, reflecting the slow easing of their grief.

The film *Muscle Memory* re-enacts this process of healing; the artist repeatedly scrubs with soap and a toothbrush a motif he has embroidered and dyed. Although some colour re-emerges in the process, the embroidery will never regain its original brilliance. Made in the aftermath of the Beirut explosion in 2020, in the context of ongoing occupation in Palestine and destruction of Gaza, *Muscle Memory* questions whether we ever heal from trauma, and embodies the arduousness of the grieving process.

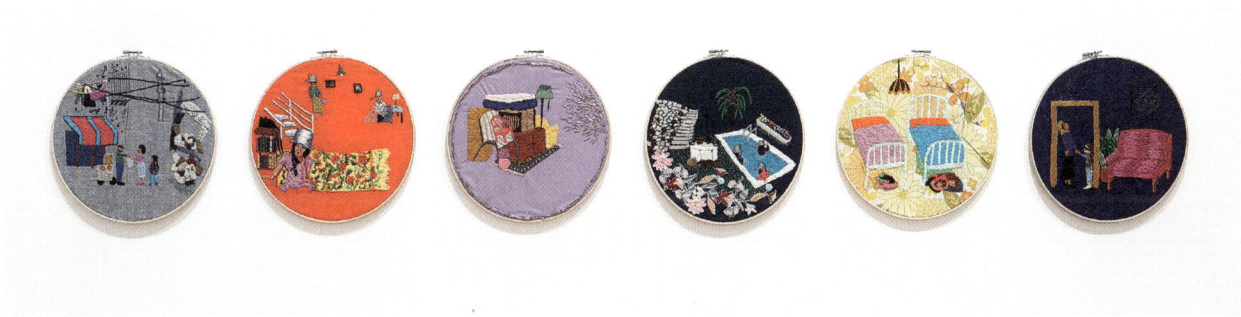

Aya Haidar, *Safe Space*, 2023. Embroidery on cotton, wooden hoops. *Material Power: Palestinian Embroidery* installation at the Whitworth, The University of Manchester (2023). Photo: Michael Pollard

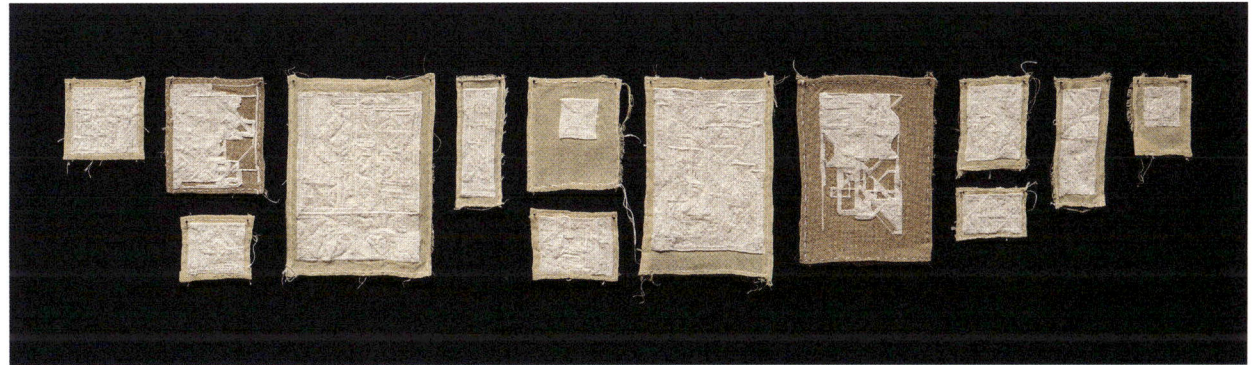

Majd Abdel Hamid, *Son this is a waste of time*, series of embroideries on waste canvas, 2015–23. *Material Power: Palestinian Embroidery* installation at the Whitworth, The University of Manchester (2023). Photo: Michael Pollard

In her installation work *Night Holes*, Mounira Al Solh intervenes on the familiar, mass-produced textiles that are common as bedcovers and blankets in family homes in Syria, Lebanon and Palestine. The artist has pierced their surface with small holes, the perimeters of which have been hemmed with thread. This gesture recalls her childhood memories of being frightened and unable to sleep during the Lebanese Civil War, when her mother would allow her to rend small tears in her pyjamas and sew them shut as a form of meditative distraction.

Suspended in the gallery like tents, under which visitors can walk, the hole-studded surface of the blankets might be read as bullet-pocked ceilings or skies full of stars. The shadows of these dance, too, on the floor at your feet.

Accompanied by recordings of children singing lullabies in many languages, and the sounds of sewing and knitting, the work speaks to the experience of refugees, and the modest comfort found in needle and thread. In its poetry and power, *Night Holes* addresses an idea at stake in all of *Material Power*, which is about how embroidery remains an articulate and meaningful medium for artists today, able to speak to the conditions of the present.

THE STRENGTH OF A THREAD

An individual thread appears vulnerable, but embroidery is ultimately a practice of reinforcement: stitching brings structure and weight to fabric, binding it more firmly to itself. Mona Hatoum's lattices of human hair reference the modernist language of the grid and the square, yet Hatoum

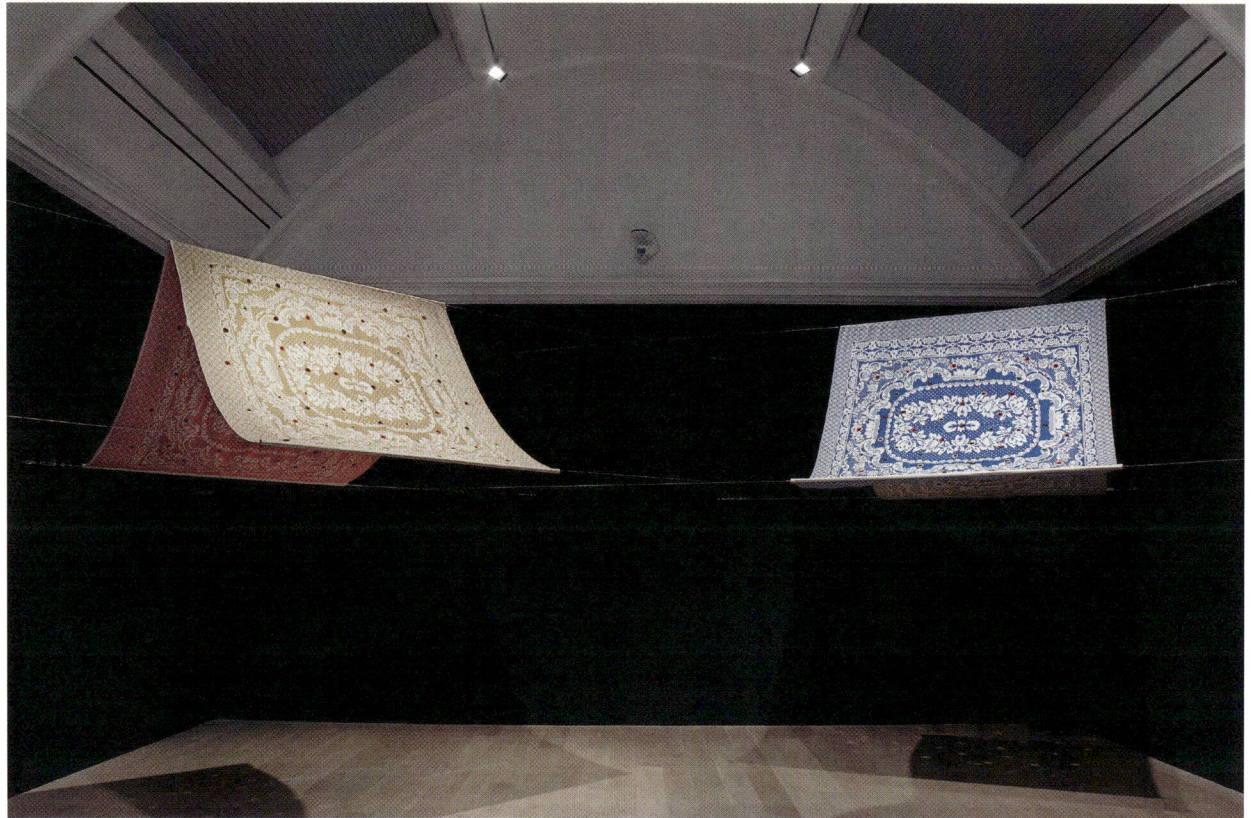

Mounira Al Solh, *Night Holes*, 2023. Embroidery on textile, audio installation. *Material Power: Palestinian Embroidery* installation at the Whitworth, The University of Manchester (2023). Photo: Michael Pollard

softens such structures (and the masculinity of their art-historical legacy) via the organic and sensual nature of her material. Although these *hair grid* works were made on small looms, they share with embroidery the intimacy of the handmade, and a connection to the corporeal – hair is an extension of the body, reflective of a changing life, its colour indicative of age. Human hair has remarkable tensile strength, yet a single strand feels weak, barely visible, like nothing. In Hatoum's woven, knotted form, however, hair embodies resilience, a refusal of dissolution.

Cloth is a universal human thing; we all have a relationship to it. Connected to the body, and the intimacy of the handmade, fabric is always familiar, and reflective of the changing emotional and political landscape of life. Whether it expresses commemoration or mourning, or embodies the political or the poetic, for contemporary artists in Palestine and beyond, embroidery is a force for critical reflection on the urgent ideas of our time.

[1] *Material Power: Palestinian Embroidery*, Kettle's Yard, 8 July–29 October 2023, and The Whitworth, 24 November 2023–7 April 2024. In 2014, the Palestinian Museum in Birzeit, West Bank, commissioned me to curate an exhibition of Palestinian embroidery in Beirut, where I was living and working as an independent curator. This exhibition, *At the Seams: A Political History of Palestinian Embroidery*, at Dar El-Nimer for Arts and Culture, Beirut, in 2016, birthed an expanded edition titled *Labour of Love: New Approaches to Palestinian Embroidery*, at the Palestinian Museum's main site in Birzeit in 2018. In between, I co-curated with Marie Muracciole an exhibition at Beirut Art Center, Beirut, titled *Unravelled*, 2016, bringing together contemporary artists from all over the world who utilise embroidery and textile in their work.

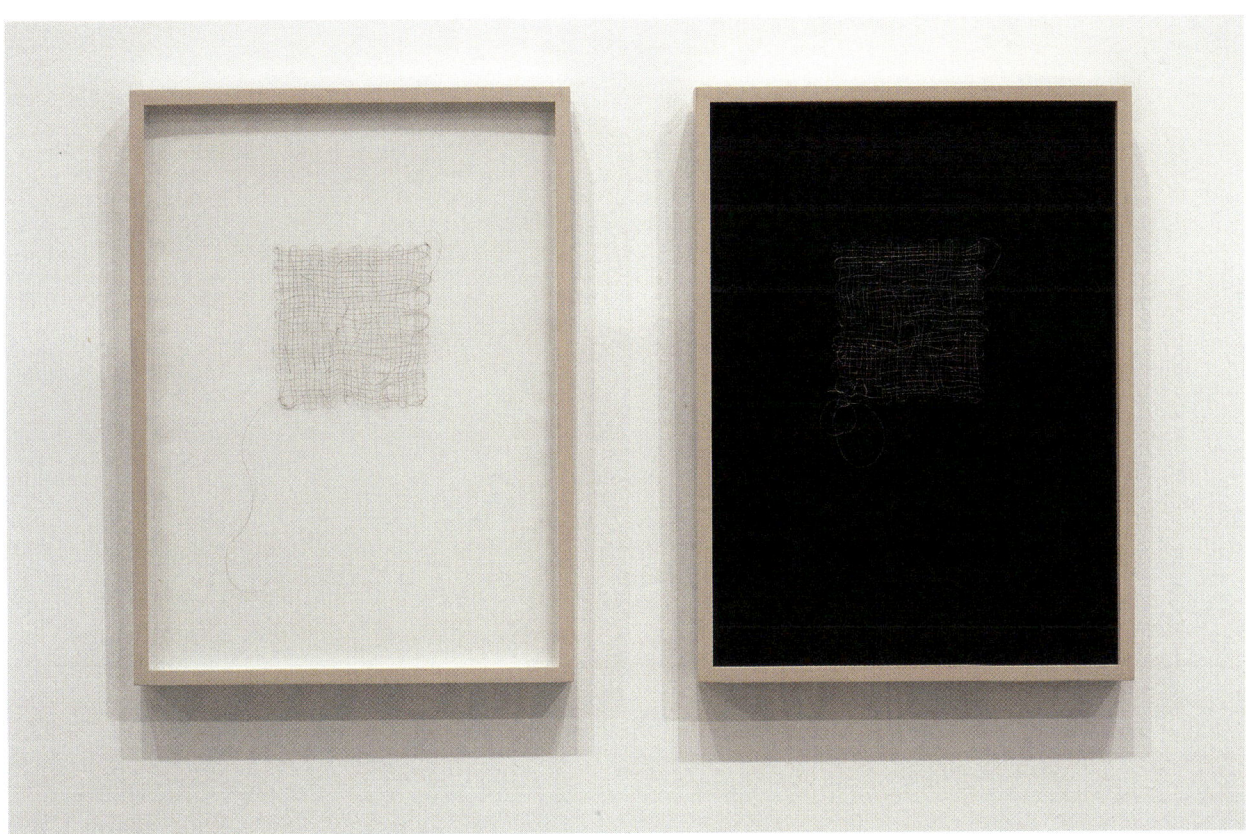

Mona Hatoum, *Untitled (hair grid with knots)* and *Untitled (grey hair grid with knots)*, 2001. Human hair, hair spray, card.
Material Power: Palestinian Embroidery installation at the Whitworth, The University of Manchester (2023). Photo: Michael Pollard

TAMAM AL AKHAL

SLIMAN MANSOUR

NABIL ANANI

CHRIS GAZALEH

MOHAMMED ALHAJ

SAMAH SHIHADI

HAZEM HARB

LARISSA SANSOUR

SARY ZANANIRI

SAMA ALSHAIBI

STEVE SABELLA

AMER SHOMALI

JOANNA BARAKAT

MAHA DAYA

MAJD ABDEL HAMID

SAMAR HEJAZI

JORDAN NASSAR

DEBORAH MULLINS

LIANE AL GHUSAIN

KIKI SALEM

MONTHER JAWABREH

SAMAR HUSSAINI

NAJAT EL-TAJI EL-KHAIRY

NAQSH COLLECTIVE

TAMAM AL AKHAL

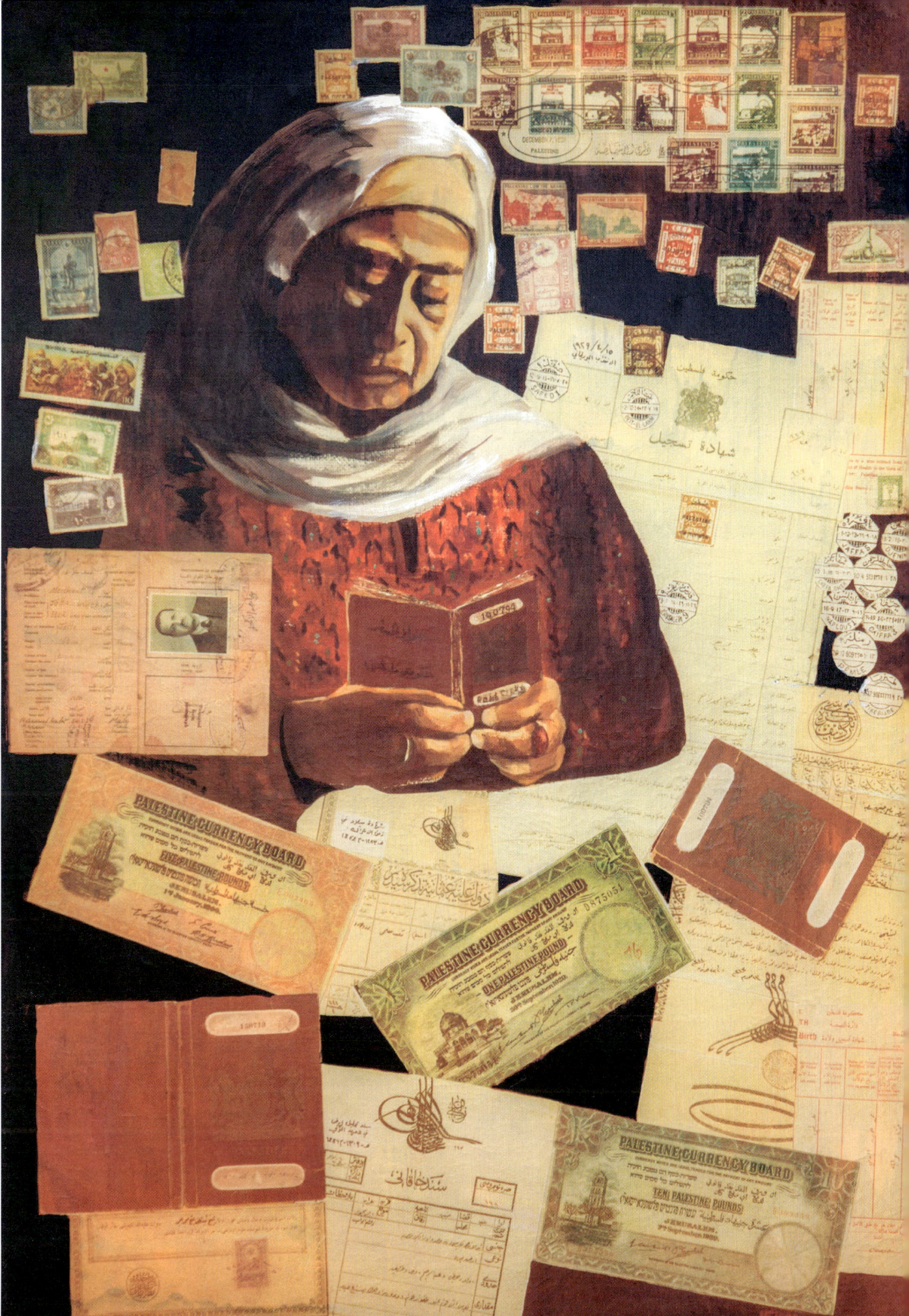

In the middle of the night on 28 April 1948, Zionist forces expelled thirteen-year-old Tamam Al Akhal and her family from their home in Jaffa, Palestine, where the artist was born and raised. Her family were among the hundreds of thousands of Palestinians escaping the violent Zionist colonisation of their homeland. While she was growing up in a Palestinian refugee camp in Lebanon, Al Akhal's talent and passion for drawing and painting created the opportunity for her to pursue a formal education in painting at the Higher Institute of Fine Arts in Cairo, Egypt, from 1953 to 1957.

She met her late husband, artist Ismail Shammout, in Cairo, where they were selected to participate in Cairo's Palestine Exhibition in 1954. In 1959 – after several attempts over a six-year courtship – they married. Al Akhal relates that, on their engagement day, 'Ismail came to me with a beautifully embroidered but old dress from the city of Majdal. He asked me to wear it for the occasion, as was his family's tradition. Ismail explained the significance of this dress and its embroidery.'

The women in Al Akhal's family and in her community wore Western-style clothing. However, in the Palestinian refugee camp in Lebanon, Al Akhal encountered women wearing embroidered dresses, as she depicted in her painting *Mothers of Heroes* (1974), where she used broad brushstrokes to suggest panels of elaborate embroidery on the dresses.

Al Akhal learned the significance behind Palestinian embroidery motifs when visiting the Palestinian Women's Union embroidery workshop in Gaza, run by social activist Yusra Berberi. Al Akhal's interest in Palestinian embroidery grew once she understood embroidery as a representation of Palestinian identity. Al Akhal states, 'I felt filled with hope and joy as I discovered our roots and who we are.'

Al Akhal began painting embroidery to explore this profound connection to her culture. She represented various regions of Palestine, depicting bridal head-dresses from Bethlehem and Ramallah, embroidery from Akka and Haifa in Northern Palestine, and the burqa and embroidered dress panels from Al-Naqab

and Bir al-Sabe' in Southern Palestine. Al Akhal explains 'These paintings resonated with me, and I was genuinely stunned that people recognised and responded well to them. As for the artist Ismail Shammout, not one painting emerged from between his fingers of a Palestinian woman without being preceded by embroidery, which increased her beauty, joy, and a sense of nation.' To Shammout, the Palestinian woman in her embroidered dress, or *thobe*, was a personification of Palestine, the motherland.

The driving force behind both Al Akhal's and Shammout's artwork was to promote the liberation of Palestine. Through painting, they captured and recorded the beauty of Palestine and its people while processing their ongoing trauma along with the collective experiences of the Nakba and Israel's violent oppression and occupation of Palestine. The couple played a significant role in the Liberation Art movement during the 1960s. In 1965, Shammout led the PLO's Department of Arts and National Culture in Beirut, and by 1969 he had become the secretary-general of the Union of Arab Artists. Tamam Al Akhal headed the Art and Heritage section of the Department of Information and Culture. Along with other artists, they constructed a visual representation of Palestinian national identity that would appeal to and inspire a Palestinian audience. They also organised travelling exhibitions that introduced the rest of the world to Palestinian embroidery.

Al Akhal painted portraits of women wearing traditional embroidered dresses. One such woman was Um Elias, a woman from Ramallah she met in Beirut. Fascinated by Um Elias's story, Al Akhal painted a life-size portrait capturing her story in brushstrokes. 'But a question remained: what was the meaning behind all the things her eyes carried? The fingers on her hands were like the fingers of a man, even with her soft and innocent face. So, I drew her and her beautiful dress and left her eyes towards the end. The answer to my question was in her eyes.' In the painting, later renamed *Mother*, Al Akhal paints the heartache in the eyes of this strong woman, whose husband abandoned her and their children for another woman in Gaza. Aside from her dress, Um Elias's hands resting on her lap reveal a farmer's life spent ploughing, planting, harvesting, and selling her crops to raise her seven children.

Al Akhal won the Golden Sail at Kuwait's 1987 Biennial featuring Arab art, for her painting *Al Talhamiya*, also known as *Our Lady Mary* or *The Virgin*. The painting comprises seven sections depicting the Annunciation as described in the Qur'an. The painting's largest and most prominent figure is the seated Virgin Mary gently holding baby Jesus in her lap. She wears the traditional Bethlehem *malak* dress with a *shatweh* headdress adorned with a halo. The colours of the striped silk panels of the dress, the ornate *tahriri* couching embroidery, and the embroidered short-sleeved *taksiri* jacket all indicate the historic Bethlehem dress. Jesus is featured in other sections as a grown man, wearing the striped Palestinian *kumbaz* and white headdress. By dressing him in Palestinian clothes, Al Akhal reminds the viewer that Jesus is a Palestinian born in Bethlehem.

The Virgin Mary is the primary subject in another painting by Al Akhal. In 1997 the mayor of Nazareth, Ramiz Jaraisy, invited Al Akhal and Shammout to visit the city. While in Nazareth, they witnessed preparations for Pope John Paul II's visit to the Church of the Annunciation and the Spring of the Virgin Mary, or Mary's Well. During renovations of the church and surrounding landmarks, restorers discovered an ancient underground spring that served as the primary water source for Palestinian villagers. Israel's refusal to allow UNESCO to claim it as a Palestinian archaeological site, along with its failed attempt to create a conflict between Christian and Muslim communities, inspired the painting *Nazareth Above All* (1999). Al Akhal describes painting 'the Virgin in her white dress preaching near the spring and all the women dressed in the embroidered dress of that region. Inscribed is the verse from the Noble Qur'an that made Jesus speak while he was in the cradle as a boy.' Nazareth's embroidery on the *jellayeh*, an open dress or long jacket worn over trousers, is delicately painted, imparting regional and temporal significance. More importantly to Al Akhal, it confirms the event as a phenomenon that happened on Palestinian land to Palestinian people.

In 2014, Al Akhal painted *The Document*, a portrait featuring actress Juliet Awwad dressed in a Palestinian embroidered *thobe* and, with a heavy heart, looking down at a passport. The *thobe* is the identity marker of where the woman and documents are from and what connects them. Spread over the background and foreground of the painting are bank notes, postage stamps and passports, including ones belonging to Al Akhal's father, brother and uncle. These artefacts from the previous century prove Palestine's collective cultural and internationally recognised national identity, pre-dating the invention of the State of Israel in 1948.

When Al Akhal painted headdresses and regional embroidery, she showcased an ancestral Palestinian cultural practice. Instead of employing the familiar symbol of the imagined rural woman, Al Akhal introduces the viewer to Um Elias, a portrait of a resilient Palestinian woman seated in front of her, sharing her tragic story. Al Akhal's depictions of the Virgin Mary create a link to time and place with the Virgin dressed in Bethlehem embroidery to reclaim her Palestinian origins. By celebrating Palestine's cultural roots, her paintings transform symbolic and nationalist iconography as she records and responds to Israeli settler colonialism and the mass dispossession of the Palestinian people.

Along with incorporating Palestinian embroidery in many of her paintings, Tamam Al Akhal wore embroidered dresses from her collection to her exhibitions and events, embodying her Palestinian heritage, culture and beauty. To Al Akhal, embroidery and other cultural traditions are evidence of Palestinian indigeneity and part of who Palestinians are as a people inhabiting their native land for millennia.

Previous spread: Tamam Al Akhal, *The Document*, 2014. Oil on canvas

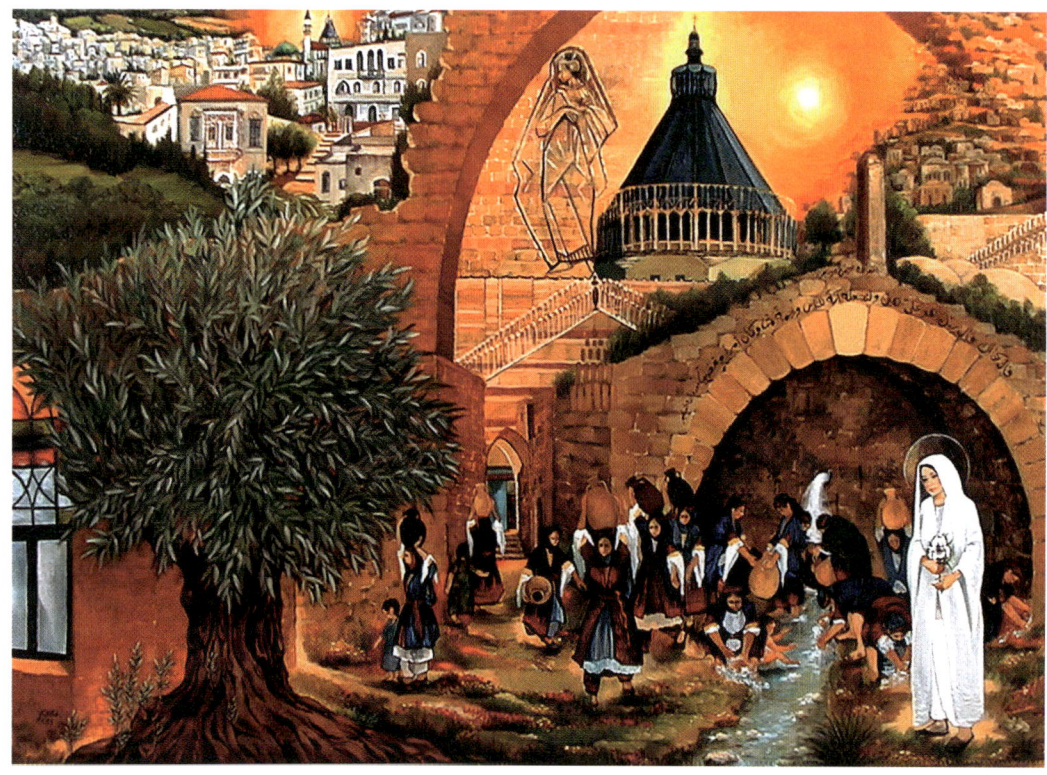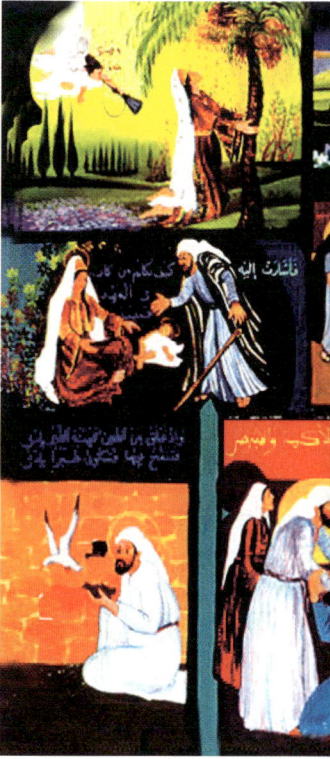

Tamam Al Akhal, *Nazareth Above All*, 1999. Oil on canvas

Tamam Al Akhal, *Al Talhamiya* (other titles include *Our Lady Mary* and *The Virgin*), 1987. Oil on canvas

Tamam Al Akhal, *The Samed Workshops*, 1978. Oil on canvas, 50 x 60 cm

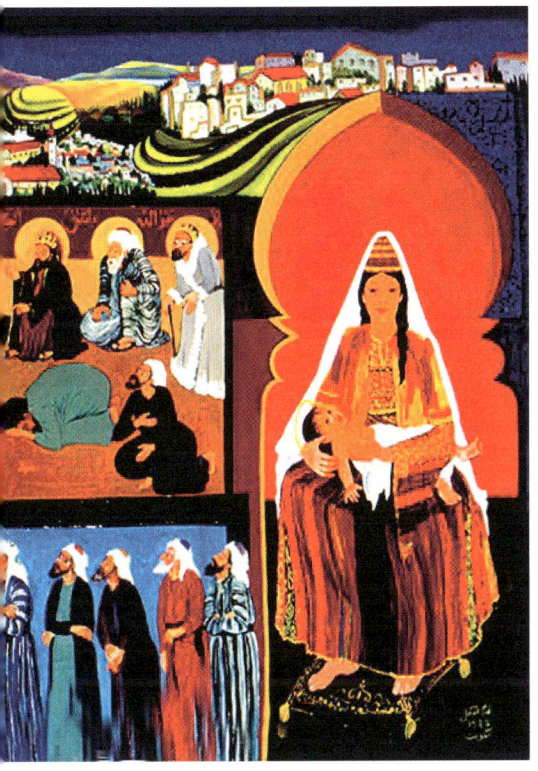

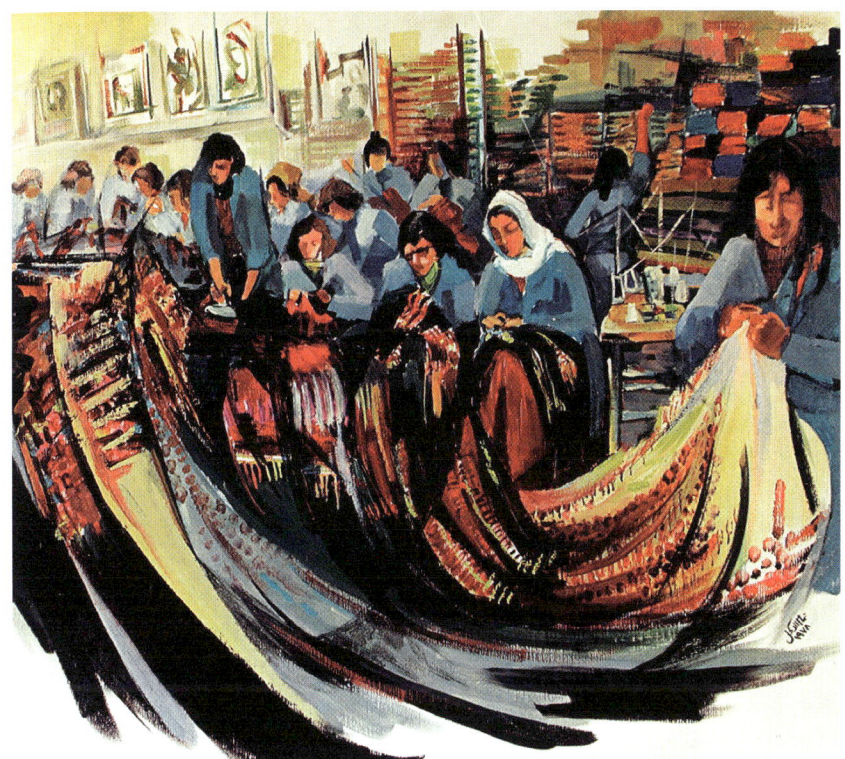

Tamam Al Akhal, *Mother*, 1969. Oil on canvas. Pergamon Museum, Berlin

Right: Tamam Al Akhal, *Mothers of Heroes*, 1974. Oil on canvas, 48 x 118 cm

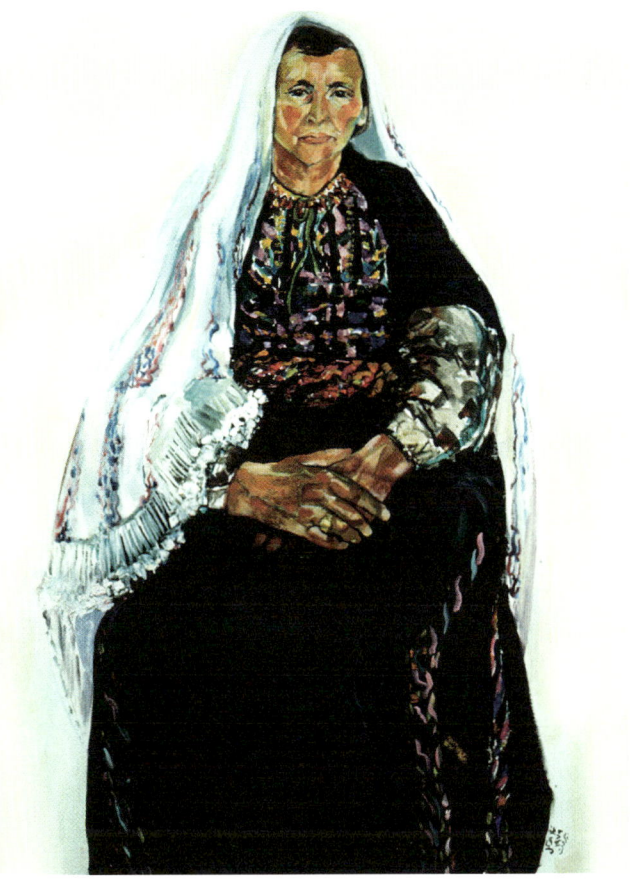

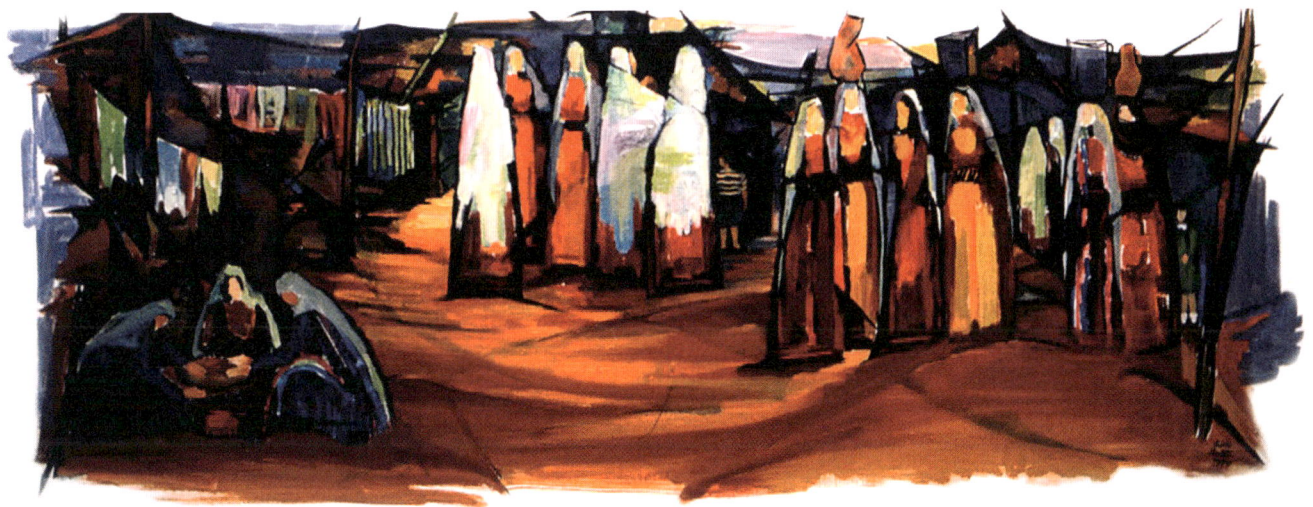

SLIMAN MANSOUR

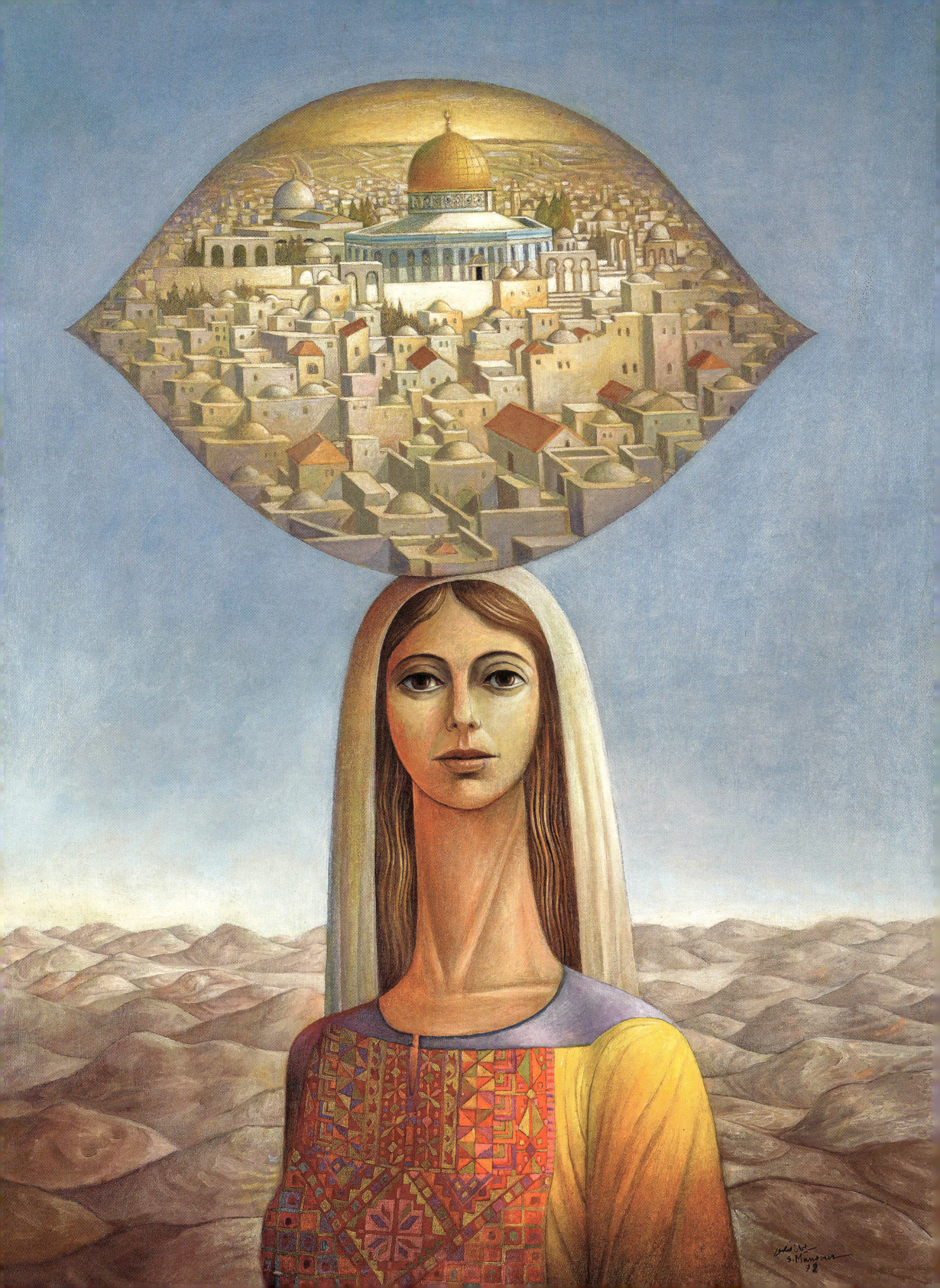

According to artist Sliman Mansour, 'Palestinian embroidery is an essential element in defining Palestinian identity because of its beauty, authenticity and roots that extend into the region's culture and ancient history.' Mansour's paintings, illustrations, posters and political cartoons were pivotal in shaping Palestinian visual language, especially through his use of symbols and iconography, such as Palestinian embroidery.

Despite Israel's forced restrictions and censorship regarding any nationalist imagery in artwork, Mansour and other Palestinian artists found innovative ways to express their cultural and national identity. They used idyllic landscapes, village and farm scenes with women in embroidered dresses as a metaphor for Palestine as a nation. This imagery evoked an emotional response in Palestinians that their colonisers could not relate to or understand.

In response to Israel's refusal to allow Mansour and other Palestinian artists to create an art union, Mansour co-founded the League of Palestinian Artists in 1972, organising exhibitions and events over the decades. These activities led to the foundation of the Al Wasiti Art Centre and archive in Jerusalem in 1992 and its opening in 1994. Mansour's prolific career as an artist, arts advocate and educator revolved around addressing Palestinian liberation, encapsulating the Palestinian experience, and preserving Palestinian culture and heritage.

Mansour was born in 1947 in Birzeit, Palestine. His painting career started in the late 1960s after he had studied at Bezalel Academy of the Arts in Jerusalem. In the 1970s, Mansour began to glorify the working class in his paintings. His work explores themes of loss, displacement and resistance, along with Palestinian identity, rootedness and connection to the land, often using the imagery of the farmer or villager woman in her embroidered dress and embroidery motifs. Mansour explains, 'Embroidery became more and more a dominant part in the paintings. We concentrated on women because women represent homeland, represent Palestine.' Mansour portrays women as beautiful, proud, energetic and, most importantly, Palestinian.

'How can we show that she is Palestinian? With the embroidery, with the dress. It's all symbolic. It's not as you see it, and that's it. There's always a meaning behind it. People ask me why I paint women's hands big. I want to show that this woman, although she is beautiful, she's a working woman who works on the land and picks olives. It's important to show Palestine as a working woman, not someone sitting in her living room.'

To Mansour, painting village landscapes and women in embroidered dresses was a way of reclaiming the narrative of Palestinian heritage and folklore. He celebrates the strength and beauty of Palestinian women, appreciating their contribution to society, family and land. As an act of preservation, Mansour's paintings of women in embroidered dresses record the different distinguishable styles from villages and regions in Palestine before the Nakba. After the mass displacement of Palestinian refugees into camps in 1948, the distinct regional embroidery motifs were replaced with mixed embroidery and a new dress style emerged. He says,

'To paint a woman from Gaza, I cared what kind of embroidery they have in Gaza, in the Hebron area, in Ramallah. Now it's mixed. It's like the language. Some years ago, if somebody from Bethlehem spoke, you could tell this dialect was from Bethlehem. Now, you can't tell. For example, many people come from everywhere to live in Ramallah. So, after one or two generations, the children speak with the same accent wherever they are from. Embroidery is the same. They lost their accent.'

In 1982, the Inaash al-Usra Society in Al-Bireh invited Mansour and his close friend and colleague Nabil Anani to be part of a research committee working on the book *Palestinian Folkloric Costume*. They worked alongside Dr Sharif Kanaana, Dr Abdul Latif Al Barghouthi, Nabil 'Alqam, Omar Hamdan and Walid Rabi'. Mansour and Anani contributed to the book's photography and layout design, and to a chapter on historic Palestinian embroidery motifs, including around 101 motifs. This chapter led to their coauthoring the well-known *Guide to the Art of Palestinian Embroidery* (1984).

Mansour recalls their enthusiasm towards continuing to source and copy motifs. 'We copied around 700 motifs, and I'm sure if we went on doing it, it would be double. We wanted to record as much as we can. Here is an example of how our folk art needs a lot of study and time spent documenting.' Mansour takes great pride in having created a book that made motifs accessible to Palestinians. He stresses the urgency and importance of taking the time to research and document Palestinian art, including folk art, created before 1948. He has also worked with other organisations, such as Sunbula in Jerusalem, to redesign patterns for embroidery.

New themes and imagery relating to resistance emerged in Palestinian art during the Intifada of the 1980s and 1990s. At the same time the Israeli military arrested artists, confiscated artwork, and shut down exhibitions. In 1987, Mansour, Nabil Anani, Vera Tamari and Tayseer Barakat formed the New Visions Movement, boycotting Israeli art materials and using only what they could find or produce locally in Palestine.

Aside from removing the physical constraints of traditional canvas and paint, the artists could express social, cultural and political concepts through their choice of medium. Mansour gravitated towards mud, a literal representation of the land, that he mixed with straw and dyed with henna and pigment powders. This medium was also personal to Mansour, connecting him to his memories of his grandmother. Mansour's mud works allowed for experimentation with form and style. When dry, the mud would crack, taking on another level of meaning, such as the fragmentation of the land and his feelings about ageing.

To Mansour, incorporating the embroidery in a mud work is like excavating an archaeological site and discovering the embroidery as evidence of Palestine. Mansour uses the names of Palestinian villages as titles for many of his abstract mud works containing embroidery motifs and his figurative paintings of women in embroidered dresses. His focus is on destroyed villages, to document and preserve them through his work. The village names

elicit a melancholic, nostalgic response for a Palestinian audience where emotions are tied to memory and place, even in those who have never visited the village or were born after its destruction.

Generations of Palestinian artists, designers and creatives continue to use and be inspired by the imagery in Mansour's artwork. Sliman Mansour's remarkable career as an artist, arts supporter and educator reflects his commitment to Palestinian liberation, expressing the Palestinian experience and safeguarding Palestinian culture and heritage. He is an advocate for preserving Palestinian embroidery, recognising its cultural and political significance. Palestinian embroidery is as integral to Mansour's artwork as his artwork is to cementing embroidery's symbolic representation of Palestinian identity.

Previous spread: Sliman Mansour, *Daughter of Jerusalem* or *Al Quds*, 1978. Oil on canvas, 121 x 92 cm. Ramzi and Saeda Dalloul Art Foundation

Sliman Mansour, *The Village Awakens*, 1987. Oil on canvas, 107 x 97 cm

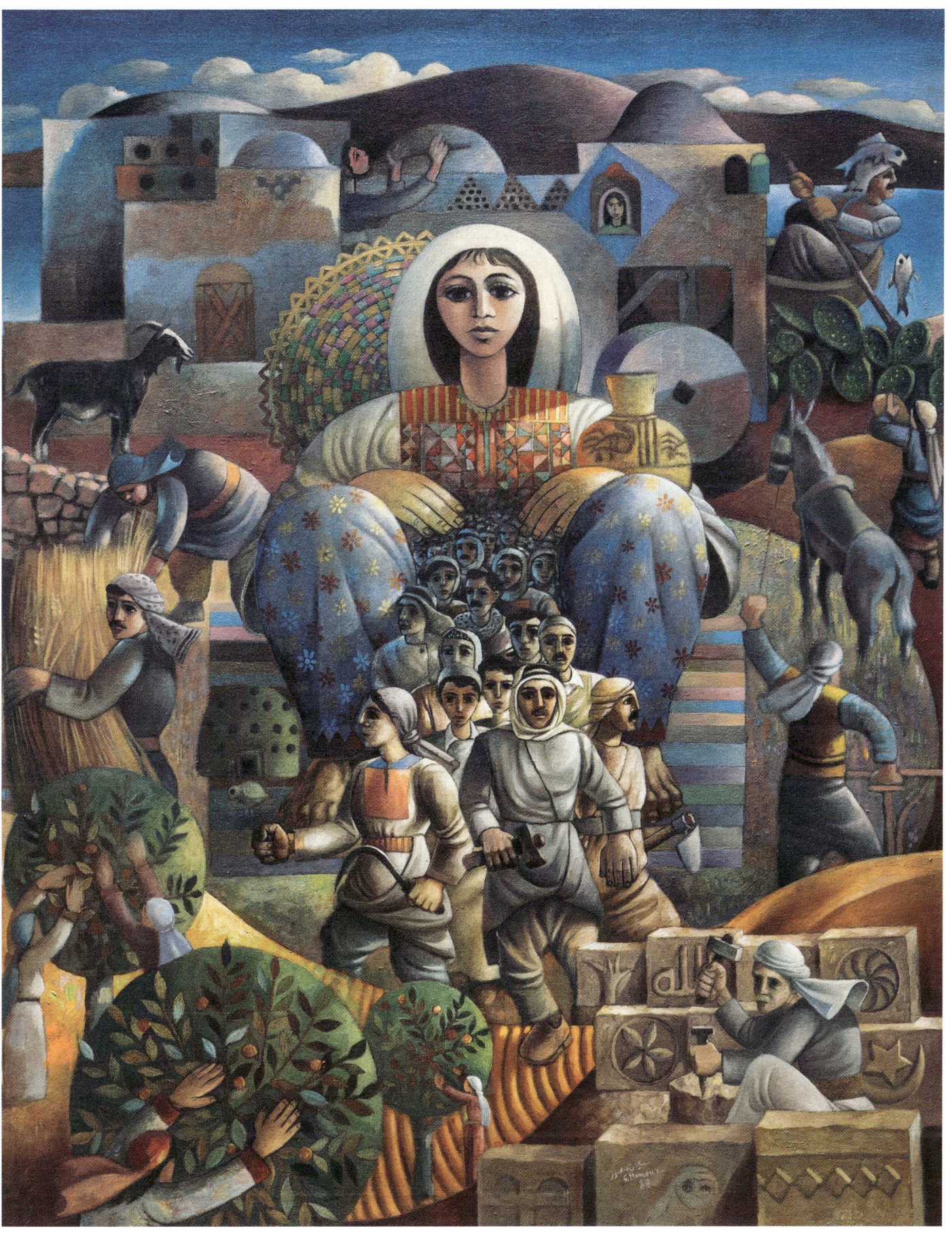

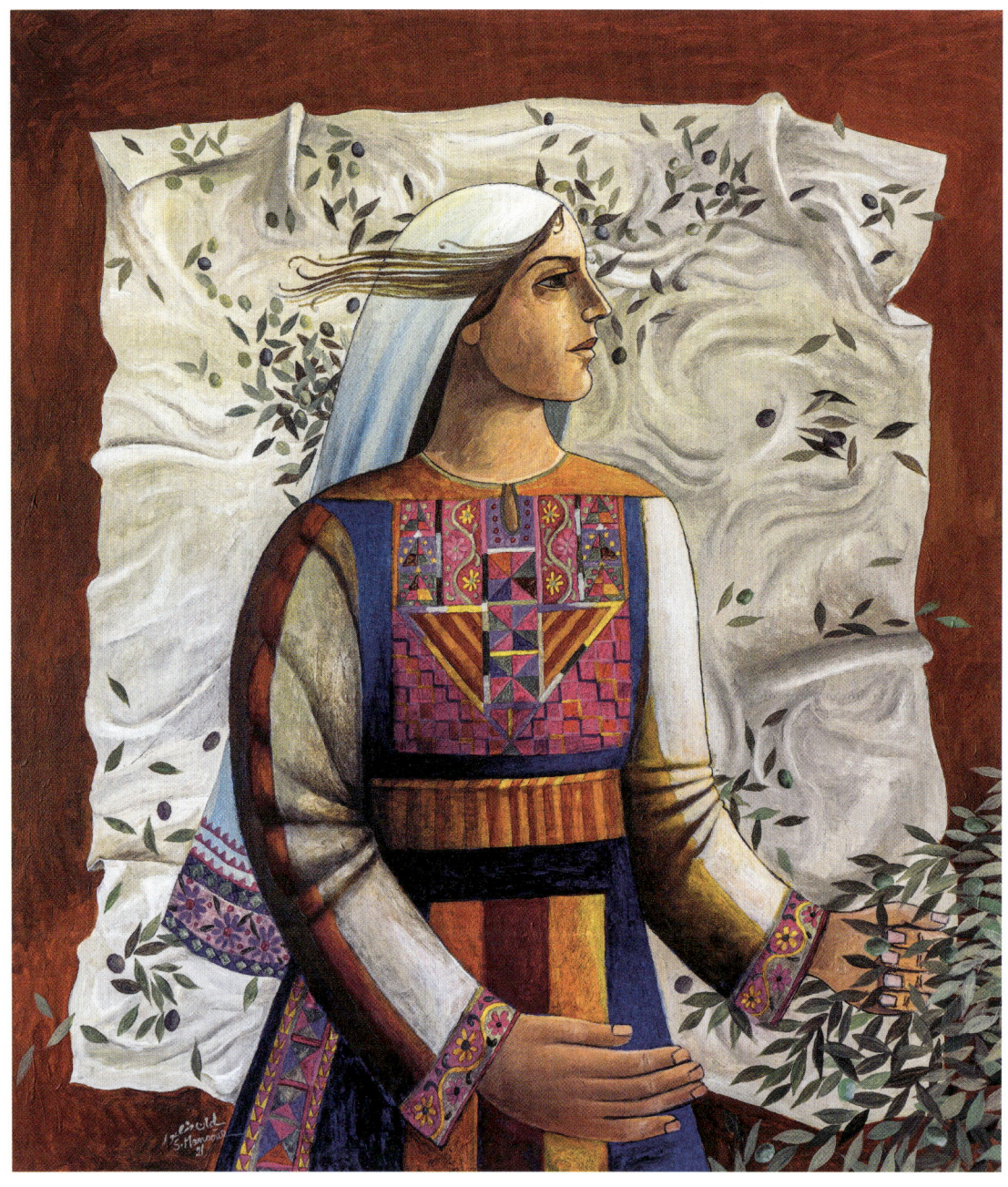

Sliman Mansour, *Olive Picking*, 2021. Oil on canvas

Right: Sliman Mansour, *Desert Tune* or *Sad Tunes*, 1977. Oil on canvas, 87 x 90 cm. Barjeel Art Foundation, Sharjah

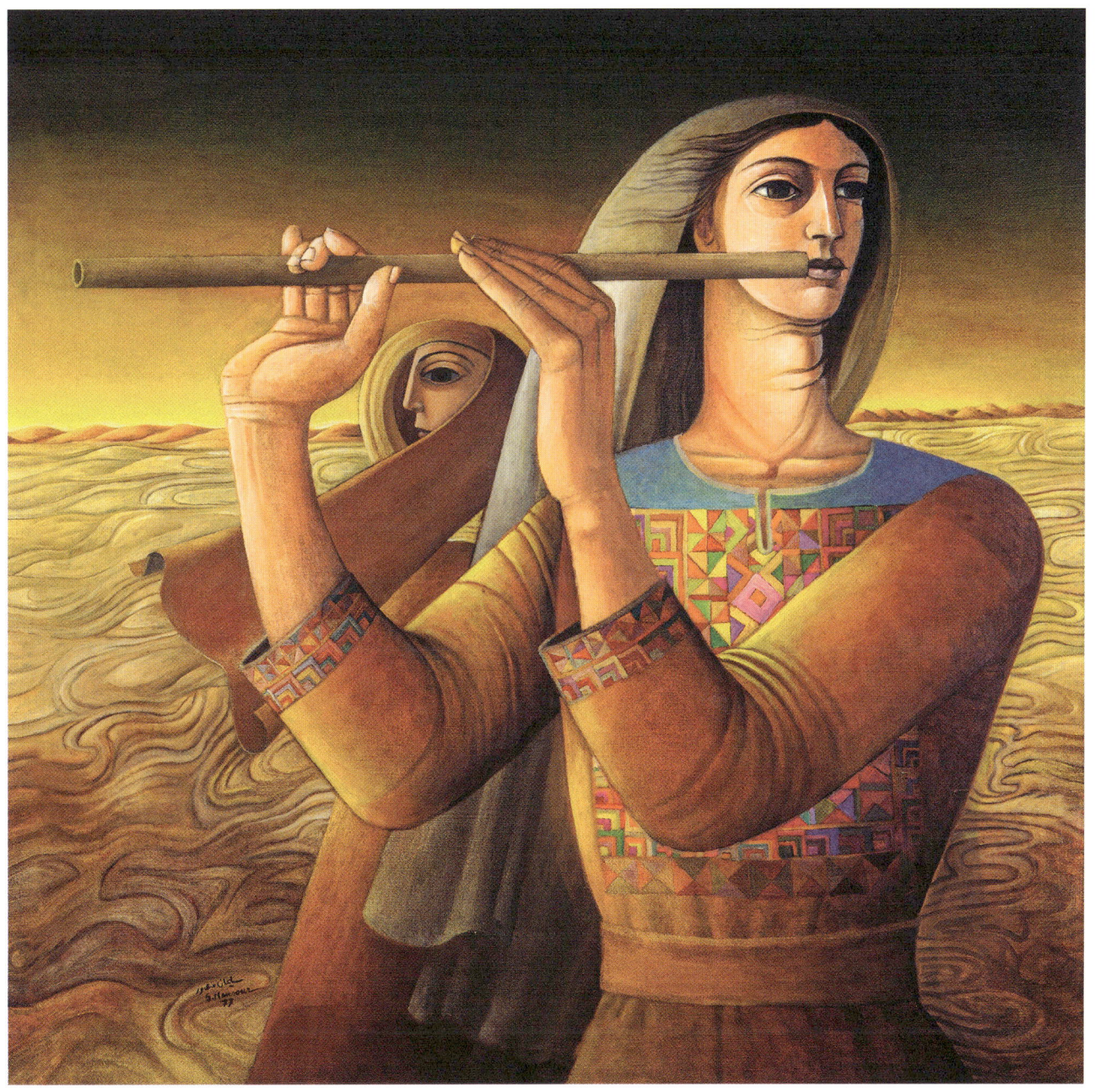

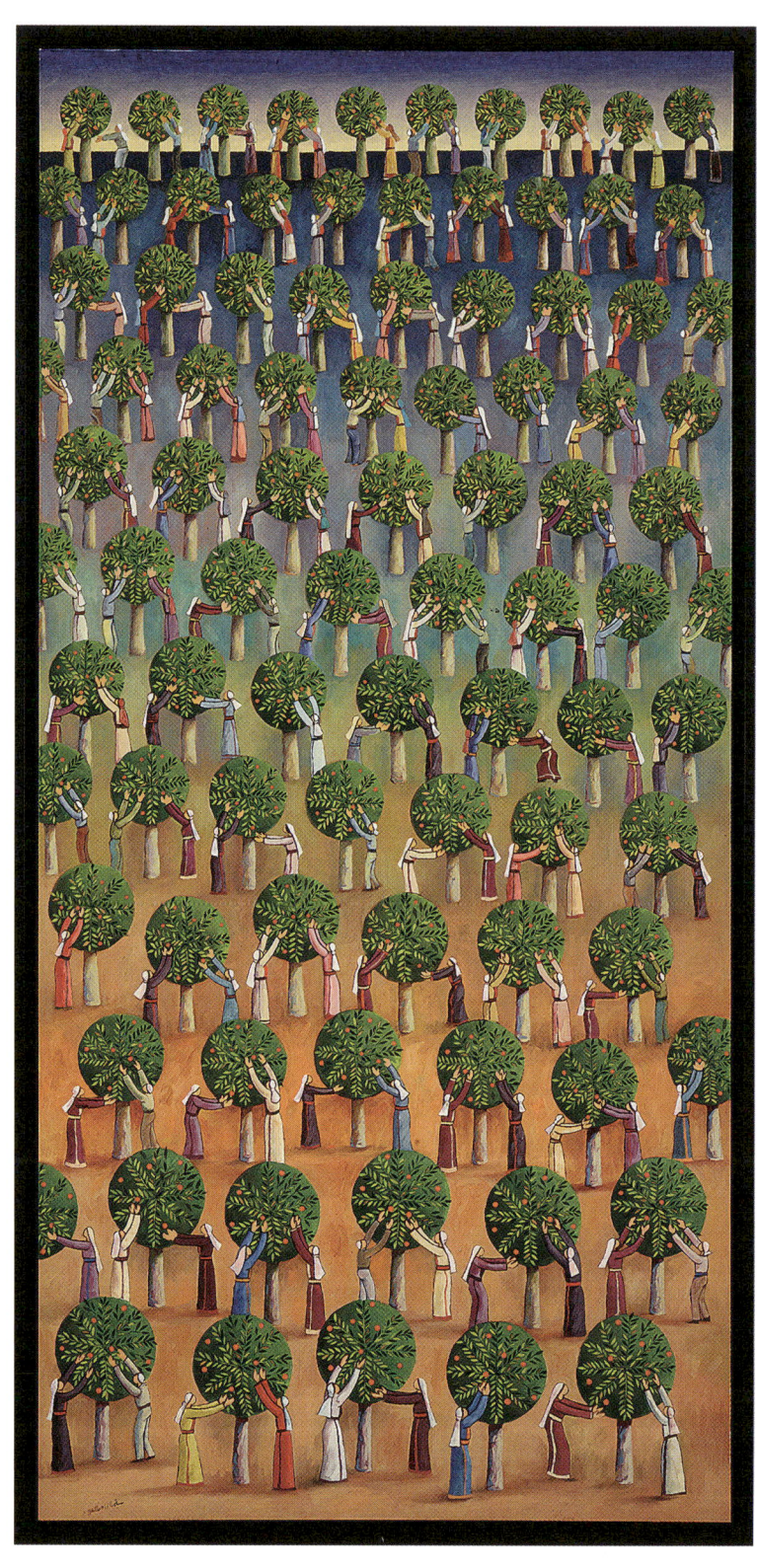

Sliman Mansour, *Orange Fields*, 2013. Oil on canvas, 226 x 329.5 cm.
Ramzi and Saeda Dalloul Art Foundation

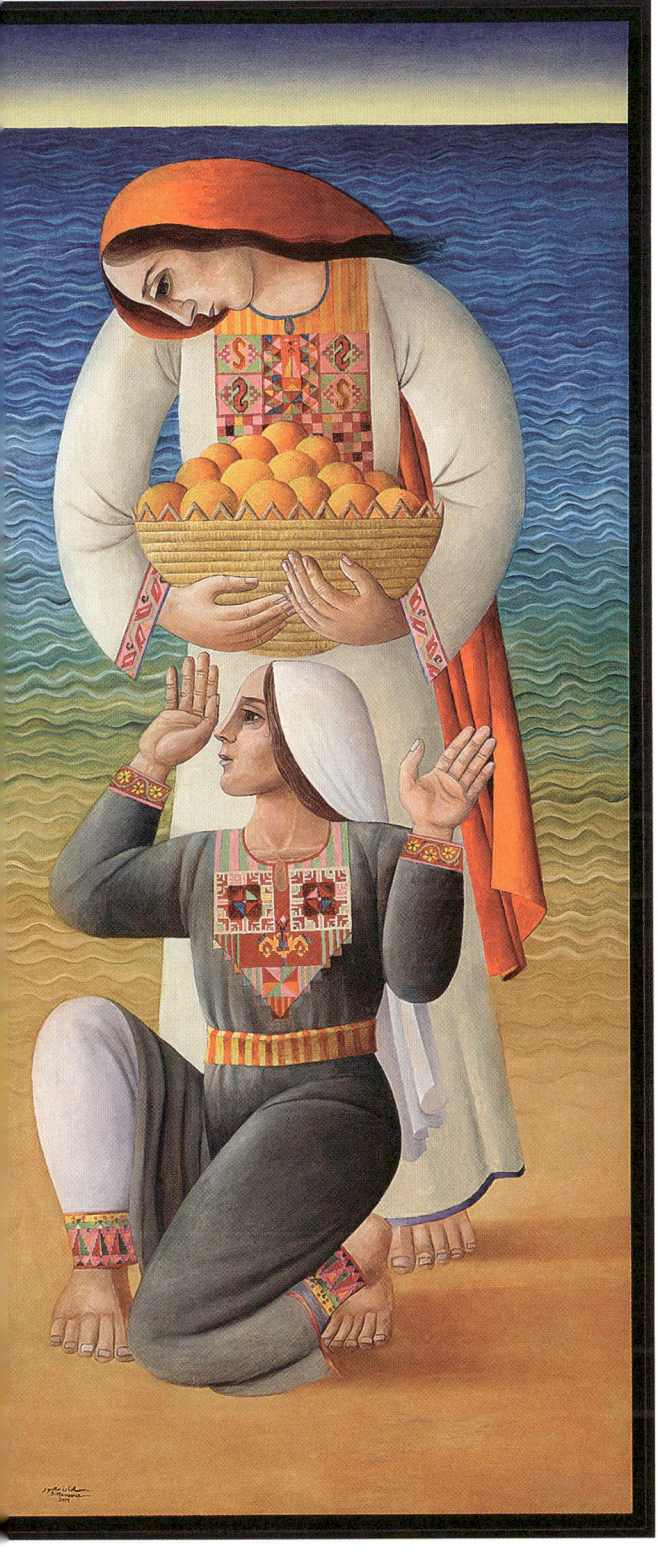

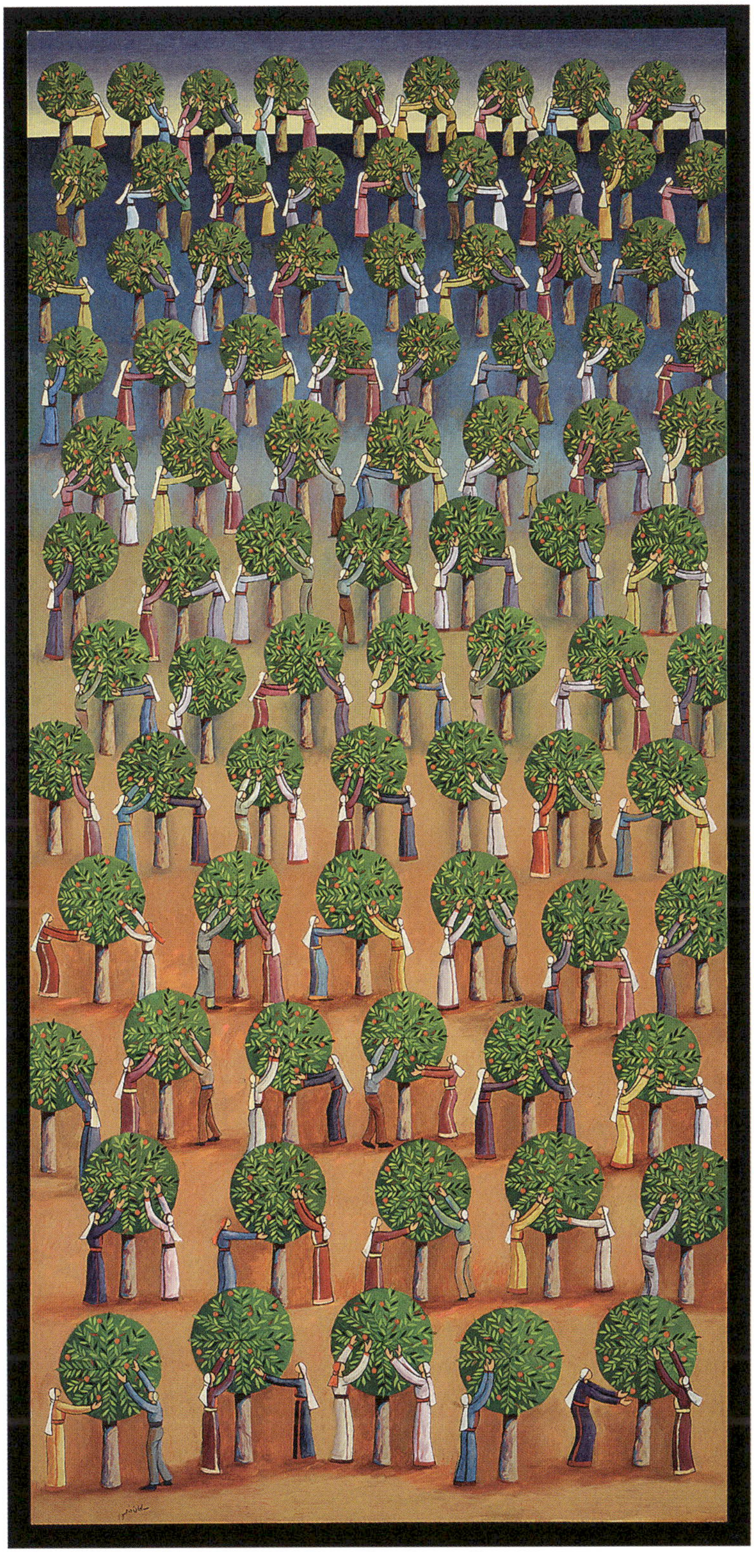

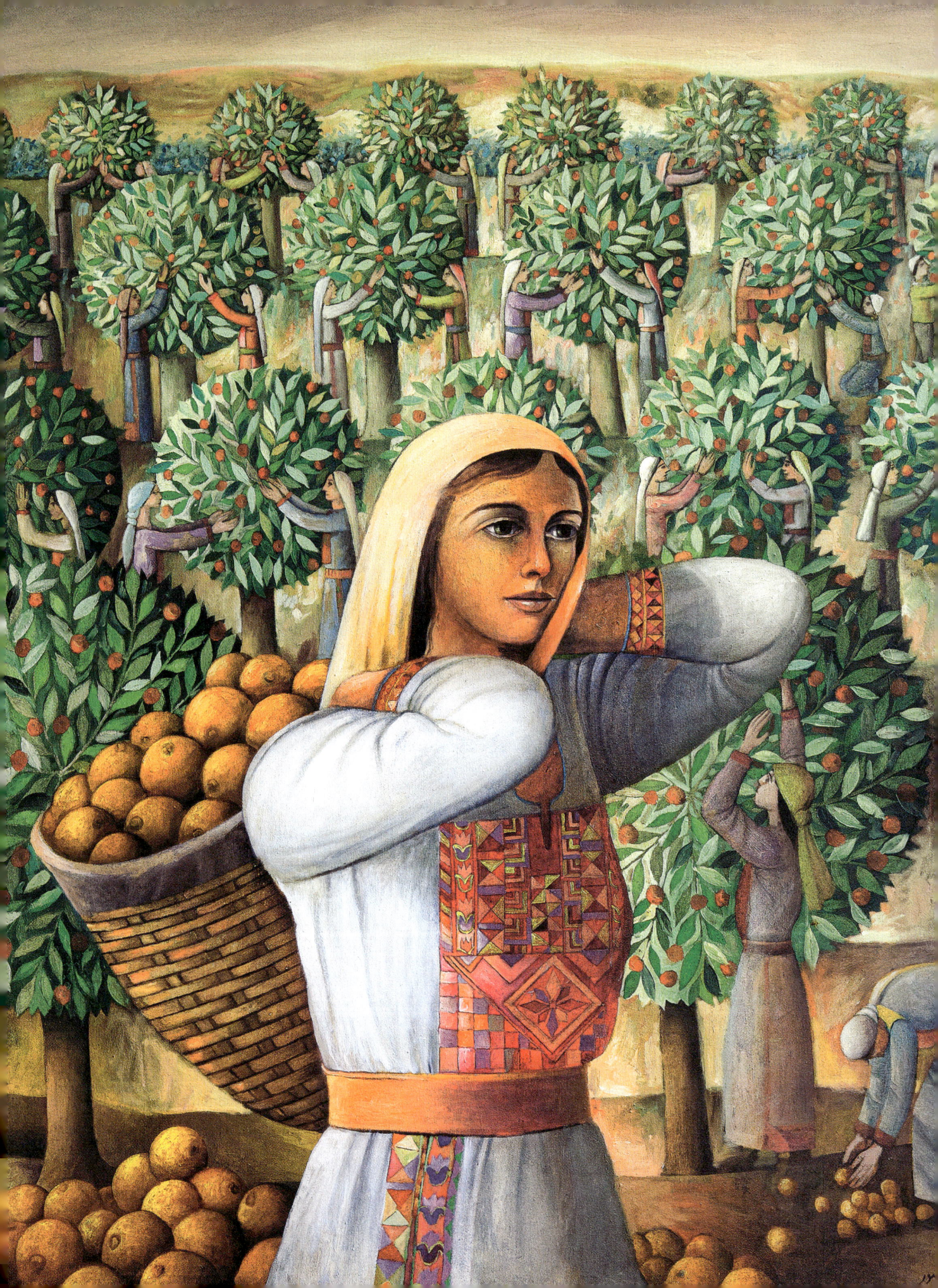

Sliman Mansour, *Yaffa*, 1979. Oil on canvas

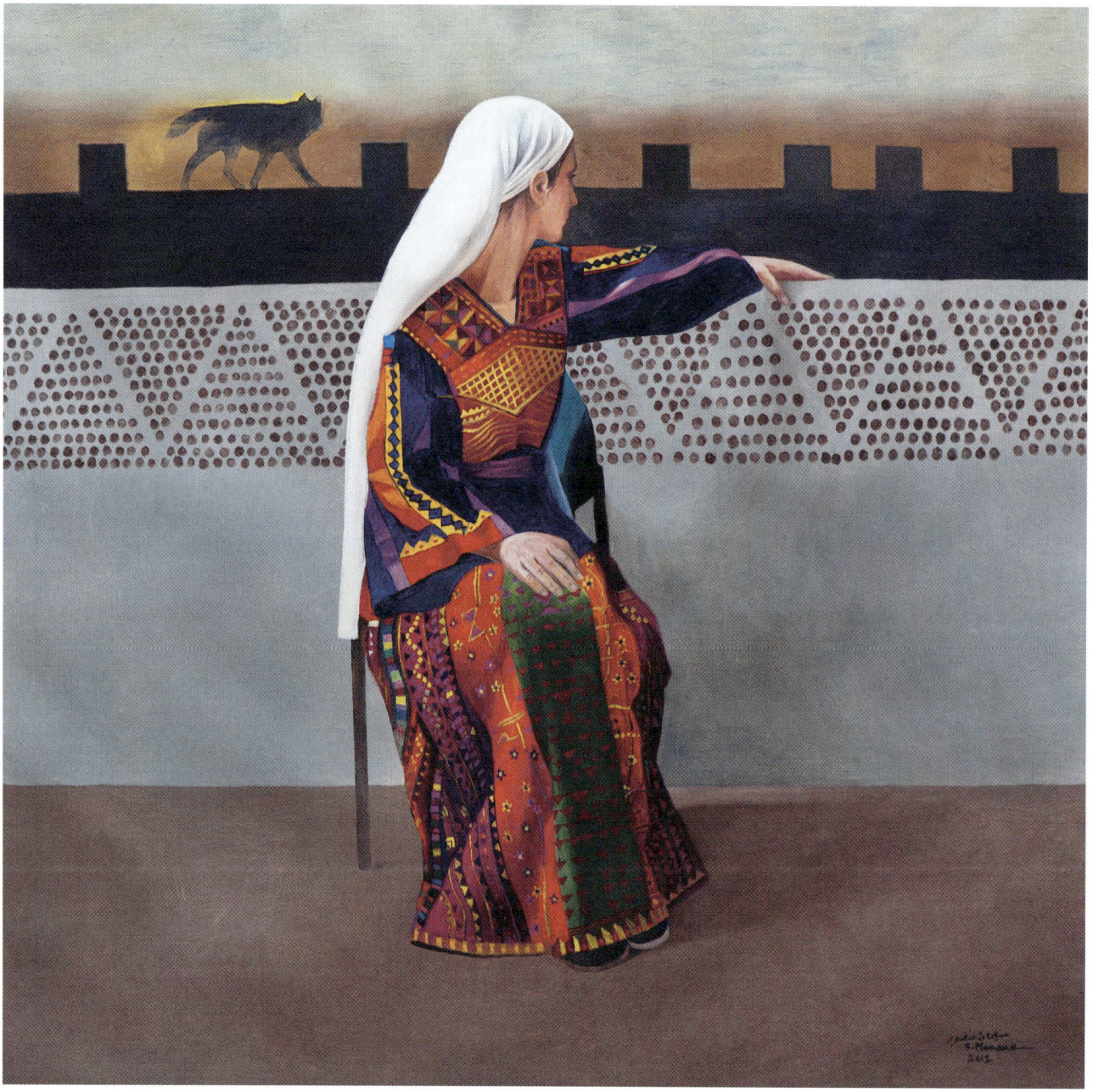

Sliman Mansour, *Jerusalem Rooftop*, 2012. Oil on canvas

Right: Sliman Mansour, *Presence of Absence*, 2019. Acrylic and mud on wood

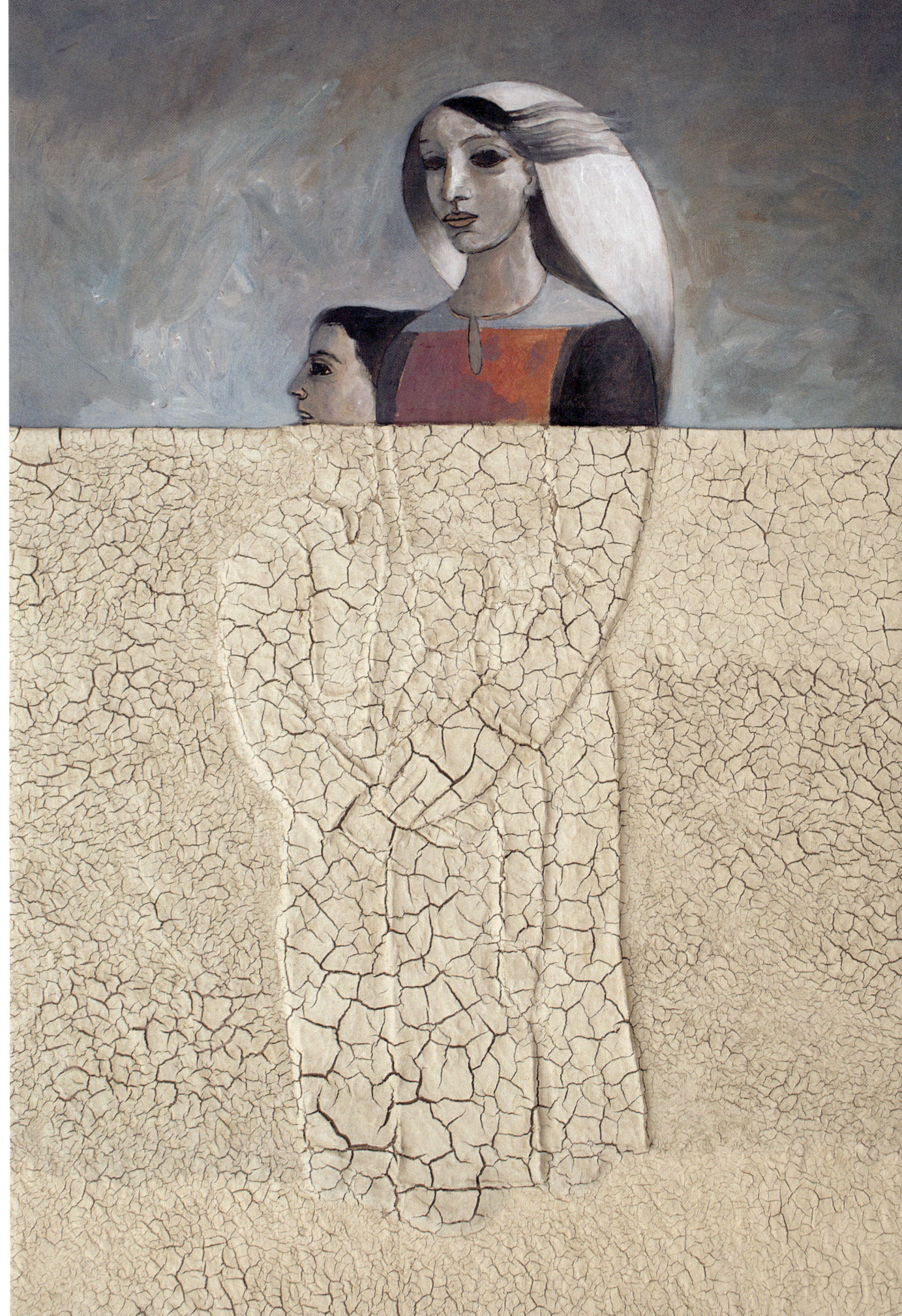

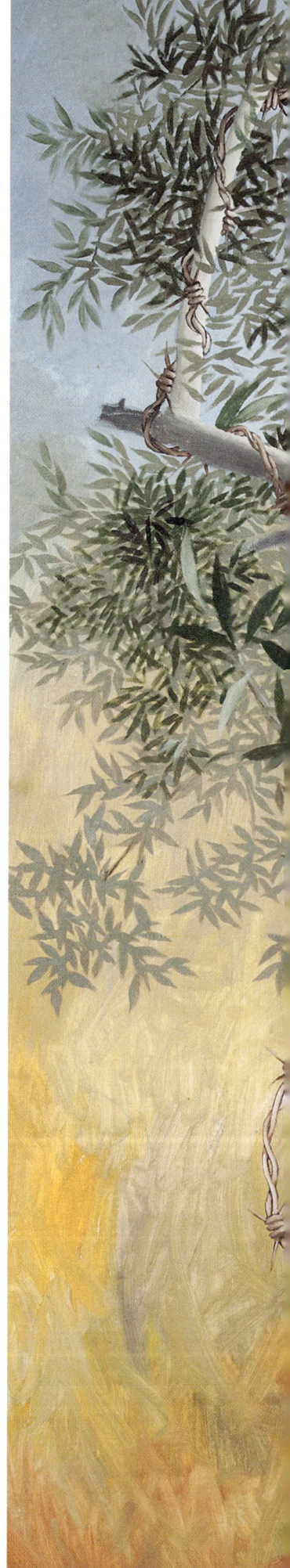

Sliman Mansour, *Quiet Morning*, 2009. Oil on canvas, 114 x 110 cm.
Barjeel Art Foundation, Sharjah

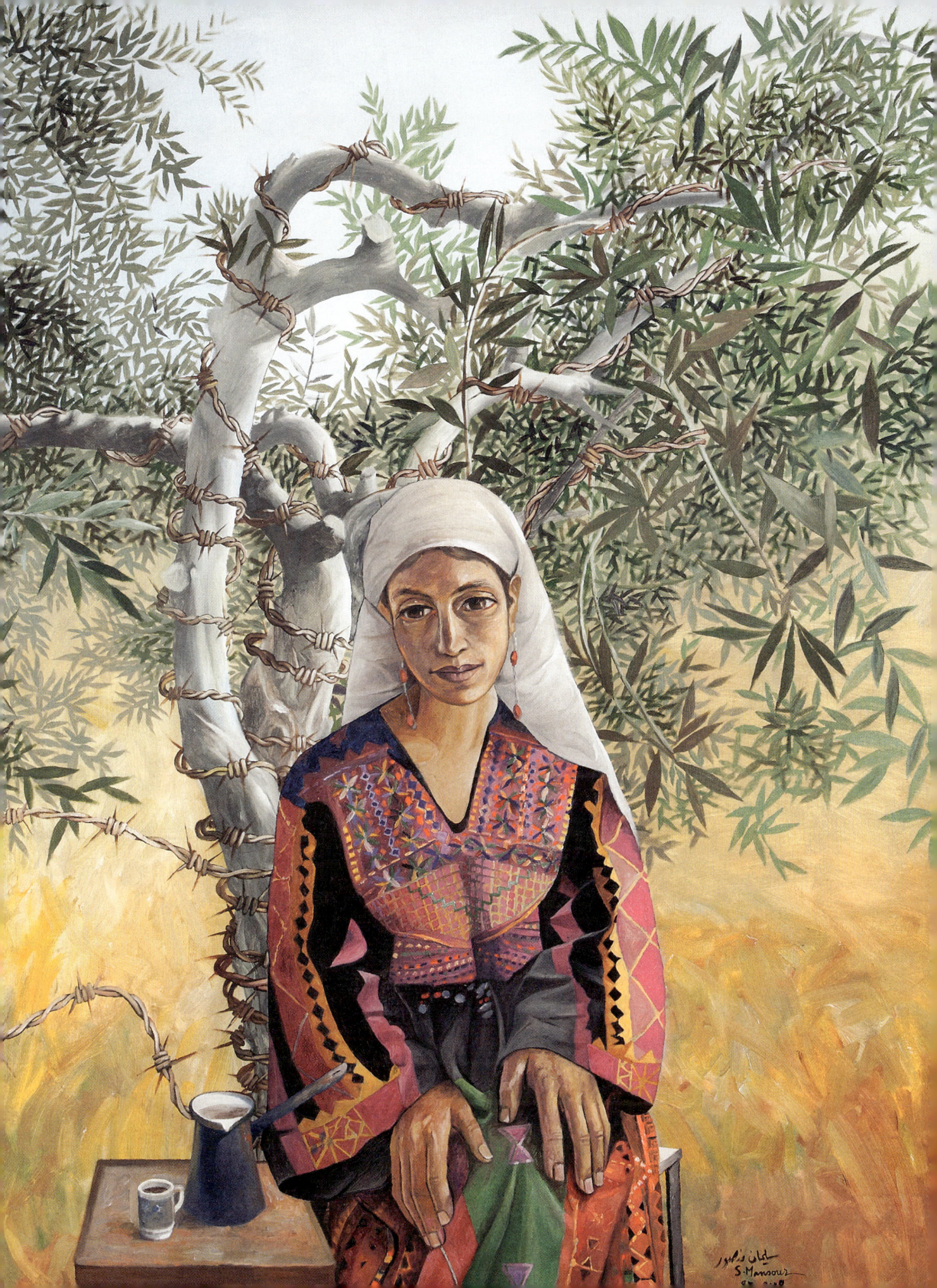

NABIL ANANI

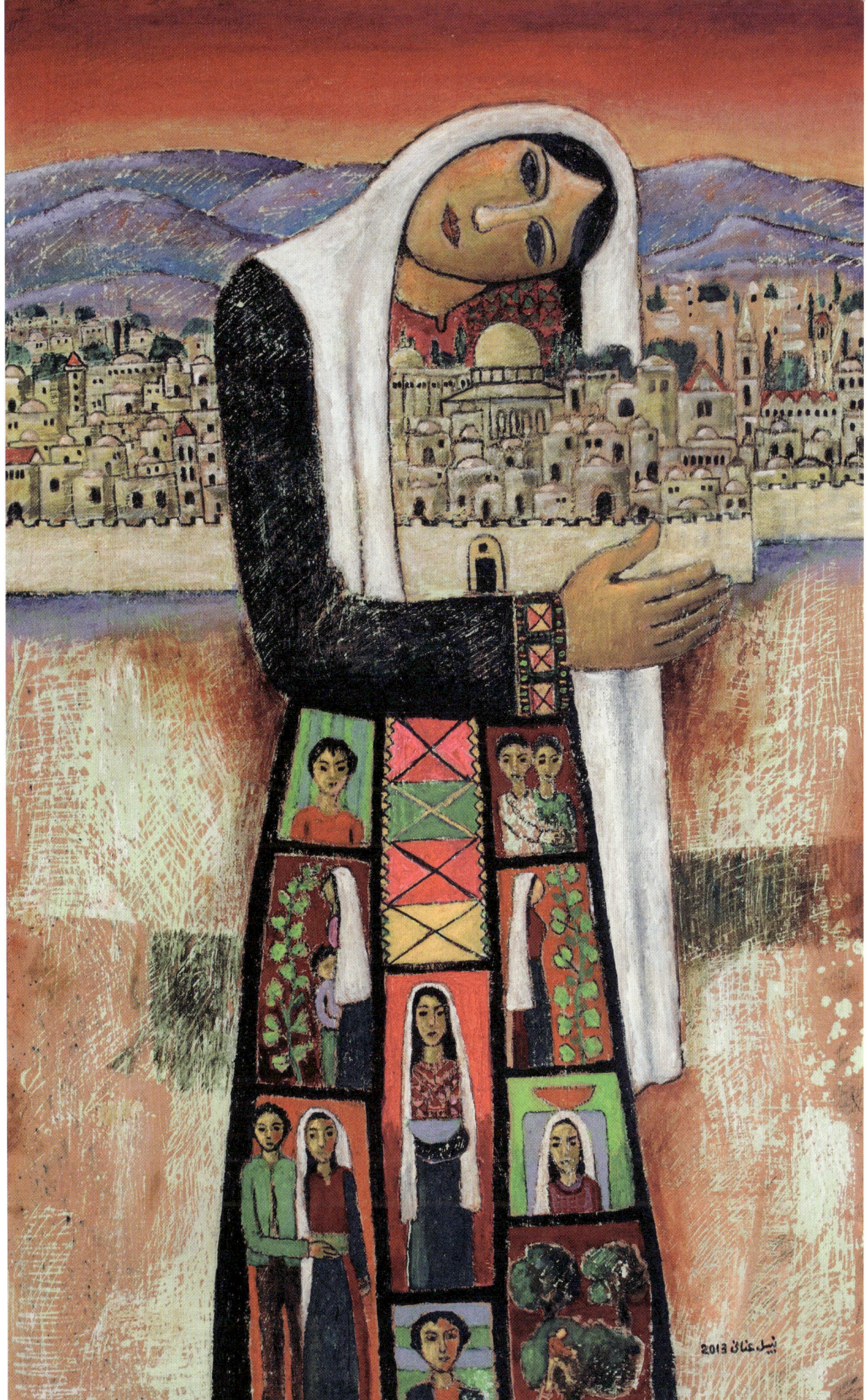

Ramallah-based artist Nabil Anani is well known for his pivotal role in Palestinian contemporary art. At five years old, in the 1948 Nakba, Anani and his family were displaced within Palestine from his birthplace of Latrun to Halhul. He graduated from the Faculty of Fine Arts at Alexandria University in Egypt in 1969, then returned to Palestine to work in arts education in Ramallah. By 1972, he had been given his first exhibition in Jerusalem and took part in forming the League of Palestinian Artists, which he later headed in 1998.

Palestine's liberation is a driving force behind Anani's work, as is reflected in his subject matter and mediums. Living under a brutal military occupation where Israeli soldiers confiscated art and shut down exhibitions meant that Palestinian artists found ways to communicate using a symbolic visual language. Anani proved that the subtle beauty of an olive orchard landscape, or a farmer in her embroidered dress, or *thobe*, would resonate with Palestinians without being explicit enough for censorship by Israel.

The woman wearing an embroidered *thobe* became an essential feature in his artwork. From the early 1980s, Anani started incorporating Palestinian embroidery and images of traditional Palestinian dress into his paintings. Additionally, Anani contributed and coauthored books on Palestinian art and folklore. In 1982, while he was on a research committee for Inaash al-Usra Society, he and his close friend and colleague, artist Sliman Mansour, contributed to the book *Palestinian Folkloric Costume*. Designing, painting and photographing while on field tours in Palestinian cities and villages led to Anani's discovery of the many uses of Palestinian embroidery. Drawn to the embroidery's beautiful and precise colours, shapes and designs, Anani was especially interested in earlier antique embroidered work characterised by abstract shapes and bright colours.

In 1984, he coauthored the *Guide to the Art of Palestinian Embroidery* with Mansour. Through this book, they aimed to introduce and identify Palestinian embroidery motifs found on dresses, shawls, handkerchiefs, bed linens, cushions and other home accessories, with their region of origin and designated numbers for the thread colours. Anani explains, 'The goal was to facilitate the task of embroidery and encourage women to practise the craft. We also named every branch or motif as told to us by the embroiderers, especially elderly ones. I was very impressed with the aesthetics of embroidery, especially chest panels [*qabeh*], side panels [*banayek*] and the lower back part of the dress [*al dyal*], reminiscent of the work of German artist Paul Klee.'

Anani worked at Birzeit University in the research centre, looking at the development of Palestinian handicrafts. 'I included embroidery in my work, along with other crafts such as straw, wood and weaving. I worked with embroidery associations to create new designs for the Palestinian women to embroider.' Anani's work with embroidery associations was instrumental in empowering Palestinian women and preserving the tradition of Palestinian embroidery. He also strove to improve how Palestinian women embroiderers could market and profit from their work. He recognised how urgent and essential preserving and continuing the tradition of Palestinian embroidery is to the Palestinian cultural narrative. His books made Palestinian embroidery motifs accessible to everyone, including Palestinian women who no longer had access to the embroidery traditions of their villages.

Preserving embroidery motifs is an act of resistance against Israel's colonisation and ethnic cleansing tactics, including attempts to appropriate and sever links to Palestinian indigenous culture and practices. He explains why the Palestinian woman became a distinguishing feature in his work: 'Her presence in the composition indicates originality and identity. In her beautifully embroidered dress, she is a symbol of heroism, identity and homeland. For this, she is the champion in my artwork. She is the mother of the martyr, sister of the prisoner, and owner of the house demolished by the occupation. You find her in the field, raising generations and resisting the occupier. Not only are there the aesthetic values in her shawl, hair and braids, but the artist can play with her shapes and elements in the composition of the painting. She isn't a specific woman – instead, she represents all women in Palestine. The embroidery isn't regionally specific but represents all Palestinian embroidery.'

In 1987, in response to the first Intifada, Anani and artists Sliman Mansour, Vera Tamari and Tayseer Barakat started the New Visions Movement. This involved a boycott of Israeli art materials, and the artists committing to using only what they could find or produce locally in Palestine. This created a significant shift in their artistic practice, as the medium became as relevant as the subject matter in expressing social, cultural and political concepts through their work. This led Anani to a factory in Khalil to experiment with and create artwork with leather. Anani and the other artists also looked to transform the familiar imagery and symbolism, creating new ways to perceive Palestinian visual language. The olive tree, calligraphy and Palestinian embroidery are still dominant features in his paintings, ceramics and leatherwork, but they are now abstracted and redefined.

Anani explains, 'This period lasted from the early 1980s to the mid-1990s and remained after the first Intifada. A new trend emerged through the New Visions Movement due to the use of different mediums and raw materials, such as leather, combined with local materials like henna, spices and dyes. Through embroidery in my work, I tackled other social issues.' In his piece *Passage into the Light* (1989), we see a shift in medium and abstract representations of the female form and embroidery motifs. The embroidery indicated on a female figure makes the work unmistakably Palestinian.

In *Mother's Embrace* (2013), he expresses the unique relationship Palestinians have with the capital city of Jerusalem. The Palestinian female figure in her embroidered *thobe*, who often appears in Anani's paintings, stands again in the foreground, lovingly cradling the city of Jerusalem over her heart. Behind her gently tilted head are purple hills in front of a pink-orange-yellow sky painted in Anani's distinct, colourful landscape style, creating a serene moment of affection and attachment. Anani tells us, 'My *Mother's Embrace* painting is an example of how to use Palestinian embroidery directly. Jerusalem is the focal point over the dress chest panel, and her bowed head expresses love for the city. I have put people instead of embroidery, especially on the sides and front of the dress.' With these portraits in place of the embroidery, the dress shares the story of the people.

Palestinian embroidery motifs also feature in Anani's more abstract works, such as his painting *Palestinian Folklore* (2020). Anani explains, 'I worked on completing some artworks inspired by Palestinian embroidery distributed within squares containing abstract motifs. It explores

and mimics the construction of a woven fabric with its harmonious forms and colours, most of which tended to be shades of red.' The eye moves around this painting, taking in the symbols and motifs that fill colourful squares.

While Anani's artwork protests against the occupation, it is also a love letter to his ancestral land, written in beautiful landscapes and celebrations of Palestinian heritage. Anani redefines what resistance looks like and plays a role in how many Palestinians imagine Palestine. With a body of work that counters the Israeli narrative, Anani fuels the collective desire for liberation, self-determination and the right of return. The incorporation of Palestinian embroidery in his work creates another layer of meaning to these remembrances, signifying the people, time, place and, most importantly, the story associated with them. His lifelong dedication to the arts and his contributions as an artist, author and educator continue to influence artists and embroiderers worldwide.

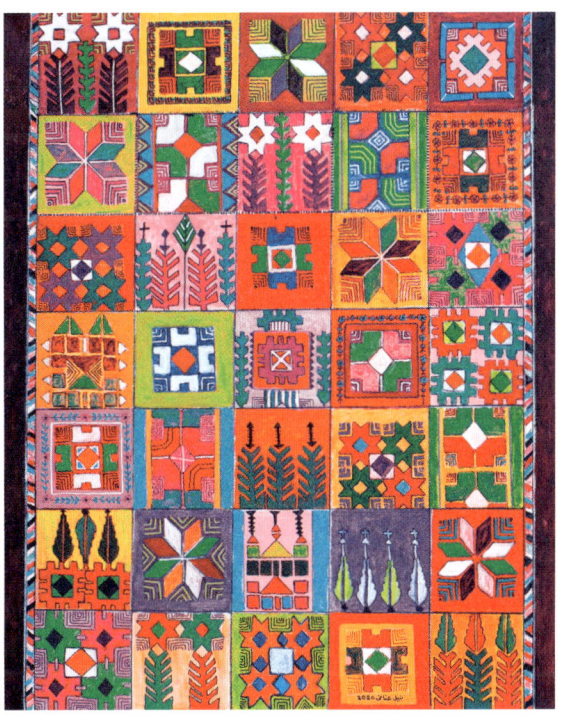

Nabil Anani, *Tatriz*, 2020. Acrylic on canvas, 100 x 80 cm

Previous spread: Nabil Anani, *Mother's Embrace*, 2013. Acrylic on canvas, 120 x 75 cm

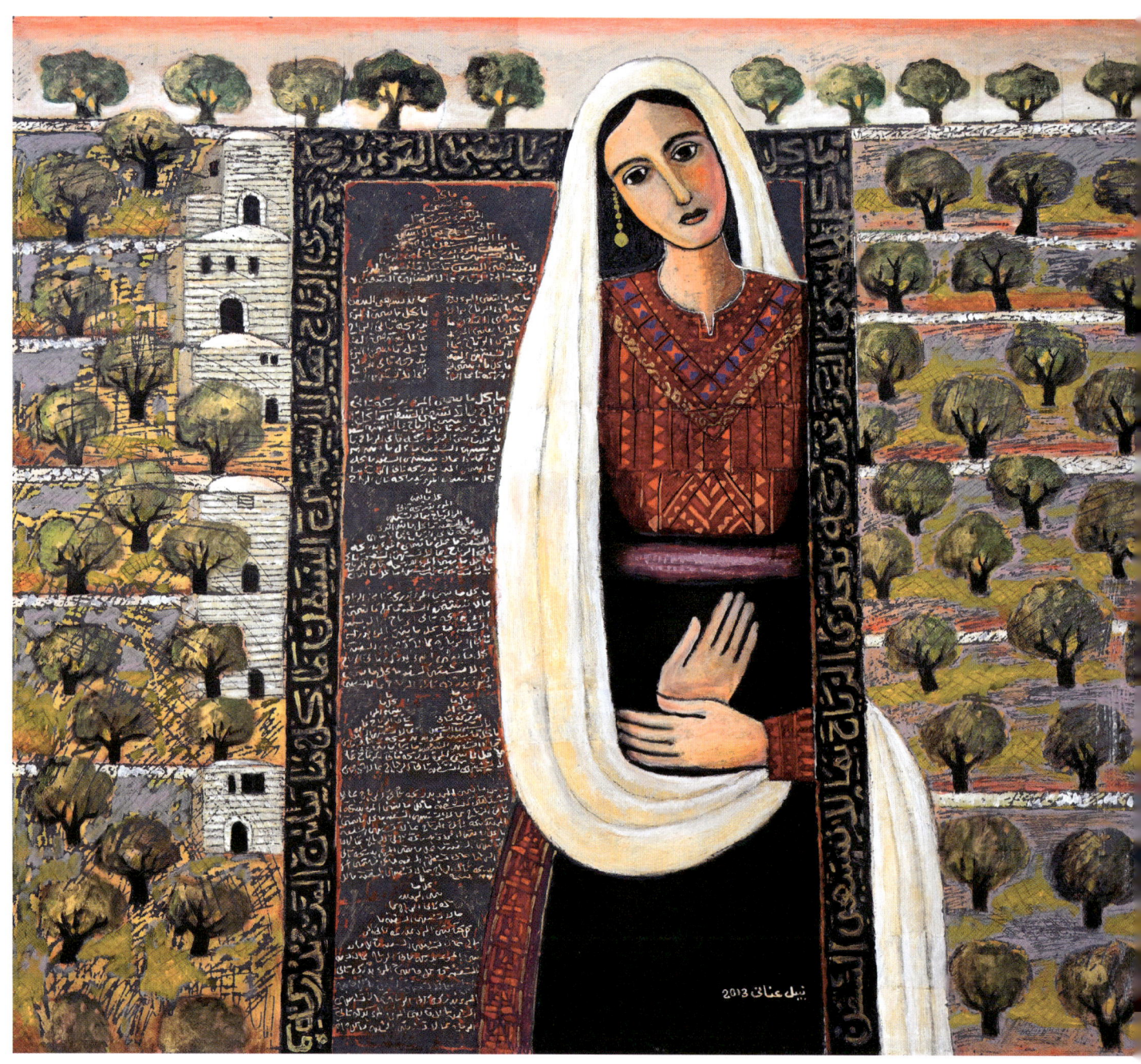

Nabil Anani, *Vision*, 2013. Acrylic on canvas, 107 x 120 cm

Right: Nabil Anani, *Homeland*, 2023. Acrylic and mixed media on canvas, 120 x 95 cm

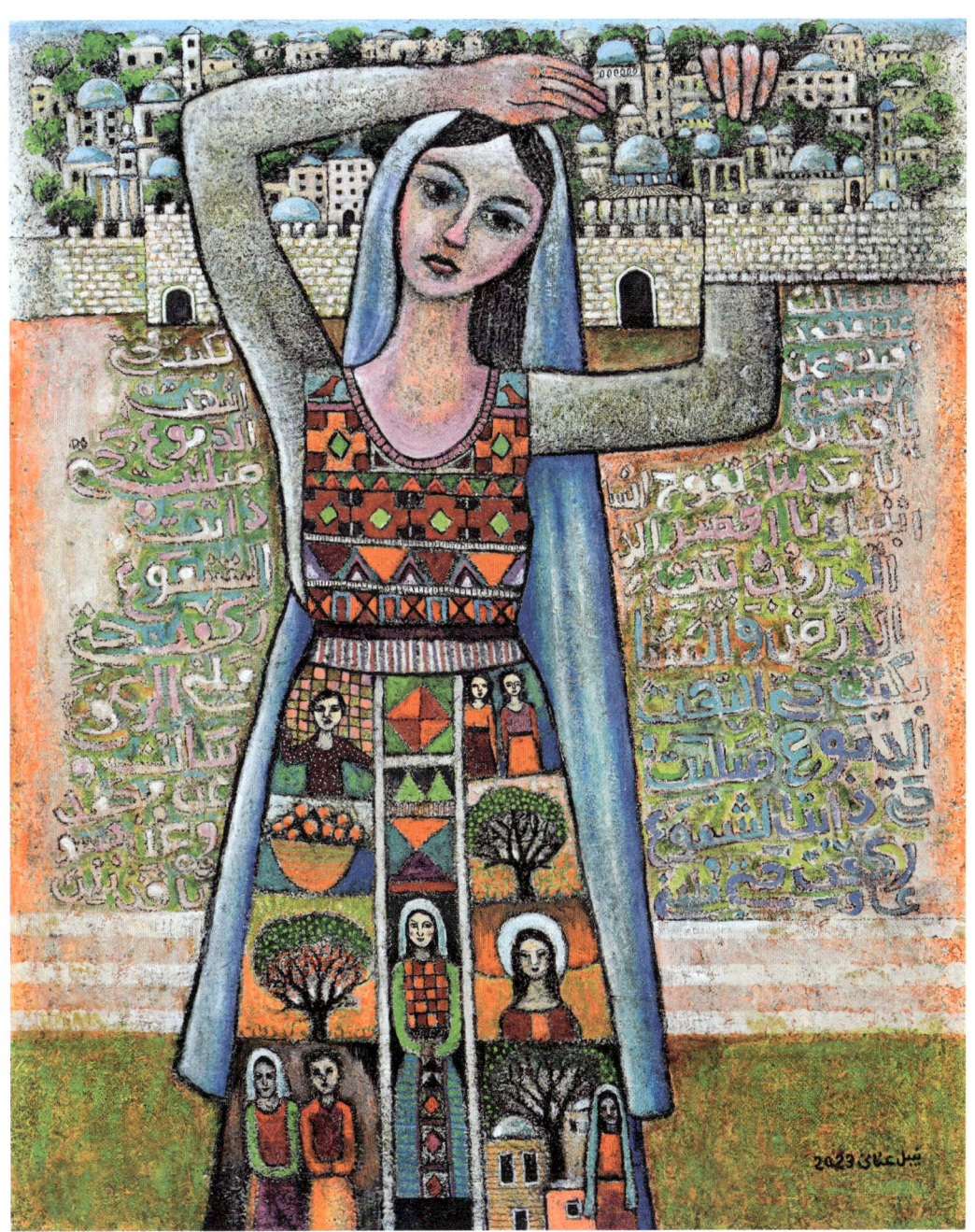

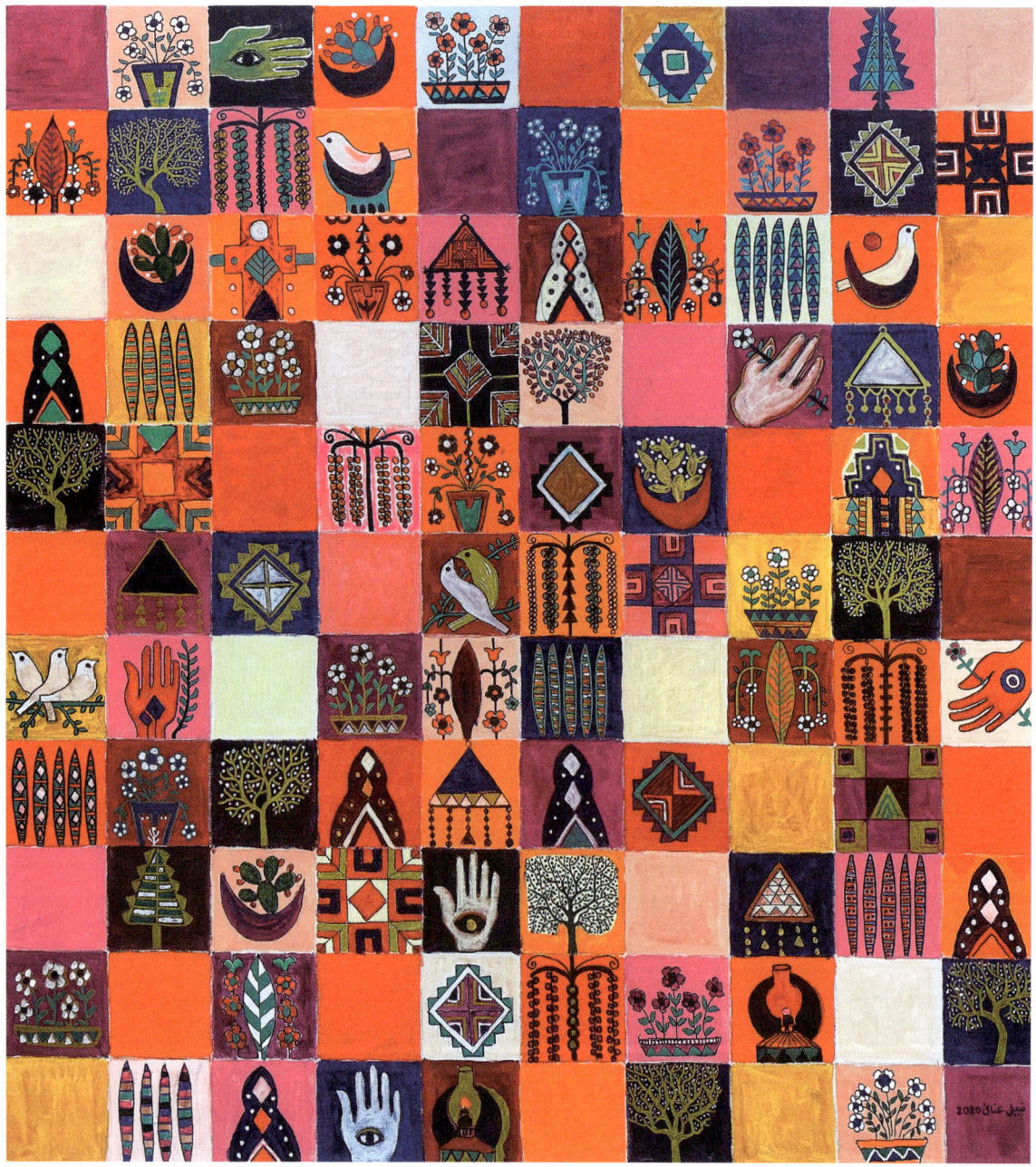

Nabil Anani, *Palestinian Folklore*, 2020. Acrylic on canvas, 110 x 100 cm

Right: Nabil Anani, *A Scene from Birzei*t, 2021. Mixed media on canvas, 97.5 x 69 cm

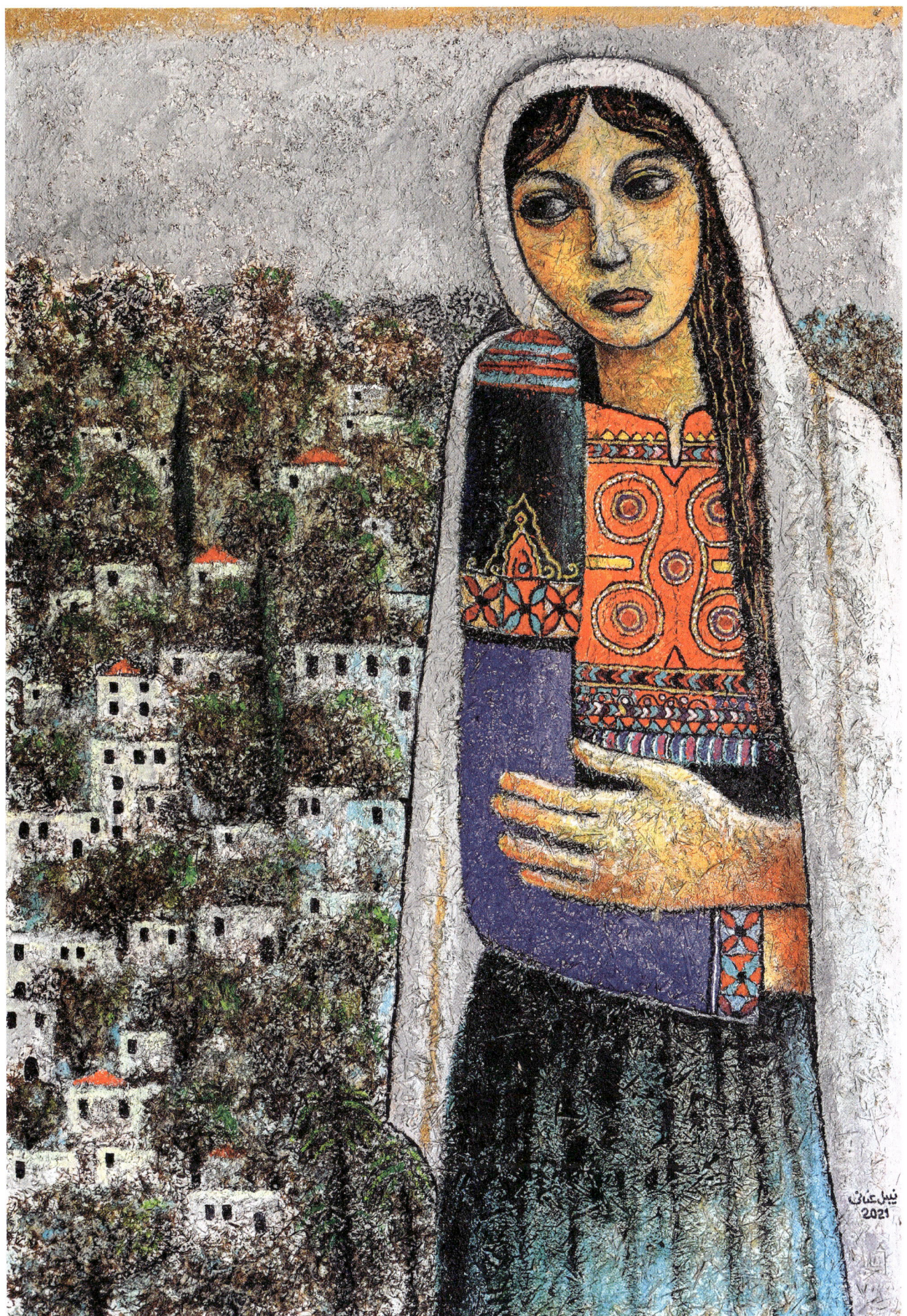

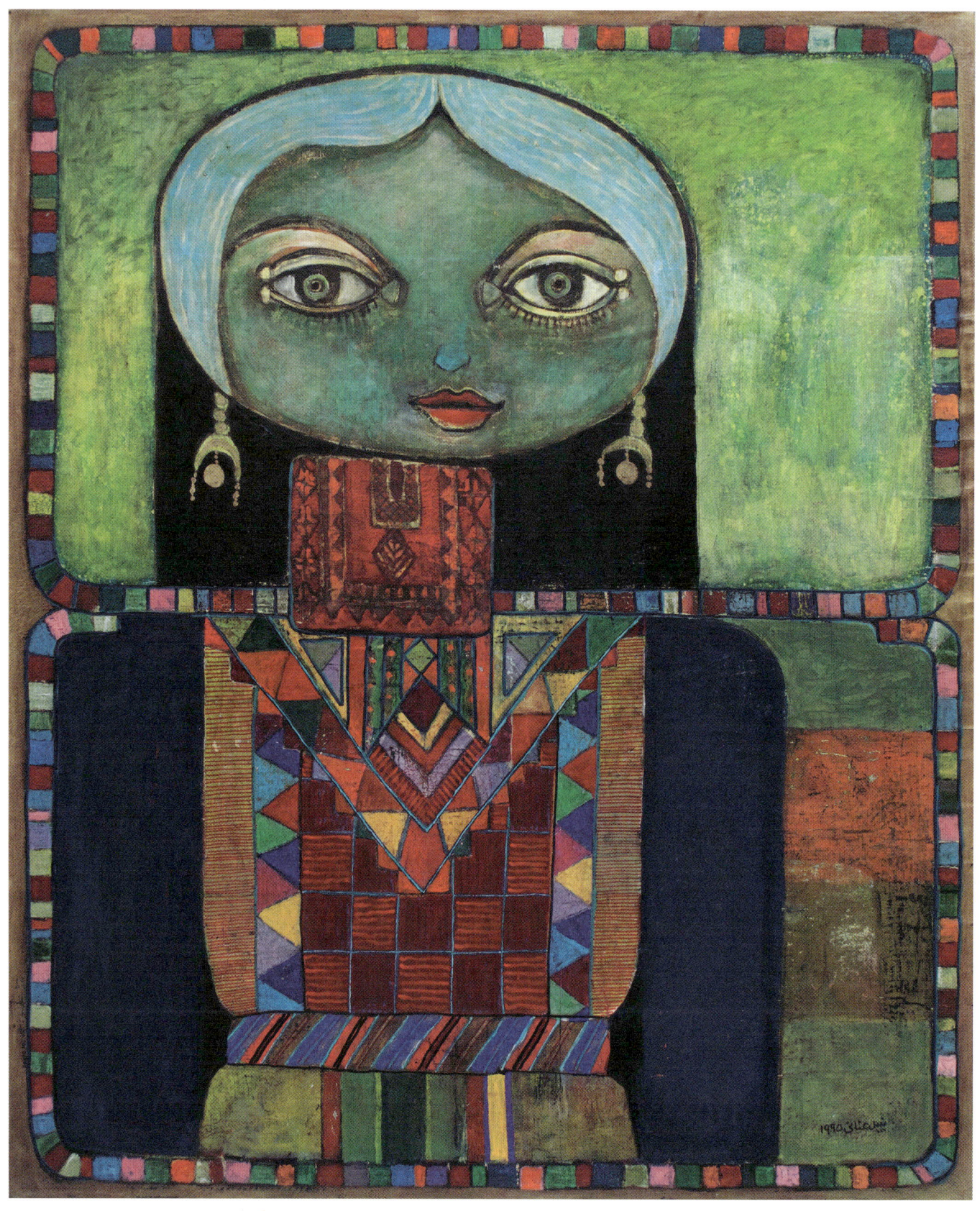

Nabil Anani, *Mother*, 1995. Oil on canvas, 124 x 105 cm

Right: Nabil Anani, *Passage into Light*, 1989. Leather and henna on wood, 80 x 80 cm

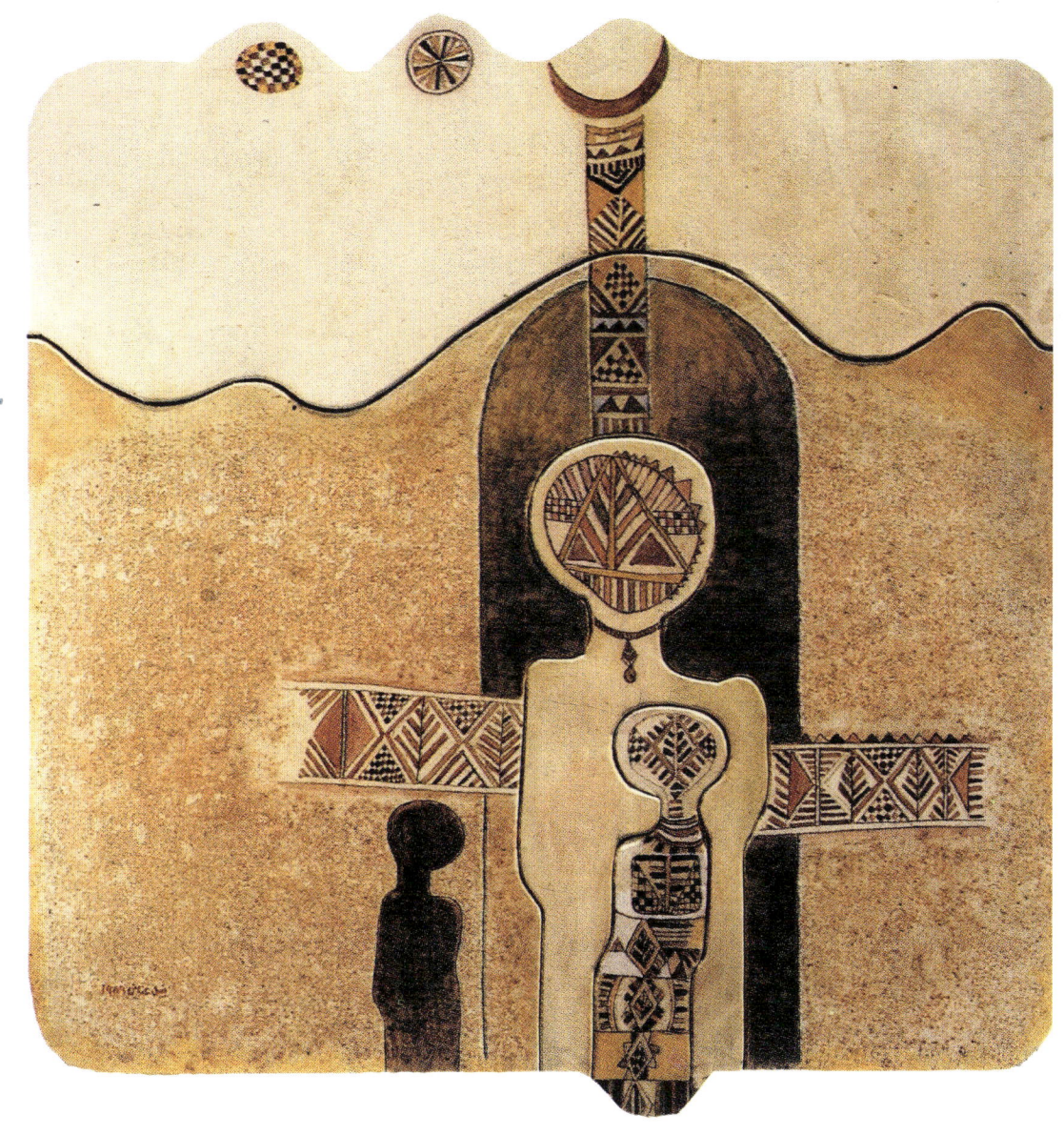

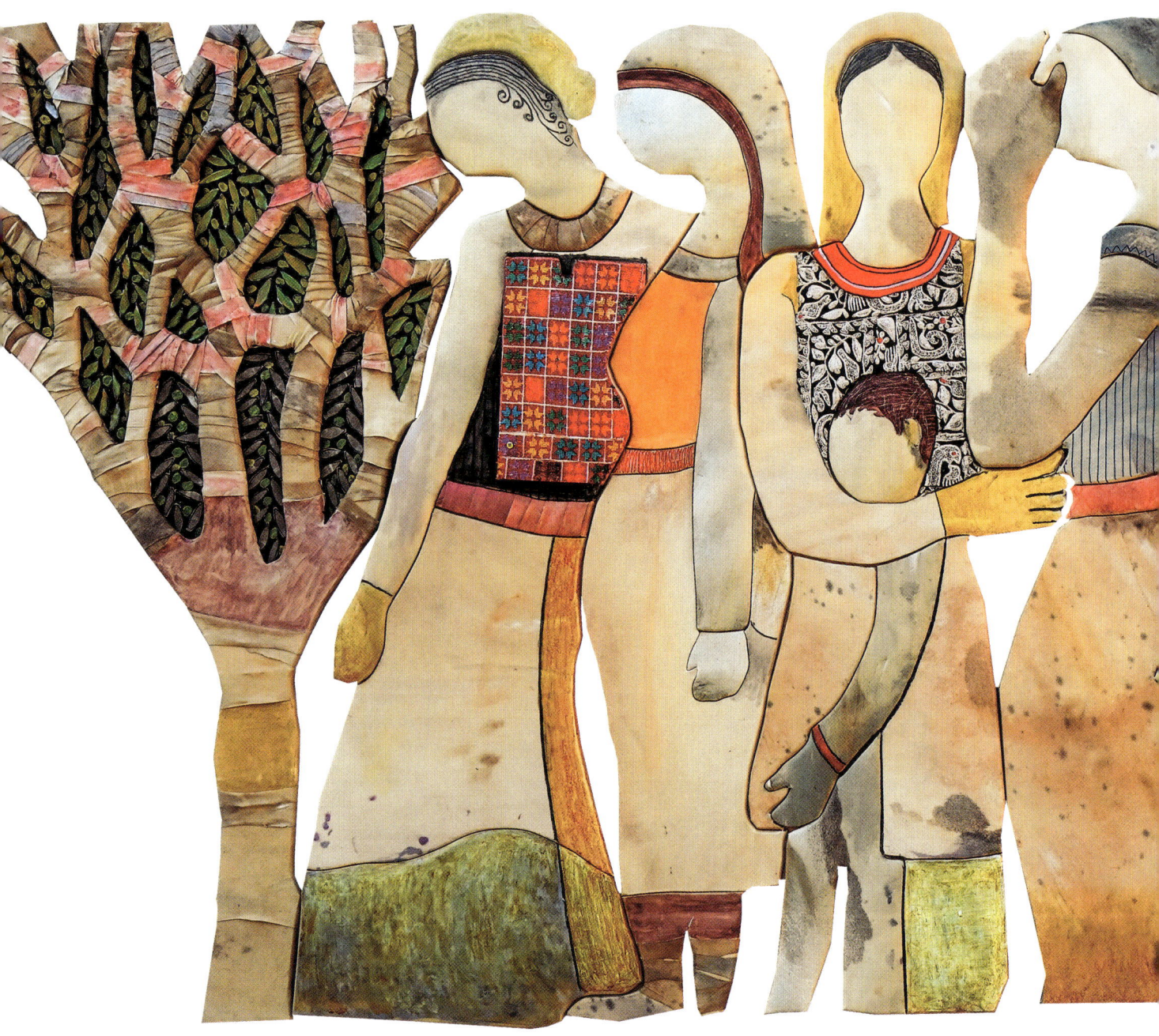

Nabil Anani, *Exit into the Light No. 2*, 2024. Mixed media on leather, 117 x 303 x 2 cm

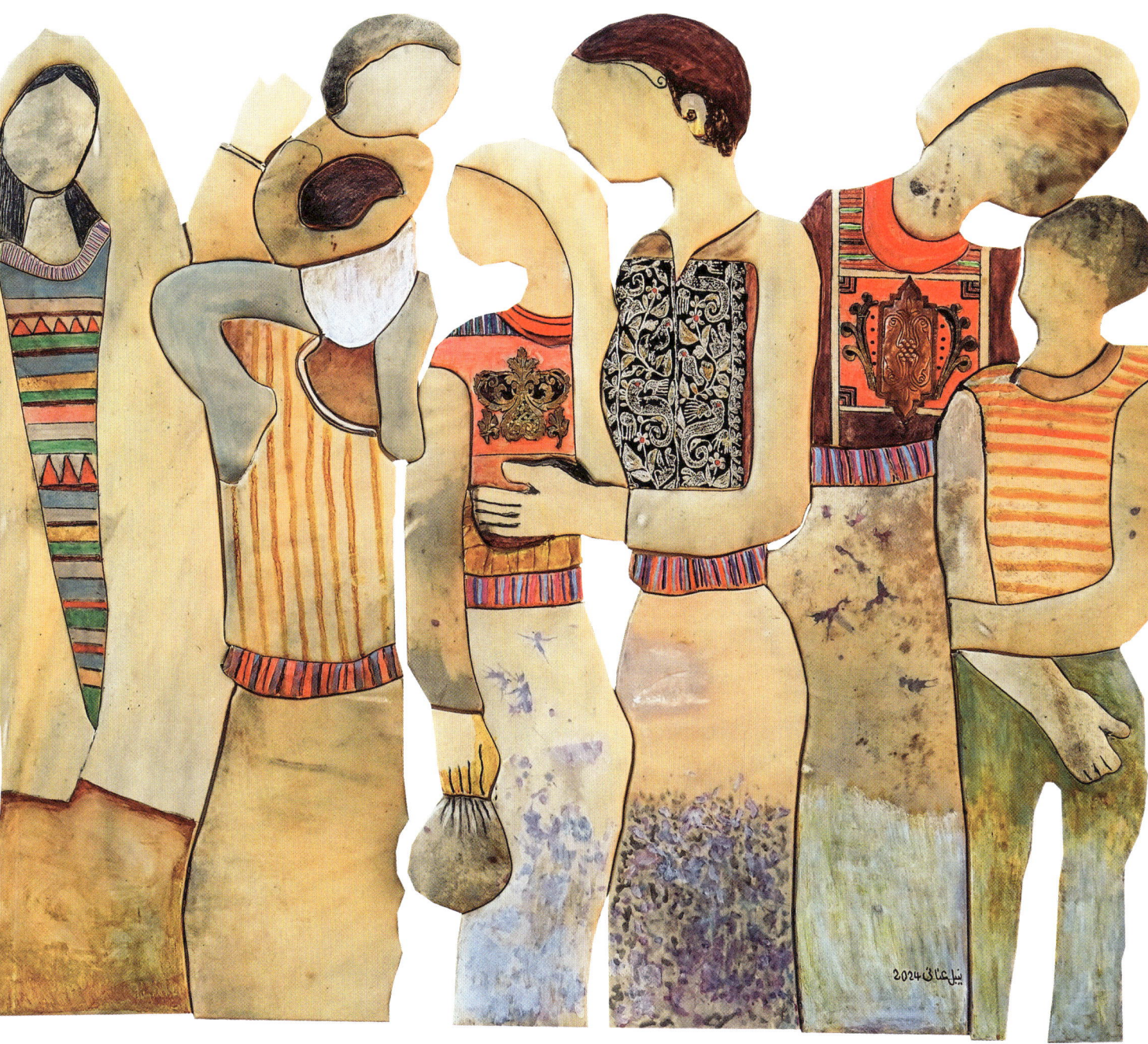

CHRIS

GAZALEH

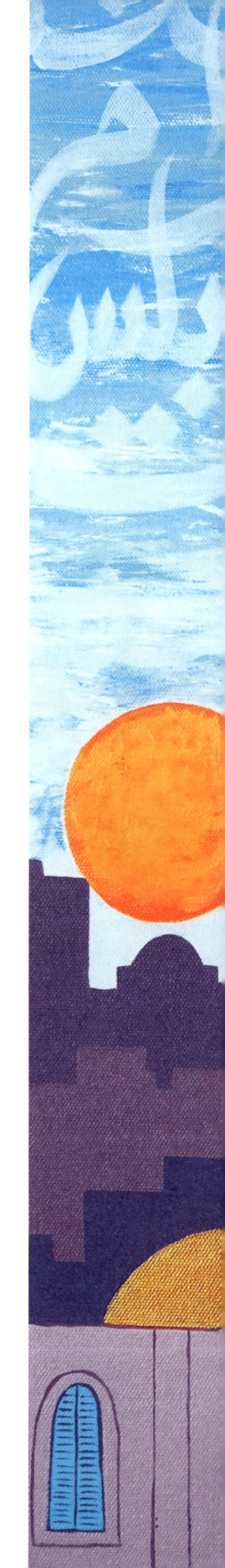

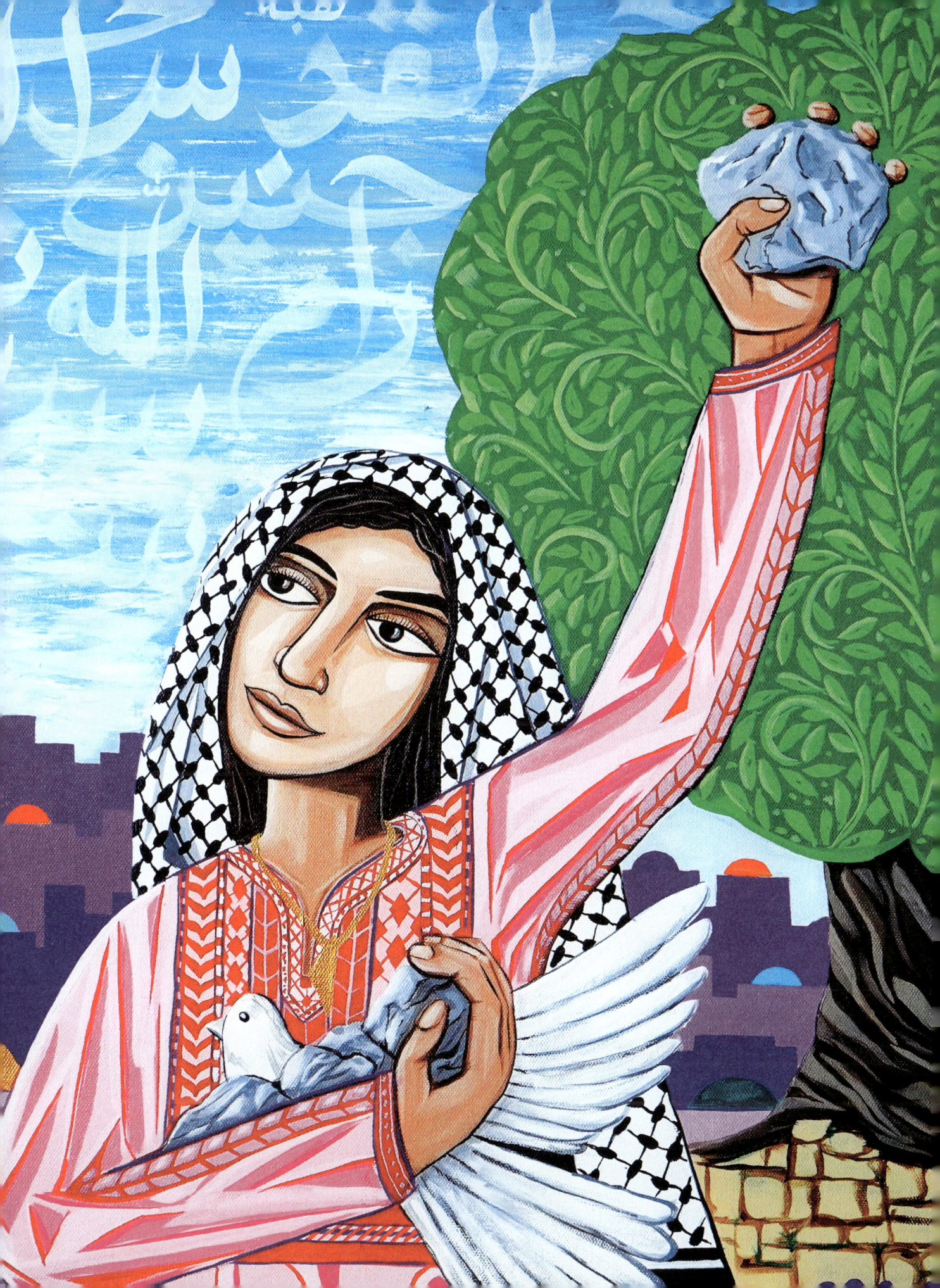

The street art, paintings and ink drawings of San Francisco-based artist Chris Gazaleh aim to raise awareness and promote conversations regarding cultural, political and social issues. His primary focus is on Palestinian liberation, fuelled by a deep-rooted connection to his Palestinian ancestry and love of Palestinian culture, history, land and people. Using street art techniques combined with Arabic calligraphy and graffiti styles, he transforms familiar symbols and imagery from Palestinian visual language into a contemporary expression of Palestinian identity.

Gazaleh often features the symbolic imagery of Palestinian embroidery in his paintings, elaborate ink drawings and murals. He feels that Palestinian embroidery represents part of Palestinian artistic culture and history. In discussing Palestinian embroidery in his work, Gazaleh says, 'In a time that our history is being erased and attacked, I see it as a symbol of resistance. Its connection to and representation of the land is a true embodiment of Palestinian culture.'

Drawn to the appearance of simplicity behind complex patterns, Gazaleh is inspired by Palestinian embroidery as an artistic practice, with its colours, patterns and imperfections. He explains that using Palestinian embroidery, or *tatreez*, in his work 'sends a message of honouring, protecting and preserving the indigenous culture of Palestine'. His family's stories, his experiences in Palestine and perspective as a second-generation Palestinian American greatly influence his artwork. He remarks, 'As a Palestinian from the diaspora, *tatreez* has always existed in my mental image of Palestine. I'm sure my family's old photographs were part of this reason. Growing up and becoming more politically involved, I learned that many women in the refugee camps would make and sell their embroidery to support their families. This made me more attached to the practice while creating my imagery.'

As is the case for many street artists committed to creating work to uplift and educate their community, Gazaleh's murals are spread throughout the San Francisco landscape, celebrating Palestinian culture while advocating for the freedom of the Palestinian people. Situated between four San Francisco neighbourhoods in the heart of the city is Gazaleh's *Humanity is the Key* mural, wrapped around an apartment building at 25 Elgin Park. Gazaleh hand painted the giant mural in 2018 with assistance from Eli Lippert. Gazaleh paints a story of resistance against Israel's oppression and occupation using traditional iconography, symbolism, and characters representing an idealised past, a current struggle, and a hopeful future where resistance leads to liberation. On one side of the building is the main character of the mural, Amal, whose name translated from Arabic is hope. She wears the headscarf and traditional embroidered dress, or *thobe*, typical to Ramallah, which shares her story on her embroidered chest panel and long vertical bands of intricate cross stitch.

'A lot of the women in my artwork wearing traditional dress represent the native, the protector, the caregiver of the land,' says Gazaleh. 'In a spiritual sense, they represent the land itself. These characters also represent strength, resilience, compassion and love. I believe *tatreez*, as a form of dress, is rich with these characteristics, celebrating the land that takes care of us as long as we love it. What we wear is political and it can be part of you – *tatreez*, in this sense, is a part of us.' Another character in the mural is Abu Falah, a farmer with his sickle, waiting for the return of his people to their native land.

In many of his murals, paintings and drawings, Gazaleh employs the imagery of the Palestinian farmer, especially the female farmer in her embroidered dress, to represent a Palestinian motherland. This imagery shares cultural information and creates an emotional response to foster understanding of the connection between Palestinians and their homeland. It also gives the viewer insight into Gazaleh's musings on what life would have been like growing up in pre-Nakba Ramallah or on his great-grandfather's orange orchards in Wadi Hunayn, before his family were forced off their land in 1948.

He says, 'The *falaha*, or farmer, is an important element of Palestinian society to represent in my art. When my *teyta* [grandmother] describes herself, she says, "*ana falaha.*" This actually makes me proud to have this lineage. I feel like I would really enjoy living in an agricultural society. I feel like it's in my blood. The duty to protect our land is deep in me. Even being born in San Francisco, I feel connected when I'm back home.' To Gazaleh, artwork, songs, stories and other cultural traditions maintain, teach and

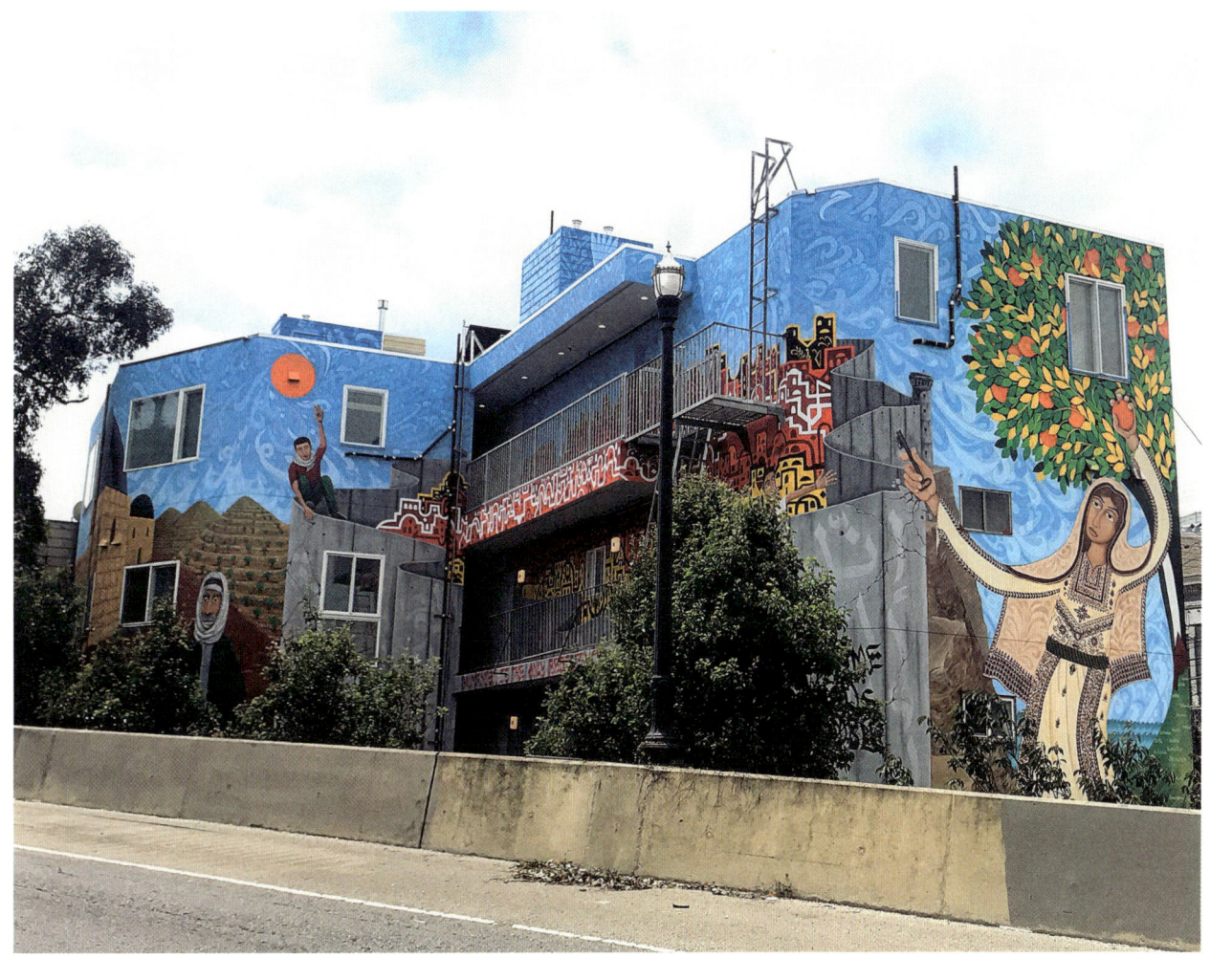

Chris Gazaleh, *Humanity Is the Key*, 2018. Wall paint and spray–painted mural, San Francisco, California, USA

Previous spread: Chris Gazaleh*, Know Peace*, 2022. Acrylic on canvas, 38.1 x 38.1 cm

celebrate this deep-rooted connection to the land passed down generationally, despite the physical distance of displacement and assimilation of different cultural practices.

Gazaleh believes that his art's universal message reaches beyond all borders. 'I create to inspire my people, give them hope and pride. These feelings cross all intersections of human identity. I think this is why my art speaks to everyone with a heart. In the end, we're all the same. Similar to music, art has no boundary or border when it comes from the soul.' His work across various mediums expresses his strong values regarding human rights, justice, freedom and peace, as well as his deep love for his culture. His experience as a Palestinian has shaped his perspectives and visual language, allowing him to convey a message aimed at raising human consciousness.

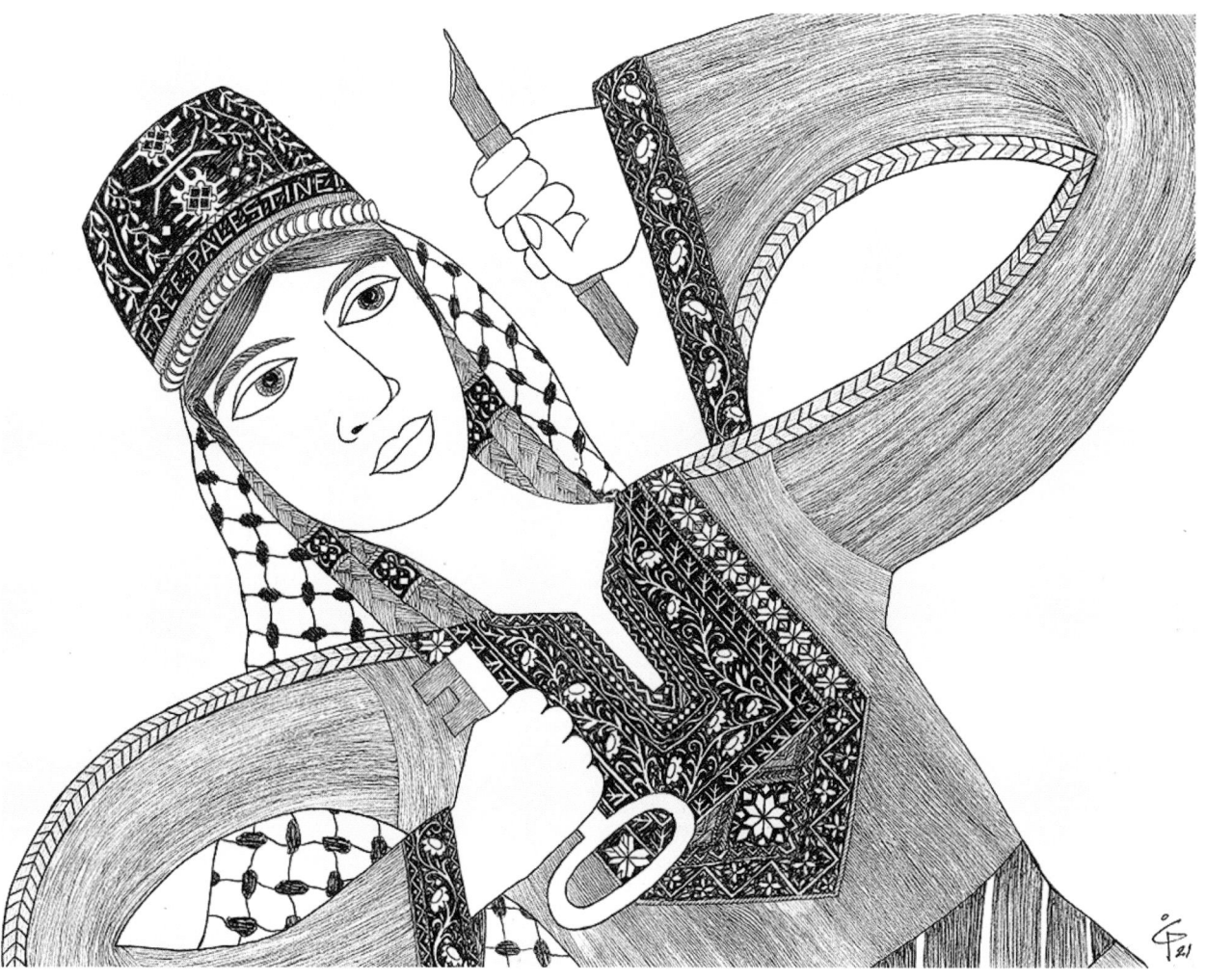

Chris Gazaleh, *Write to Resist*, 2021. Ink on paper
Right: Chris Gazaleh, *Inkifada*, 2019. Ink on paper

Next spread: Chris Gazaleh, *Heart Shaped Rocks*, 2023. Wall paint and spray-painted mural

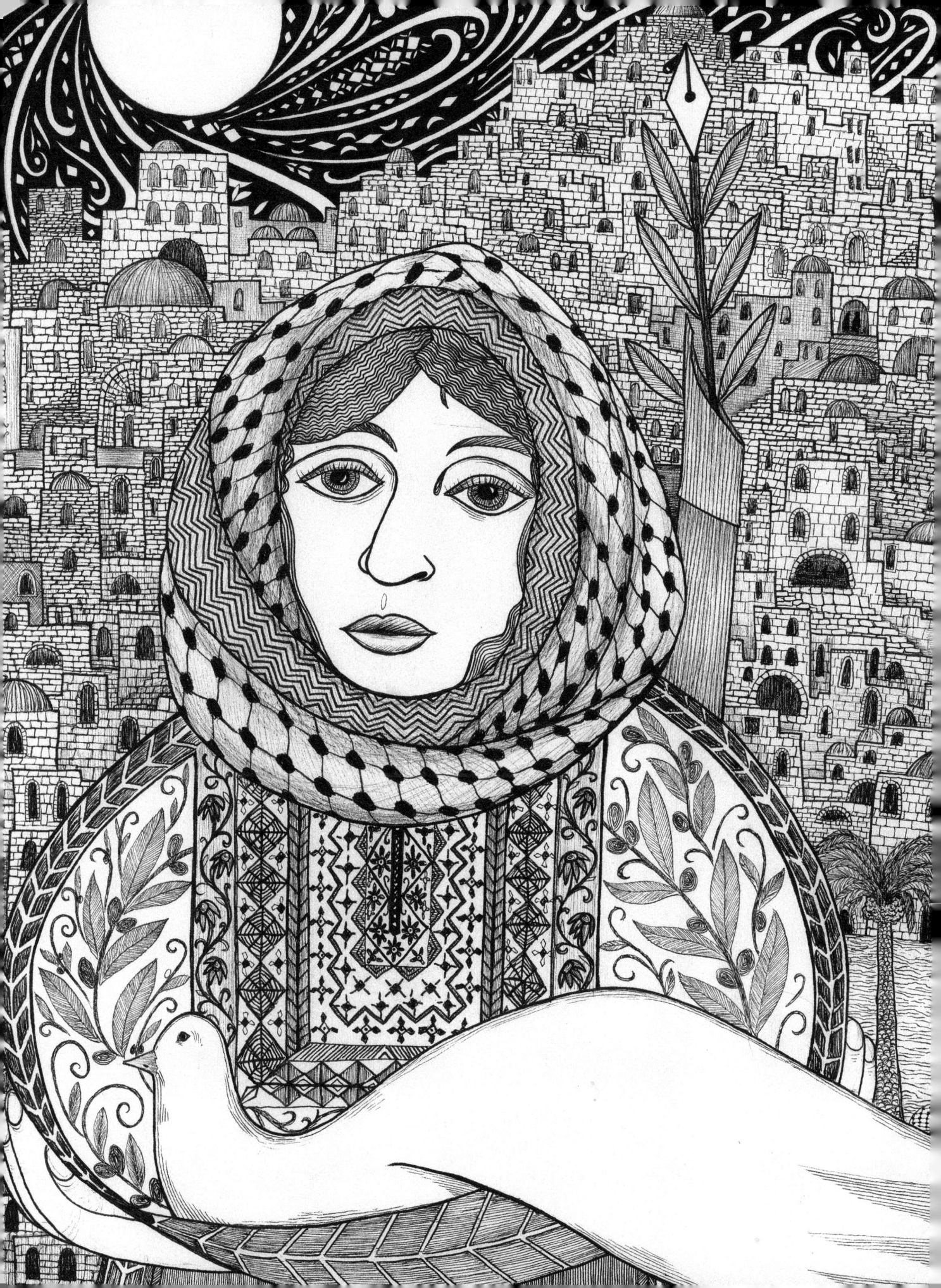

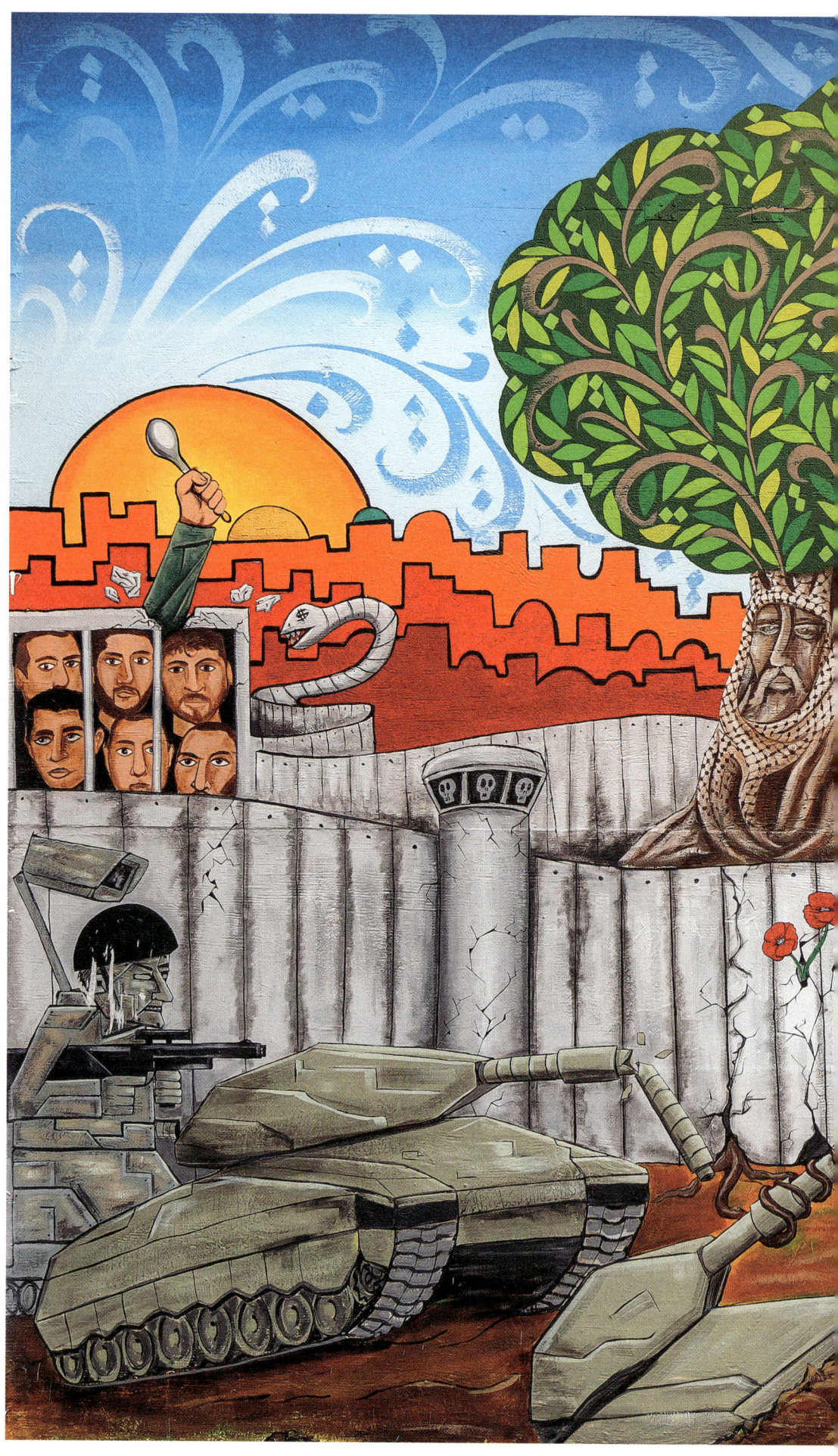

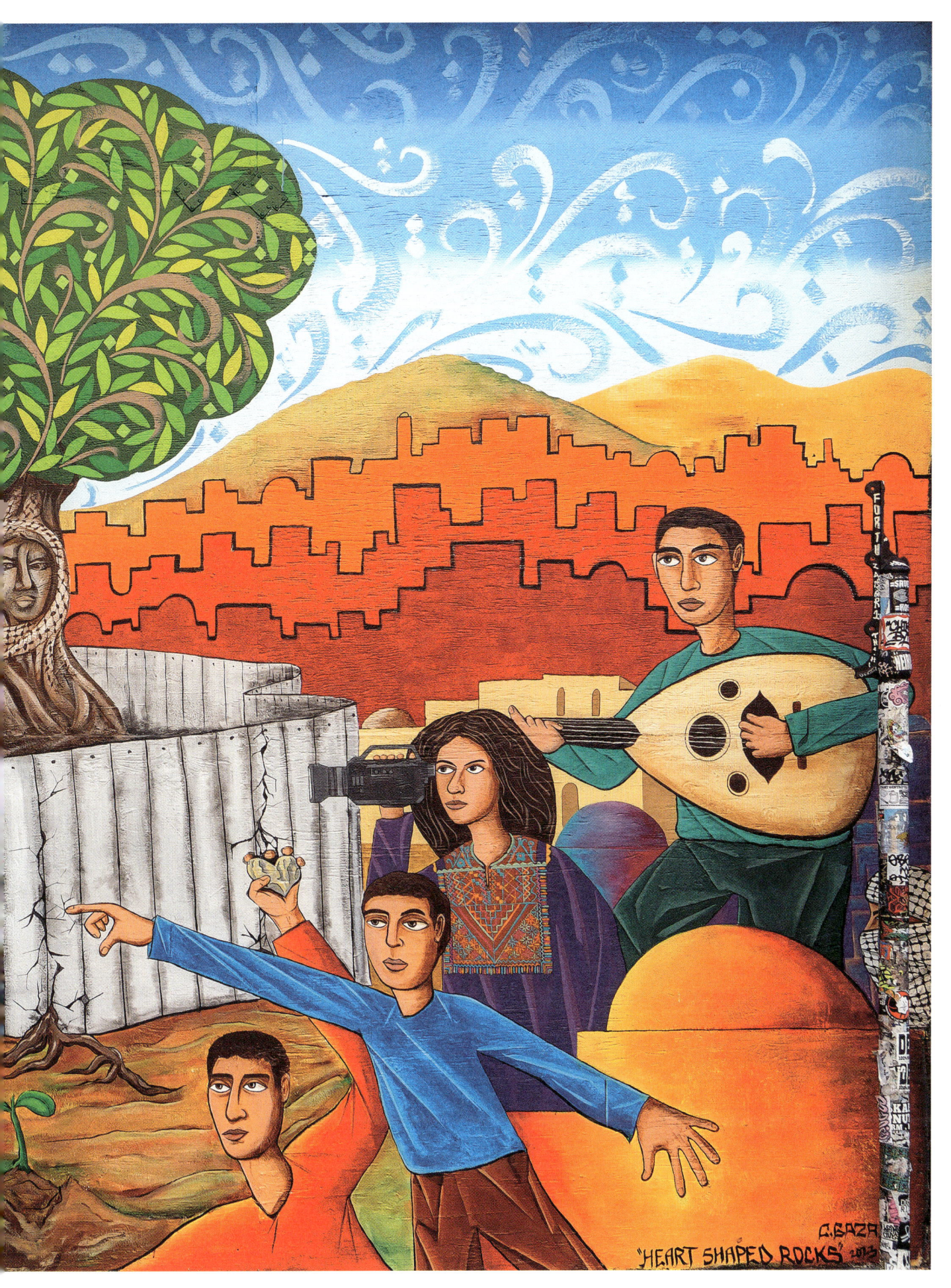

"HEART SHAPED ROCKS" 2013

MOHAMMED
ALHAJ

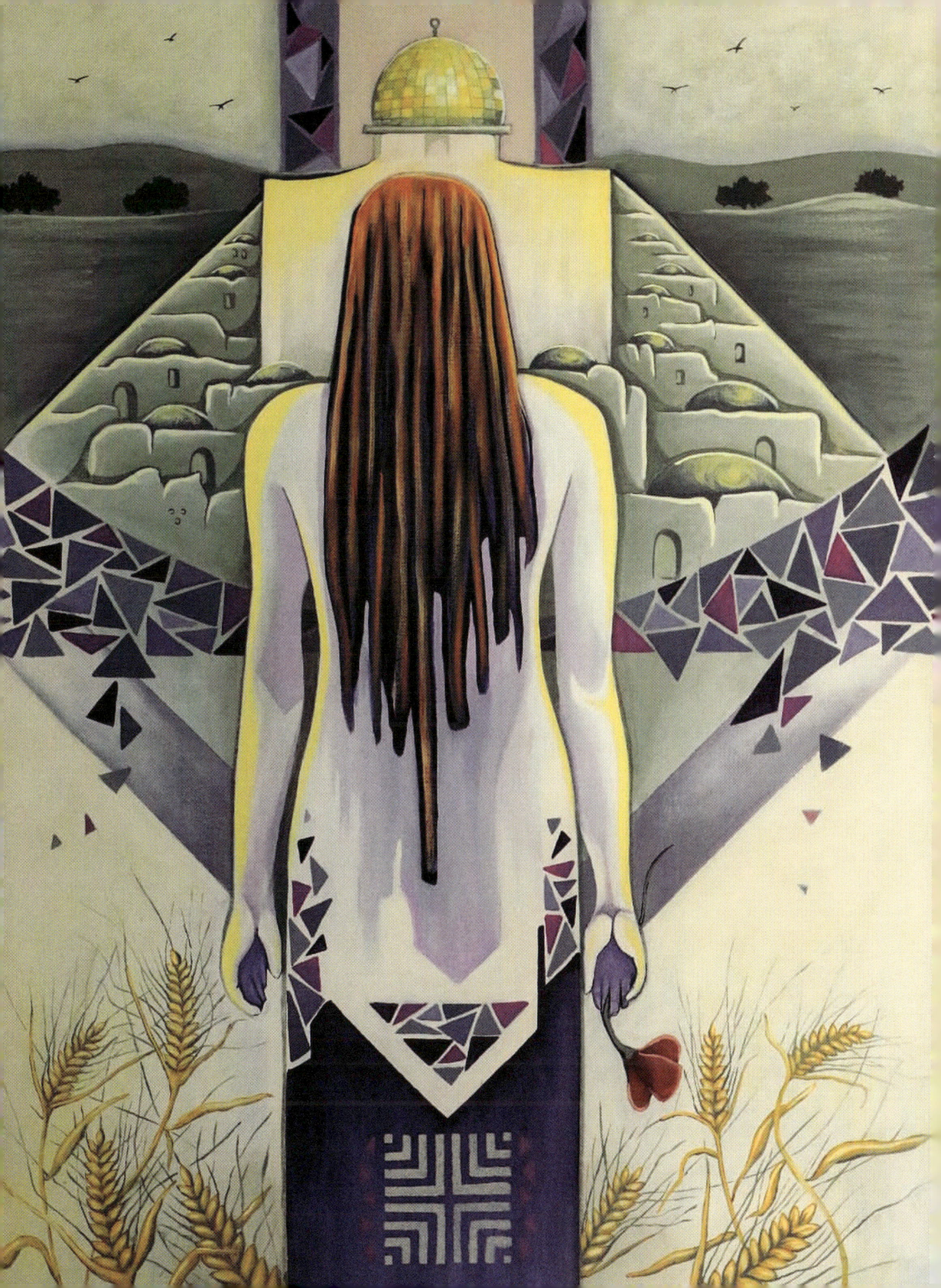

Gazan artist Mohammed Alhaj places Palestinian embroidery motifs in many of his drawings and paintings to signify Palestinian heritage and national identity. Alhaj was born in Libya in 1982, the son of Palestinian refugees, and returned to Gaza, Palestine, in 1995. In 2004, he graduated with a degree in art education from the Faculty of Fine Arts, Al-Aqsa University in Gaza City. There, he presented a graduation project under the supervision of Kamel Al Moghani, a prominent artist who inspired Alhaj to include patterns in his work.

Soon after, Alhaj maintained his art practice while working as an art teacher. Over the past twenty years, he has worked in various mediums and styles, his work having been exhibited in solo and group exhibitions. In his first exhibition in 2006, *Palestinian Features*, he used mixed-media relief sculpture work expressing national and heritage symbols. Alhaj found this symbolism inspirational and he continues to employ it in his artwork.

Alhaj recognises the significance of producing work with a strong sense of Palestinian visual identity, where he explores themes relating to identity, memory and displacement. Beginning in his youth, he would draw geometric and foliage designs and patterns, which led him later to add decorative elements and symbols to help convey concepts. He makes it a point 'to link heritage with national identity and to add a Palestinian touch' to his artwork.

In deciding which patterns or motifs to add, he says, 'I choose them carefully either for an aesthetic touch or for an expressive connotation that suits the nature of the content of the artwork. As I said, adding these symbols displays Palestinian national identity to the viewer, regardless of the viewer's nationality. Art is a visual language that doesn't need a translator. Therefore, I felt obligated to focus on heritage in some of my works.' Alhaj frequently adds rows of embroidery motifs or individual motifs deliberately placed in the composition.

From his parents' forced displacement, to living through Israel's cruel seventeen-year blockade on Gaza, to Israel's horrific genocide of Palestinians in Gaza, Alhaj's work has reflected his interpretation of the physical and psychological effects of Israel's permanent and cruel siege on Gaza. His work addresses and reflects the suffering, isolation and trauma brought about by forced displacement. Embroidery motifs re-establish a remembrance of indigenous cultural practices. They tile across some works in a row; in others, the motif frames the subject within. On paintings and drawings featuring women, such as *You Shall Not Die* (2022) from the *Wheat* series, motifs on their dresses indicate their Palestinian identity, steadfastness and connection to the land. In Alhaj's landscapes, embroidery motifs decorate the sky and buildings, designating them as Palestinian.

During Israel's genocide of Palestinians in Gaza, Alhaj, along with his wife and children, escaped Israeli bombardments multiple times, leaving them internally displaced in a tent, with no resources. His home, studio, and life as he knew it, were left behind under the rubble. He explains, 'Through my works, I try to provide visual messages about the time and place I belong to. It is also an opportunity to fight against the occupation through art, especially since we are here in Gaza exposed to an unprecedented genocide that has even led to the annihilation of heritage, history and art. Our artwork is threatened and in danger unless it is saved. Art plays an important role in bearing witness to this occupation, which does the unimaginable to obliterate our heritage through plundering, stealing and appropriating.'

By reinforcing symbols relating to heritage and capturing the effects of mass displacement in his artwork, Mohammed Alhaj resists Israel's cultural erasure and ethnic cleansing of Palestinians. Despite the destruction and loss of his artwork in Gaza, Alhaj's surviving work continues to communicate his message.

Right: Mohammed Alhaj, *Broken Into*, 2023. Acrylic on canvas, 40 x 40 cm

Previous spread: Mohammed Alhaj, *You Shall Not Die*, from the *Wheat* series, 2022. Acrylic on canvas, 80 x 60 cm

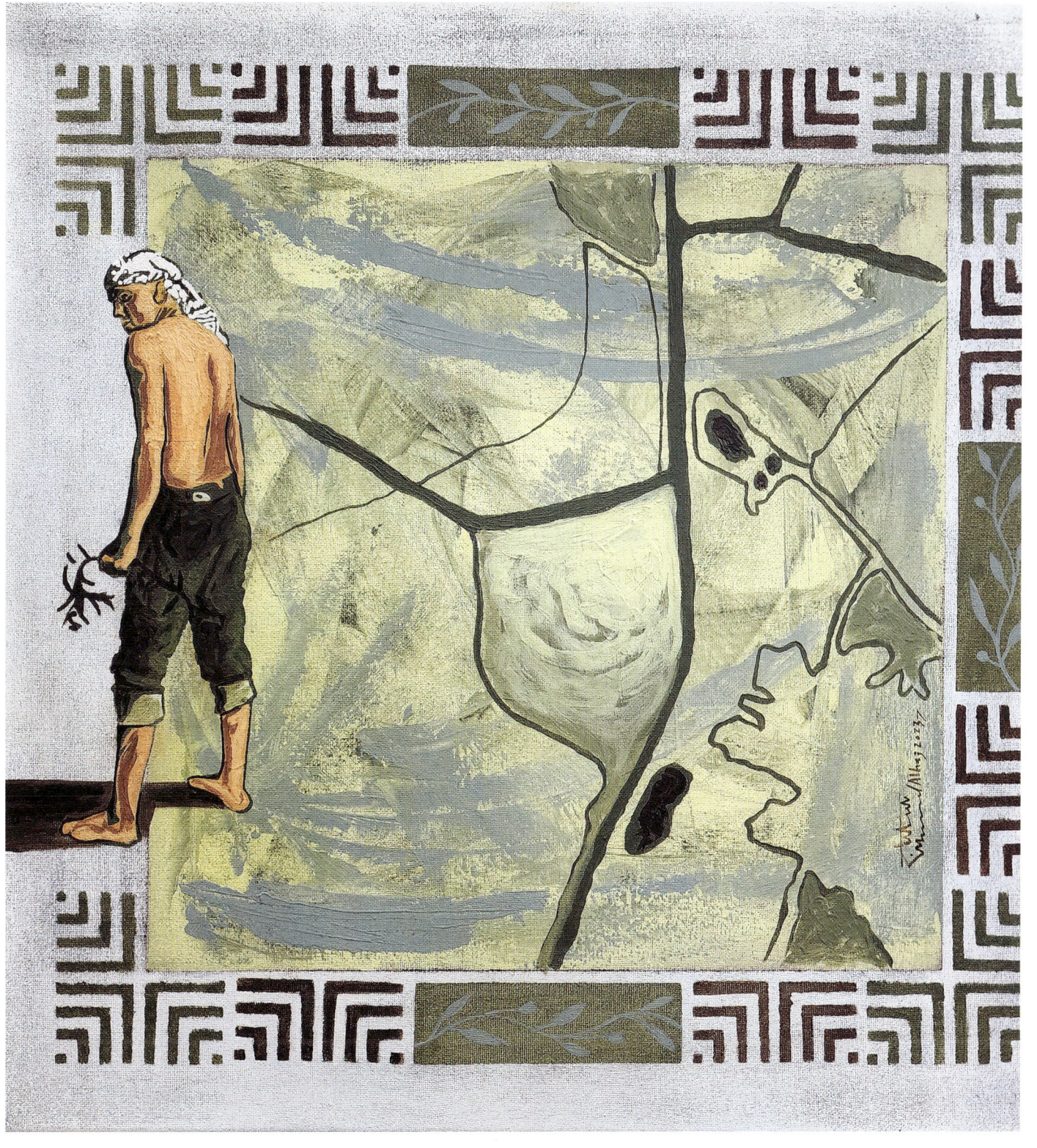

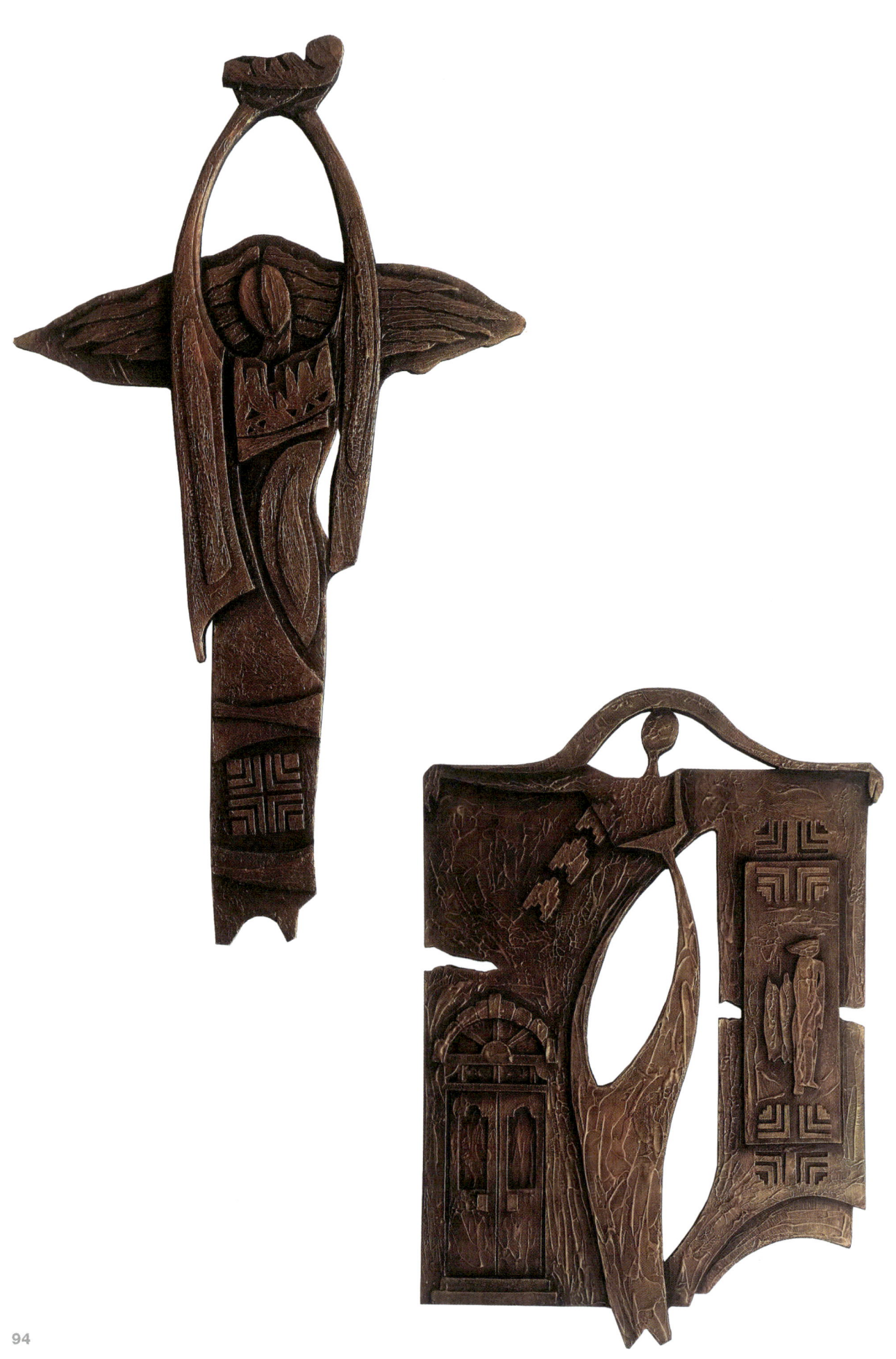

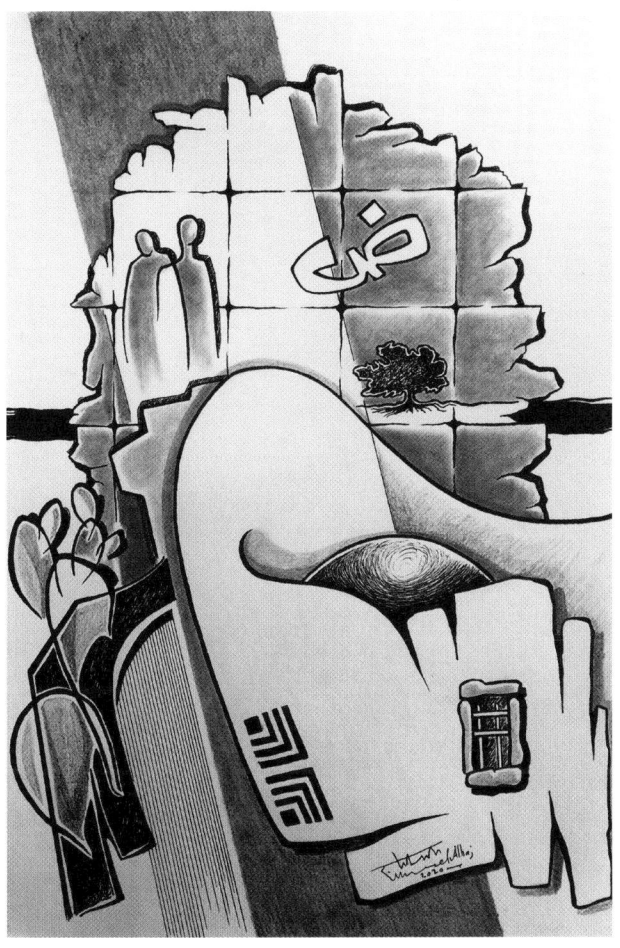

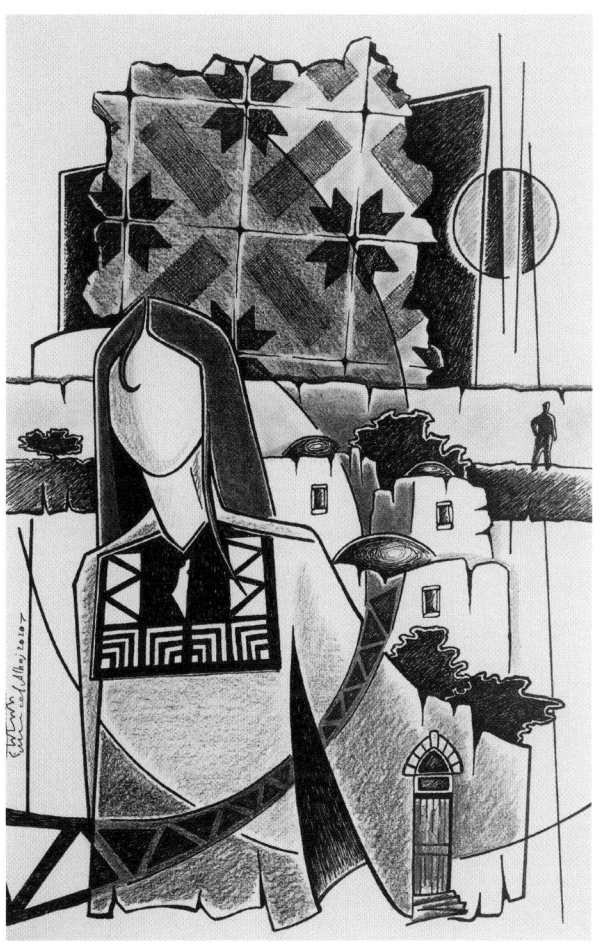

Mohammed Alhaj, *Yearning*, 2020. Ink and pencil on paper, 38 x 28 cm
Mohammed Alhaj, *Village Girl*, 2020. Ink and pencil on paper, 38 x 28 cm

Left: Mohammed Alhaj, *Birth*, 2020. Mixed media on wood, 50 x 30 cm
Mohammed Alhaj, *Birth*, 2020. Mixed media on wood, 70 x 50 cm

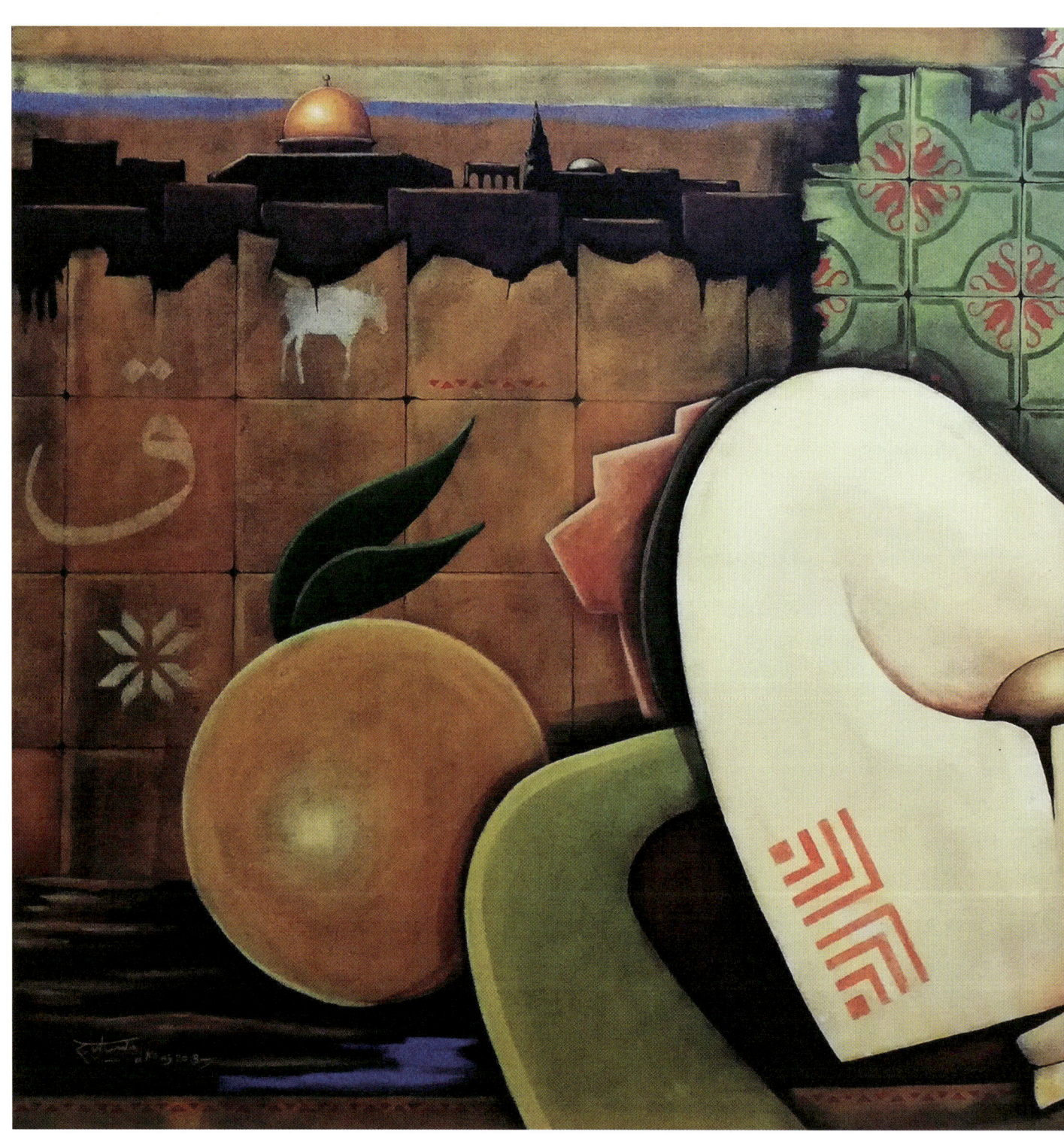

Mohammed Alhaj, *From Gaza to Jerusalem*, 2019. Acrylic on canvas, 200 x 100 cm

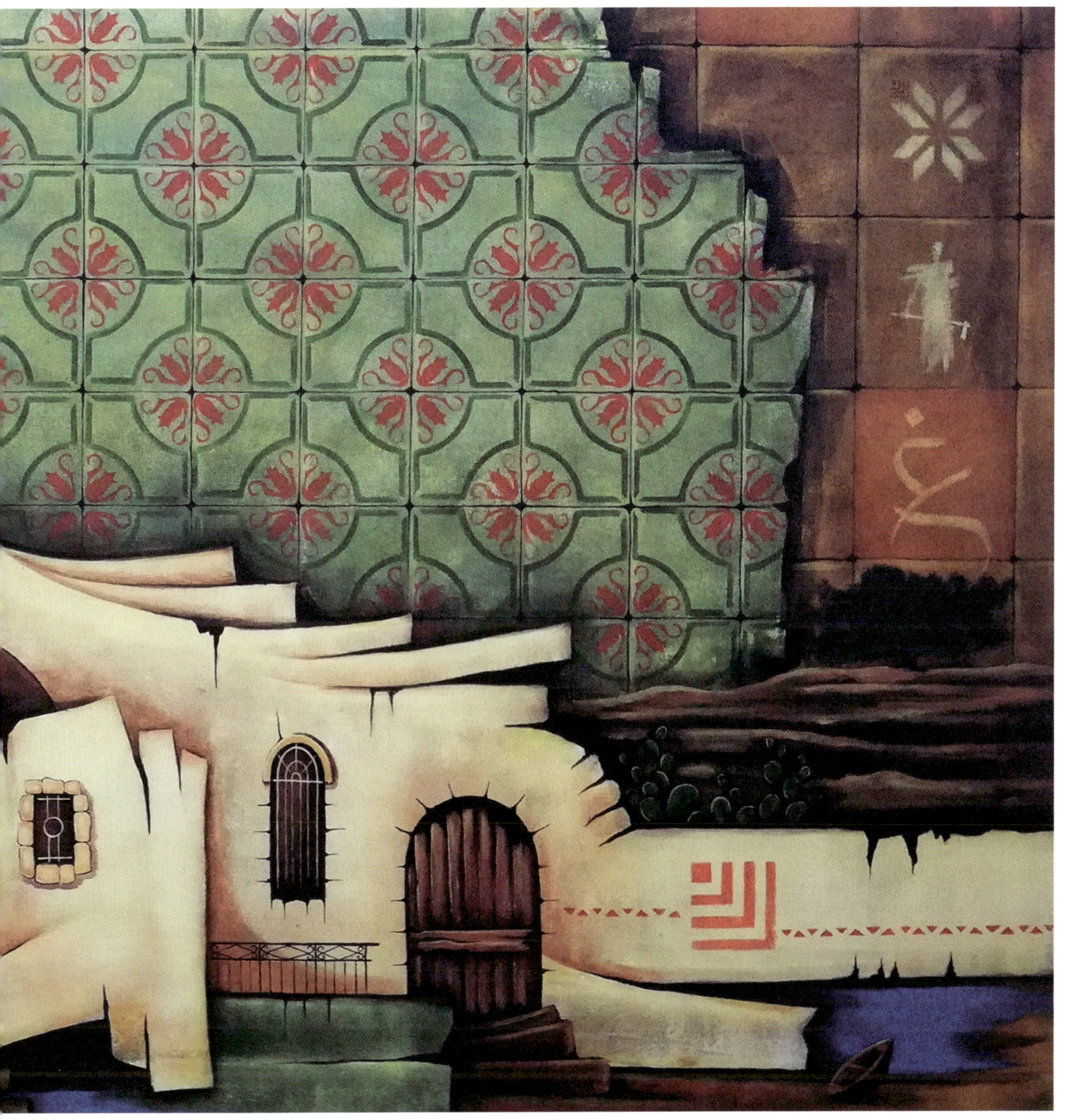

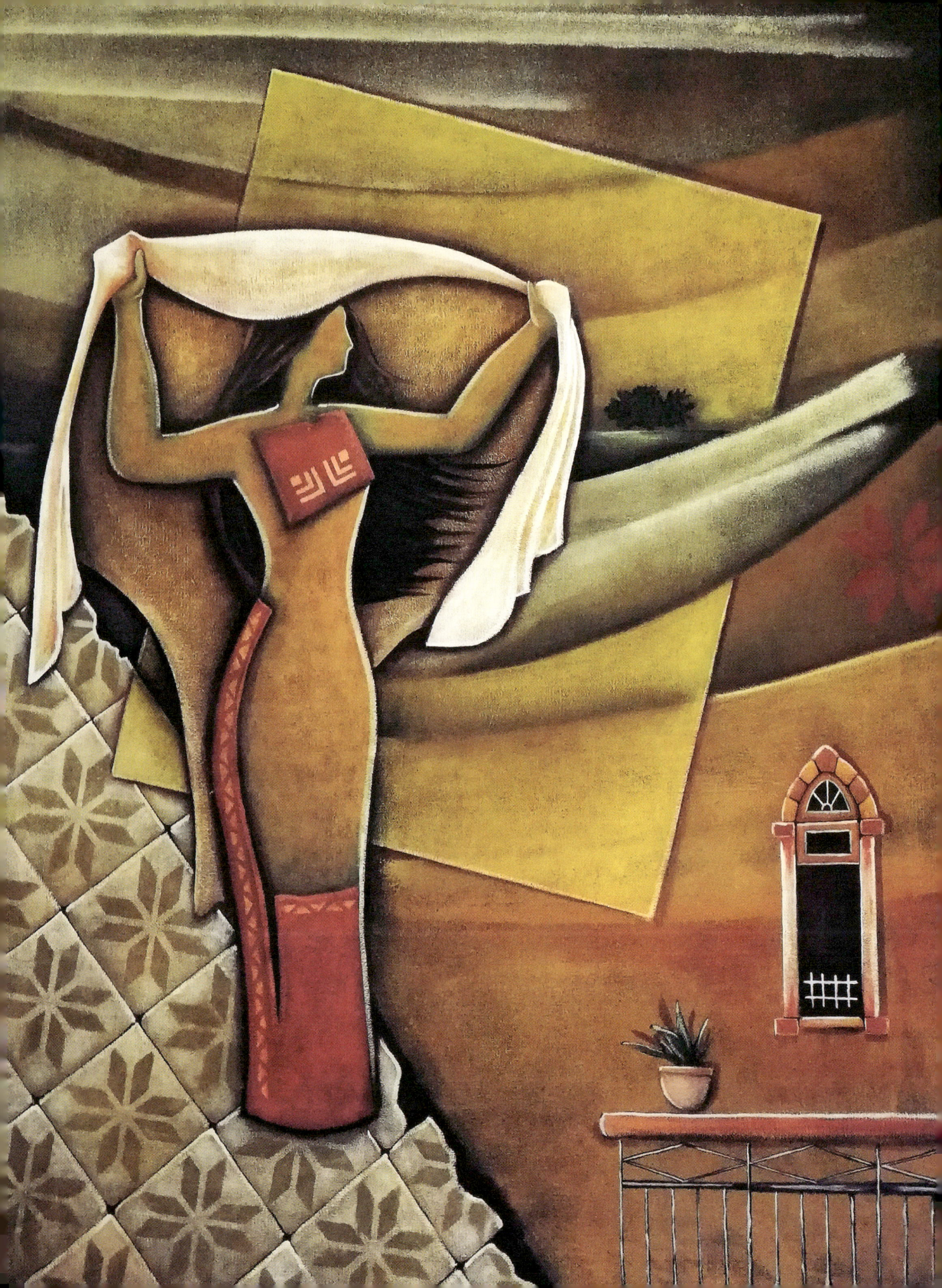

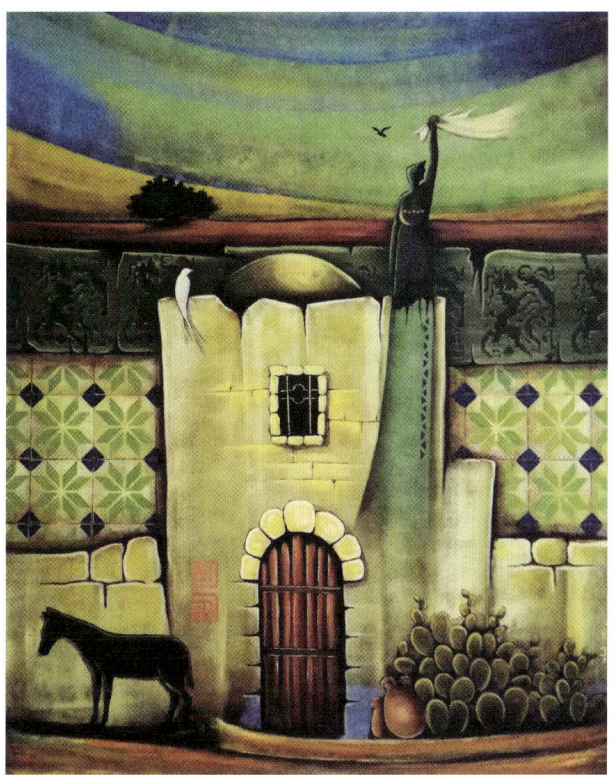
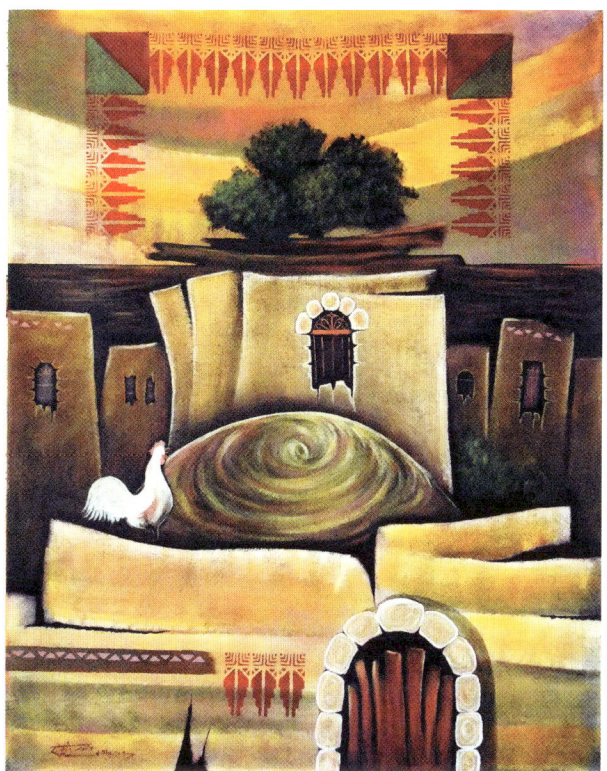

Mohammed Alhaj, *Wave* or *Looming on the Horizon*, 2019. Acrylic on canvas, 120 x 100 cm
Mohammed Alhaj, *Cock*, 2018. Acrylic on canvas, 100 x 80 cm

Left: Mohammed Alhaj, *Troida Is North*, 2020. Acrylic on canvas, 100 x 80 cm

SAMAH

SHIHADI

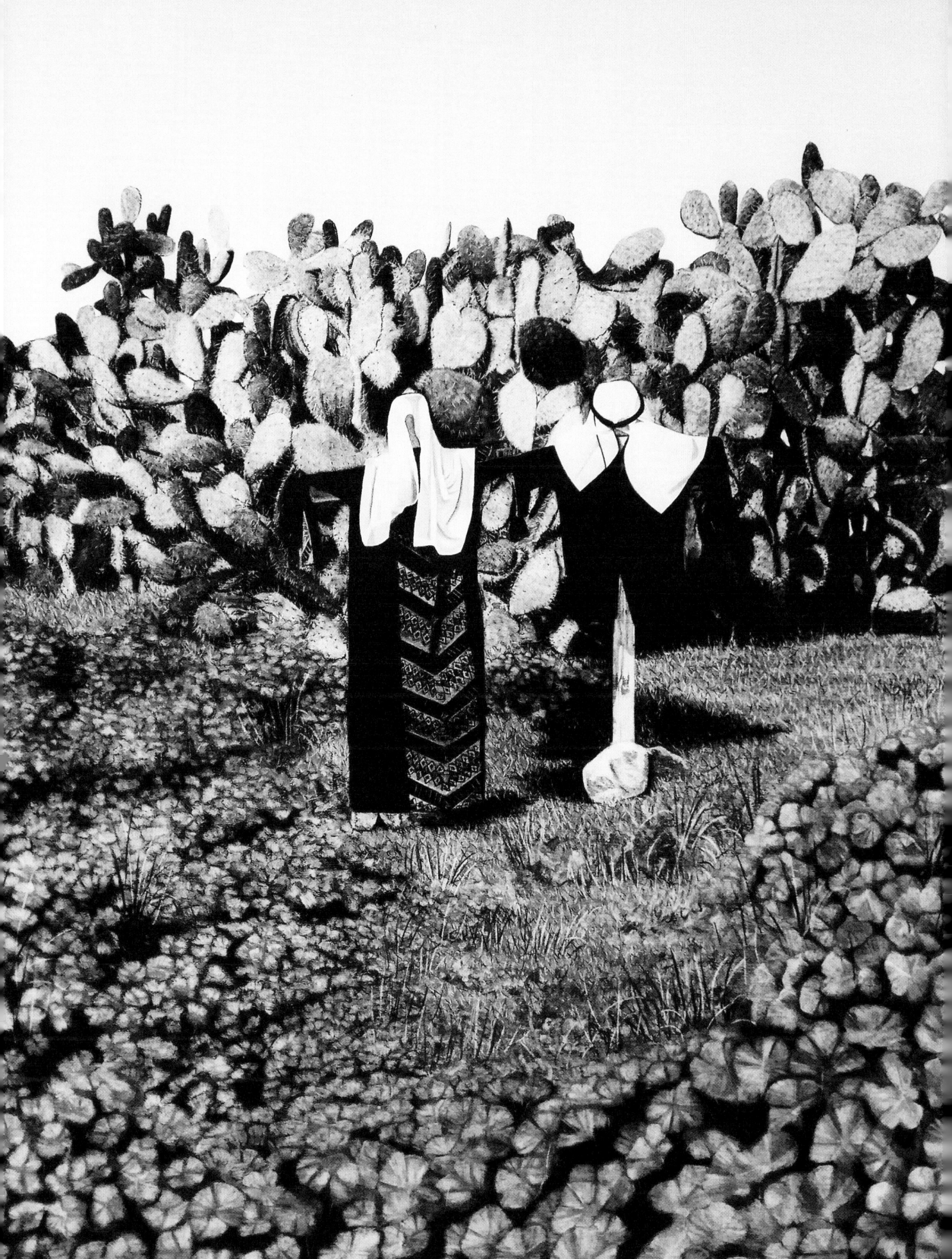

'Despite the sadness that stems from the artwork, I hope the viewer will appreciate the beauty in the landscape, the embroidered dress, and the richness of our heritage,' says Haifa-based artist Samah Shihadi. In her hyperrealistic pencil and charcoal drawings featuring Palestinian embroidery, she captures all these elements with meticulous precision.

The imagery of the embroidered dress has become integral to her art practice. Shihadi explains that the challenge and complexity of drawing fabric, especially embroidery, 'requires a loosening and untying of threads in order to understand them'. In her work, Shihadi uses the symbolism of Palestinian embroidery as a signifier of Palestinian identity, commenting on women's societal roles in Palestinian culture centred on themes of memory, nostalgia, and displacement after the Nakba. Like snapshots capturing moments of physical space and time, her drawings reflect her family's experiences, encompassing a collective story viewed from the observer's perspective.

Shihadi explains the role of symbolism in her work: 'Like the cacti and ruined homes that appear in my artworks, these symbols play an essential role in documenting the abandoned villages and the memories of families who suffered the Nakba in 1948. The important thing for me is that the viewer sees the reality and truth of what happened in Palestine in 1948. Symbols, including clothes, cacti and characters, always appear in the same place, and represent our permanent attachment to our beloved land that was stolen from us.'

In *Scarecrows* (2018), the faceless figures with outstretched arms stand straight, side by side, in front of a wall of tall cactus plants that demarcate the borders of one plot of land from the next. Shihadi says, 'The scarecrows wear the traditional dress, as if they were a Palestinian woman and a Palestinian man protecting their country and lands, standing steadfast in the face of the enemy.' As in all her drawings, we see Shihadi's masterly use of light and texture. The female and male scarecrows are the focal point of the drawing, where the contrast of the white headscarf and *hatta* against the dark fabric of the embroidered dress and jacket draws the viewers' attention to their protective stance.

In her work, Shihadi presents her mother, Zahra, in an embroidered dress. Zahra is featured in the *Cactus Harvest* series, tending the land or resting. Shihadi explains, 'Every time I take photographs to prepare for a work, my mother immediately puts on the embroidered dress. The dress is very important in highlighting and showing who she is as a Palestinian woman from a family displaced from their village. It appears as support, strengthening the work in meaning and significance while adding beauty.'

The mother figure also represents the connection with the motherland, a multigenerational relationship tied to the landscape and expressed through embroidery. *Mother and Daughter* (2019) is an example of this generational bond. Zahra, wearing her embroidered dress, stands next to a large, fully grown mulberry tree in the barrel where Shihadi's grandmother planted it. Her hand rests on the tree trunk in a poetic embrace like an extended branch. The powerful exchange between the two figures is a reminder of the familial connection that cannot be severed despite the trauma of displacement, loss and time.

The village of Mi'ar was destroyed in 1948, including Shihadi's mother's family home. *My Mother's House* (2020, 2021) consists of two finely detailed charcoal works where Shihadi depicts Zahra solemnly sitting near where the mulberry tree was originally planted on her family's land on the site of their destroyed home, where only a portion of a wall still stands. Shihadi revisits the dialogue between her mother and the mulberry tree, with the absence of the tree as a poignant reminder of their uprooting and displacement. Unlike the tree, Shihadi's mother would return to the site of her original home, pick herbs for tea, and connect to the land and its memories. Shihadi is driven by a sense of duty as a Palestinian woman and daughter of a family displaced from their village 'to speak out and tell our story, our memories and our lives in our country.'

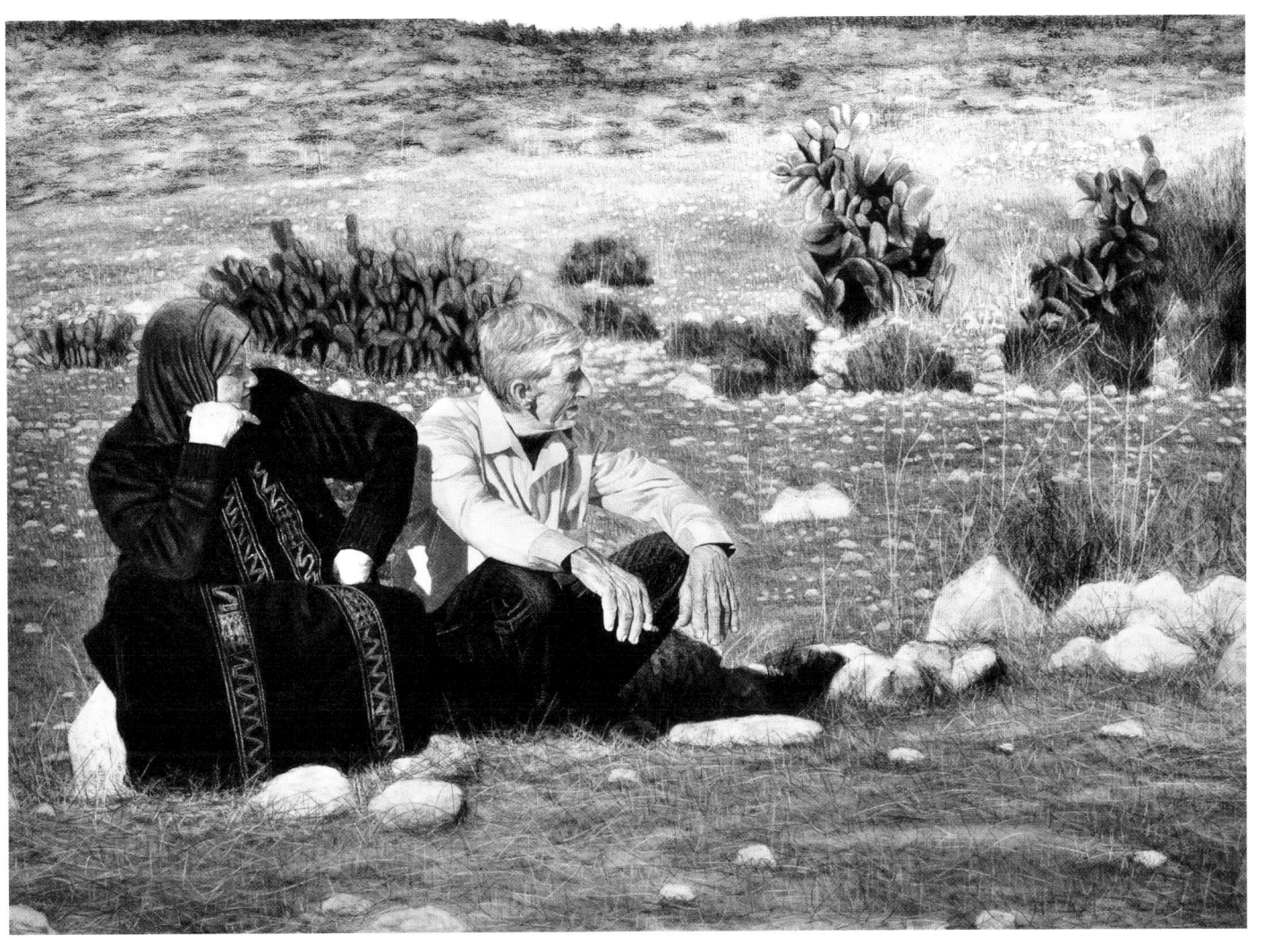

Samah Shihadi, *Harvest Break*; *Cactus Harvest* series, 2017. Charcoal on paper, 70 x 100 cm

Previous spread: Samah Shihadi, *Scarecrows*, 2018. Charcoal on paper, 150 x 100 cm

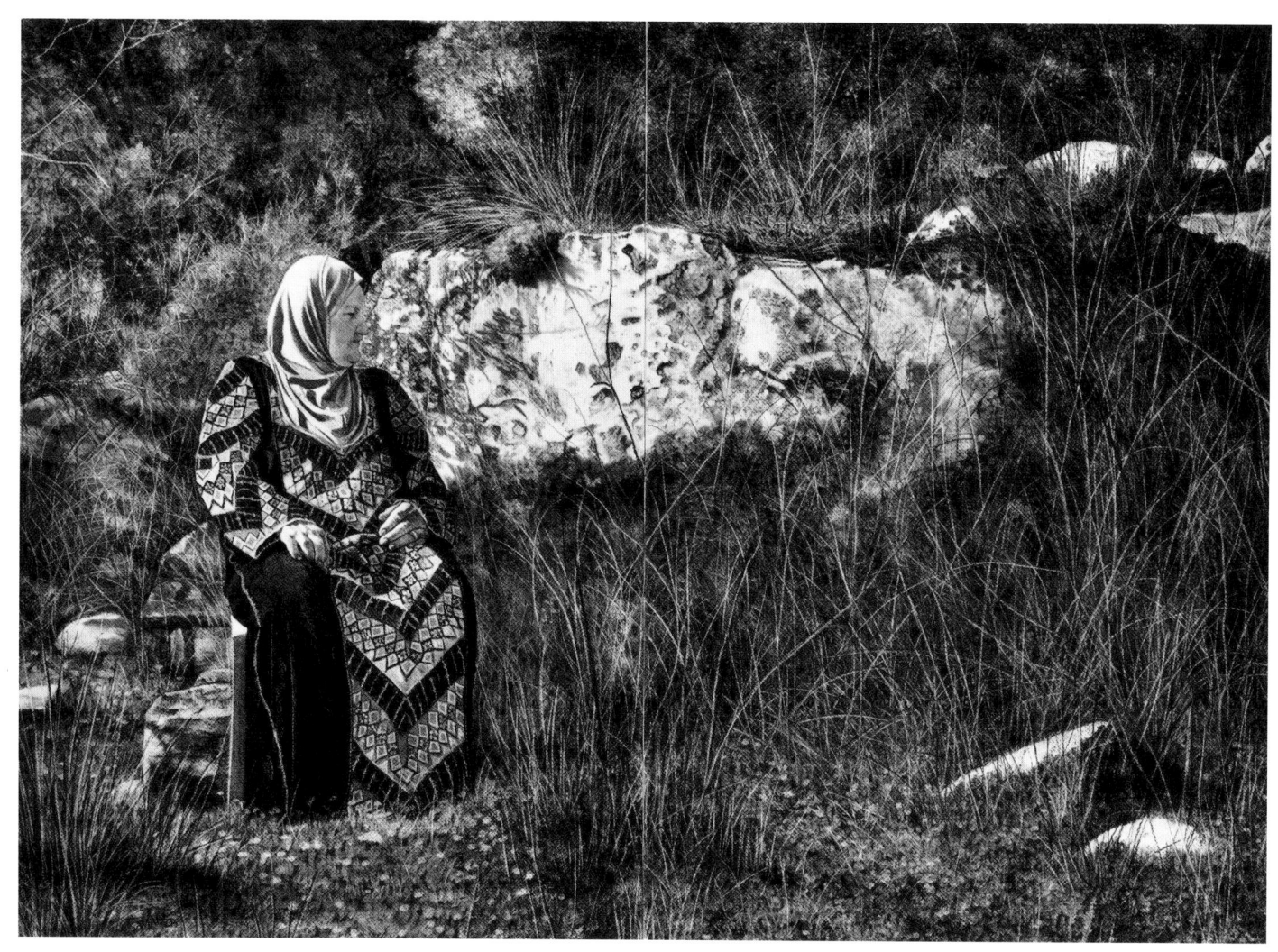

Samah Shihadi, *My Mother's House*, one of a series of two works, 2020. Charcoal on paper, 100 x 70 cm
Right: Samah Shihadi, *Cactus Harvest 1*; *Cactus Harvest* series, 2017. Charcoal on paper, 56 x 76 cm

Next spread: Samah Shihadi, *Mother and Daughter*, 2019. Charcoal and paper, 190 x 140 cm

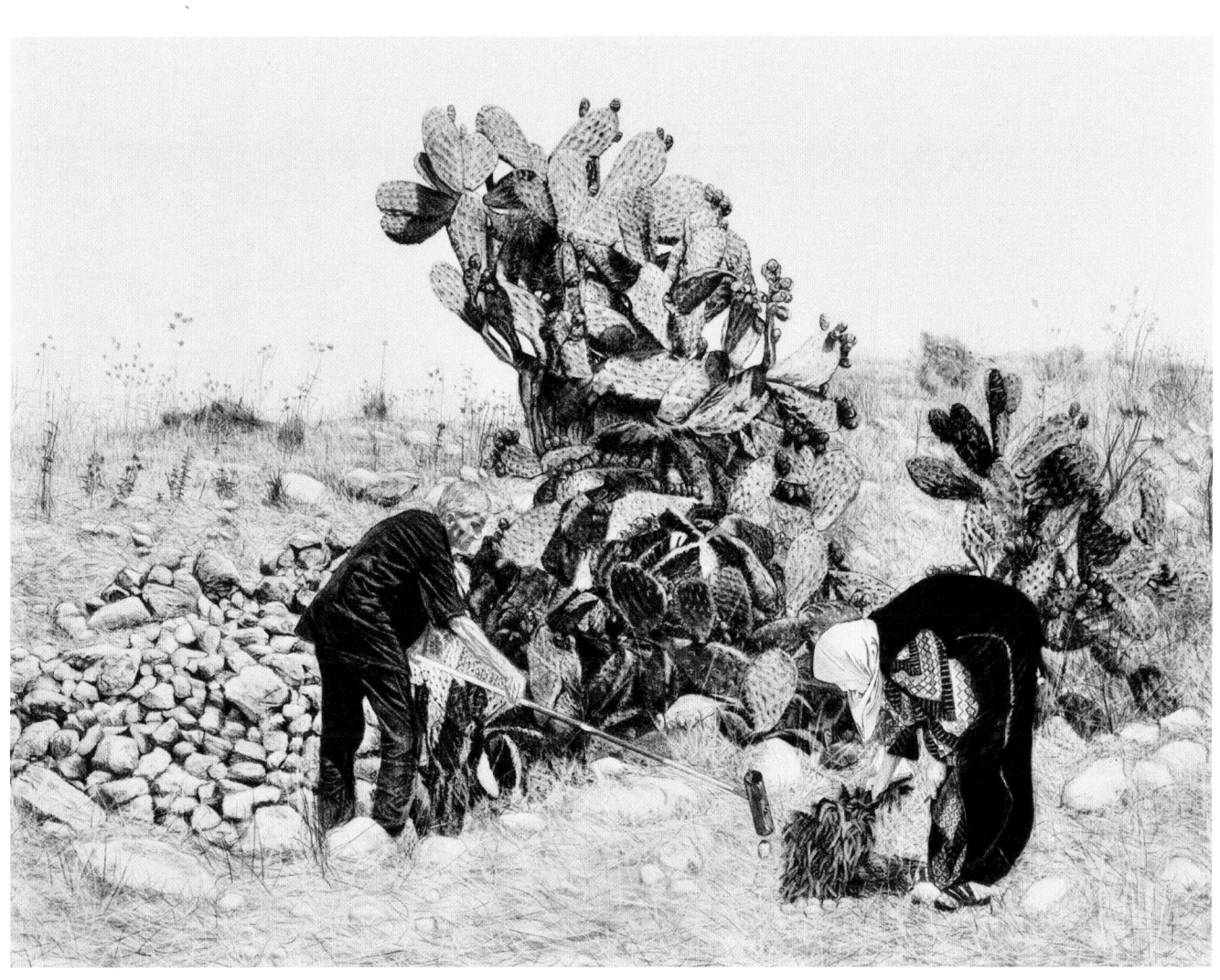

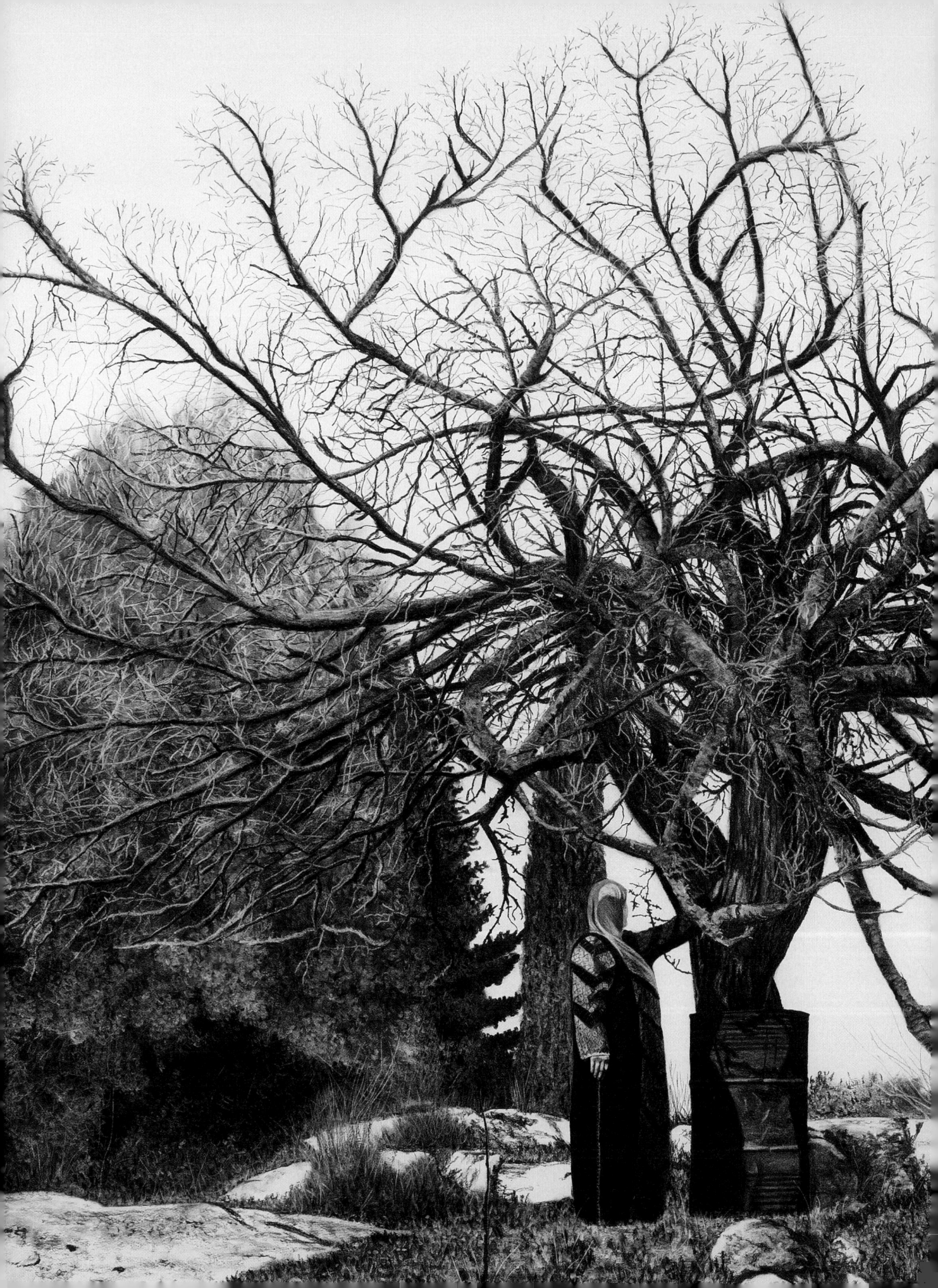

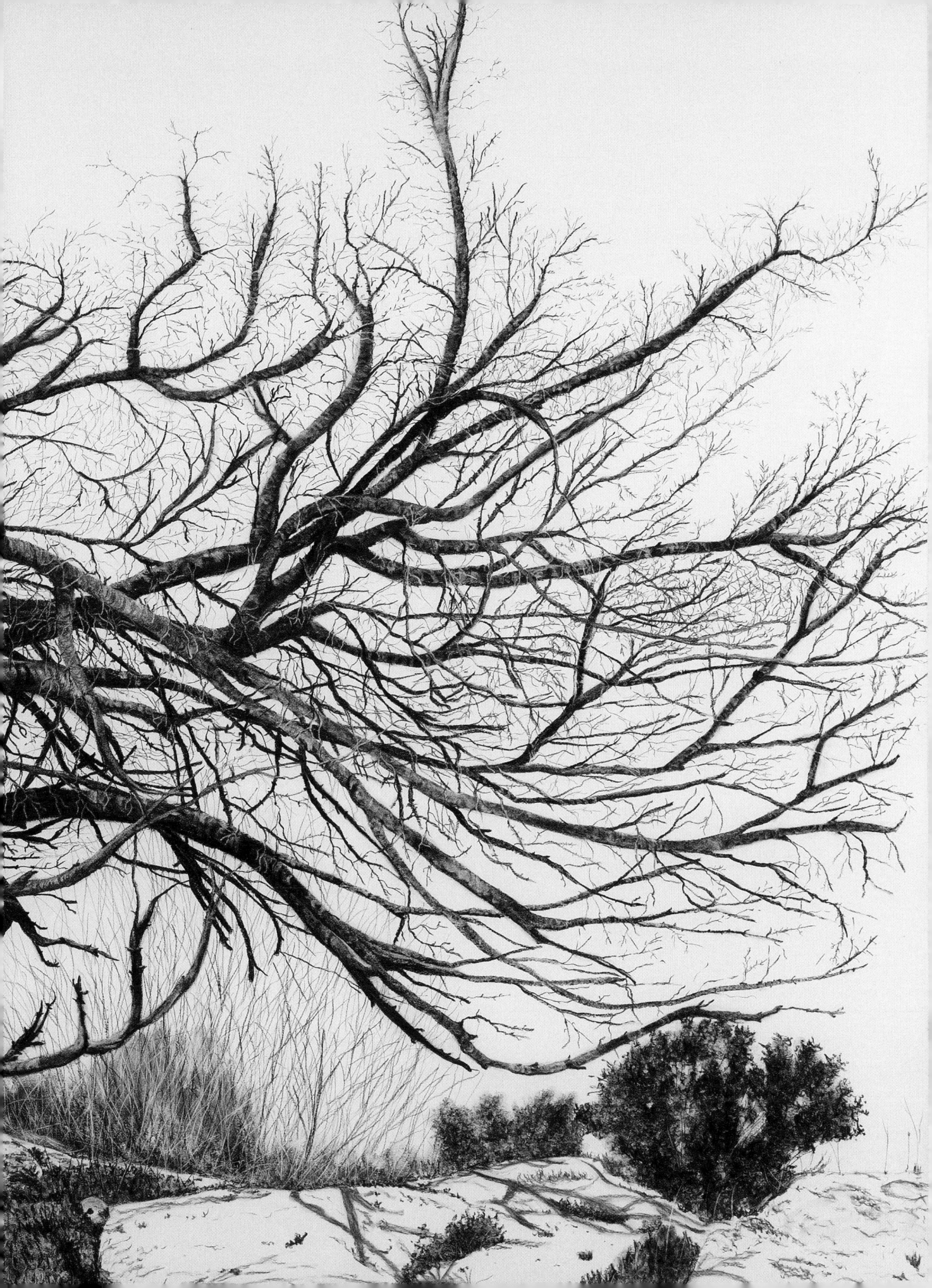

HAZEM
HARB

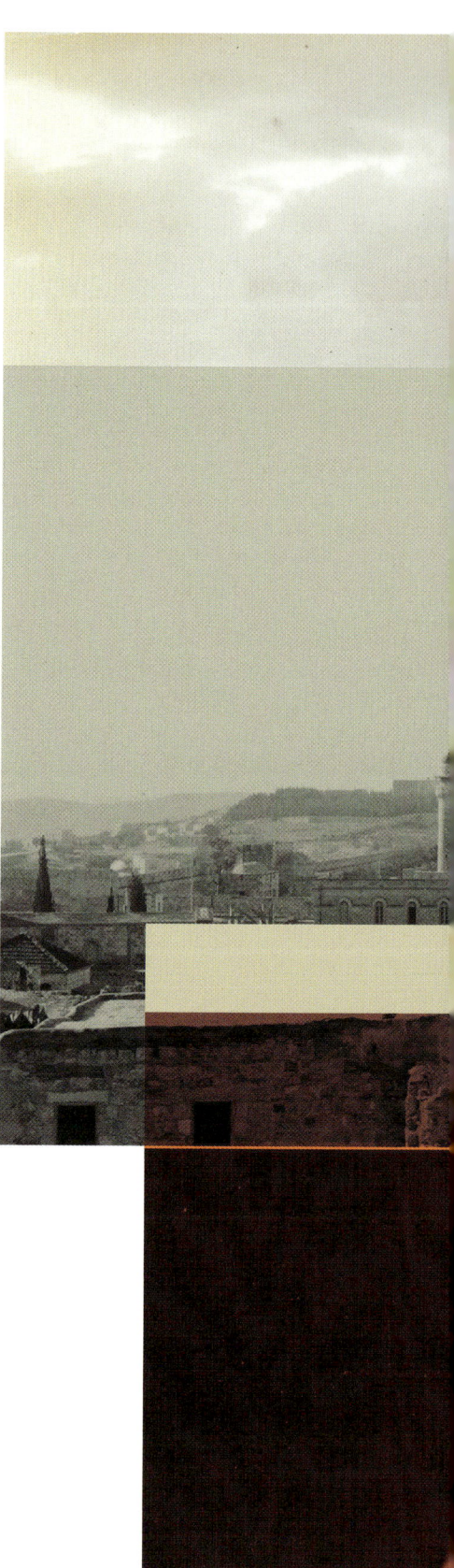

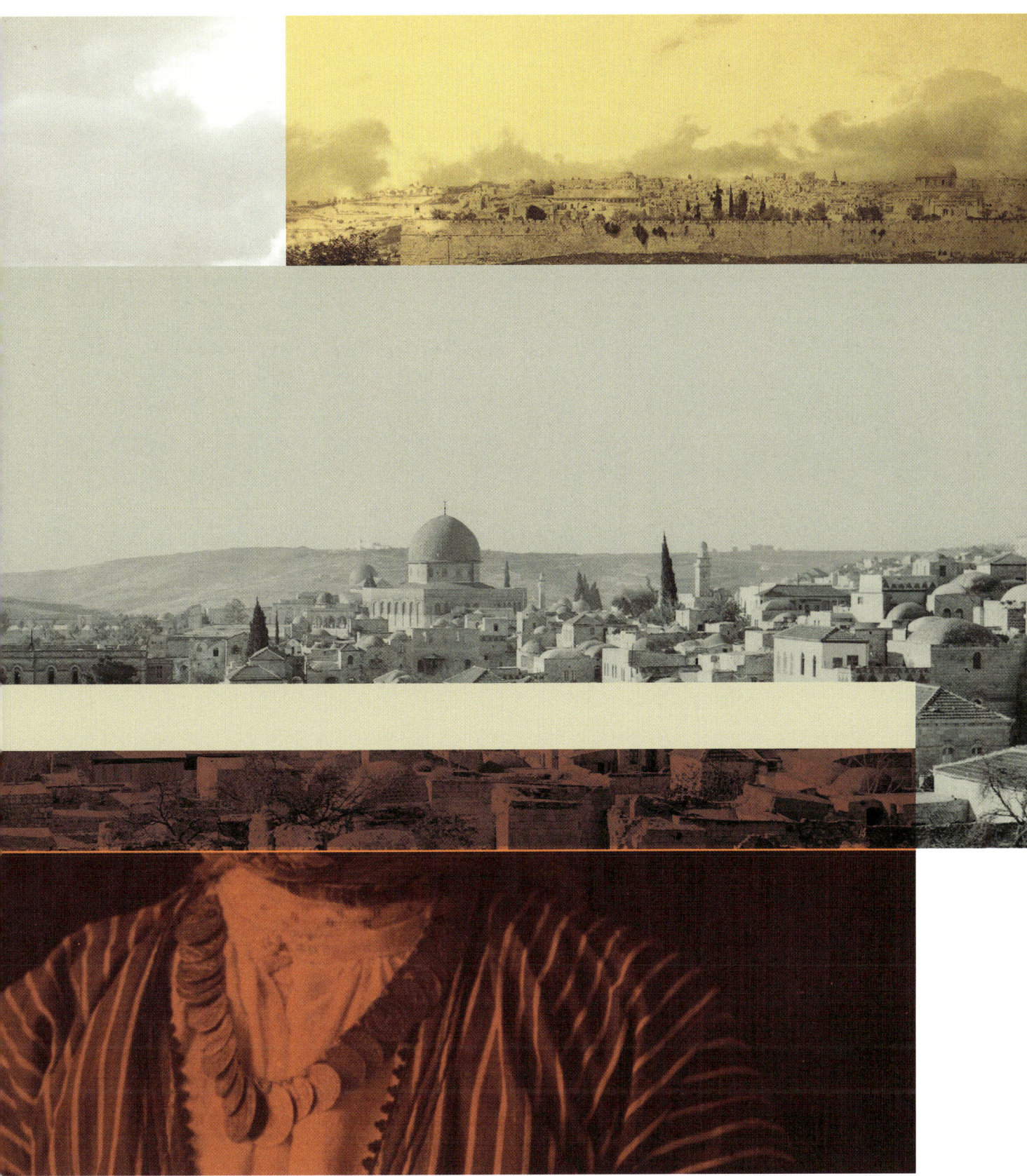

Well known for his collage, installation and conceptual art, artist Hazem Harb explains why he includes imagery of Palestinian embroidery in his work: 'As an artist, I observe Palestinian embroidery through an anthropological lens, understanding it as a trace of culture in terms of Palestine's tangible, aesthetic heritage. It is also a way in which we can understand Palestinian social identities more deeply.'

To Harb, born and raised in Gaza, Palestinian embroidery represents memories of his family and community. It also informs how he views himself and shapes his visual language. He says, 'Embroidery, as both a practice and a product, is deeply rooted in Palestinian culture. It's a marker of Palestine and the various communities that form it. The patterns vary from place to place, but the practice of creating these designs unites the women of Palestine. The images and geometric shapes that reflect the Palestinian embroidery that forms elements in my artwork relay historical evidence and the aesthetic intricacies of the community seldom seen by the masses. As artefacts reimagined, the images show how women engaged with society and how their clothes became an expression and celebration of their national identity. It is all the more important to communicate this, as this identity is regularly under threat and denied.'

Harb's research focuses on Palestinian archives dating from 1890 to just after the 1948 Nakba period. He believes that photographs and ephemeral materials offer insight into details of Palestinian life beyond biased historical written records. In his collaged compositions, Harb brings together archival photographs, coloured plexiglass, paper and other materials. He describes his process in choosing the images he includes in his work: 'I examine these images to know my country before the occupation. By lifting these pictures out of the archival context, I cast a fresh gaze upon them, showing that these visual materials remain relevant in the contemporary moment. In my art I often borrow from the various structural forms these designs entail, using the embroidery patterns to inform slices and shapes in my collages.'

Along with his large-scale collages, Harb produces work using various multimedia and mixed-media resources, such as drawing, sculpture, installation and video art, to best relay his concepts. He uses photographs depicting Palestinian embroidery combined with neon lights and raw materials, including multiple images on wood and strings in Palestinian national colours, denoting textiles and Palestinian currency from 1936.

Harb explains how the Library of Congress released pictures, documents and books related to the history of Palestine that illustrate the violence and massacres committed in Palestine under British occupation followed by those of the Zionists. He says, 'My interest is to search in detail for what Palestine was geographically, demographically and socially. My work is an excavation of these images and a detailed examination of all the elements inside the photos, from people, homes, clothing, culture and the geography of places. I rewrite them differently rather than offering up a simple nostalgic review.' The archives raised essential questions for Harb, causing him to examine how architecture became an expansionist colonial tool used for the erasure of Palestinian villages. This led him to reimagining these archives. He continues, 'I searched for pictures of Palestinian embroidery because of its strong representation of heritage and history and its ability to evoke questions about the realities of people and places.' Palestinian embroidery as a distinct cultural signifier in Harb's work creates a space for remembering and reimagining Palestine.

In discussing his *The Place Is Mine* series (2018), Harb explains that the original scene and its image typically inspire the colours he foregrounds. He introduces colours to reflect and underscore the natural colour of the land, such as the green of Palestine's olives. In some works, there is a revival of the colours of the Palestinian flag, as seen in *Dear Lord* (2016). In his diptych *The Silk Line of Identity* (2020), a unified image emerges from two tinted photographs collaged in an alternating pattern. The photographs depict posed studio portraits of women dressed in traditional embroidered dresses from Bethlehem. Harb explains, 'I sliced and collaged it, forming an unprecedented pattern which recalls its roots in Palestinian heritage and the mechanics of embroidery. The model, fixed to the centre, comes to form a monument imposed upon the landscape. The notion has preoccupied me and regularly features as an icon in my art.'

The embroidery in Harb's collages dates to when the embroidered dress expressed a personal localised identity, specific to a time and place, before it transformed into a symbol of the Palestinian collective and its deep-rooted connection to the land. Harb elaborates: 'Sociologists have long explored the relationship between sartorial choices and trends and their ability to communicate about individual and group identities. In the Palestinian context, this is highly pronounced. By introducing these images to the contemporary art context, I push forward the diversity, intricacies and lesser-seen elements of Palestinian culture. These images contest the framing of Palestinian women as a homogenous group. The embroidery designs are rich and varied, as well as the information they would reveal to the observer about the wearer, communicating where she's from.' The inclusion of imagery of women in traditional dress communicates the vital information Harb needs to express his concept, echoing how Palestinian women shared their personal stories through the embroidery on their dresses.

Harb's art reframes and transforms the viewer's notions of history, place and memory while addressing migration, displacement and borders. 'My work reformulates the archives and places them in a context that resonates with the present time. The danger in remediating images is that they can come across as sentimental or nostalgic.' Although his art centres on the Palestinian case, he notes how the subject matter also connects to collective experiences. Harb crafts a visual language that communicates outside the mass-media narrative and engages and resonates with audiences worldwide.

Previous spread: Hazem Harb, *The Place is Mine, Series #5*, 2018. Handmade layers of collage archival fine art printed photography on MDF wood, 150 x 120 cm

Hazem Harb, *Places and Existence*, 2021. Sepia photographic print mounted on MDF board with neon light, 200 x 138 cm

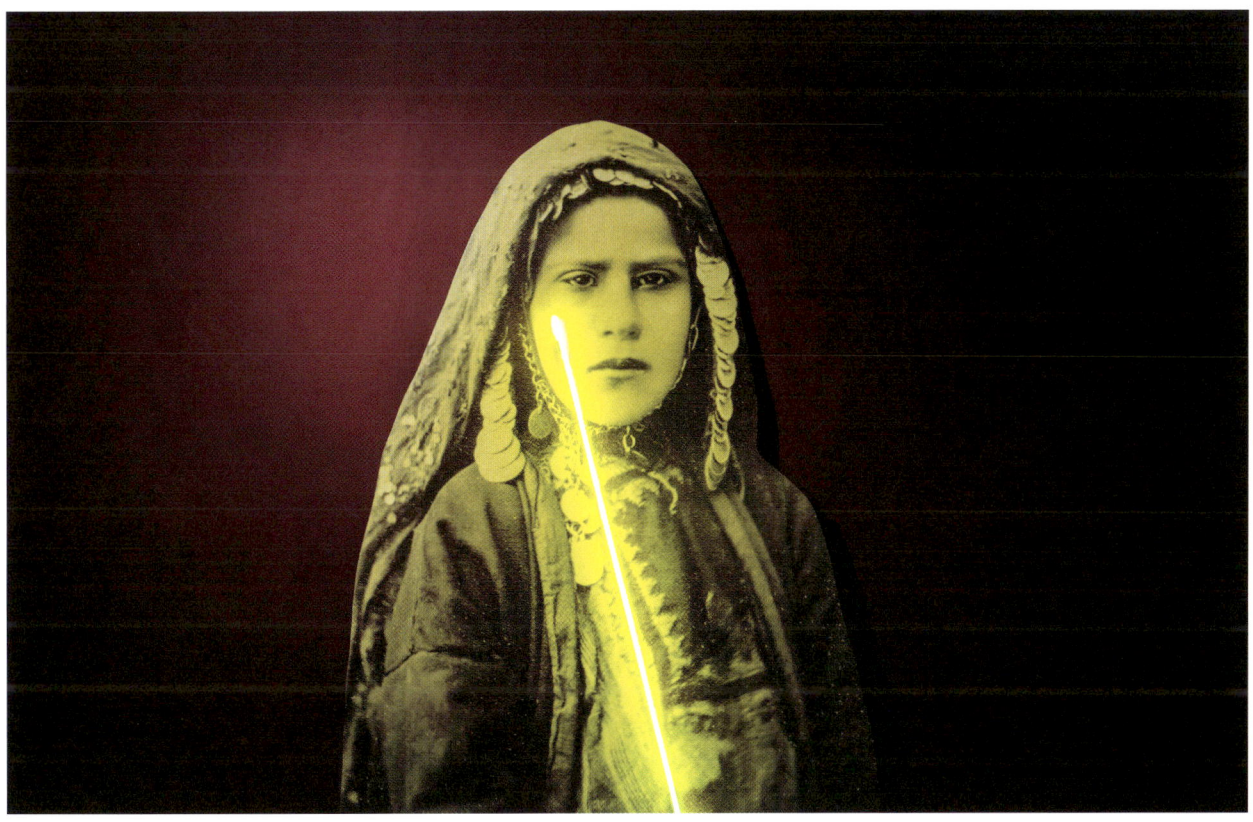

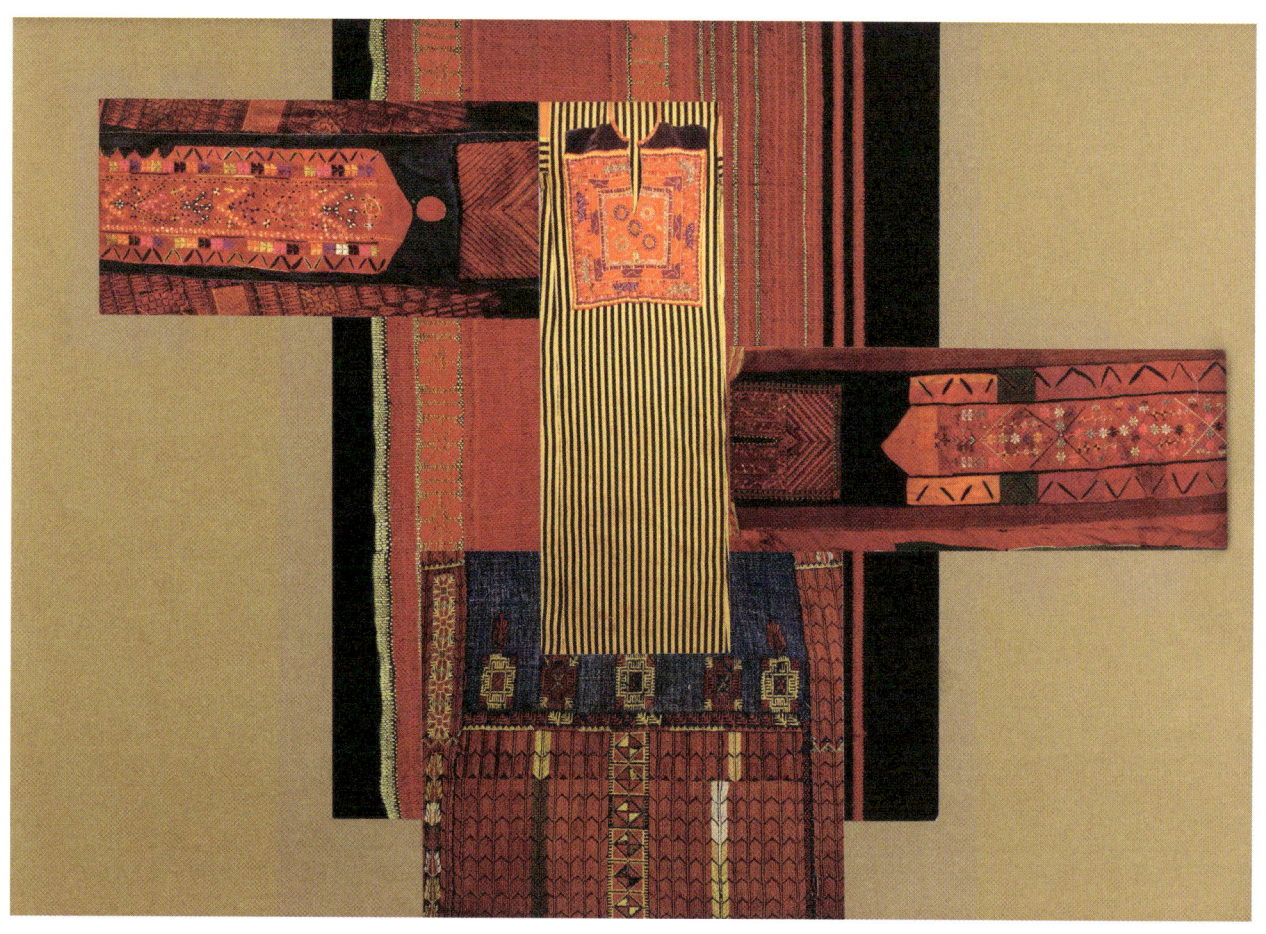

Above and facing page: Hazem Harb, *Stitching Unity*, series of eighteen, 2024. Handmade collage on fine art paper, 32 x 45 cm

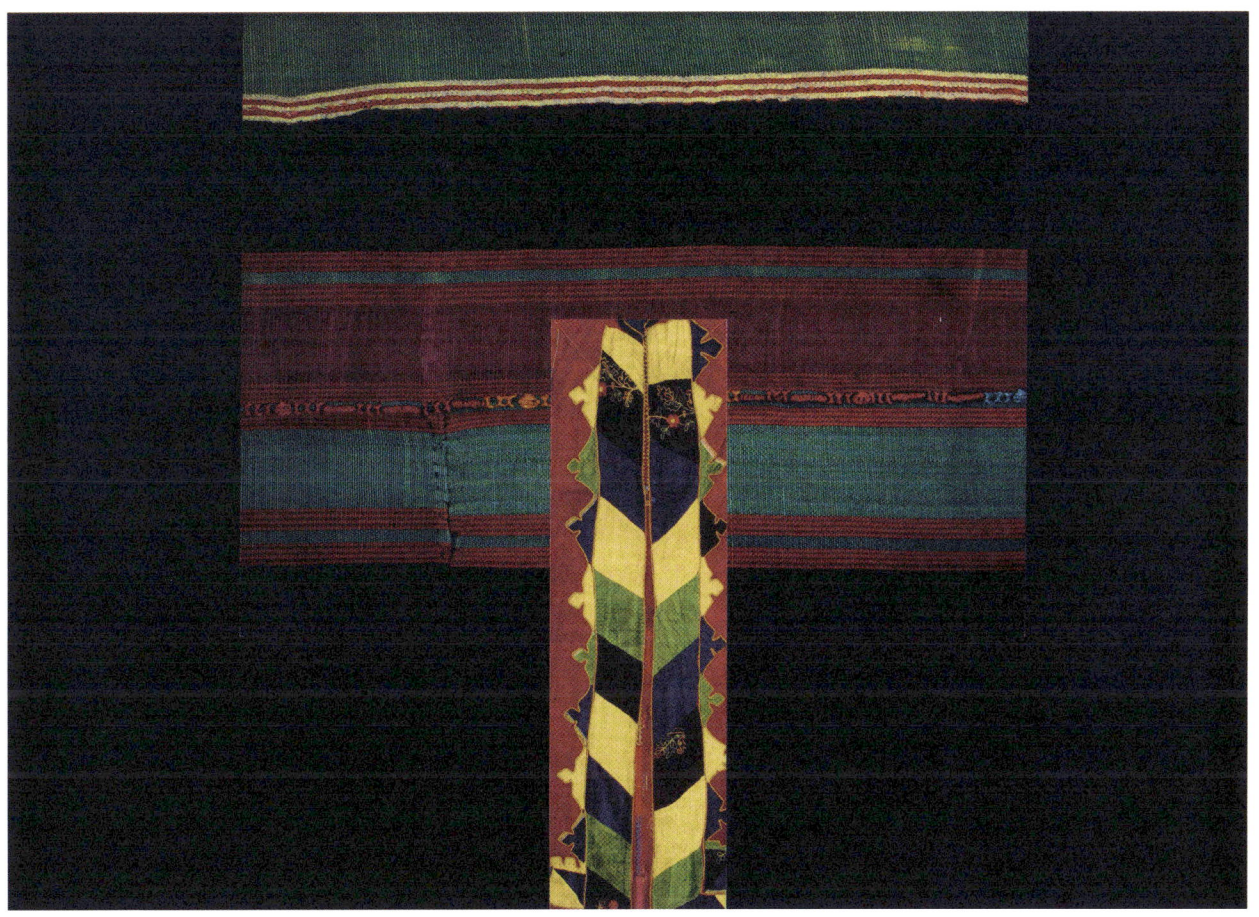

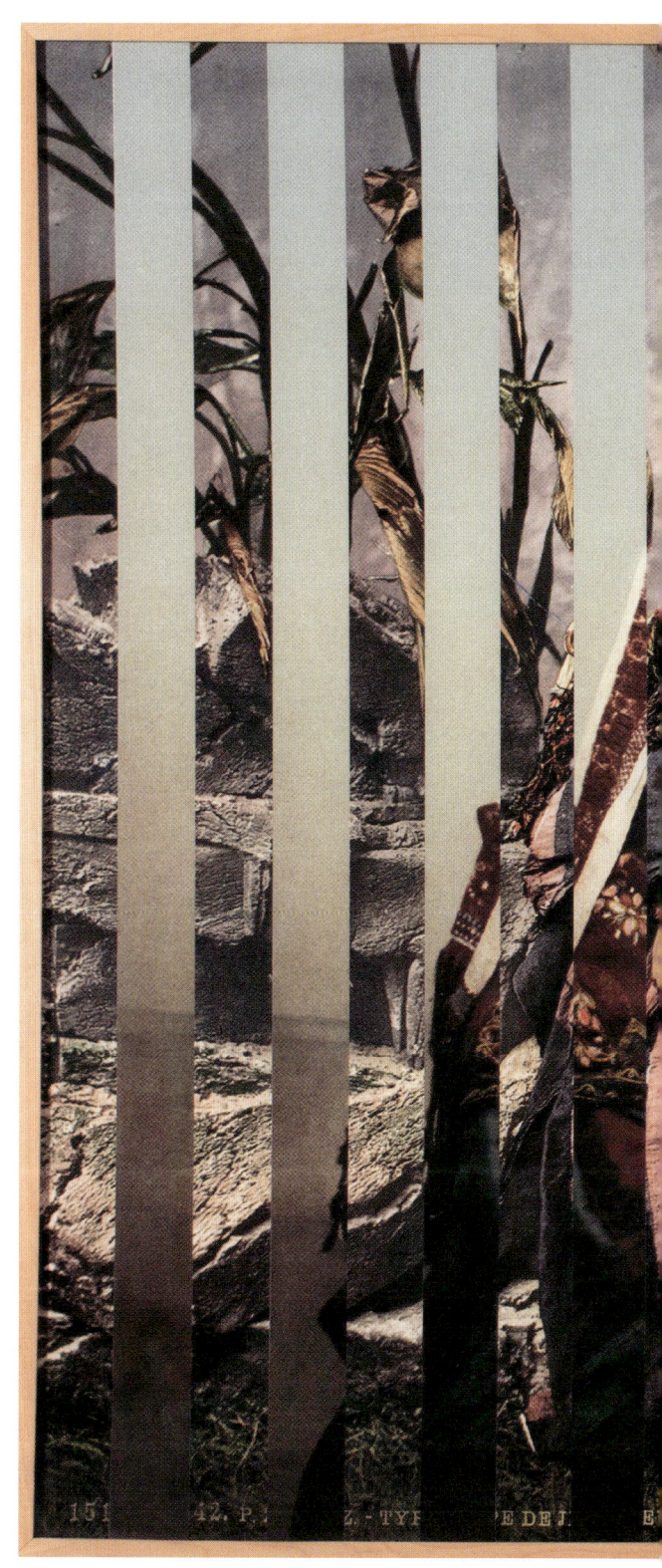

Hazem Harb, *The Silk Line of Identity*, diptych, 2020.
Handmade layers of collaged archival photography fine
art prints on MDF wood, 300 x 200 cm

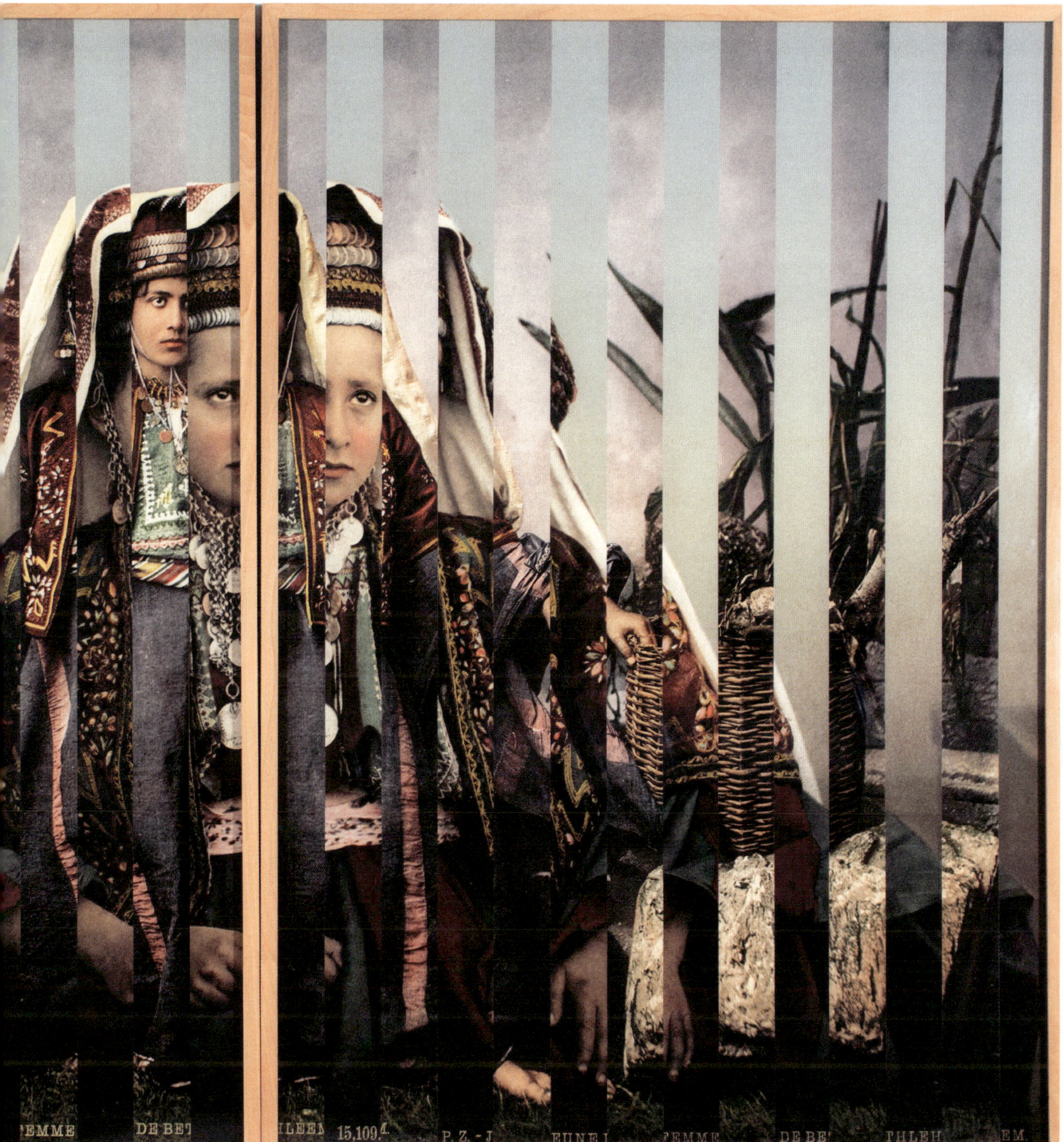

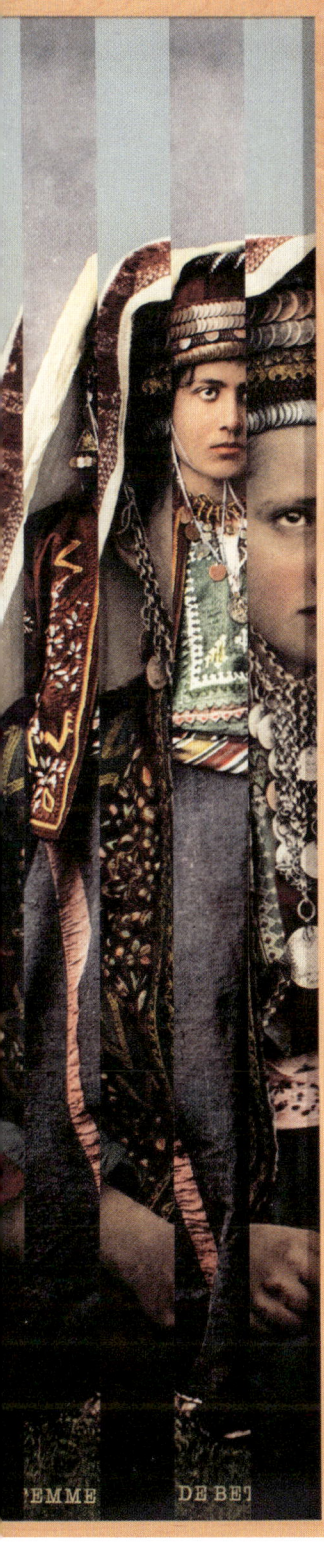

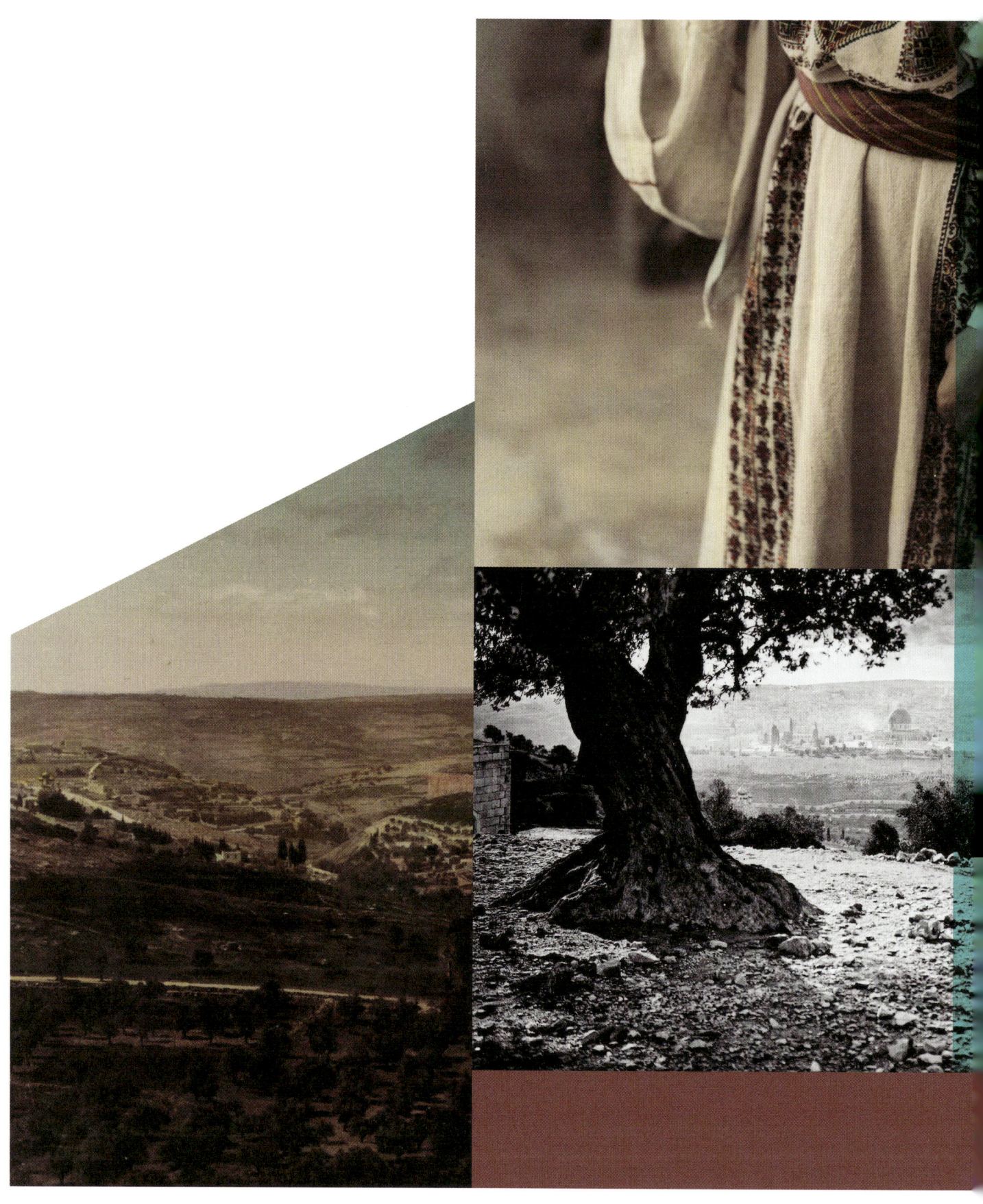

Hazem Harb, *The Place is Mine, Series #4*, 2018. Handmade layers of collage archival fine art printed photography on MDF wood, 150 x 120 cm

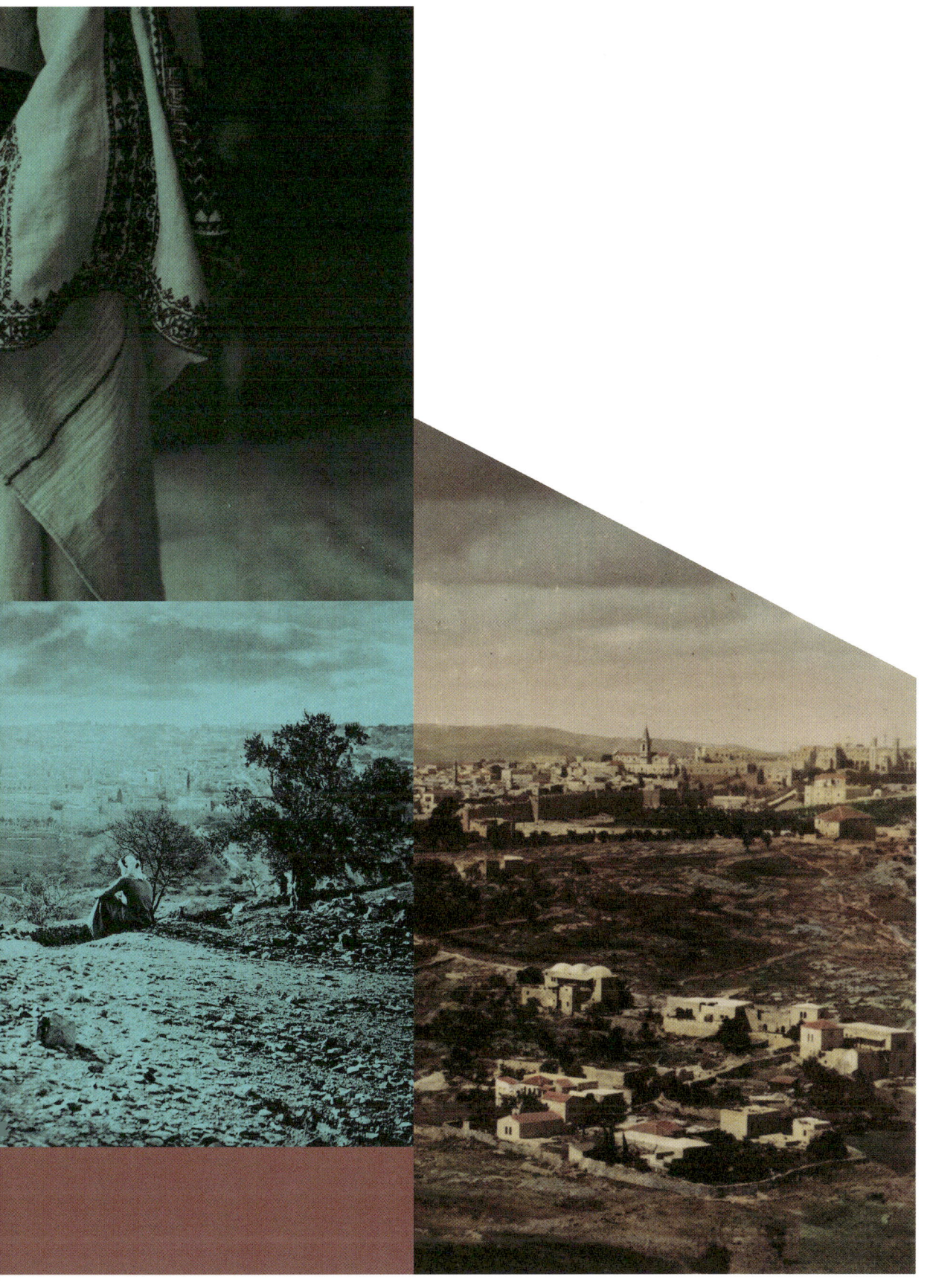

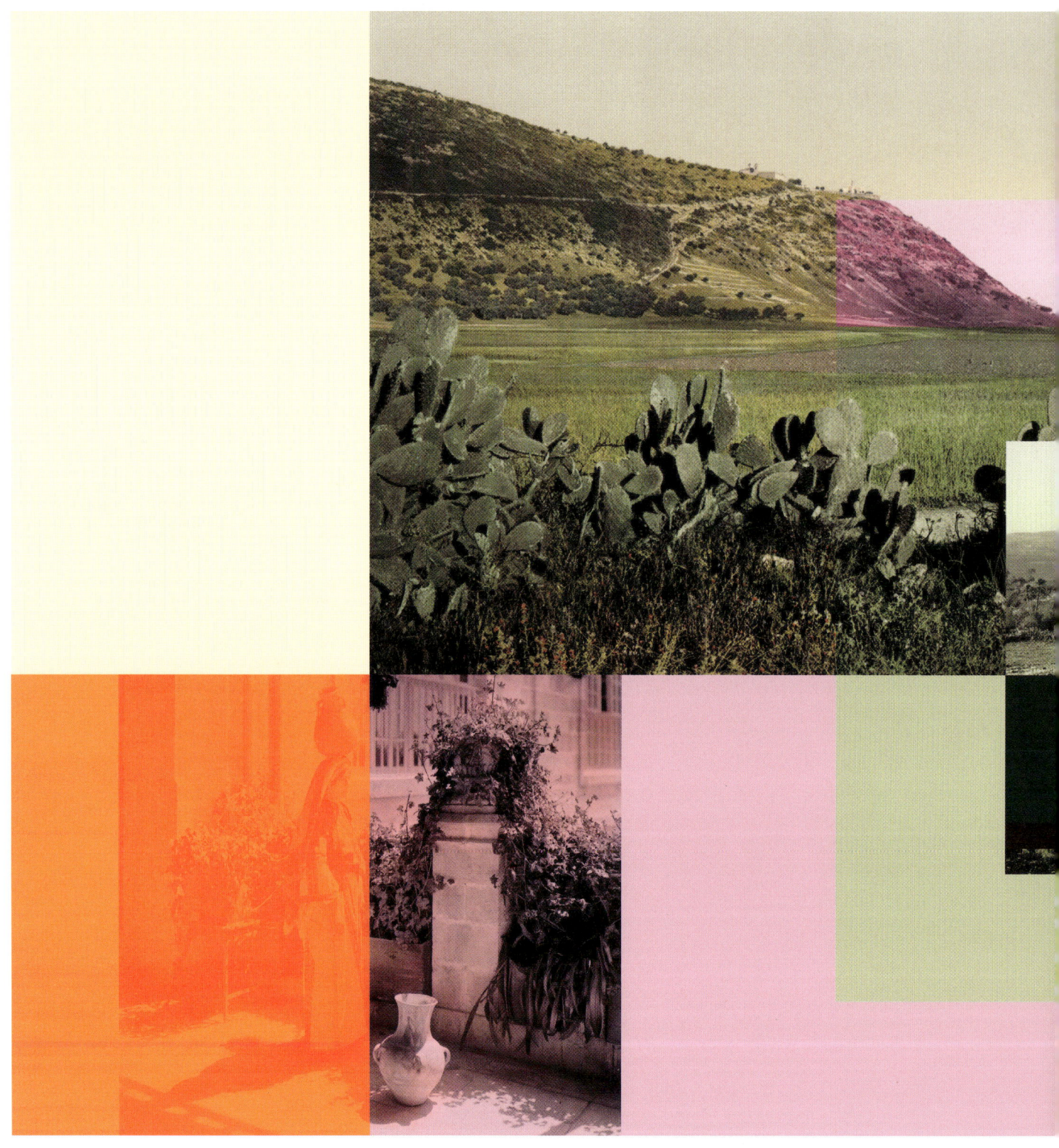

Hazem Harb, *I Am the Land and the Land Is You*, 2023. UV fine art unique prints, layered collage on acrylic, 400 x 200 cm. Collection of Nisreen Bajis

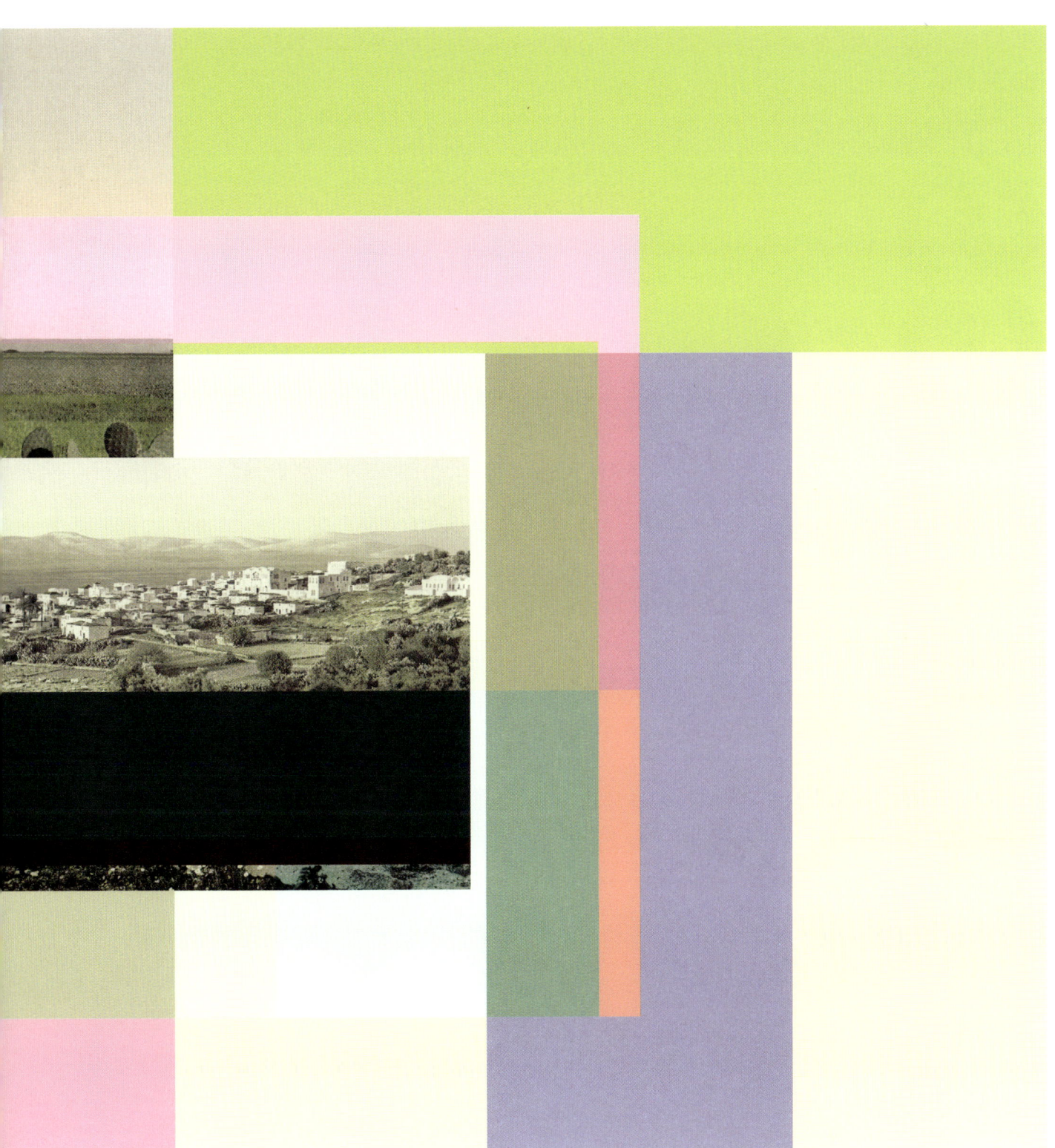

LARISSA SANSOUR

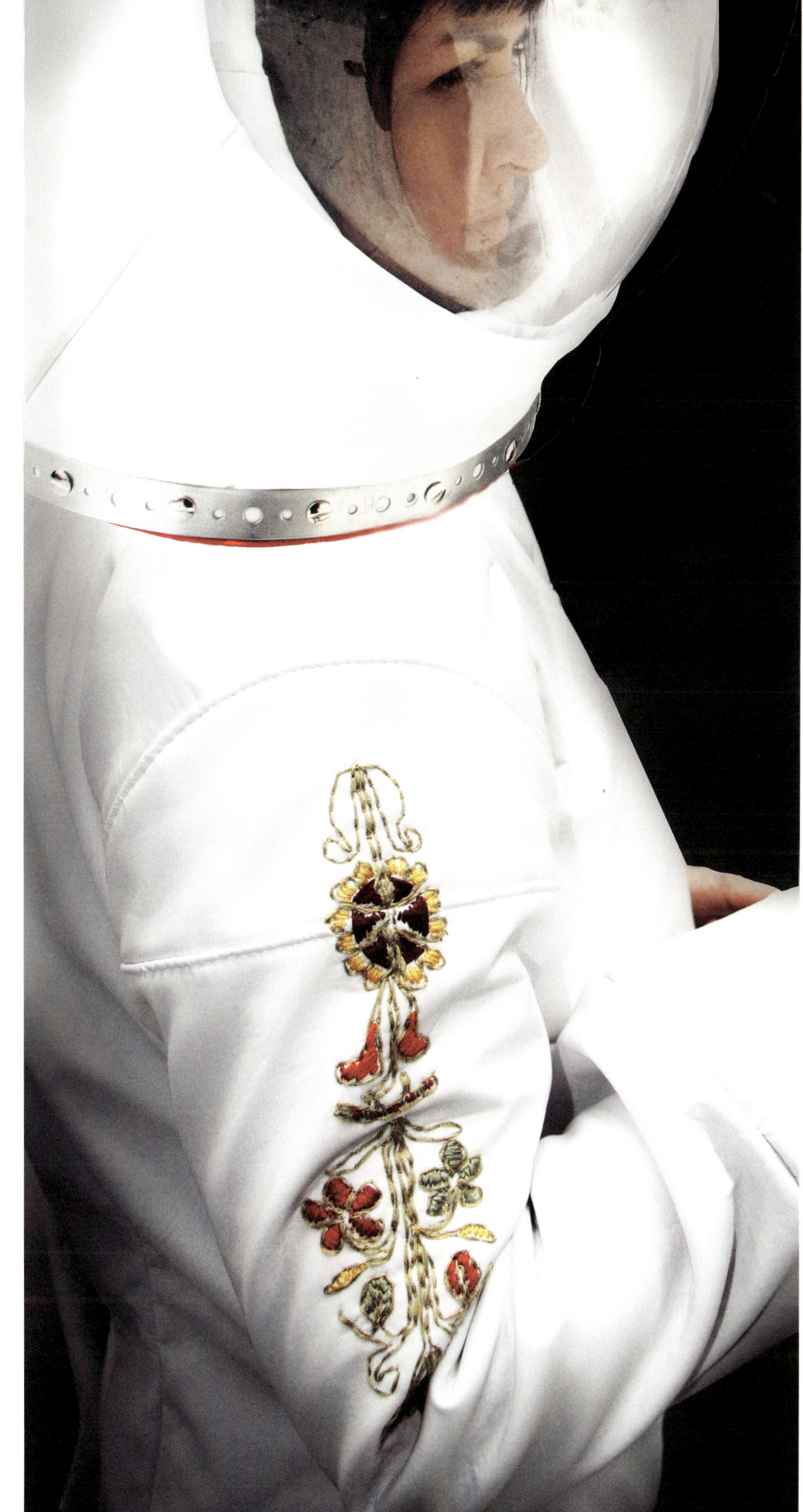

Filmmaker Larissa Sansour sees Palestinian embroidery as an identity marker. She uses it to reference 'Palestinianness' rather than the craft of embroidery itself. She says: 'I have been dealing a lot with issues of the Palestinian psyche and how it is inextricable from a rupture in historical time, due partly to the exodus of Palestinians from their land in 1948. Temporality is blurred in most of my work, and the element of trauma permeates various decades of experience, interlinking past, present and future. On a never-ending revolving reel, specific signifiers make their appearance over and over again.' Sansour demonstrates this in her films *A Space Exodus* (2009), *Nation Estate* (2012), and her films made with Søren Lind, *In the Future, They Ate from the Finest Porcelain* (2016) and *In Vitro* (2019).

Sansour works closely with costume designers to create clothing that the characters in her films wear. She incorporates embroidery which, she says, 'usually sits tightly in the framework of the whole concept, costume and film in general, rather than act as an afterthought or decoration'.

In *A Space Exodus*, Sansour is an astronaut in space or, more specifically, the first Palestinaut landing on the moon, and Bethlehem-style couching embroidery features on the sleeve of her spacesuit. Sansour explains that it 'had to be feminine and indicative of cultural belonging. The film flips gender and ethnic power roles, presenting space exploration as a female and Palestinian achievement. The idea is that I get lost and trapped in space, unable to reach Jerusalem or land on the moon, and hence unable to free myself from my attachment to Earth. And so, the embroidery on my spacesuit's sleeve was central to delineating this kinship.'

The Palestinian embroidery in *Nation Estate* ventures beyond the confines of Sansour's costume, designed as a large cross-stitch pattern with Bethlehem couching embroidery on the pocket. The star cross-stitch motif decorates the floor, travel documents and clothing, serving as a logo or branding tool for Palestine in this world composed of one high-rise building. Sansour says, 'It subverts the traditional form of embroidery, indicating a new context in which to perceive this craft. I wanted

the cross stitch to cease being a repetition of a lost past and to take on an active role in forming a future narrative. In the film, I enter a hi-tech skyscraper that functions as a Palestinian State with all Palestinian cities and towns distributed across the floors. The building is sparse, cold and sterile, mimicking the atmosphere of a museum.'

Sansour points out the numerous references to Palestine, such as the olive tree, flag, *keffiyeh*, holy landmarks and embroidery. She explains, 'These appear as empty vessels, mere artefacts on display. The mechanical affiliation mantra of these symbols has long had a numbing effect on our present-day Palestinian reality, an existence that oscillates between past and future but never the present. This retro-futurist existential void serenades its past, begrudges its future prospects, but excludes its present. The overwhelming use of the star motif in the film, on my sleeve, lobby floor and passports, reiterates the Palestinian traumatic bond to definitions of national identity.' The cross-stitch star motif repeatedly used in the film is found stitched on dresses from regions across Palestine. Today, this recognisable embroidery motif is a visual signifier of the nationalism Sansour describes.

Sansour transforms another instantly recognised symbol of Palestinian nationalism – the *keffiyeh*. 'In *In the Future, They Ate from the Finest Porcelain*, the *keffiyeh* pattern functions as a cultural DNA in the outlandish archaeological project of the main protagonist. A rebel leader calls herself a narrative terrorist – her mission is to change the course of history or the historical narrative. The *keffiyeh*-patterned plates and bowls in the film are based on the utensils introduced in *Nation Estate*. The idea explores the role of myth in chronicling our stories by using objects from a fictional film. The rebel group buries these porcelain plates in various parts of historical Palestine for future archaeologists to find. How many years do these fictional objects have to stay in the ground before they become real?'

Aside from the presence of the *keffiyeh*, characters in the film also wear traditional dress. In the film *In the Future, They Ate from the Finest Porcelain*, two sisters alternate between wearing traditional folkloric Palestinian dresses and school uniforms. Describing them, Sansour says,

'This reshuffling of costumes muddies the distinction between personal, collective and state memory.' She continues, 'The younger sister, who dies at the age of nine, appears in various imagined or dream-like states of negotiation: [these are] attempts by the living sister to overcome or comprehend her present predicament as well as deal with her grief. This exclusive tragedy is slowly inter-threaded with the national catastrophe of loss. The folkloric dresses take these girls from their actual everyday recollections of school days into the realm of a tale weaving across the generations. They are not reminiscing about their pasts but those of all who came before them.' The traditional dresses are the vehicle that transports the characters across time to embody their Palestinian ancestors. While the dresses from *In the Future, They Ate from the Finest Porcelain* indicate a feeling of a Palestinian past, in Sansour's film *In Vitro*, scenes including embroidery are specific to Bethlehem.

In *In Vitro*, the juxtaposition of archival film footage of Manger Square and the current setting of a bunker under the city of Bethlehem blurs the linear function of time. Sansour explains that a group of scientists escape an environmental disaster that renders the earth uninhabitable, and they retreat to this bunker. The bunker includes a sophisticated orchard and an elaborate cloning farm where scientists have created clones from the DNA of their children killed in the apocalypse. The film switches between scenes in the bunker and old memories before the disaster. We see Dunia, the dying leader, speaking to Alia, the clone of her deceased daughter, her successor. Alia, born and raised in the bunker, is haunted and confused by her memories of the surface she has never seen and events she has never experienced. In the film, Dunia tells Alia to guard these images that she keeps in her memories, even though the memories are alien to Alia and are originally Dunia's memories and stories.

Sansour tells us, 'Dunia is the generator of this world above the earth with all its images that include archival footage, lived experiences and thoughts. The images of the past, present and future seamlessly fluctuate as though belonging to an uninterrupted temporality. The past is often imagined with the nostalgic zeal of bucolic scenes, archives of women in romantic Palestinian folklore and childhood memories. In contrast, the present takes place in a Brutalist bunker.

'At some point in a heated argument, Alia becomes resentful of Dunia's dismissal of their current world as transient and unreal. The footage of the women in their embroidered dresses in Bethlehem is over 100 years old. Old Bethlehem appears in the context of the future after the disaster, when our world ceases to exist. In the film, we revisit the same places in Bethlehem with all its reincarnations in the present and in the future, especially in the case of Manger Square. These reiterations are there to accentuate our encapsulated state of no belonging, forever suspended and rejected from historical time, tending only to repeated tropes we dig up from the past and refusing to let go to rethink a future.'

In her films, Sansour challenges the perception of cultural symbols and expands her audience's visual understanding of Palestinian embroidery. Sansour honours Palestinian embroidery's cultural significance in the present by allowing her audience to witness it as a remnant or artefact while also imagining it repurposed for the future.

Previous spread: Larissa Sansour, *A Space Exodus*, 2009, film still. Costume designer Line Frank

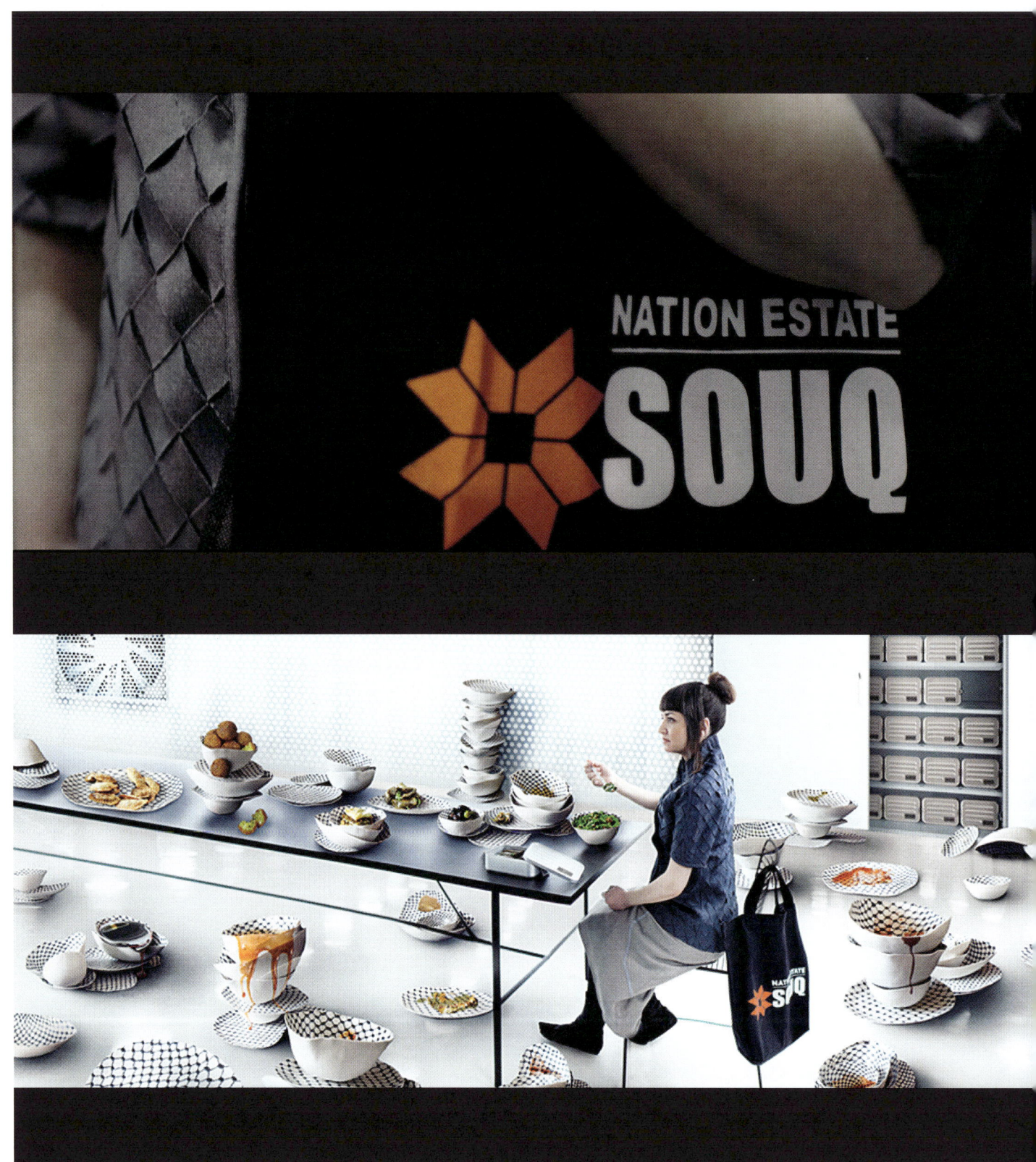

Larissa Sansour, *Nation Estate*, 2012, film stills. Costume designer Line Frank

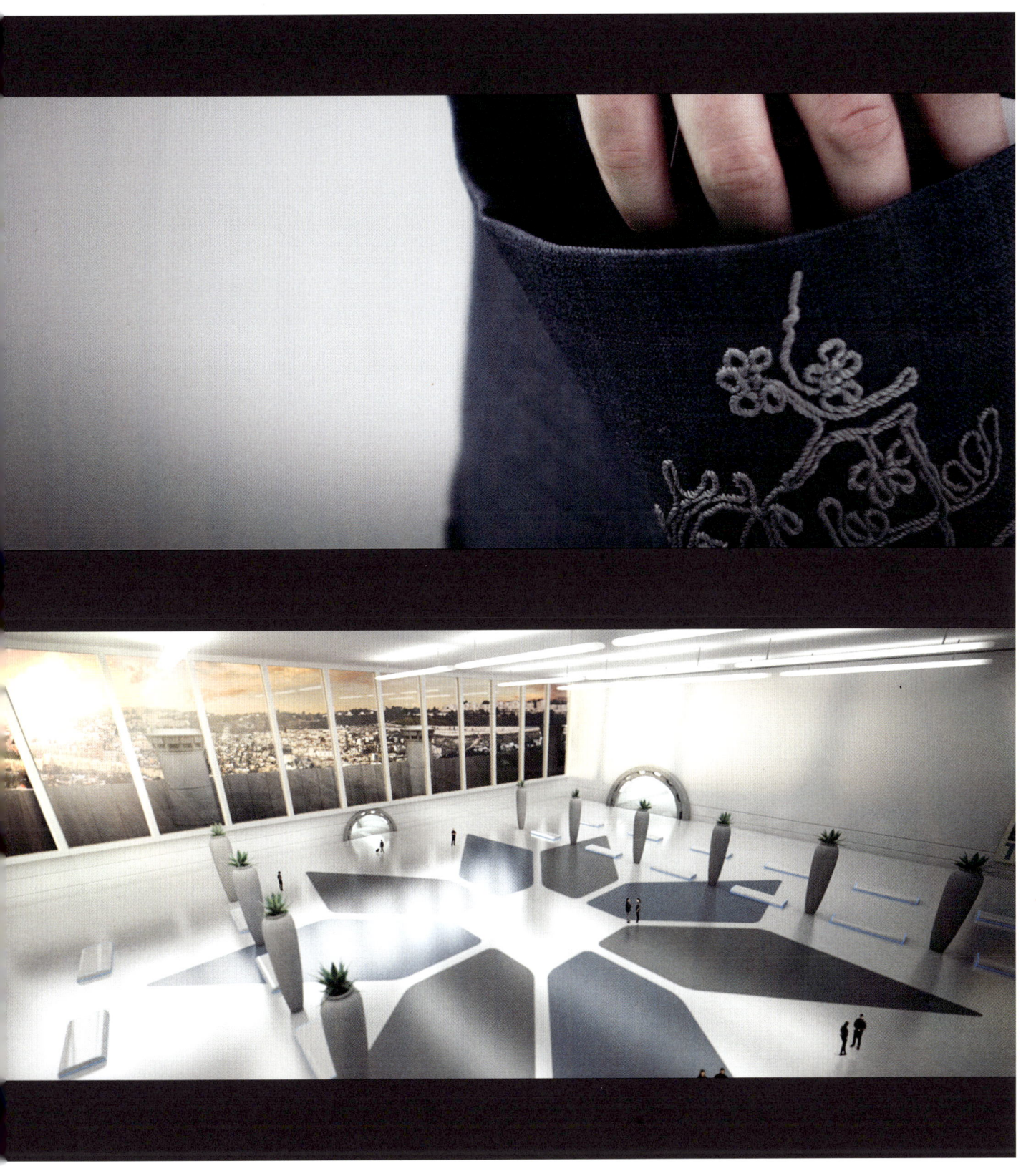

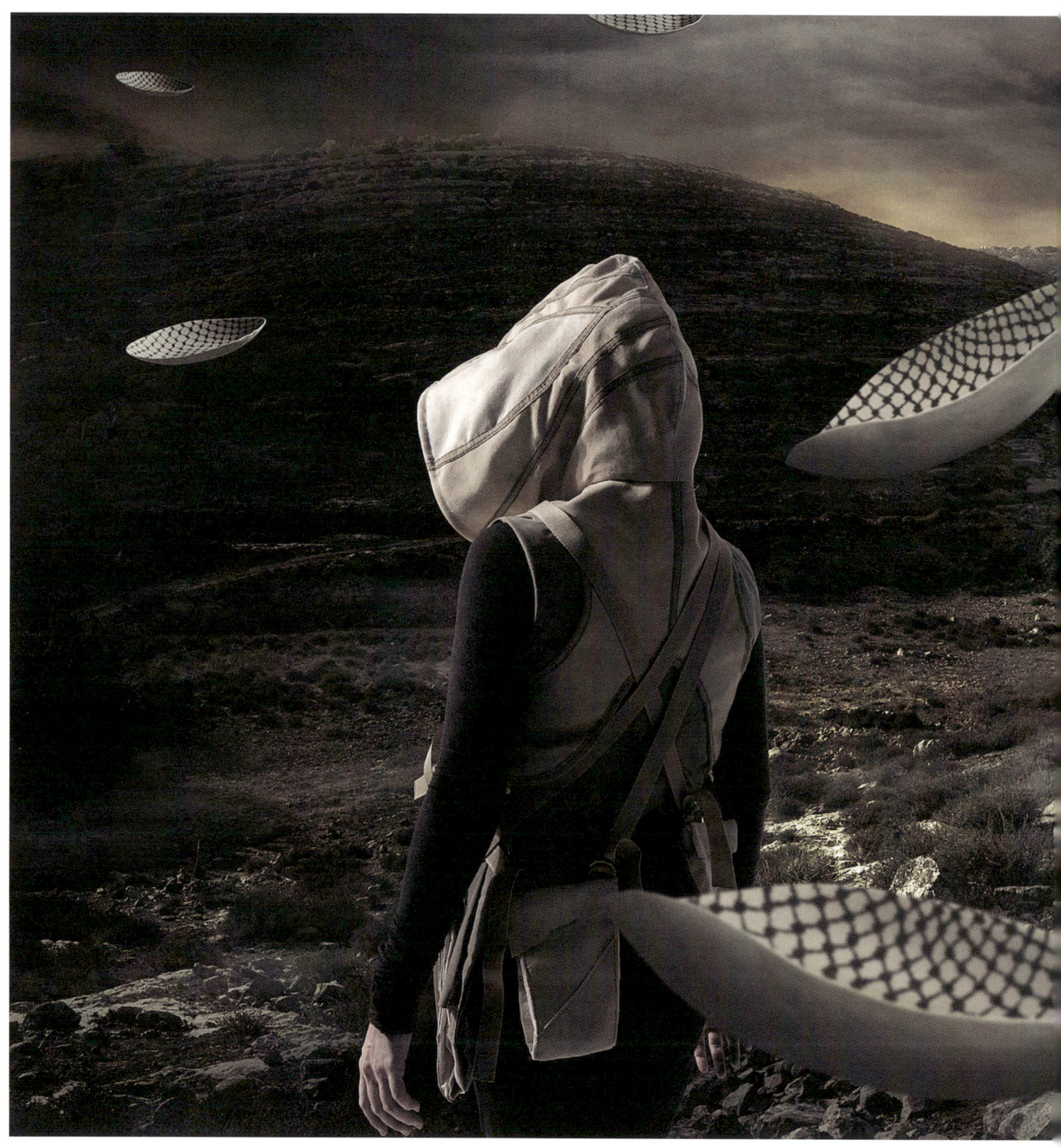

Larissa Sansour and Søren Lind, *In the Future, They Ate from the Finest Porcelain*, 2016. Film still

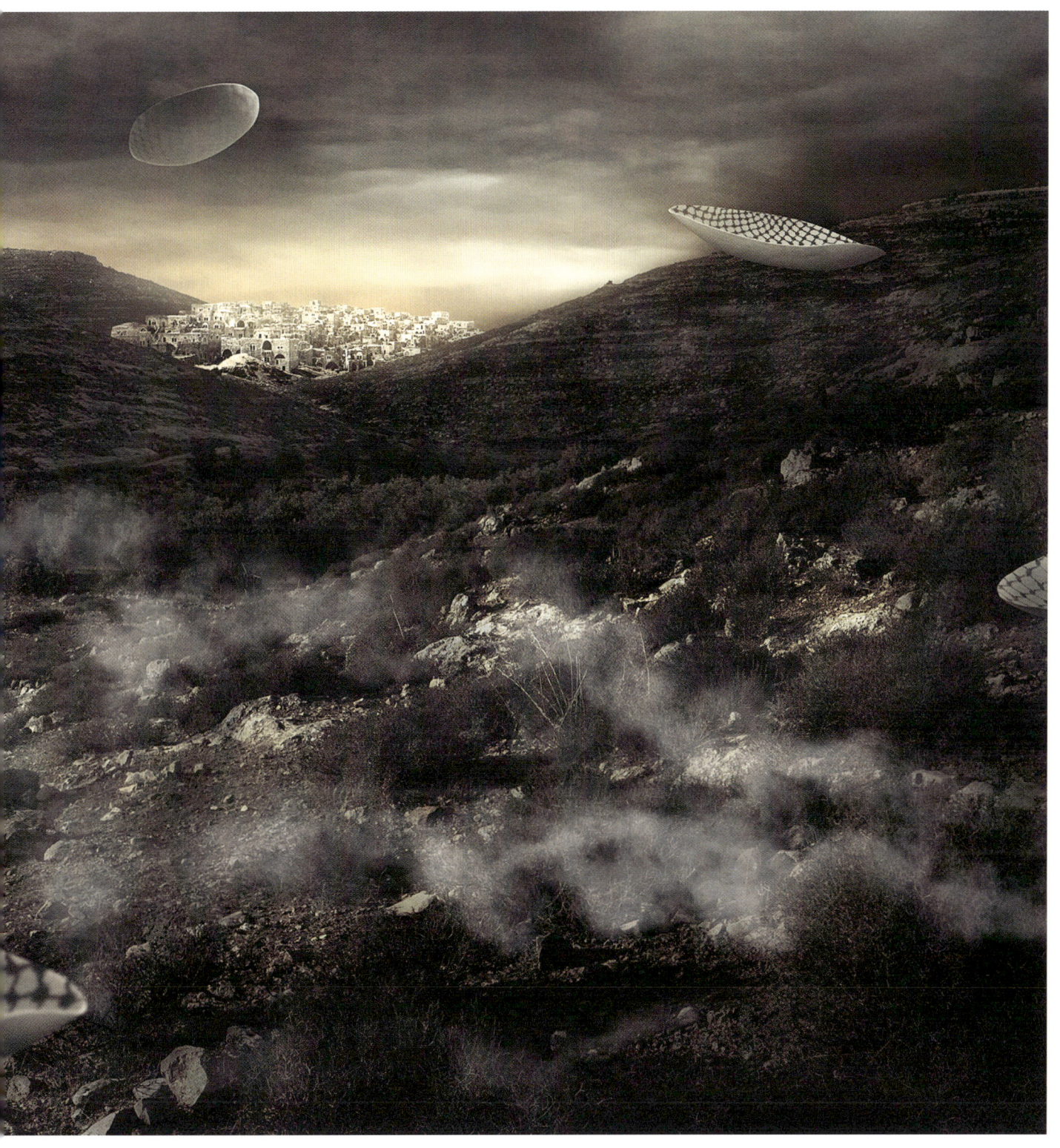

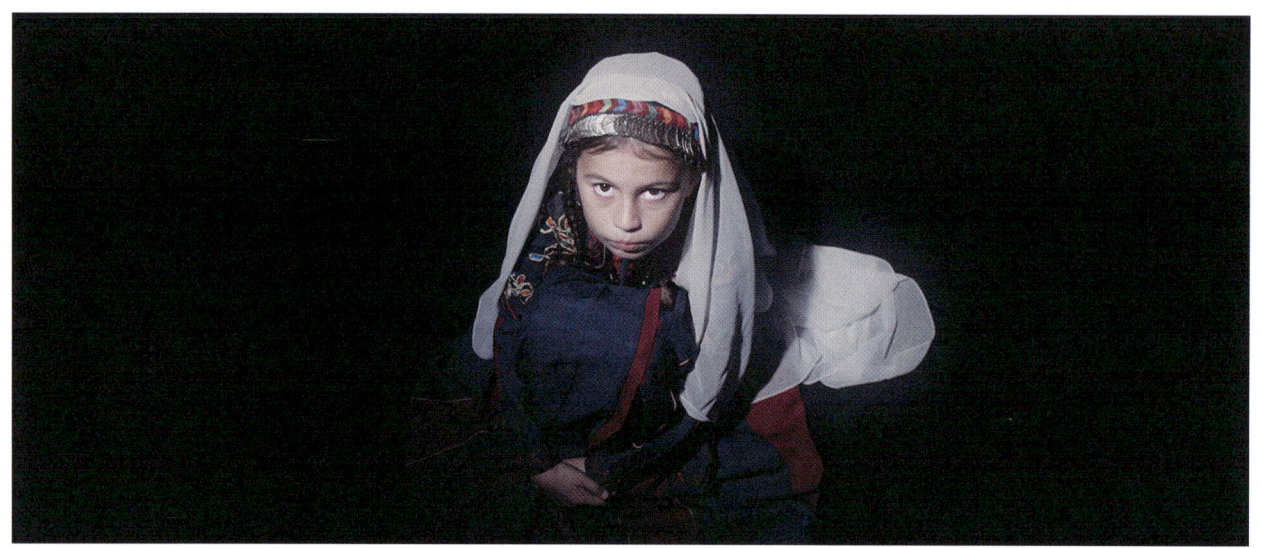

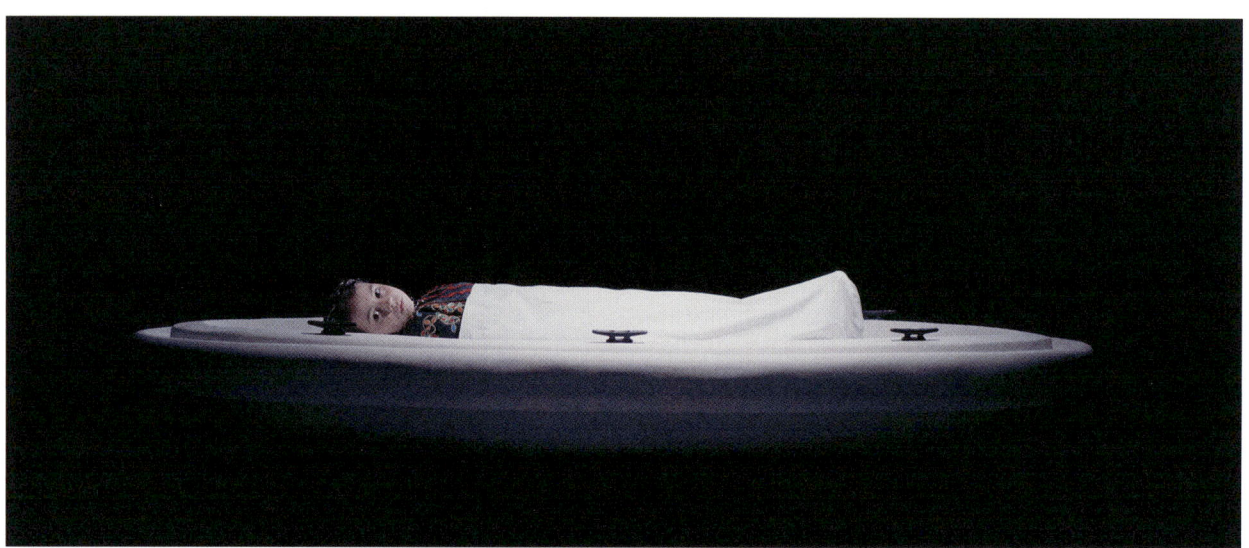

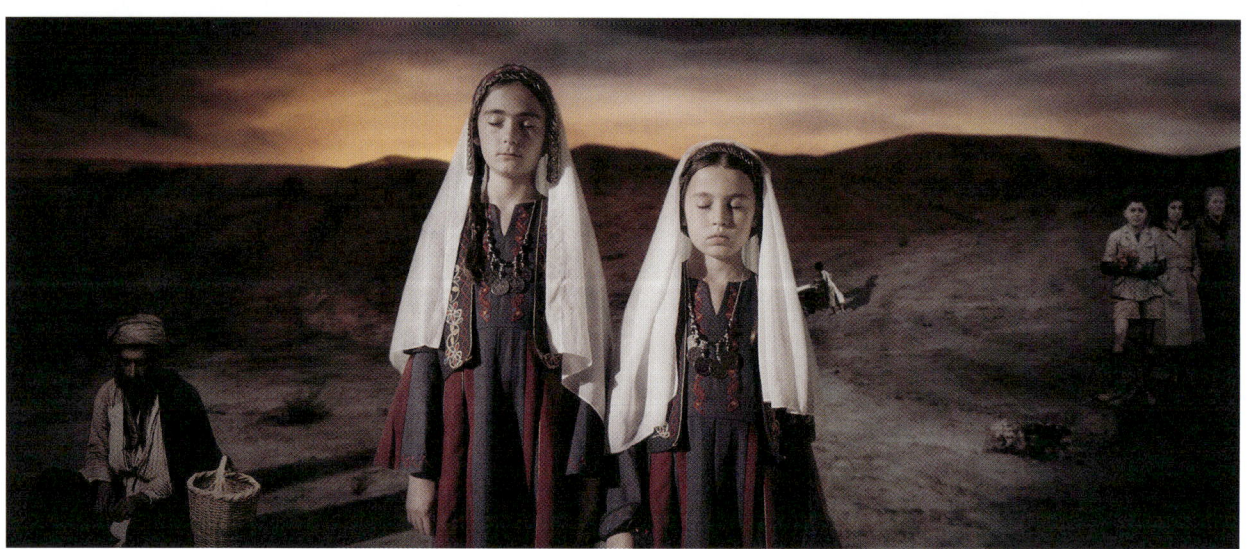

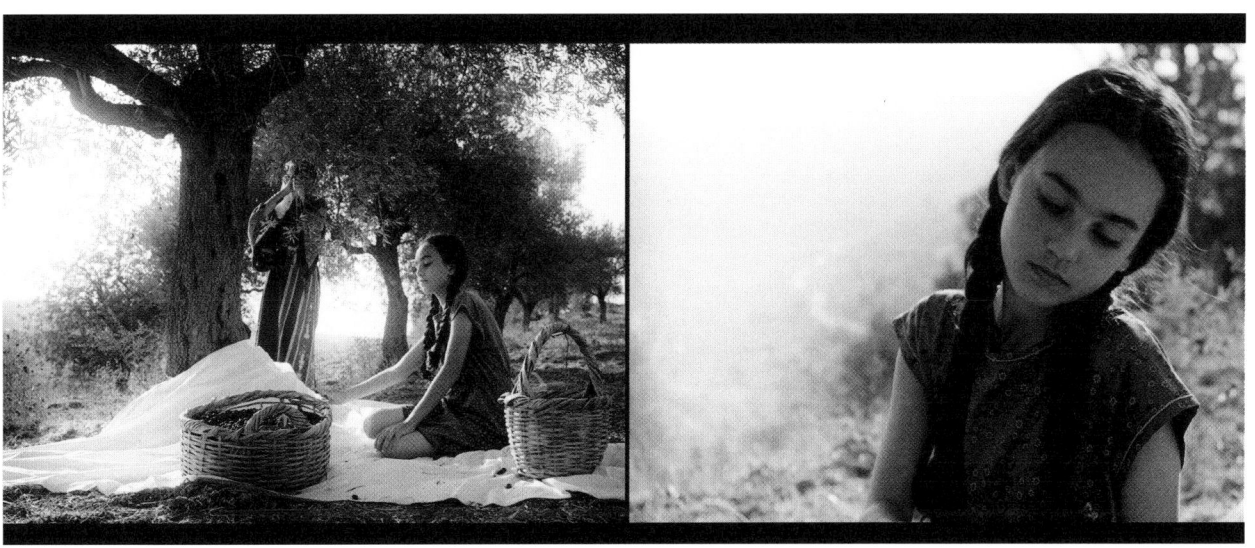

Larissa Sansour and Søren Lind, *In Vitro*, 2019. Film stills. Costume designer Anne Sofie Madsen

Left: Larissa Sansour and Søren Lind, *In the Future, They Ate from the Finest Porcelain*, 2016. Film stills. Costume designer Line Frank

SARY ZANANIRI

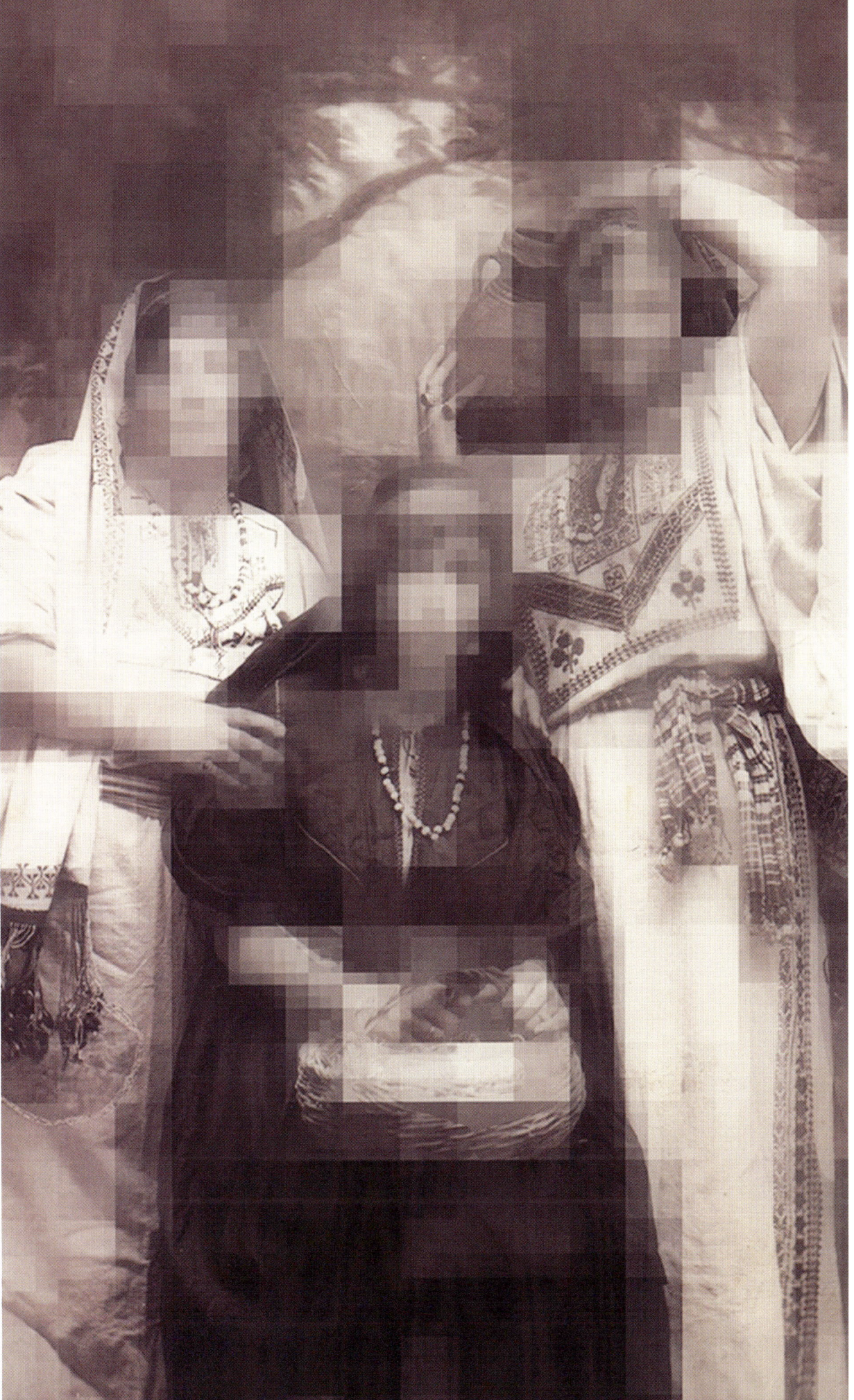

Artist and cultural historian Sary Zananiri asks, 'How do we view the past? What is it that we see as authentic? And how do we consider notions of historical change?' Regarding his series *Performing Self, Performing Other*, Zananiri reports that it 'began with a singular photo of my grandfather, a Jerusalemite, dressed in a *thobe* as a woman, pictured beside a friend dressed in a men's *abayeh* with *keffiyeh* and *agal*. It's an image that I had grown up with and one that was treated with much humour within the family.' His manipulation of archival photographs in this series challenges notions of class and gender expression in Palestine.

Through his research, Zananiri discovered similar photos in other Palestinian family archives, particularly those from urban centres. He gratefully acknowledges the generous cooperation of many people, families and archives, without whom the project would not have been possible.[1] He found literature referencing 'cultural cross-dressing', a phenomenon where photography studios of the Middle East offered to take portraits of people in 'traditional' dress provided by the studio. In the context of Palestine, this mainly focused on drawing from Ramallah, Bethlehem and Bedouin costume styles. The studio produced these images as photo postcards or *cartes de visite* shared between friends and acquaintances as a form of social currency.

Zananiri highlights the importance of acknowledging Arab participation in cultural cross-dressing. It has been predominantly analysed from the perspective of European tourists visiting the region. Zananiri explains, 'For Palestinians from urban centres like Jerusalem, Jaffa and elsewhere, who typically wore the modern fashions of their European counterparts, the decision to be photographed in "traditional" costume was a suspension of self and the articulation of another identity.' Zananiri's *Performing Self, Performing Other* series engages with the complex set of social, cultural and political histories of Palestinian modernity. It considers this through the lens of the *thobe*, *tatreez*, portrait photography and class, while revealing how modernity impacted the projection of self and authenticity from the 1920s and 1930s, the heyday of Arab nationalism during the British Mandate period. The series also engages

with how such images are misread today, obscured by Orientalist readings of history.

'Reading these images from the present day, it would seem they are a vision of the social life of the past, and indeed they are. However, for the people involved in such studio photographs, rarely were such clothes a part of their daily life. The decision to don these clothes and memorialise the act of "dressing up" with a photograph was an assertion of identity in a period of nationalism born in response to the British colonial administration and the growing threat of Zionist migration.' Zananiri goes on, 'This is not to say that they are not an authentic vision of a historical reality, but authenticity here relies on the enaction of nationalism in wearing Palestinian symbols such as *tatreez* and the *thobe* it adorns, not the garments themselves. A matrix of class and modernity, both as a lived experience and ideological framework, distanced urban middle-class Palestinians from such costumes that, by this period, were predominant in rural working communities.'

This practice demonstrates how urban Palestinians could articulate their link to land and culture and their links to the rural *fellahin* and Bedouin compatriots, when identifying as Palestinian was becoming increasingly important. Zananiri explains, 'The act of putting on "traditional" clothing for these middle-class Palestinians was, in fact, a transgressive act, not so much from a cultural perspective as with their Western counterparts, but in terms of breaching the class and urban-rural divides that informed Palestinian society at the time.' Zananiri's interest lies in the misconstruing of these images today as authentic visions of either 'the Orient' or 'Holy Land' from a Western perspective, or as a mode of Palestinian nostalgia and identity formation. He draws attention to the need for more understanding of the modern urban middle classes who commissioned and sat for these photographic portraits. He explains how the temptation to read photos at face value, without knowledge of the day-to-day lives of these photographic subjects, would be to obscure the modern histories that informed their production.

In *Performing Self, Performing Other*, Zananiri challenges contemporary assumptions about these photographed portraits. These assumptions distort the meaning and therefore the original images themselves. He describes how this parallels scholarship about the region in this period. He examines examples of studies from the nineteenth century focused on Late-Antiquity Christian mosaics in Palestine and Jordan, especially those altered during the seventh-century shift from Byzantine to Umayyad rule. These early studies revealed that the tesserae, the small tiles that make up the mosaics, had been lifted and re-laid to remove the figures of animals, replacing them with patterns or designs of foliage. Western scholars of the nineteenth century attributed the re-laying of mosaics to the imposition of Muslim proscriptions against the depiction of figures. However, later comparisons with Umayyad art of the same period, which often featured animal and human figures, debunked earlier Orientalist assumptions of an Islamic imposition upon Christian art. Instead, contemporary scholarship proposes that these churches were more likely shared spaces of worship during conversion periods.

The pixilation used to obscure figures in this new series of photographic works disrupts the act of spectatorship, disguising faces and bodies while referencing the tesserae of the Late-Antiquity mosaics. Through this series, Zananiri questions 'how archaeological or ethnographic knowledge is generated – ostensibly modern, objective and academic – and the ways such knowledge has coloured popular perceptions of the region in the West'.

Performing Self, Performing Other reflects on the historical understanding and misinterpretation of the region, particularly in times of great cultural and political change. The original photographs are drawn from family archives from the British Mandate period in Palestine, which marked the end of Ottoman rule. Similarly, the re-laying of the church mosaics demonstrates the shift from Byzantine to Umayyad rule. By conjuring the mosaics through pixilation, this series attempts to draw a longitudinal correlation between Palestinian bodies and their erasure over periods of rapid cultural change. So doing effects a layering of the very modern preoccupation with the past.

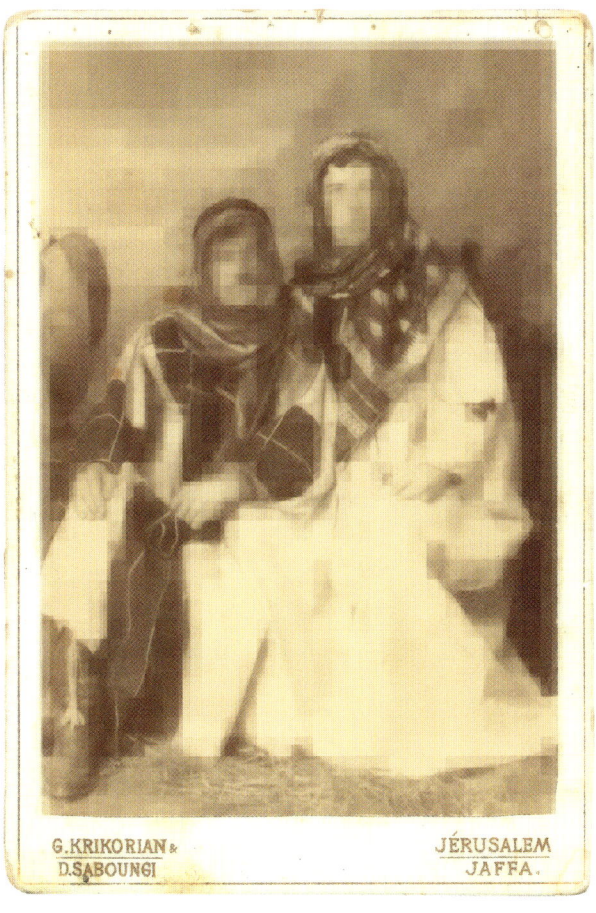

Sary Zananiri, *Performing Self, Performing Other 6*, 2023. Manipulated archival photograph, 14.1 x 20 cm

Previous spread: Sary Zananiri, *Performing Self, Performing Other 3*, 2021. Manipulated archival photograph, 12.1 x 20 cm

1   In particular Joseph Malikian and the Malikian family, Laila Abbas at the Palestinian Museum Digital Archive, Micaela Sahhar and the Sahhar family, and Eddie Zananiri and the Zananiri family.

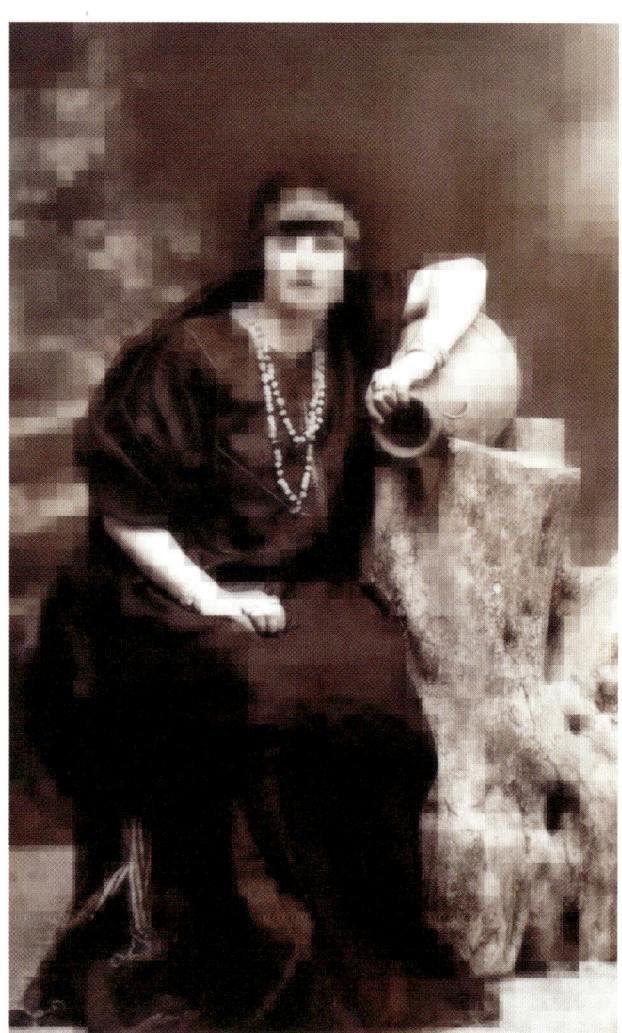

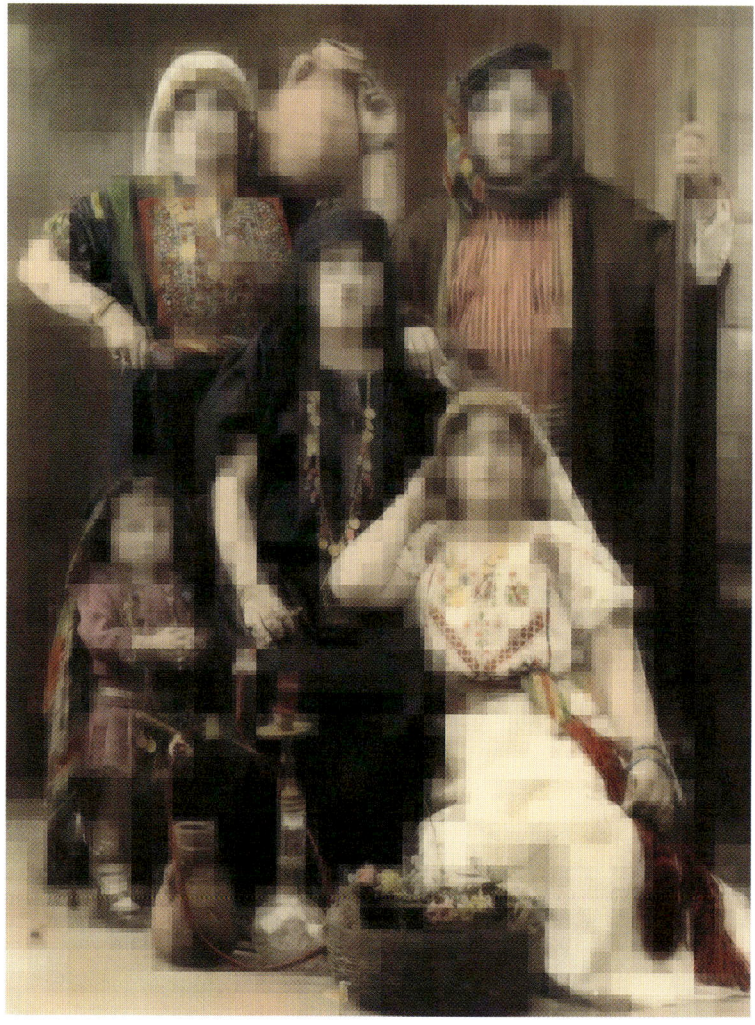

Sary Zananiri, *Performing Self, Performing Other 2*, 2020. Manipulated archival photograph, 12.7 x 20 cm
Sary Zananiri, *Performing Self, Performing Other 5*, 2023. Manipulated archival photograph, 15.2 x 20 cm
Right: Sary Zananiri, *Performing Self, Performing Other 4*, 2021. Manipulated archival photograph, 20 x 13.1 cm

Next spread: Sary Zananiri, *Performing Self, Performing Other 1*, 2020. Manipulated archival photograph, 20 x 12.5 cm

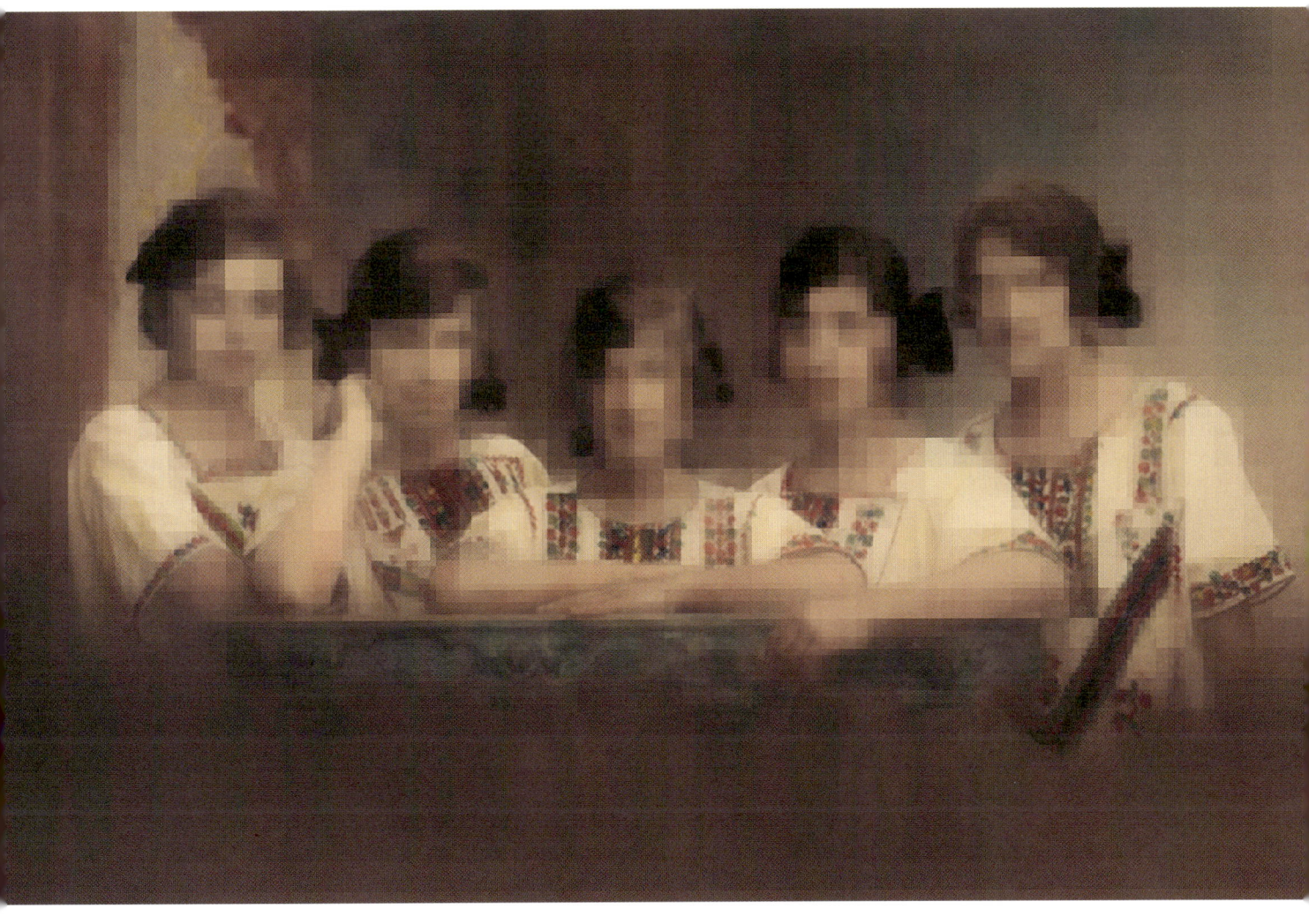

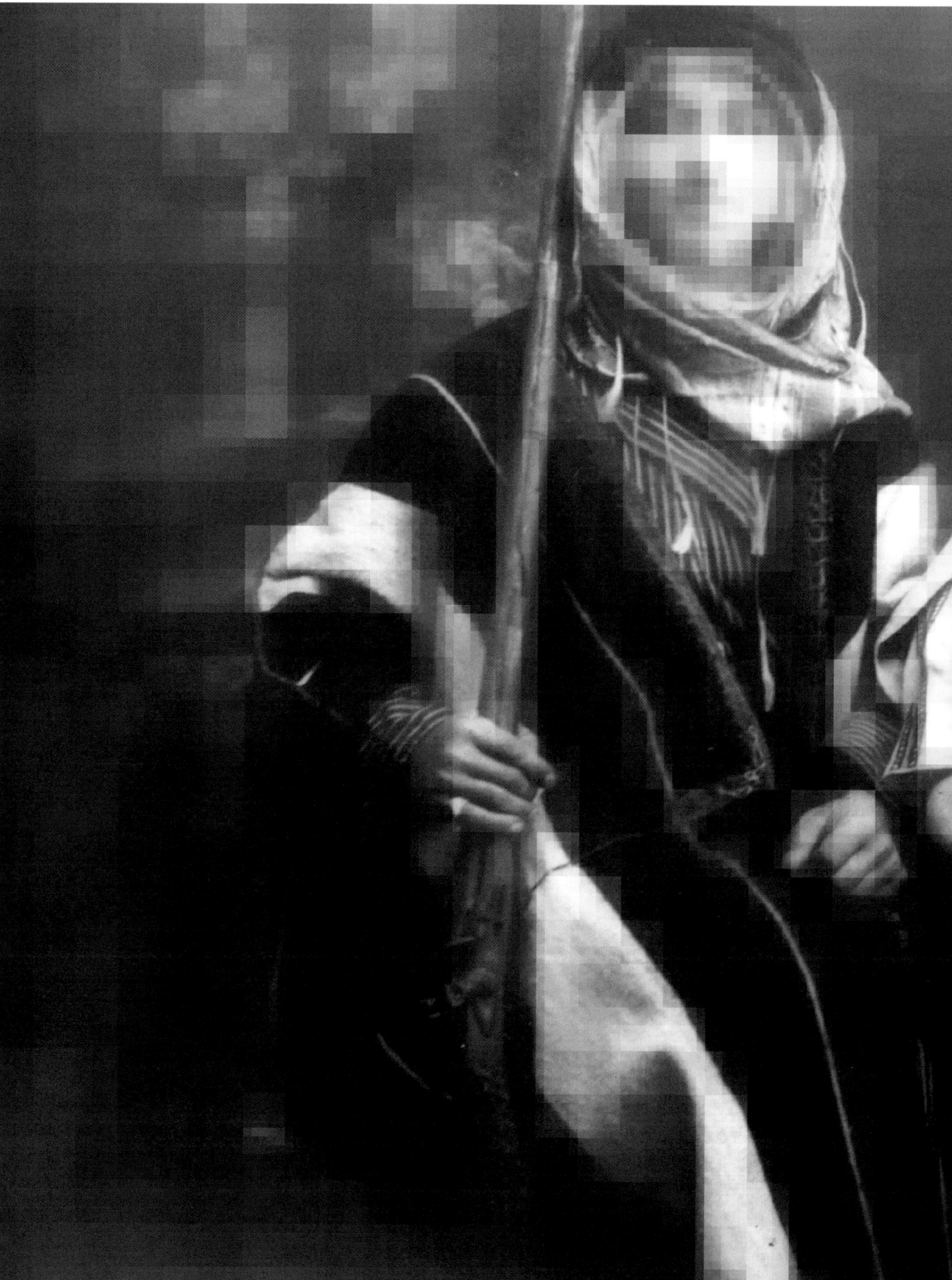

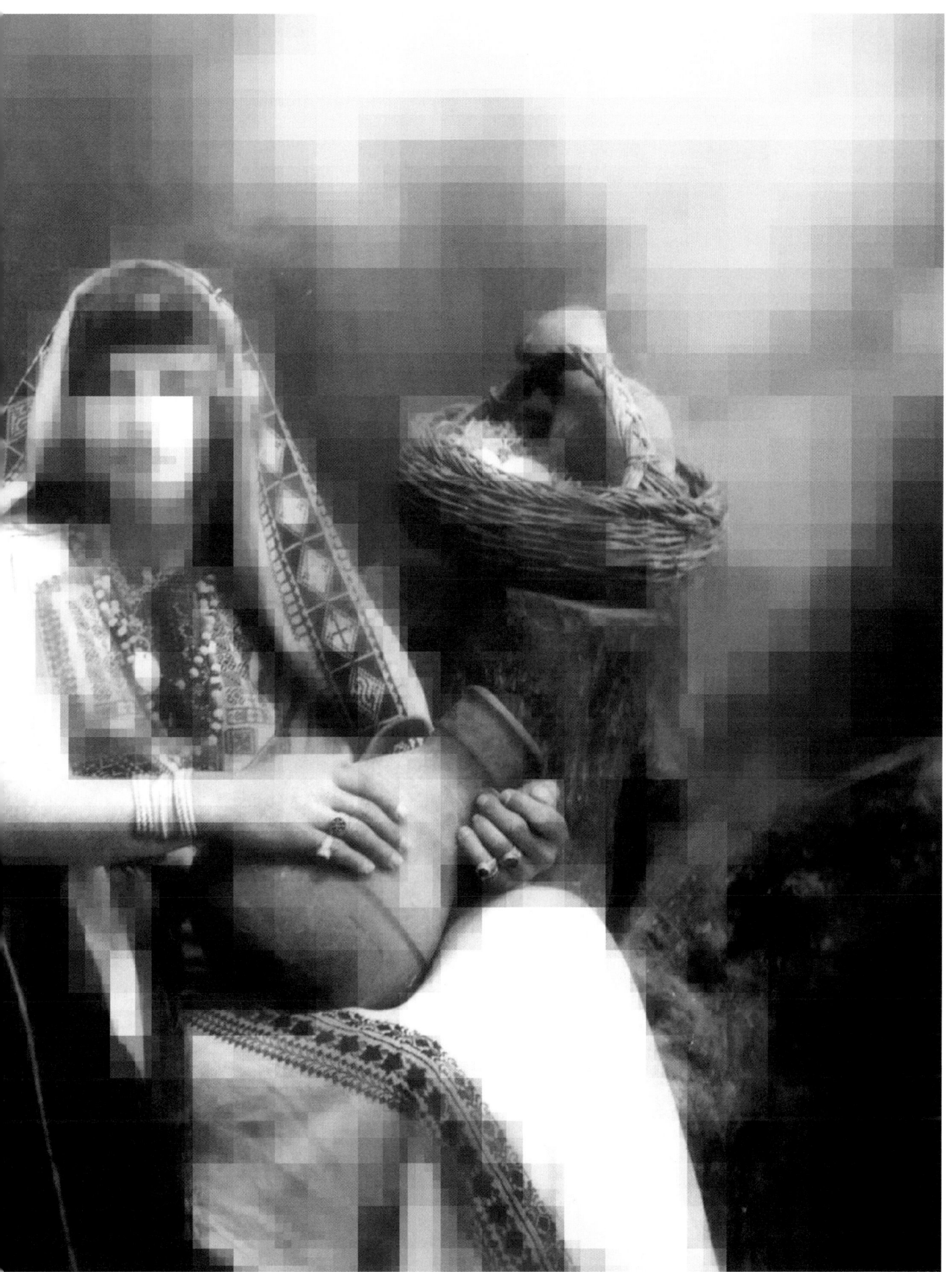

SAMA ALSHAIBI

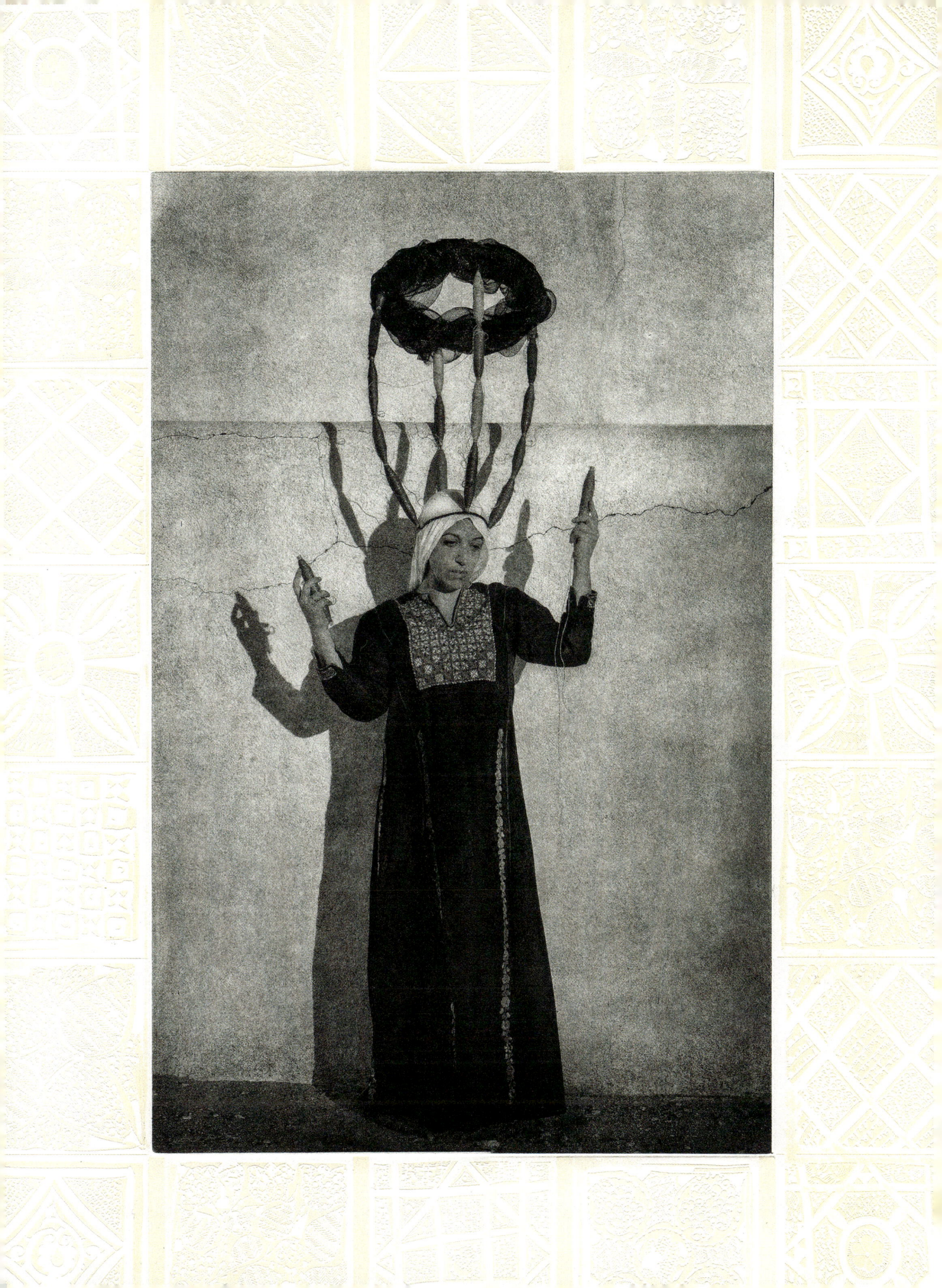

Through her photography, video and multimedia installations, Sama Alshaibi challenges viewers to rethink the Arab woman's body and positionality. She reframes ideas concerning exile, memory, power structures and representation. With her image and body as the subject, Alshaibi employs devices like Palestinian embroidery to create context within her work, and directly engages the body politics of the Palestinian woman.

The tailors and seamstresses from Sama Alshaibi's mother's family play a crucial role in influencing how she approaches costume, embroidery and traditional cultural dress in her art. 'I see my mother and her mother's work as a manifestation of identity, those who embroidered, stitched, cut, knitted and clothed our history, memories and future hopes through their handiwork.' Her mother designed and sewed the costumes featured in Alshaibi's photography. She says, 'By working with my mother and the skills she learned from her family, I'm presenting Palestinian narratives through the material processes of producing textiles and dresses. I perform these narratives by wearing them on the body. Sometimes, the stories are obvious. Sometimes, the knowledge is more hidden, in that the expertise of Palestinian craft is known only to my mother and me. Wearing her work honours the legacy and resilience of Palestinians, especially women's labour.' Alshaibi's mother's participation in the work and the process behind it makes the work inherently personal and intergenerational.

Alshaibi's *Birthright* series (2004–05) rethinks how the refugees and the Palestinian diaspora engage with memory. *The Disinherited: A Counter Memorial to Exile* (2005) is fashioned after the historical Palestinian embroidered headdress with dowry coins, worn by a bride on her wedding day and then daily after marriage. Alshaibi based this piece on her mother's memories of her grandmother and the longing to inherit the headdress, which was instead sold after she died. On her headdress, Alshaibi minted images from visas and passports on the coins as permanent markers of Alshaibi's family's memories of exile. She creates a performative memorial to the land, events, and even the headdress that women stopped wearing after 1948. The memorial is no longer a monument structure on land but a wearable object, moving with the body from site to site.

In another piece in the series, *Worthless Possession* (2005), Alshaibi is peering through an old key, wearing an embroidered dress from Ramallah. The dress identifies the wearer as Palestinian and the key as a redundant object tied to a bittersweet memory of loss and unwavering hope of return.

Alshaibi brings together her paternal Iraqi and maternal Palestinian lineage in *SWEEP* (2010). Under the billowing black *abaya* from Iraq, she wears a Palestinian dress where she can 'carry both sides of my identity – and I've struggled – even if our communities' challenges are very different'. Wearing an *abaya* made for her by her father's cousins represents her Iraqi father, her birthplace in Basra, and stories about her paternal aunts, grandmother and Iraqi women. Wearing the *abaya* also made her reflect on women's experiences in Iraq after the US invasion, and how women became targets of sectarian violence.

In the *Carry Over* photography series (2018–19), Alshaibi presents her longstanding interest in the image of the Arab female figure, especially when viewed as a rich and complicated aspect of Palestinian visual culture. Referring to Orientalist photography practices dating back to the 1890s, the photographs in this series feature Alshaibi as the subject, carrying oversized objects over her shoulder or on her head. In this series, the image and process involved in producing albumin, photogravure and gum historical printing echo the multitude of archival photographs documenting Palestinian women up through the British Mandate period. They posed with a large water jug on their heads or over their shoulders, a vessel used for filling water at the local water spring. Ironically, many people have mistaken these photos of urban upper-class Palestinians taken in photography studios as documenting natural rural life. The photos were similar to those taken by tourists visiting Palestine who wished to construct an image of Palestine and Palestinian women fit for the Western gaze and biblical imaginings.

The Western lens romanticising and fetishising Arab women, including rural Palestinian women, became a practice employed by Palestinian artists too. Alshaibi mentions that this was demonstrated in mid- to late twentieth-century Palestinian art with depictions of Palestinian national resistance expressed through a feminised homeland.

She states, 'In *Carry Over*, I wanted to unpack how the female peasant woman came to signify the motherland, while also critiquing Orientalist images that framed women, and therefore our region, as the passive, exotic other.' Alshaibi comments that, even though these images are beautiful, they don't tell the whole story. She continues: 'Tina Sherwell claims that Palestinians were very aware of the kind of image the West assigned them. The woman's body, the water vessel and her traditional clothing were the only way commercial studios wanted to photograph Palestinian women. It froze them as a distant and historical "other".' Her series examines and challenges the presentation, regulation and construction of the Palestinian woman's body through the colonial lens.

By assigning her body to bearing the weight of colonial violence, war and exploitation, Alshaibi rewrites the incomplete story of the Palestinian female into one of strength rather than passivity. In *Water Bearer* from the *Carry Over* series, we see Alshaibi as the subject in a white dress and headscarf, carrying a grenade- or wasp-nest-shaped water jug over her head. The body posture and expression relay that the large vessel is heavy and, on closer inspection, the viewer discovers a hole. Alshaibi explains that the hole in the vessel makes the container 'dysfunctional to its form and intended use. By blurring the boundary between decorative and dysfunctional, my images become metaphors for how Orientalism functions. The symbolic weight of signifiers is attached to everything. I imply the subject is the bearer of the absurd and irrational – a direct critique of the Orientalist photographs.'

In the same photograph, she belts her dress with a *keffiyeh* tied around her waist. Palestinian farmers traditionally wore the *keffiyeh* headdress, which was later adopted and made iconic by Yasser Arafat and other PLO fighters. In *Water Bearer*, Alshaibi acknowledges it as an enduring symbol central to the Palestinian liberation struggle. She also points out how the *keffiyeh* 'reflects the challenges when the world sees your cause through a

symbolic garment that is very simple for them to dismiss or politicise. The protagonist in white is a warrior. She is resistance itself. *Thobe*, army fatigues, everyday clothing – it doesn't matter. The struggle is always carried on our bodies over time and place.' The Palestinian embroidered *thobe*, or traditional Palestinian dress, appears in *Spools* and *Threads*, and an embroidered shawl in *Before Us* and *Eternal Love Song*, where the embroidery becomes part of the conversation shared by the subject, a Palestinian woman's body, with the viewer.

In 2020, Alshaibi was one of ten women artists nominated to participate in the *100 Years /100 Women* exhibition for the Park Avenue Armory in partnership with the National Black Theatre in New York. The show celebrated the centennial of the 19th Amendment's ratification. Alshaibi's commissioned project, *Adjudicating the Jezebel* (2020), a work presenting the Palestinian *thobe* as a moment of Palestinian-American pride, was inspired by congresswoman Rashida Tlaib's Palestinian embroidered dress worn to her 2019 swearing-in ceremony at the US House of Representatives. By sewing images on linen, Alshaibi collaged Palestinian embroidery patterns, historical political posters of resistance, and her photographs, 'to construct a tension between cultural identity, gender, and intersectional feminism seen in the 2018 election. The trailblazing paths of Tlaib and women like her honour the sacrifice and labour of the suffrage movement and the enduring fight for a democracy that serves us all.' In this piece, Tlaib's embroidered dress is a proclamation of her Palestinian identity and a celebration of the shift in representation in American politics.

In her work, Alshaibi reconstructs the notion of the physical memorial and how memories of exile, loss and displacement, though relevant to a specific place, move with the body wherever it goes. She reclaims the image of the Palestinian Arab woman, creating a space for recognising the ongoing trauma and exploitation of that body through settler colonialism, war and patriarchy. She critiques Orientalist and colonial imagery of Arab women and transforms the visual representations of the Arab female, reclaiming her power despite the illogicality she faces within these imposed systems.

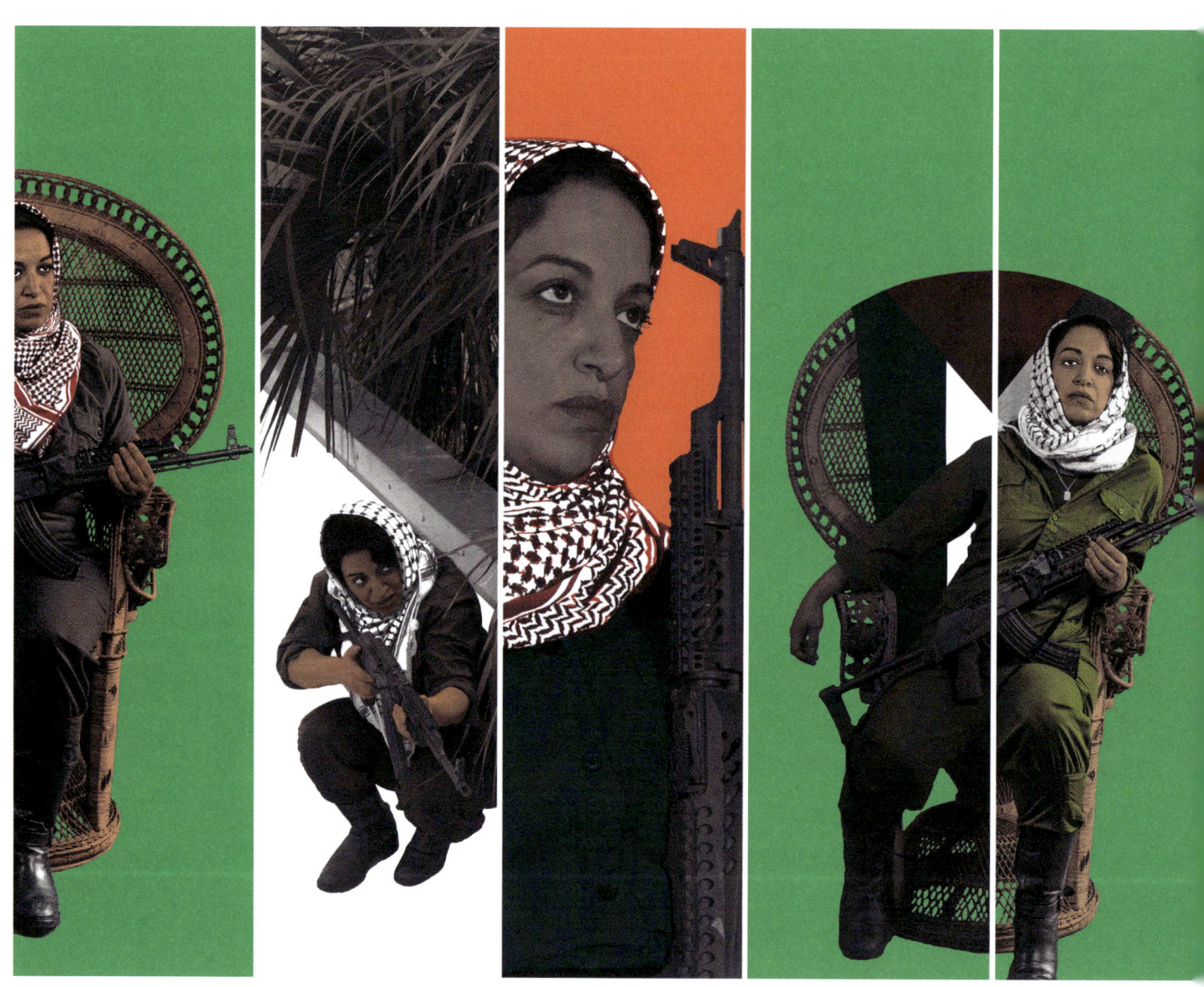

Sama Alshaibi, *Generation After Generation*, 2019. Digital print on Hahnemühle 100% cotton white paper, 233.6 x 609.6 cm

Pages 138–139: Sama Alshaibi, *Spools*; *Carry Over* series, 2019. Photogravure print, blind embossing with transparent ink relief rolled on Stonehenge White 100% rag, 63.5 x 50.8 cm

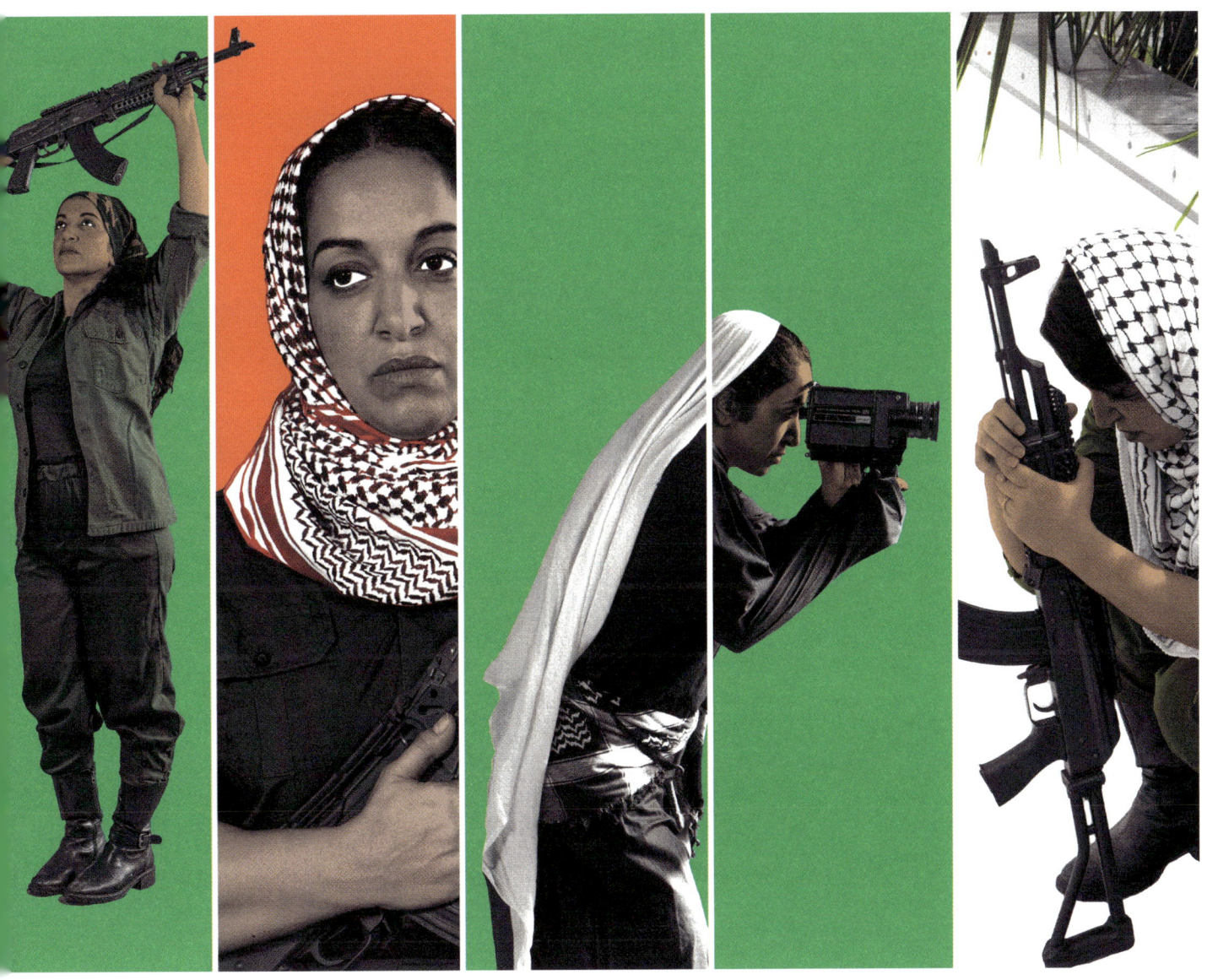

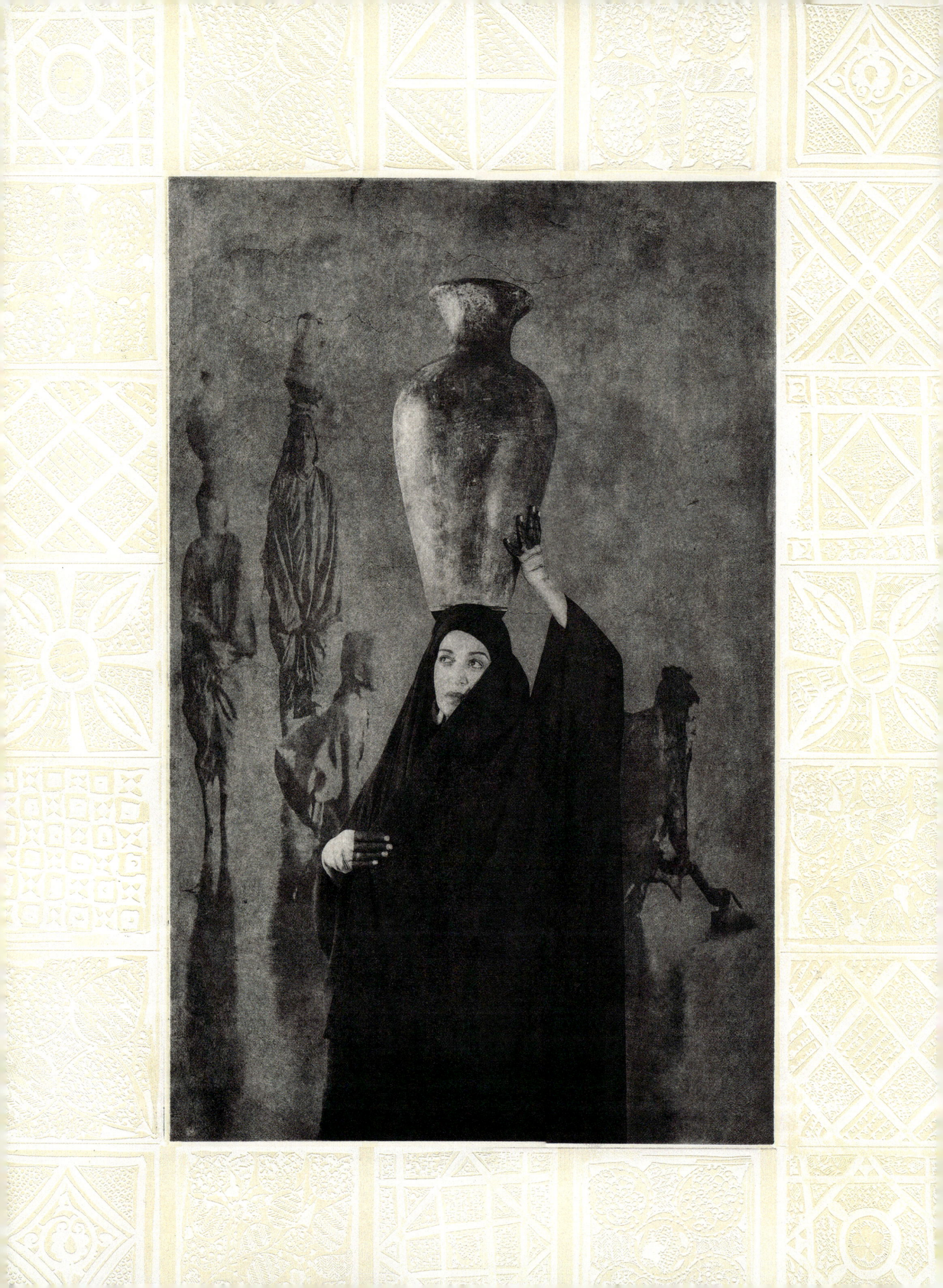

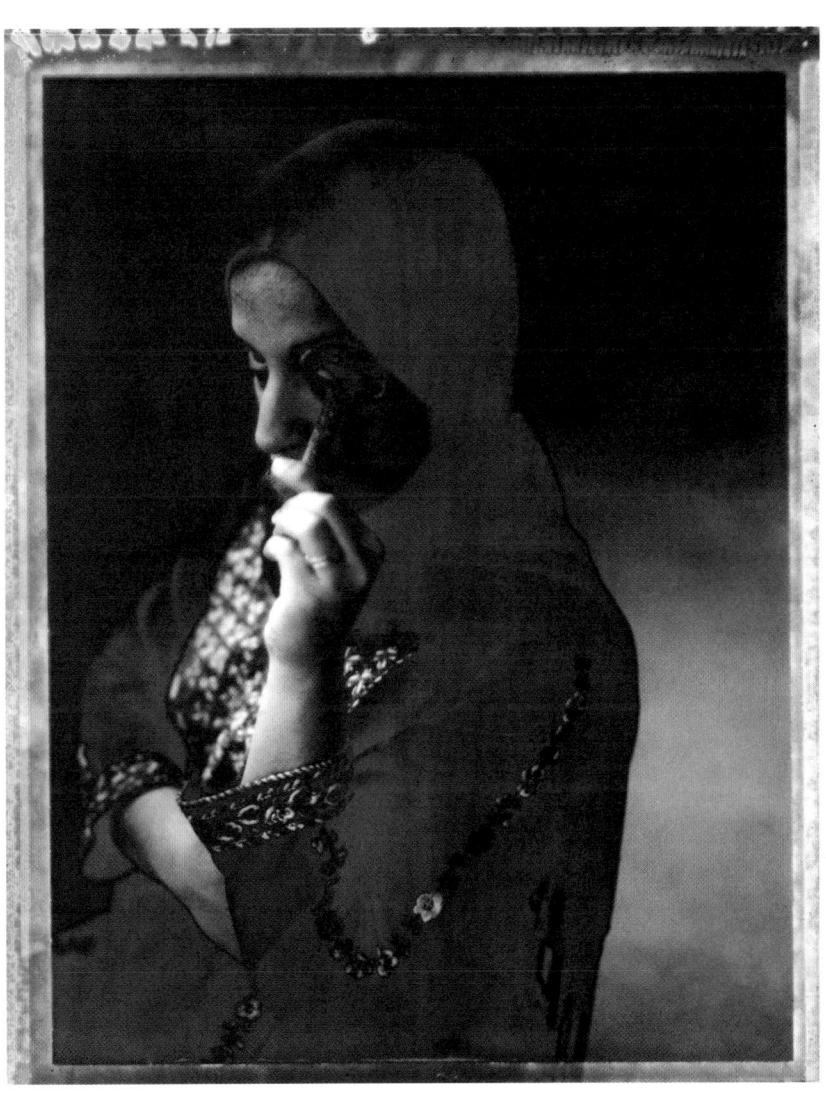

Sama Alshaibi, *Worthless Possession*, 2005. Digital archival print

Left: Sama Alshaibi, *Standing River; Carry Over* series, 2019. Photogravure print, blind embossing with transparent ink relief rolled on Stonehenge White 100% rag, 63.5 x 50.8 cm

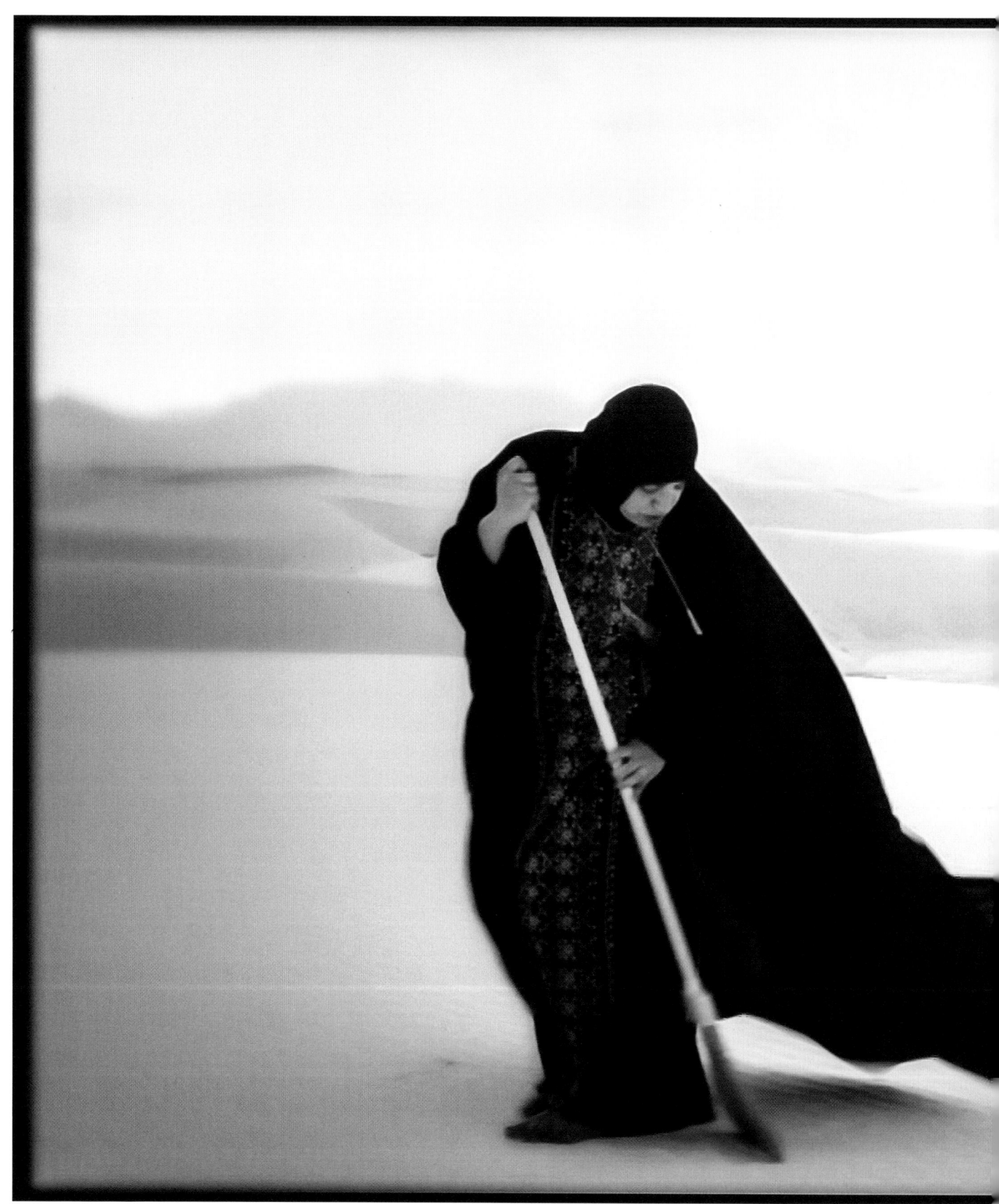

Sama Alshaibi, *SWEEP*, 2010. Video still

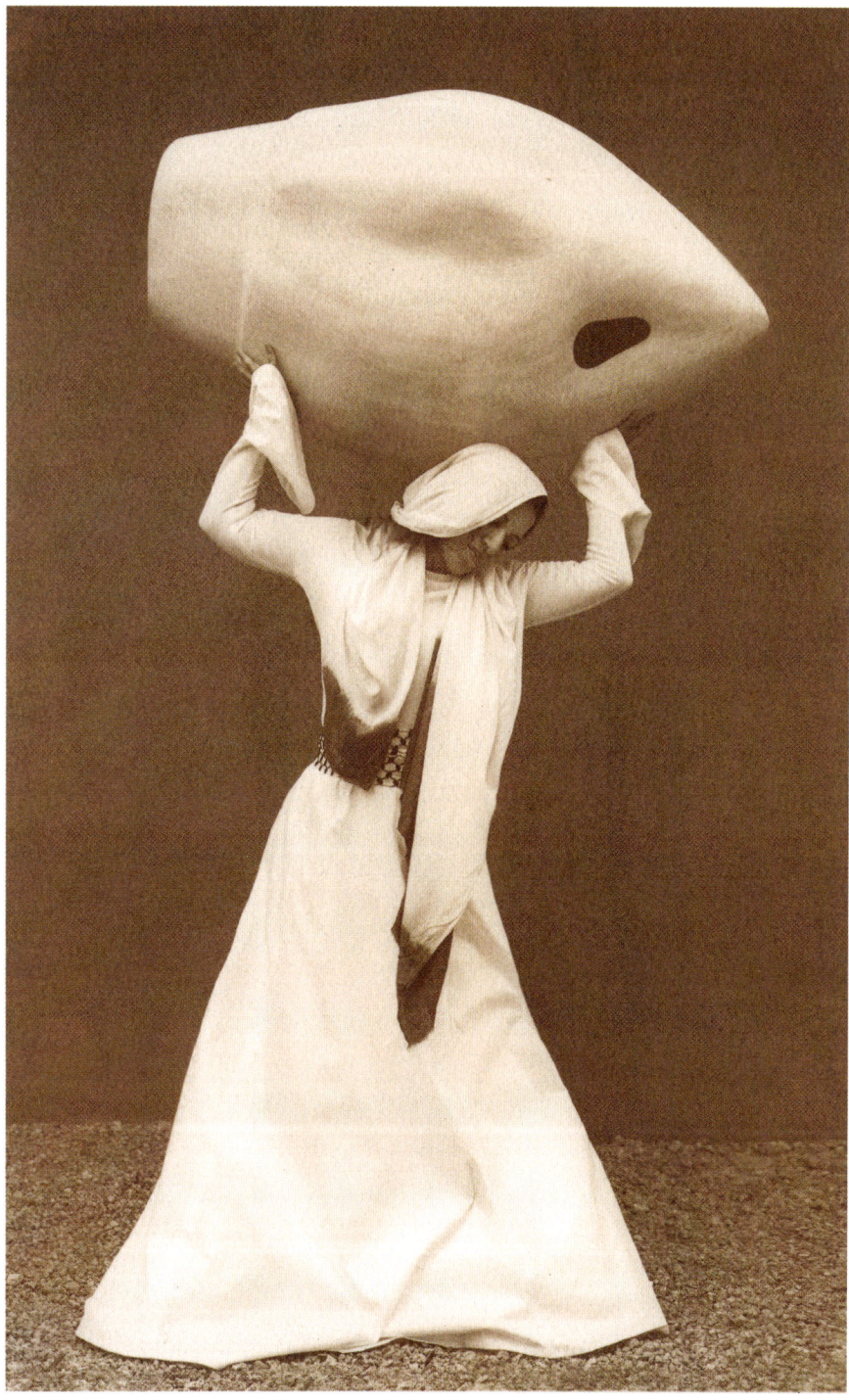

Sama Alshaibi, *Water Bearer*; *Carry Over* series, 2018. Albumen print on Somerset Satin White 100% rag, 53.3 x 35.5 cm

Right: Sama Alshaibi, *Before Us*; *Carry Over* series, 2019. Albumen print on Somerset Satin White 100% rag, 53.3 x 35.5 cm

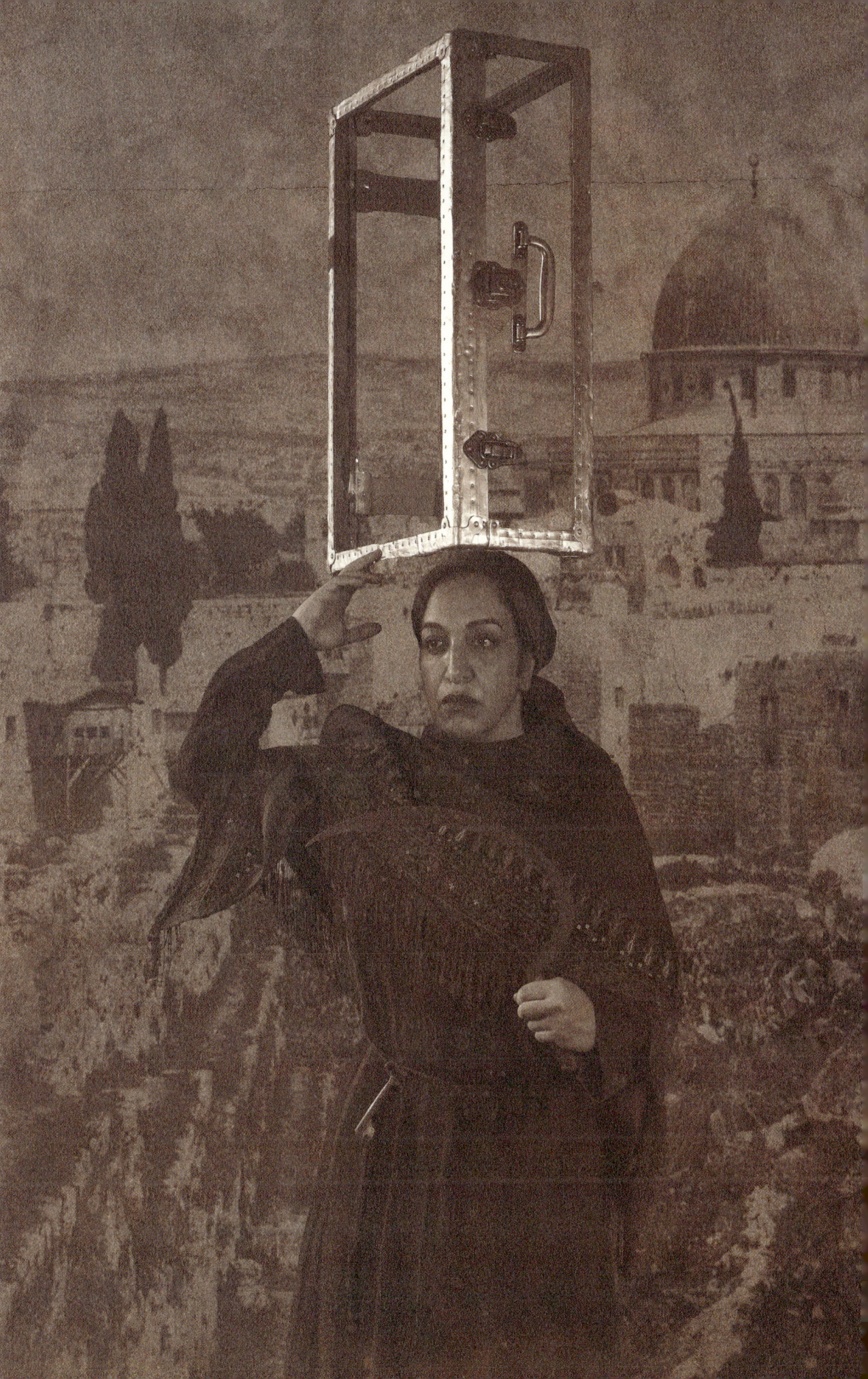

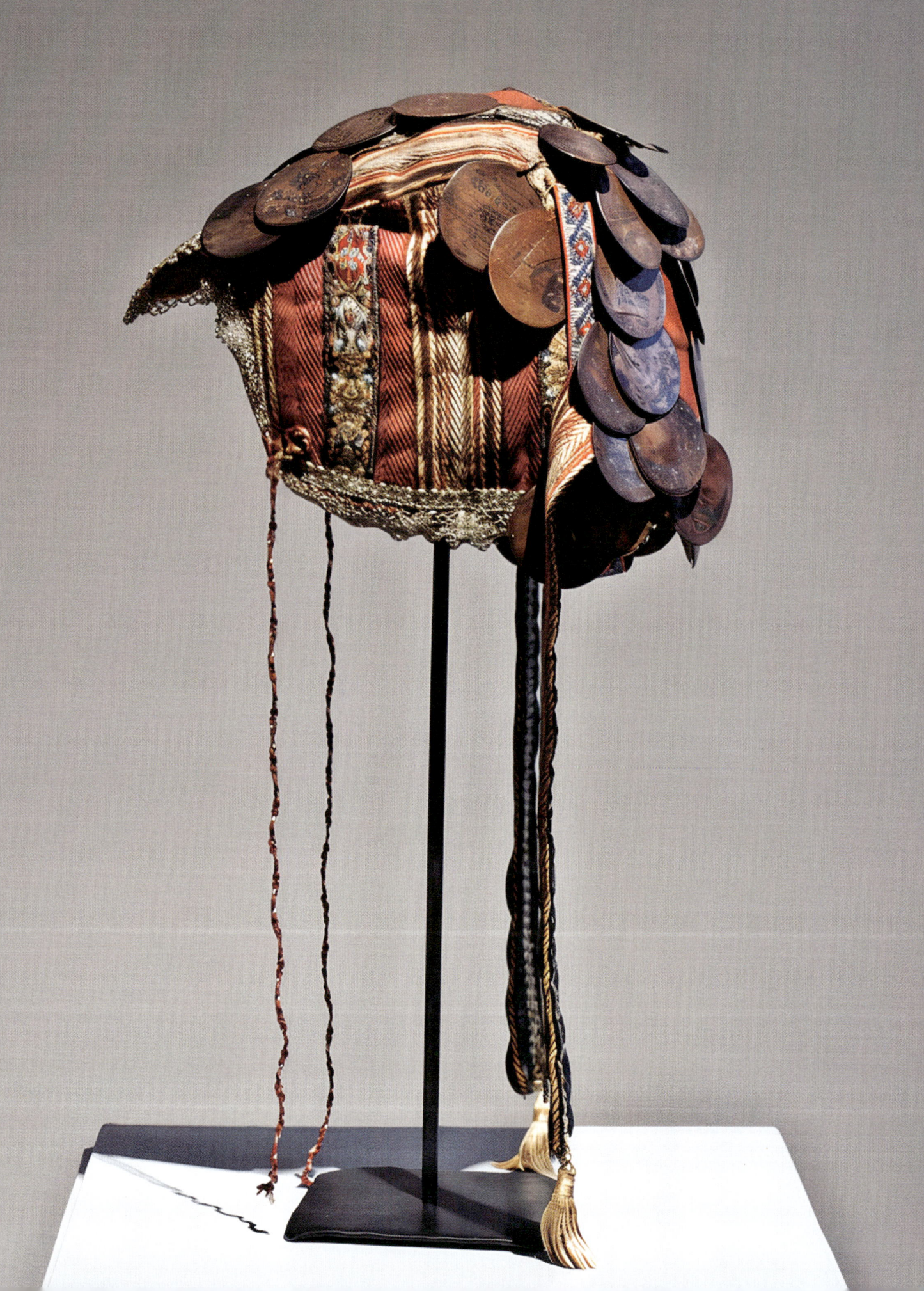

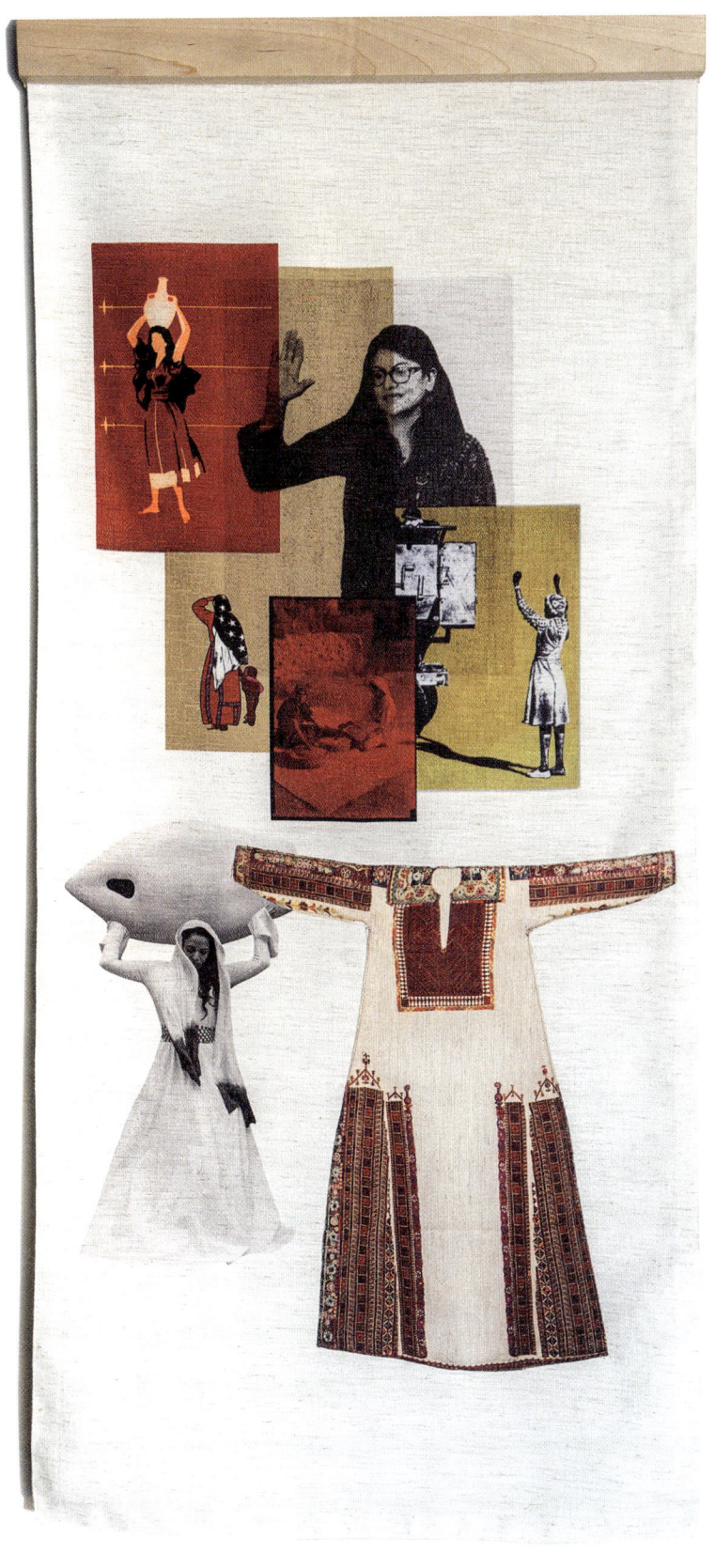

Sama Alshaibi, *Adjudicating the Jezebel*, 2020. Mixed media on linen, 121.9 x 60.9 cm

Left: Sama Alshaibi, *The Disinherited: A Counter Memorial to Exile*, 2005.
Copper, fabric, beads and thread

STEVE SABELLA

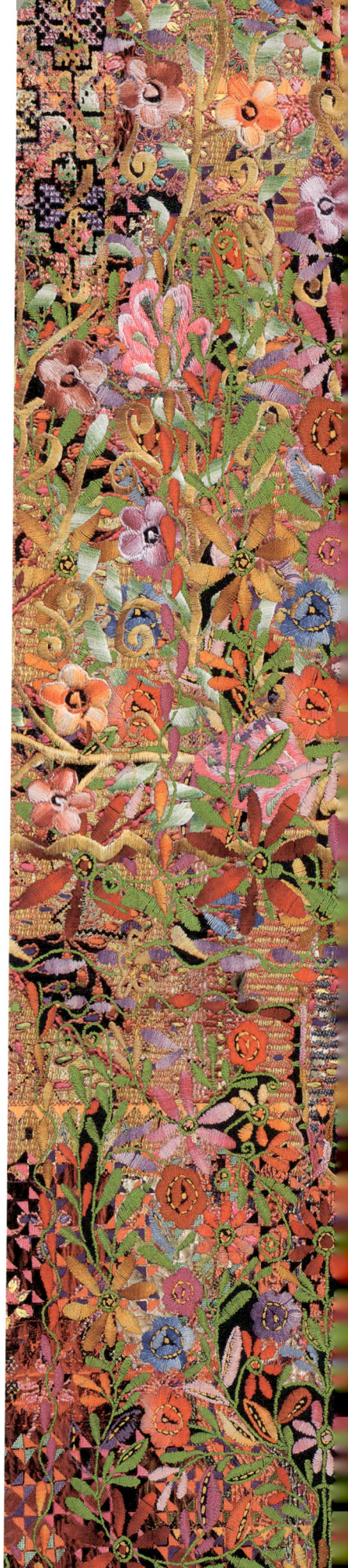

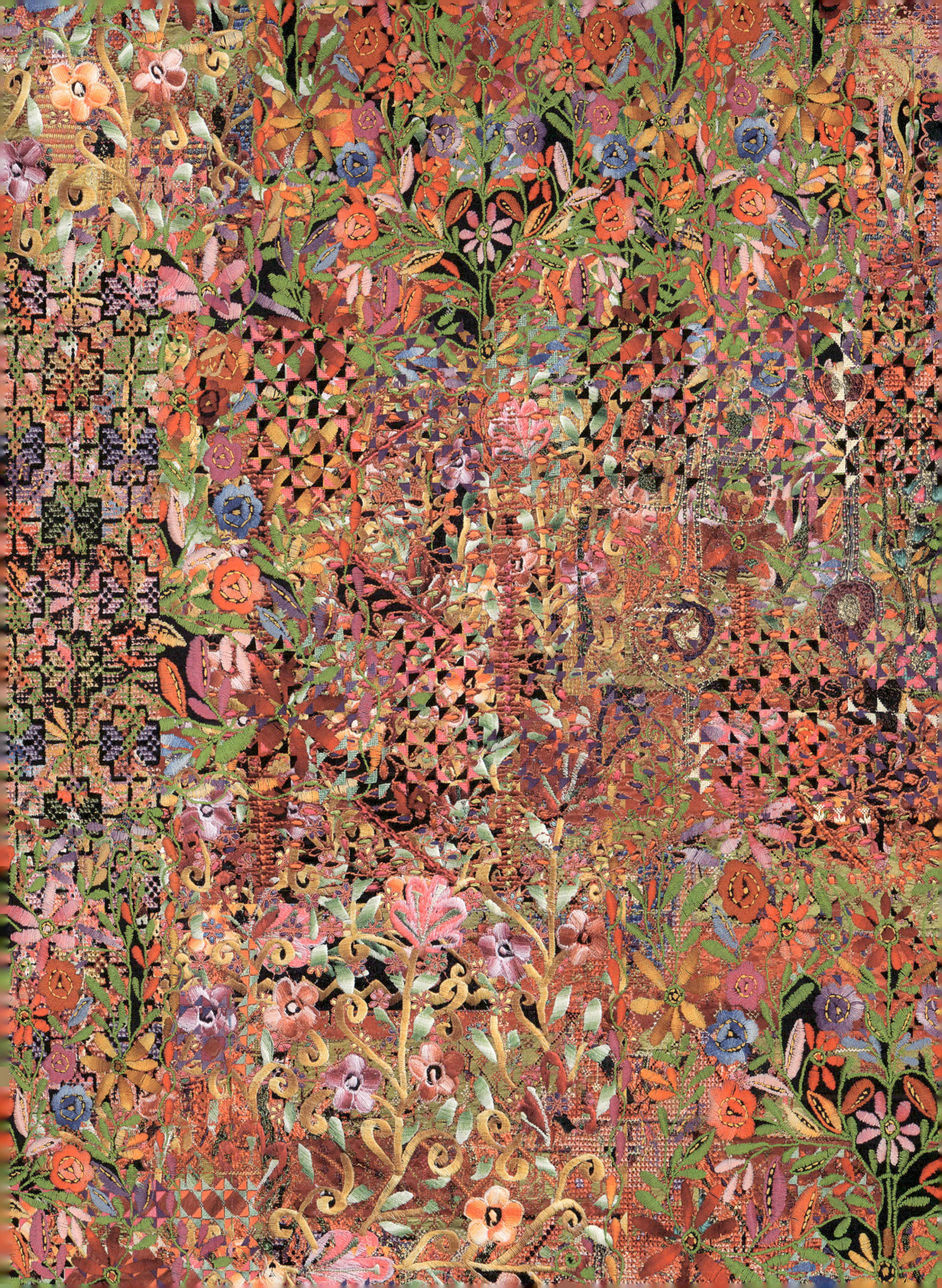

Born and raised in Jerusalem and now living in Berlin, Steve Sabella remarks in his memoir *The Parachute Paradox* (Kerber Verlag, 2016), 'I wanted an identity of my own, embroidered with my own life philosophy and stitched with my own threads.' He later elaborates on his perspective of identity and the role Palestinian embroidery plays in relation to it. 'I never saw my identity as a label but as a process, fluid, changing every day. If light falling on Earth is always new, how can we stay the same? After all, we are creatures of light. And the light shines in all the colours of the world. Now imagine these colours as the threads of your life where it is up to you how you weave them. This results in the creation of a self that is always new, unique, original.'

Childhood memories of his mother and sisters practising embroidery in his family home in the Old City of Jerusalem reminded Sabella of his photo collage technique. 'Palestinian embroidery is recognition of collective identity and narrative that gets renewed, awakened every time we see or touch its beauty. But given Palestine's history, the beauty pierces the heart.' He continues: 'In many ways, I see a lot of similarities between my collage process in general and the practice of embroidery, where I sit endless hours piecing images together, penetrating their realities. I sometimes resort to images that have Palestine in their history, and piecing them together creates a space for Palestine to emerge in a renewed way. Embroidering threads or realities together, looking at them, going through them, is healing. And, from there, only beauty can emerge.'

Sabella describes how the process of Palestinian embroidery relates to this work. 'I found great meaning when they explained how embroidery should look fine woven inside out. I saw the method as one of meditation, of spending countless hours travelling from one almost invisible square to another, hopefully in the right direction. The shaping of vibrant colours entices one to enter a trance state and explore the self and its inner truths.'

In his project *Cécile Elise Sabella* (2008), he expresses his relationship to his daughter using the idea of the two sides of the embroidered fabric. When Cécile was four years old, he cut her clothes into squares and photographed them from both sides, which Sabella has explained was 'to mirror her universe and mine. I wanted to convey the fact that there can never exist a single, one-sided piece of cloth. There is always the other side. Similarly, and no matter what, regardless of our language barrier or origin, Cécile and I will always be connected.' He carefully stitched the photos on canvas or paper. The biggest surprise for Sabella was what happened on the other side, where one knots or secures the stitch. He says, 'The threads created a landscape of their own, of coloured sprouts as if growing, flowers as if dancing, birds flying in an open sky. The threads were part of the whole, the bigger picture.'

Sabella joined an international co-action creative group to counter extremism through arts and culture. From their first meeting, the group focused on reimagining and transforming the world and, in that process, themselves too. Sabella recounts an instance before being picked up to go to the airport. 'The sun was shining in the blue sky, warming the cold street corridors. I put my sunglasses on and looked at the sun with my eyes closed. And then I felt this thought of mine echoing in a very different way, genuinely believing that, as long as there is one person left who imagines a better world, life has a chance. I was in a state of bliss. And the moment my studio found me, I transformed that state of bliss into *Everland*.'

The name of the artwork emerged from group sessions where participants were tasked with creating and naming an imaginary home or island. 'One word led to the other, from Noland to the inverse of Neverland – Everland. *Everland* is every free land, including the land of Palestine we all dream of, one with roots in every other culture.' In *Everland* (2020), Sabella marries photography, collage and embroidery to landscape his utopian vision.

By collaging his photographs of Palestinian embroidery, Sabella creates a beautiful new world while maintaining the harmony in colour and textural quality that is valued in the original embroidery. He explains, 'I like the dimensions between perceived reality and illusion, between image and imagination. I did not stitch with cotton, wool or silk but with digital threads woven on a new fabric of life. *Everland* celebrates all the charm that comes out of Palestine, a place where everything gets disrupted. Yet, the connecting technique enables the different stitches to penetrate deep

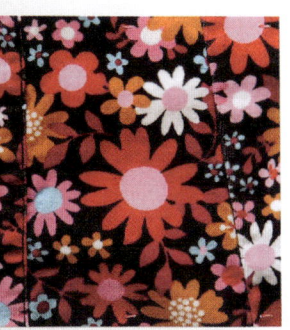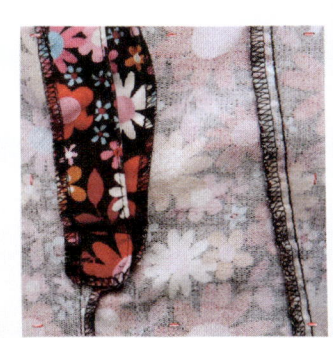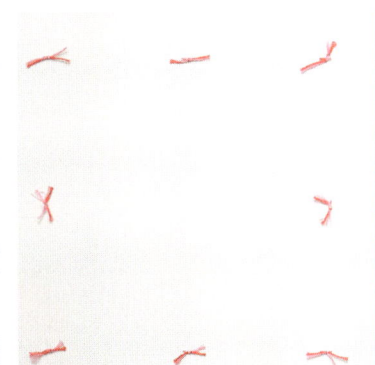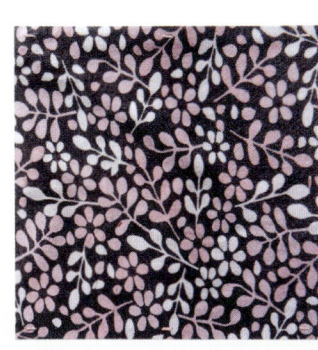

into new borders, creating unique designs that look as if they represent every other culture.' Sabella seamlessly pieces together the various images of embroidery to appear naturally connected. Various bright colours and types of stitch overlap, creating a sense of depth. An organic flow allows the eyes to travel around the piece, taking in the flowers, stars and geometric motifs.

Sabella explains how *Everland* reconnects the fragmented reality of Palestinian land through using various stitches from different regions of Palestine. 'If the occupation has the power to separate people, then imagination has more power to reunite them in different ways and forms. *Everland* is a study on the archaeology of the future, the archaeology of the image. Buried in these embroidered patterns are many stories with roots in the past, carrying information. And the collage allows for a renewed spirit to emerge. I also saw a parallel to when I wrote in my memoirs, *The Parachute Paradox*, when I stitched my wounds with barbed wire. In *Everland*, green threads replaced the barbed wire.'

Sabella's view is 'that there is an Other in all of us. Each – Other. And, through combined efforts, we should stop drawing borders and start drawing our future. And without justice for Palestine, the world cannot be at peace.' This sense of reconnection is reiterated in Sabella's decision to make the collage a series of squares that can be arranged and displayed in any formation or 'in different constellations'. Sabella opens a space for the collective imagination to

consider Palestine in terms of possibilities like the countless visual possibilities that emerge from *Everland*.

Sabella dedicated *Everland* to artist and art historian Kamal Boullata. To Sabella, 'Kamal was an expert on the literature of the soul. Every conversation with him was about essence, about true being, whether we spoke about art or life. *Everland* celebrates all the beauty that comes out of Palestine. The way I see it, to be born in Jerusalem or anywhere else always means you are becoming a citizen of Earth. We are all from everywhere and nowhere. Poetically, we are all from elsewhere. This is the *Everland* we are all searching for. And getting there is an extraordinary journey of limitless discovery.' Through *Everland*, Sabella leaves us contemplating the endless possibilities of a better, more beautiful world.

Steve Sabella, *Cécile Elise Sabella*, 2008. Hand-stitched Lambda print

Previous spread: Steve Sabella, *Everland 1*, 2020.
Photo collage, Lambda print mounted on matt Diasec, 80 x 80 cm

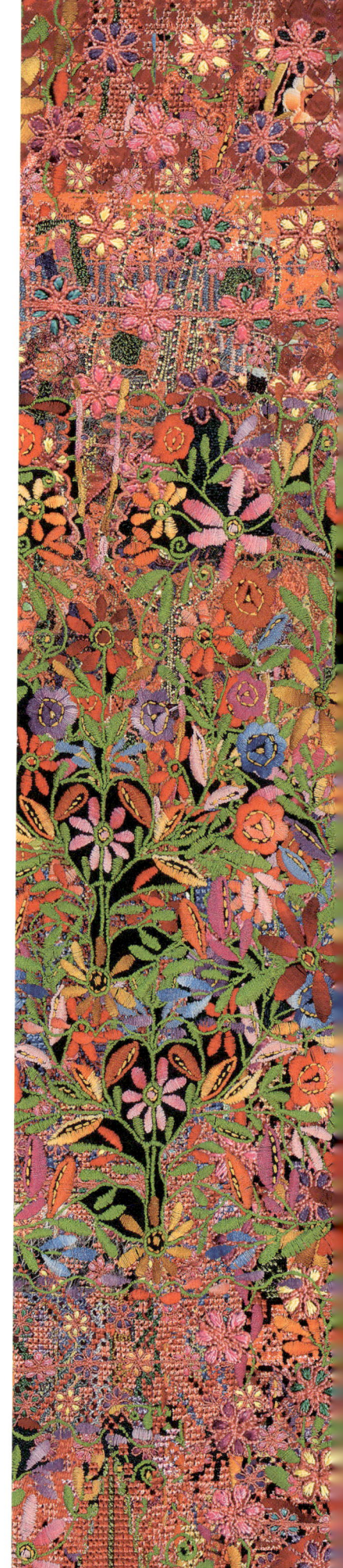

Steve Sabella, *Everland 8*, 2020. Photo collage, Lambda print mounted on matt Diasec, 80 x 80 cm

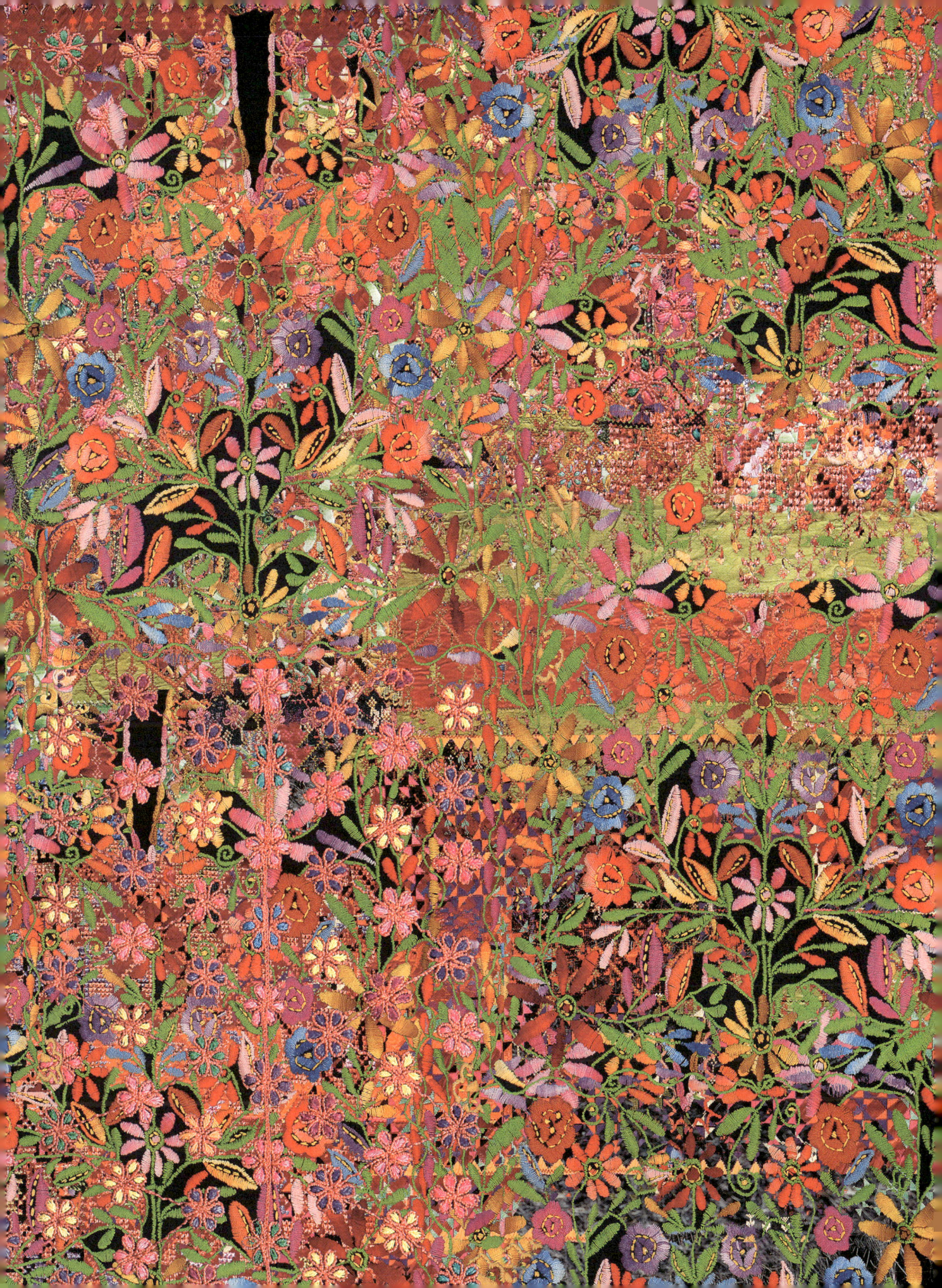

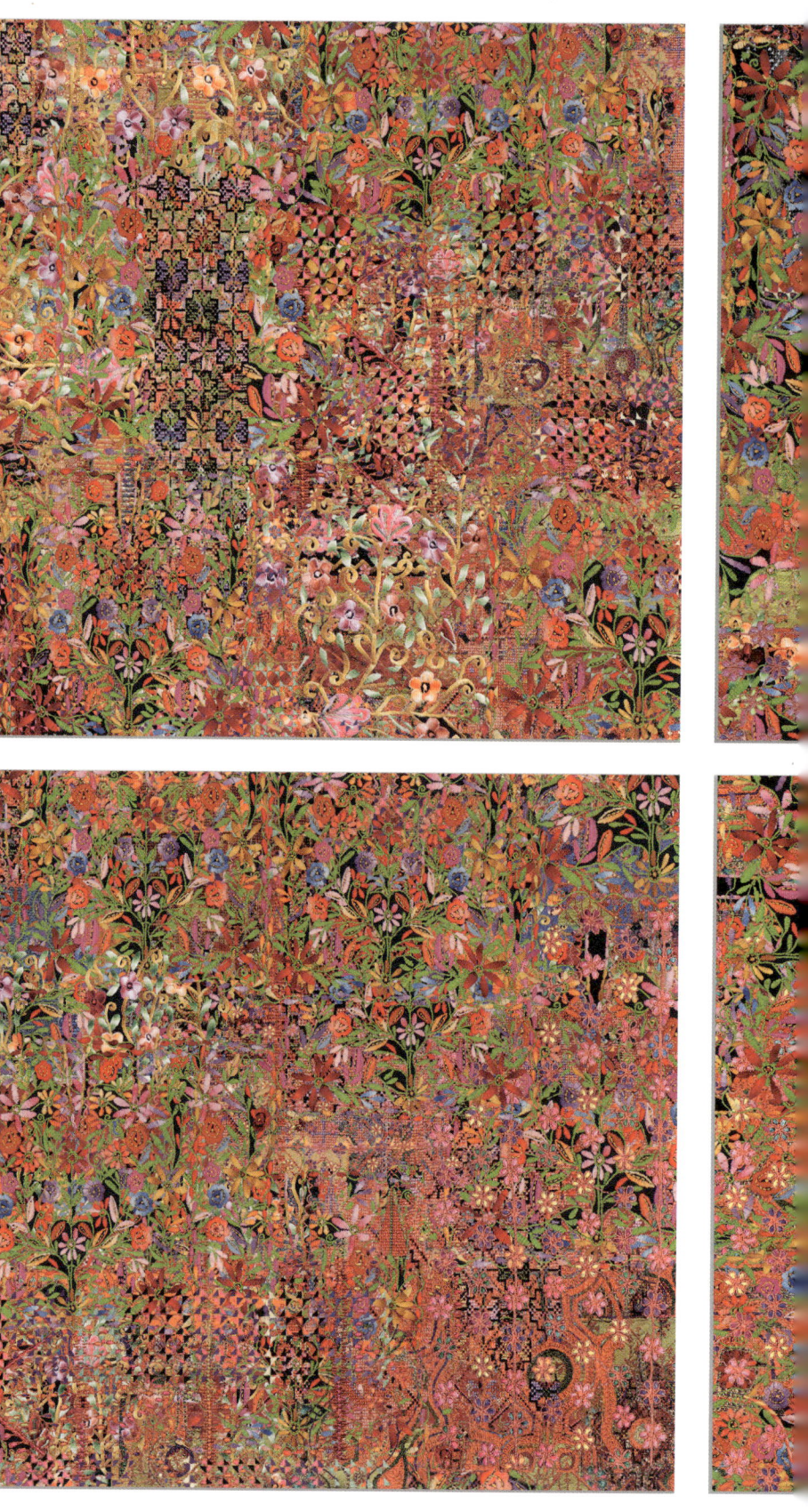

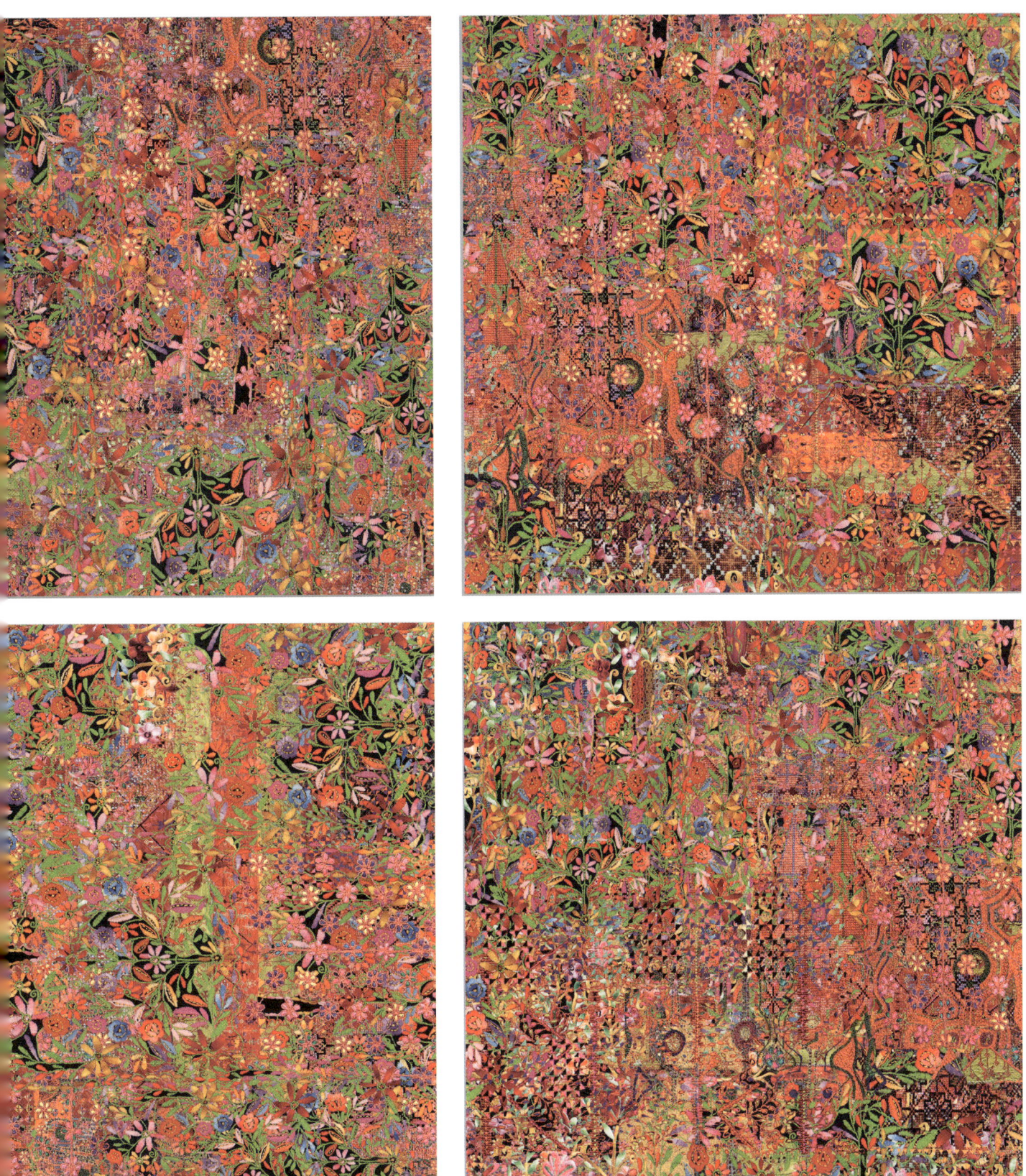

Steve Sabella, *Everland 1–6*, 2020. Photo collage, Lambda print mounted on matt Diasec, 80 x 80 cm

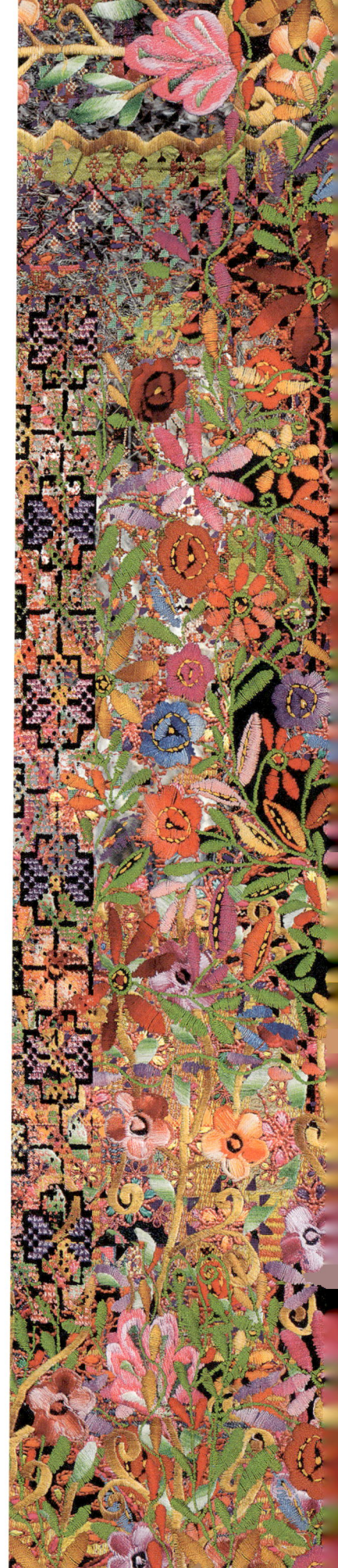

Steve Sabella, *Everland 9*, 2020. Photo collage, Lambda print mounted on matt Diasec, 80 x 80 cm

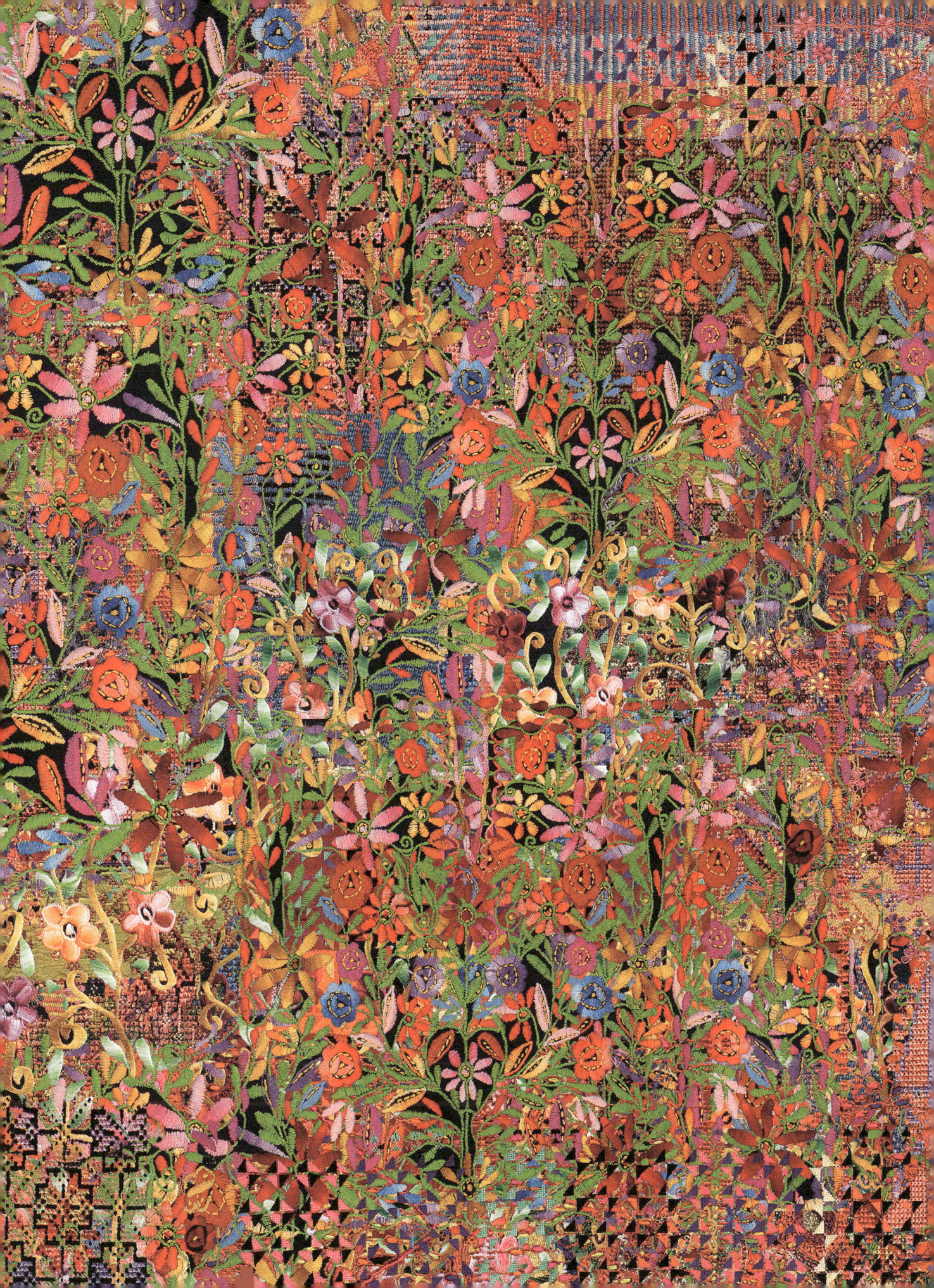

AMER

SHOMALI

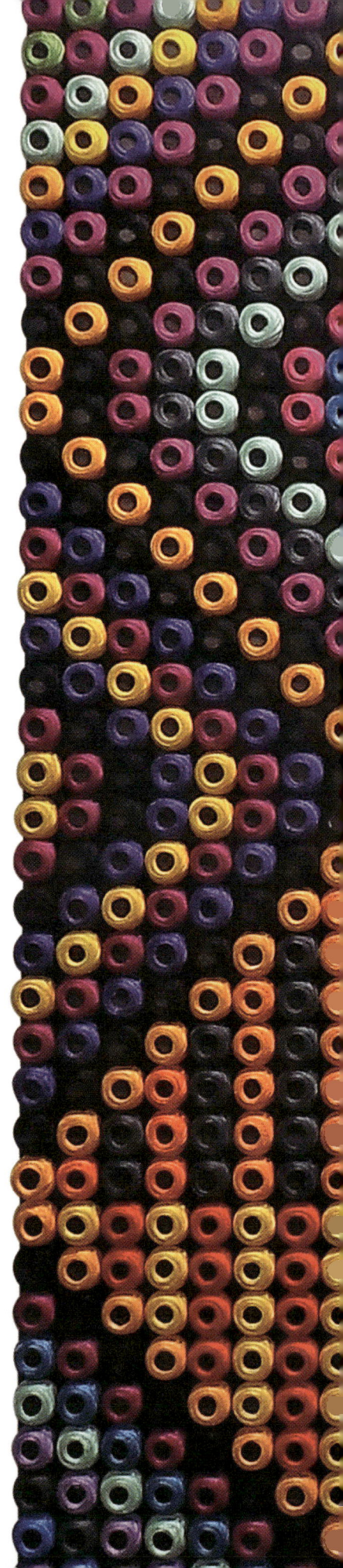

With a background in animation, graphic design, architecture and engineering, multidisciplinary artist Amer Shomali incorporates and transforms Palestinian iconography to serve as sociopolitical commentary on Palestine. We see this in his application of Palestinian embroidery motifs in his *Broken Weddings* series (2018). The inspiration behind this series came from an antique, embroidered Palestinian wedding dress that was up for sale in an Israeli auction house in 2017.

Shomali contacted the auction house to inquire about the unworn wedding dress and discovered that the seller was an Israeli who had inherited it from his father, a member of the Haganah militia. His father claimed that he had found the dress in one of the abandoned Arab houses during the Nakba in 1948 when Zionists destroyed and ethnically cleansed Palestinian villages. Zionist militia groups, like the one the dress seller's father belonged to, attacked, depopulated and razed 530 Palestinian villages. These groups killed approximately 13,000 Palestinians and left more than 750,000 Palestinians displaced after being forcefully expelled from their homes, like the home in which the seller's father found this dress. The dress sparked questions for Shomali. 'I started wondering why a bride would leave behind a dress that she spent years embroidering. Was her fiancé a fighter turned martyr, and that's why she abandoned the dress, a burden of memories, to run to a shelter? Perhaps she was in her home and killed by the man who stole the dress? In all cases, the wedding never took place.'

When approaching any of the works from the *Broken Weddings* series from a distance, we encounter enormous Palestinian cross-stitch motifs. As we get closer to the work, we realise that the stitches of the embroidery motif are made from brightly coloured unused balls of embroidery thread, coming together like a pixelated image. In most of Shomali's artwork, he employs one medium, which becomes the subject of his work. He says, 'By rearranging thousands of the same item, I change its meaning, a little bit like embroidery.' When stitched on a dress, tiny cross stitches make up individual motifs that measure around a few centimetres; they are now presented on a monumental scale when replaced with balls of thread. The scale and the medium of balls of thread serve as a reminder of the

tremendous loss and trauma that has permeated Palestinian life since the beginning of the ongoing Nakba.

Shomali explains, 'I reconstructed details of dresses from several depopulated villages using balls of thread. I replaced each stitch with a whole new ball that had never been used. Like the dresses not yet embroidered, broken weddings, unperformed songs, unbuilt homes, unborn children. The balls of thread aligned like gravestones, like bags of corpses after a disaster, like abandoned beehives, like dried wells. Threads unable to liberate themselves from their balls to say what they have to say: *Broken Weddings*, witnesses of the possibilities of the amputated lives of 1948.'

Shomali has produced seven pieces in this ongoing project, with motifs from dresses from the villages of Beit Jibrin, Deir Nakhas, Dawayima, Ramleh, Salameh, Lifta and Bir al-Sabe'. His research included visiting George Al Ama's dress collections and studying books on Palestinian embroidery by Widad Kawar and Shelagh Weir. The inclusion of embroidery in Shomali's work taps into the fundamental human element left out of conversations about the Israeli occupation of Palestine. When discussing *Broken Weddings*, Shomali says, 'I am inviting the viewer to reconsider the Palestinian refugees as humans whose lives got ruptured, rather than the prevailing statistical interest. I ask people to shift their focus from the United Nations' statistics and to zoom into the lost lives, dreams, and weddings.'

His recognition of Palestinian embroidery's familiarity and universal appeal allows his work to communicate his message more effectively. Shomali adds, 'Each culture has its own embroidery. Differing in the techniques, colours and patterns, they all consume time and demonstrate intimacy. People from different backgrounds appreciate embroidery because it will tickle a soft spot somewhere in their memories. Palestinian embroidery has yet another advantage, which makes it contemporary, as it resembles geometric abstraction art. I think that Palestinian embroidery is deeply rooted in a local context yet speaks to a wide audience. This is the ultimate objective of art, becoming international while still being locally rooted.'

Shomali also incorporates embroidery in his paintings *Postcolonial 'Palestine'* (2013) and *Postcolonial 'Harvest'*

(2014). The women in embroidered dresses in these paintings reference two oil paintings from the 1970s by Sliman Mansour: *Palestine* (1979), featuring a woman holding oranges, and *Harvest* (1977), where a woman holds spikes of wheat. Shomali draws attention to how Mansour's paintings resonated with Palestinians in the late 1970s when Palestinian farmers were united with the land and played a crucial role in pushing forward the production cycle.

Instead of the entire figure of a farmer in her embroidered dress, Shomali recreates Mansour's paintings by cropping the image so that the hands become the focal point. The objects are spotlighted in colour, while the hands and chest panels of the dress are monochromatic and recede into the black background. He replaced the oranges with Israeli Tapuzina orange juice bottles and the wheat spikes with Israeli Berman's bread, as these brands are popular among Palestinians working as cheap labour in Israeli factories. Shomali says, 'They are the descendants of the Palestinians who used to own the orchards of Jaffa oranges and wheat fields in Palestine. They lost their land and its produce.'

While Mansour's paintings reflect a romanticised utopian past represented by the personified motherland and her bounty, Shomali's paintings comment on the effects of Israeli settler colonialism by focusing on what is now left in the hands of the people. By intentionally blacking out the colourful embroidery, Shomali transforms them into mourning dresses representing 'the Palestinian women who lost their land, their hope, and their families'. Rendering the embroidery in this way invites conversation about Israel's attempts at erasing, destroying and replacing Palestinian cultural and agricultural production.

In the *Broken Weddings* series and *Postcolonial Palestine* paintings, Shomali uses Palestinian embroidery to bring the discourse back to the Palestinian people and their lived experiences, contrasting with the oppressive dominant narrative. His *Broken Weddings* series marries the medium to the message, inviting contemplation on the potential that precedes devastating loss. The *Postcolonial Palestine* paintings reveal the direct effects of settler colonialism on the Palestinian people. In both works, Shomali engages the viewer with Palestinian embroidery and shares the story of loss resulting from brutal settler colonialism and ethnic cleansing.

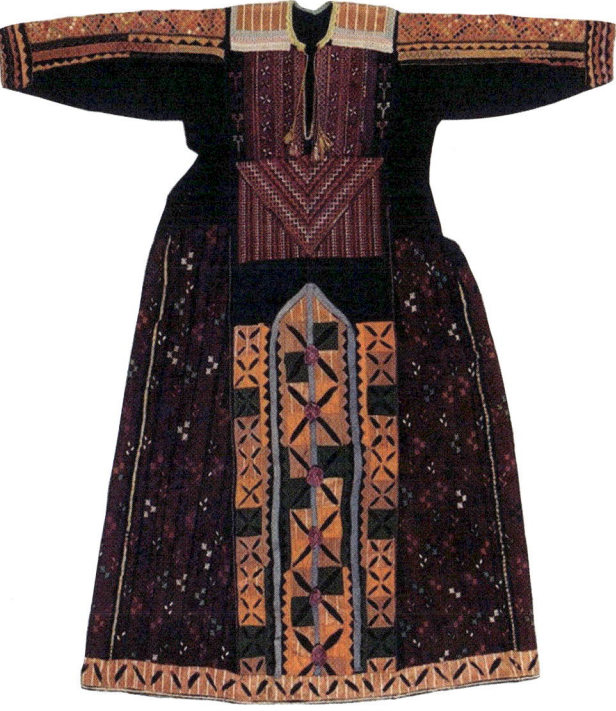

Antique Palestinian embroidered dress up for sale in Israeli auction; it inspired the *Broken Weddings* series

Previous spread: Amer Shomali, *Broken Weddings in Al Dawayima*, 2018. 1,296 DMC spools mounted on aluminium and wood base, 166 x 166 cm

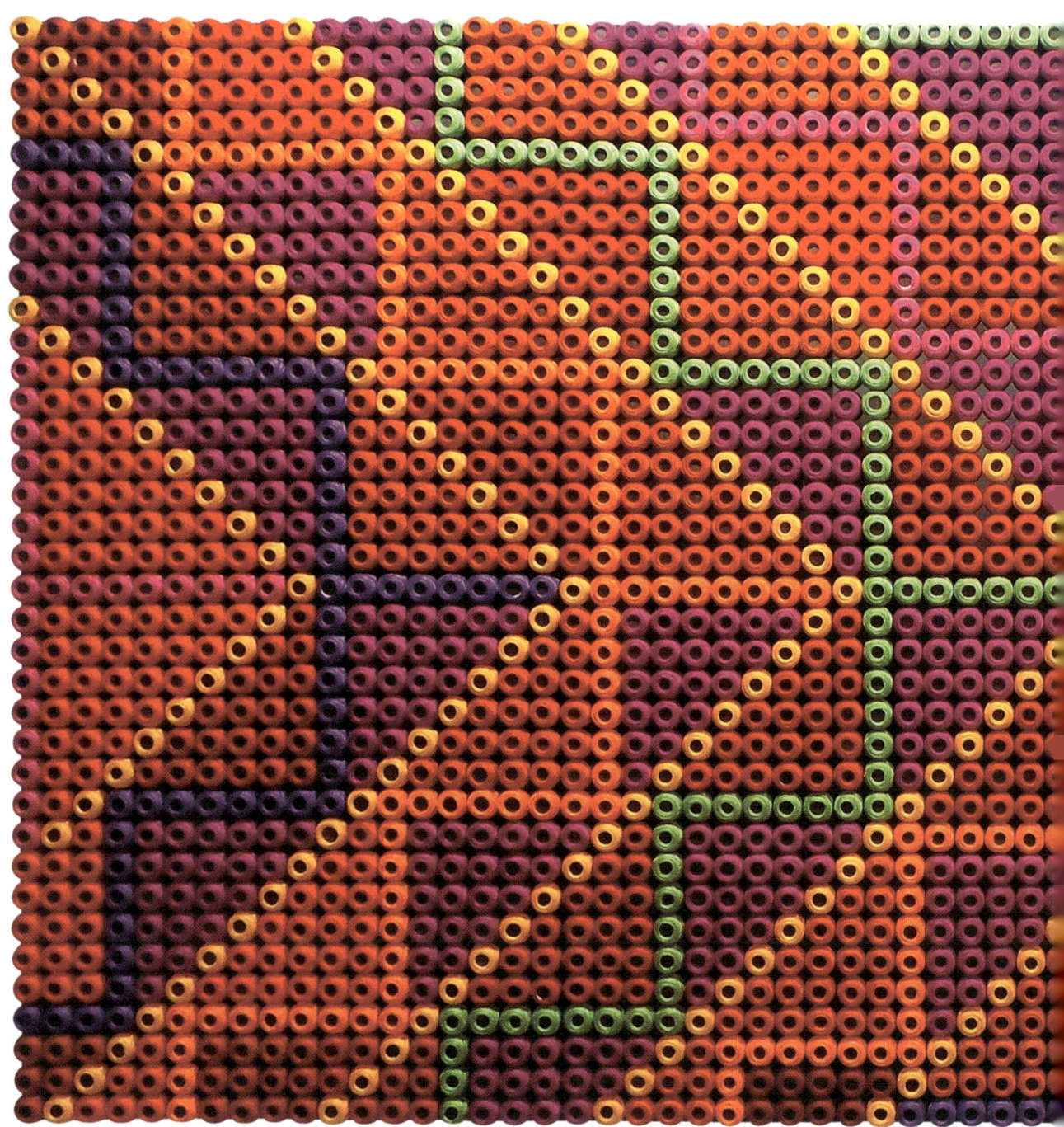

Amer Shomali, *Broken Weddings in Deir Nakhas*, 2018. 2,592 DMC spools mounted on aluminium and wood base, 332 x166 cm

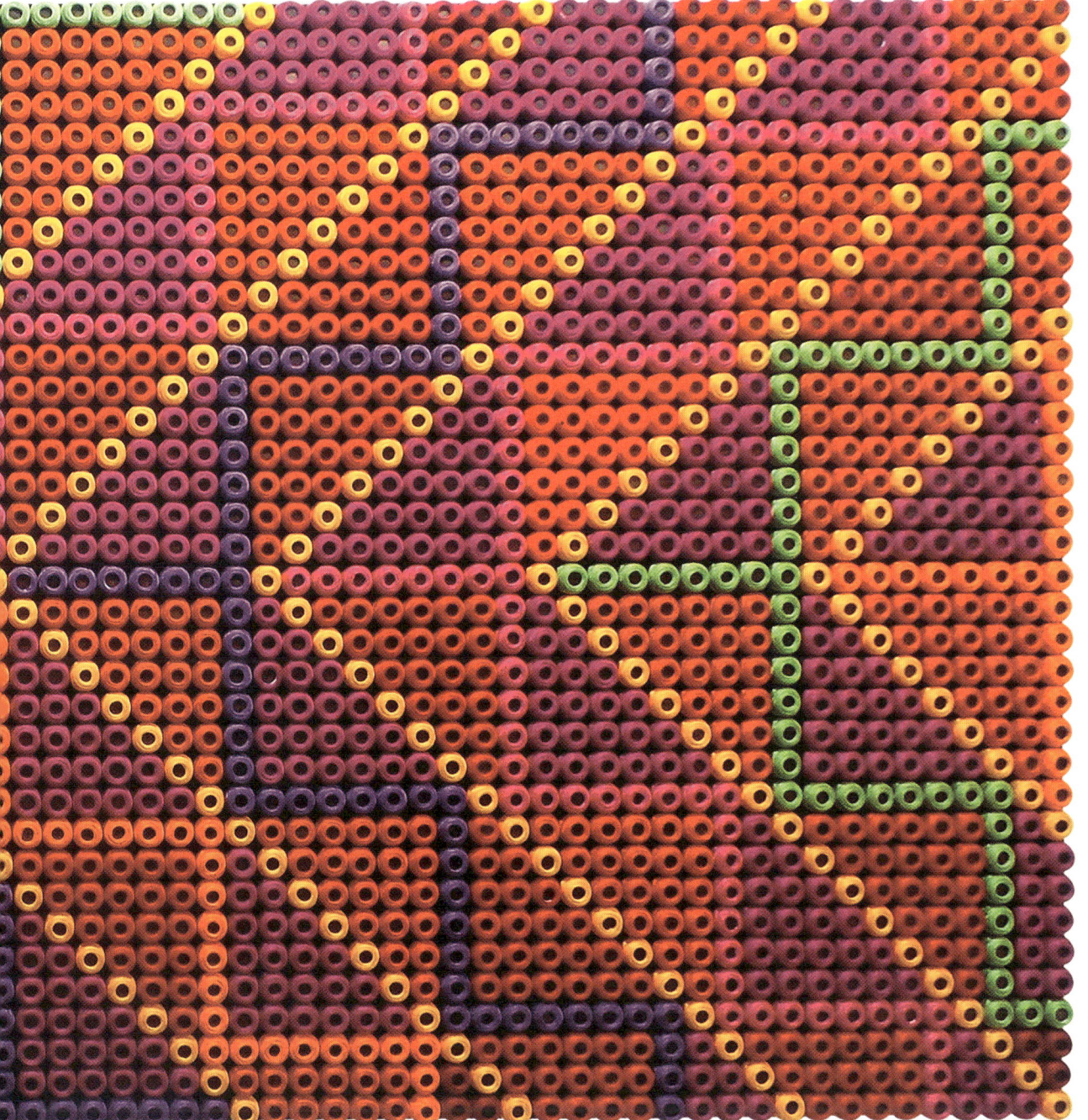

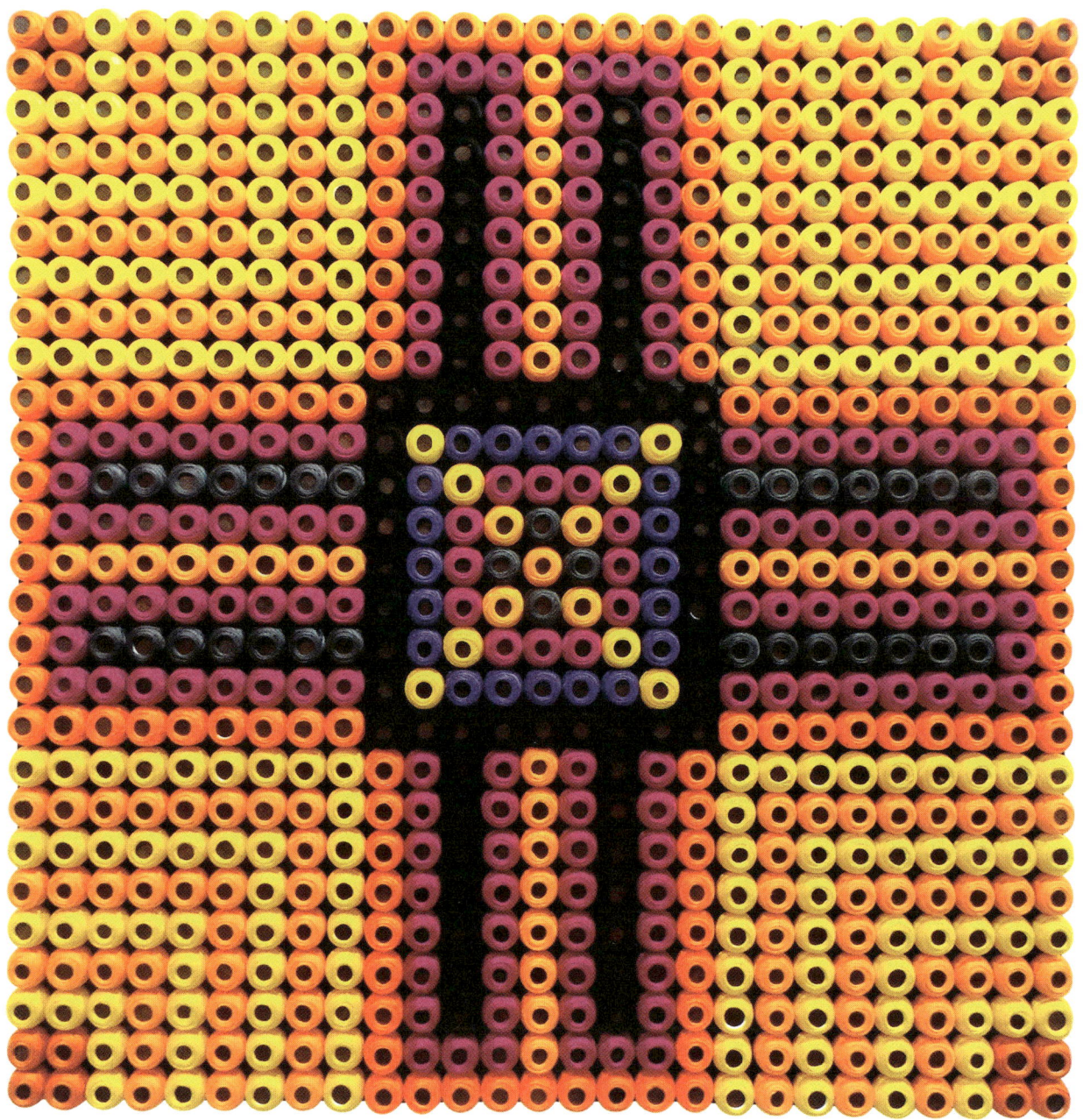

Amer Shomali, *Broken Weddings in Ramleh*, 2018. 729 DMC spools mounted on aluminium and wood base, 124.5 x 124.5 cm

Right: Amer Shomali, *Broken Weddings in Beir Al Sabe'*, 2019. 2,304 DMC spools mounted on aluminium and wood base, 220.8 x 220.8 cm

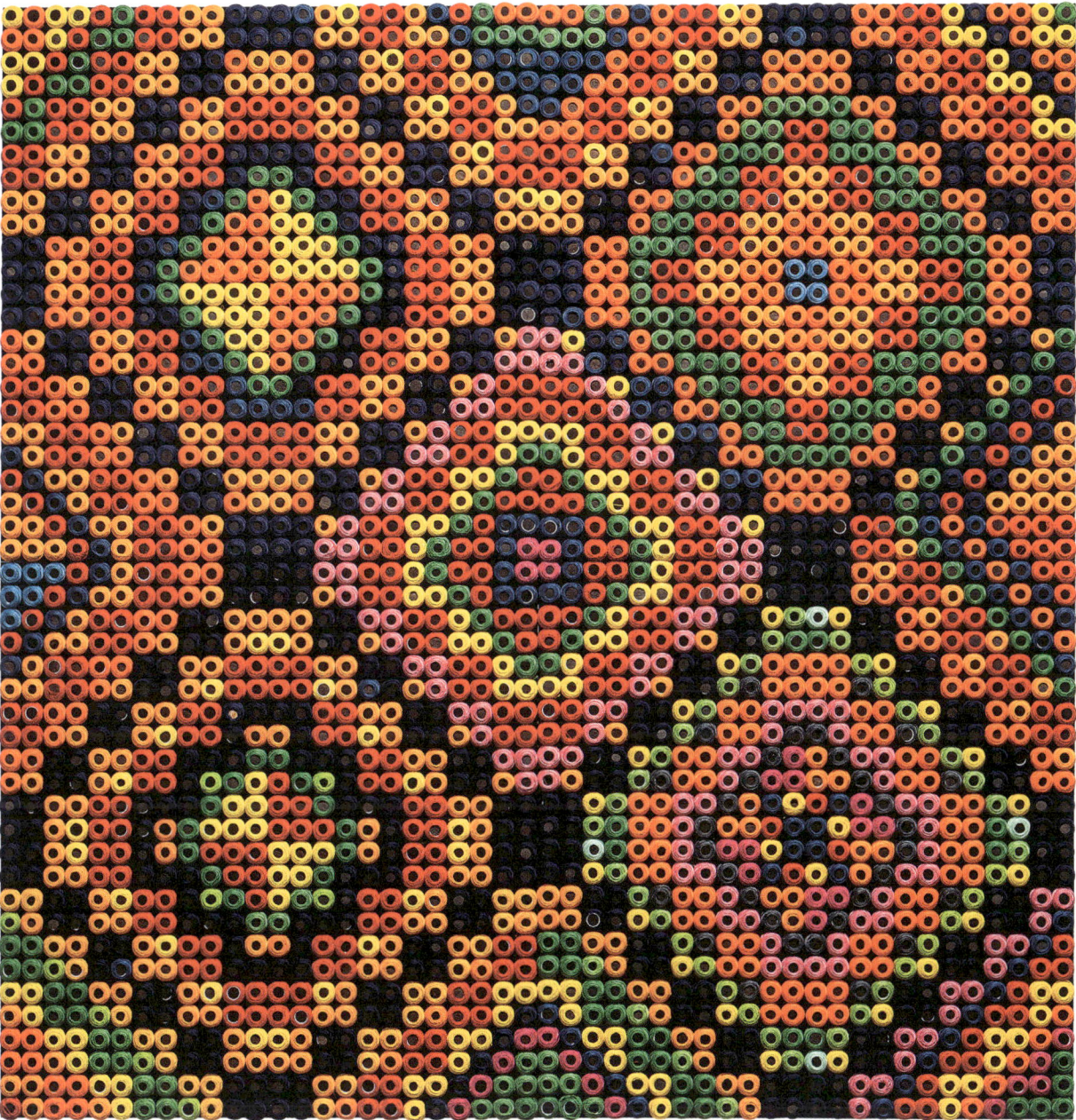

Right (detail): Amer Shomali, *Broken Weddings in Al Dawayima*, 2018. 1,296 DMC spools mounted on aluminium and wood base, 166 x 166 cm

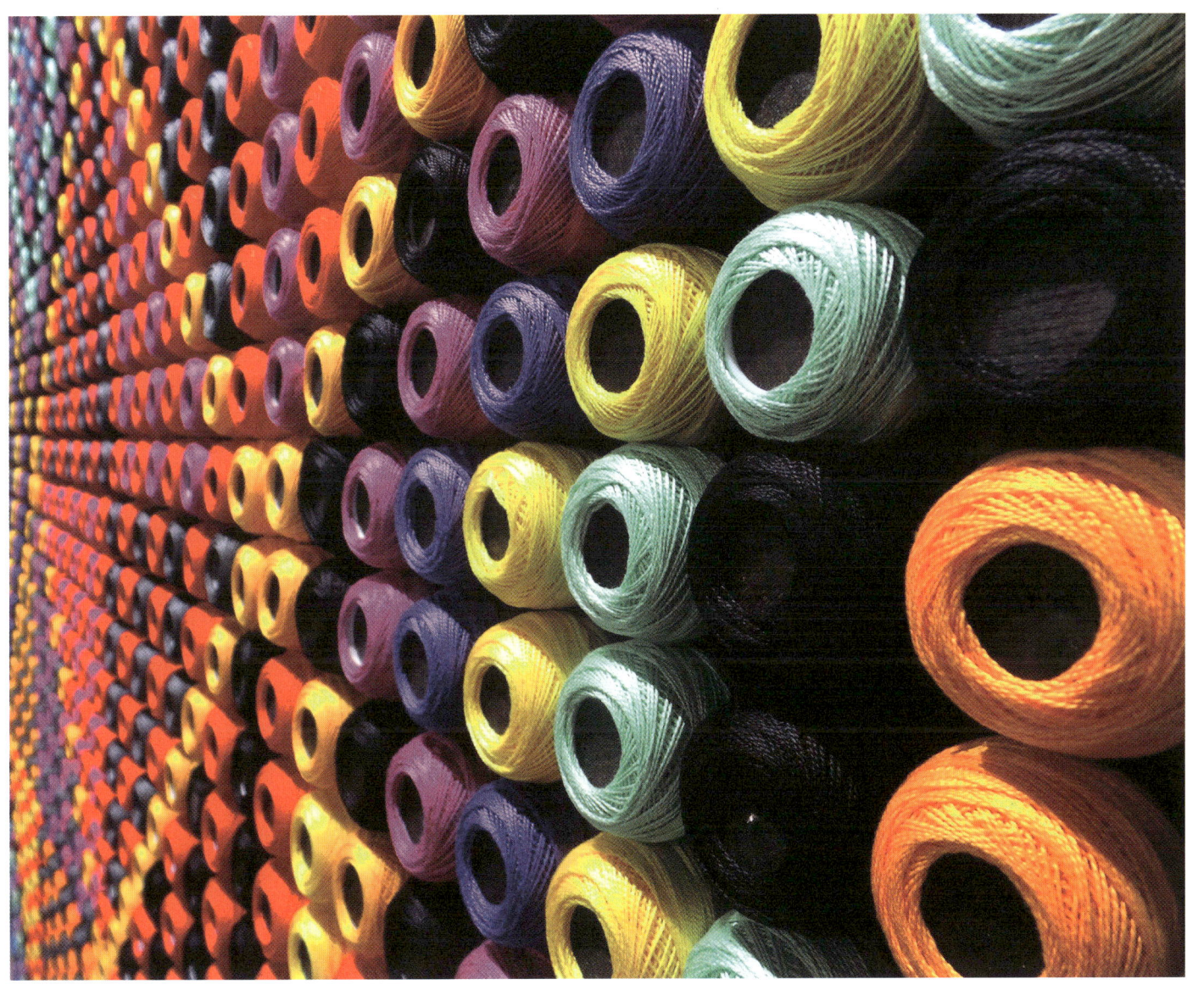

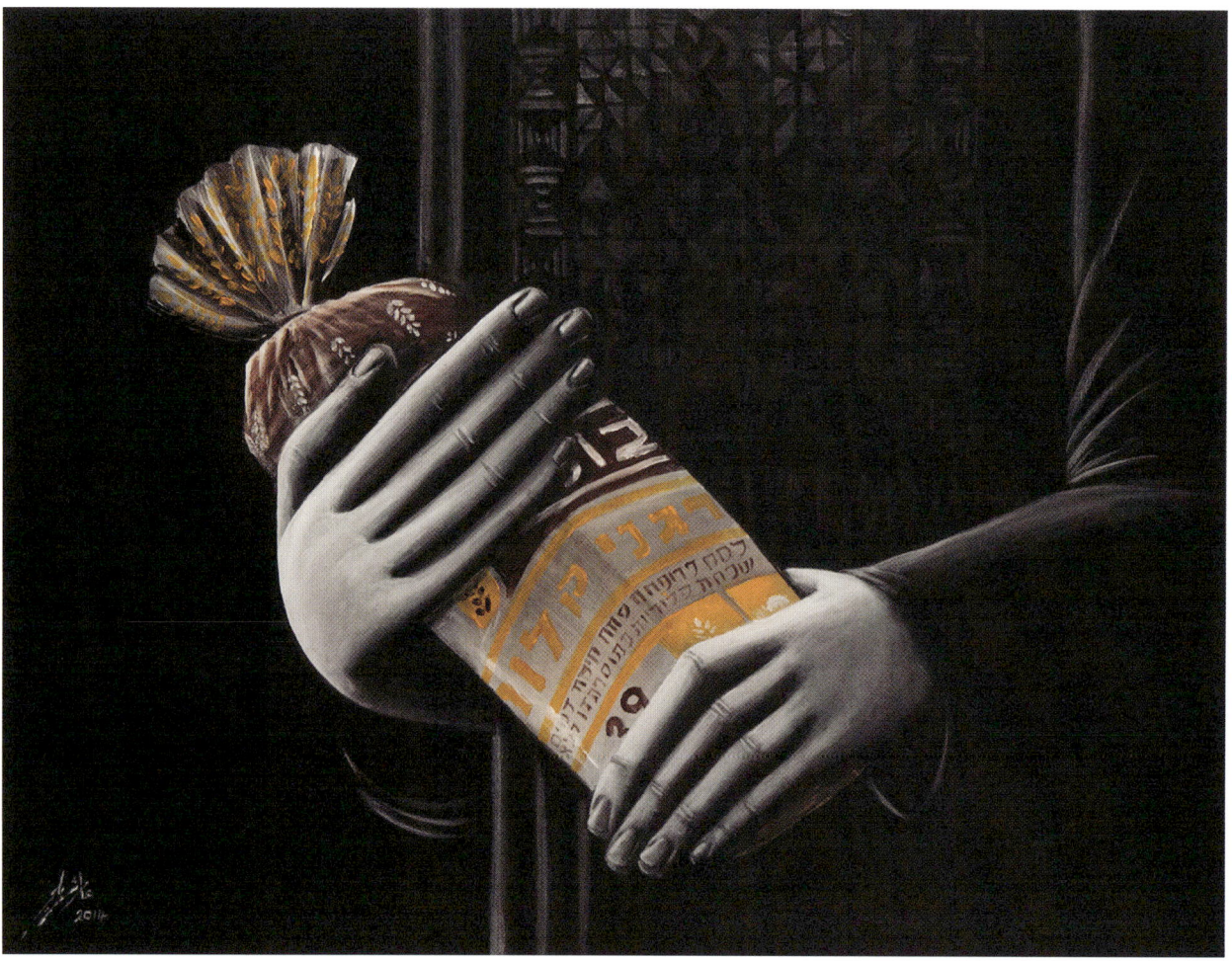

Amer Shomali, *Postcolonial 'Harvest'*, 2014. Acrylic on canvas, 60 x 80 cm

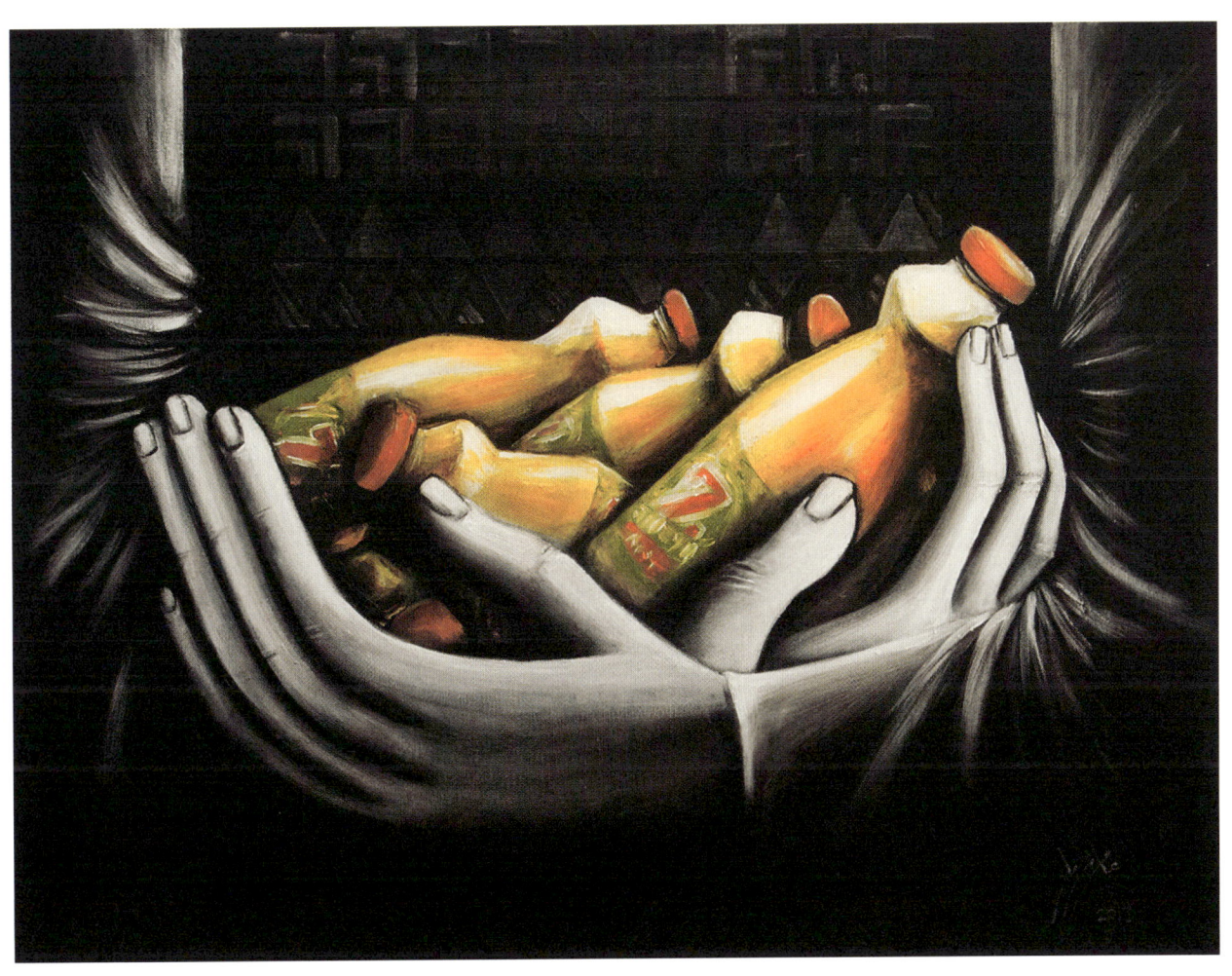

Amer Shomali, *Postcolonial 'Palestine'*, 2013. Acrylic on canvas, 60 x 80 cm

JOANNA
BARAKAT

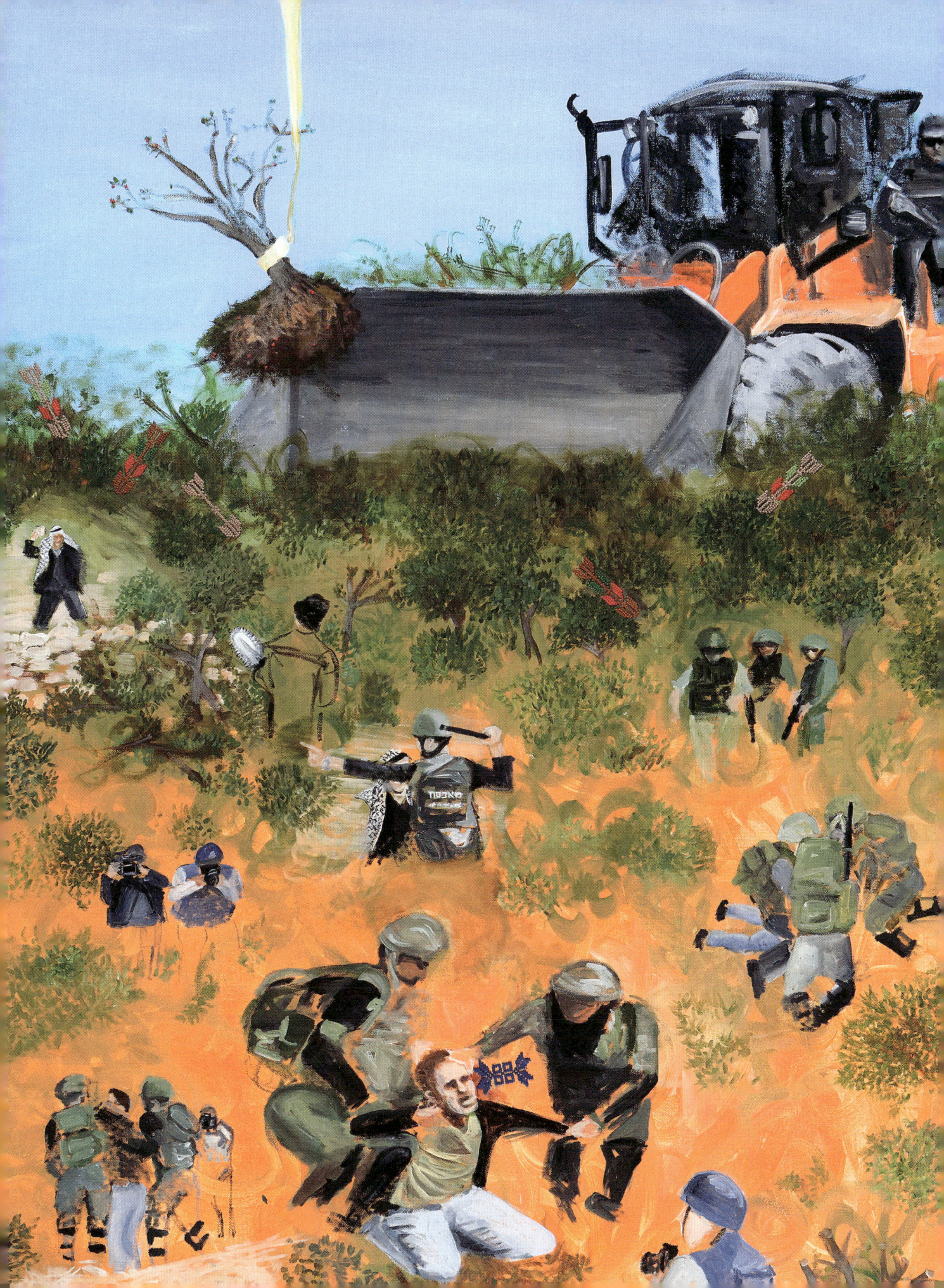

In her hand-embroidered paintings and textile artwork, Joanna Barakat approaches Palestinian embroidery as a language to relay messages and concepts, and to create space for connection and conversation. Her preoccupation with Western propaganda and concern over the dehumanisation of Palestinians drive much of her work. Employing the language of Palestinian embroidery as a medium and conceptually, Barakat's artwork articulates a deep-rooted connection to her Palestinian heritage and challenges Western colonial narratives, myths and stereotypes.

After extensive research, and having discovered the storytelling capability of Palestinian embroidery, Barakat developed a technique of hand stitching traditional Palestinian embroidery motifs directly onto painted canvas. Palestinian embroidery became central to her art practice after her visceral self-portrait painting *Heart Strings* (2017), where she depicts herself looking down pensively as she stitches her bare skin. Barakat says, 'It was the first time I hand embroidered directly on a painting. This work reclaims and re-embodies my story as a diaspora Palestinian, with the embroidery representing a longing to return to indigeneity. Through embroidery, I can finally speak a native Palestinian language fluently instead of broken Arabic, which always left me feeling like an outsider.' In the painting, she wears the traditional white headscarf, as a display of modesty in contrast to her naked skin – symbolising what one hides or reveals about oneself.

Her work *American Nakba* (2017), where she hand embroidered Palestinian embroidery motifs on a spraypainted American flag, speaks to similarities between the plight of Indigenous peoples of America and that of the Palestinians. Barakat recalls, 'Growing up in America, you are indoctrinated through media and education to glorify the white settler colonial myth, where the dehumanised Indigenous population stands in the way of the settler hero. Even as a child, it all seemed like a farce to me. The genocide and continued violence against the Indigenous population felt too familiar. At the time when I made *American Nakba*, I intended it as a call for Palestinian Americans to stand in solidarity with Indigenous communities and advocate loudly for Indigenous rights in America.' Today, we see examples of solidarity and allyship where Palestinian groups stood with Indigenous communities in opposition to the Dakota Access Pipeline, and when Indigenous communities and activists participated in protests and other forms of activism calling for Palestinian liberation and an end to the genocide in Gaza.

In another of Barakat's hand-embroidered paintings, *The Witness* (2018), a scene unfolds with an olive tree torn out of the ground. She explains, 'It bears witness to generations of a Palestinian man's family who loved, nurtured and cared for their olive trees for centuries. It danced and swayed to the songs they sang during the olive harvest. It now watches as the man's elderly father throws stones at Israelis with chainsaws and bulldozers, trespassing on his ancestral land to steal the trees. It watches the soldiers pinning the man to the ground while he cries, "My olives, my olives," translated into Palestinian embroidery hand-stitched to the canvas. The tree also watches the Israeli soldiers arrest the man and take him away.'

Barakat borrows the scene from news footage from the early 2000s. The work speaks to Israel's ongoing land theft over the past seventy-five years, and Israeli soldiers arresting innocent Palestinian men, women and children, holding them indefinitely without charges or trial to humiliate, torture and traumatise them. The violence against Palestinians and their land also comes from settlers in nearby illegal settlements, who attack Palestinians, steal their trees and set trees and orchards on fire.

In her mixed-media work *There's No Place Like Home* (2018), Barakat focuses on the concept of the Palestinians' right of return to their homeland after being forcibly displaced. She references Dorothy's journey to find her way home in the story of *The Wizard of Oz* in both the title and the symbolic imagery featured in the work. The central character wears a traditional Palestinian embroidered dress and red shoes, alluding to Dorothy's ruby-red slippers. The Yellow Brick Road from the story is also referenced in the artwork, with the background made up of a repeated embroidered house motif. Barakat intentionally omits the stitches which fill the house motif to depict the empty homes of Palestinians following their violent eviction by Israeli occupation forces, starting in 1948 and continuing ever since in the ongoing military occupation, settler colonisation, theft and usurpation of the land.

In *The Water Spring* (2019), Barakat uses Palestinian embroidery motifs to tell the story of Israel's water restrictions on Palestinians. Historically, Palestinian women collected water from the local spring, which they depicted on their dresses with the water spring embroidery motif. In this work, the disappearing Palestinian embroidery motifs of the water spring and cauliflower, representing regional plants, are enclosed by the barbed wire embroidery motif, representing Israel's restriction of clean and safe water sources for Palestinians and the devastating effect on agriculture in the West Bank.

Israel controls all water and water-related infrastructure in East Jerusalem, the West Bank and Gaza. Over 97 per cent of Gaza's water has been contaminated and unfit for human consumption for decades. With 90 per cent of the West Bank Aquifer diverted to Israel, Israeli settlers living in illegal settlements in the West Bank consume four times the amount of water as Palestinians, who are consuming less than the World Health Organisation's daily minimum recommendation. These same Israeli settlers also violently damage water pumps and pipes leading to Palestinian villages and cities in the West Bank. Israel intentionally destroys Palestinian agriculture and economy by strictly restricting their usage of the remaining 10 per cent. Barakat states, 'Here is a peek into the near and ominous future where Israel continues to deny Palestinians their human right to water for agriculture and domestic use, adding climate refugees to the pre-existing Palestinian refugee crisis and further aiding in the genocide and settler colonial dispossession of the indigenous population.'

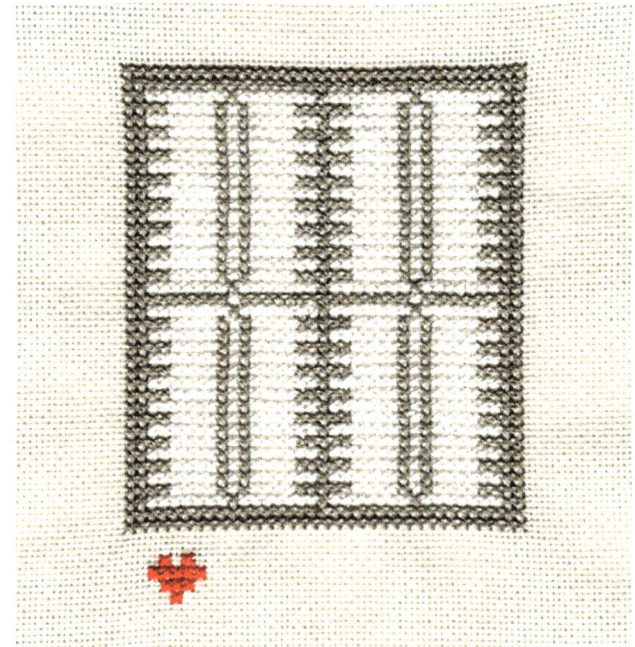

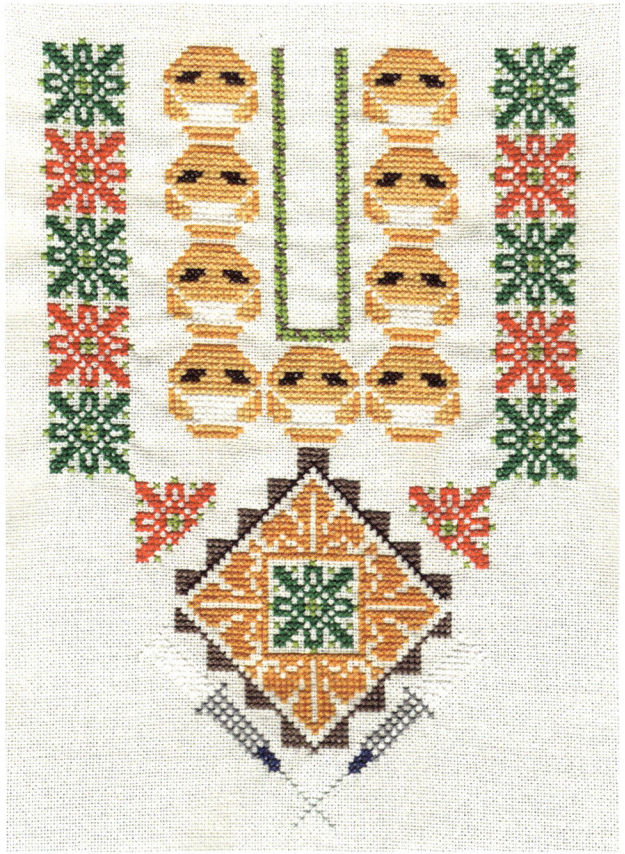

Joanna Barakat, *Like*, 2024. Cotton thread on cotton, 12 x 12 cm
Joanna Barakat, *2020*, 2022. Cotton on cotton fabric, 21 x 28 cm

Previous spread: Joanna Barakat, *The Witness*, 2018. Acrylic and cotton thread on canvas, 101 x 76 cm. Photo by Jonathan Gibbons

Barakat's art practice also delves into her inner world, sharing transcendental ideas through embroidery and mixed-media works. In *The Return* (2018), Barakat represents the Qur'anic verse 'to Allah we belong and to Allah we shall return', often used by Muslims to express grief over the loss of a loved one. She describes the abstract work as 'all energy spiralling back to the source of creation', where she spray painted the background spiralling towards a white, hand-embroidered Palestinian cross-stitch motif.

Another of her hand-embroidered works, *Entanglement* (2019), relates the concept of quantum entanglement to human connection with another person, group of people, place or idea. Threads emerge from and connect to four squares centred in each motif, resembling the heart's four chambers. She explains, 'Visualising entanglement in symbolic terms creates an opportunity to contemplate this connecting force, removing the illusion of separateness and emphasising an idea of oneness.'

Inspired by talismanic shirts and amulets, Barakat focuses on faith and its profound impact in *Amulet* (2021). The work features two hands in *sujood*, or prostration in prayer. One hand holds a protective amulet, which she hand embroidered using Bethlehem's *tahriri* or couching stitch, emulating the protective amulets depicted in couched roundel embroidery motifs found on Palestinian embroidered dresses and jewellery. Resembling glyphs of an ancient language, simplified Islamic prayer postures can be read in rows down the other hand. Barakat presents the postures as a conduit for heightened energy frequency and flow during prayer.

In *2020* (2022), Barakat draws a comparison between Palestinian embroidery motifs and emojis when reflecting on the way people turned to online platforms for communication and connection during the COVID pandemic. Historically, Palestinian women documented their surroundings and significant life events on their dresses with various embroidery motifs representing things and ideas, in a way similar to our use of emojis today. Barakat states, '*2020* brings together two visual languages and tells a story about a significant moment in time that humanity collectively experienced. Like

the chest panels on dresses of historic Palestine, *2020* documents a significant moment in our lifetimes.' The artwork is composed like a traditional Palestinian dress chest panel: rows of embroidered masked-face emojis are repeated around the neckline, with a Palestinian crown disc embroidery motif and vaccine injections below it. Within the crown disc is a stylised virus emoji representing the coronavirus. Rows of the same virus emoji frame the masked emojis on the chest panel.

In *Like* (2024), Barakat looks at how people consume social media content about Israel's genocide of Palestinians in Gaza on social media. 'Social media played a monumental role in waking up the world to Palestine. It unveiled Western mainstream media's blatant propaganda and the imperialist agendas it serves. I wanted to capture the obscure way people interact with the violent content on social media. I'm curious about the mental compartmentalising that occurs when scrolling through the usual cute pet videos, funny memes, sports highlights and makeup tutorials to viewing Israel's unimaginable destruction and violence happening in real time to Palestinians in Gaza. To raise awareness, we like, share and repost this content, an act previously reserved for posts that brought pleasure, not pain. It's strange seeing little red hearts under such horrific photos. I wonder how people in the future will look back and comprehend the "liking" of this violent content.' The hand-embroidered work depicts a square filled with the grave embroidery motif and a red heart, resembling a 'liked' Instagram post.

Barakat draws inspiration from Palestinian embroidery techniques and implements them in her work as a way of documenting events and sharing ideas. Though initially drawn to Palestinian embroidery as a language and storytelling device, she values how it facilitates connection and community while creating opportunities for conversations and activism. Her artwork embodies her personal connection to her Palestinian heritage and addresses socio-political issues such as Western propaganda, colonial narratives, and the ongoing struggles faced by Palestinians.

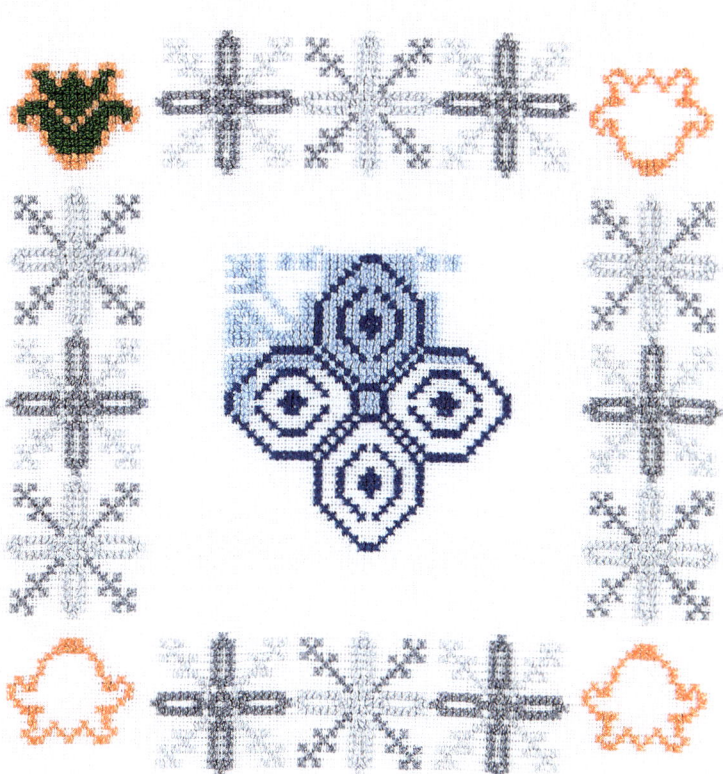

Joanna Barakat, *The Water Spring*, 2019. Cotton thread on linen, 31 x 31 cm.
Photo by Jonathan Gibbons

Next spread: Joanna Barakat, *Heart Strings*, 2017. Acrylic, spray paint and cotton thread on canvas, 61 x 91 cm.
Photo by Jonathan Gibbons

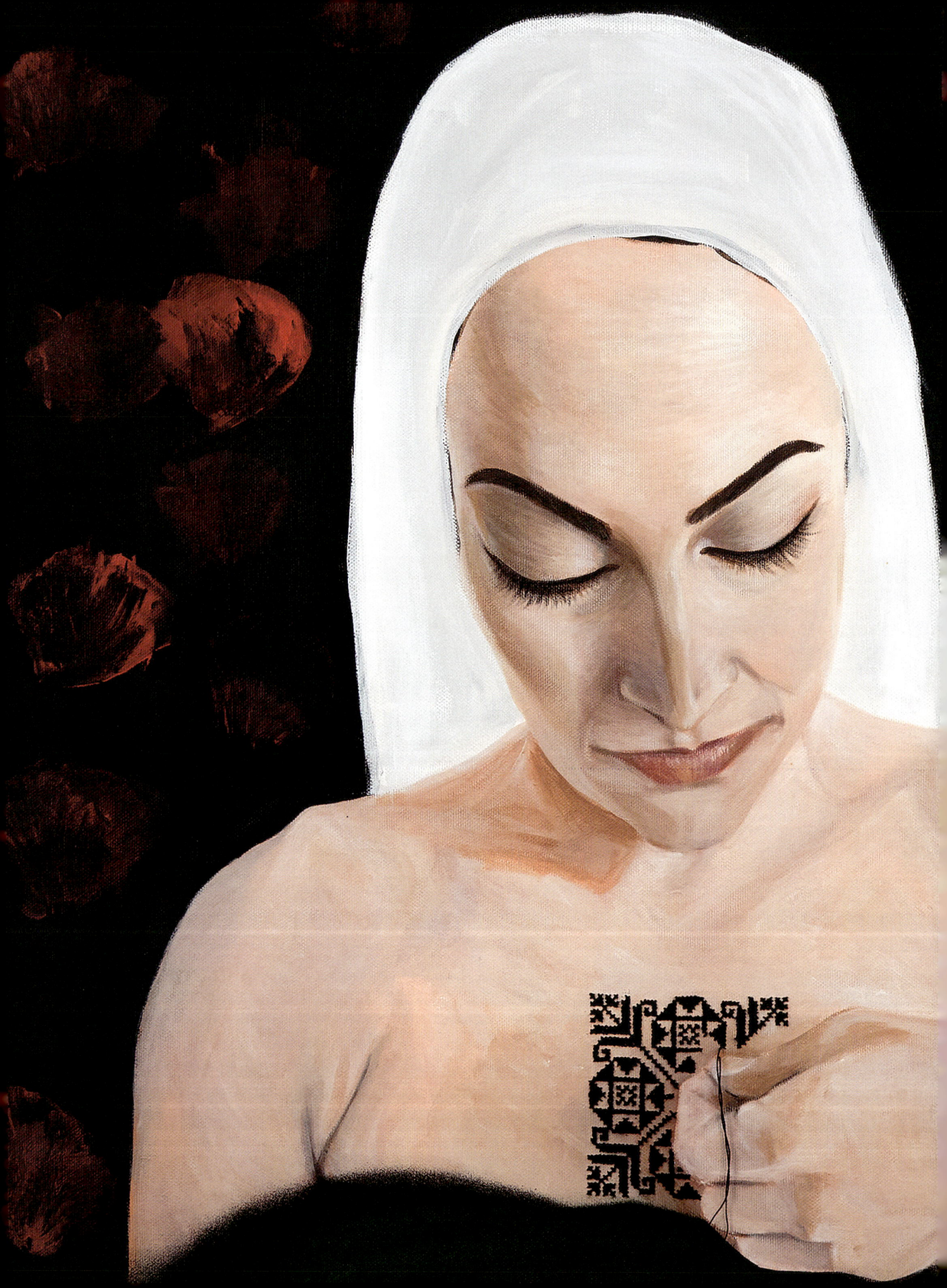

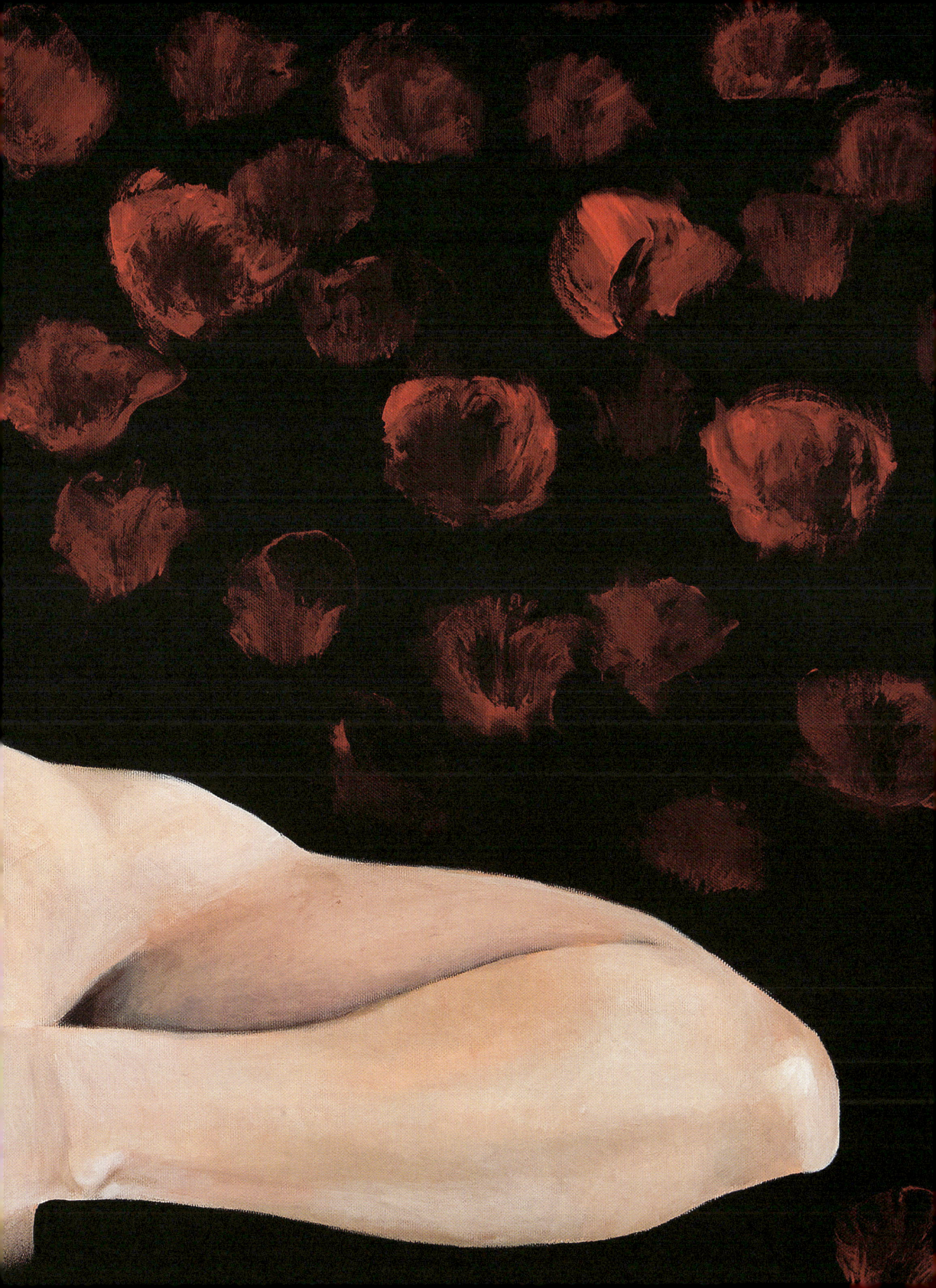

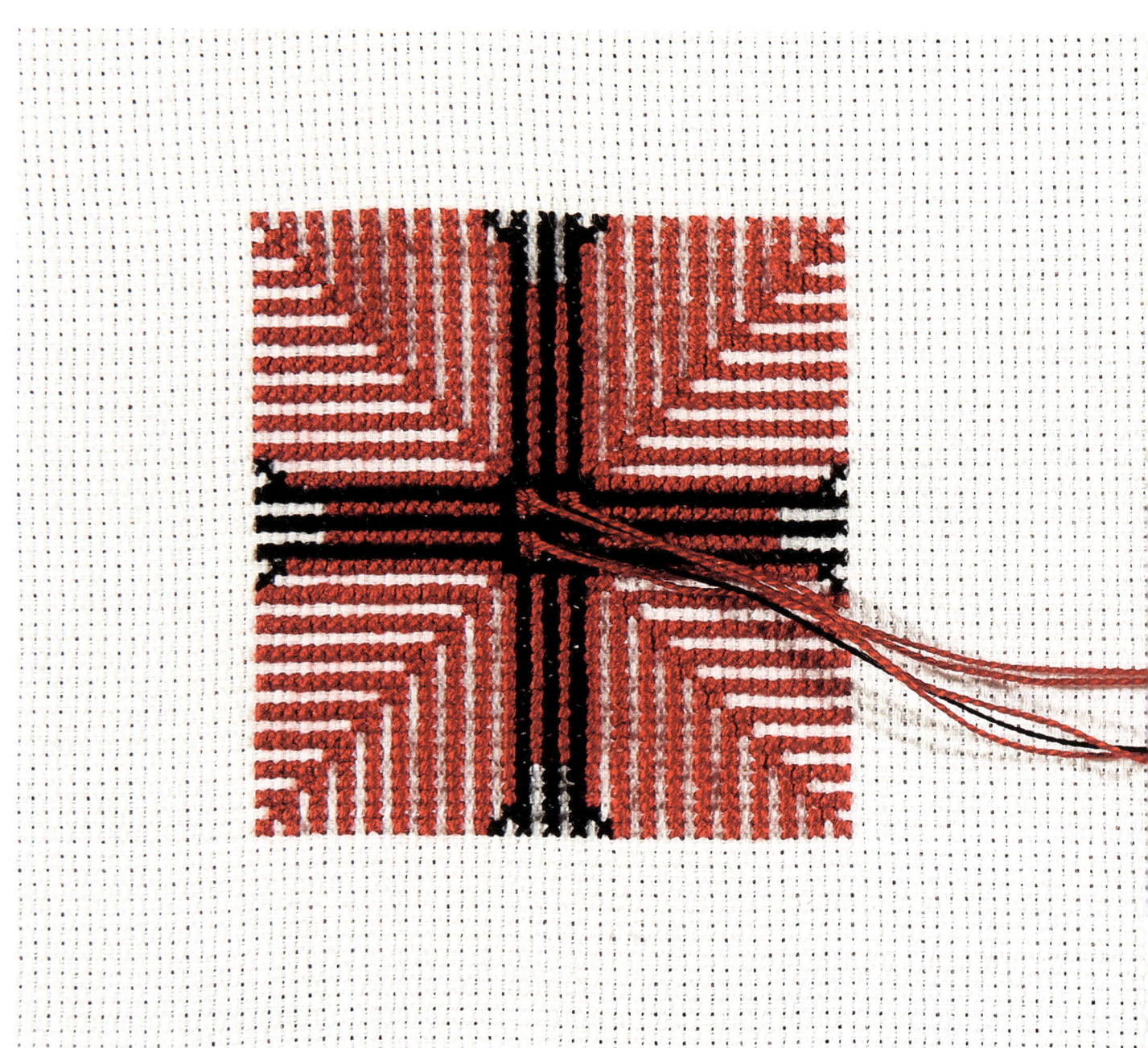

Joanna Barakat, *Entanglement*, 2019. Cotton thread on cotton, 15 x 30 cm. Photo by Jonathan Gibbons

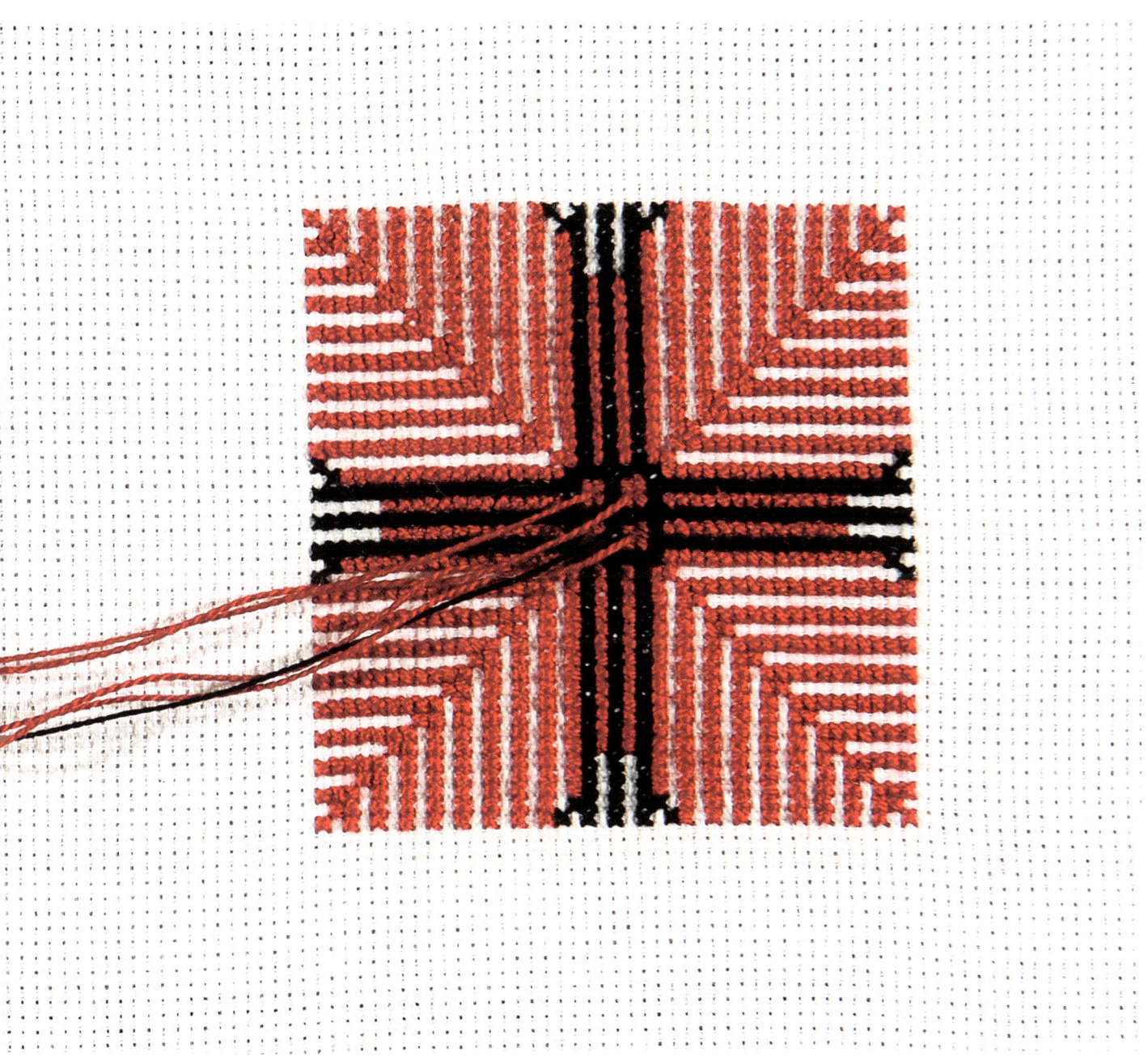

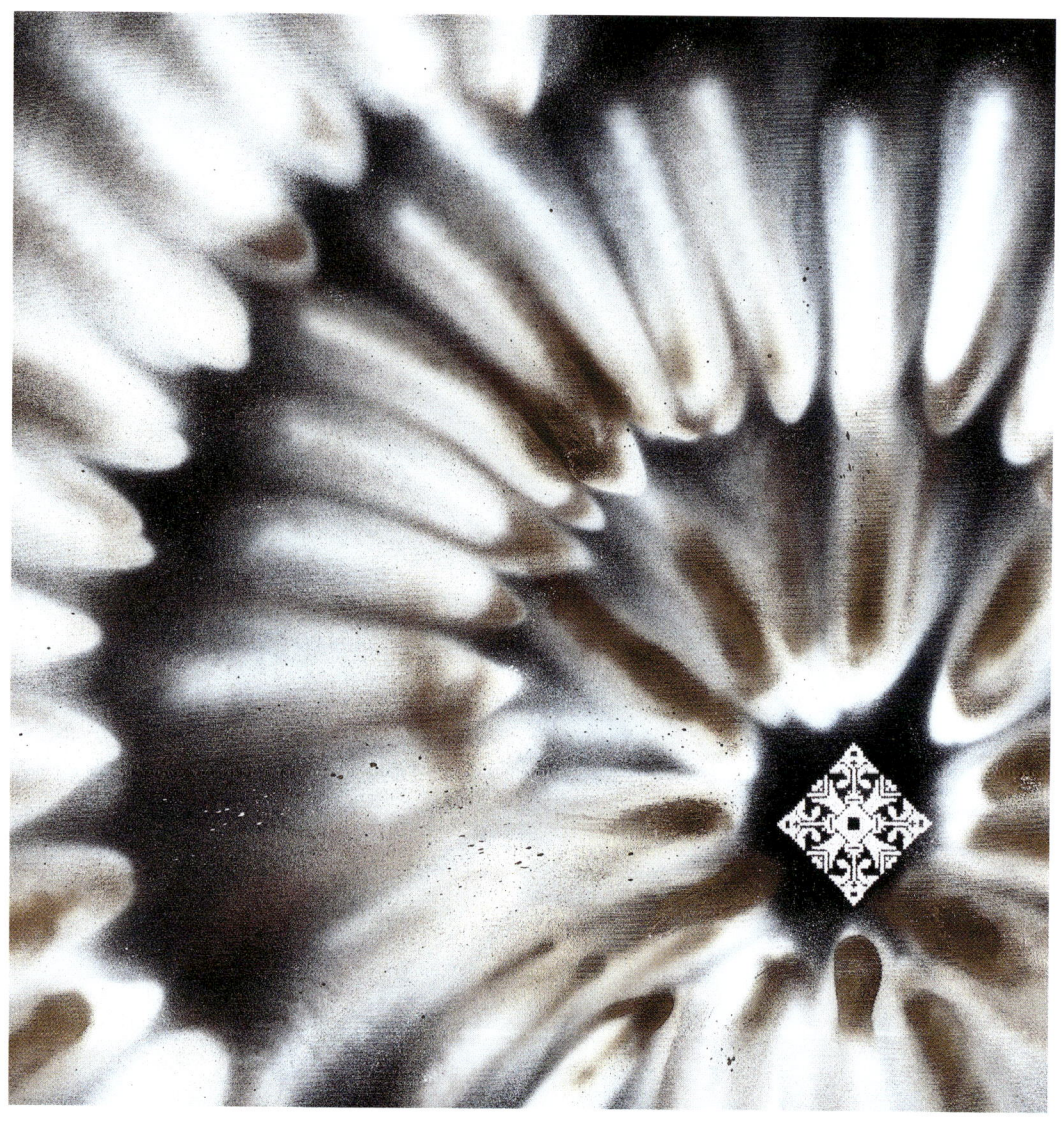

Joanna Barakat, *The Return*, 2018. Spray paint and cotton thread on canvas, 70 x 70 cm. Photo by Jonathan Gibbons
Right: Joanna Barakat, *Amulet*, 2021. Fabric paint, metallic thread on cotton, 30 x 39 cm. Photo by Jonathan Gibbons

Next spread: Joanna Barakat, *American Nakba*, 2017. Spray paint and cotton thread on canvas, 76 x 101 cm. Photo by Jonathan Gibbons

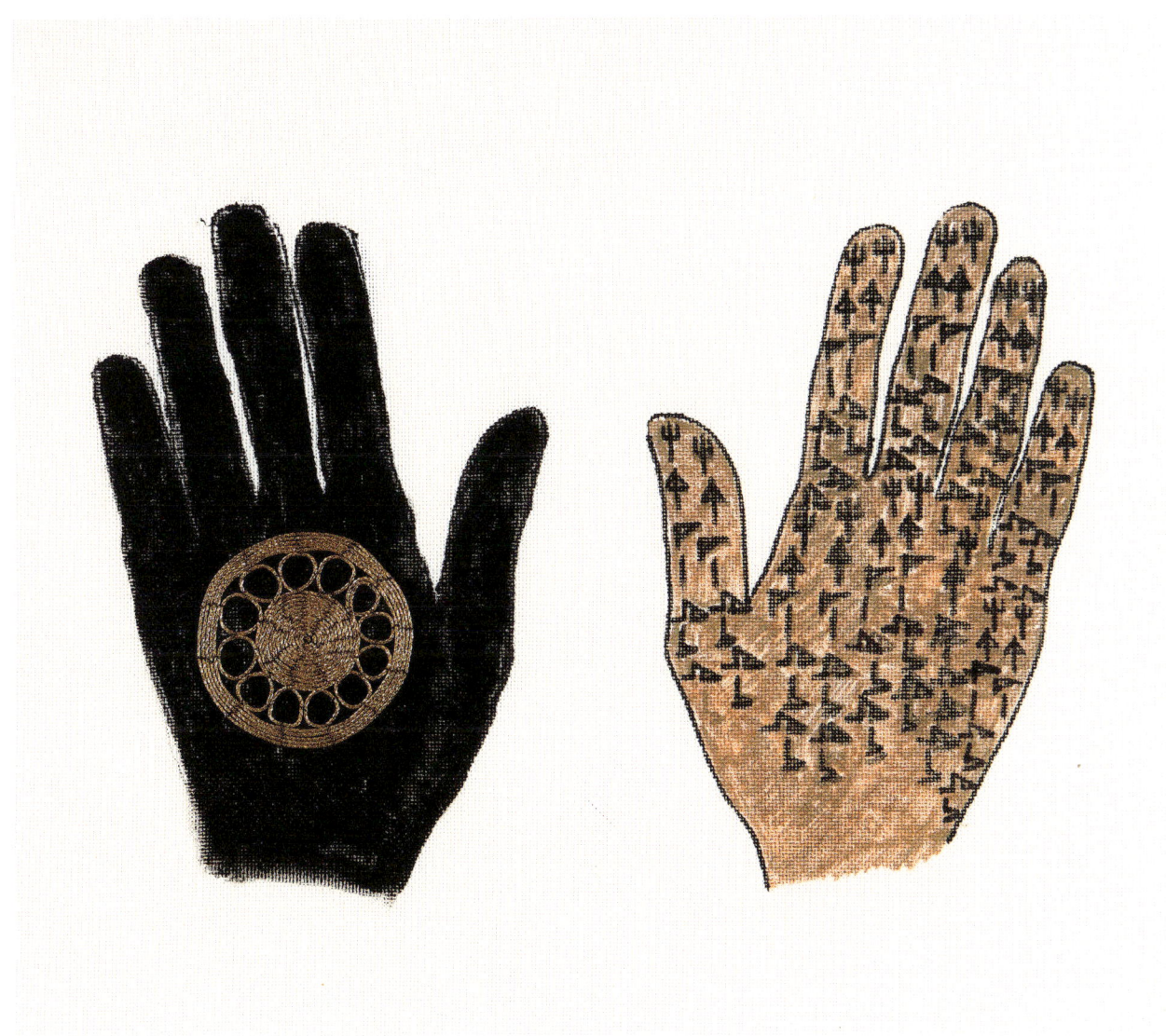

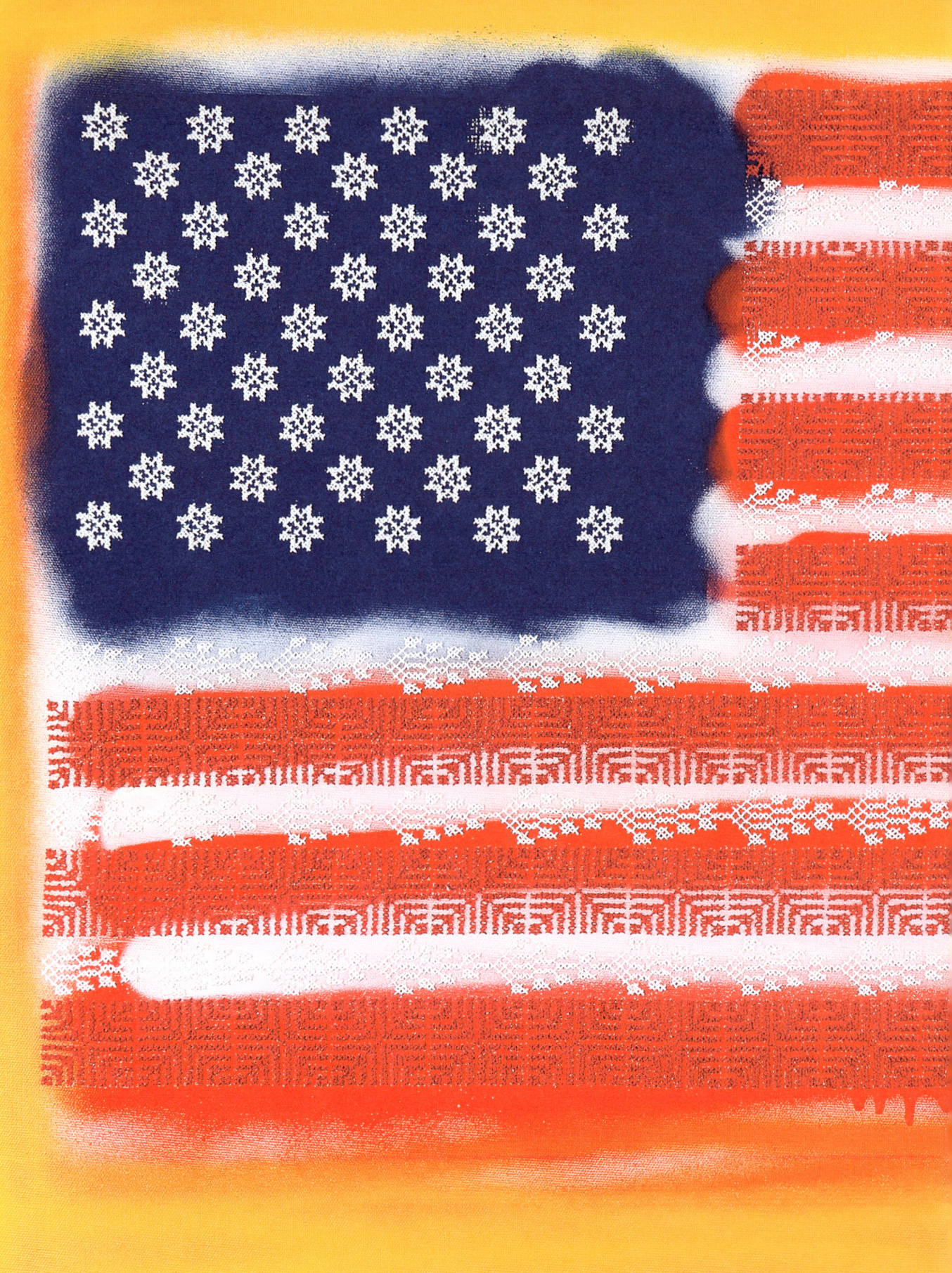

MAHA

DAYA

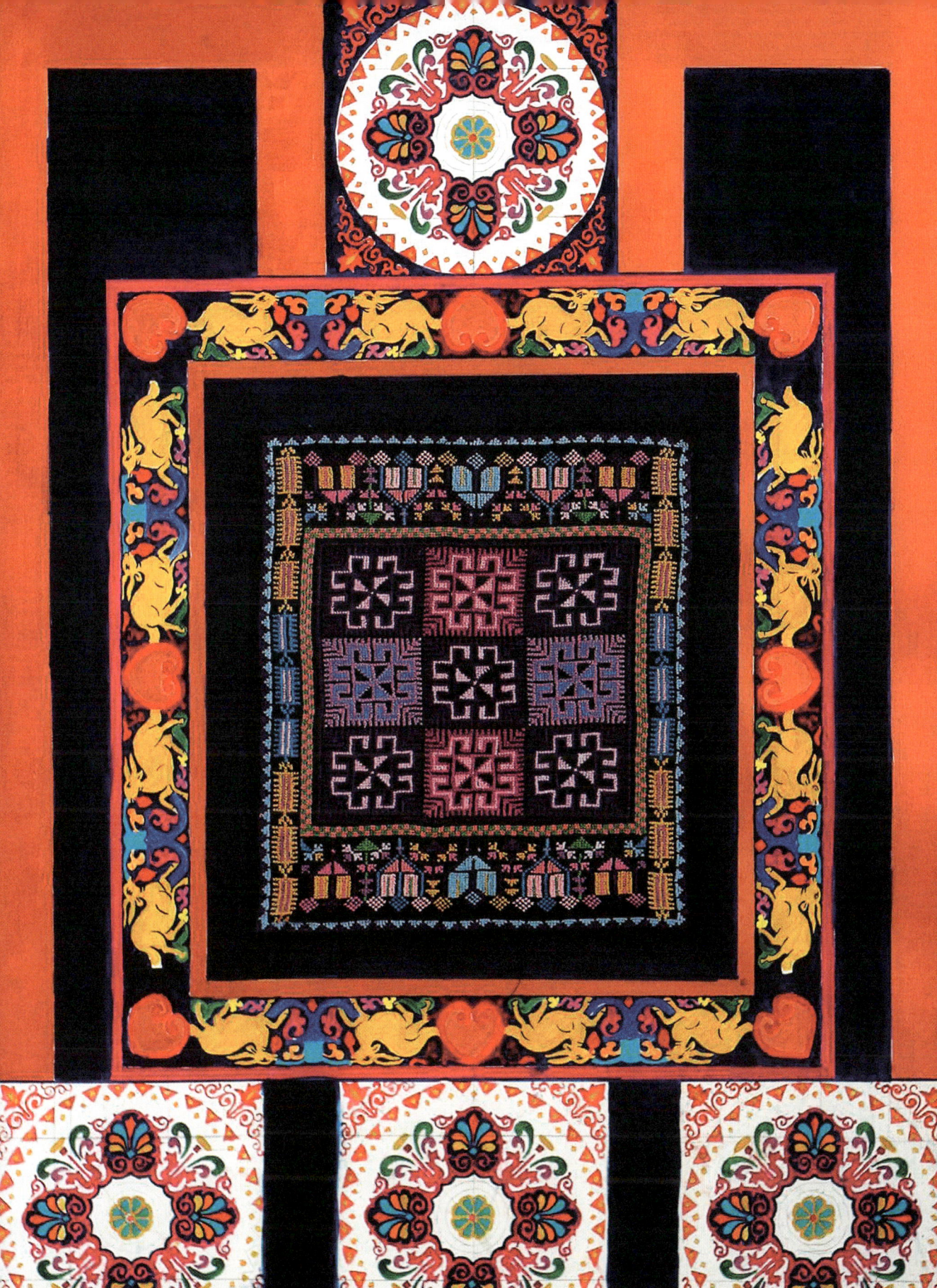

Gazan artist and designer Maha Daya incorporates Palestinian embroidery in her visual art and fashion design. Since her childhood, Daya has loved to embroider, draw and paint. Her early experiences observing how women wore regionally specific clothing and accessories from different areas of Gaza deeply ingrained in her the importance of preserving this art, and reinforced her passion for her cultural heritage. Her mother gave Daya her first traditional Palestinian embroidered dress, or *thobe*, with Gazan motifs, when she was six years old. Daya credits her mother for cultivating her love for embroidery: 'My mother was skilled in embroidery, and she would tell me that, when they immigrated in 1967, she would embroider flowers painted on soap wrappers. She was my first mentor. She doesn't know I took all the information from her and kept it in my memory archives as a reference for the long term.'

From a young age, Daya understood the cultural significance of her neighbour's navy *thobe*, which had two turquoise and dark-pink stripes that she wore with a gold necklace. She remembers the women wearing traditional Palestinian embroidered dresses on family occasions, and her mother taking her to the market, where she saw women wearing plain black dresses, some with little embroidery. She asked her mother about the gold necklace they wore and her mother explained that the necklace with olive-shaped golden beads is called *hobeya*. 'I realise now that this necklace is specific to Gazans, especially in the areas of Zeitoun and Shujaiya.' Her love of Palestinian embroidery's beauty, diversity and creativity, along with her recognition of its essential role in cultural heritage and history, motivated her to research it and master the skill, eventually bringing it into her work as an artist and designer.

Her path in reimagining and incorporating Palestinian embroidery in her fashion design started in 2002. She began searching for old, embroidered dresses, some to save for her collection and others to upcycle, using traditional embroidery to create new contemporary styles. She would share her collection of dresses from across Gaza, including al-Majdal, Isdud, Dimra and Khan Younis, to educate people on how the dress evolved after Israel's military occupation of Palestine in 1967. Palestinian embroidery connects Daya's fashion design and art practice through her use of motifs that share the same patterns and meanings.

To Daya, Palestinian embroidery 'is not just a decoration, but carries deep meanings associated with Palestinian history, identity and culture'. In her first painting featuring Palestinian embroidery motifs, *Palestine* (2009), she reconfigures the motifs to create new geometric patterns and shapes. She innovates and transforms the traditional into an abstract representation of the familiar through various mixed-media techniques and oil painting on cross-stitch fabric. She explains, 'Including embroidery in paintings contributes to preserving this traditional art and its transfer to future generations. I use it in my paintings to deliver a socio-political message expressing our resistance and steadfastness. A unique aesthetic distinguishes it, and the use of these shapes, patterns and geometric motifs in paintings makes it visually beautiful and enhances the value of the artwork.' Though Daya reinvents embroidery patterns in her paintings, her approach to painting embroidery motifs reflects her admiration and respect for traditional heritage.

Daya's inclusion of Palestinian embroidery in her practice began with drawing then painting the pattern. It then evolved into attaching embroidery from old dresses to her paintings, or her hand embroidery on black fabric. She says, 'It developed through work, practice and continuous research on this historical art form, so the techniques in the painting changed.'

Daya creates multiple dimensions and textural qualities in her mixed-media paintings. Her extensive research includes searching for books on the history of Palestinian embroidery and collecting images of embroidery motifs for reference. She studies the symbolism and meaning behind the motifs and points out that 'choosing the appropriate embroidery style reflects the story or idea embodied in the painting'. She continued using Palestinian embroidery in her art to represent Palestinian identity and culture. Daya says, 'This choice can be a powerful way to communicate with the public and deliver important messages through art.' She implements the storytelling capability of Palestinian embroidery, emphasising regionally specific motifs.

To cope with years of Israel's incessant bombardments on Gaza, Daya turned to her art practice. 'In previous wars, I was overcome by fear and depression, unable to draw or embroider for a long time until I could recover. Since the difficult and harsh 2021 war, I decided to draw, challenge myself and document what I see of buildings that refuse to fall, fixed and firm – places and memories that left with those who left.' Daya started a new series of paintings documenting the recurring situation of the relentless bombardments on Gaza, based on photographs by Gazan journalists. In these paintings, she expresses the tragedy that befell the residents of buildings affected by the bombing. Since 2007, Israel's siege on Gaza, with its land, air and sea blockade, has also made it difficult to obtain fabrics, threads and needles, 'as most of the destruction and siege led to a lack of resources and basic materials needed to practice embroidery'. Daya describes how the incredible loss and widespread destruction of Israel's horrific genocide of Palestinians in Gaza has affected her. 'There is a terrible psychological impact caused by the exodus and mass displacement from my city of Gaza to the city of Khan Younis in the southern Gaza Strip, leaving behind all my material possessions, paintings, embroidery, all my dreams and future projects. Our departure to the unknown was strenuous and gruelling. I tried to restore myself by bringing a sketchbook and trying to draw. I brought sewing threads and a shawl, where I embroidered the tree of life motif. When we were displaced to a tent in the Mawasi area, I painted embroidery patterns on our tent with charcoal extracted from firewood used for cooking.' Before the genocide, Daya was preparing her embroidered clothing line for a fashion show. With her fashion ambitions on hold, Daya continued to embroider despite her circumstances.

In *All Eyes on Rafah* (2024), Daya hand embroidered the Pasha's tent embroidery motif in the centre, surrounded by the phrase 'ALL EYES ON RAFAH'. This phrase circulated on social media during Israel's brutal bombardment of Rafah, which they had falsely proclaimed to be a 'safe zone'. Daya expands on why she chose these motifs: 'I chose Pasha's tent, since it is a Palestinian embroidery motif which references the tent I lived in in the Mawasi area of Khan Younis, and symbolises the tents where people were burned alive west of the city of Rafah. I also used the motif of the olive leaf branch pattern found in the Palestinian *keffiyeh*, which symbolises peace for a land that has never seen peace.' She continues to explain Rafah's significance to her: 'The city of Rafah has great geographical, strategic and cultural importance. It is located on the border between the Gaza

Strip and Egypt, symbolising steadfastness and defiance. The Gazans name it the South Citadel. Rafah had a great impact on me. The first time I entered the city and wandered its streets was in this war. I lost my father in it. He was buried there. *All Eyes on Rafah* expresses interest in a city that faces many challenges, making it the focus of the world's attention, especially when displaced people were burned alive in tents. The world stands helpless before this afflicted city.'

Daya presents the *Roadmap* series, cross-stitched maps based on the evacuation maps printed on leaflets dropped on Gaza from Israeli planes. She explains, 'In *Roadmap*, I refer to the peace plan first proposed in 2003 for a permanent solution, which aimed to establish an independent Palestinian state living in peace on the other side. But, here, the vision differed by becoming the roadmap of evacuation and displacement. It demonstrates how Israeli warplanes throwing leaflets on how to evacuate targeted areas forcibly displaced people of the Gaza Strip. They do it to ensure it reaches all residents given the electricity and communications interruptions, as they are maps showing paths residents can use to reach areas the Israeli maps claim to be safe.' Daya's hand-embroidered *Roadmap* series serves as a powerful commentary on the daily realities, traumatic struggle and tragic displacement faced by Palestinians in Gaza since the beginning of the genocide. Like a diary of embroidered entries, Daya's embroidered works after the *Roadmap* series document and respond to Israel's genocide of Palestinians in Gaza as she experienced it first-hand.

Daya invites the viewer to interact with her artwork 'emotionally and intellectually, and to appreciate the exerted effort and applied skill in it, enhancing understanding and appreciation of Palestinian heritage'. Her work addresses meaning and making to ensure that the viewer is aware of the value of Palestinian embroidery's heritage and cultural significance, and the urgency of its preservation. She feels inspired by 'preserving Palestinian identity, national belonging, documenting and transmitting heritage to future generations'. Daya's passion for her cultural identity and commitment to representing it through her artwork is a powerful testament to the beauty, diversity and enduring significance of Palestinian embroidery.

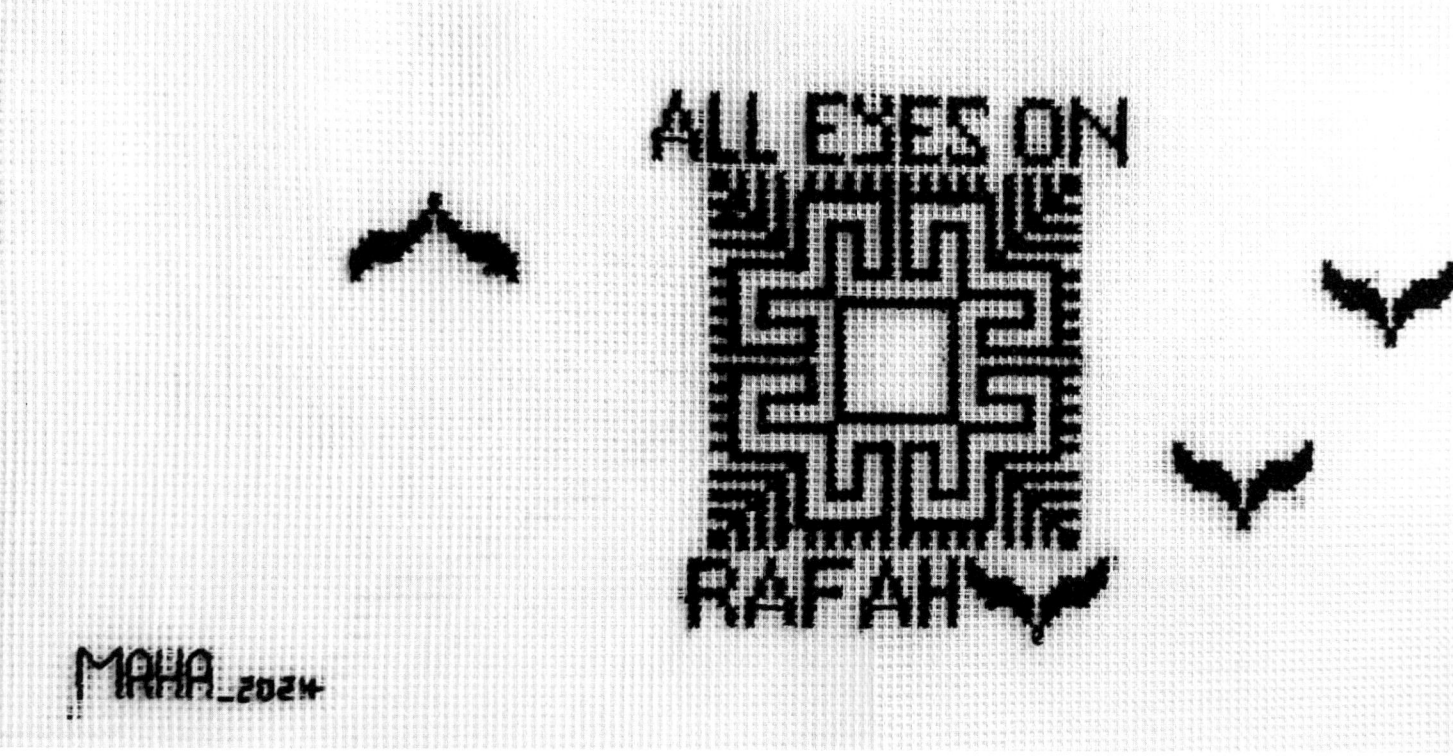

Maha Daya, *All Eyes on Rafah*, 2024. Cotton thread on cotton fabric, 15 x 35 cm

Right: Maha Daya, *Ships*, 2024. Cotton thread on cotton fabric, 40 x 50 cm
Maha Daya, *Church*, 2024. Cotton thread on cotton fabric, 40 x 50 cm

Page 189: Maha Daya, *Pasha's Tent*, 2017. Oil on canvas, 90 x 110 cm

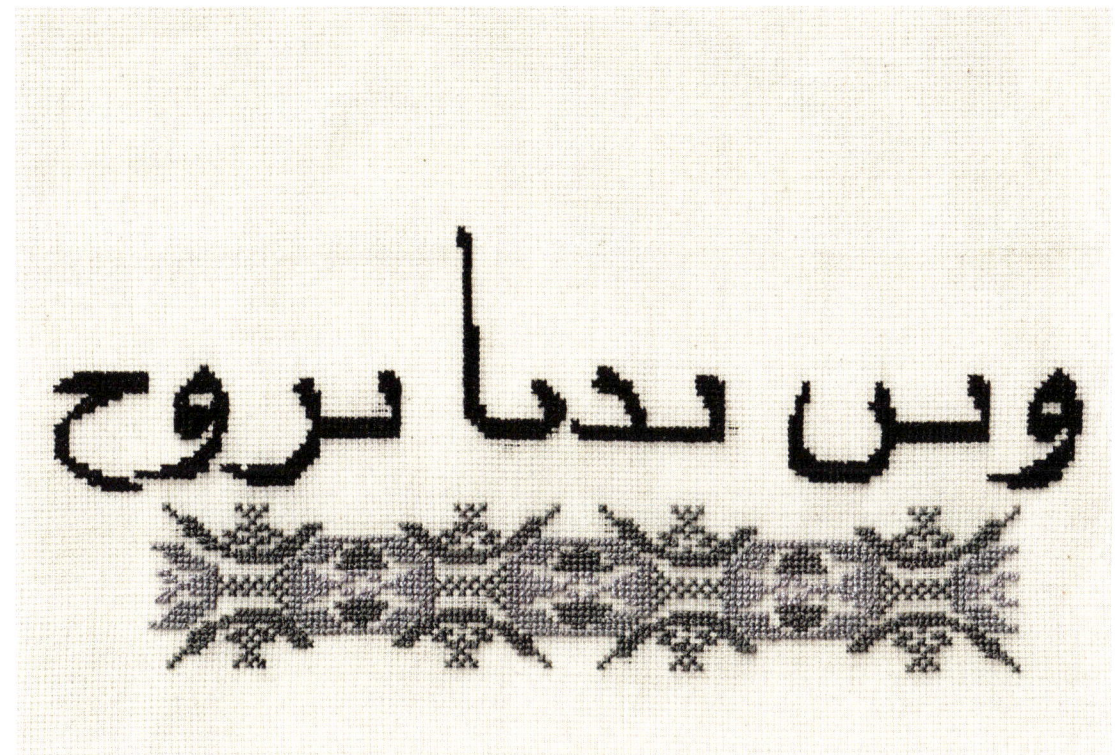

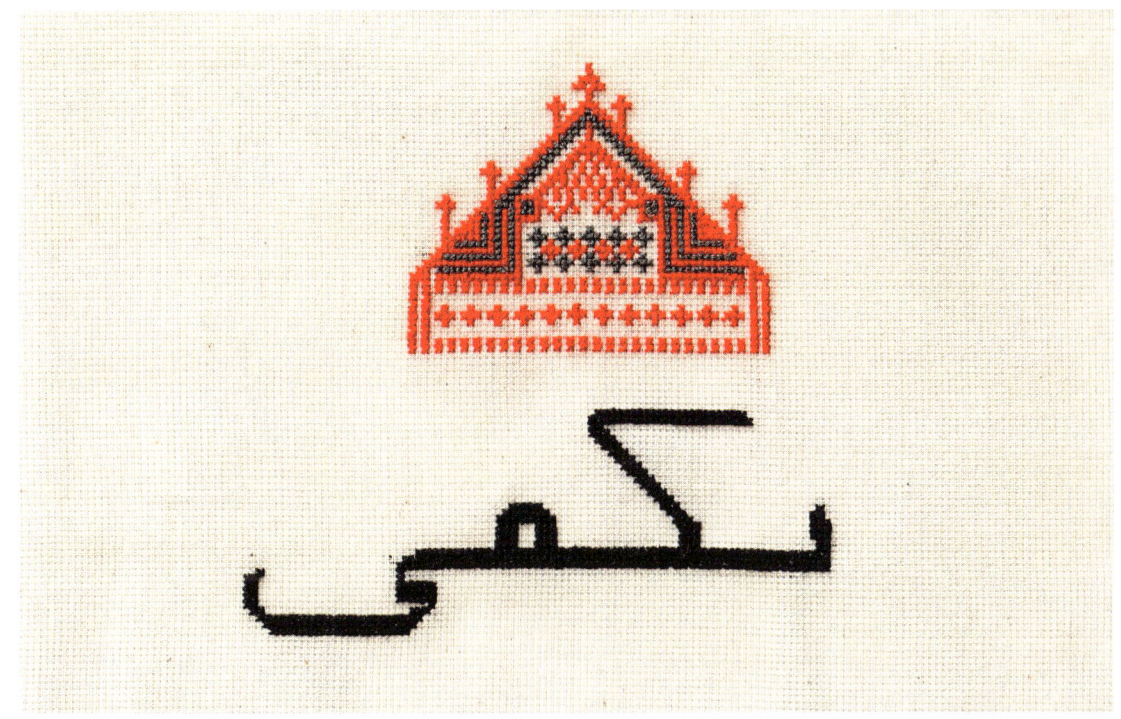

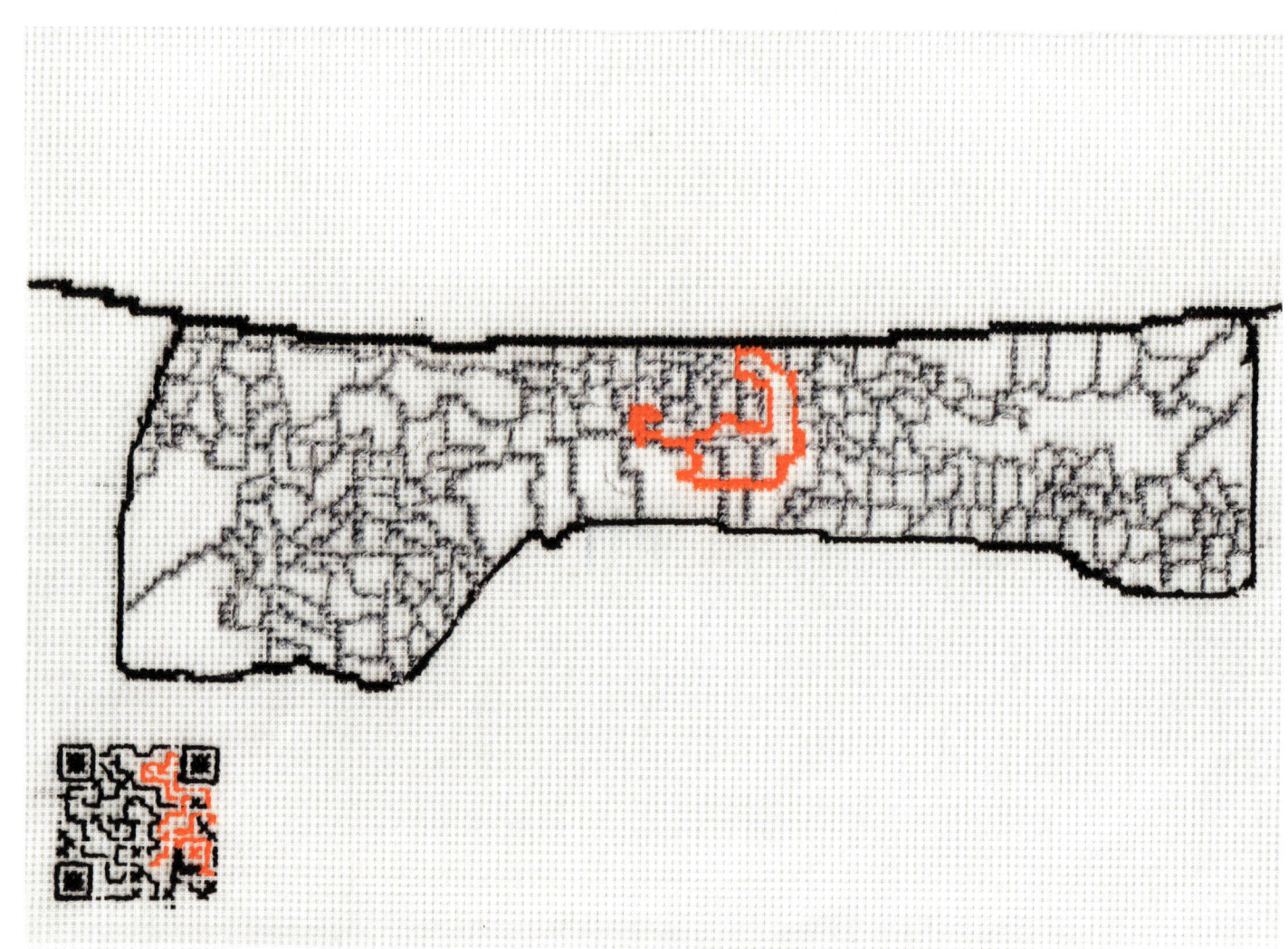

Maha Daya, *Roadmap 1*, 2024. Cotton thread on cotton fabric, 30 x 20 cm

Maha Daya, *Roadmap 2*, 2024. Cotton thread on cotton fabric, 30 x 20 cm
Maha Daya, *Roadmap 3*, 2024. Cotton thread on cotton fabric, 30 x 20 cm
Maha Daya, *Roadmap 4*, 2024. Cotton thread on cotton fabric, 35 x 20 cm
Maha Daya, *Roadmap 5*, 2024. Cotton thread on cotton fabric, 38 x 28 cm

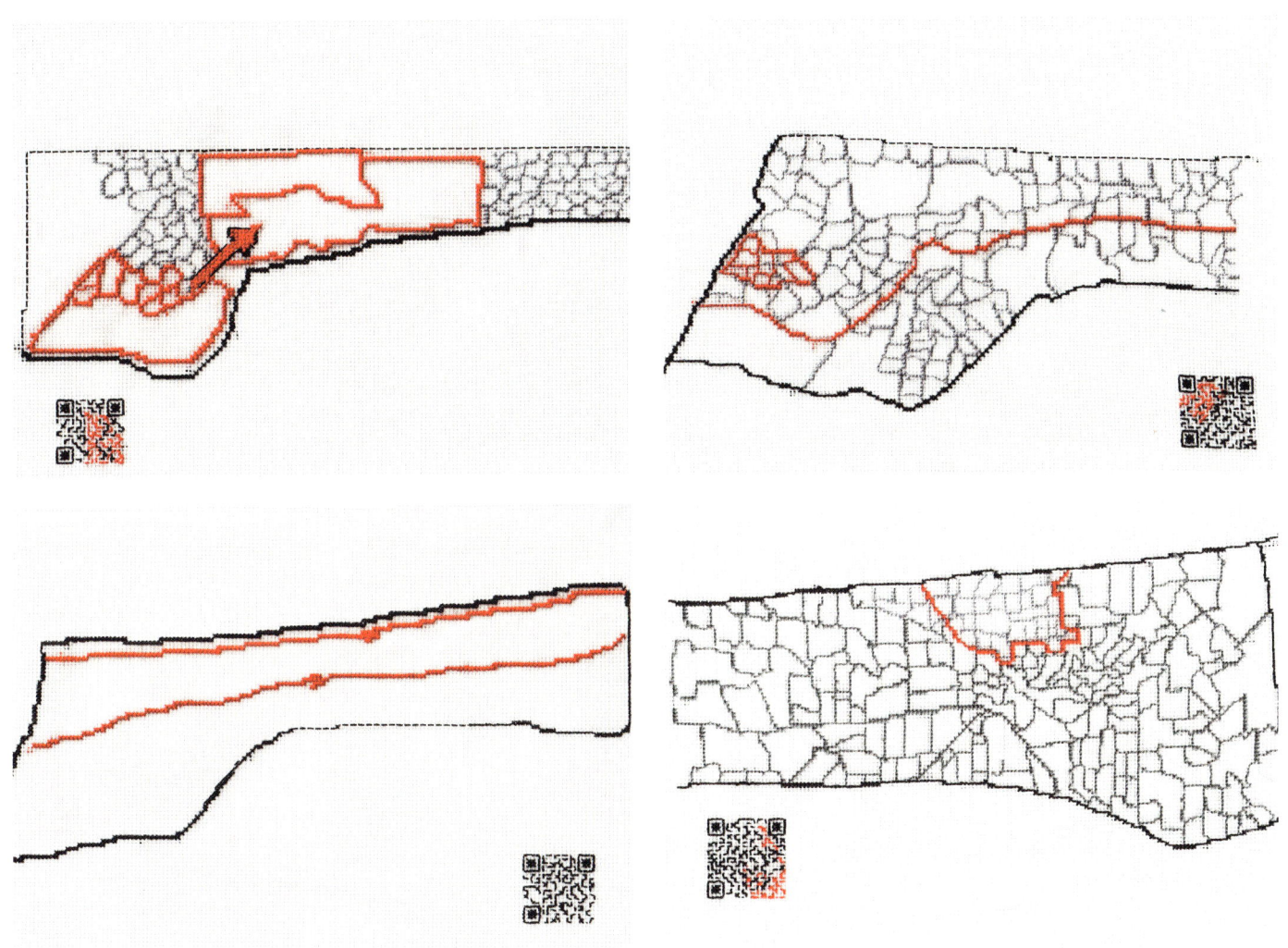

MAJD ABDEL HAMID

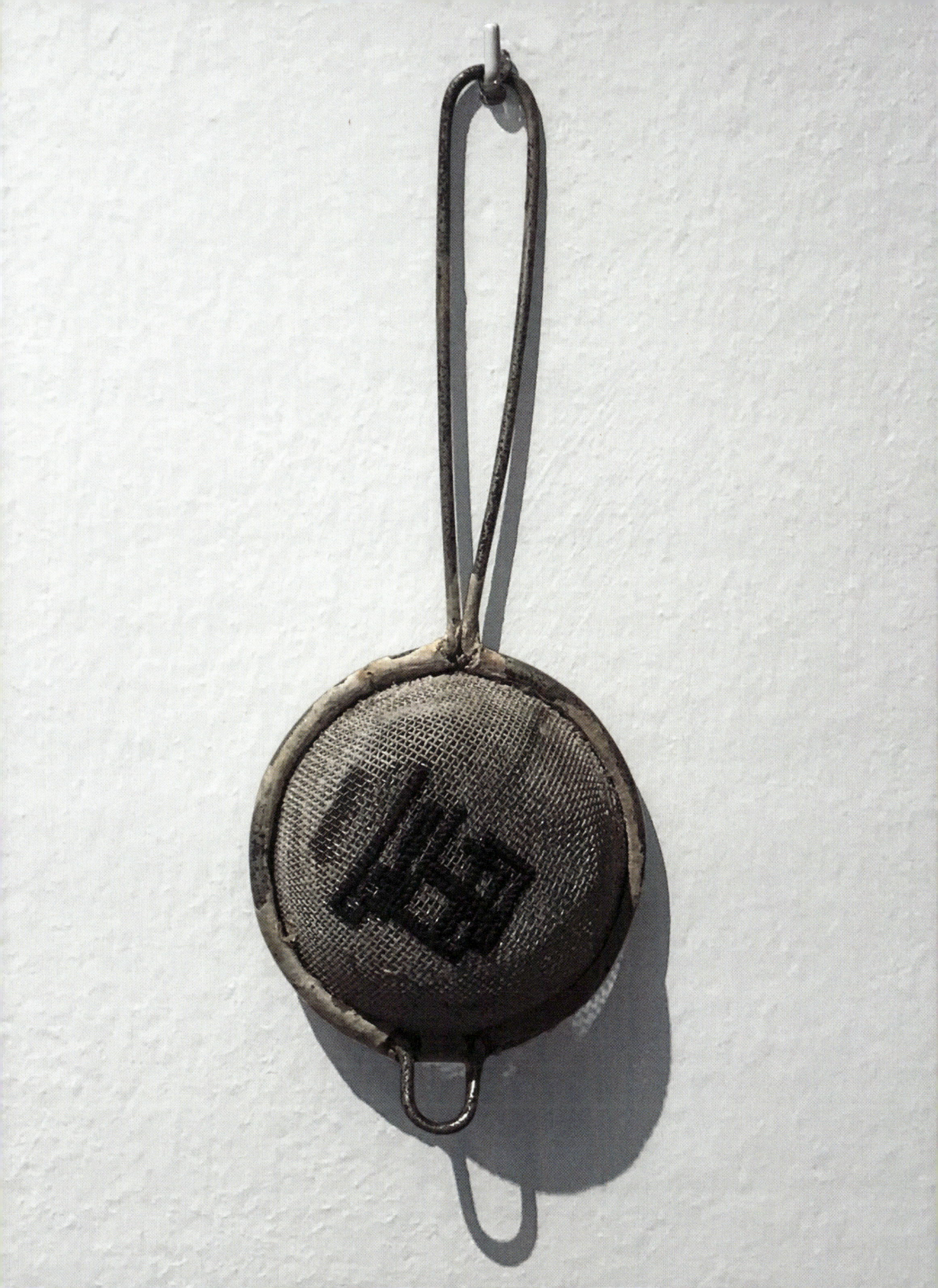

Drawn to Palestinian embroidery's cultural and collective value, artist Majd Abdel Hamid states: 'I feel like embroidery is this comfortable space where layers of inherited identity around being Palestinian is not about nationalism. It's a cultural heritage that you're part of.' Abdel Hamid was born in Damascus, Syria, and has lived in Jordan, Palestine, Lebanon, Sweden and France. From 2007 to 2009, he studied at the esteemed International Academy of Art Palestine in Ramallah, and then at Malmö Art Academy in Sweden, graduating in 2010. Trained as a multidisciplinary artist working in various mediums, Abdel Hamid unlearned constructs regarding art to create a practice built on exploration, patience and time, one that investigates complex themes such as violence and grief.

After learning the basics of Palestinian cross-stitch embroidery, Abdel Hamid started to experiment. He loved the repetition, portability and tactile nature of what he considered a humble and modest medium. Embroidery created a container with physical and temporal limits that Abdel Hamid prefers to work in, allowing him time to process his ideas and contemplate themes in his work. He describes how he approaches the medium with humility, sensitivity and respect. 'I don't want to represent the practice. I borrow from it. I work with it. I'm trying to impersonate my great-grandmother's experimentation with embroidery. This is my relationship to it.' He points out that he exists in the context where 'there is this practice and you're doing something within the practice'.

In 2015, Abdel Hamid approached a Palestinian embroiderer to commission a white embroidery piece based on Kazimir Malevich's *White on White* painting. Her response to his request was, 'Son, this is a waste of time.' Despite his disappointment, Abdel Hamid set off to create the work himself, reflecting on the shift in embroidery's perceived value after its commodification after 1948. This resulted in an ongoing series of white cross-stitched compositions.

Abdel Hamid's *Screenshots* (2016) series examines how people interact and relate to the extreme violence viewed on their phones. He collected images for this series from screenshots of video footage of the Syrian civil war. He says, 'It's how we use images of violence that leads people to become desensitised to this pornography of violence. In this

relationship, you scroll, seeing 10,000 images on your phone, and you have to touch it to unsee it, which is counterintuitive to photography that you never touch.' He explains his interest in embroidery as pixels, examining the mechanics of the image and researching YouTube and low-resolution video formats. 'The first video was 144p, and then it became this idea of embroidering all these pixels.' He abstracted the embroidered images with backgrounds of solid blocks of colour, allowing for the anonymity of the individuals featured in the work while still relaying enough visual information. To Abdel Hamid, the depiction of violence in his work looks at the collective memory of these events. He points out the work is not about his reaction to violence but a way of recording a relevant event in time experienced by the spectator and the people in the screenshots.

After ISIS bulldozed the border between Syria and Iraq in 2014, Abdel Hamid grew fascinated with the idea of open borders, investigating people's attachment to national identity and sovereignty. Referring to the Sykes–Picot Agreement, *Borderlines* (2017) draws attention to borders drawn up in 1914 by the West for division and colonisation of the Middle East. Made up of multiple colourful, tightly layered stitches that pull and distort the white fabric they are stitched on, *Borderlines* invites reimagining these man-made national borders.

In *Tadmur* (2019), Abdel Hamid revisits the theme of violence, creating on domestic objects over 100 repetitions of the blueprint of Tadmur Prison in Syria, a site of extreme torture and violence. Interested in the possibilities of abstraction, Abdel Hamid says, 'I started repeating this map on every possible object I have at home. I thought this would be like recording this site without recording it as a site of horror, without referencing the direct history of who blew it up,[1] or the people who were there.' Despite accepting the existence of violence, he refuses to normalise the horror.

During the COVID pandemic in 2020, Abdel Hamid continued work on *Son This Is a Waste of Time* (2015–ongoing), a somatic expression of time where he records the hours, days and months it takes to complete the white cross-stitched compositions. Work came to a concerning halt with the devastating Beirut Port explosion on 4 August 2020, which left him with a severe head injury. He panicked when he could not work on the white cross-stitch series which, for Abdel Hamid, was tied to a sense of security and order.

In a spirit of experimentation, he completed *Compositions* (2020), five colour embroidery pieces. Through his intuitive and experimental approach, he refers to his colour pieces as sketches in thread. He would work on various pieces he carried around, measuring how many he completed in months rather than minutes. When discussing experimenting with embroidery, Abdel Hamid speaks of its minimalism and relevance to contemporary art. He says, 'This idea that minimalism is strictly a Western mode is simply not true. Even if you look at the Kaaba, it's very minimalistic. There was a black cube in the desert way before the white square.'[2] After completing five coloured works, Abdel Hamid returned to his white cross-stitch series, the resumption coinciding with a back operation and the intensity of that situation. To Abdel Hamid, 'It's not just work I'm doing, it's what I'm living.'

The *Muscle Memory* (2022) series reflects a dynamic and emotional relationship with a city. The destruction and devastation caused by the Beirut Port explosion, followed by the collapse of the economy, left Abdel Hamid in a state of mourning for Beirut. For him, the crucial role embroidery plays in this relationship is one of healing and repair. It is through slow, repetitive stitching that he can process his thoughts and feelings. 'I thought that to love this city again, not have resentment and get over this, I needed to grieve, and then I could fall in love again. You can have a new rhythm. You can have a new thing.' When referring to his complicated relationship with familiar areas in Beirut, he recognises that projecting his Palestinian identity is unavoidable. He borrows the historical mourning ritual of widowed Palestinian Bedouin women, who would dye their embroidered dresses in indigo, turning the vibrant red and colourful embroidery to dark blue. The dark dye fades after many washes, revealing the colourful embroidery once again. Fascinated by the processes involved, Abdel Hamid states that this 'do-it-yourself guide to grief' is 'a very complicated mental and emotional process that is suddenly abstracted into time, being patient, washing and life. How much time would you need to wash again?'

He created a sketchbook of intuitive embroidered compositions with colourful threads. He took photos of the embroidery details and noticed possible emerging motifs that he could repeat. The accompanying forty-two Polaroid photos were a compilation taken over ten years that complemented photos of the embroidery. He explains, 'It's muscle memory because the eye is a muscle. Seeing is a way of exercising your eye, and, when you look, you're not trying to see something in the space. You look at the patterns. You look at the shape, which is also what embroidery is about. It's a way of reflecting on it, which is also art.' As Abdel Hamid's understanding of grief evolved, so did the concept and process of his art. He expands on this: 'We can heal, we can reconstruct, but it's not going to be the same. I learned this after I finished.' He recorded a one-hour video of the ten hours spent washing the indigo dye out of the embroidered fabric with a toothbrush. He hoped to reach a moment of catharsis since the sink was in his home studio; whether in Beirut, Ramallah or Paris, his locality dictates how he interacts with the process.

Abdel Hamid's use of Palestinian embroidery is a testament to the potential to address complex themes and conceptual ideas through embroidery. *Thread Box* (2024) was born from an abstract idea of a safe space, questioning to whom a safe space is accessible. Abdel Hamid's safe space has become smaller and portable, symbolised by a white outline of the flattened DMC thread box replicated in silk thread. Abdel Hamid responds to the relevance of Palestinian embroidery and how one engages with the intimate through embroidery: 'When you see embroidery, you feel a lot of warmth. You can relate to it. When you see textiles – in the family house with layers of blankets or mattresses piled on top of each other – it's a depository of intimacy. This is not a reaction to violence and occupation. This is who we were before this happened.' He continues, 'It's not about originalism or going back. It's a continuum. There's a rupture. It's very violent and it's not stopping. I feel this is mentally necessary for people to build on because we exist regardless of occupation, and wars do not define my existence. This is something ongoing, and it will stay. It doesn't end. So embroidery, even though it became political, became about nostalgia. It is about a way of living. It's a way of seeing. It's a way of abstraction.'

---

[1] In 2015 the prison buildings were destroyed with explosives. They were by that time in the hands of ISIS.
[2] Kazimir Malevich painted his influential *White on White* in 1918.

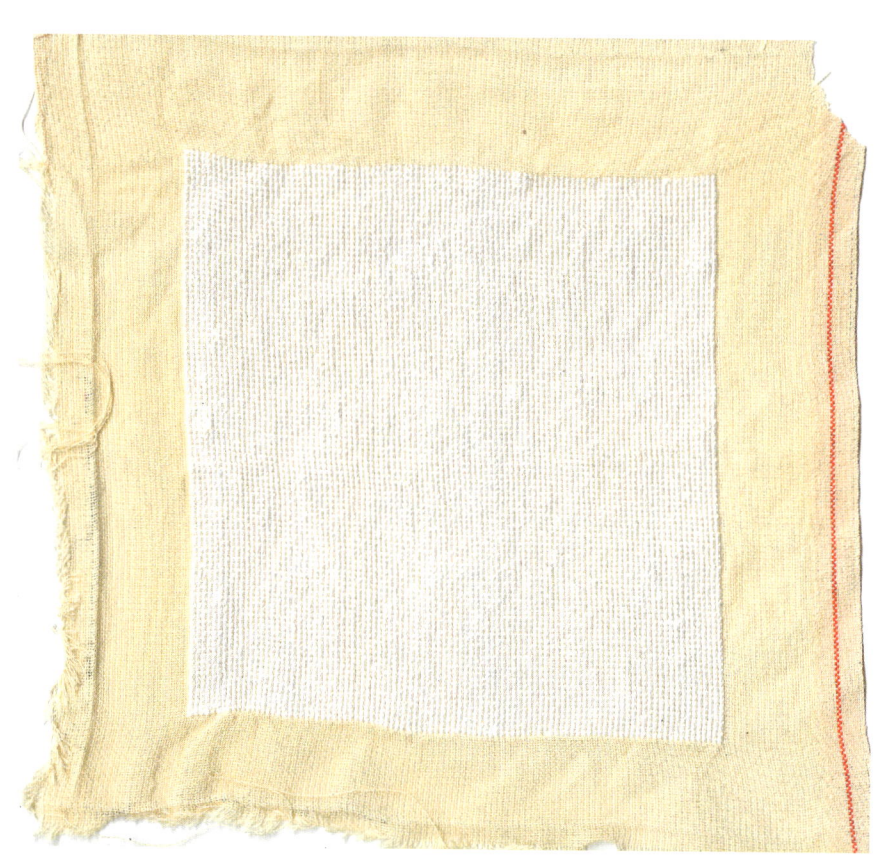

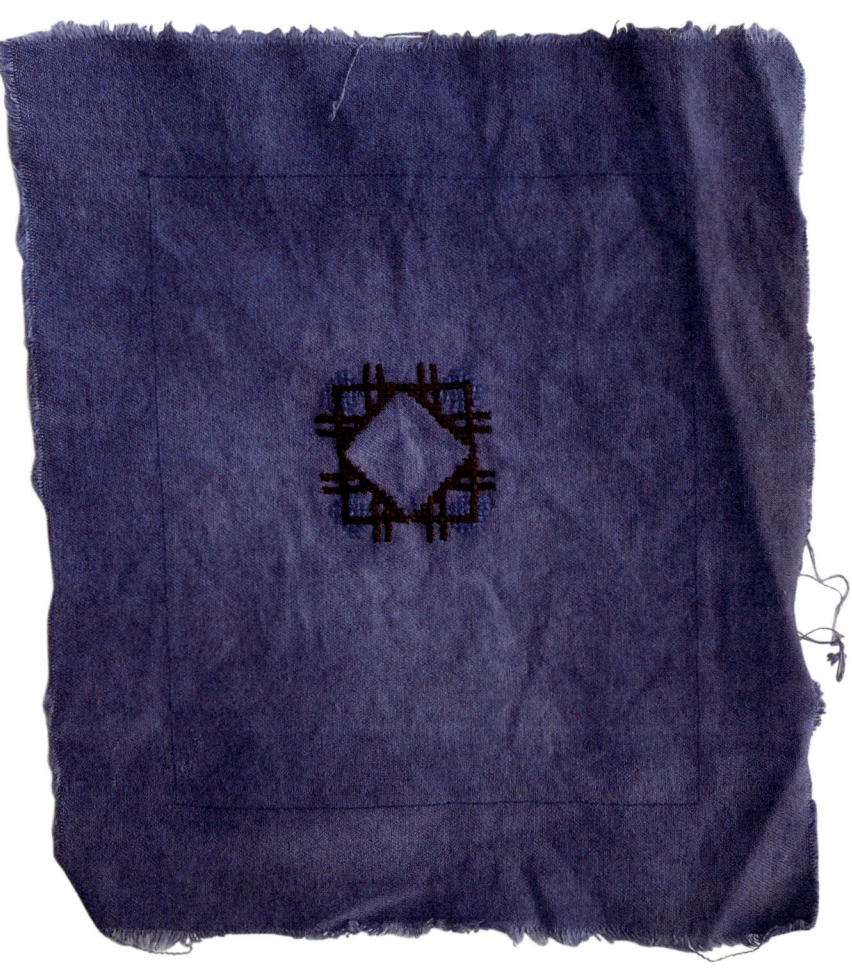

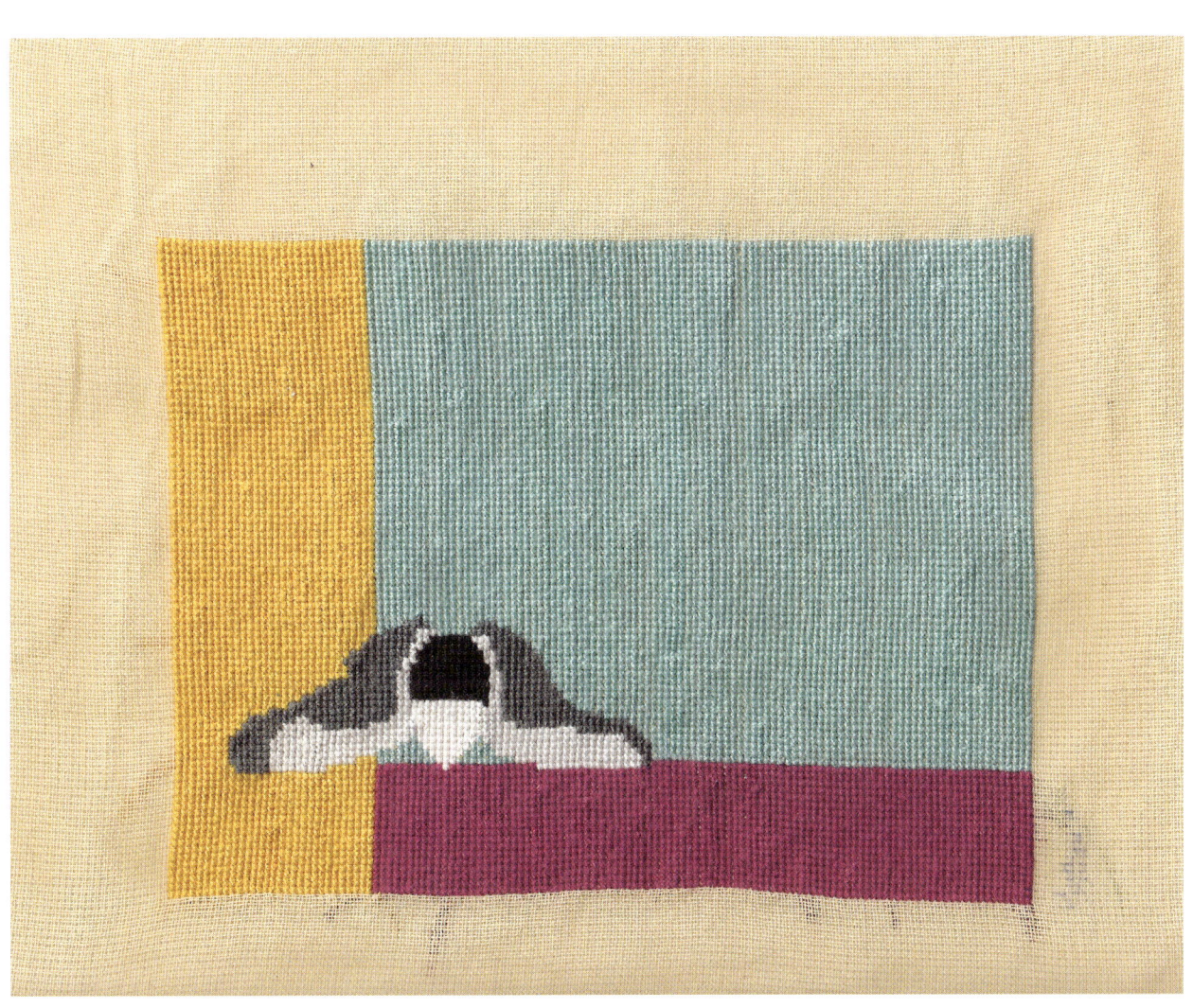

Majd Abdel Hamid, *Screenshots* series, 2016. The scene depicts a man on the ground after the military opened fire on protestors Dar'a, Syria, in 2011. Cotton thread on cotton fabric, 19 x 14 cm

Left (top): Majd Abdel Hamid, *Son, this is a waste of time*, *White on White* series, 2015–23. Cotton thread on cotton fabric
Majd Abdel Hamid, *Muscle Memory*, 2022. Cotton thread on indigo-dyed cotton fabric

Pages 196–197: Majd Abdel Hamid, *Palmyra Prison*, *Tadmur* series, 2019. Cotton thread on metal strainer

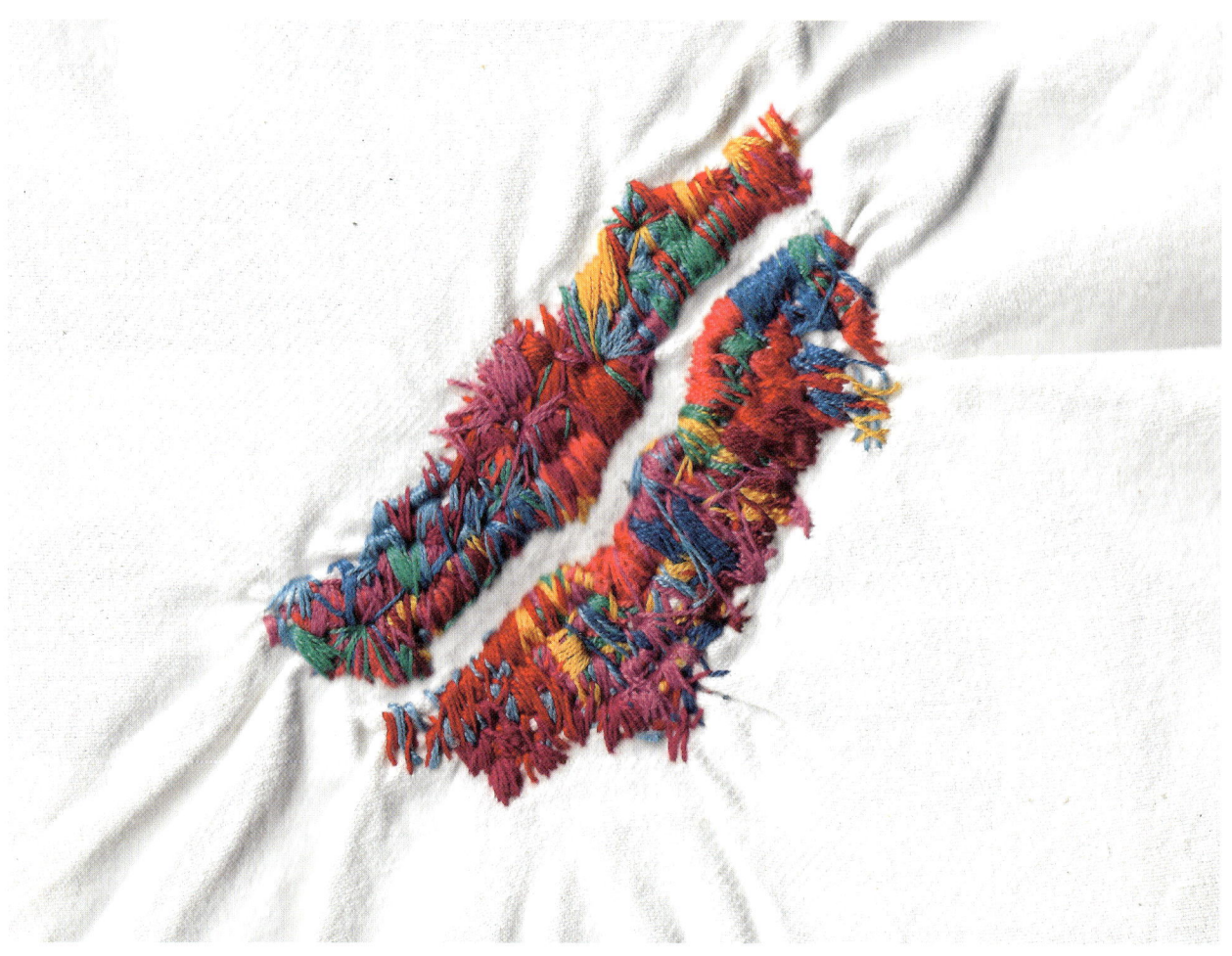

Majd Abdel Hamid, *Borderlines: Syria–Iraq Border*, 2017. Cotton thread on cotton fabric

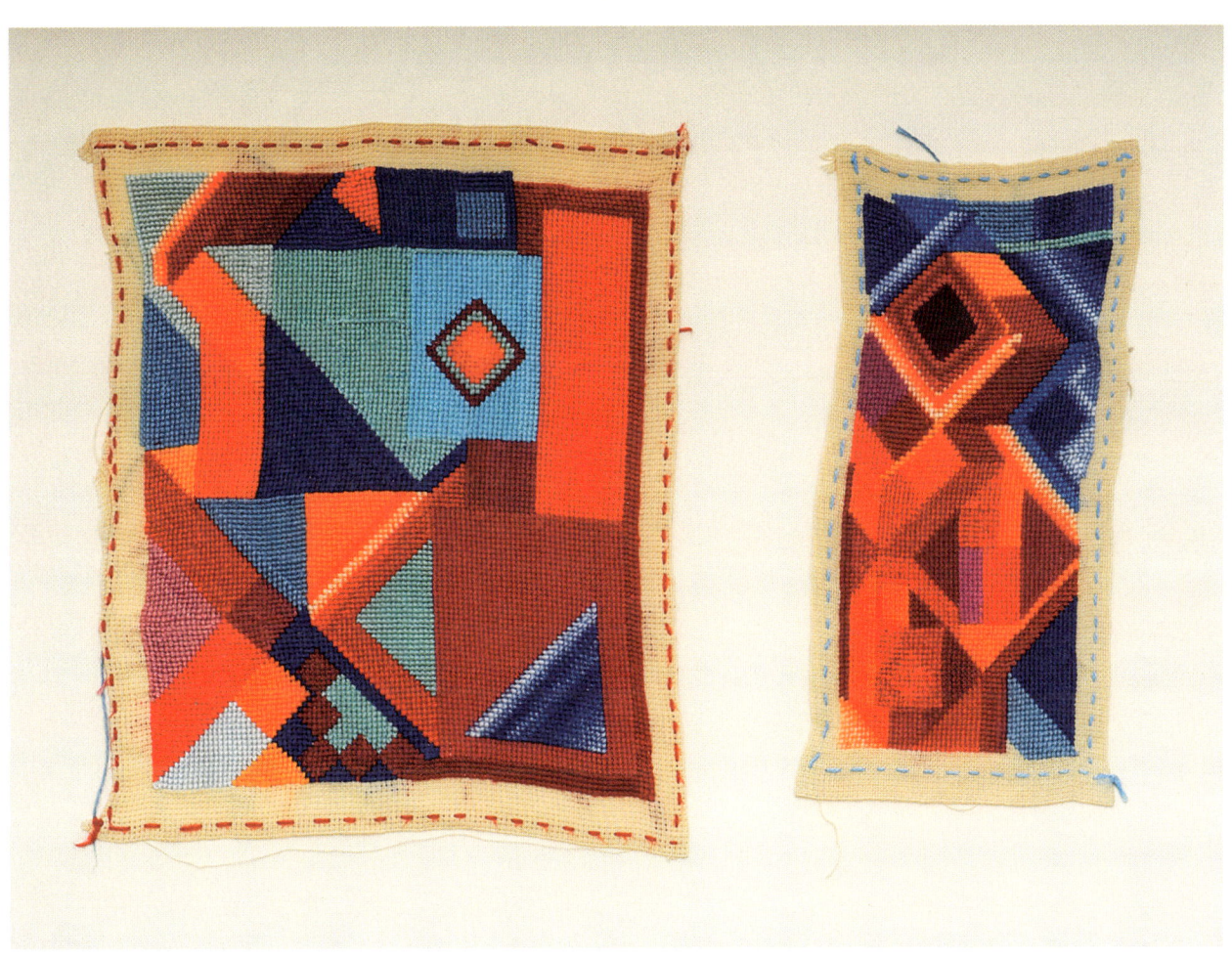

Majd Abdel Hamid, *Post Blast Abstractions*, 2020. Cotton thread on cotton fabric. Barjeel Art Foundation, Sharjah

SAMAR

HEJAZI

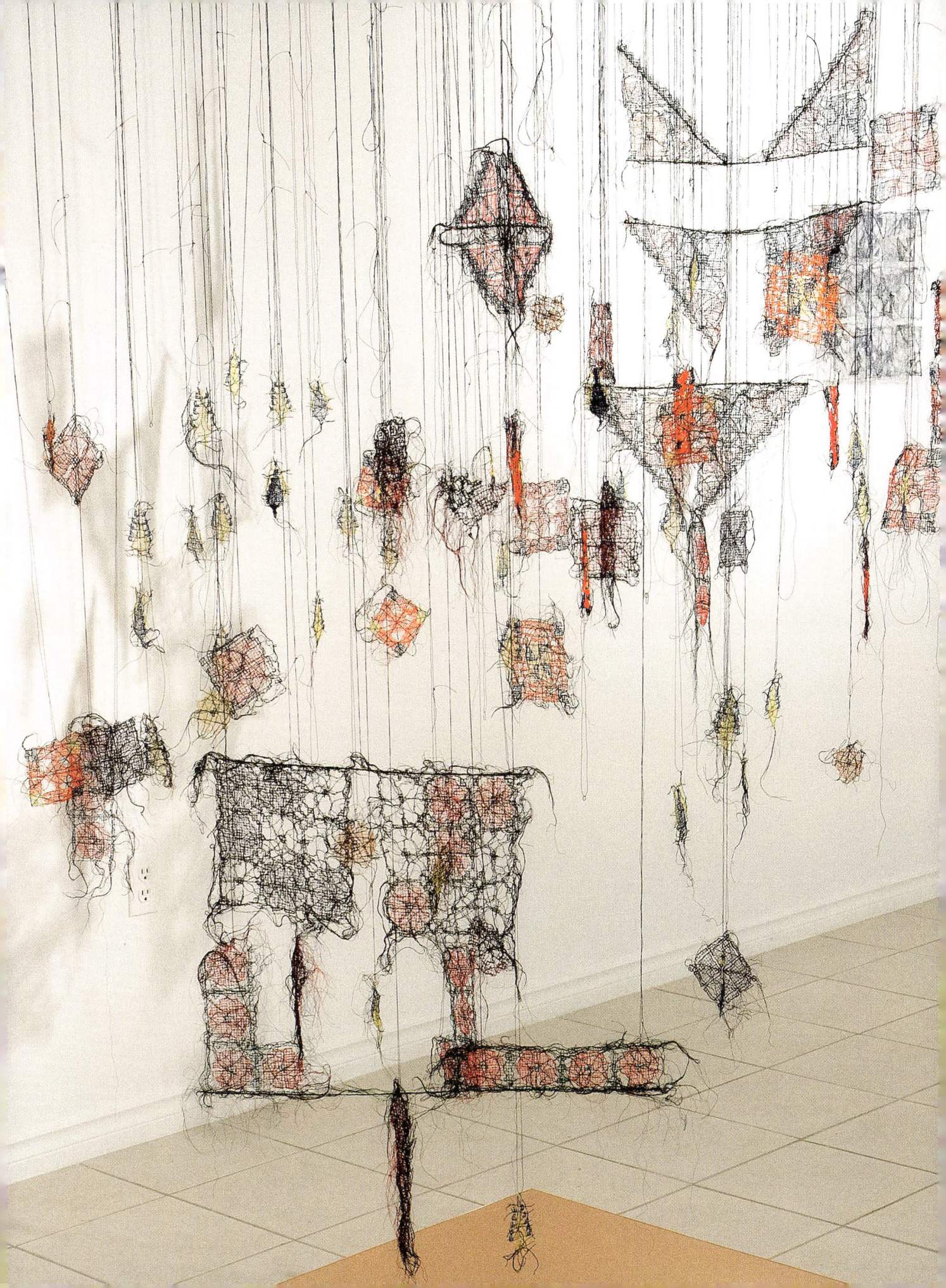

Samar Hejazi's art, utilising textiles, sculpture and printmaking, transforms Palestinian embroidery into artwork that examines the constantly changing interpretations of meaning and perception. Hejazi describes her relationship to embroidery, or *tatreez*: 'All the places I considered home were adorned with *tatreez*. I always understood that, beyond being an aesthetic choice, Palestinian embroidery was representative of its national and societal stories.' To Hejazi, learning how to embroider was intuitive and eventually conceptual. With regard to using Palestinian embroidery in her art practice, Hejazi states, 'It is an act that permits me to open the hypothetical doors of conceptual questioning. I see it as text, a source of knowledge from which I can draw information.'

Inspired by diverse craft and textile practices, Hejazi looks to broaden the inherent limits of creating meaning. Living among various cultures, she is always discovering how the nature of perception, meaning and subjective truths change depending on context and historical narratives. She reflects: 'It inspired me to try to create work that exists without history or place. How do I make work that only exists in the encounter between itself and the viewer?' Influenced by various craft traditions, Hejazi uses light, shadow and movement to create an immersive, multidimensional experience that examines perception's fluid nature.

Hejazi found the behaviour surrounding *tatreez* fascinating, 'the emphasis on following a set of rules concerning technique and method, the repetition of specific choreographies to reiterate motifs and the repetition of motifs to create patterns. I wondered if this adamance could be metaphorical if it were a reflection of patterns of thought. I felt that, through *tatreez*, I could investigate if these behaviours related to social ideologies and, if so, how these belief systems were embedded into this practice of rhythmic, repetitive movements.' In the *Geometries of Difference* (2019) series of embroidered and printed works, Hejazi transfers repeated motifs from Palestinian embroidery to echo patterns of behaviours which make up acts of identity. The work critiques the assimilation within society rather than celebrating individuality. Hejazi

intentionally leaves out stitches in the repeated motifs, creating individual and unique motifs within the composition. The manipulation of embroidery motifs is a metaphor for meaning, which Hejazi challenges conceptually and physically.

Regarding *Coiled* (2019) and *Poetics of Separation II* (2020), she explains, 'I am interested in the performative aspects of colour and its changing qualities. When I work with the motifs, I read them as if they are text, pulling them apart, distorting them and playing with shadow and scale. This is a way in which I negotiate with them.' Both works feature a mirrored *makhalah* (*kohl* bottle) motif, stitched on fabric that has been pulled apart and held together by red embroidery threads. The resin on the part of the motif suspended by strings in *Poetics of Separation II* and on one of the two pulled-apart sections of *Coiled* changes the texture to transform the soft thread and fabric. By splitting the motif, Hejazi invites the viewer to question what it means to be whole and remain connected when split or pulled apart from an origin. This work articulates how the diaspora redefines ideas about culture, home and identity.

The Intricacies of Wholeness (2019) is a colossal embroidery motif pulled apart and connected only by strings, followed by a print series on paper (2021). Using the style and language of Palestinian embroidery motifs, Hejazi critically addresses how national, colonial and imperial narratives shape and influence identity construction.

She explains, 'The stitches that are undone represent the imposing hand of the oppressor – the "modifier" and "disintegrator" of the ancestral narrative. The undoing of the stitches leaves behind a blurred abstraction of what once was – a representation of the effect of settlers and colonisation on nations and national narratives. This piece explores how empire has exploited tradition and culture to construct a specific national identity. It articulates the suppression and distortion of the voices of those who are native to a land, who tell their stories through their craft and who are oppressed and used for the construction of a national project.' Thread plays a vital role as the visual and conceptual connector.

Hejazi transforms thread again in *TB1* (2019) and *TB4* (2020), using a sewing machine to stitch embroidery motifs onto a water-soluble fabric. When the fabric dissolves, the motifs remain intricately connected by the stitched threads. She reimagines this traditional practice conceptually and materially to explore how we interpret meaning based on our perspective. Additionally, the shadows cast against the wall behind *TB1* and *TB4* create another layer of dimensionality, colour and meaning. They shift depending on where the viewer is standing and the light in the space.

When speaking about Palestinian embroidery transforming over time based on history and context, Hejazi says, 'I enjoy the contrast between the urge for it to remain the same in terms of technique while observing the shifts in its meaning. I wonder about the way Palestinian identity exists in relation to the world and how it expands and contracts based on the perception of those who define it. I feel that it transgresses the boundaries delineated by the concept of a "nation", which leads me to realise that most defined things transgress the boundaries of identification.'

In Hejazi's installation *Transgressed Boundaries* (2020), thread holds together the Palestinian embroidery motifs suspended from the ceiling. The absence of fabric to support the embroidery makes the viewer aware of our internal narratives and fleeting thoughts. She also questions how people exist without land, referencing the embroidery without fabric to other dimensionalities and meanings.

She installed another iteration of *Transgressed Boundaries* at the Sharjah Art Museum in 2023, comprising two artworks. The first is made up of black-and-white outlines of the Pasha's tent embroidery motif, loosely connected by threads floating in a rectangular composition near the wall. The second work consists of white interlacing squares, typical of traditional Islamic patterns, suspended from white threads, gently rotating to create a new piece at every glance. In both works, the shadows cast against the wall create another layer of dimensionality through light and shadow.

Samar Hejazi's innovative and intuitive approach to Palestinian embroidery involves delving deep into the traditional art form through extensive exploration and experimentation. By pushing the boundaries of conventional techniques, Hejazi aims to expand the inherent limits of creating meaning within the embroidery, ultimately expressing the evolving nature of perception.

Previous spread:
Samar Hejazi, *Transgressed Boundaries* installation, 2020. Thread and mirrored acrylic plastic, approximately 1.5 m x 1.5 m x 2.5 m

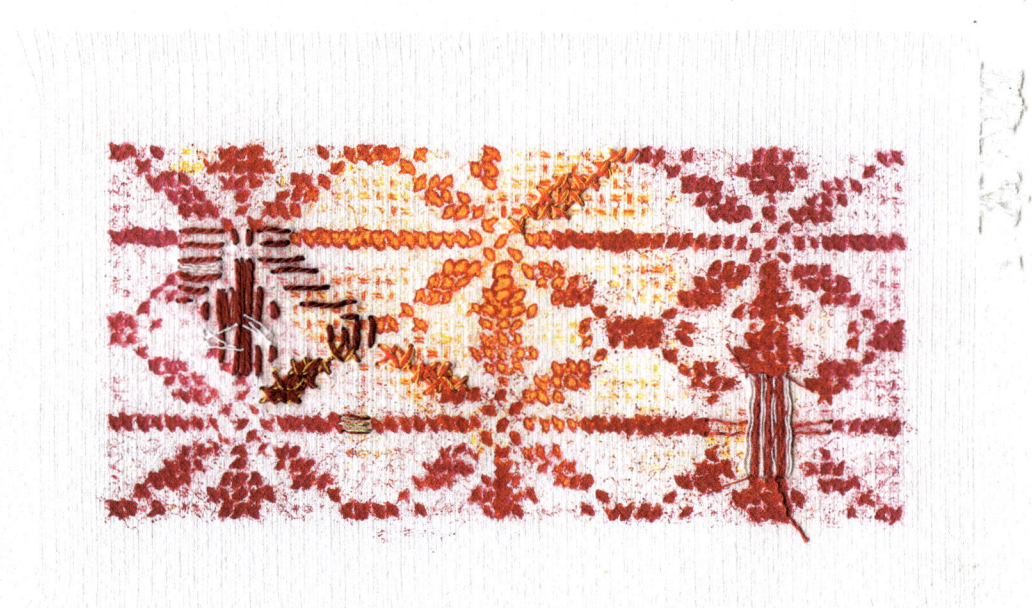

Samar Hejazi, *Geometries of Difference*, 2020. Ink and thread on paper, 16.5 x 24 cm
Right: Samar Hejazi, *The Intricacies of Wholeness*, 2019. Textile, 210 x 86.5 cm

Next spread: Samar Hejazi, *TB1*, 2019. Thread, 19 x 30 cm

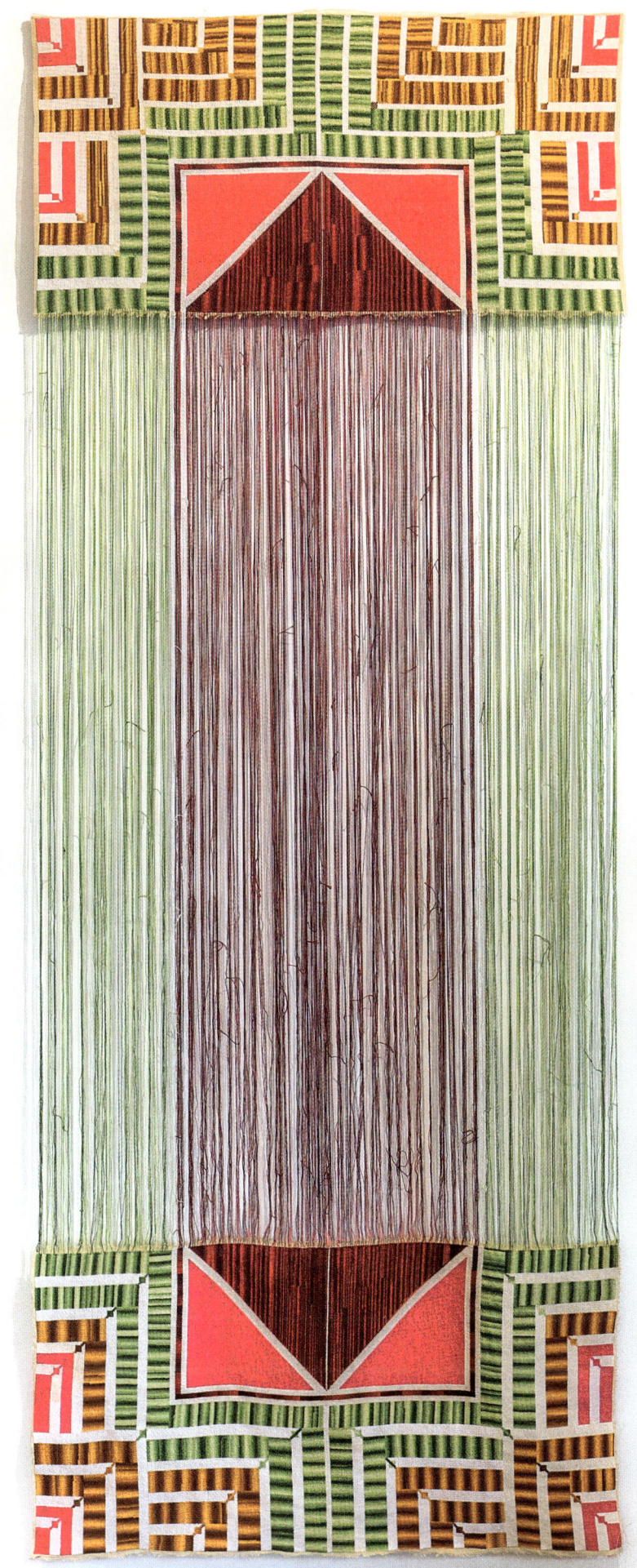

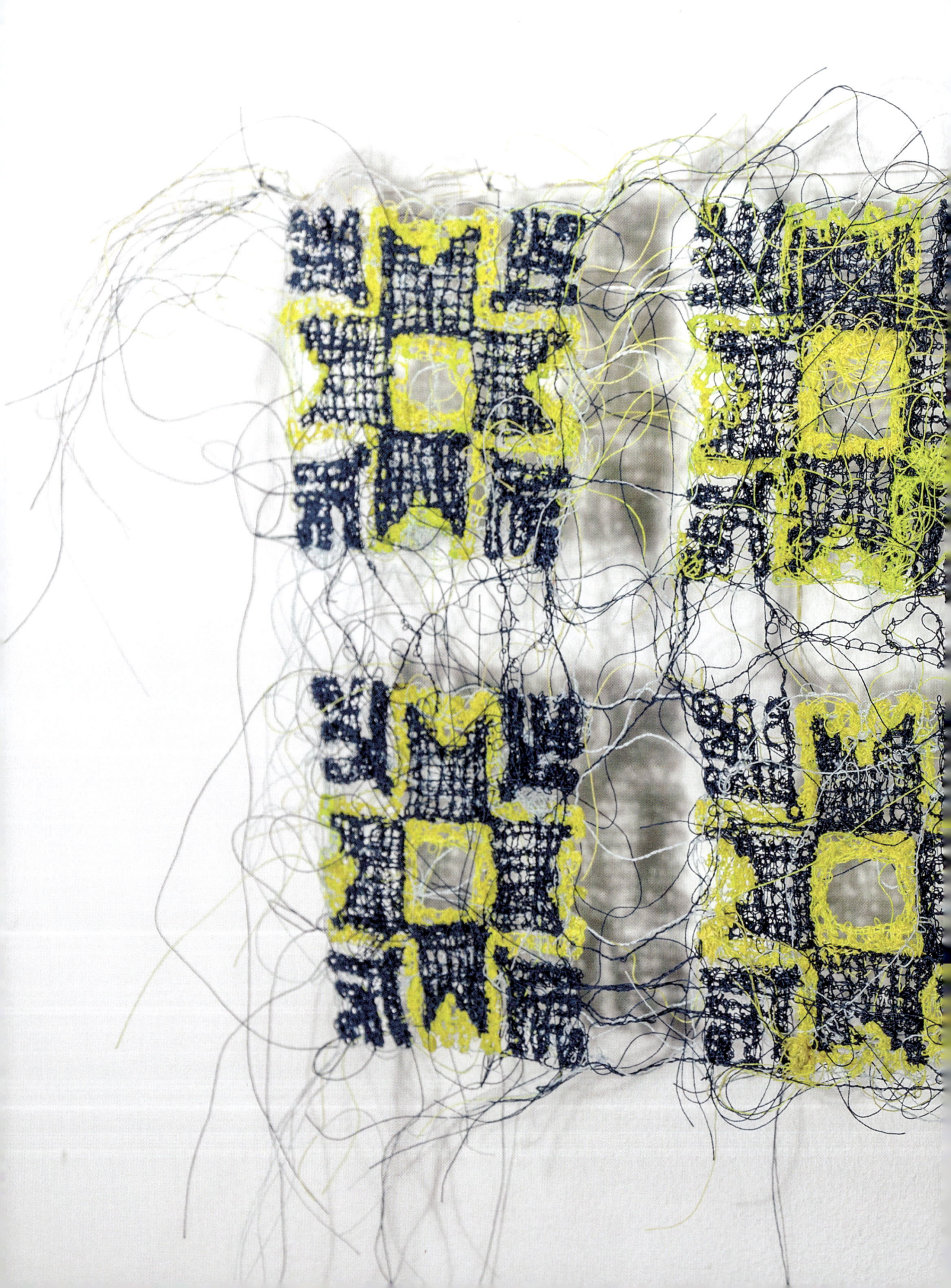

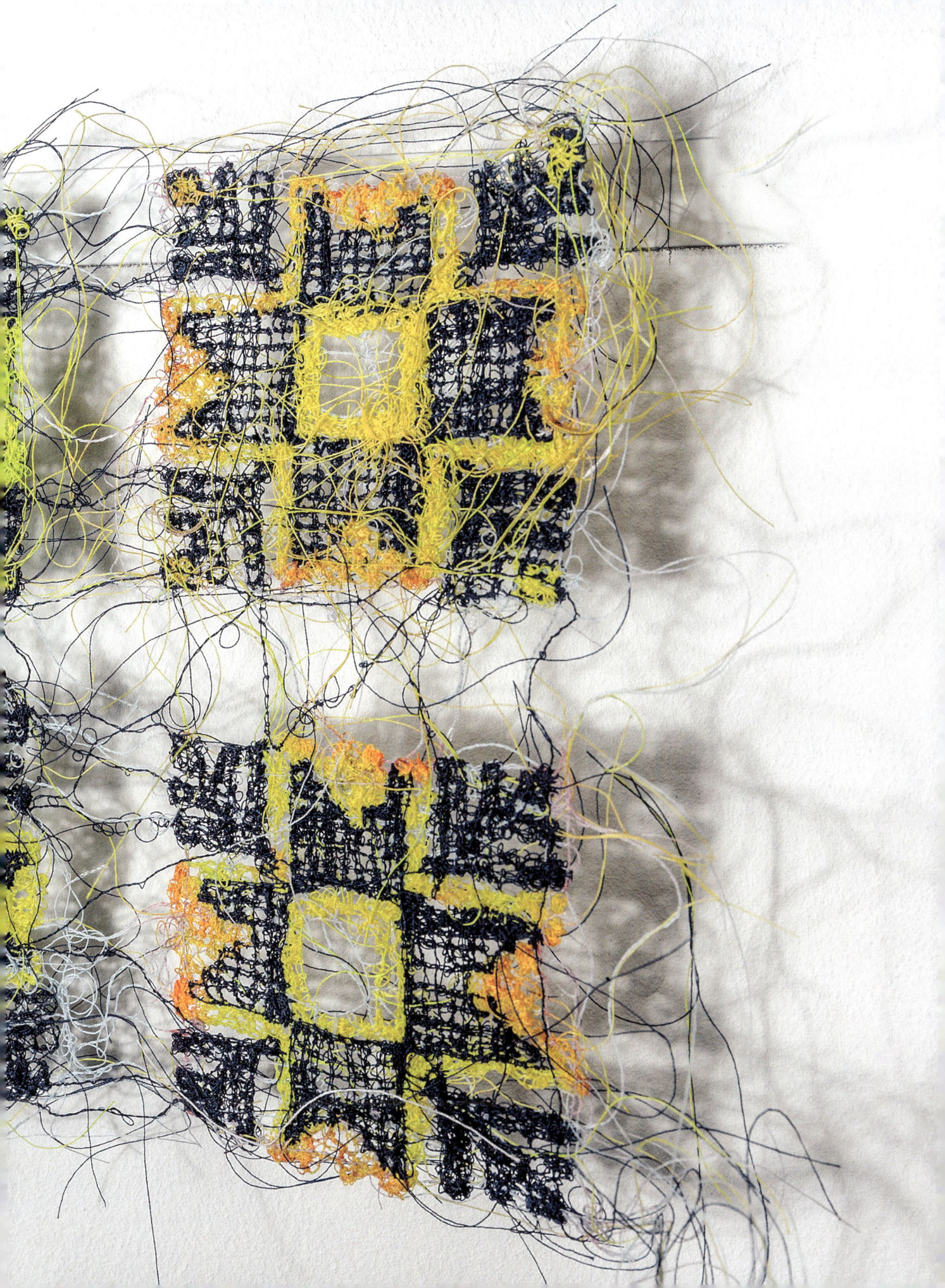

Samar Hejazi, *Poetics of Separation II*, 2020. Cotton thread, cotton fabric and resin, 25.5 x 20.5 x 3.2 cm

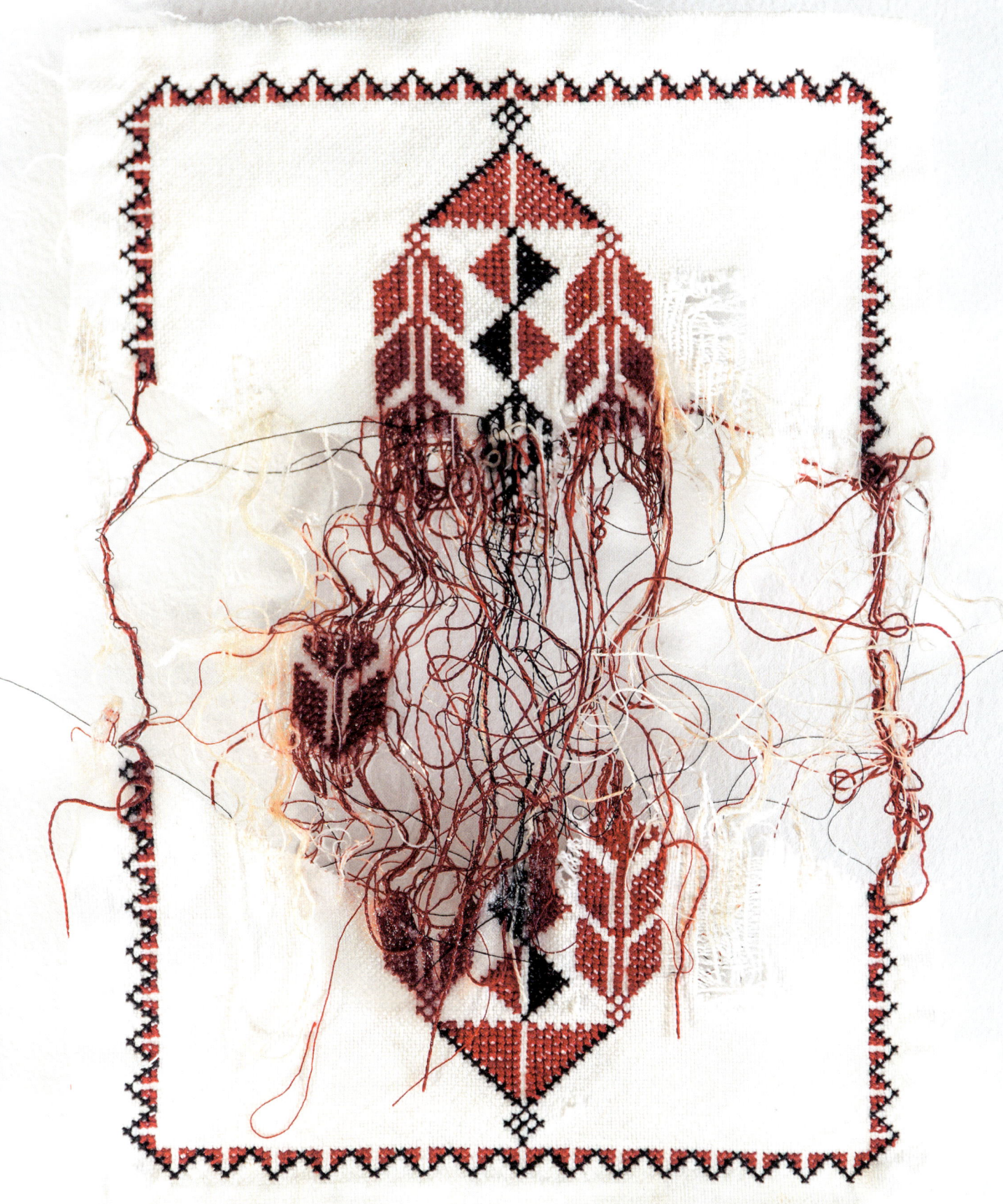

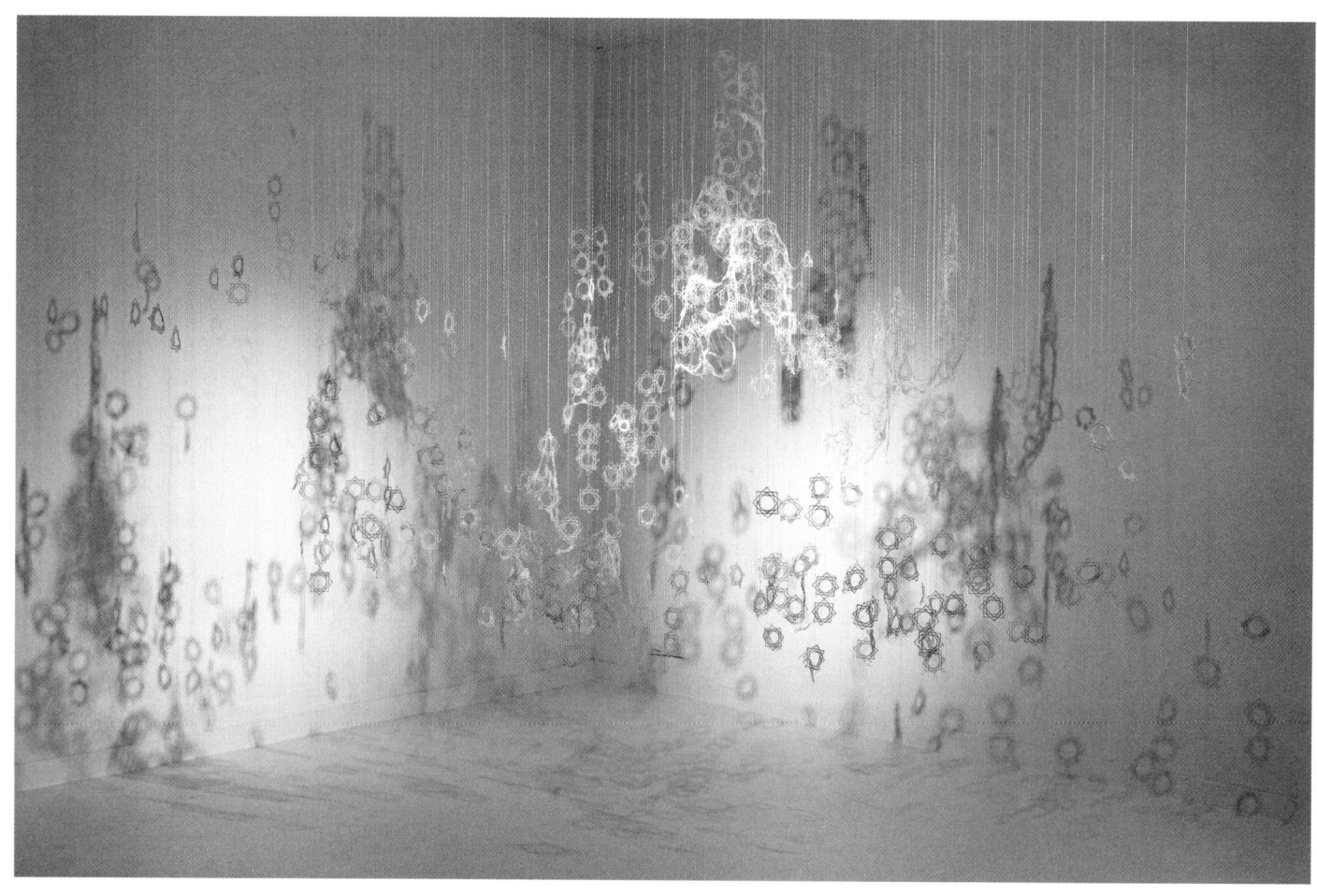

Samar Hejazi, *Transgressed Boundaries II*, exhibited in the Sharjah Islamic Art Festival 2023.
Thread, wire, light, shadow, paint and laminate, 250 x 400 x 200 cm

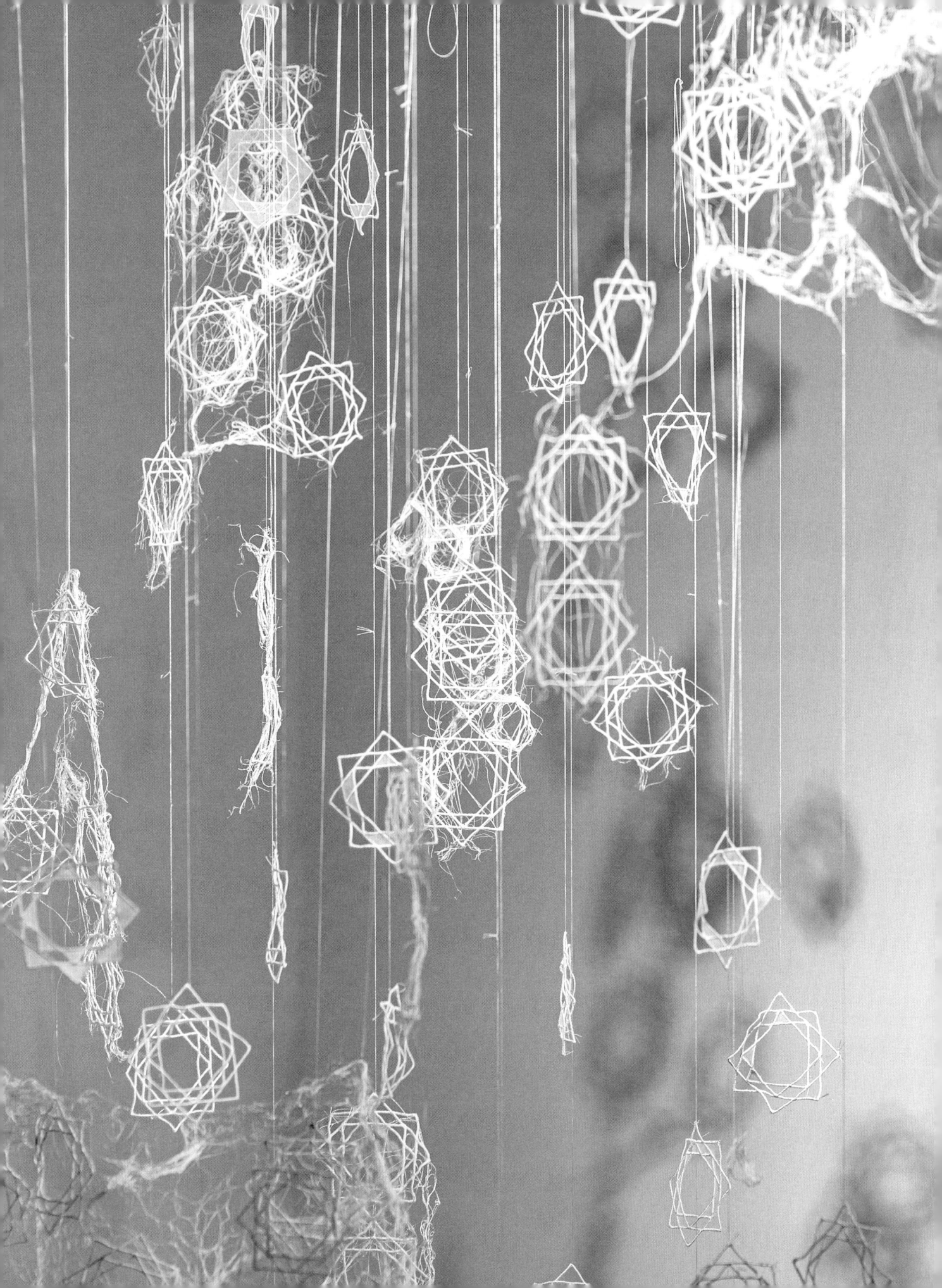

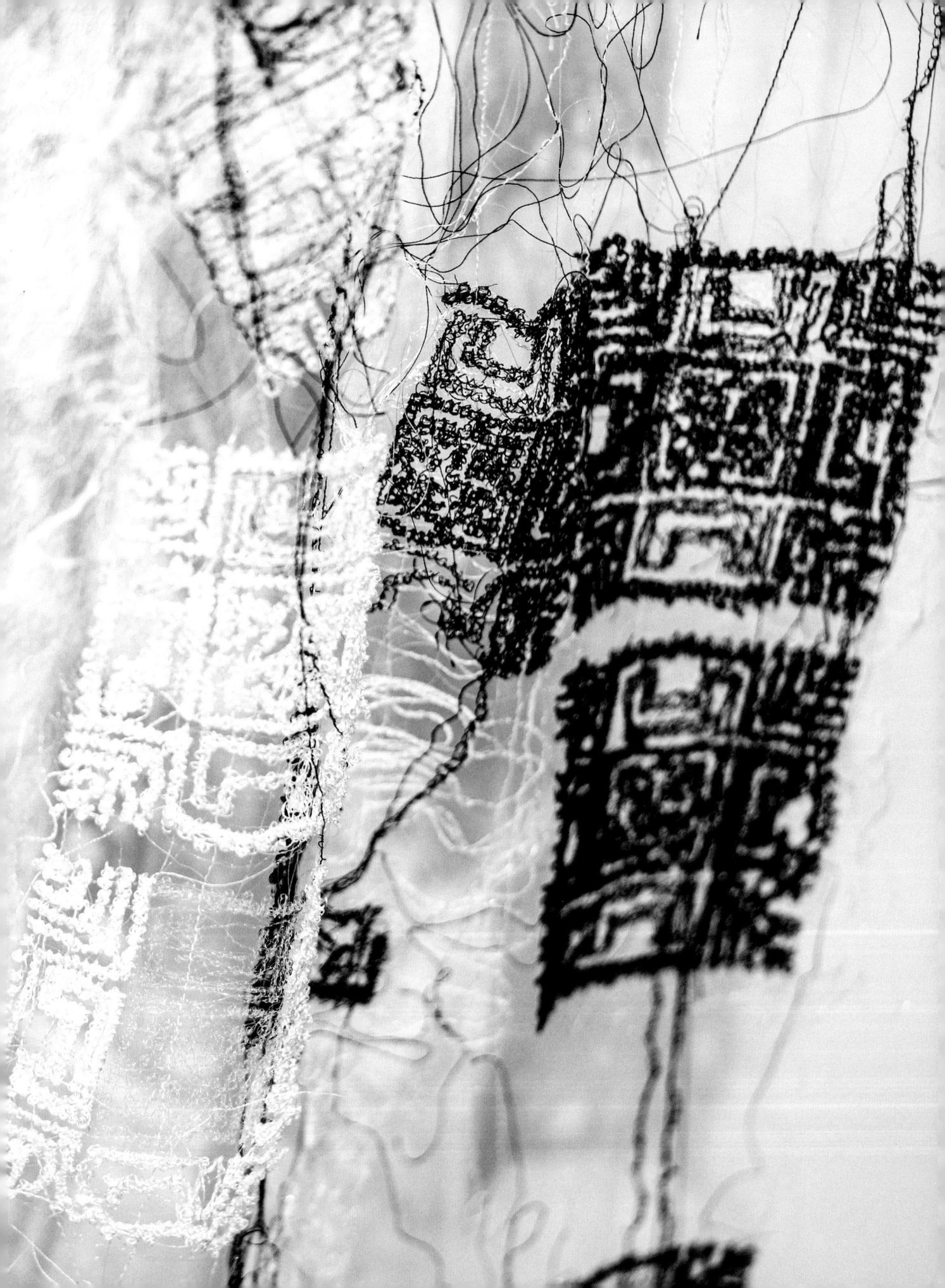

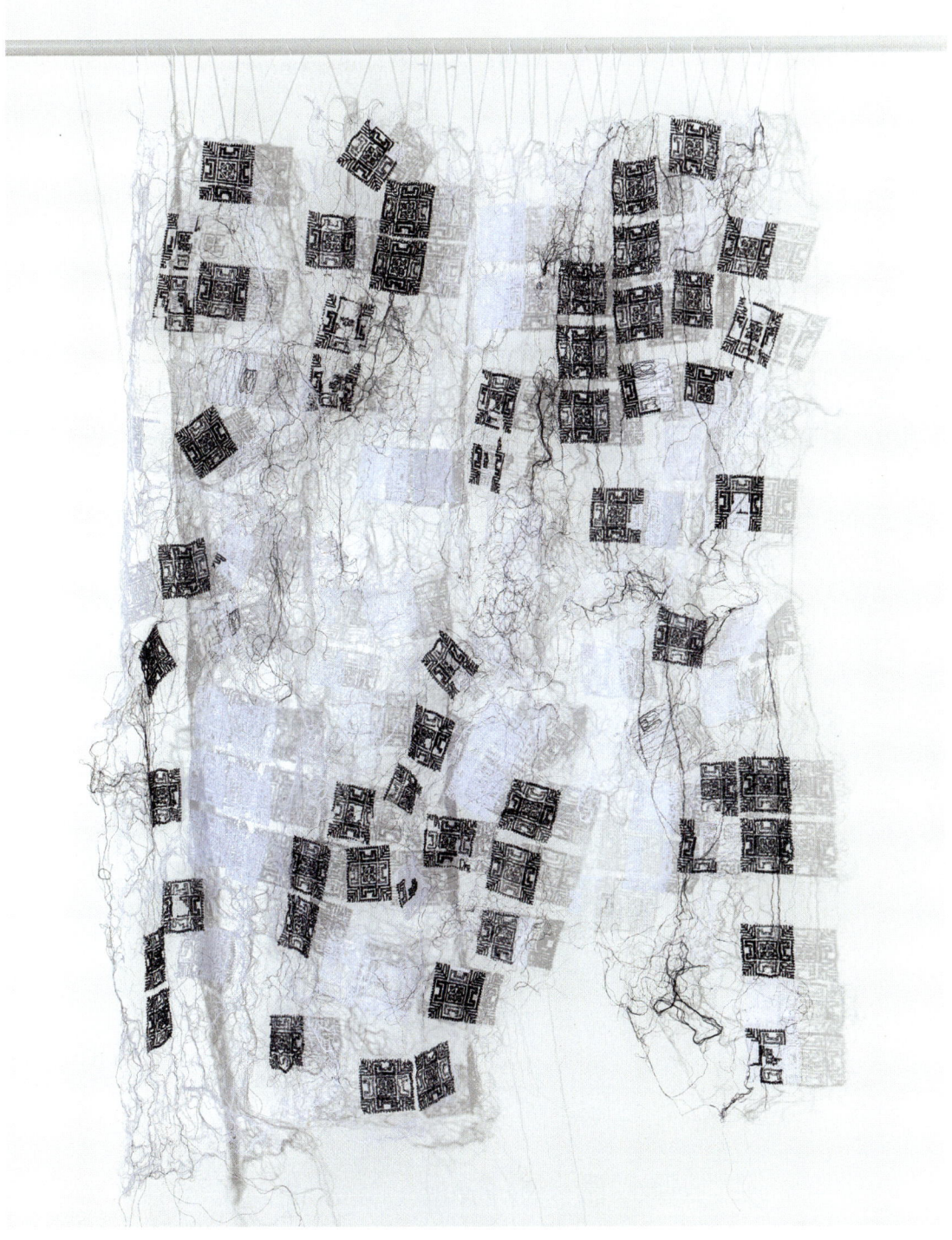

Samar Hejazi, *TB9 B&W*, exhibited in the Sharjah Islamic Art Festival 2023.
Thread, PVC pipe, light, shadow, 182.8 x 122 x 25.4 cm

JORDAN NASSAR

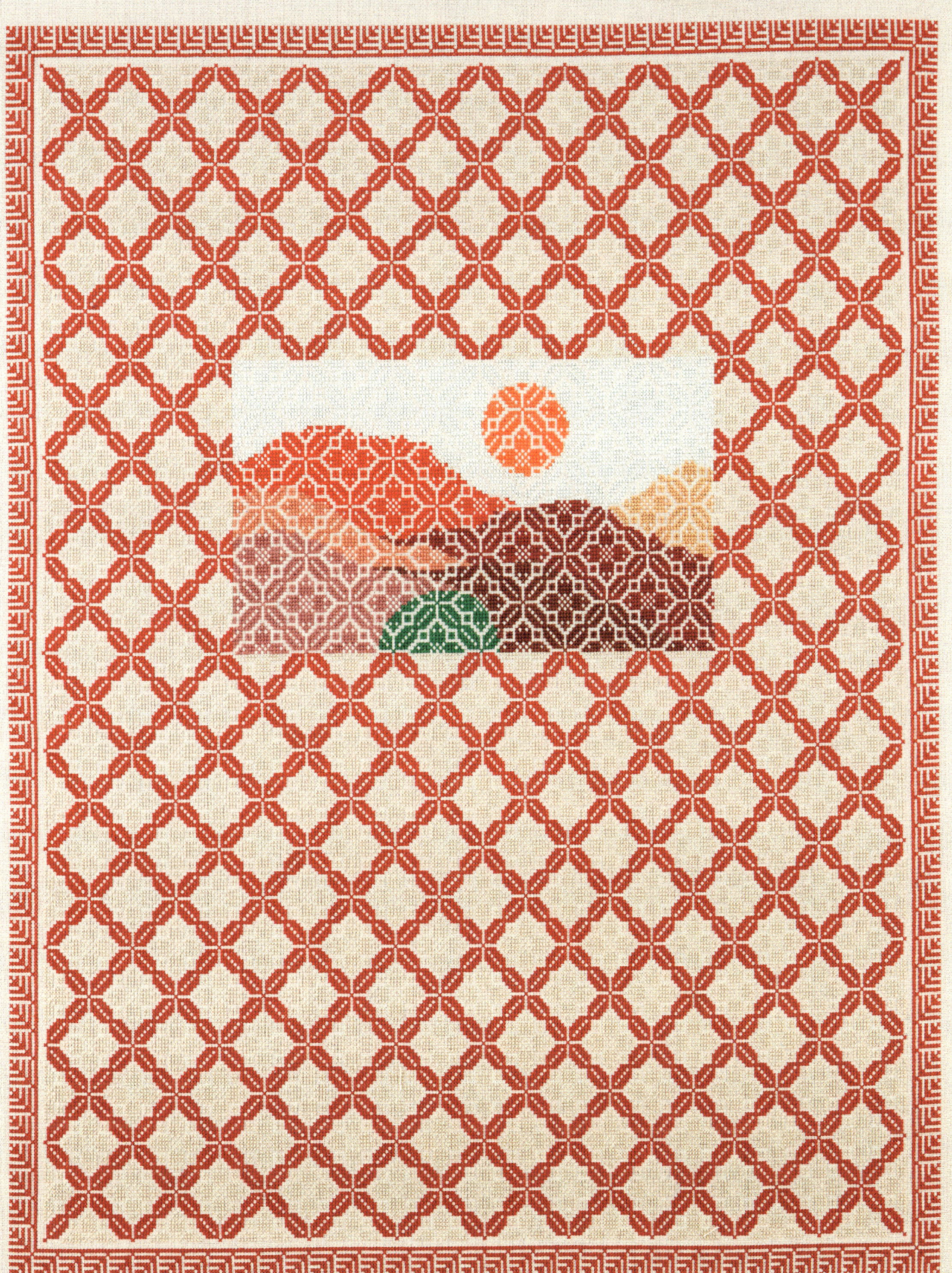

New York-based artist Jordan Nassar's upbringing and his family's influence shaped his worldview, sparking a curiosity about Palestinian embroidery, or *tatreez*. He tells us, 'My father was Palestinian-American, and my brothers and I were raised to identify as such, which took precedence over my mother's Polish heritage. Born and raised in Yonkers, New York, my father never spoke Arabic. Yet, of all four siblings, he was the only one who travelled to Palestine as an adult. He felt a deep connection there and embarked on human rights work in the region before I was born. Our family home was littered with souvenirs that he would bring back from Palestine, along with yellowed photos of traditionally dressed Arab ancestors. Stories and dinner table anecdotes featured idyllic tales of the homeland and our family's exploits in the New World after coming to New York.' Following his father's example, Nassar became the only one among his siblings to travel regularly to Palestine.

Growing up, Nassar had yet not developed his strong sense of belonging and attachment to the region. The biased messaging from American media, along with attending school in the Upper West Side of New York, left him confused about his relationship with Palestine, especially after 9/11. When Nassar lived in Berlin after college, he was exposed to different ways of thought and expression in Europe, including supporting Palestinian human rights. Nassar recalls, 'I gradually felt the need to explore, and assert, my Palestinian heritage, thereby better understanding my relationship to Palestine and Palestinian-ness.'

Through his desire to reconnect to Palestine, Nassar, who was already experimenting with crafts like weaving and crochet, discovered Palestinian *tatreez*. He says, 'The beautiful thing about *tatreez* is the modesty of the materials – a needle and thread and some fabric are all you need to begin. And so, I began.' Nassar researched the history of Palestinian embroidery and discovered the wide array of Palestinian cross-stitch motifs, compositions and colour combinations. He says, 'I began embroidering, mastering the material and eventually putting my twist on it. I started to "paint" landscapes across the traditional patterns and compositions. Through *tatreez*, I discovered that I paint, just with thread.'

Practising and designing *tatreez* work also satisfies what Nassar describes as the part of his brain that yearns for pattern. He says, 'I imagine compositions of colours and shapes across the repetitive rows of stitches. Varying combinations of patterns or isolating one pattern and repeating it across a whole canvas gives each piece a distinct mood and recalls a different region of Palestine. Changing the coloured threads can make two identically stitched pieces appear completely different. The possibilities are endless.'

Nassar explains why he includes landscapes in many of his works. 'On a formal level, landscape serves as a vehicle for colour work and, in that sense, it could have been anything. Conceptually, of course, the topic of land is central to the issue of Palestine. In my case, I arrived at the landscape from a different direction. My first inspiration came from Etel Adnan's paintings.'

Nassar's interactions with other diaspora Palestinians reinforced how he approached landscape in his work. He realised that many people spoke about Palestine in 'a fantastical way, dream-like, utopian, much the way my father and grandparents had painted images of the homeland for us in stories. It was always rolling hills, sweet honey, fragrant herbs, olive trees, young fuzzy almonds, goats and sheep wandering the terraced valleys, and so on. It is a place that exists – in this way – only in the imaginations of the diaspora. The reality in Palestine is much harsher but, even at its happiest, it is a normal place on earth. Yet this imagined, perfect, abundant paradise of Palestine is something that struck me as special and beautiful and something that belongs to us, to the diaspora. A resulting sensation spurred by the pain of being separated from the homeland is that we dream of Palestine. I began to interpret my work as formal works of colour, as well as depictions of these dreams.'

'*Tatreez* connected me to Palestine, as a proverbial connection of the brain and the heart, and, ultimately, it would also lead me to real-life connection and collaboration with Palestinian embroiderers,' says Nassar. He commissioned embroidery from women living in Dheisheh refugee camp in Bethlehem, Beit Ummar near Hebron, and other places around Palestine. Nassar designs pieces for them to embroider and instructs them to leave a section unembroidered for him to complete. He says, 'This process was conceived so that each piece would become a collaboration. The women would use their sense of colour and choose where to apply each colour on the pattern. I responded to the aesthetic choices with my selection of colours and compositions.

'Although I still make pieces entirely on my own, the ongoing body of collaborative pieces is recognisable because they feature traditional patterning surrounding an inset landscape. I love the feeling of the women's traditional style of *tatreez* pressed up against and surrounding my landscapes, with the patterns seamlessly continuing across the whole piece.' He continues, 'It is incredibly meaningful to me to create artworks that were embroidered by the hands of women in Palestine as well as by my own hands. It has been an honour to get to know and feel at home in their communities, as well as the broader Palestinian embroidery community. For a half-Palestinian American that set out to connect to my heritage, this is one-thousand-fold more than I could have dreamed.'

Nassar views heritage as the crux of his work. While his practice centres on Palestinian embroidery, he also creates glass-beaded artworks in the style of glasswork from Hebron and woodworking with brass inlay in the Levantine style. Nassar states, 'With all of these crafts, it is imperative for me to learn how to do them myself and, by extension, my hands and my body learn these ancient traditions.' Nassar points to examples where the notion of heritage is present in other ways, such as in the titles of his artworks and exhibitions. He takes inspiration for titles from Palestinian, Arab and Arab-American literature, such as the writing of Ghassan Kanafani, Etel Adnan, Khalil Gibran or the lyrics of Umm Kalthoum songs. Nassar says, 'Arab writers, poets, artists and musicians provide us with a cultural heritage that transcends language, borders, and time. I draw on these heritages and imbue my work with them as often as I can.'

Nassar spends hours embroidering daily, and some of his works contain over 100,000 stitches. 'I like to imagine that the way I spend my day embroidering mirrors a peaceful day for a Palestinian and makes me feel closer to my heritage and my ancestors. My hands perform the same motions as theirs did. My days and theirs are aligned. In between waking up and going to bed, we embroider. In between tasks and chores, we embroider. In between meals and errands, we embroider. I embroider every day, often while in transit. *Tatreez* is a way of life for me, as I imagine it is for Palestinians around the world. It is a daily habit, an occupation for fidgety hands, and an outlet for creativity. This is a Palestinian tradition we are proud to not only keep alive but also to innovate and explore, to reinvent and carry on.'

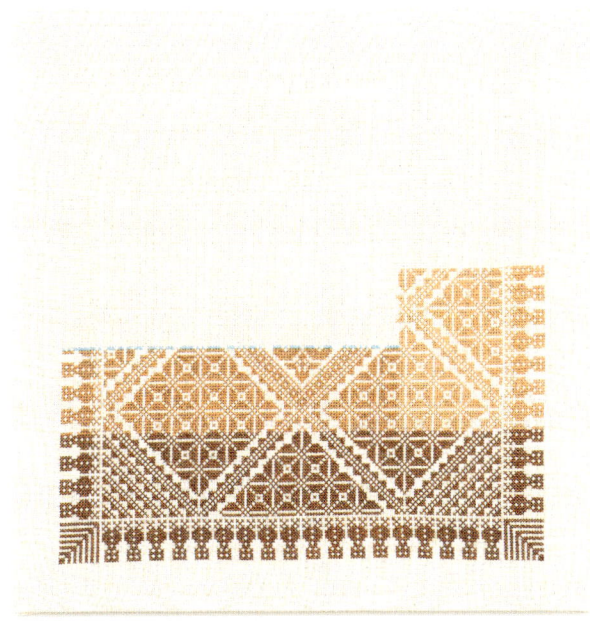

Jordan Nassar, *My Fruit Shall be Gathered*, 2018.
Cotton thread on cotton fabric, 50.8 x 50.8 cm

Previous spread: Jordan Nassar, *In the Heart of the Rose*, 2020.
Cotton thread on cotton fabric, 97.8 x 76.2 cm. Collection of Stacey Jordan Cook and Ryan Cook. Photo by Phoebe d'Heurle

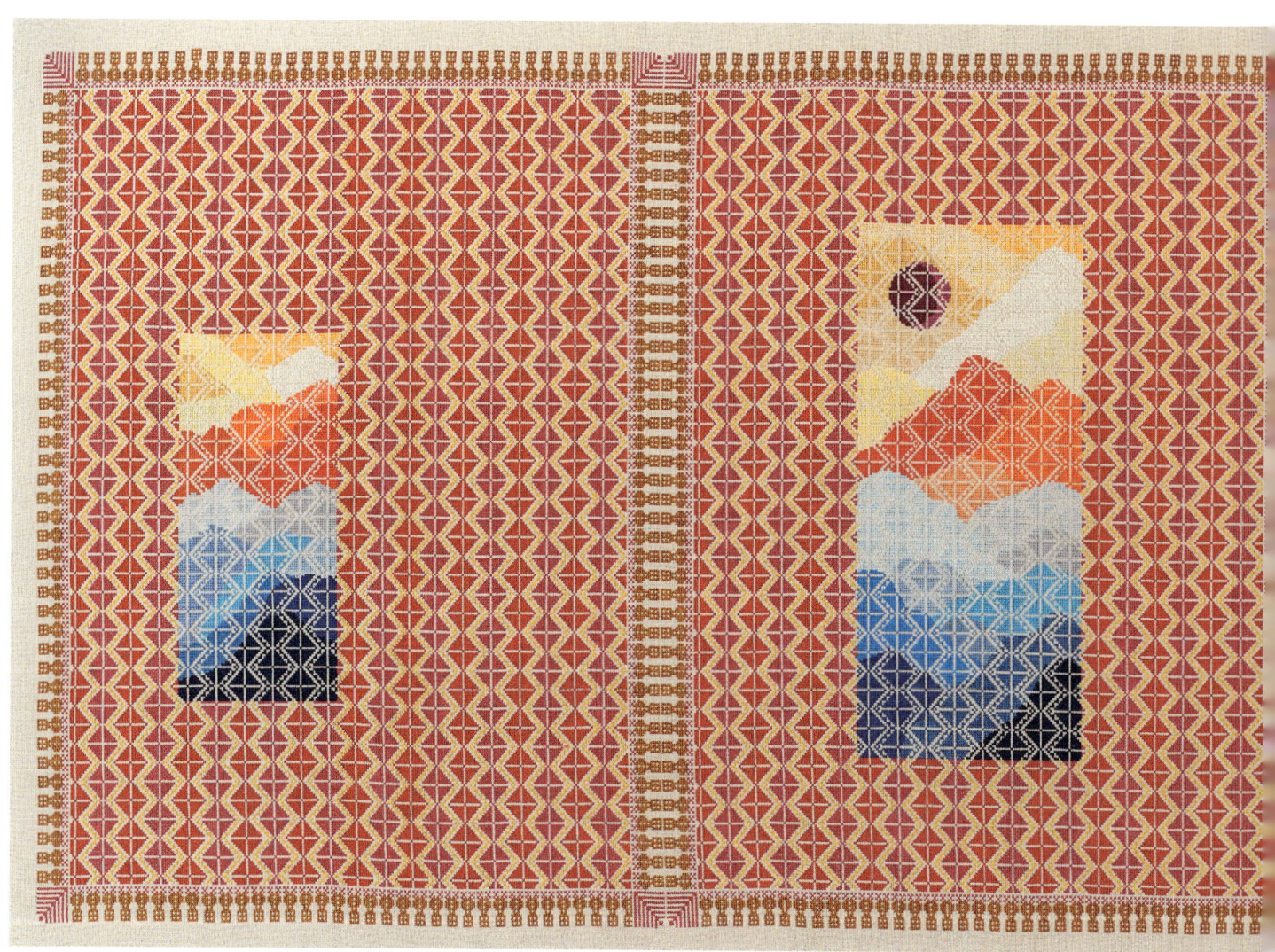

Jordan Nassar, *Saw Tornadoes Covered with Flames*, 2020.
Cotton thread on cotton fabric, 98.3 x 278.6 cm. Collection of Lizbeth and George Krupp.
Photo by Phoebe d'Heurle

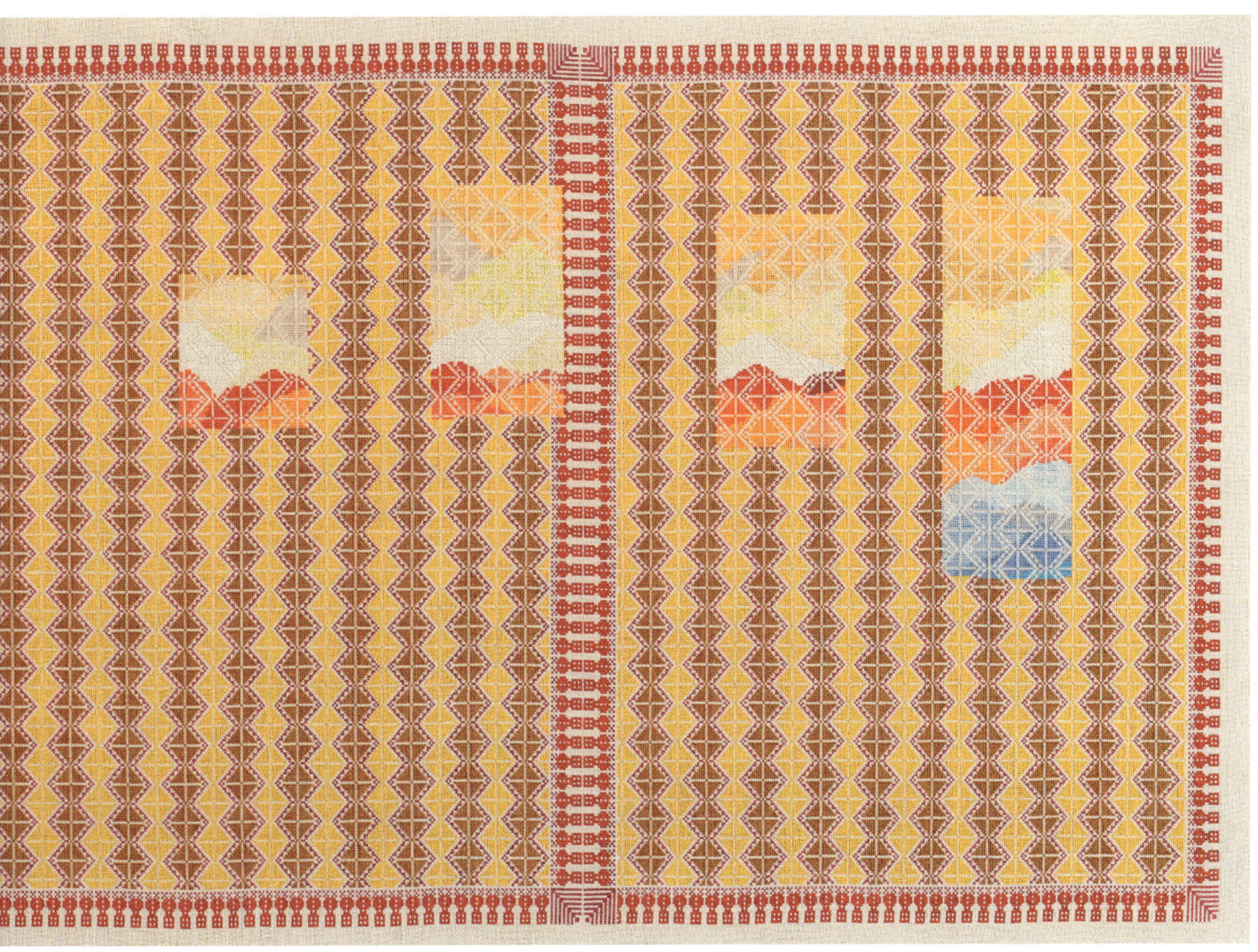

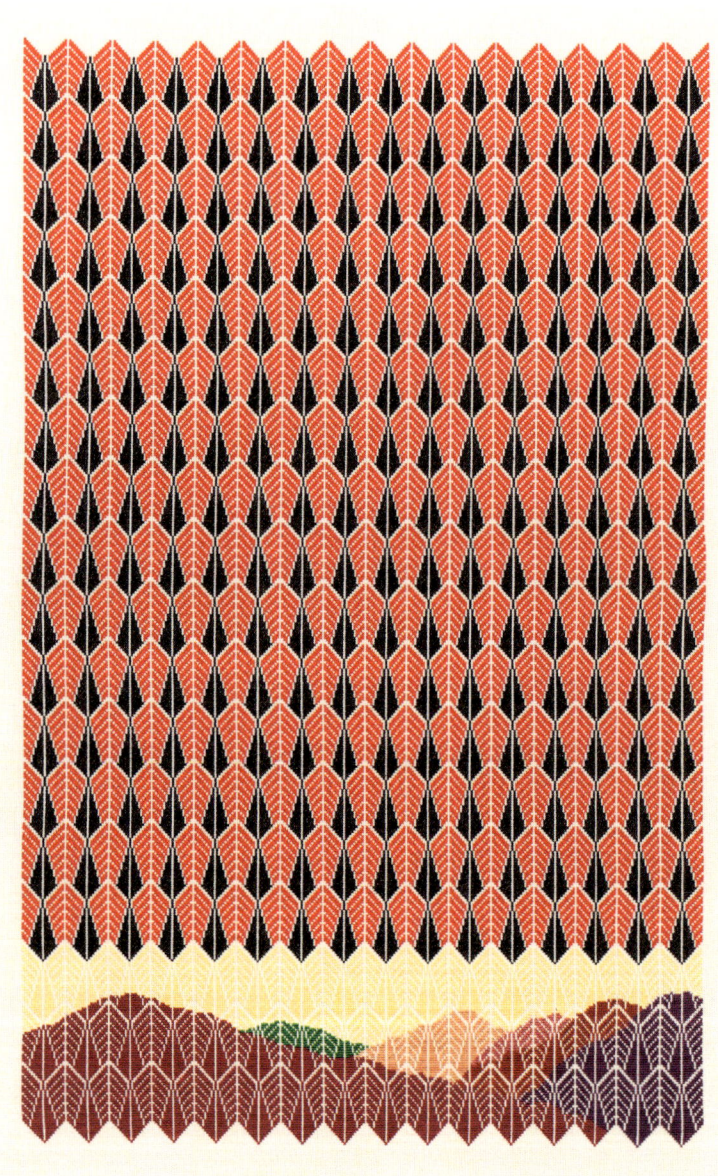
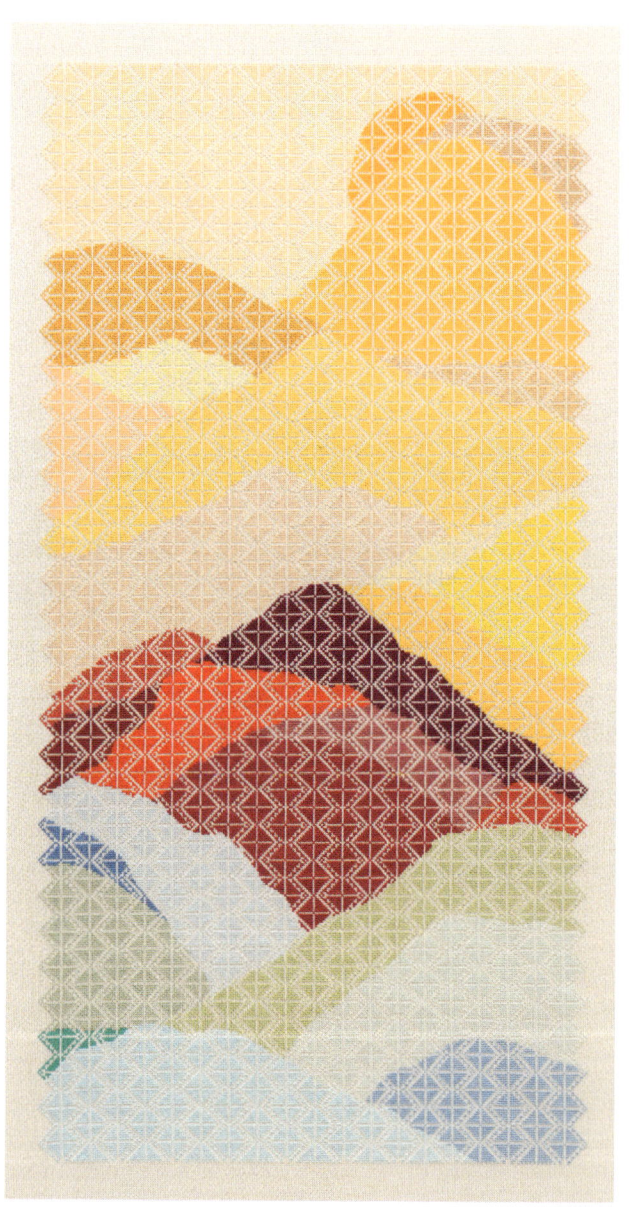

Jordan Nassar, *The Sun Has Sulfuric Dreams*, 2019. Cotton thread on cotton fabric, 119.4 x 80 cm.
OZ Art NWA, Bentonville, Arkansas. Photo by Matthew Kroening

Jordan Nassar, *To Go to the Mountain*, 2019. Cotton thread on cotton fabric, 129.5 x 71.1 cm.
The Museum of Contemporary Art, Los Angeles. Photo by Phoebe d'Heurle

Right: Jordan Nassar, *The Sun Watching*, 2019. Cotton thread on cotton fabric 120.7 x 91.4 cm.
Private collection. Photo by Michael Underwood

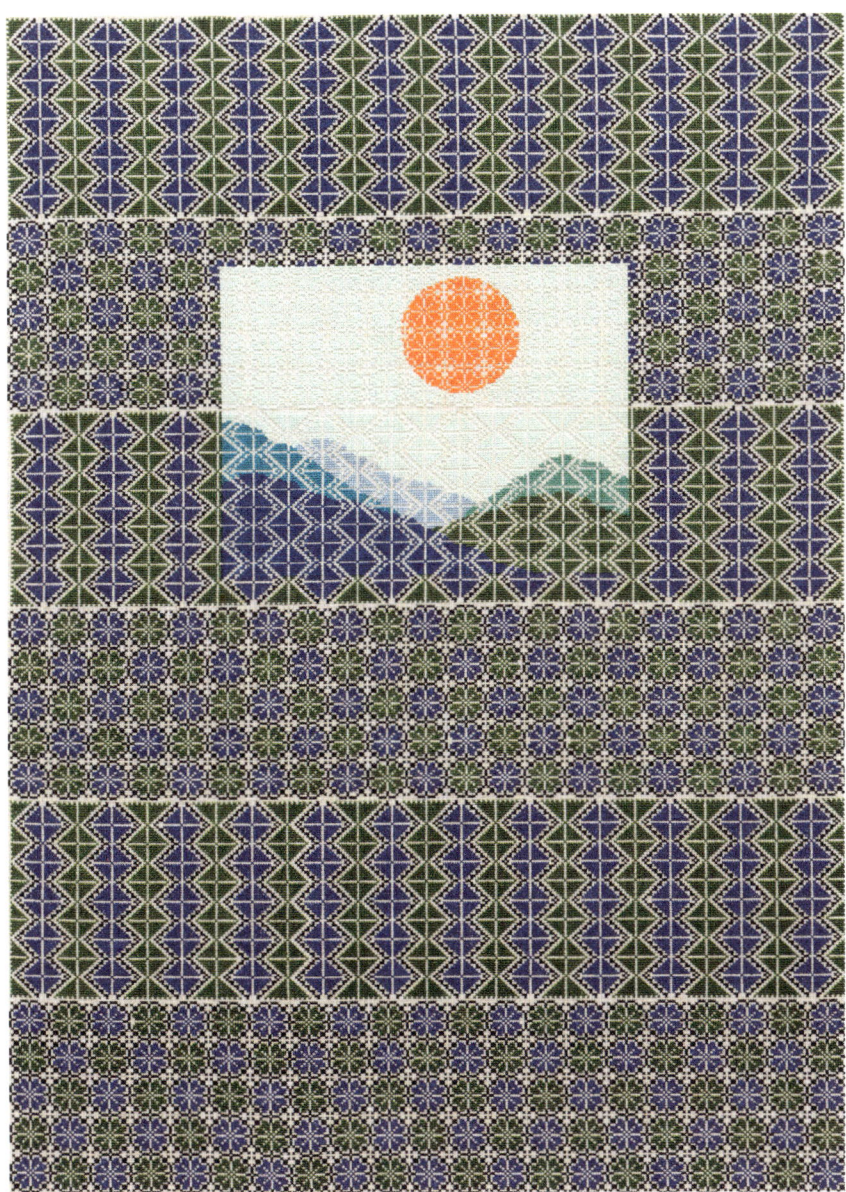

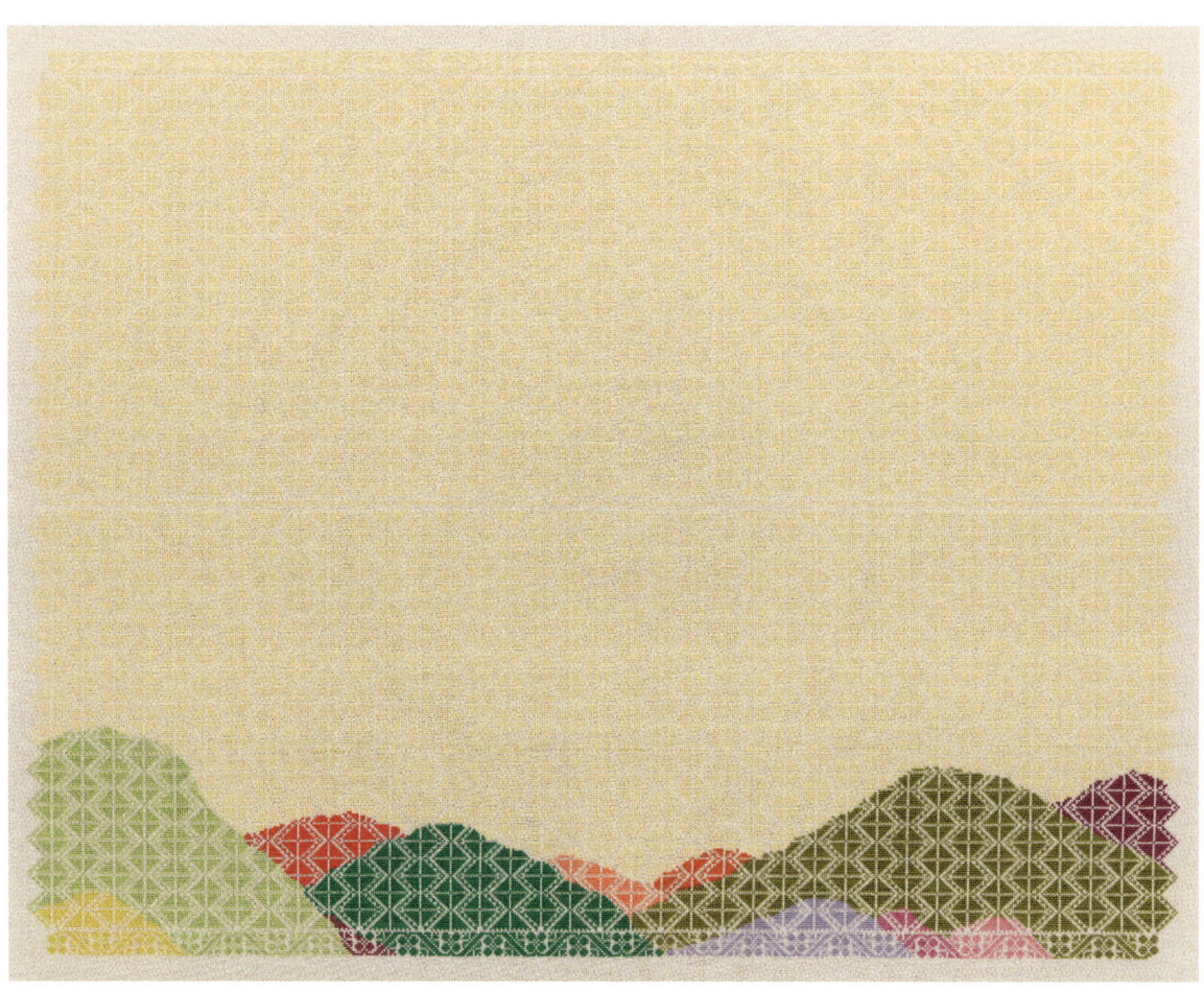

Jordan Nassar, *A Sun to Come*, 2022. Cotton thread on cotton fabric, 106.7 x 138.4 cm.
Private collection. Photo by Matthew Kroening

Right: Jordan Nassar, *A Lost Key*, 2019. Cotton thread on cotton fabric, 126 x 82.9 cm. Whitney Museum of American Art,
New York, gift of Avo Samuelian and Hector Manuel Gonzalez 2019.388. Photo by Phoebe d'Heurle

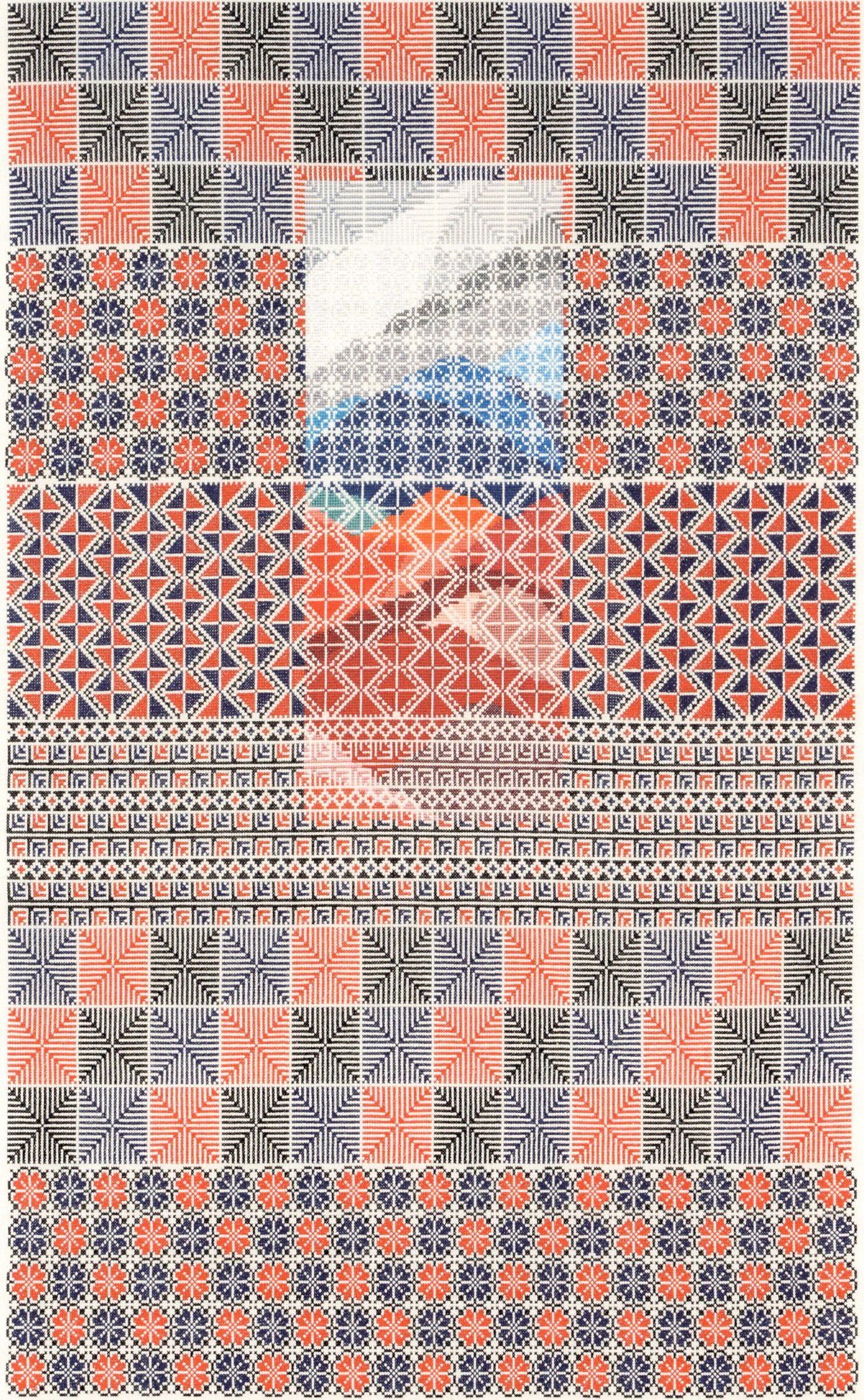

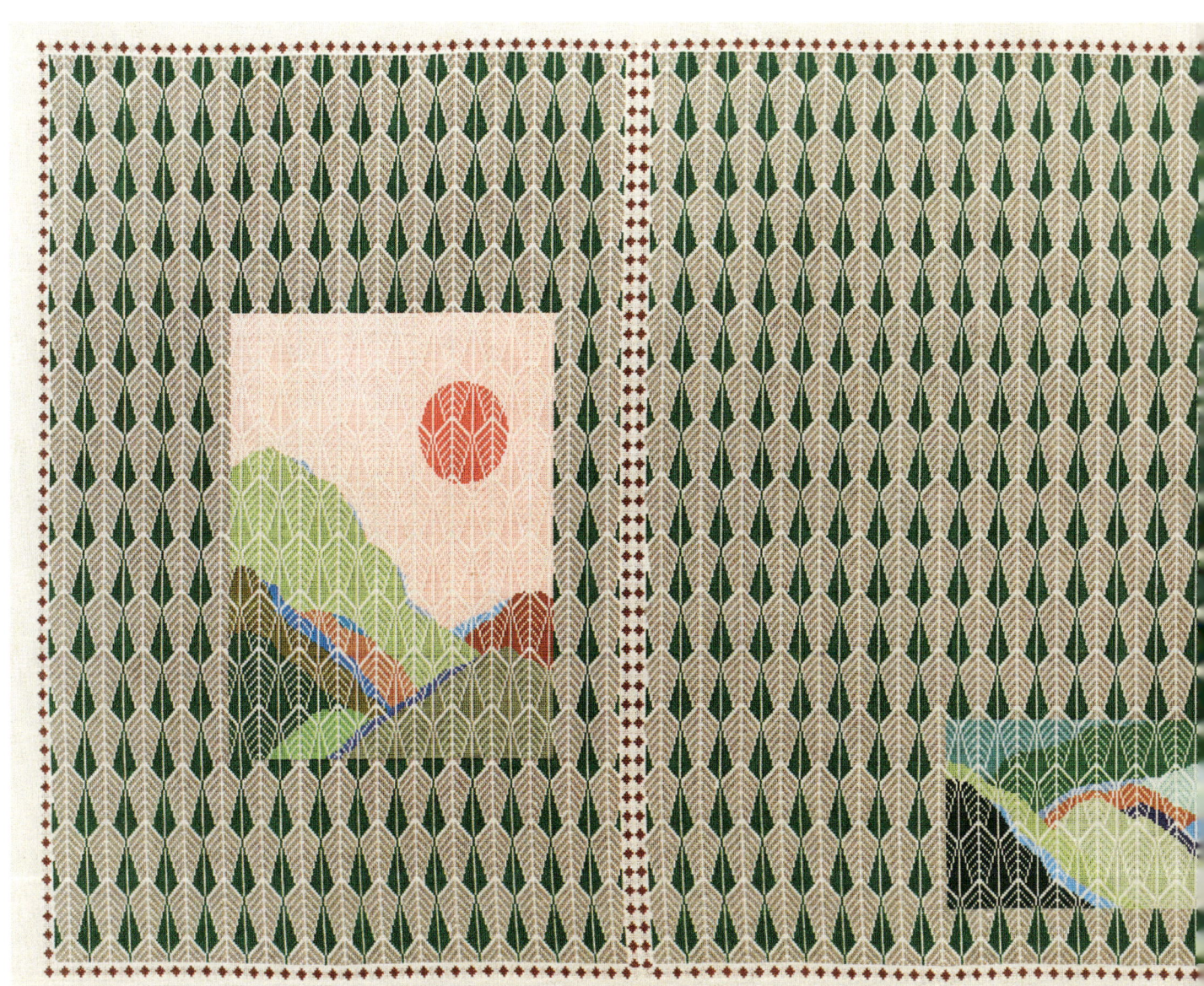

Jordan Nassar, *A Stream Is Singing Under the Youthful Grass*, 2020,
Cotton thread on cotton fabric, 106.7 x 275.6 cm. Private collection.
Photo by Phoebe d'Heurle

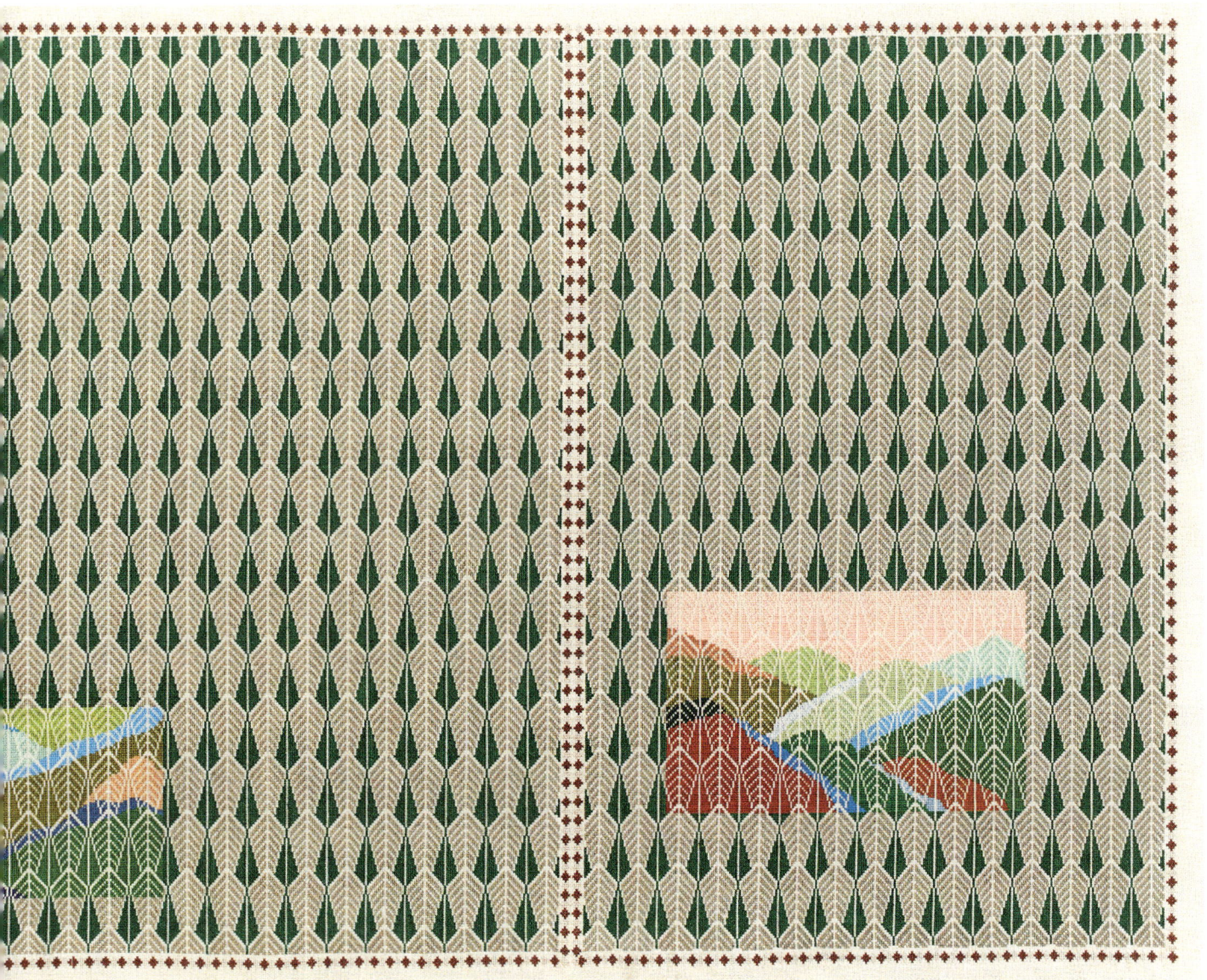

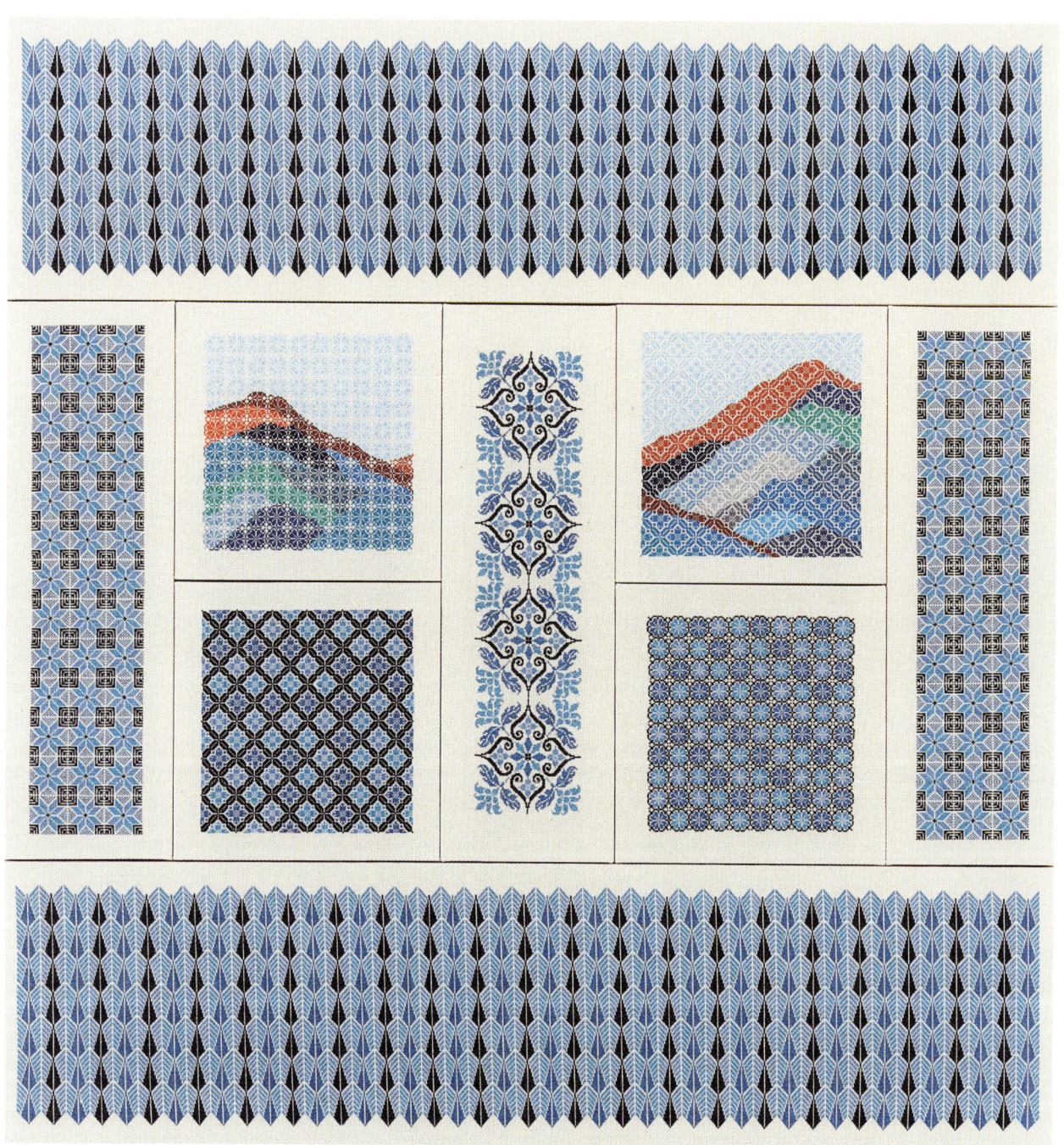

Jordan Nassar, *Beyond Boundaries*, 2022. Cotton thread on cotton fabric, 213.4 x 205.7 cm. The Alfond Collection of Contemporary Art, Rollins Museum of Art. Photo by Phoebe d'Heurle

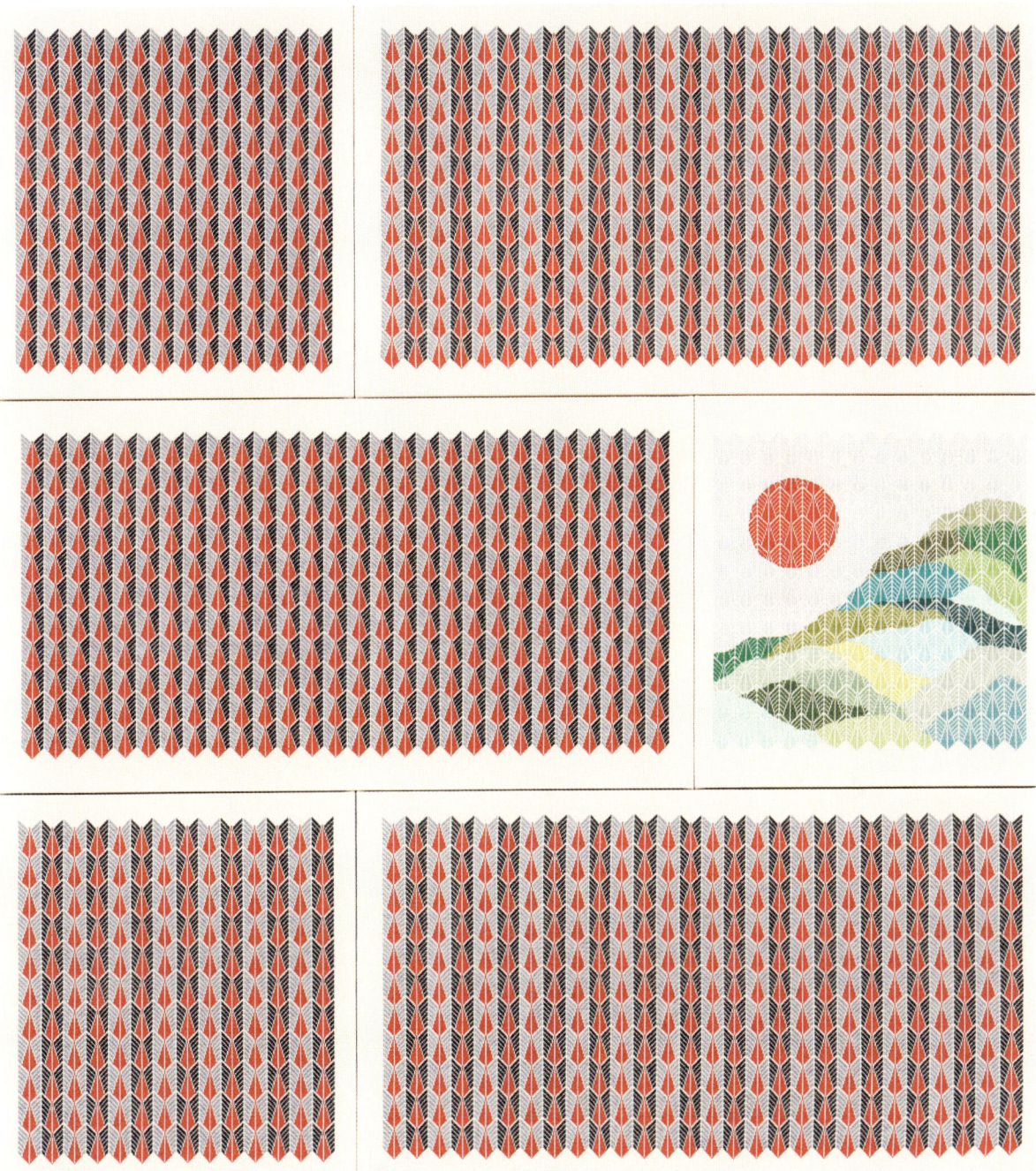

Jordan Nassar, *Brick Walls and Closed Windows*, 2022. Cotton thread on cotton fabric, 236.2 x 218.4 cm. Collection of Deborah Green and Clayton Aynesworth. Photo by Phoebe d'Heurle

DEBORAH MULLINS

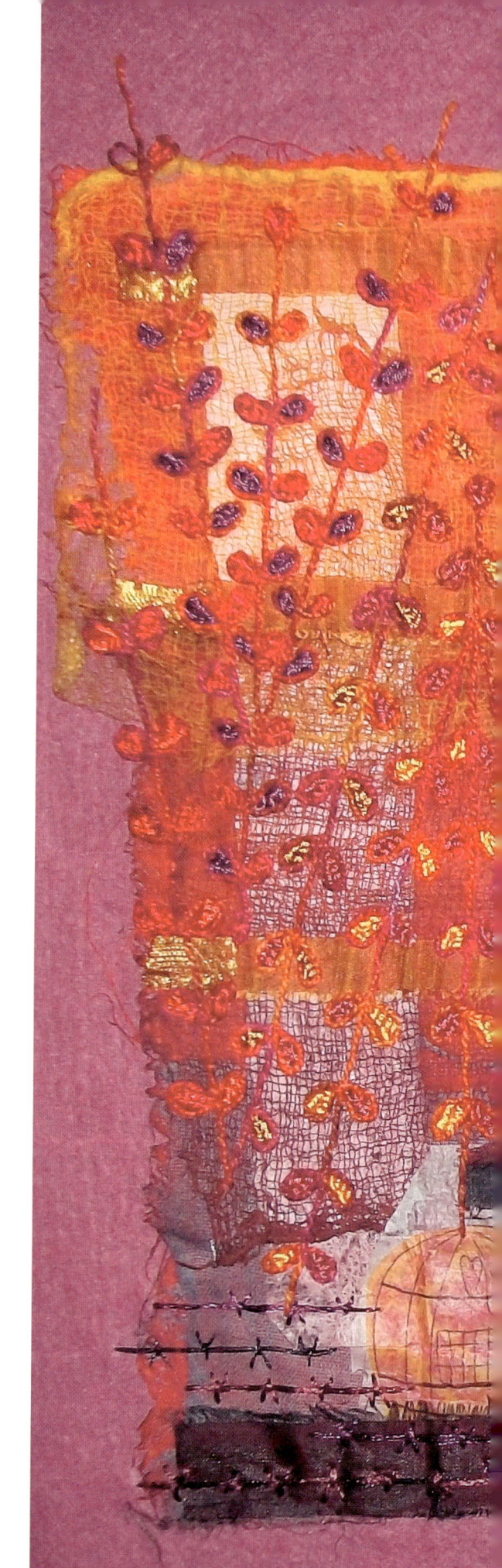

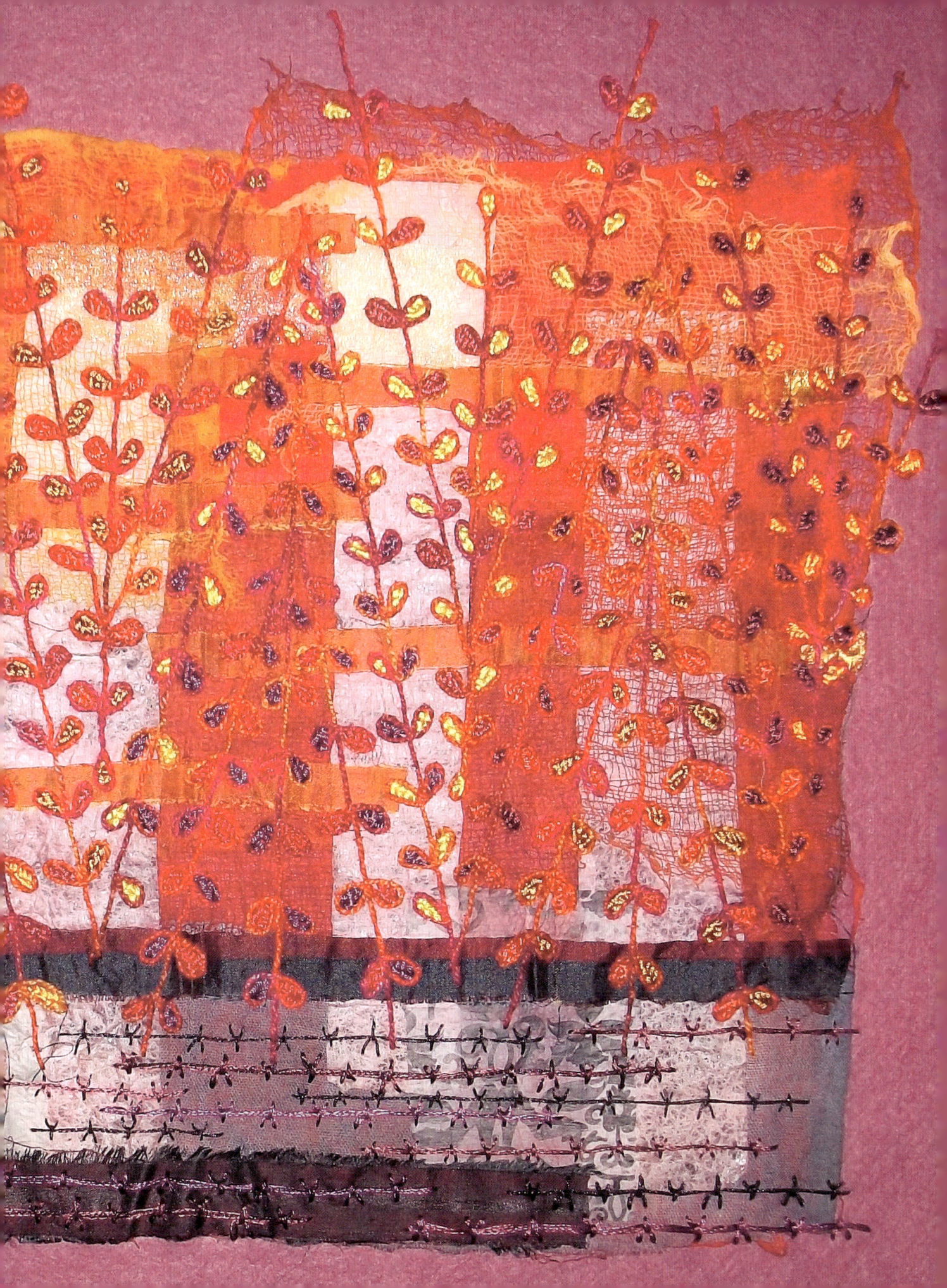

In 2013, Deborah Mullins's life took a new direction following a three-month sabbatical with her husband, Revd. Canon Peter Mullins, at the Tantur Ecumenical Institute, overlooking Checkpoint 300 and the separation wall in Palestine. On this trip, Mullins discovered the range of Palestinian embroidery, particularly Bethlehem's *tahriri* (couching) stitch, at Maha Saca's Palestinian Heritage Center, the Bethlehem Arab Women's Union and Beituna Al Talhami Museum. She says, 'What I had felt, the people I had met, the injustices I had seen and heard about during and following that first stay in Palestine ignited a burning desire and compulsion to respond creatively.'

Upon returning to the UK, she was diagnosed with breast cancer. After completing treatment and surgery, she signed up for a creative textiles course to inspire a positive and creative response to her experience in Palestine. With a background in patchwork and quilting, she taught herself the *tahriri* stitch she fell in love with and began to hand embroider. 'I truly believe that without the time at Tantur and the breast cancer, I would not have had the drive or the inspiration to be creating in the way I have been over the past six years. The final push came as I was awarded two prizes for my work and met the Princess Royal,[11] to whom I spoke about my motivation and the "issue" of Palestine. Without this last step, I may not have had the confidence to accept that my work was artistically valid. After that, I started calling myself a textile artist and gradually came to believe it.'

After completing the course and being inspired by Leila Sansour's film *Open Bethlehem*, Mullins produced her series of the same name, wherein she simplified designs of the Bethlehem dress chest panels. Mullins explains, 'I felt that these pieces could represent the opening up of the town itself, its freedom from constraint, as well as freeing up the regularity of traditional Bethlehem embroidery.' In describing the materials and colours used, she shares how she 'revelled in the fact that handmade felt does not produce straight lines demarcating the different colours. Allowing the borders to ebb and flow, not to be regular and straight, suggested an element of freedom and openness.' She continues, 'I have usually chosen colours that I liked together, with little regard to whether they were the traditional colours, though *Open Bethlehem V* consciously tries to mix the orange, pink and green that are often found together on a Bethlehem dress. Wire is available in many different thicknesses and colours and, as I dye many of my threads, I could choose quite freely which colour palette to use.' Mullins returned to Bethlehem in 2018, where she spent time at Beituna Al Talhami and the Women's Child Care Society in Beit Jala. In her research into late nineteenth-century and early twentieth-century Bethlehem dresses in the British Museum archive, she discovered how the actual scale of the intricate embroidery from that period differed from the oversized and less refined contemporary *tahriri* embroidery available commercially. In her *Borders* series, she successfully reproduced a range of border designs on the same small scale as those she researched from books and dresses. Mullins says, 'I value making beautiful and intricate pieces with a second, deeper or more political meaning.'

Of her piece *Border Crossing* (2018), she explains that it is 'in one sense just a network or grid of interlocking borders, designed to be aesthetically pleasing. However, many people do not notice the black couched line that meanders its way across the piece, at one point almost enclosing an area of the design. I thought of Qalandiya [checkpoint] and people I met in Bethlehem, the Anastas family, living near Rachel's Tomb, surrounded on three sides by the separation barrier that looms over their house and blocks light and their view. There is no logic to the positioning of the separation barrier, other than oppression and land grab, so there is no logic to the progression of this black line across the piece.'

Referring to *Checkpoint* (2019), another piece in the series, Mullins explains that it 'is based on a photo of the revolving gates at a checkpoint, designed to slow down or prevent progress across an artificially imposed border. Again, aesthetically pleasing but based on something so ugly and repressive, which is why I had to give it a subtitle: *Borders Where There Should Be No Borders*.'

After working with *tahriri* borders, she created two chest panels to original scale, representing and incorporating elements from Bethlehem and Jerusalem, the two places that meant the most to her on her trip to Palestine. The first, *Qabbeh* (2020), uses the Key to the Heart design in the centre panel and *tishrimeh*, zigzag appliquéd edging. The second one, *Al Quds Qabbeh* (2020), is less traditional in style. It features a lino-print motif from the stonework on the Haram al-Sharif – the sacred compound that contains Al-Aqsa Mosque and The Dome of the Rock Mosque.

Jerusalem and Bethlehem are referenced elsewhere in in her work. In *Nativity Church, Bethlehem* (2016), Mullins incorporated elements such as the ancient Byzantine mosaics, pillars and lamps from her photographs of the Church of the Nativity in Palestine. Another piece inspired by Bethlehem is *Star of Bethlehem*, after the Palestinian cross-stitch motif, filled with *tahriri* border designs rather than cross stitches. Within *Haram al-Sharif I* (2015), she applied beading to capture the light more effectively on top of lino-printed and stitched fabric. Inspired by the shapes and colours of the Haram al-Sharif, she hand dyed the background and layered elements of the stitched design, creating a complex construction with an effect of some areas seen through others.

Mullins describes the inspiration behind her work *Tears Over Gaza* (2015): 'If the original time I spent in Palestine in 2013 was seminal to my whole future life as an artist, the Israeli bombing offensive on Gaza in 2014 is inextricably linked with my chemotherapy treatment during that summer. Had I been experiencing the same cancer in Gaza at that time, I would not be alive now.' The background fabric of *Tears Over Gaza* is constructed from paper, printed tissue, ribbon, gauze and muslin, bonded together to make a stitchable fabric. The paper used in creating the fabric was taken from a series of pages from *National Geographic* magazine with photos of Gaza's beach at sunset, crushed and kneaded using the Japanese *momigami* technique. The main couching stitch motif is known as 'almond branch' in Jaffa, but in Gaza is called 'tears'. Mullins says, 'The tears, the barbed wire representing the blockade of Gaza, and the empty birdcage representing the hope of escape and freedom, combined to express my feelings at the time about both Gaza and my health.'

A later artwork titled *All That Remains* (2016) was inspired by the stories of Palestinian families expelled during the Nakba who retained the key to their family's house in their home village. The title comes from Walid Khalidi's book about the histories of the Palestinian villages destroyed in 1948. Mullins

describes transferring the key's rust to the fabric and threads to 'represent stages of memory – not necessarily the memory of the key owners, but of the society around them'. Mullins was also moved and inspired by the *Key of Return* above the entrance to Aida refugee camp in Bethlehem. She constructed a 140-cm-long key from recycled bottles and heavy cardboard, covered in wadding and dyed calico. She describes each section as 'graffitied with all the names of the villages ethnically cleansed of their Palestinian inhabitants and either demolished or "re-purposed"'. Like the original flanking the entrance of Aida camp, this *Key of Return* focuses on longing and the right to return.

Though the metastasis of breast cancer to her bones restricted her mobility, she could still sew both *Qabbeh* (2020) and *Talhami Fantasy* (2020). To Mullins, *Talhami Fantasy* was a reaction to COVID-19 restrictions and her new physical limitations. She explains, 'I wanted to allow the *tahriri* borders to meander and travel beyond the restrictions of straight lines. I also enjoyed exploring and playing with the many circular motifs found in both the Bethlehem chest panels and the *taqsireh* (short-sleeved jacket) worn over the dress.'

Through her exhibitions, workshops and talks to the Embroiderers' Guild and other groups, Deborah Mullins found various ways of thoughtfully engaging with a British audience about Palestine, allowing for deep conversations and questions in a non-confrontational manner. She says, 'Palestinian embroidery embodies for me the creative spirit of Palestinian women through the ages, their connection to the places where they lived and the communities to which they belonged. It is their resilience and determination to retain and promote their cultural identity that shines through their embroidery. My overriding principle is that I do this work to honour and show respect to the many creative Palestinian women of the past and present who work towards preserving their heritage and history. I hope that my work can play a small part in that.'

Deborah Mullins passed away in 2020, leaving behind a legacy of textile artwork honouring Palestinian cultural tradition and showcasing her passion for humanity as an ally to the Palestinian cause.

[1] Princess Anne of the British Royal Family.

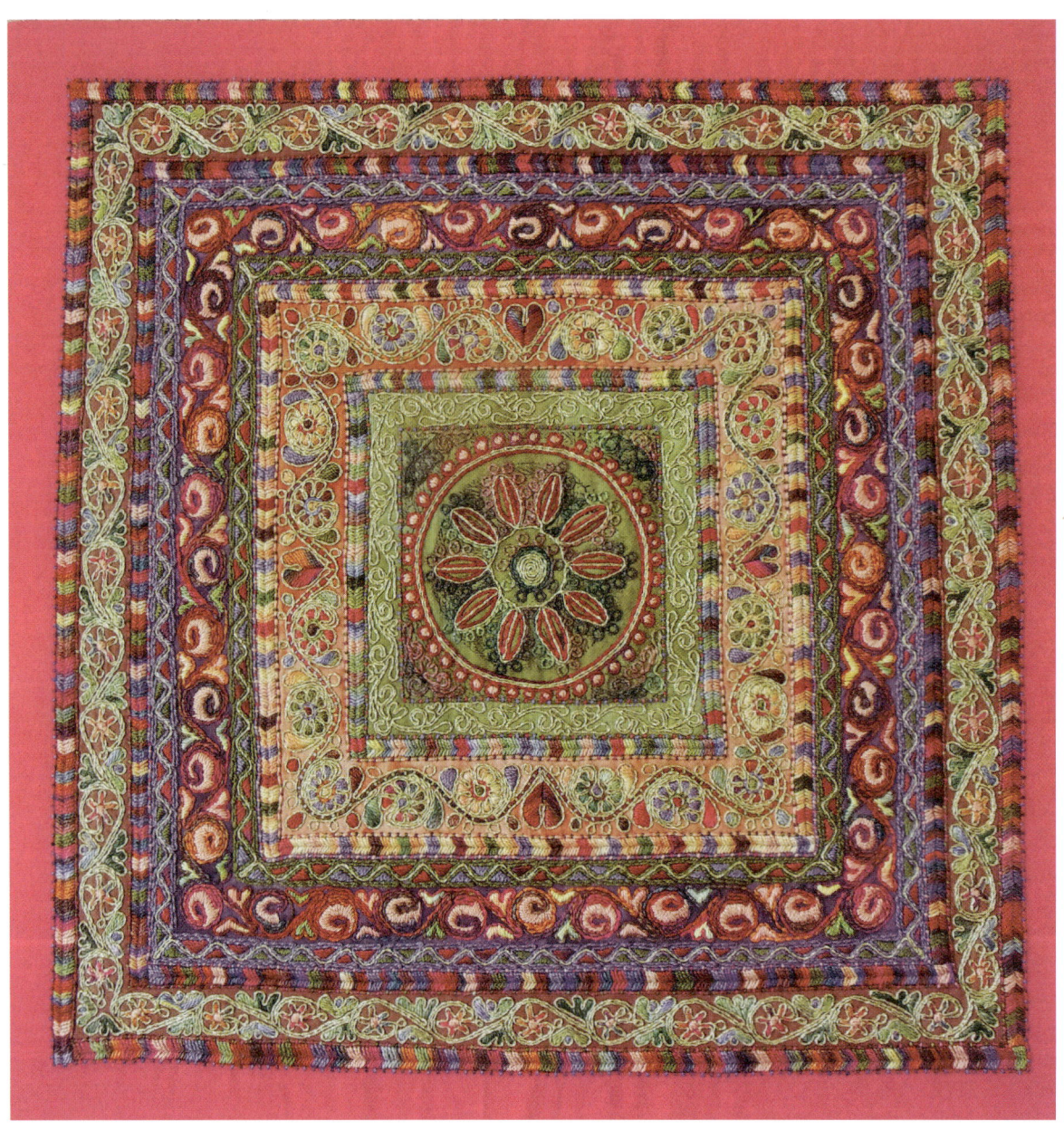

Deborah Mullins, *Al Quds Qabbeh*, 2020. Hand-dyed threads, wire and lino-print on fabric, 65 x 65 cm
Right: Deborah Mullins, *Star of Bethlehem*, 2019. Hand-dyed threads on hand-dyed fabric, 58 cm x 58 cm

Pages 232–233: Deborah Mullins, *Tears Over Gaza*, 2015. Mixed media, 40 x 40 cm

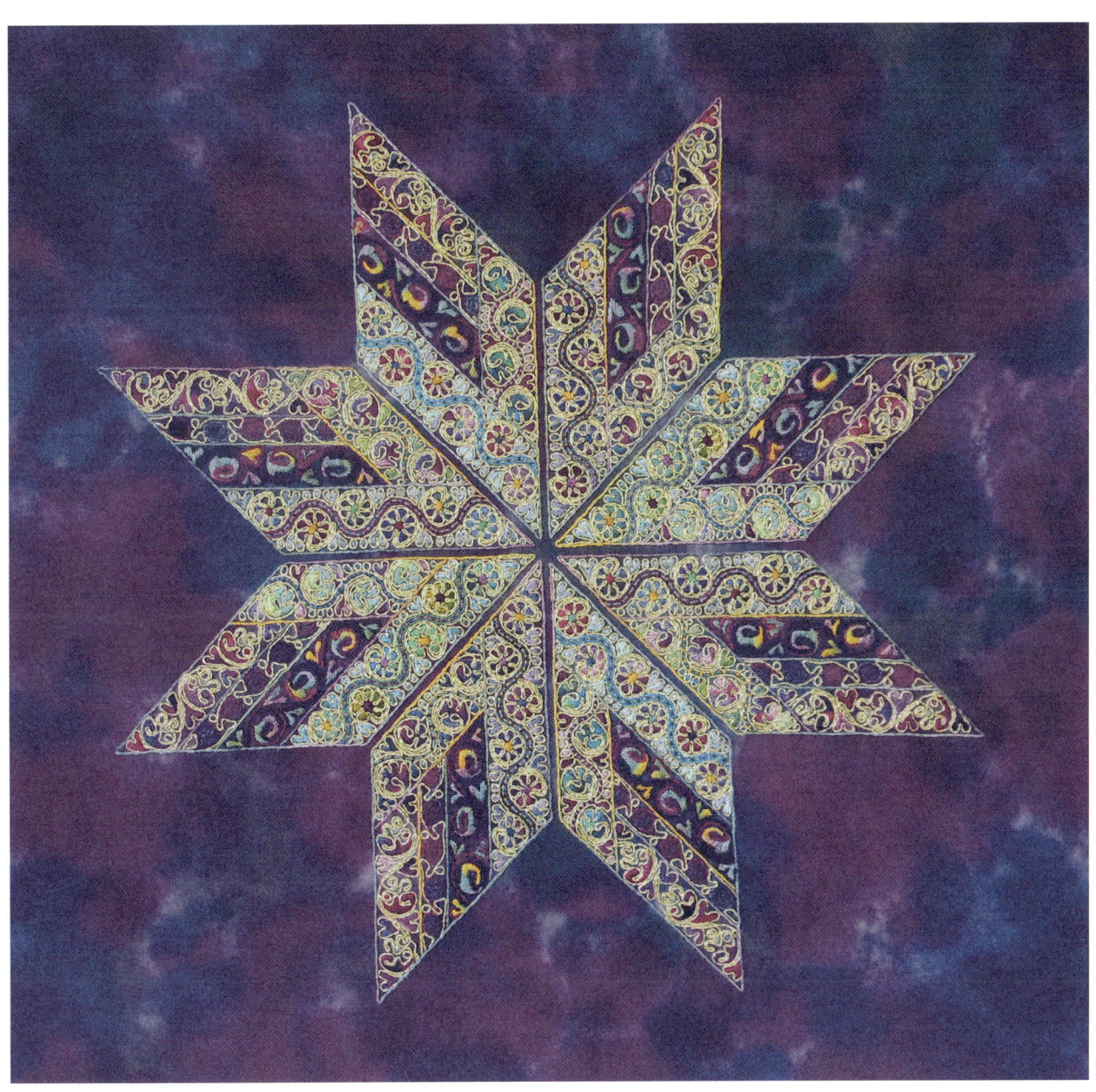

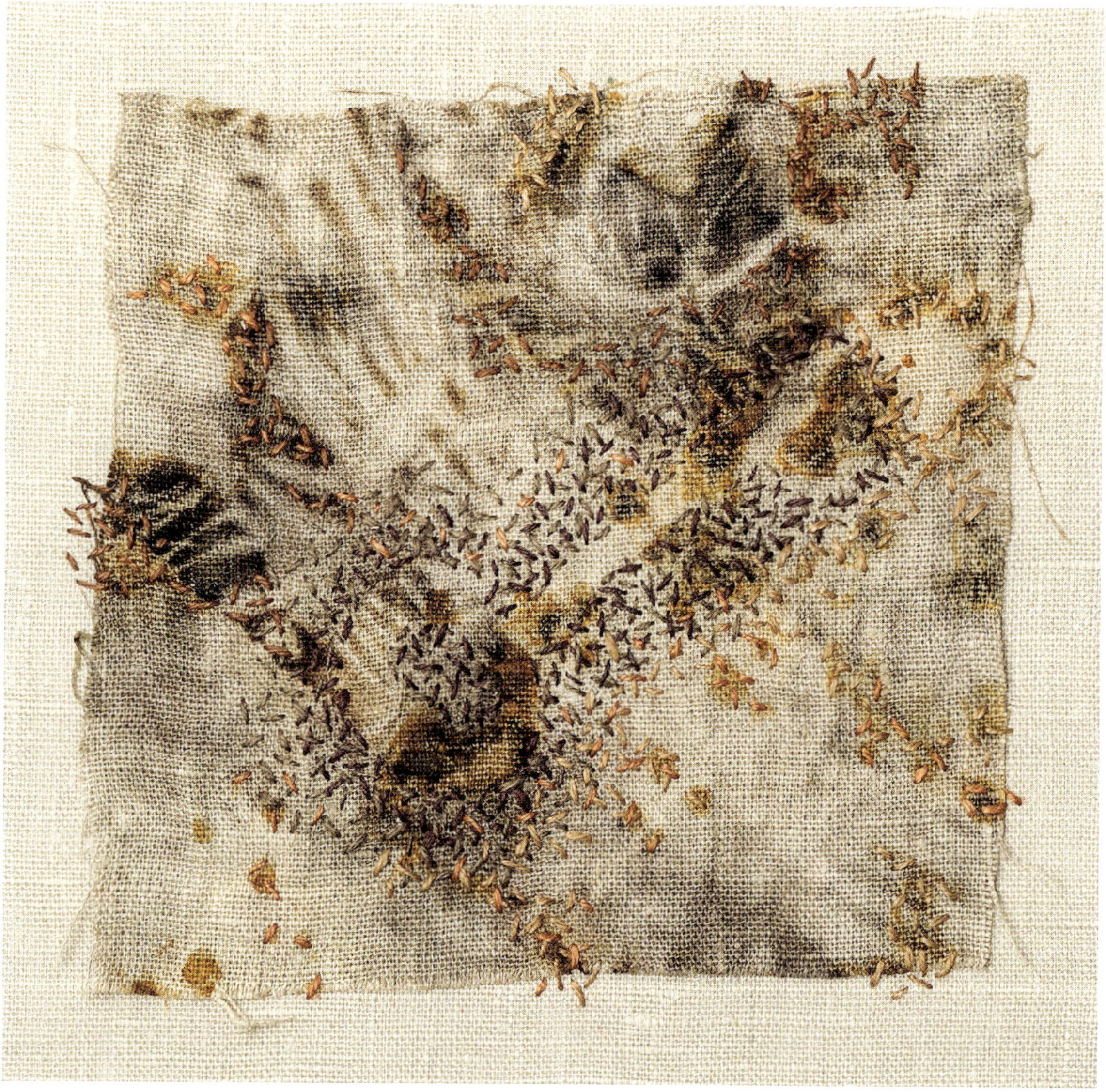

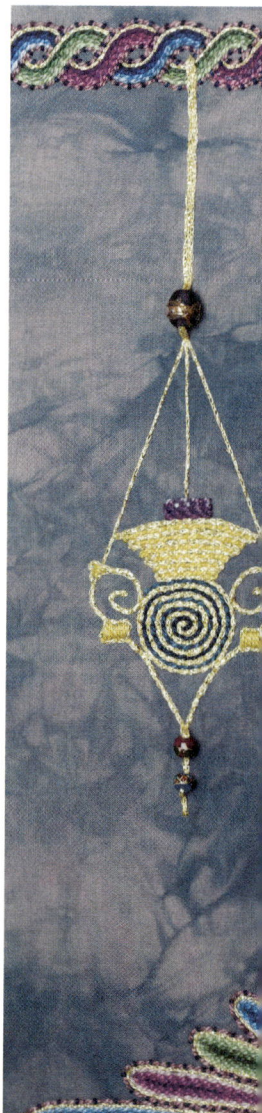

Deborah Mullins, *All That Remains*, 2016. Thread and rust on linen, 21 x 21 cm

Right: Deborah Mullins, *Nativity Church, Bethlehem*, 2016. Hand-dyed thread and mixed media on hand-dyed fabric, 63 x 39 cm

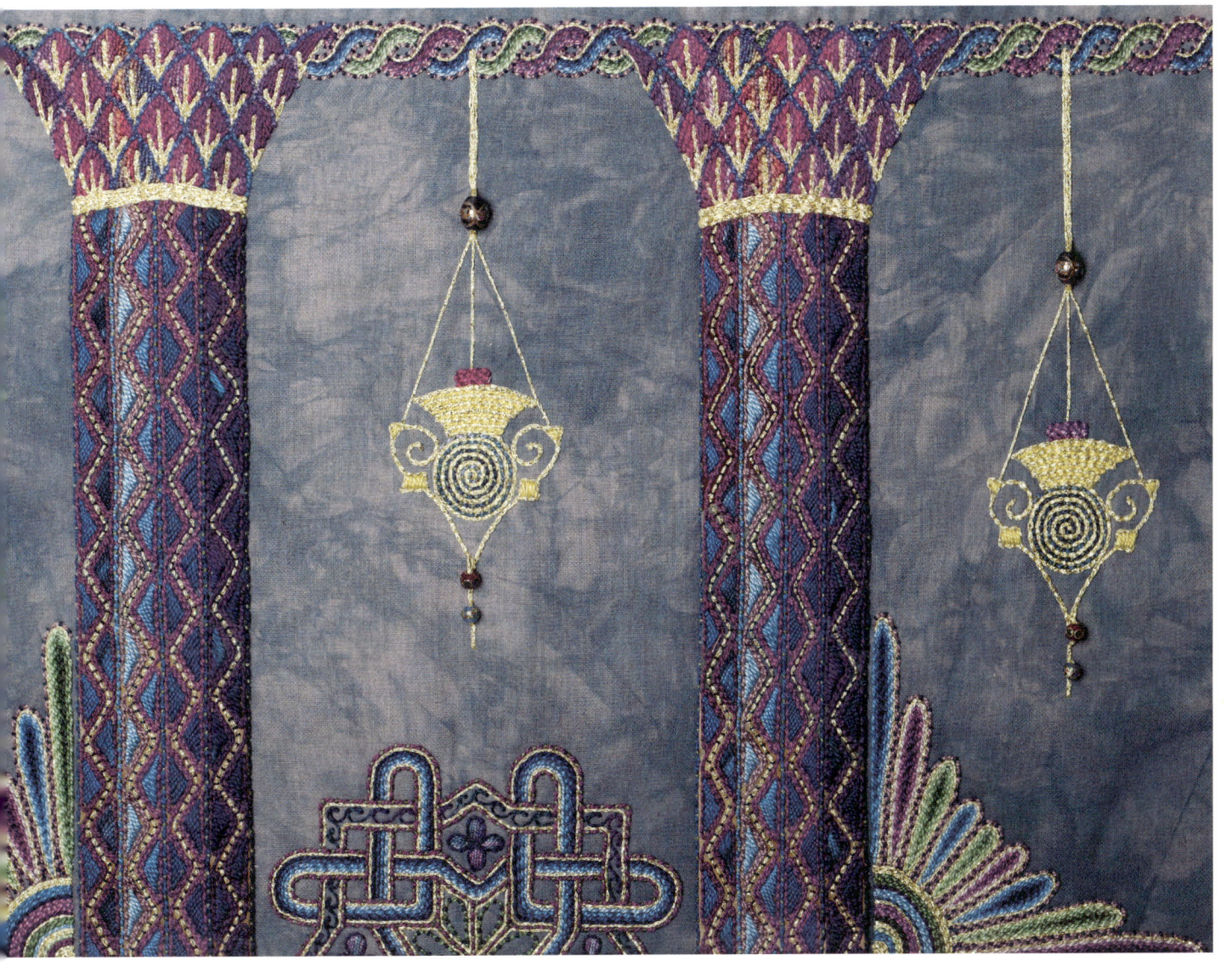

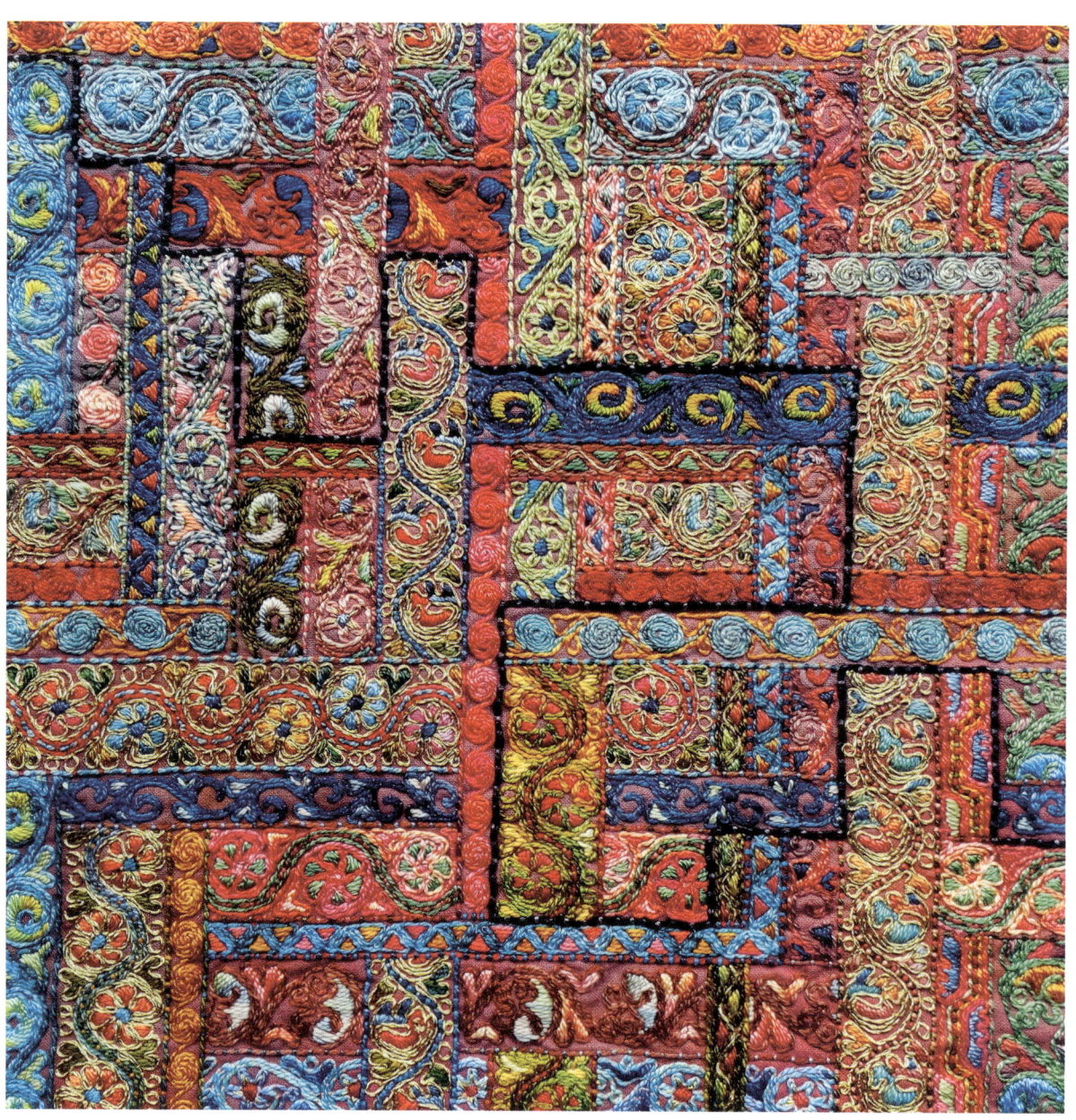

Deborah Mullins, *Border Crossing*, 2018. Hand-dyed threads and wire on hand-dyed fabric, 29 x 29 cm

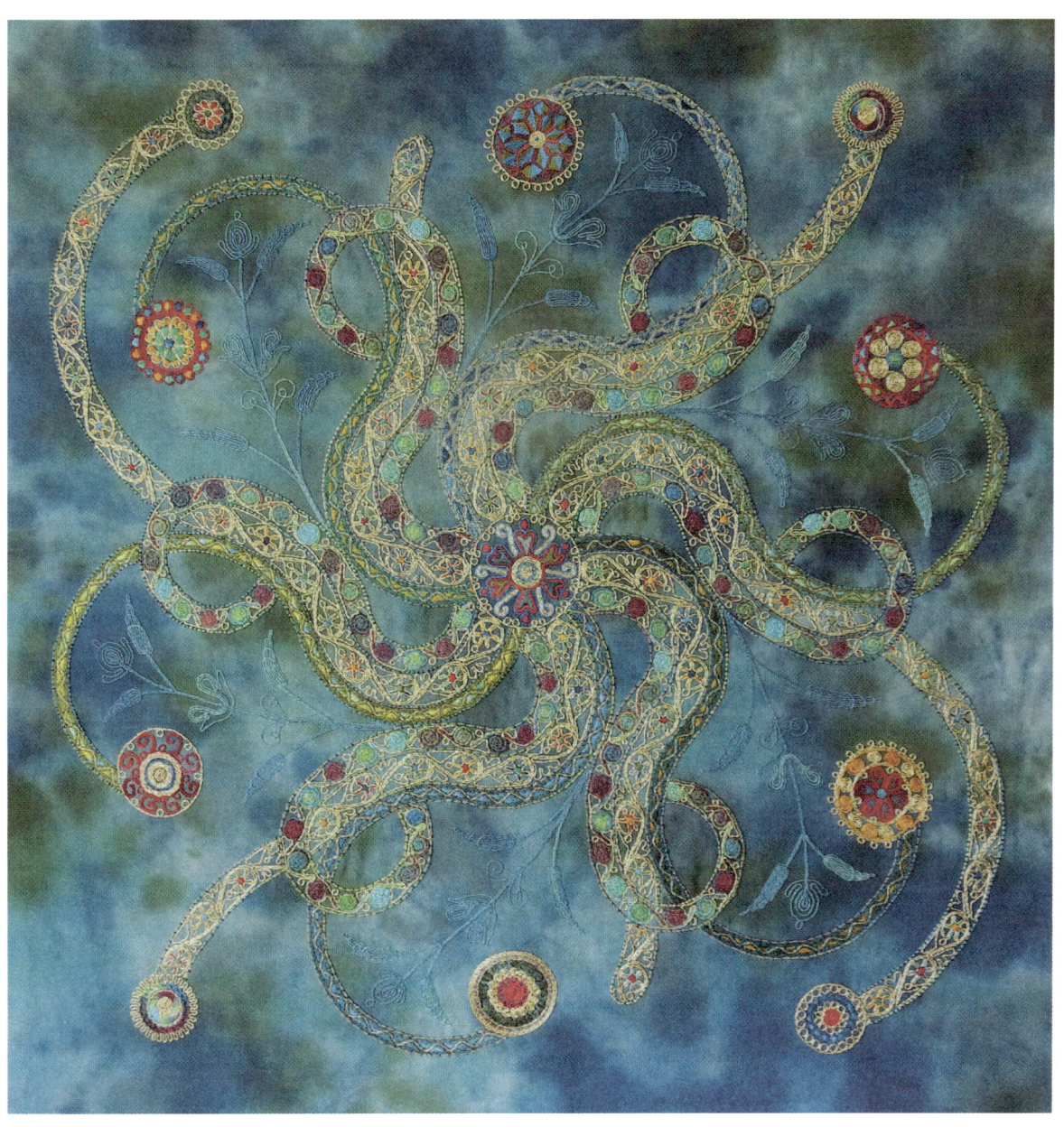

Deborah Mullins, *Talhami Fantasy*, 2020. Hand-dyed threads on hand-dyed fabric, 63 x 63 cm

LIANE AL GHUSAIN

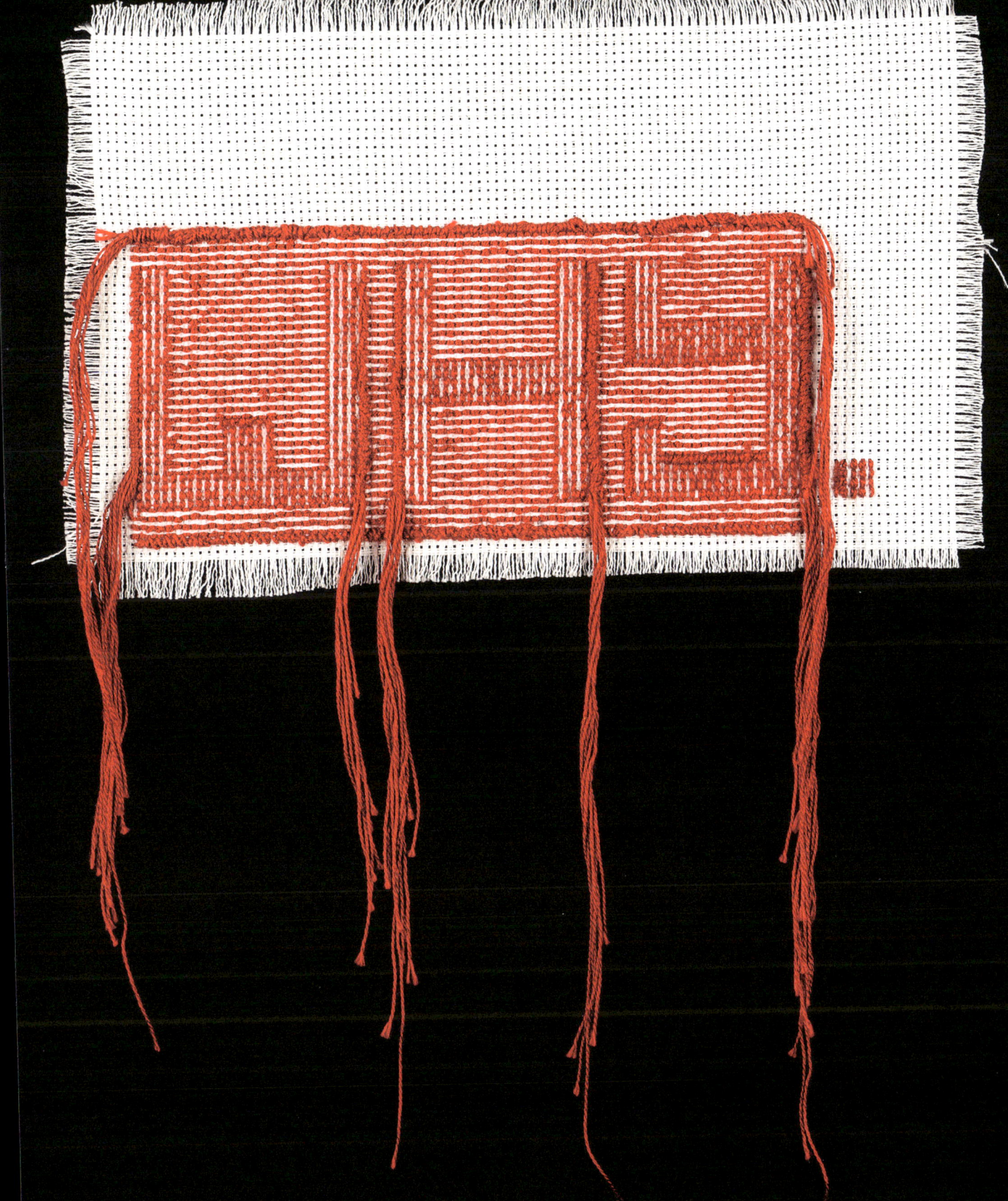

Liane Al Ghusain started to embroider in 2020 under curfews and lockdowns. She describes the feeling of familiarity with the practice of Palestinian embroidery: 'I had muscle memory for it, yet I had never done it before. My only explanation is mirror neurons, firing throughout a lifetime of watching my grandmother knit and stitch. In the corners of my childhood memories, she sits cross stitching tapestries and even upholstering entire armchairs in her own embroidery. As she hooks threads, she sees out of the corner of her eye the mere intention of a rowdy grandchild to make mischief, calling out before we even gained the speed it took to jump on a couch or bully a younger cousin. Somewhere in a house in Kuwait furnished exactly like a living room in Palestine, my developing brain is unconsciously watching, programming me with the patience for threading needles and counting stitches. Coding the craving for that particular exhilaration of flying through a row of diagonals, then crossing back only to do it again, stopping finally to read the raised X's like the most guttural braille.'

Al Ghusain was interested in how the women would examine the back of their embroidery to judge the embroiderer's skill. She discovered how some women would inspect the embroidery of their son's potential bride in this way, to determine whether she was a suitable candidate – since meticulous stitches reflected competence in taking care of her home.

Al Ghusain explains, 'The organisation of stitching serves as a metonym for one's capability to run a household. I observed that, if my cross stitches were pre-planned, I could make short, straight dashes on their reverse, as opposed to diagonal ones – this saves both time and thread, i.e., it is the most direct route between points A and B. I'm sure this was something to consider by Palestinian mothers-in-law, for imported cotton thread is expensive and hard to come by.'

Al Ghusain began to approach cross stitch as three-dimensional, viewed from the front and the back. To successfully articulate her concepts, she kept the work minimal, with fewer motifs and colours. *Why* (2021) is a two-sided embroidered work with cross stitches forming a red rectangle on the front of the fabric and straight stitches on the back revealing the word 'why'. Al Ghusain explains, 'Once I developed my *tatreez* skills, I realised that cross stitches manifested neat dashes on the back of the canvas when they were done uniformly. Then, I realised that I could control the direction the dashes would go, which meant I could hide secret messages at the back of my work. In an embroidery series titled بلا عقد, or *Without Issues*, I imagined my future mother-in-law would look at the back of my canvas and find a message there for her.' Her exploration of cross stitching to convey hidden messages and reflections of societal expectations illuminates the subtext in her work.

Another work created for her future mother-in-law is *Letter to Salwa* (2021), composed of wedding and fertility embroidery motifs such as the bridal comb and the pomegranate. The two birds facing each other references a story from Wafa Ghnaim's book *Tatreez and Tea: Embroidery and Storytelling in the Palestinian Diaspora* (2018), in which a woman has sent an unfinished embroidery to her friend with a bird facing inwards. If her friend stitches another bird facing inward, she knows that she is happy and sees eye-to-eye with her mother-in-law who lives with her. If she stitches a bird facing the other direction, it indicates that they are not getting along. With birds facing each other in this work, Al Ghusain sends a hopeful message to her future mother-in-law that she is looking forward to a harmonious relationship.

Al Ghusain is now married, but she completed *Why* and *Letter to Salwa* before having a mother-in-law to send stitched messages to, and made a *Letter to the Unborn* (2023) for her son, Rami, while still pregnant with him. On black-cotton, cross-stitch embroidery fabric, green stitches come together to form the question in Arabic, 'How Can We Blossom While Palestine Wilts?' This work came as a response after Israel's genocide of Palestinians in Gaza, which left Al Ghusain in a state of grief and anguish at the sight of thousands of slaughtered children shared on social media.

In *Sacred Compound* (2021), Al Ghusain improvised an abstracted, free-form cross stitch depicting a spiralling genesis or Big Bang. Zigzagging staircases lead to the focal point of an aerial view of the sacred compound housing Haram al-Sharif and Al Aqsa Mosque in Jerusalem with a repeated archway pattern. Al Ghusain also features Palestinian embroidery in her installation work. An example is *Practicing Devotion* (2022), in which a stitched textile piece accompanies a three-channel video installation. Inspired by Sufi devotional and healing practices that invoke the ninety-nine names of Allah in Arabic, Al Ghusain cross-stitched thirty names of Allah for the thirty days of Ramadan in black thread on pink cross-stitch fabric. Al Ghusain stitched 'NOTHING IS EVER LOST IN THE KNOWLEDGE OF GOD' in red English letters running up the side with the border.

Liane Al Ghusain's journey into the world of Palestinian embroidery is a profound exploration of heritage, identity and womanhood. She aims 'to integrate demanding, laborious practices rooted in identity and womanhood, and yet to speak the most developed, contemporary visual lexicon I possibly can while remaining true to my work'. Through her art, she seeks to connect with her legacy as a craftswoman while challenging traditional perceptions of embroidery by incorporating contemporary visual language. Her ability to weave personal and societal narratives into her work, and experiment with hidden messages in her embroidery, adds depth and complexity to her art.

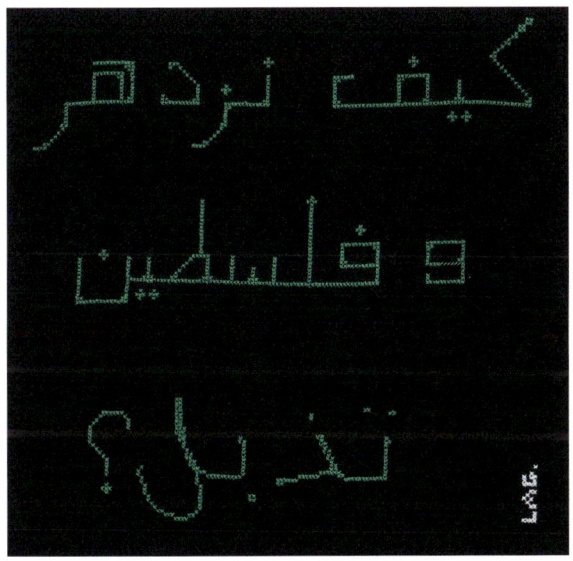

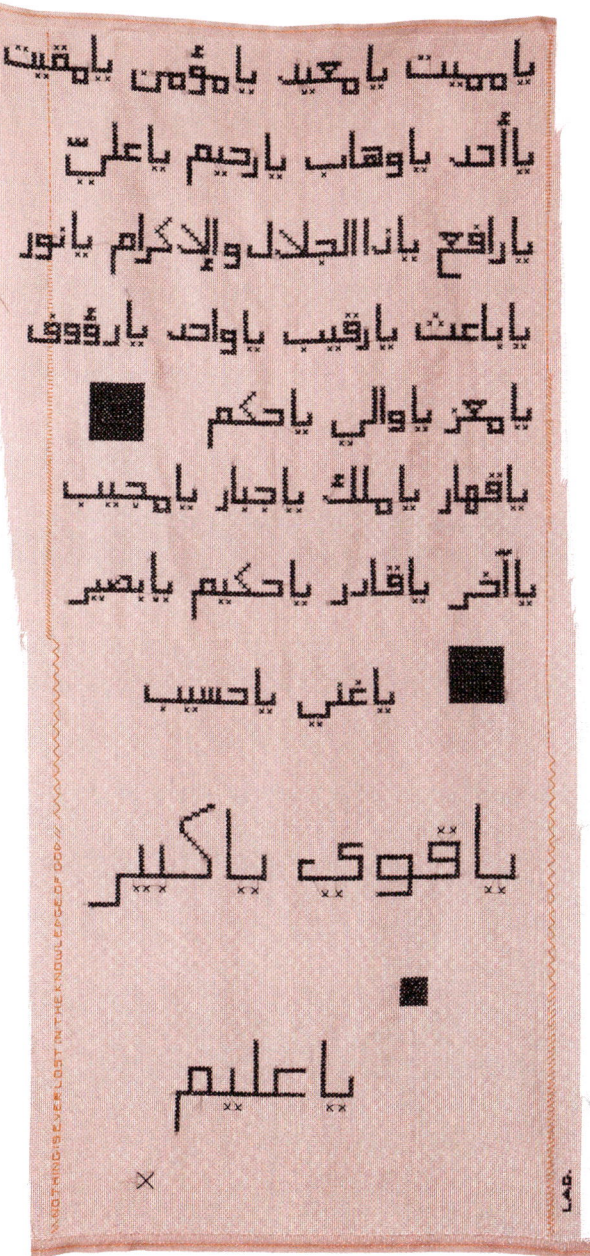

Liane Al Ghusain, *Practicing Devotion*, 2022.
Cotton thread on aida fabric

Left: Liane Al Ghusain, *Letter to the Unborn*, 2023.
Cotton thread on aida cotton fabric, 40 x 40 cm

Previous spread: Liane Al Ghusain, *Why*, 2021.
Cotton thread on aida cotton fabric

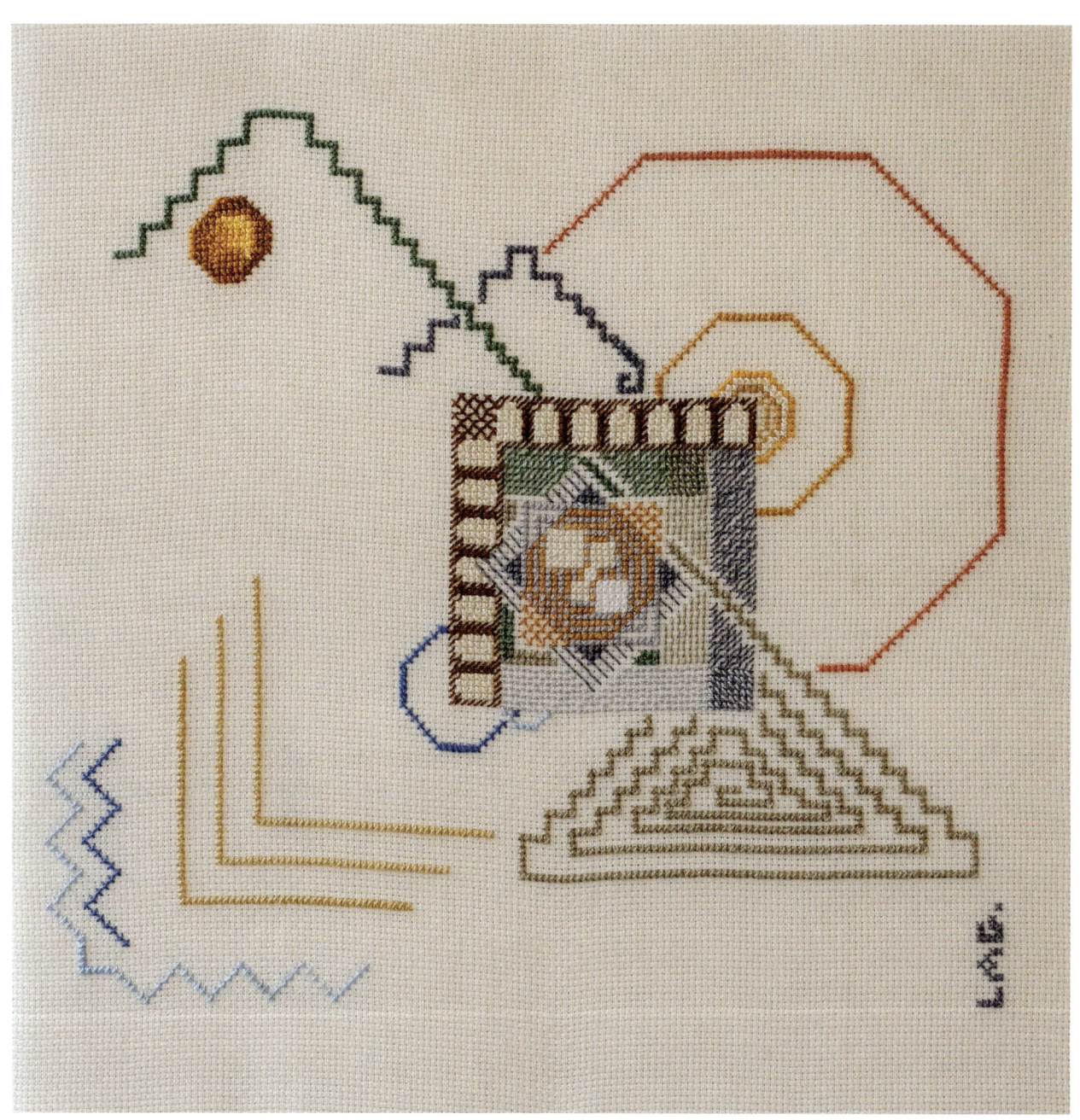

Liane Al Ghusain, *Sacred Compound*, 2021. Cotton thread on aida cotton fabric, 40 x 40 cm

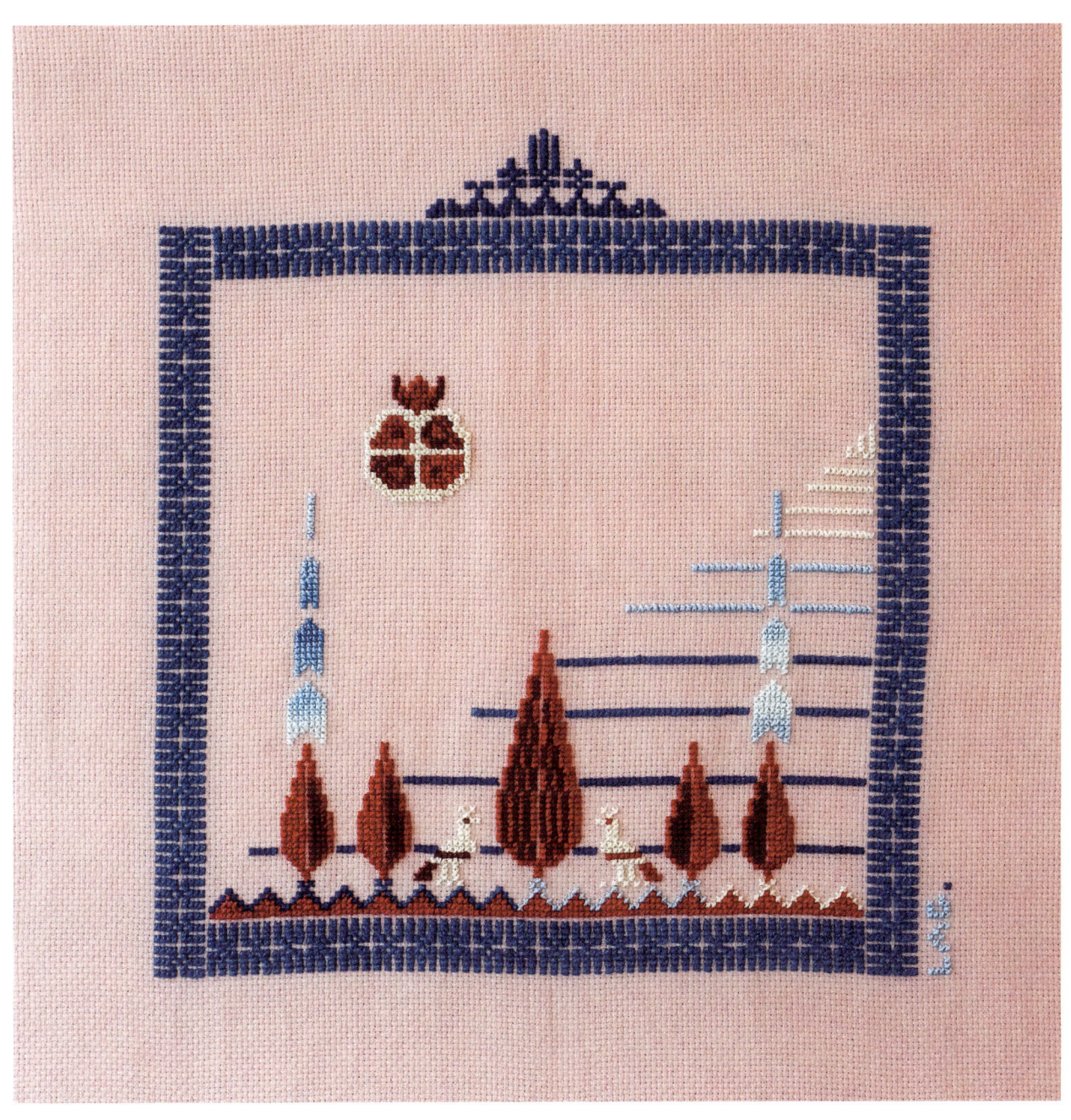

Liane Al Ghusain, *Letter to Salwa*, 2021. Cotton thread on aida cotton fabric, 40 x 40 cm

KIKI

SALEM

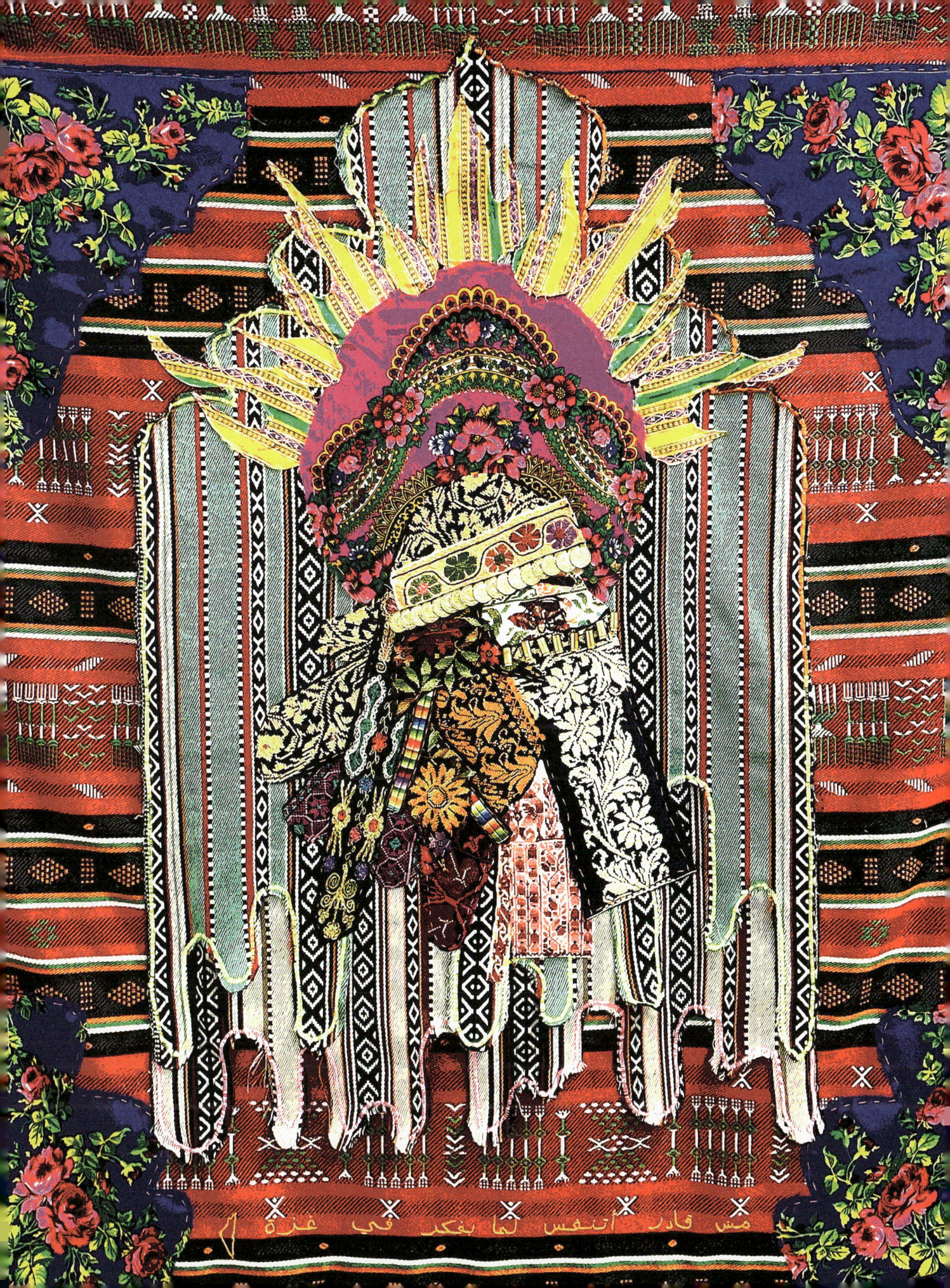

مش قادر اتنفس لما بفكر في غزة

Now living in St Louis, Missouri, Kiki Salem was born in Al-Bireh, Palestine, and spent her childhood in her family's home village of Beitin. From a young age, she would use art and craft to cope with living under Israeli military occupation. She recalls, 'I witnessed some traumatic events as a child at the hands of the Israeli army. I remember having trouble sleeping, and my mother bought me crayons, colouring books, and beads to make jewellery. I'm not sure if she knew at the time the impact that would have on me, especially with the beading, the repetitive minuscule actions that you get lost in during the process… This all leads to a highly rewarding product when completed, and is still very much prevalent in my practice.'

The more she understands the integral role played in Palestinian women's lives by Palestinian embroidery, the more she feels destined to be involved in the practice. 'There is an ancestral blueprint that was left behind by women before me,' she says. 'When I think about it, that is a gift, an inheritance. For a people who have had so much stolen, from land and property to culture and autonomy, this practice is our generational wealth, something that can never be taken from us even when our homeland is. I use elements of *tatreez* in my work as a form of resistance to the colonial powers that aim to annihilate us.'

Her work explores themes of escapism, experimental visual pattern development, linguistic hybridisation, Western cultural influence, Orientalism and the issues relating to Palestine. Salem uses a variety of mediums and disciplines in her murals, paintings and animations, focusing on textile and pattern making, including Palestinian embroidery. She remarks, 'More recently, I've begun distorting the *tatreez* patterns, mainly when I paint larger-than-life murals. The melting and distortion are a visual metaphor for the experience I have in the diaspora, where so much of our identity is being stripped from us the longer we stay away from home, making us unrecognisable to ourselves and our people who have stayed in the homeland.' By merging tradition with innovation, Salem's artwork and murals in Palestine and across the United States transcend borders.

Her Palestinian and Brazilian grandmothers were talented textile artists and dressmakers. Her Palestinian grandmother, Fatima, wore traditional Palestinian embroidered dresses daily, practised embroidery for decades and created embroidered work highly sought after by other Palestinian women. Despite growing up surrounded by embroidered dresses, Salem was not interested in having one until she reached adulthood; she now buys them second-hand. When she was ten years old, she was first captivated by the practice of Palestinian embroidery when she saw her aunt, Najwa, stitching in Beitin. It was Salem's aunt Najwa who taught her the fundamentals of cross stitch.

Salem started incorporating Palestinian embroidery motifs in her work while attending the School of the Art Institute of Chicago. When speaking of her love of geometric patterns and tessellation, she reveals, 'I've always been bad at paying attention in sterile classroom environments, so instead of taking notes I would doodle in my notebooks. I remember starting to draw patterns and decided to pick up some embroidery supplies. I would look at and recreate *tatreez* patterns during lectures and found that it helped me focus better. Anything noteworthy the professor would say, I'd jot down and keep embroidering. I became obsessed with the patterns and started applying the motifs to my projects in my studio courses as well. I would print them massively onto fabric, code them into a weaving structure, or animate them on the computer. Every time I'd finish a project that had *tatreez* involved in it, I'd find more and more that it made sense to continue the practice that is my birthright.'

This was at the time before Palestinian embroidery gained popularity on social media and before internet resources were made available worldwide. She says, 'I didn't know how many people from younger generations were paying attention to our indigenous textiles. I felt a strong sense of duty to preserve our culture and history, as it's constantly being stolen and erased. Over time, I began developing new means of using the patterns beyond embroidery, effectively advancing our culture beyond 1948, where everything feels like it has stopped and held its breath.'

Her research on Palestinian embroidery is primarily visual. In Palestine in 2022, she visited elders from her family in their homes and asked to see their embroidered dresses, where she photographed the patterns. She also spent time with seamstresses and embroiderers, observing their techniques. She found books on Palestinian embroidery at the Ramallah Library and in fabric and haberdashery shops. In the US, Salem conducted most of her research online. She also read books by Wafa Ghnaim, which provided Salem with the historical context of the connection between the practice and the land.

Salem describes extracting patterns directly from the embroidered dress in person or from a photograph. She says, 'From there I will draw it, either in a gridded notebook or on the iPad. I use Procreate for most of my digital works. I find it easier to play around with the colours on that app. Colour is such an important part of my work. As much as I love the traditional colours used in *tatreez*, I feel with the technology and resources available, I can push the boundaries of the practice through colour and distortion.'

Salem's deep connection to Palestinian embroidery, and her dedication to preserving and evolving the practice, reflects her passion for and commitment to her cultural heritage. Salem wishes the viewer to keep an open heart and mind when taking in her work, knowing how it can provoke joy or sadness depending on who is looking at it. When discussing her work, she explains that, 'It all comes from a place where love and rage have sat hand in hand within me for the majority of my life. As far as conversations go, I always want people to talk about Palestine, talk about our struggle, ride for our resistance movement, and help us work towards our liberation and, more broadly, the liberation of the Global South and its diaspora. If my work can be a catalyst for those conversations and hopefully actions, that is the ultimate goal.' Through her artwork, murals and creative explorations with Palestinian embroidery, Salem pays homage to the ancestral legacy of Palestinian women and uses it as a form of resistance against the erasure of her people's identity.

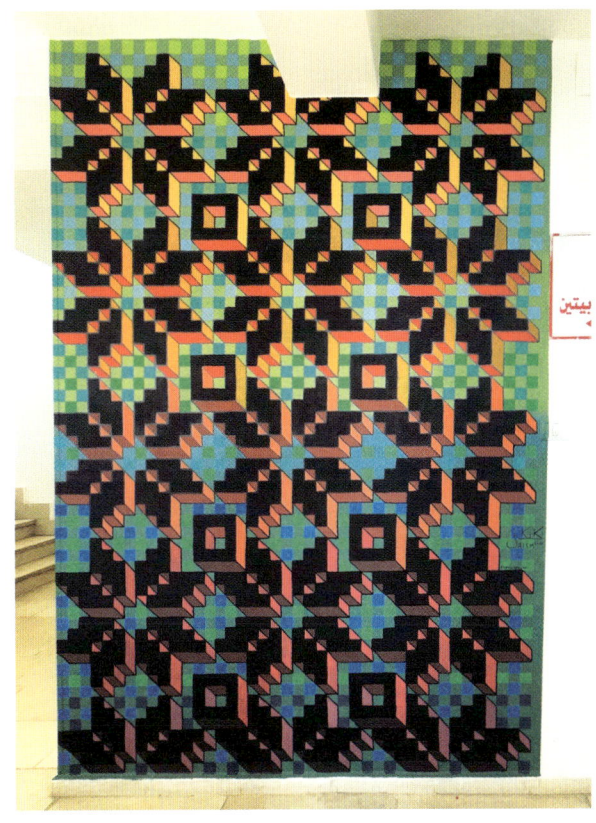

Kiki Salem, *Tatreez Mural*, 2022. Beitin, Palestine. Wall paint and aerosol spray paint, 3.3 x 5.1 m

Previous spread: Kiki Salem, *I Can't Breathe When I Think of Gaza*, 2024. Mixed textile, brass coins, 9-mm brass bullet shells, tassel trimming; and hand-embroidered *tatreez* scraps donated by Rania 'Um Fouad' Hamed, a seamstress in Beitin, Palestine, 142.2 x 114.3 cm

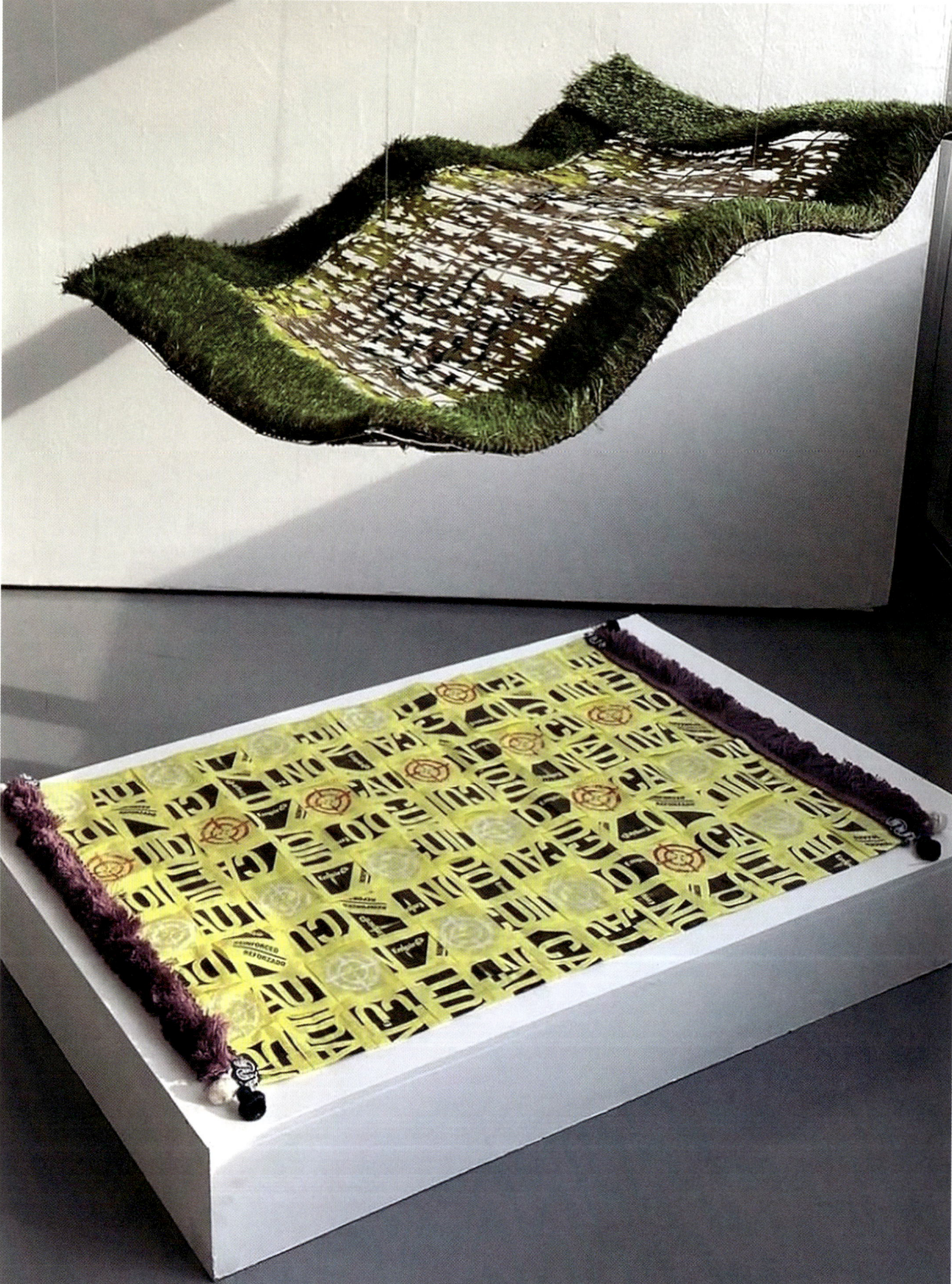

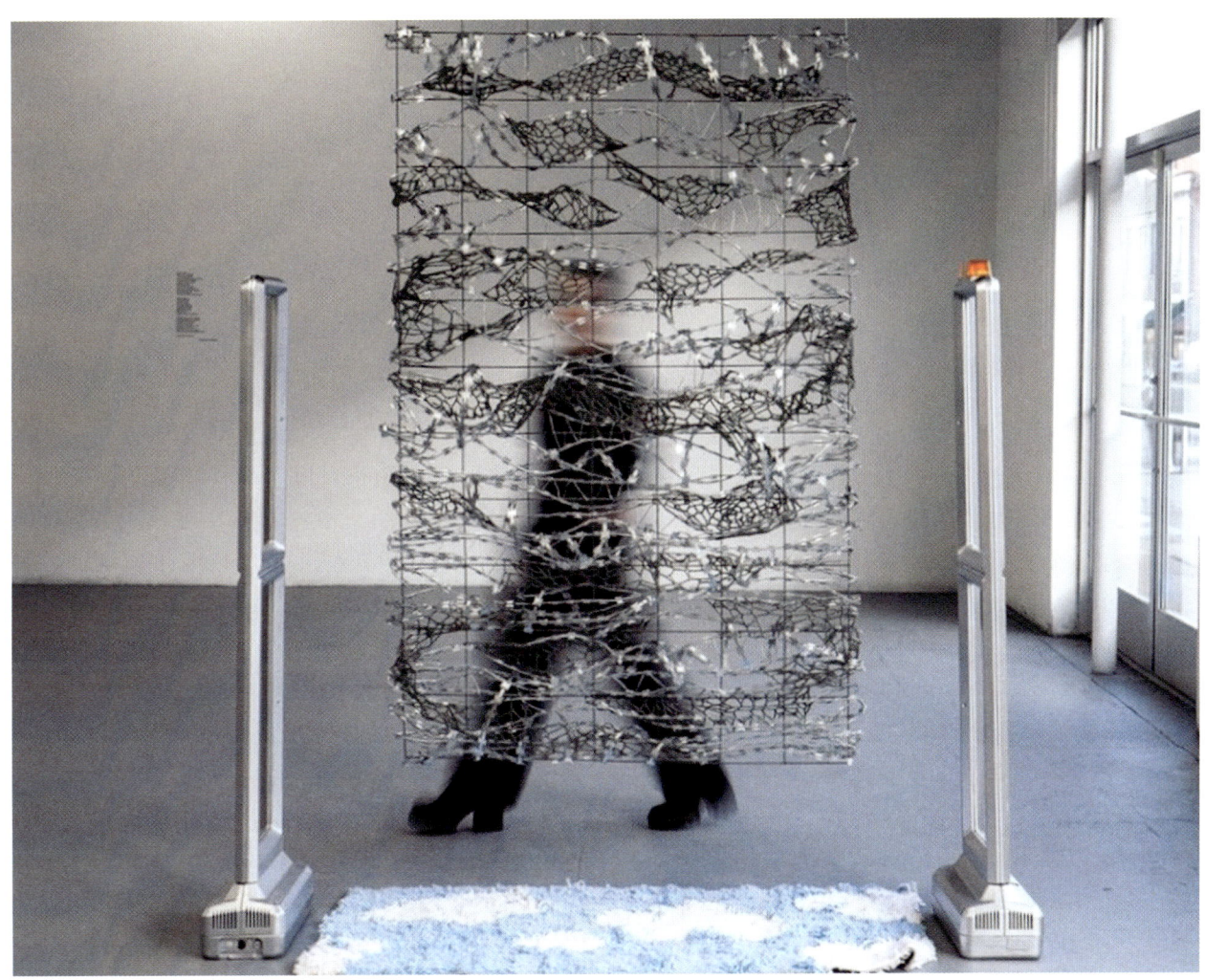

Kiki Salem, *The Silver Lining We Don't Need*, 2020. Razor wire, steel, mixed fibre and metal detector, 1.2 x 2.7 m. Photo by Virginia Harrold

Left: Kiki Salem, اذكر الله, *Remember God*, 2022. Razor wire, synthetic turf and aerosol spray paint, 76.2 x 121.9 cm
They Watch Where We Pray, 2022. Caution tape, ink and tassel trimming, 76.2 x 121.9 cm, installation exhibited in the Cincinnati Art Museum, Ohio

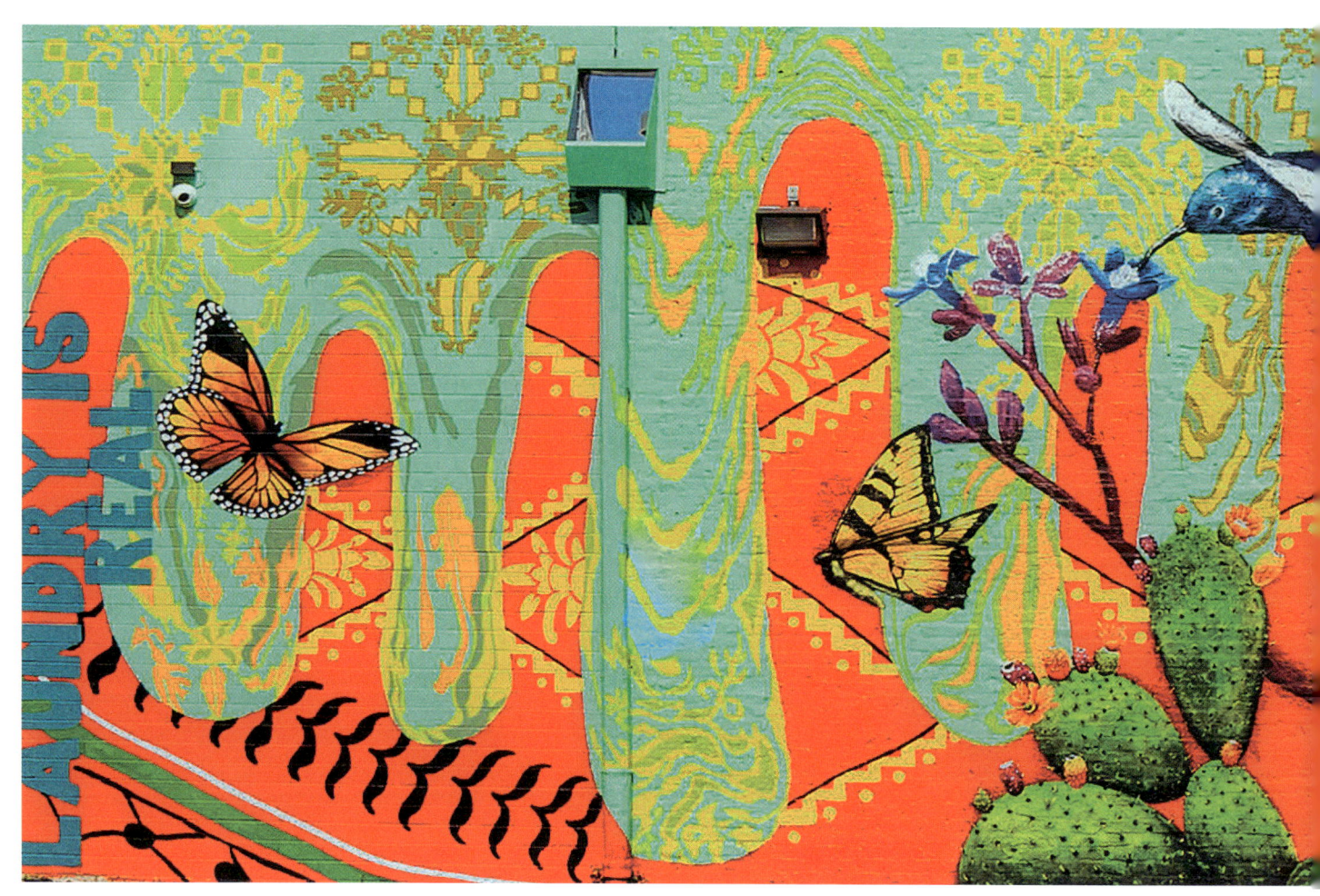

Kiki Salem, *A Palestinian and a Mexican Get Together and F*ck Up a Wall*, 2024. Wall paint and aerosol spray paint, Chicago, Illinois. 14.6 x 4.8 m. Made in collaboration with Mario Mena. Photo by Pedro Ramirez

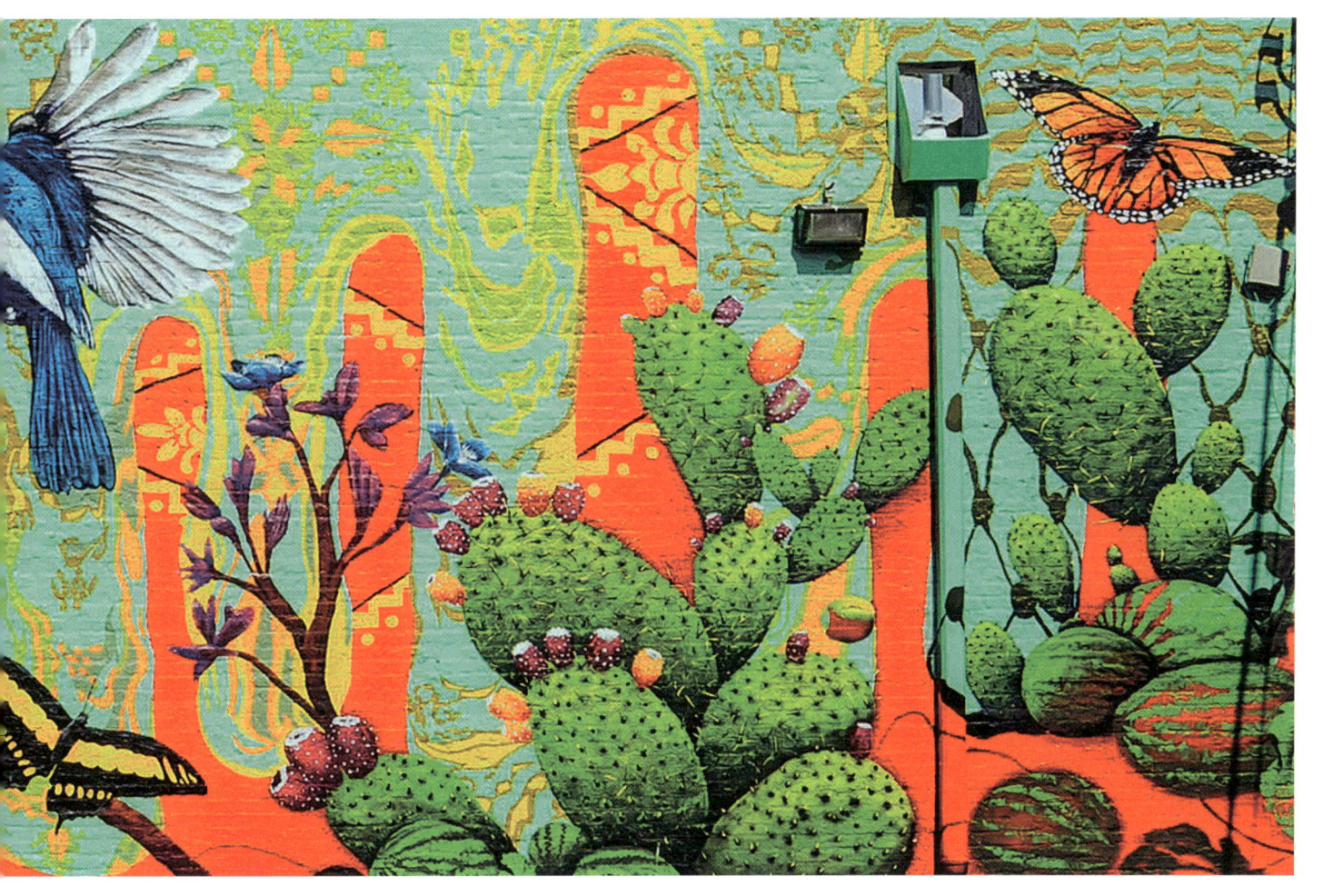

MONTHER JAWABREH

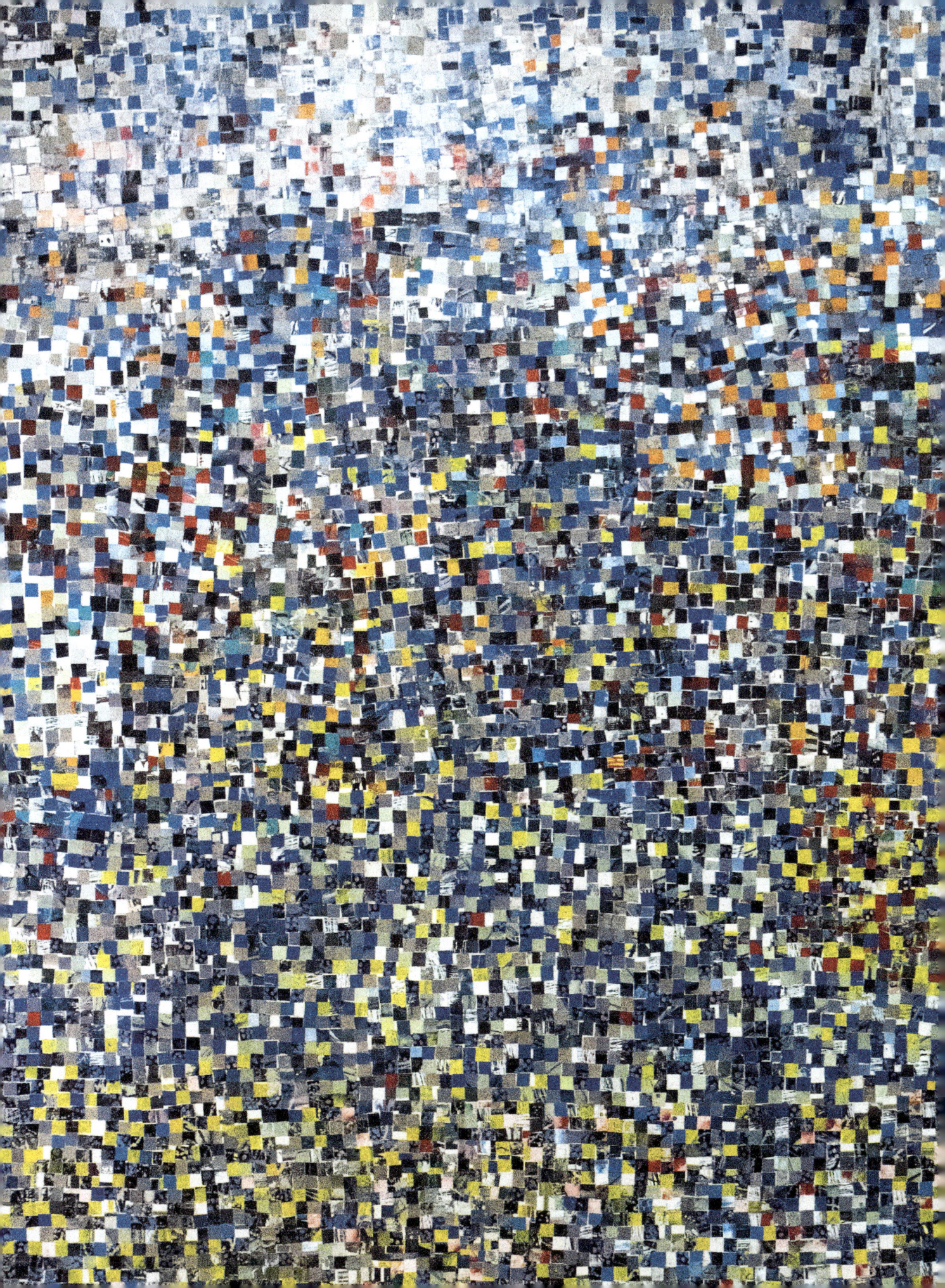

In his artwork, Monther Jawabreh explores various concepts and processes that revolve around memory, place and time. He explains how he 'deconstructs these concepts through the material, re-exploring them and their ability to adapt and captivate, linking this to the Arte Povera style and its philosophy of reusing raw materials liberated from notions of dominance and subjugation, and resisting commodification in the bourgeois sense'.

Jawabreh's work involves time-consuming, repetitive labour that echoes the time and effort required to create a Palestinian embroidered dress. Jawabreh is inspired by and incorporates Palestinian embroidery in his mixed-media artwork, installations, and community projects to decolonise the Palestinian narrative through the arts. He has demonstrated this in his embroidered *The Last Image* series, *Elevation* installation, mixed-media works, community street art initiatives and the *Edge*, where he took apart and reconstructed original work.

Jawabreh's *The Last Image* series consists of portraits of Palestinians killed by Israel's incessant bombardment and tank shelling of Gaza between 7 July and 26 August 2014. Israel killed 2,251 Palestinian men, women and children, leaving 11,231 people wounded and 100,000 unhoused and internally displaced. In this series, Jawabreh experimented with multiple embroidery techniques and elements of printing and weaving. His 2017 *Elevation* installation exhibited in Tunisia explored the theme of repetitive physical exertion, as in the embroidery process, where he replaces thread with twisted metal wire. With over 10,000 handmade pieces, Jawabreh's process echoes the redundant and time-consuming nature of life under Israel's military occupation of Palestine, while showing appreciation for the slow nature of Palestinian embroidery and weaving.

Jawabreh works to reincorporate elements of Palestinian embroidery into aspects of modern-day Palestinian life through community-based art initiatives. Jawabreh comments, 'The motivation behind this was to reinspire the embroidery's legacy and to retain its cultural significance while actively combatting colonial, capitalist and Zionist influences on contemporary Palestinian life.' Jawabreh, a lecturer at the Palestine Technical University

and Dar al-Kalima University College of Arts and Culture, undertook his largest community project taking designs inspired by Palestinian embroidery and printing them on the walls and doors in Qatanna in Jerusalem, Beit Sahour in Bethlehem and the Palestine Technical University in Al-Aroub.

In 2018, with Elbirou Gallery and support from the A. M. Qattan Foundation, Jawabreh also decorated village neighbourhoods in Sousse, Tunisia, with designs inspired by Palestinian embroidery. He describes this project as 'the interpretation of Palestinian embroidery as a humanitarian, historical and patriotic representation of Palestinian identity, especially given the loss of the human touch as we witness pervasive technological advancement and the invasion of external commercial industry. I'm bringing back this legacy, making it present in our daily lives and using it to uplift its cultural and aesthetic role by bringing it into designs on home murals and the doors of commercial shops.'

He is responding to 'the loss of an integral part of our identity with the coloniser's settlement architecture impacting Palestinian architecture, and how its blatant capitalist identity has destroyed the history and value of these places, disregarding the rules of the environment, as if it were dropped down onto us from somewhere else.' He adds, 'This theme was a matter of interest to the press, institutions, and most importantly, the local community who initiated the participation and interaction in this activity with their collaboration and transferring it to their homes.' He hopes the project will bring joy to local communities and draw domestic tourism to these areas while preserving Palestinian heritage and history.

When Jawabreh discusses the anticolonial nature of his work, he parallels the Palestinian struggle with that of Indigenous peoples worldwide. Jawabreh comments, 'Today, Palestinian embroidery is considered a political line of defence when confronting the Zionist narrative.' He applies this same conceptual framework to its inclusion in his artwork. In discussing the similarities of preserving heritage by Indigenous populations subjected to ethnic cleansing, Jawabreh notes that 'The use of embroidery in the Palestinian counternarrative correlates with Indigenous

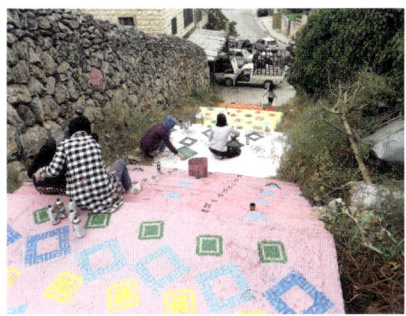 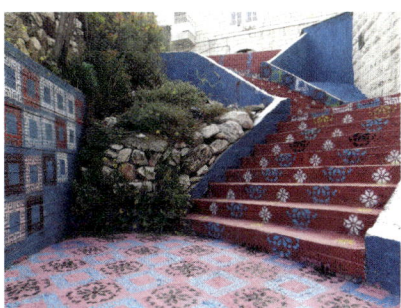 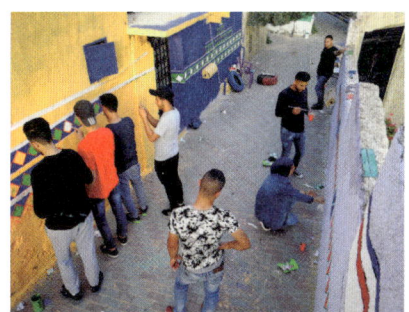

history in America, Canada and Australia, and how they have used their indigenous textiles and handicrafts as a continuing testament to their identity and existence in the face of extermination.' Palestinian embroidery also stands as a testament to Palestinian indigeneity and the existence of the people and their rich culture, refuting the Zionist national rhetoric and mythology.

The comparison to Indigenous peoples in America can also extend to land stewardship, as the embroidered dress worn by rural women in Palestine documented the deep connection to the land and agricultural society. Jawabreh states, 'Even now, Palestinian embroidery has played an active role in resistance and resilience.'

In Jawabreh's *Edge* series (2019), he deliberately tore apart his original paintings created and exhibited between 2005 and 2018. They include paintings from *The Last Image* series and *Fractured Time* series. He states that, after a period of reflection, he 'decided to rebuild these works, liberating them from the emotional and temporal dominance of their original production time, allowing the work itself to build its identity through contemporary methods. This transformed the pieces into historical autobiographies within themselves.'

In the two-part project, exhibited in 2019, Jawabreh first deconstructed and then reassembled installations, merging two works into one or incorporating two or three works into a single artwork. A one-metre by one-metre piece took him over eighty hours to create. Jawabreh revisits the process of weaving in 2019 in his *On Progress* series and again in 2021 in his *Prologue* series. The

destruction of a decade's worth of his original artwork and the rebuilding that occurs by weaving them into new works can be viewed as signalling the destruction and dismantling of oppressive colonial systems and the creative potentiality of rebuilding and redesigning them into something new. Despite being imperceptible, the old stories are still present in their integration in the new artwork's configuration.

Jawabreh says that he views his method of working as bringing us closer to the idea of embroidery and its creation, its reasons and methods, its relationship with place and people and how it has managed to shape the identity of peoples and nations. Through his process and artwork, he draws attention to the importance of culture and heritage while centring the conversation on time and material, inviting the experience of the present moment.

Community art initiatives bringing Palestinian embroidery into public spaces in Palestine. Photo taken in Al-Doha in Bethlehem, Palestine, with Dar al-Kalima students. 2018

Community art initiatives to bring Palestinian embroidery into public spaces in Palestine. Photo taken in Bethlehem, with Marsam 301 and Dar al-Kalima University students' spaces. 2018

Community art initiatives to bring Palestinian embroidery into public spaces in Qattana and Ramallah in Palestine, with support from A. M. Qattan Foundation. 2018

Previous spread: Monther Jawabreh, *Edge* series, 2019. Cut acrylic paintings reassembled on canvas, 200 x 200 cm

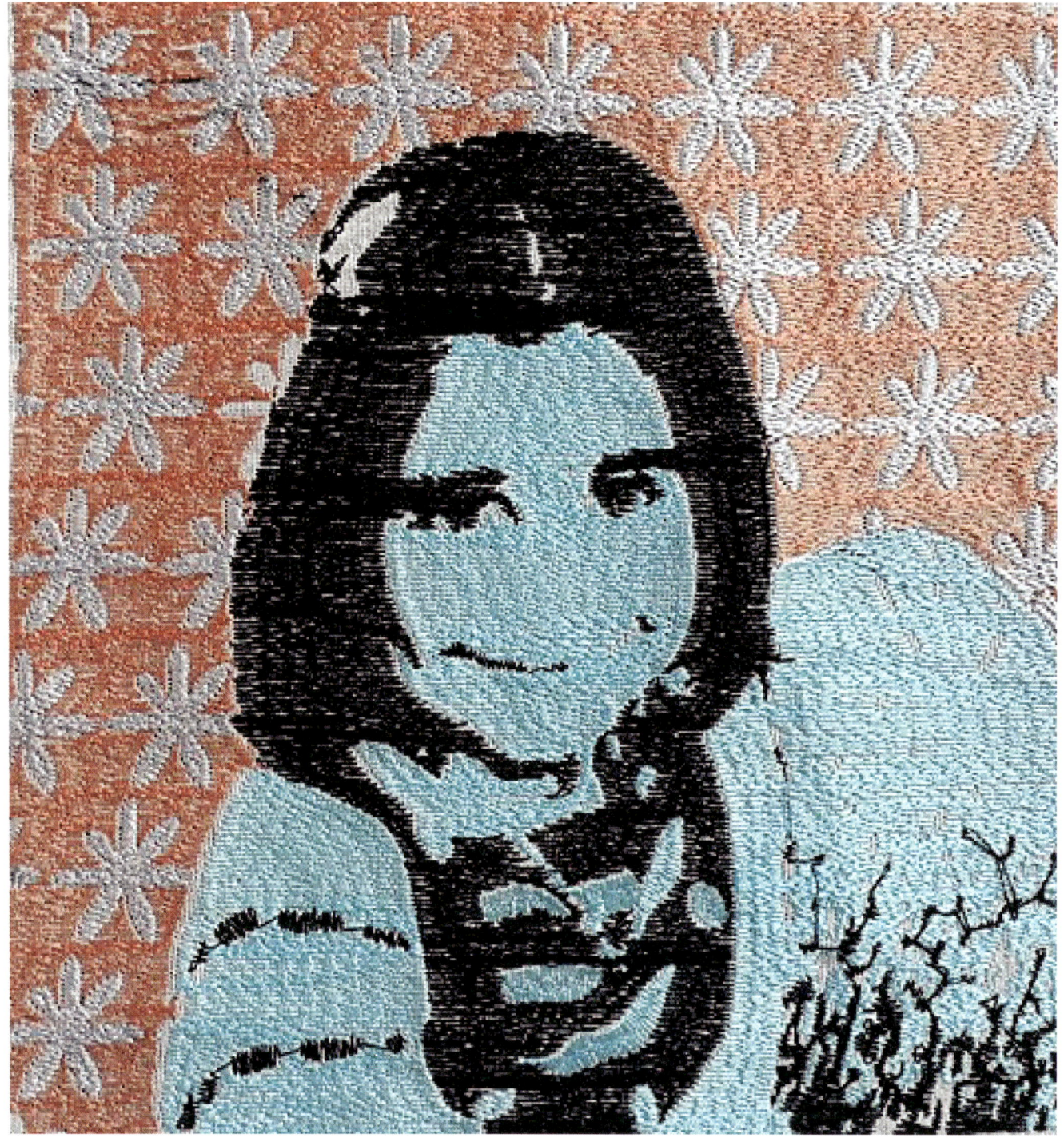

Monther Jawabreh, *The Last Image*; *What is Known exhibition*, 2015. Embroidery on canvas, 20 x 20 cm

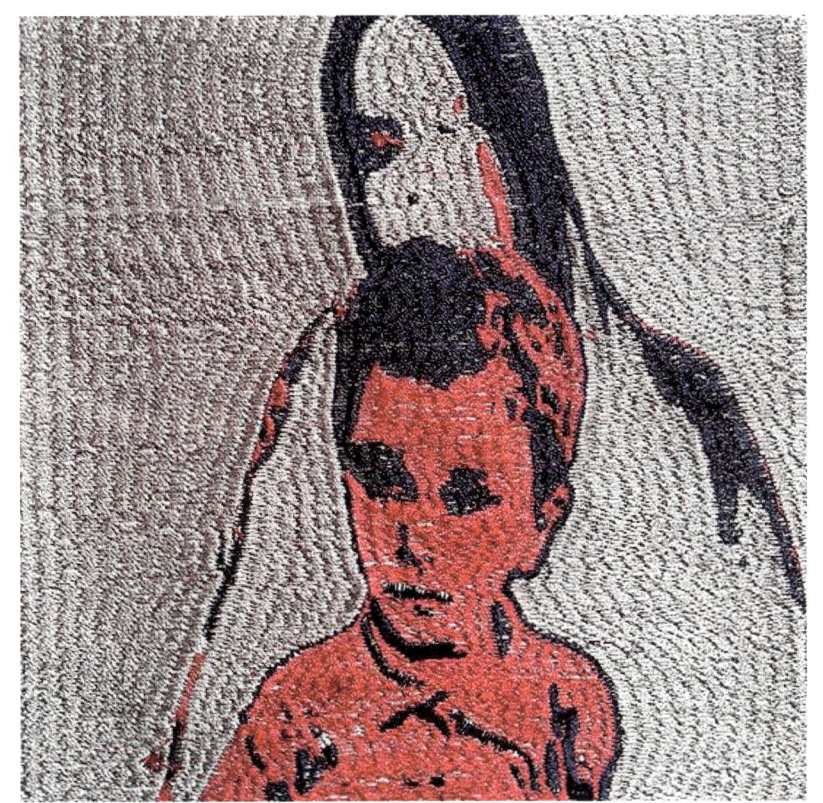

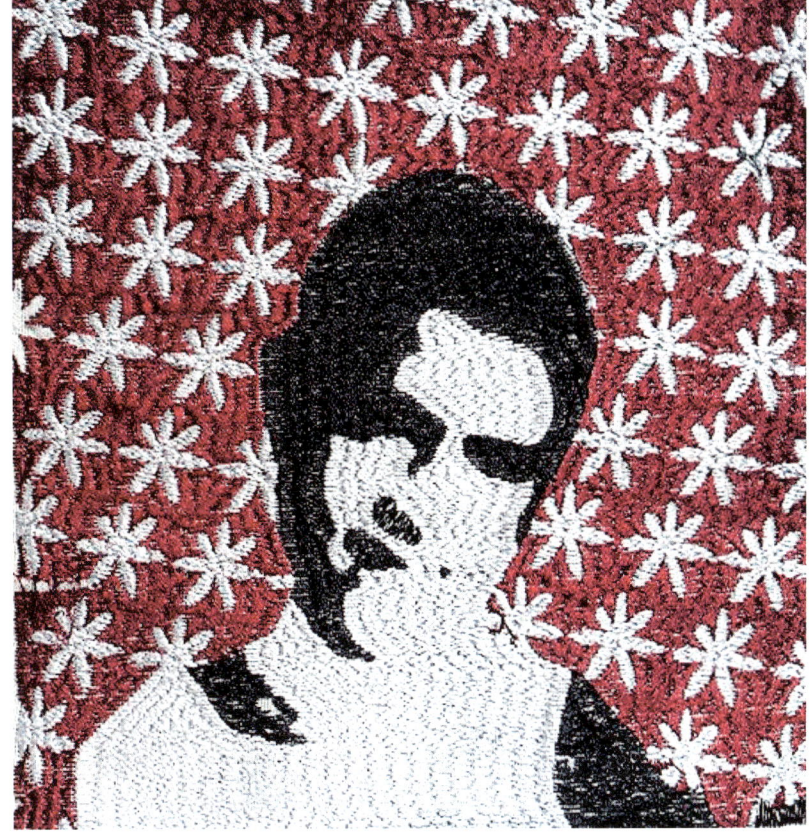

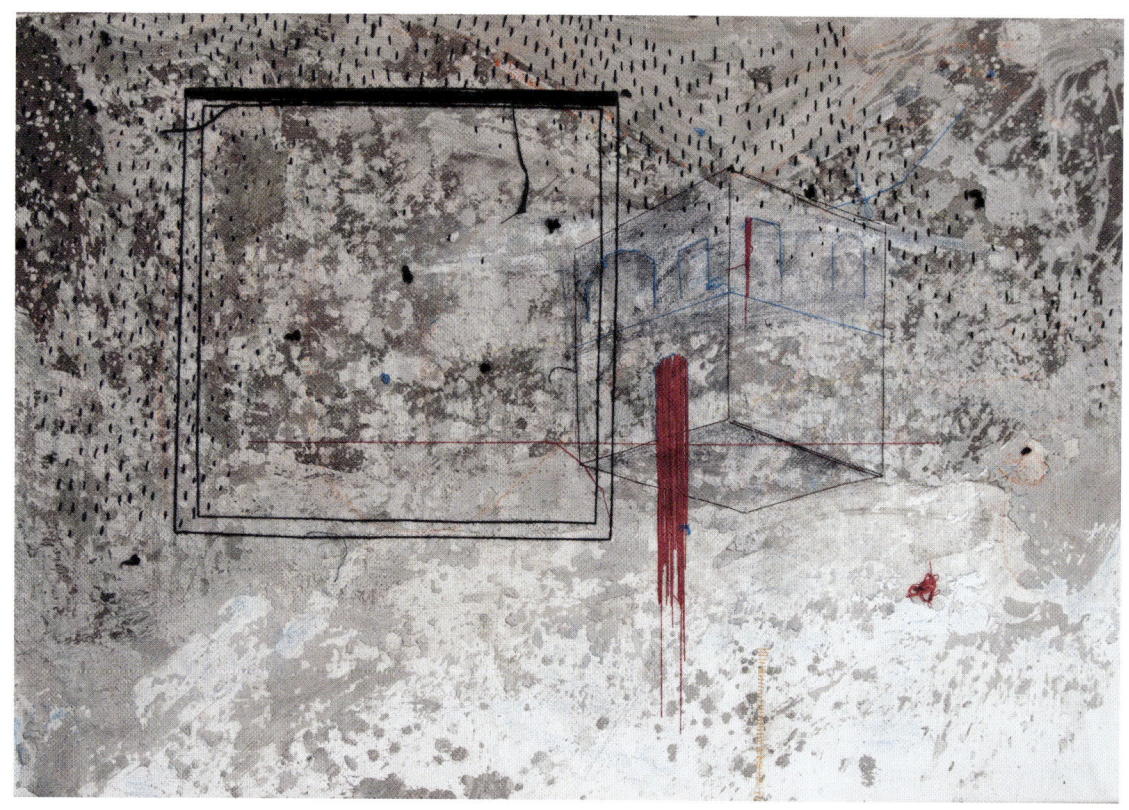

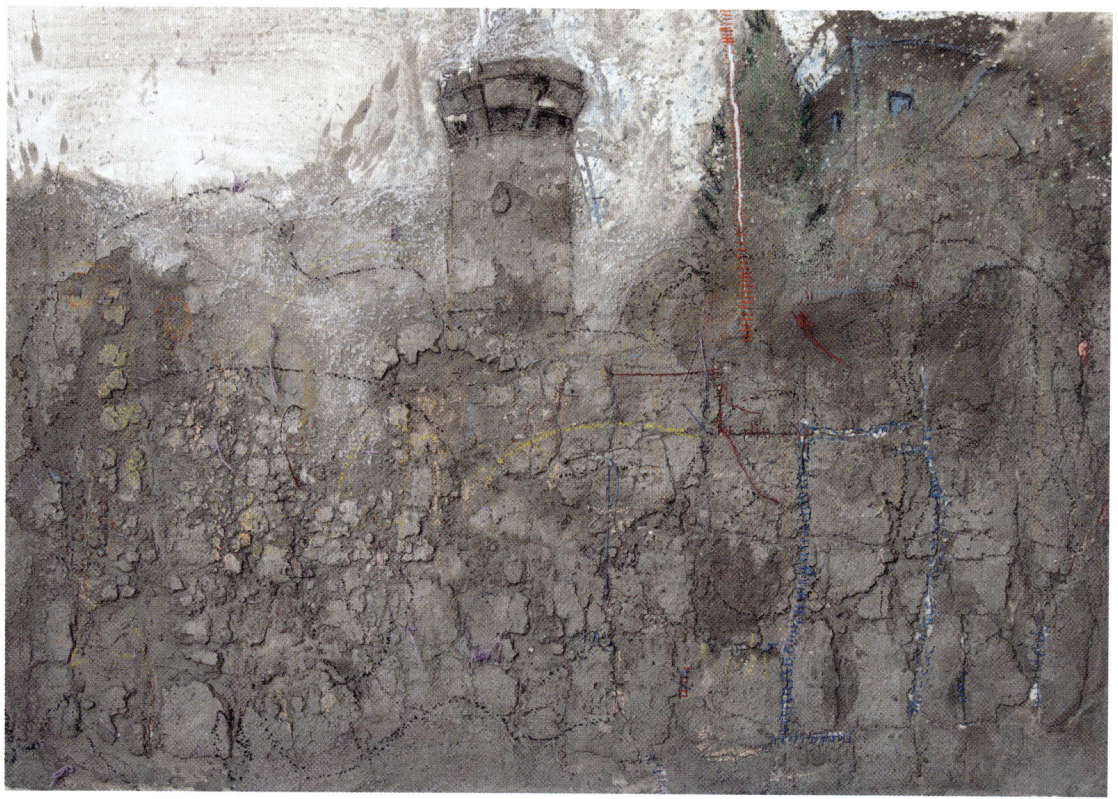

Monther Jawabreh, *The House Flies*, 2022. Flexible and fixed cement, thread and mixed media on canvas, 114.5 x 77 cm
Monther Jawabreh, *Untitled*, 2022. Flexible and fixed cement, thread and mixed media on canvas, 114.5 x 77.5 cm

Right: Monther Jawabreh, *Fractured Time*, 2016. Embroidery on canvas, 60 x 60 cm

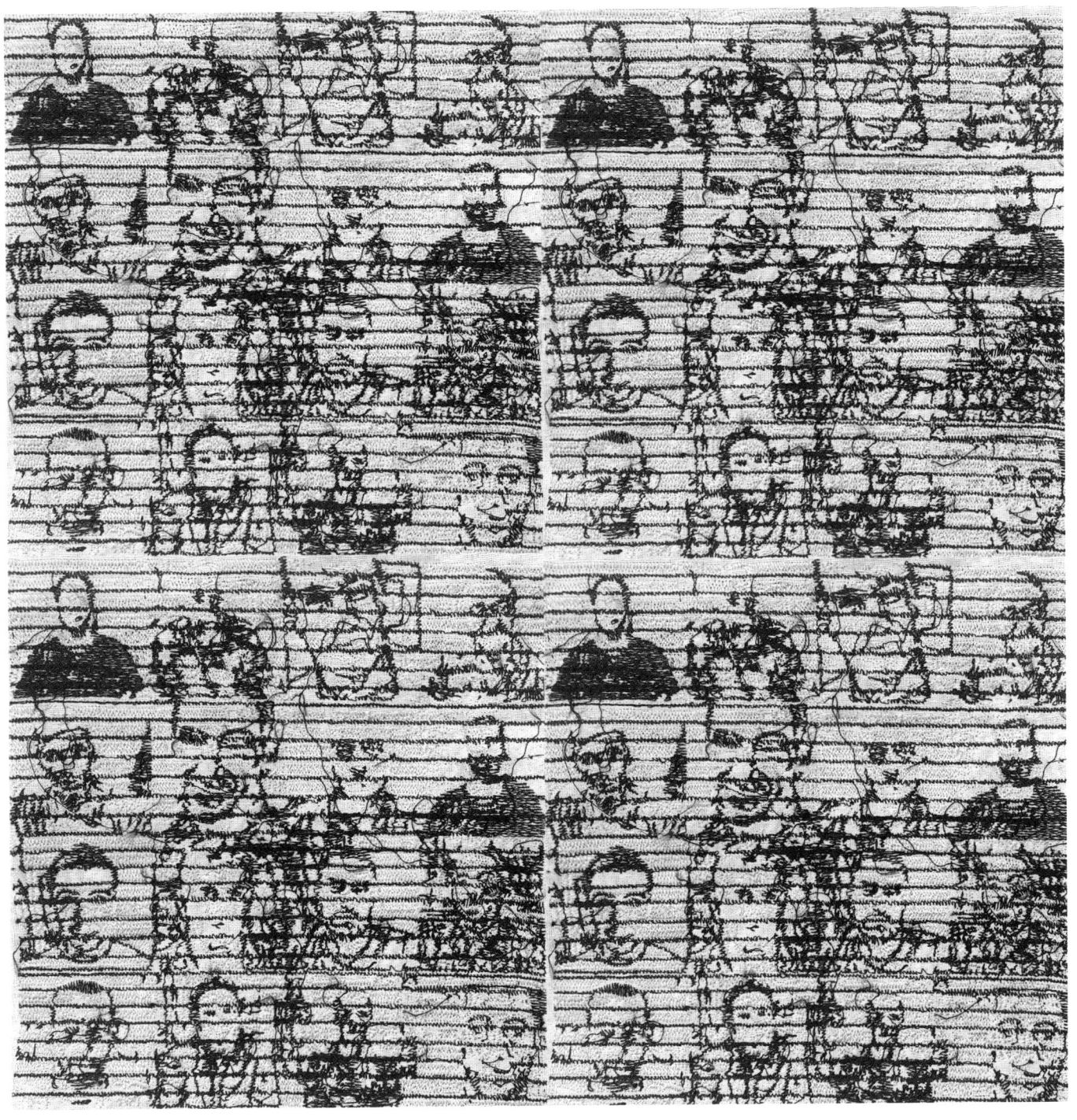

Monther Jawabreh, *Fractured Time 6*, 2015. Acrylic and wool on canvas, 155 x 121 cm

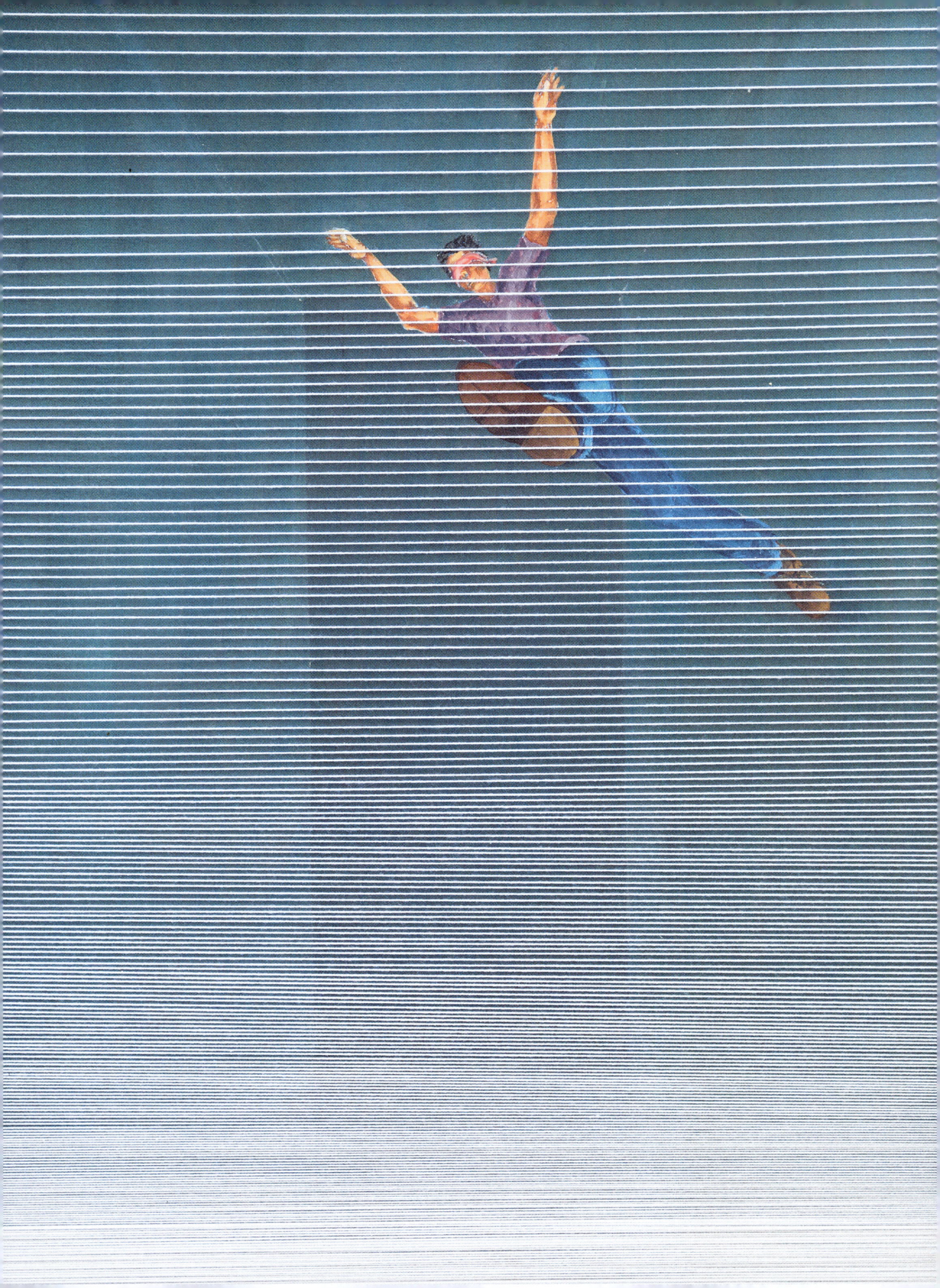

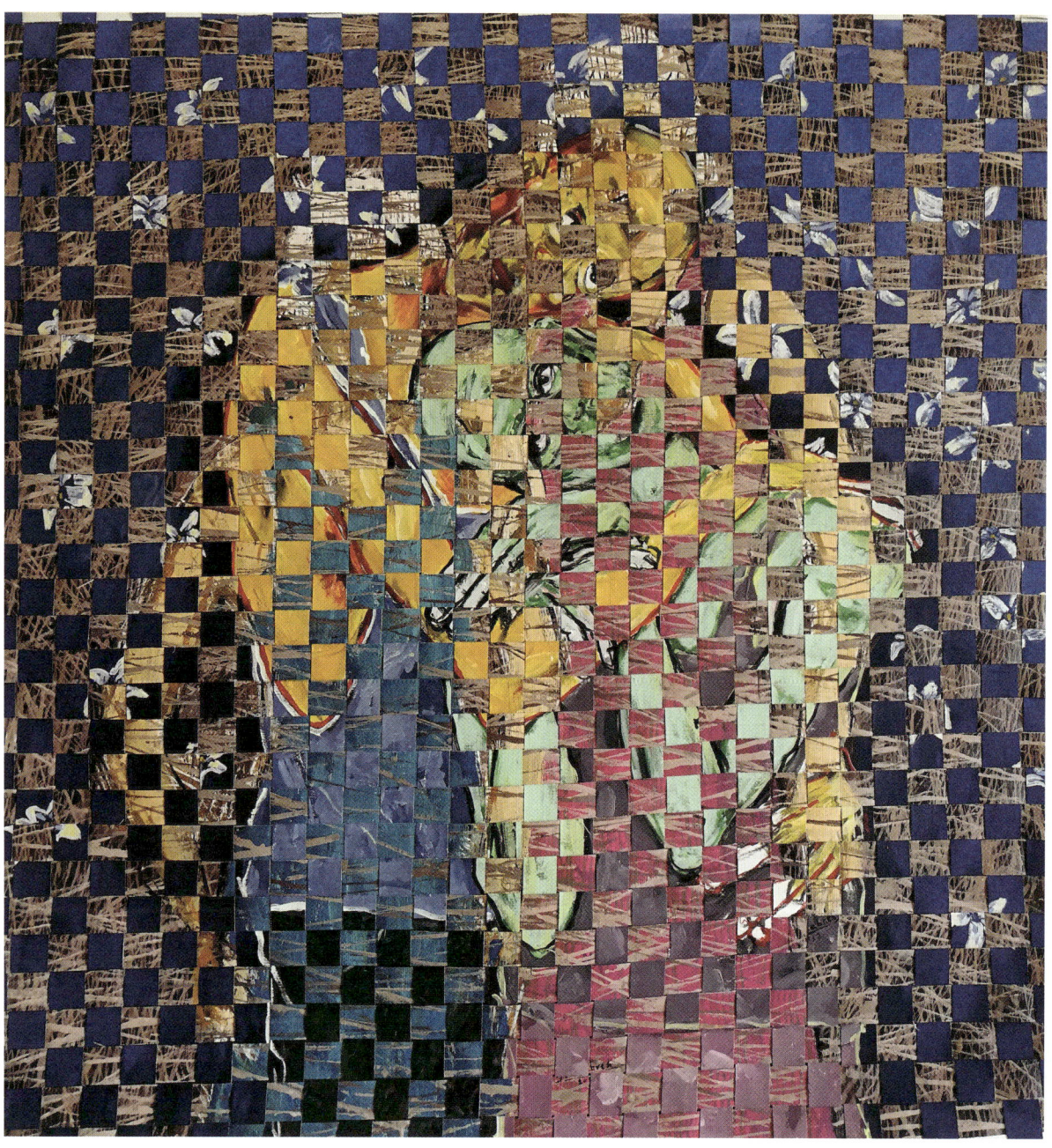

Monther Jawabreh, *Edge 1*, 2019. Woven acrylic paintings on canvas, 100 x 100 cm

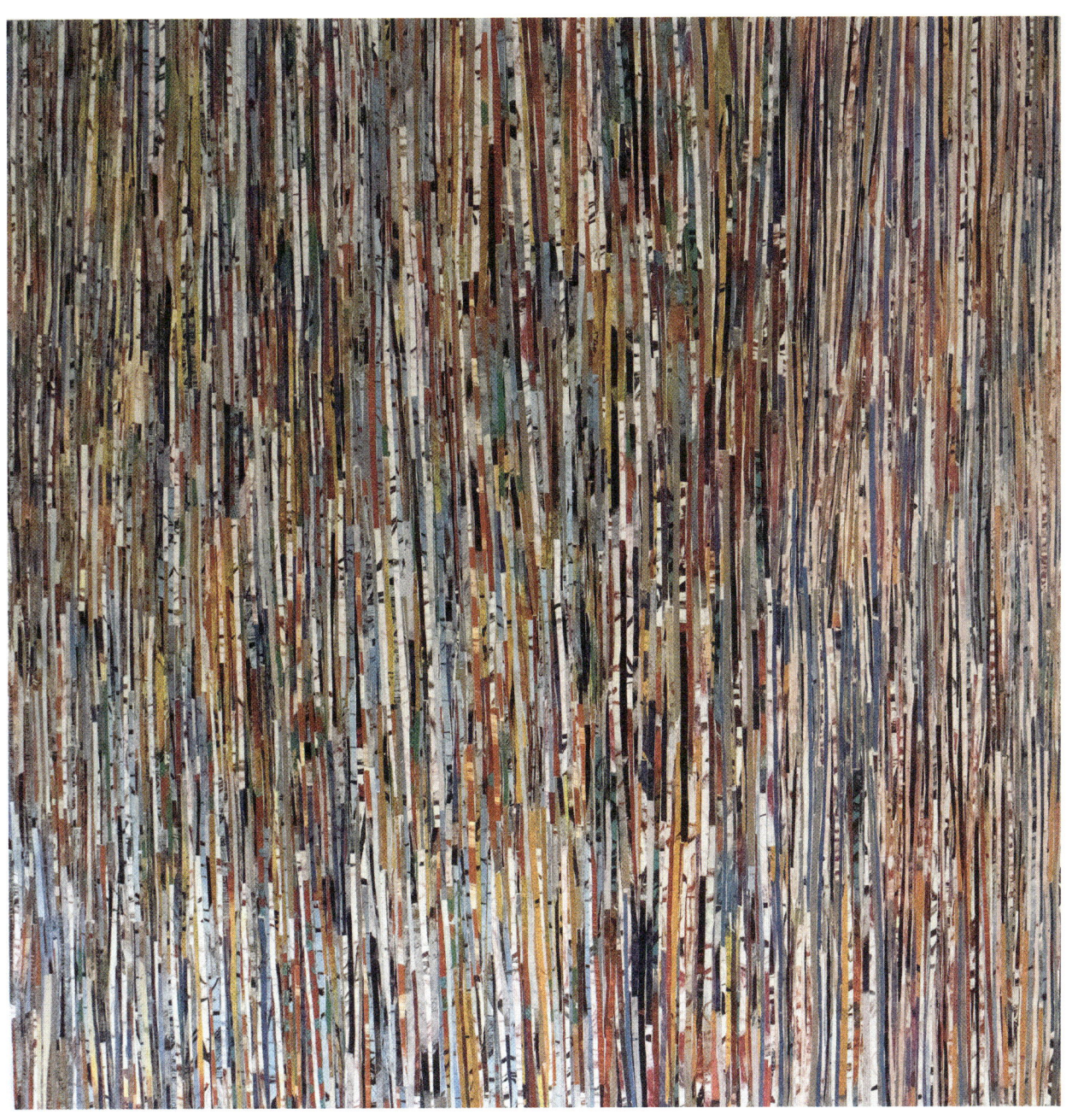

Right: Monther Jawabreh, *Edge* series, 2019–2020. Cut acrylic paintings reassembled on canvas, 200 x 200 cm

SAMAR HUSSAINI

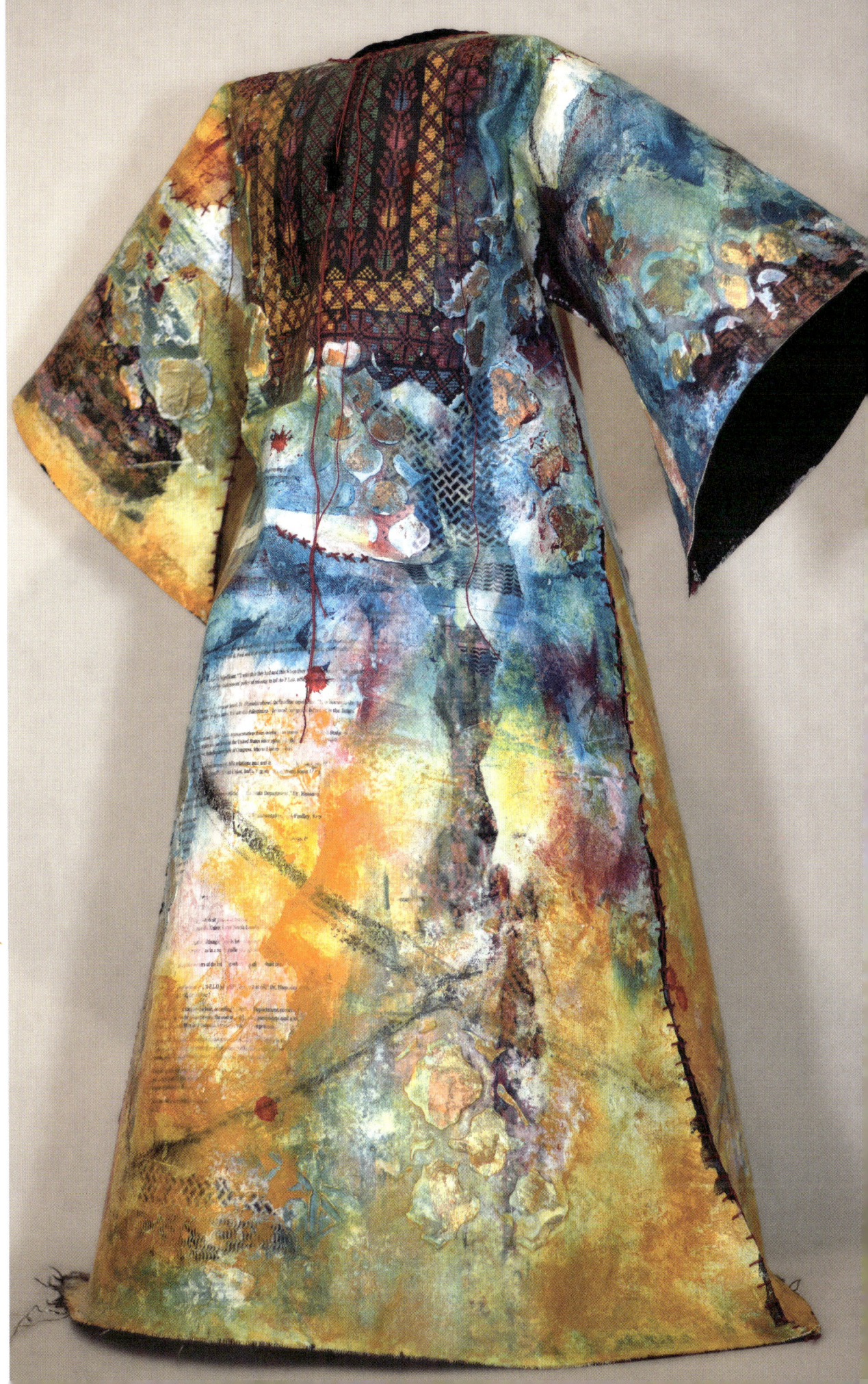

'My grandmother Ulwiyya al-Hussaini taught me the basics of Palestinian embroidery and the ties that bind us as Palestinians,' recalls Palestinian-American artist Samar Hussaini when reminiscing about her childhood trips every summer to East Jerusalem and the West Bank to visit her family. 'My grandfather, Dr Ishaq Musa al-Hussaini, a scholar, taught me the importance of our history. My father, Dr Hatem al-Hussaini, a political activist, instilled the importance of Palestinian justice and integrity. My mother, Lama al-Hussaini, imparted the most valued Palestinian traditions: the importance of education, and strength in the face of adversity.' Samar Hussaini's family and ancestry are pivotal in shaping a sense of pride and connection to her Palestinian culture. These core values passed down through her family became the compass with which Hussaini navigates her life and artwork.

'Over forty years later, my family's journeys have passed to me. Through my art, I share our story to show Palestinian culture in a positive light. I want my children to know where our family came from, the hardships they endured, their strength, and the beauty of our culture.' Hussaini's work detailing Palestinian tradition encourages dialogue, compassion and solidarity. It also points to the struggle for self-determination, cultural identity, and a way of life that endures systematic eradication. She says, 'I incorporate tatreez into my work to share our expressive tradition ingrained in hundreds of years of history. I share it with my children so they will one day pass on the tradition, history and knowledge to their children. My art is a record of my Palestinian identity, and every viewer is part of my achievement.'

Her Palestinian heritage and culture inspired Hussaini's artistic style by blending academic studies with her work in art and advertising, to generate a layered perspective on identity and design. In her abstract and mixed-media works, she uses acrylic paint, ink, charcoal, graphite, thread and collage. She layers Palestinian embroidery, or tatreez, and Arabic graphic designs in her abstract paintings, including the iconic patterned keffiyeh, and Hussaini's father's writing related to evoking empathy.

From afar, the viewer sees the painting's colours and distinctive movement – only to realise, upon closer inspection, that hidden layers and details evoking the Palestinian story are revealed. In her paintings, Hussaini incorporates designs and cultural symbols of Palestinian heritage to illustrate its multitude of challenges. Her abstract mixed-media work on canvas superimposes traditional cross-stitch embroidery motifs and Islamic patterns to construct a visual metaphor for identity. Building on her previous work, she created a print-on-fabric installation piece Ahlan – With Open Arms (2022) for the Palestine Museum US's exhibition From Palestine with Art, a collateral event for the 2022 Biennale Arte in Venice.

Hussaini's sculptural dress series imparts the multifaceted Palestinian story by incorporating Palestinian embroidery, her father's writing and Palestinian design elements. 'The embroidery represented in my work derives from tatreez passed down to me from my grandmother, mother and other women in my family.' The construction of the thobe, a traditional Palestinian embroidered dress, is reimagined as a mixed-media sculpture. 'All are intertwined with mixed-media layers of acrylic paint, charcoal, ink, collage and gold leaf, anchoring my present identity to our history. The reinterpreted thobe dresses are inspired by dresses that were given to my mother as wedding gifts from my mother's aunt, Hind al-Husseini, who was a pioneer of education and established Dar Al-Tifel orphanage in 1948. My colour palette is influenced by family tatreez pieces and Palestinian landscapes remembered from childhood memories.'

Hussaini's sculptural dresses create the illusion of a body filling the space under the painted canvas thobe. 'By taking notice of the absence of the human form, the thobe series reflects on Palestinian identity by asking the question: without a country or homeland, how does one's cultural identity survive? The sculptural pieces express the beauty of Palestinian culture that dates back centuries, and the resilience of its people to carry on despite difficulty and suffering. Our identity survives and grows even in the face of adversity, oppression and discrimination. It's my way of preserving Palestinian practice and identity passed down from mother to daughter while reinterpreting those traditions in the present-day diaspora.'

Hussaini inspires cultural and socio-political awareness through her work and creates a dialogue about Palestinians living in occupation and exile. 'Each painting and sculpted dress represents the story of scattered refugees with a fragmented culture and way of life, a diaspora, and a collective future in jeopardy. It embodies families experiencing the tragedy of losing their homes, land, and traditions passed down from generation to generation. Yet, conviction and strength reveal a drive that no amount of injustice can stop, the drive for self-determination and pursuit of hope for a better future despite hardship.' She encourages the viewer to look beyond the misinformation in the media to learn more about the many challenges faced by a nation of scattered people who remain united by their history, culture and love of their homeland.

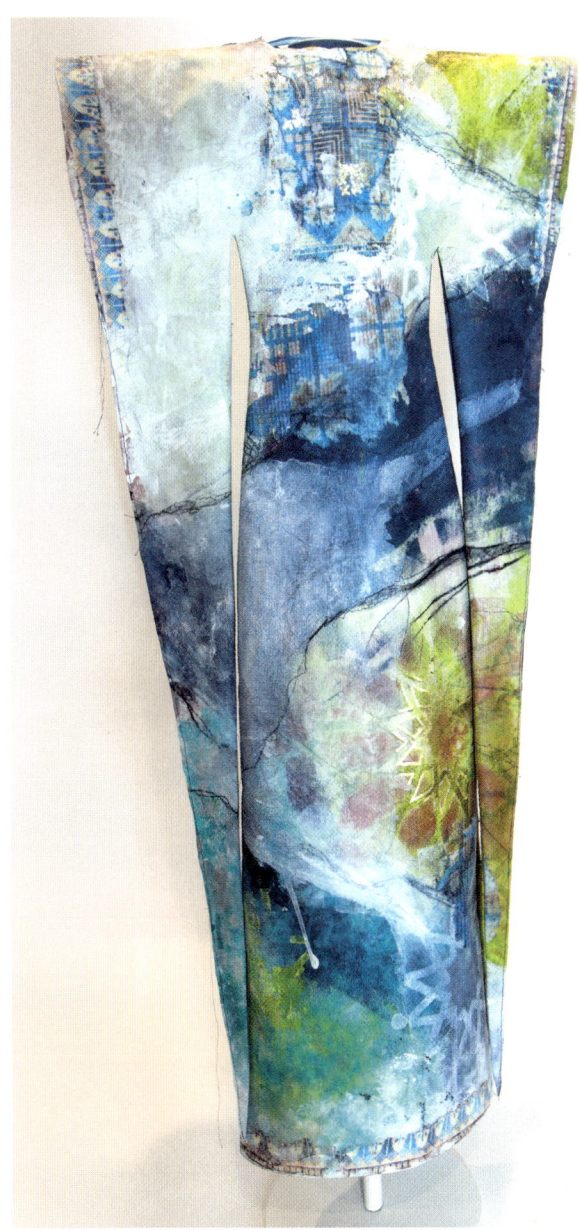

Samar Hussaini, *Woven View 2*, 2022. Mixed media, 106.6 x 50.8 cm

Previous spread: Samar Hussaini, *Resilient Legacy 2*, 2016. Mixed media on canvas

Next spread: Samar Hussaini, *Woven View*, 2021. Mixed media, 167.6 x 106.6 cm

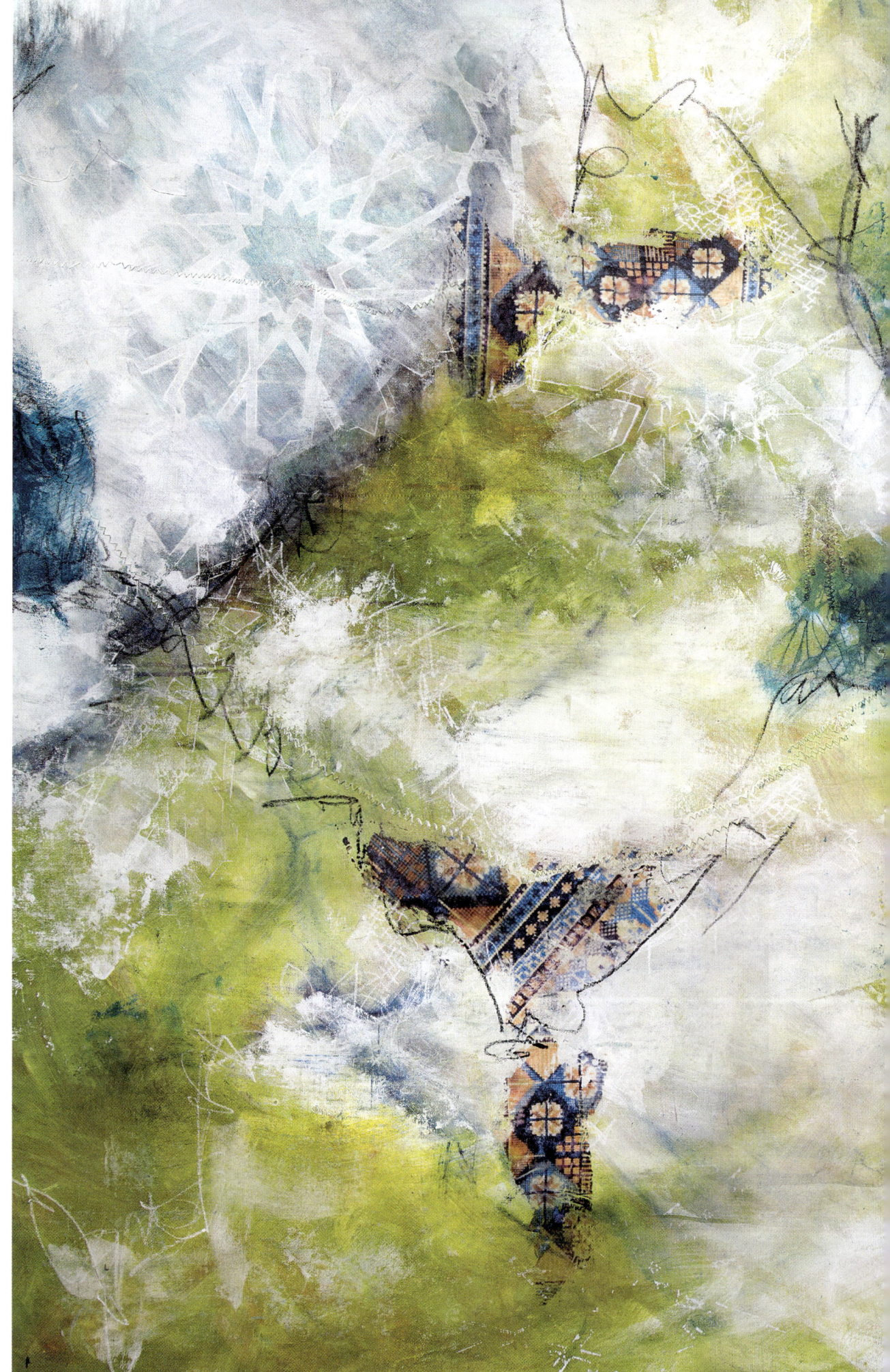

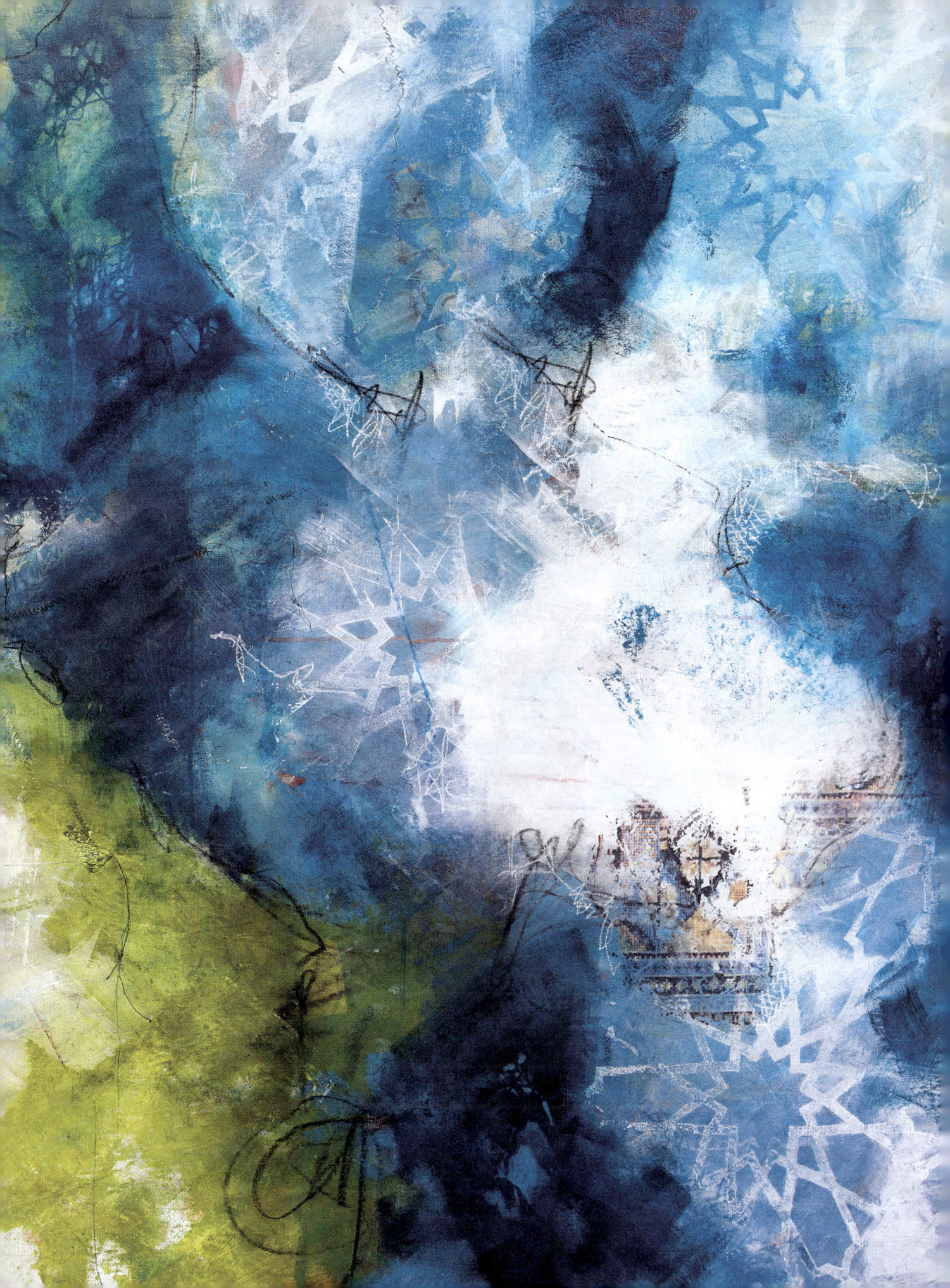

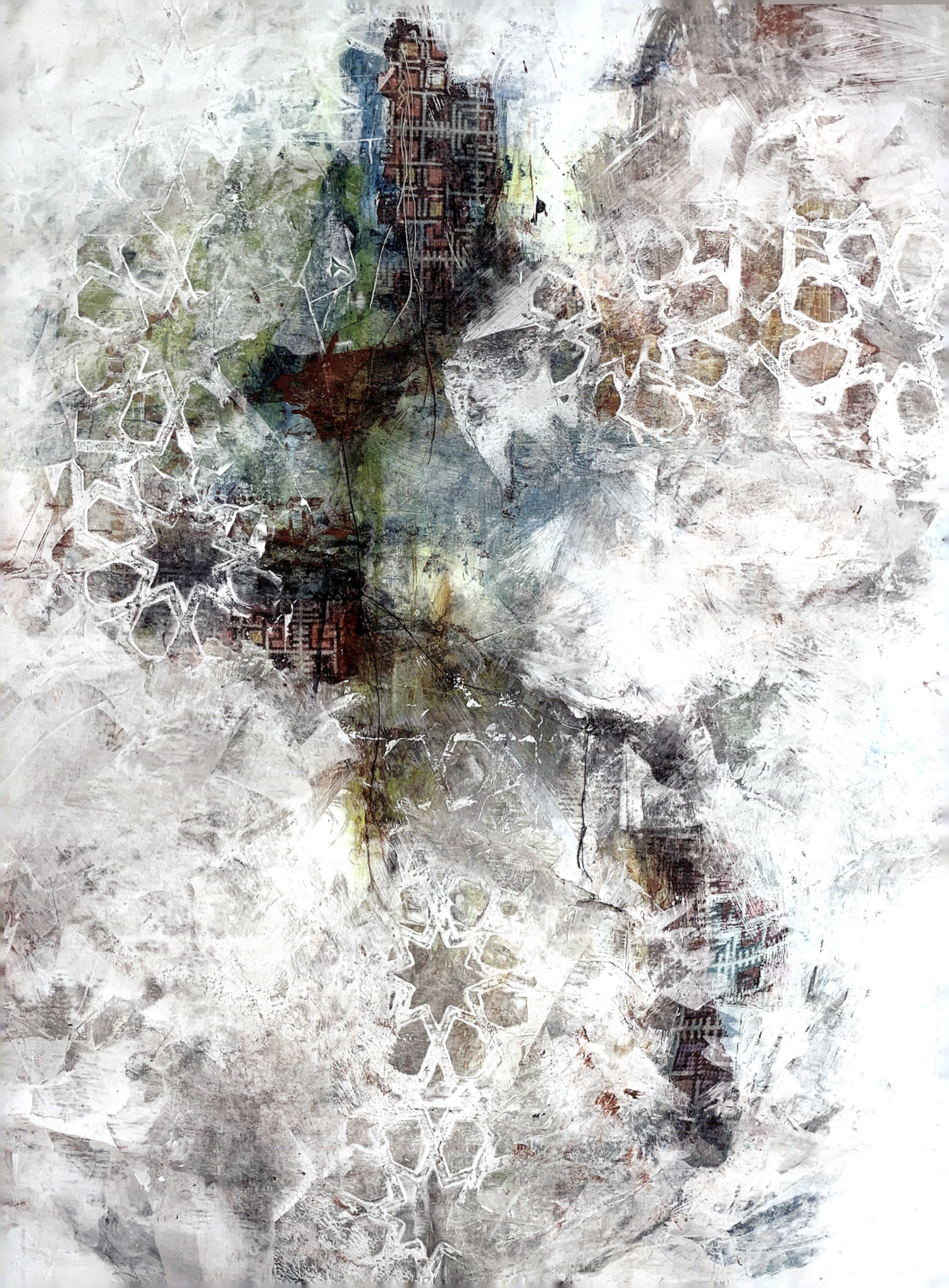

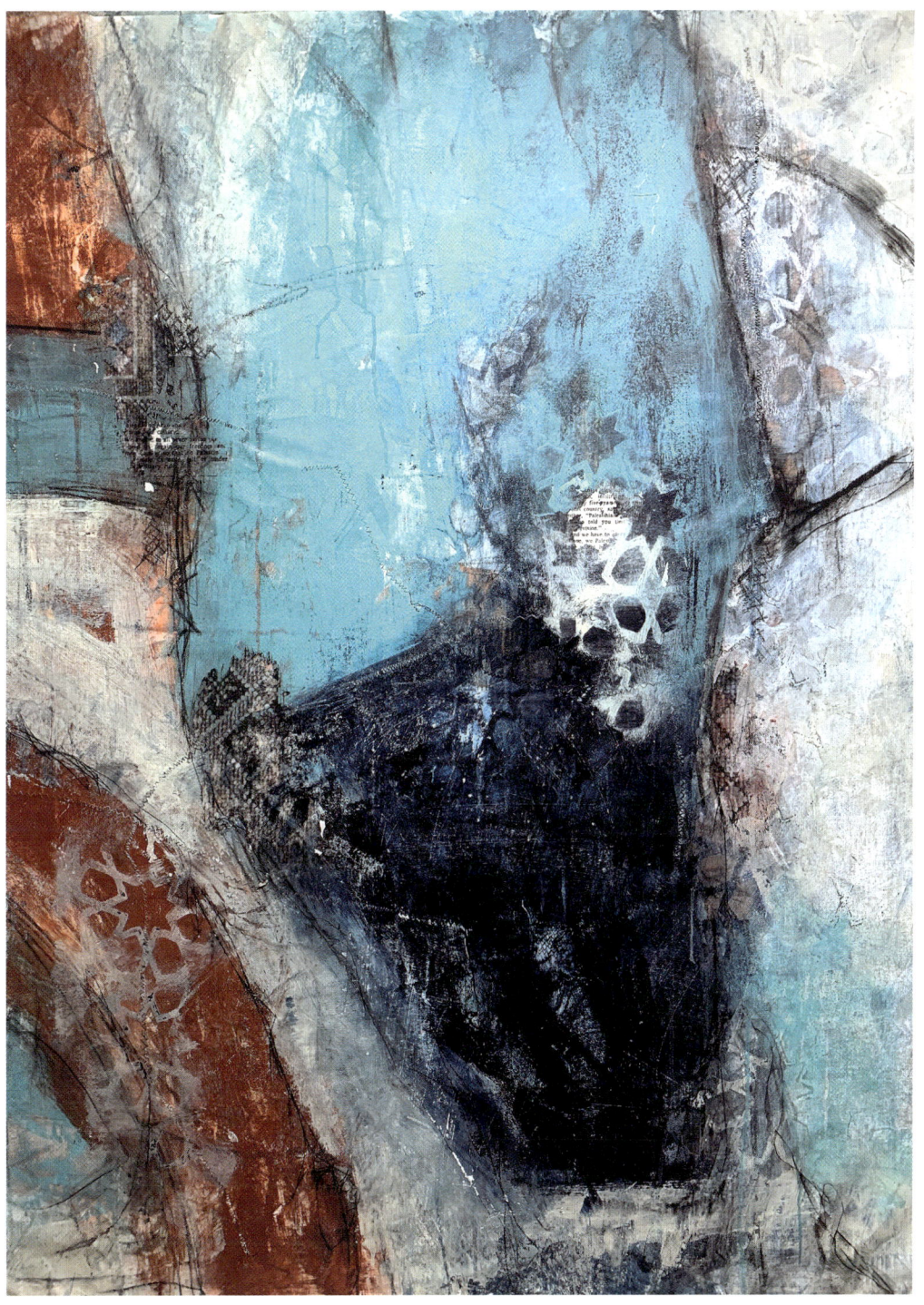

Samar Hussaini, *Links to Homeland*, 2020. Mixed media, 127 x 111.7 cm

Left: Samar Hussaini, *Connected Thread*, 2020. Mixed media on paper

NAJAT EL-TAJI EL-KHAIRY

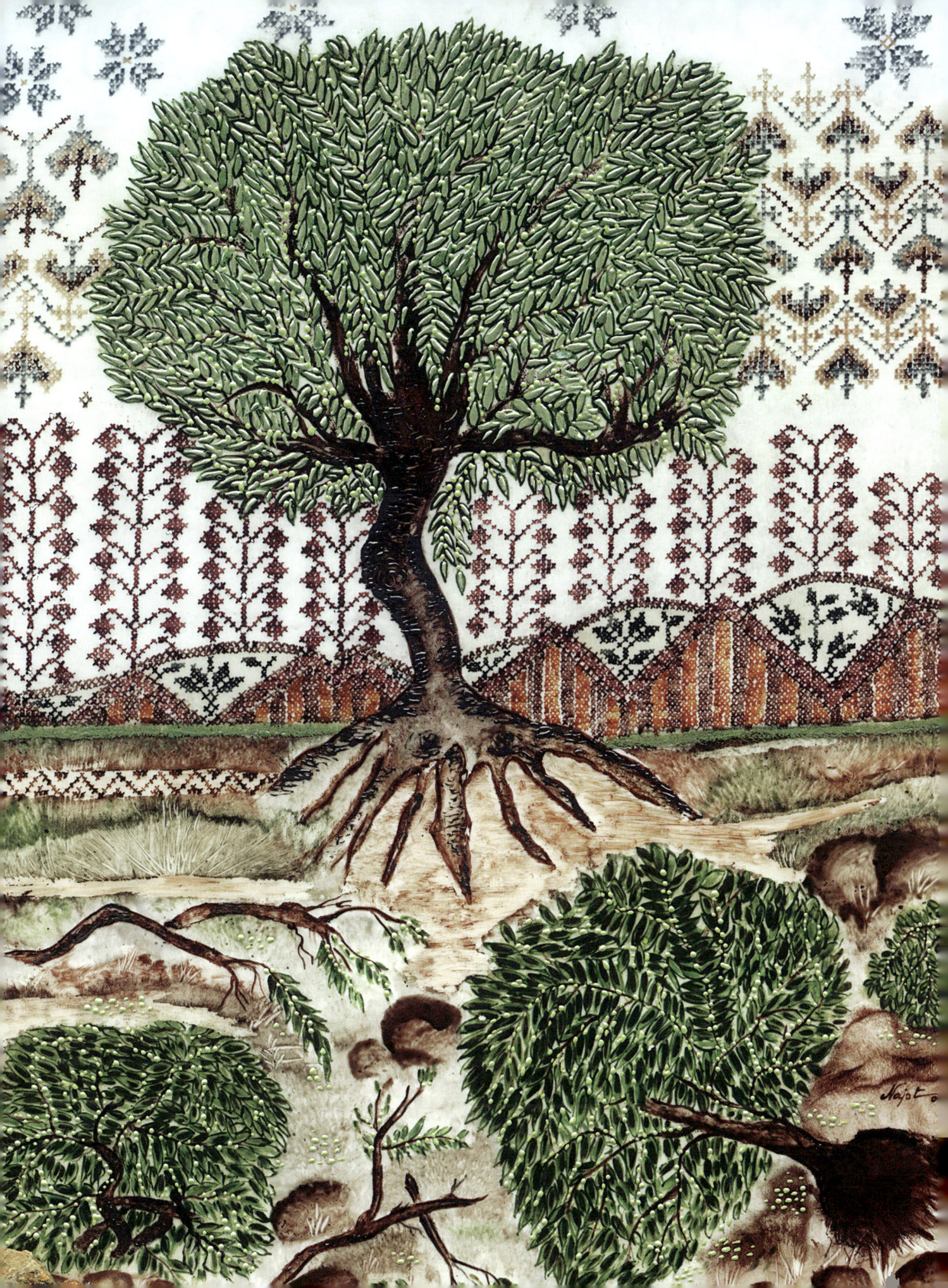

Porcelain artist Najat El-Taji El-Khairy describes the drive behind her art practice: 'My artistic mission has always been to preserve and promote Palestine's art forms by asserting our Palestinian identity and existence. We need to document our history, geography, culture and heritage, as well as everything that defines our people living on their native land and in the diaspora. This includes safeguarding Palestinian *tatreez* embroidery, crafts, poetry, oral storytelling, folkloric dance, song and music, all of which protect our narrative for future generations.'

El-Khairy feels that, being born in 1948, the year of the Nakba, and given the name Najat, meaning rescue and survival, has shaped and defined her life's journey as an avid collector of Palestinian art and crafts, artist, researcher, lecturer, curator and strong advocate of Palestinian art and heritage.

From childhood, she has had an affinity with the intricate and colourful embroidery decorating her family home, pieces that her mother salvaged from Palestine. She recalls, 'Since then, I have been fascinated by and in constant conversation with the threads that manage to create distinct patterns and speak volumes about the history and culture belonging to my ancient land of Palestine.'

El-Khairy describes the defining moment that pushed her into focusing on preserving Palestinian embroidery. 'Following the theft of land came the systematic appropriation of our culture, including our precious embroidery. My mission was magnified when I found out that our distinct Palestinian designs, which had been passed on for generations from mother to daughter, were stolen and used boldly for an Israeli El Al airline flight attendant uniform. This grave robbery created a *malaise* feeling in me that pushed me to reclaim our heritage. My integrity led me to help put an end to this blatant usurpation by unveiling and recognising the real people behind these treasures.' El-Khairy held conferences and exhibitions showcasing Palestinian embroidery, art and crafts to reverse the West's negative stereotype of Palestinians. These events allowed the audience to engage in dialogue and better understand Palestinians as 'cultured, peace-loving people with a tremendous background who desire nothing but to live in their legitimate homes and

lands'. At the same time, she worked as a porcelain artist for over twenty-five years.

In 2005, after having predominantly worked in the European Dresden ceramic technique, El-Khairy developed her 'Renaissance: Embroidery on Porcelain' technique, which married her preferred art forms: Palestinian embroidery and painted porcelain. El-Khairy explains, 'Since material and fabric wear out with time, I came up with the idea of eternalising the patterns on a more durable medium. I used special hand-painted techniques for different cross-stitch embroidery motifs that graced the village women's apparel for centuries. I replaced the *tatreez* tools – fabric, needle and thread – with porcelain tiles, pen and paint, respectively.'

With great concentration and precision, El-Khairy employs the same process of counting and painting each stitch in geometric and floral embroidery motifs with a fine pen. She says, 'I also follow and count the chosen patterns, draw them cross by cross with my pen, using the appropriate coloured paint, onto the porcelain surface. The tile undergoes several firings in a kiln to permanently stabilise my work. When I picked up my very first *Ramallah* chest panel artwork out of the kiln, I felt totally elated. I sensed the fulfilment of the essence of my being, my purpose, my *raison d'être*. With my new creation, I was contributing, ever so slightly, to preserving our distinct Palestinian motifs and patterns on the solid and durable stone-like surface. To me, this medium symbolises Palestinian resistance, resilience, tenacity and everlasting existence.' She continued painting embroidery samplers and dress chest panels from different villages, presenting various embroidery patterns and thread colours from each region.

Embroidered dresses are inspired by the natural environment surrounding the Palestinian village woman who recounts her story in its stitches. El-Khairy employs the same narrative treatment to her porcelain tiles, to tell stories, relay messages and share ideas. She borrows patterns and references for embroidery motifs and dresses from books by her good friend Widad Kawar, the renowned collector of Palestinian embroidery and Middle Eastern textiles. She says, 'I naturally get inspired by my own embroidered collection. My work ethic entails respecting the old motifs that graced the village women's embroidered dresses for ages, with the aim of safeguarding the original Palestinian *tatreez* designs from any addition or alteration. To ensure the survival and authenticity of Palestinian embroidery, I am especially diligent in documenting and conveying the significance behind all patterns used in my creations.'

Yesterday (2008) recreates the front and back view of a traditionally embroidered dress, or *thobe*, and a shawl that would be worn as a headscarf, copying the intricate cross-stitch embroidery found on the chest, front, side, back and sleeve panels. *Yesterday* inspired El-Khairy to create *Tomorrow* (2008), which she describes as a contemporary presentation of a floral V-shaped path leading to a promising open future. The tile features motifs symbolising the right of return, and doves representing hope for peace, contrasting with lines of dense embroidery which she describes as the harsh and inhumane checkpoints awaiting eradication.

In another pair of tiles, El-Khairy presents Palestinian female and male *Yin* (2010) and *Yang* (2010). She describes the work: '*Yin*, the female, is represented by the triangular shape in the centre, symbolising femininity, birth, and a protector of generations. It asserts the divine importance of the woman in Palestinian society. She is the yin, characterised by soft depictions of delicately coloured floral motifs, their roots entrenched in her native land of Palestine. *Yang* is the square representing the male: the *fellah* (farmer) who ploughs the fields, plants the cypress trees, palm trees and orange groves, all depicted in cross-stitched motifs. His blue eye in the centre reaches the horizons of his land to protect it from the evil eye. Amulets guard the four corners of his fields. He is yang: strong, focused, and masculine.' Here, El-Khairy employs imagery inspired by Palestinian embroidery, such as protective amulets and representations of an innate tie to the land.

El-Khairy was angry when Israel built its oppressive separation wall across the West Bank, despite the disapproval and protests of human rights organisations worldwide. She explains how her artwork *The Wall – The Return of the Soul* (2007) encapsulates that time. 'After all, it is a heinous segregating apartheid wall designed to grab

more lands from its indigenous people. A poisonous snake was on the loose in the Holy Land, slithering along, intending to strangle Palestinians by making their lives unbearable. My message to the world in creating this art piece was to express my feelings towards this monstrous wall of separation.

'I chose the superstitious number thirteen for the number of panels making up the wall to assert that it will most definitely fall. The depiction of the Palestinian soul, returning to engrave its identity on *The Wall*, attests that the wall's construction through stolen Palestinian land is to separate people and families from one another – the farmer from his land, the children from their schools, people from their work – and to deprive them of access to hospitals, places of worship, and even essential water resources. No matter how high and imposing, this ugly wall will be unable, indeed incapable of preventing Palestine's growth. Her flowers rise onto the wall, empowering it with designs that graced her gorgeous traditional village dresses for centuries.'

In response to Israel's attacks on Gaza in 2008–09, El-Khairy's empathy for the suffering and agony of the Palestinians in Gaza drove her to create the *Gaza* series. El-Khairy shares the message behind the eight-tile series exhibited at the Jerusalem Fund in Washington, D.C.: 'Every stitch painted told them to resist and be strong, and that I stand in solidarity until liberty. This artistic expression brought me closer to Gazans by exchanging letters with artists living there during the making of this exhibition. Rendering the Majdal dress with its typical fuchsia-, green- and orange-striped fabric colours and patterns is one of the most inspiring experiences I've had.

'Majdal is a place where weaving flourished. It is also known for its typical cross-stitch patterns, embellishing the fabric with shades of pink, violet, green and turquoise. cypress trees, tall palm trees, chevron, arches, saw, and amulets are among the popular motifs in this area. Shawls from Isdud in minuscule cross stitches formed part of this collection. It was a challenge to imitate the original thick thread of the fringe, so I opted for raised enamel work to create an authentic appearance.' This same raised enamel technique is applied in her detailed depiction of each leaf on the olive trees, using light and texture to add dimension to her porcelain tiles.

Along with Palestinian embroidery motifs, El-Khairy employs well-known symbols associated with Palestinian identity, such as the olive tree. She explains, 'Embroidered cross stitches were destined to reach my *Olive Fields* series. They establish Palestinian existence and reclaim history. Motifs like walls of Jerusalem, road to Nablus, road to Jerusalem, old man's teeth, cypress trees, olive leaves, star of Bethlehem and flower of Ramla – my hometown – all form the breathtaking landscape.' In her works *Olive Harvest – Forbidden Colours* (2016) and *Olive Season* (2017) in the *Olive Fields* series, she represents the festivities around olive harvesting. She describes the scene: 'The *keffiyeh* spread on the ground is ready for annual olive picking. The villagers wearing embroidered dresses enjoy picnics of authentic foods like *ma'aloubeh*, *mussakhan*, *falafel*, *hummus* and *knafeh Nabulsieh* under the olive trees. After year-long hard labour, it is time to sing and dance the folkloric *dabka* to celebrate the olive harvest season.'

The olive tree also appears in her earlier work *The Rebelled Spirits* (2008), where a steadfast olive tree is the subject; embroidery motifs fill the sky in the background and uprooted trees are strewn across the foreground. El-Khairy explains that the scene 'describes the tenacity of the majestically standing olive tree refusing to be uprooted. Its obstinate willpower is the Palestinian in flesh and soul. Its roots are anchored profoundly in the land to secure its survival for generations.'

In *Nostalgia* (2014), El-Khairy articulates her yearning for her homeland. She says, 'Its fields are playing music to our ears with cross-stitch motifs and flowers from our hometown underneath the olive tree, all of which embody peace, harmony and serenity. I used the raised-work enamel technique to paint my olive trees to give each leaf a special luminous effect and give them valuable life status. Olive trees symbolise peace and resilience, representing Palestinian resistance, endurance and determination. Look closer between the ancient branches of my olive trees – the map of beloved Palestine is always present for no one to erase.' These works convey El-Khairy's great love for Palestine, mirrored by the motifs and symbolism she expresses in her work.

Dunes of Palestine (2012) is a three-tile series where El-Khairy vividly recalls visiting Palestine in 1997. With her brush and pen on porcelain, she captures the dunes near the Jordanian border. She says: 'The Palestinian cross-stitch embroidery designs found their way amid the golden sands of the ancient land. They adapted their usual bright colours to the shades of the desert dunes to blend and survive in the magnificent Palestinian landscape, recounting to the passerby the daily life stories of the Holy Land.'

For El-Khairy, preserving Palestinian art and heritage is a joyful obligation that led her on her artistic journey. She tells us, 'Helping preserve Palestine's artistic heritage was a destiny driven by my instinctively innovative spirit, which led to conceptualising "Renaissance: Embroidery on Porcelain". I take pride in having created a merger of the two art forms and sense a great deal of pleasure when my audience, from all ages, is greatly interested in our native land. Whenever my work is recognised, generating curiosity and admiration, I feel truly fulfilled. We owe it to our homeland to hold on to every precious embroidered detail as it tells the noble story of our revered land of Canaan, Palestine.' Through her meticulous porcelain painting technique, she celebrates the rich and diverse beauty of Palestinian embroidery on tiles, preserving it for ages to come.

Right: Najat El-Taji El-Khairy, *Yang*, 2010. Hand-painted porcelain, 30.4 x 30.4 cm

Pages 276–277: Najat El-Taji El-Khairy, *Rebelled Spirits*, 2008. Hand-painted porcelain, 40.6 x 30.4 cm

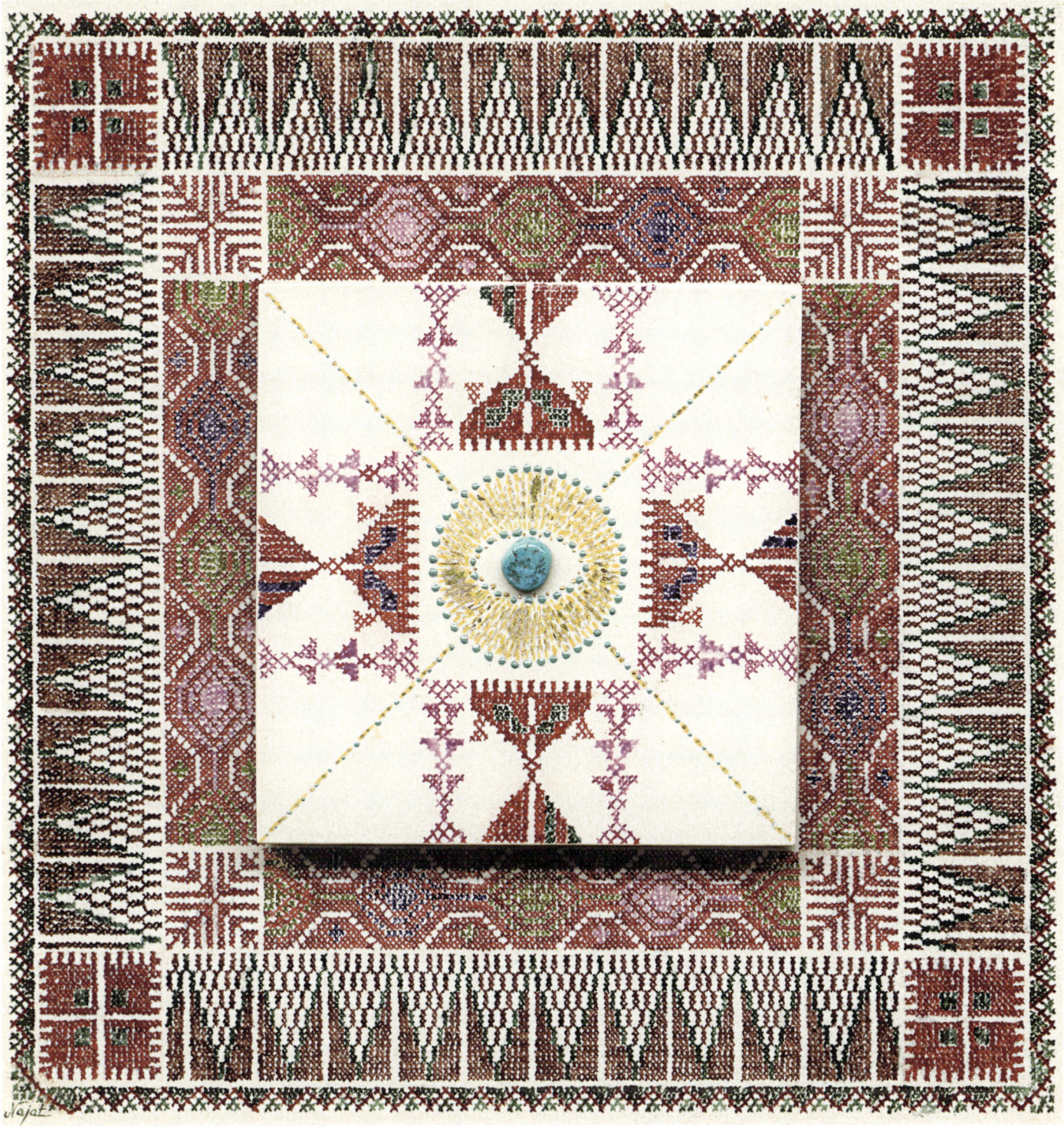

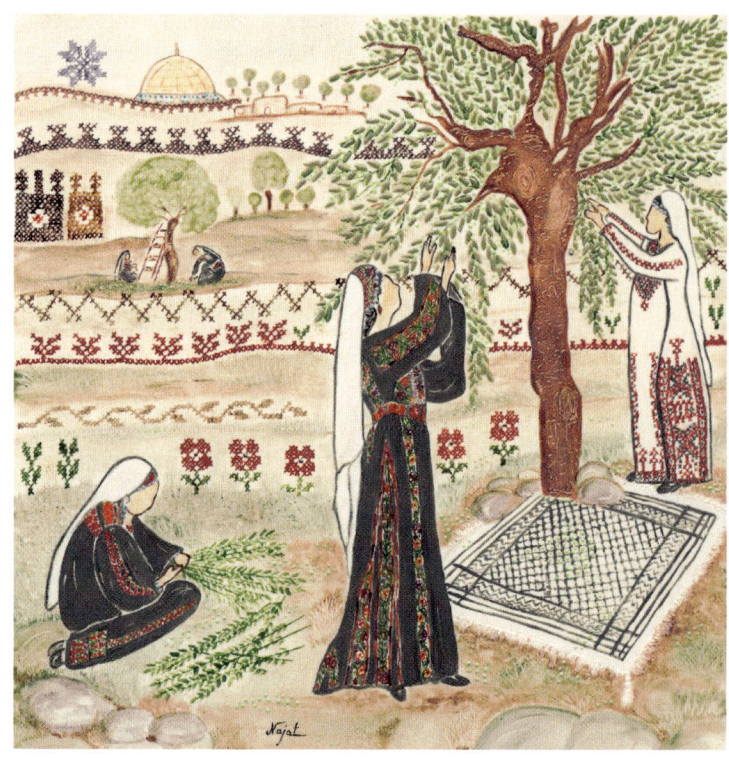

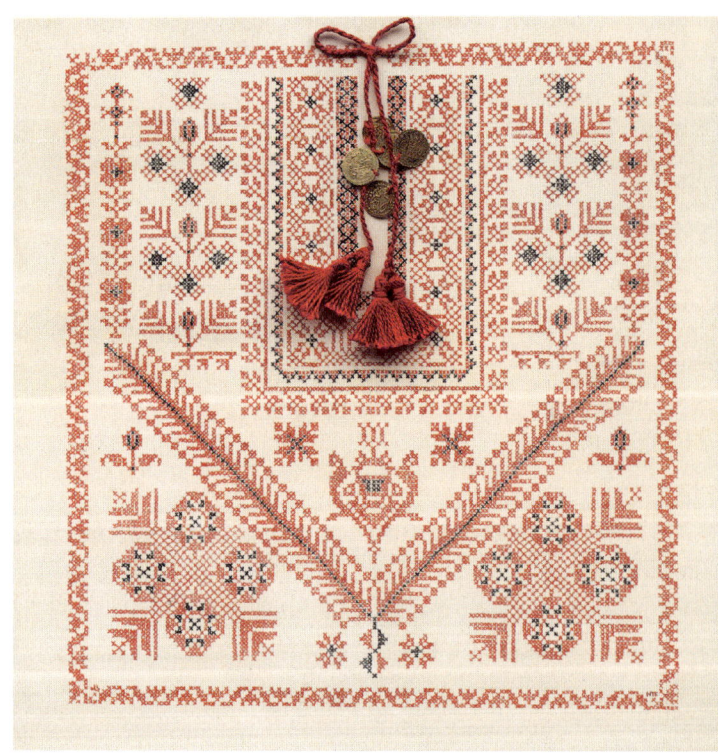

Najat El-Taji El-Khairy, *Olive Season*, 2017. 30.4 x 30.4 cm
Najat El-Taji El-Khairy, *Dunes*, 2012. 30.4 x 30.4 cm
Najat El-Taji El-Khairy, *Majdal Dress, Back Panel*,
Gaza series, 2009. 30.4 x 30.4 cm

Najat El-Taji El-Khairy, *Ramallah 1*, 2005. 30.4 x 30.4 cm
Najat El-Taji El-Khairy, *Nostalgia*, 2014. 30.4 x 30.4 cm
Najat El-Taji El-Khairy, *Yin*, 2010. 30.4 x 30.4 cm

All works hand-painted porcelain

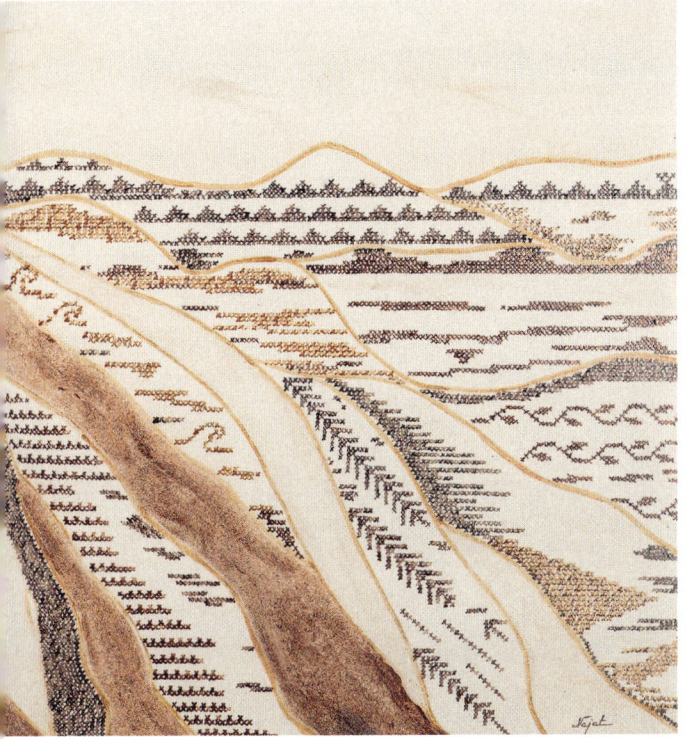

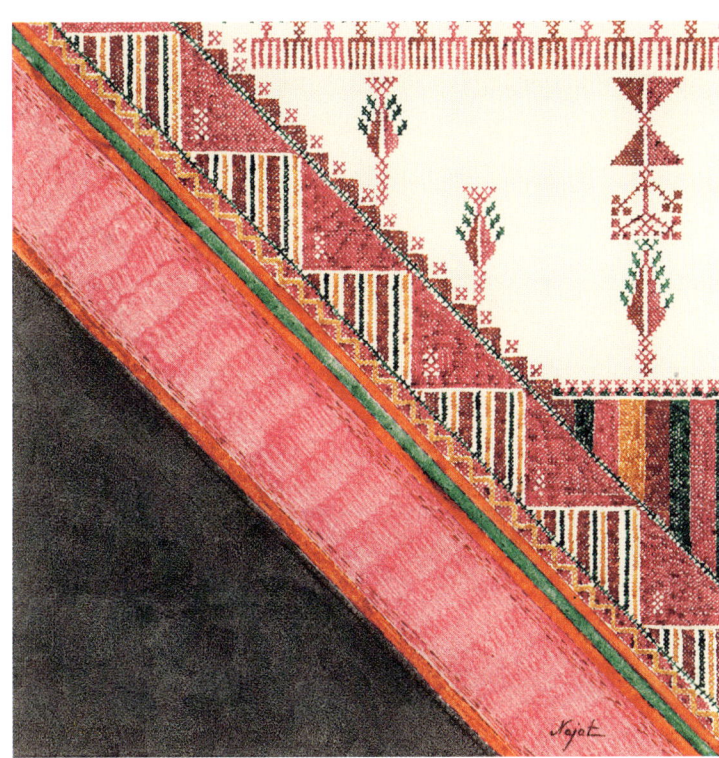

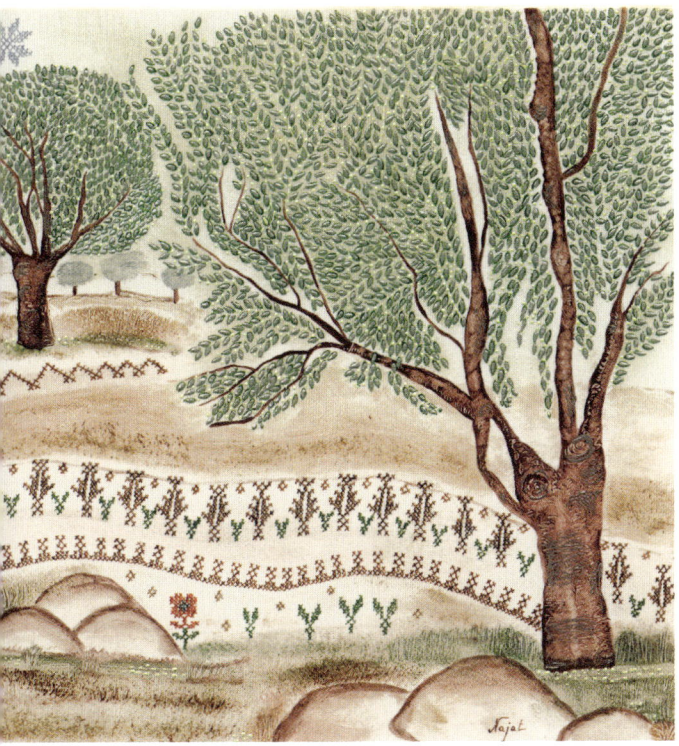

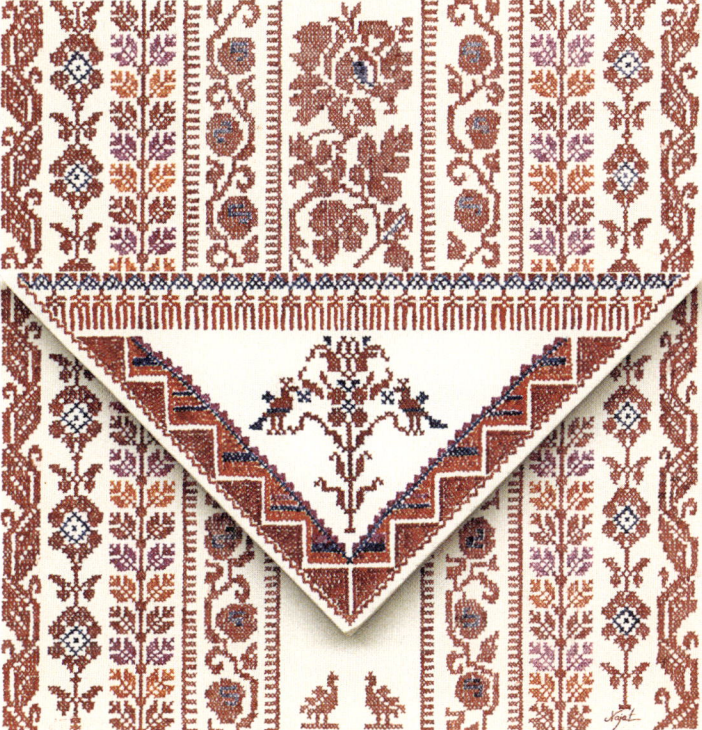

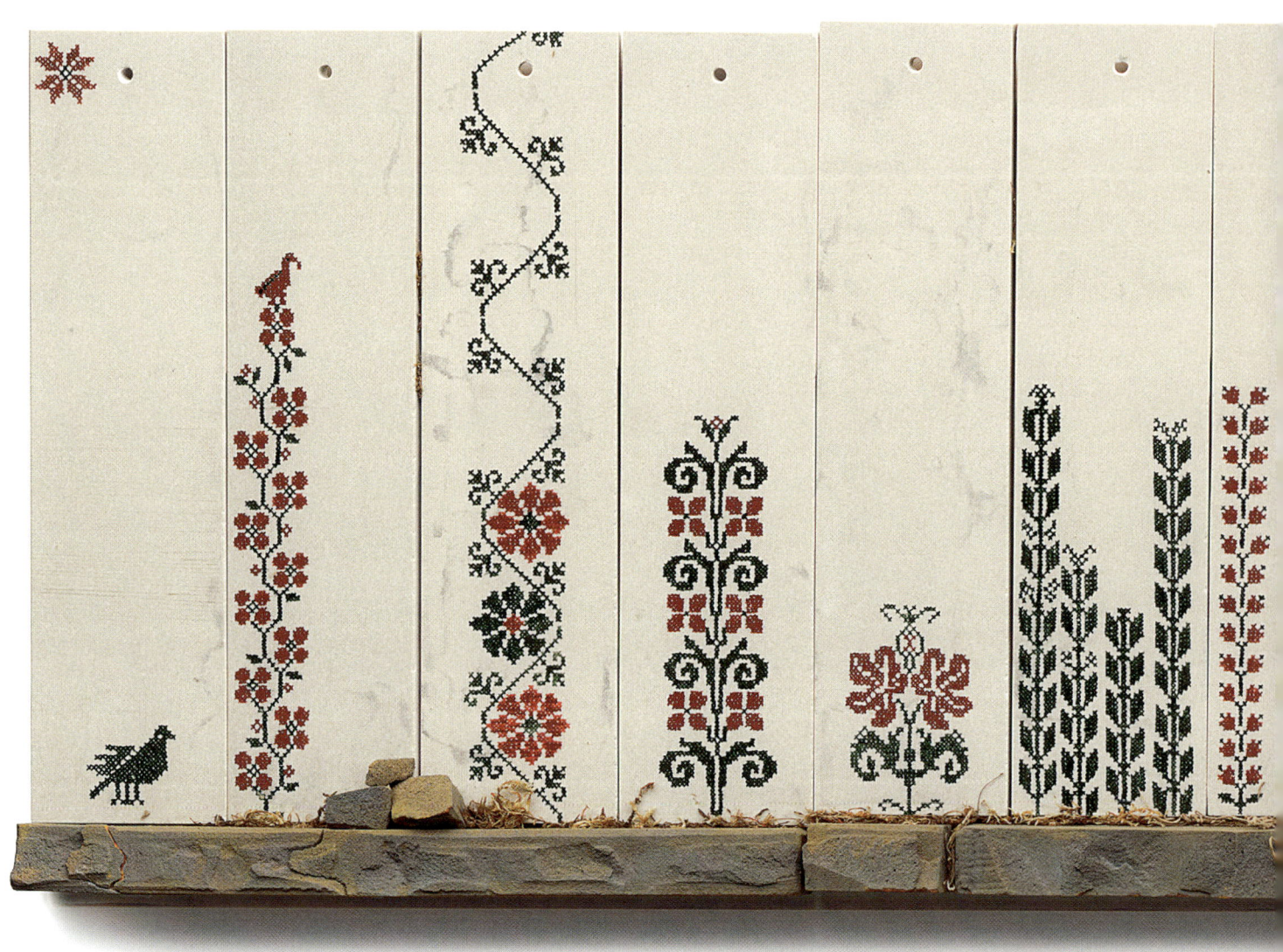

Najat El-Taji El-Khairy, *The Wall – The Return of the Soul*, 2007. Hand-painted porcelain, 106.6 x 10 cm

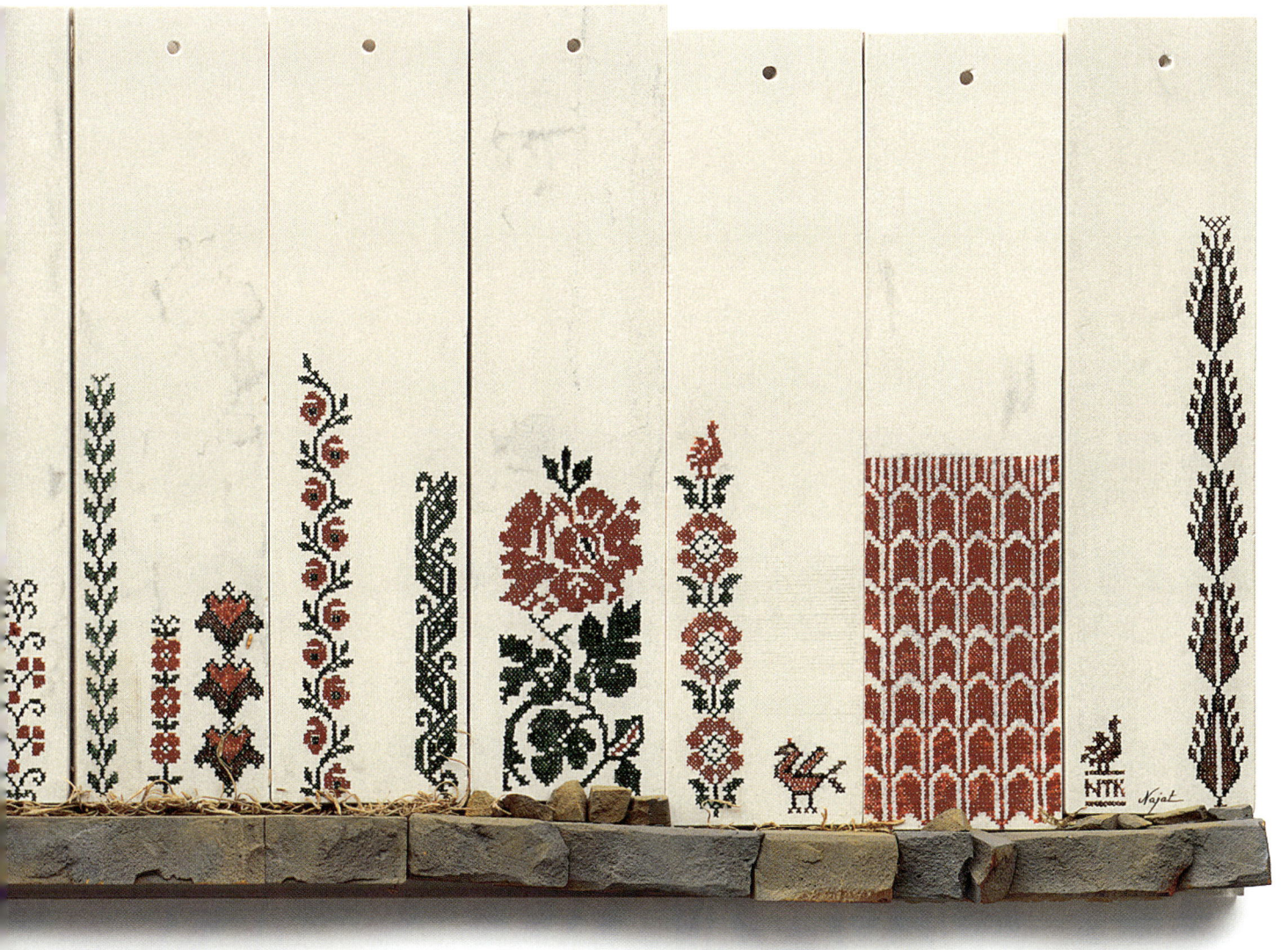

NAQSH COLLECTIVE

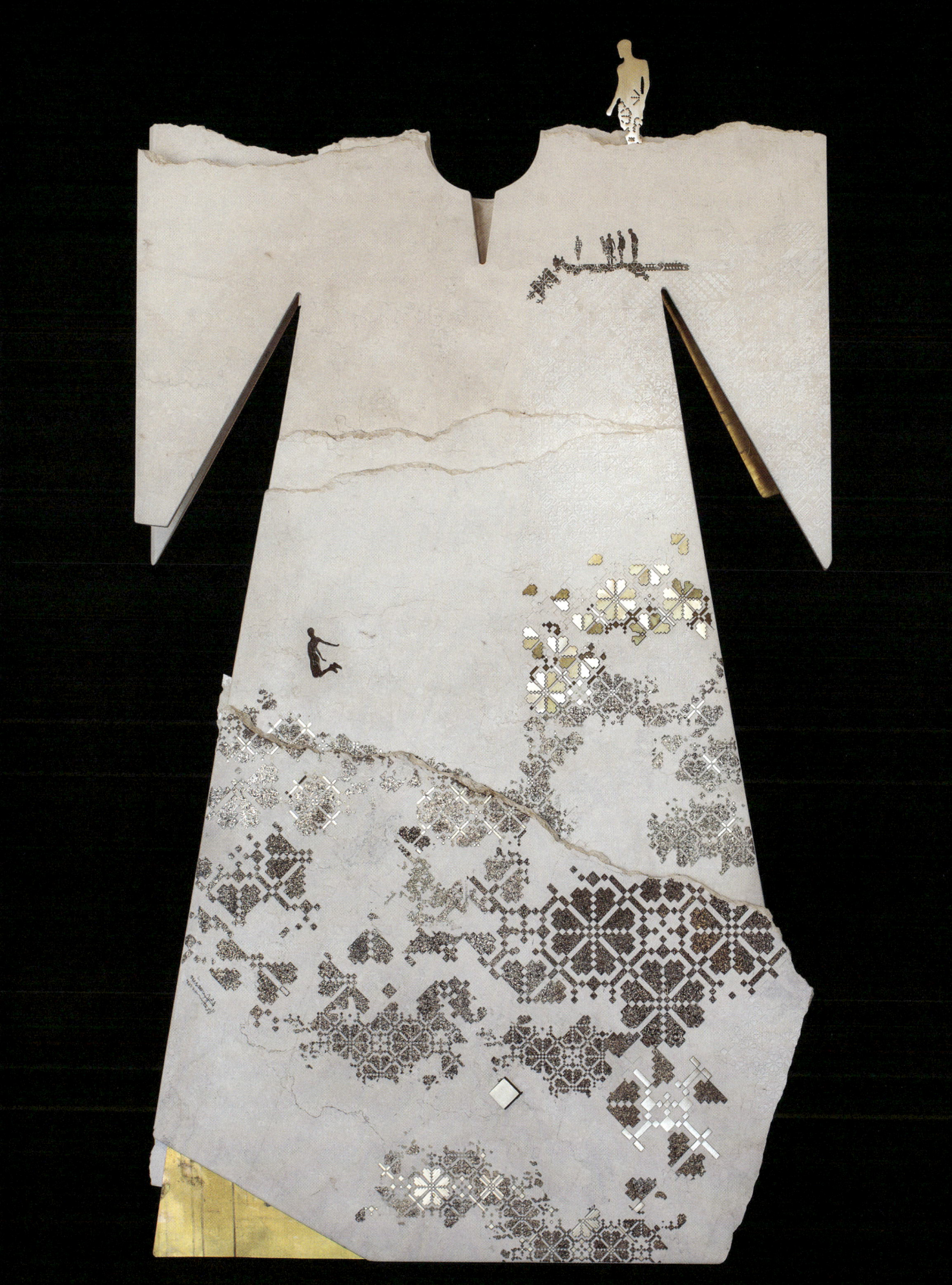

In 2009, sisters Nisreen and Nermeen Abudail founded Naqsh Collective. In their Amman-based design studio, Nisreen's architecture background and Nermeen's graphic design practice come together to create design-art pieces made predominantly in marble, stone, wood and brass. The main thread that ties their work together is the recurrent presence of engraved Palestinian embroidery motifs.

The Arabic word *naqsh*, meaning to engrave, is their method of preserving their heritage. They explain, 'The everlasting nature of building and carving motifs in stone gave us the confidence to select materials that will stand the test of time, retelling our stories for centuries to come.' By incorporating Palestinian embroidery in their work, Naqsh Collective shares and records stories of Palestine, capturing its beauty and evoking a feeling of permanence despite Israel's attempts at its erasure.

The Abudail sisters view Palestinian embroidery, or *tatreez*, as integral to Palestinian collective memory. 'We share memories of sitting with our mother and grandmother, embroidering different motifs together, such as flora, fauna and other patterns they taught us. Embroidery is an essential element in our culture for sharing our ancestors' stories. We approach design from a point where we want to reflect some of our DNA and origins. The final pieces that we present to the world tell our original stories with elements, like *tatreez*, from our background. We saw potential in *tatreez* like no other in terms of strong geometries and aesthetics in colours.' The research for their extensive archive of Palestinian embroidery motifs used in their work includes referencing books on Palestinian embroidery and studying examples of antique dresses in Widad Kawar's collection at the Tiraz Centre in Amman, Jordan.

A nostalgic feeling emerges in the Abudail sisters when they recreate old and familiar objects, such as the embroidered pillow, table runner or shawl. Their artworks, like *The Shawl* (2015), *Cushion* (2018) and *Wall Runner* (2019), are crafted of solid walnut wood with rows of engraved embroidery and inlaid brass. For Naqsh Collective, blending traditional elements with innovative designs breathes new life into each series, imbuing it with a unique theme and narrative.

The motifs play an essential role in the storytelling. *Yaffa Chair* (2017) tells the story of the women of Beit Dajan, a prosperous village in the Yaffa, or Jaffa, region of Palestine. Dresses from Beit Dajan told stories about the orange orchards, with the orange blossom embroidery motif, and from daily life with the couch embroidery motif. For the *Yaffa Chair*, the sisters carved the couch motif out of the marble seat and the orange blossom motif out of the brass supporting the left side of the chair. Naqsh Collective highlights the agricultural and industrial sectors of Palestine that are often overlooked and negated by Israeli and Western narratives.

The sister design team created *The Bride's Carpet* (2017), the beginning of a fictional tale of a bride who buries her mother's wedding present, a hand-embroidered carpet, to protect it from Israeli forces. This story mirrors the real-life experiences of displaced Palestinians who hid their valuables and fled their homes having planned to return. With only large motifs showing, hundreds of smaller motifs carved out of basalt stone are buried under a layer of brass shavings. The bride's story continues with the nurturing and blossoming of seeds left behind from the carpet in *The Onyx* (2018) and *Flora and Fauna* (2018) sculptures, featuring embroidery motifs of flowers, branched foliage and birds cut out of sheets of brass appear to be growing out of stone.

Naqsh Collective's *Wihdeh Collection* (2019) comprises a series of 75 x 75 cm stone works, each focusing on a different Palestinian embroidery motif. Engraved and inlaid with brass, the repeated patterns of embroidery motifs appear to radiate brass beams in some areas and disappear into the stone background in others. *Wihdeh Wa Shatat* (2018) is an open-air exhibit in a wheat field in Jordan, overlooking Palestine. It features 180 sundials representing the Palestinian diaspora spread worldwide. The sundials are a metaphor for the Palestinian relationship with time since 1948, where the diaspora is held in limbo, waiting for a return home. The fragile limestone base with the strong brass gnomon speaks to what the sisters call 'showing the tension we experience as a resilient people in a state of fragility'. The sun streams through the engraved Palestinian embroidery motifs on each sundial gnomon, reflecting the enduring beauty of Palestinian culture and its influence in various geographies.

In 2020, the Naqsh Collective collaborated with social enterprise 81 Designs to create *A Thobe Story*. Working closely with Palestinian embroiderers from Ain al-Hilweh refugee camp in South Lebanon, they created a series of ten embroidered *thobe* dresses that translated their distinctive style and stories from stone and wood to fabric. That same year, Naqsh Collective made *Wa Mashat* (2020), in brass on marble, which depicts a Gazan woman wearing an embroidered dress and coin headdress, walking through a wheatfield. The sisters imagine the walk from Palestine to Jordan without the series of imposed borders. They based *Heavy Road to Damascus* (2020) and *Heavy Road to Egypt* (2020) on the two Palestinian embroidery motifs historically found on women's dresses that originally celebrated a trip taken to buy the bridal trousseau; after 1948, displaced Palestinians traversed those same roads after their forced expulsion by Israel to Damascus and Egypt.

Palestine's seaside city of Yaffa inspired the *Yaffa* series (2022). The Abudail sisters describe the series as 'a combination of real photos with imagination, weaving the embroidery into old images of Yaffa.' The seaside landscape, with its port and surrounding buildings, is made up of Palestinian embroidery motifs carved into natural stone and inlaid with brass. With Yaffa being the ancestral home of the Abudail family, the coastal city holds a special significance for the sisters.

Combining the shape of *A Thobe Story* (2020) with the themes and imagery from *Akka* (2018), *Stone Thobe*

(2023) sees Naqsh Collective illustrate the story of the Akka cliff divers, on a *thobe* made from Botticino marble. The marble land and sea are made up of engraved and inlaid brass embroidery motifs that also decorate the brass divers patiently waiting for their turns. One brave diver who has already jumped off the cliff into the sea is caught in motion midair with arms and legs suspended behind him.

A common visual representation across all Naqsh Collective's artwork is Palestinian cross-stitch motifs disappearing or fading into the background, symbolising the attempted erasure of Palestinian identity through ethnic cleansing and assimilation to the cultures of host countries in the diaspora. The sisters explain, 'It reflects the present status of embroidery and the struggle that Palestine is going through. It is growing very difficult for Palestinians to protect their culture, as they are busy trying to survive under this occupation and the daily struggles it creates for them.' Through their work, Nisreen and Nermeen Abudail honour their ancestors' memories, struggles and resilience, ensuring Palestinian narratives survive for generations.

Previous spread:
Nisreen Abudail and Nermeen Abudail of Naqsh Collective,
Stone Thobe, 2023. Botticino marble and brass, 165 x 120 x 50 cm

Nisreen Abudail and Nermeen Abudail of Naqsh Collective, *Akka*, 2022. Stone and brass

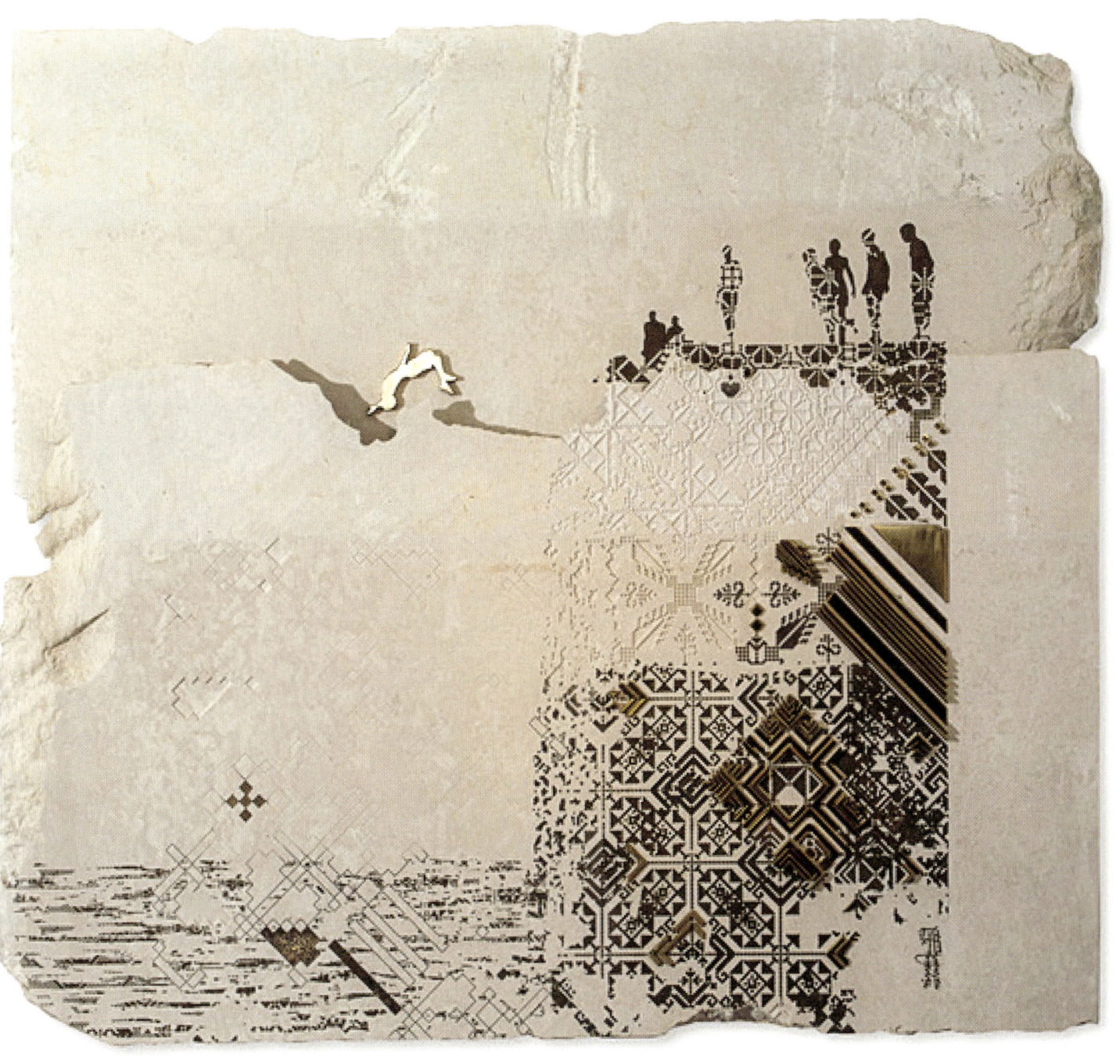

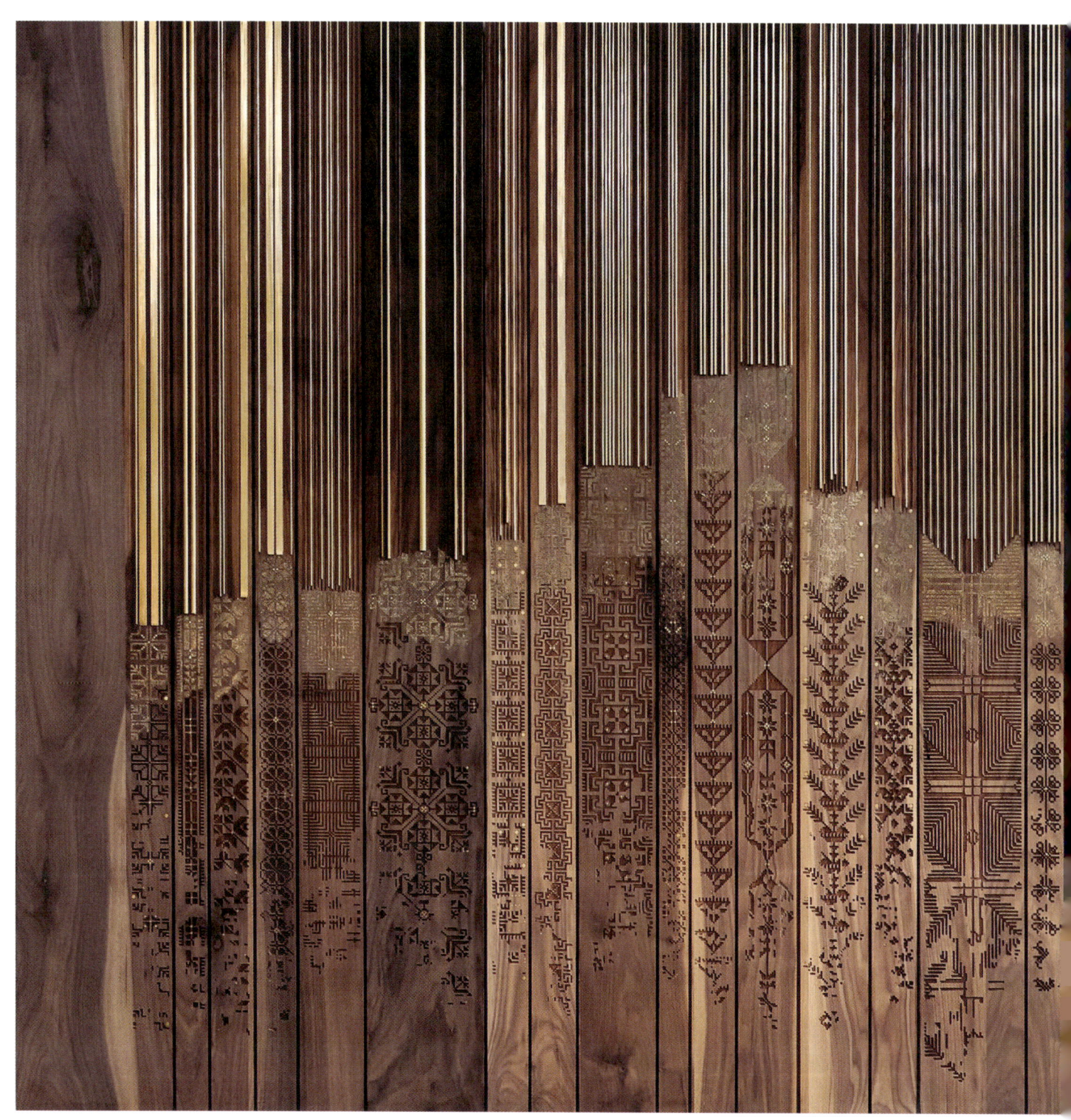

Nisreen Abudail and Nermeen Abudail of Naqsh Collective, *Shawl*, 2015. Walnut wood and brass, 225 x 375 cm

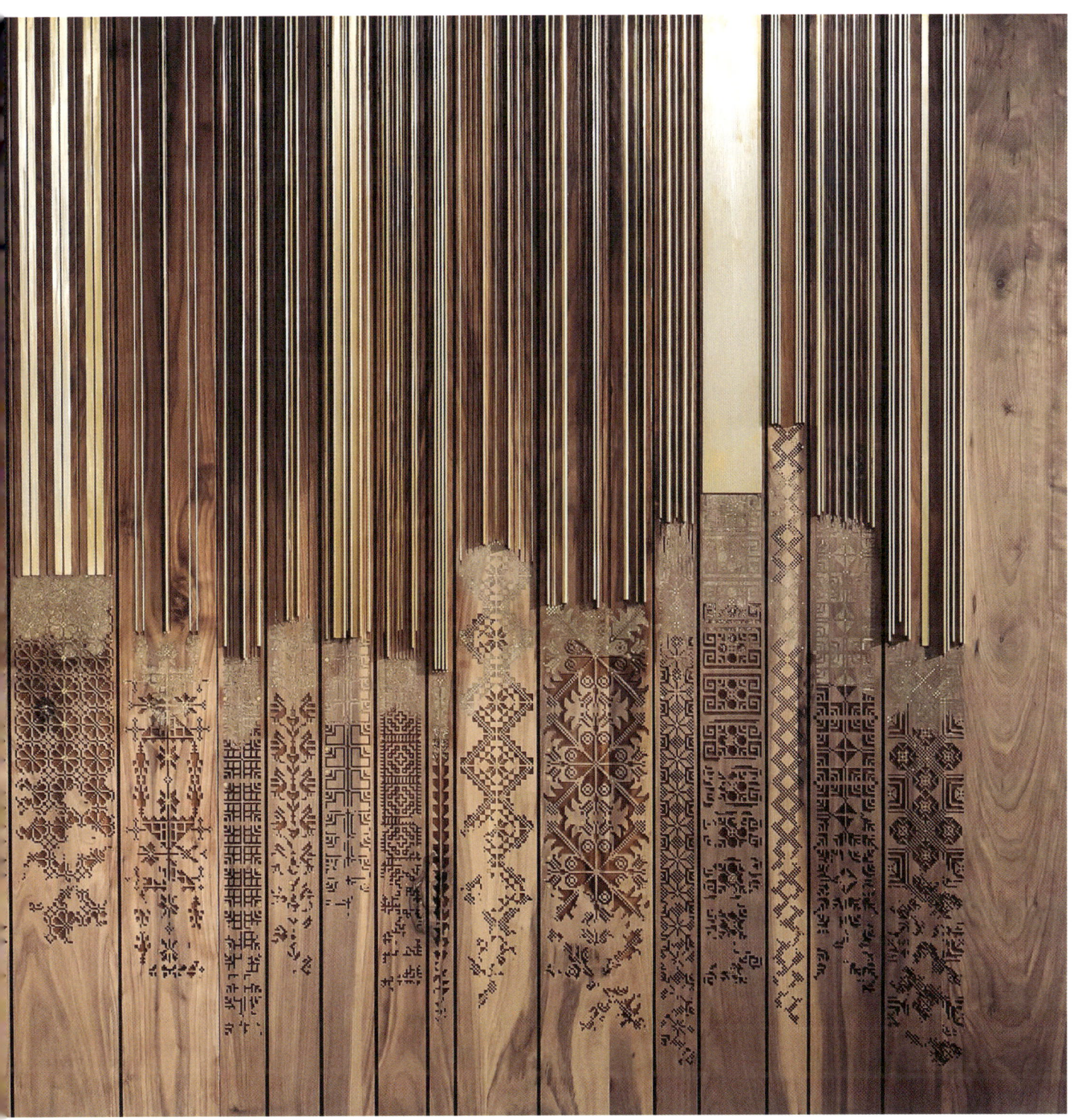

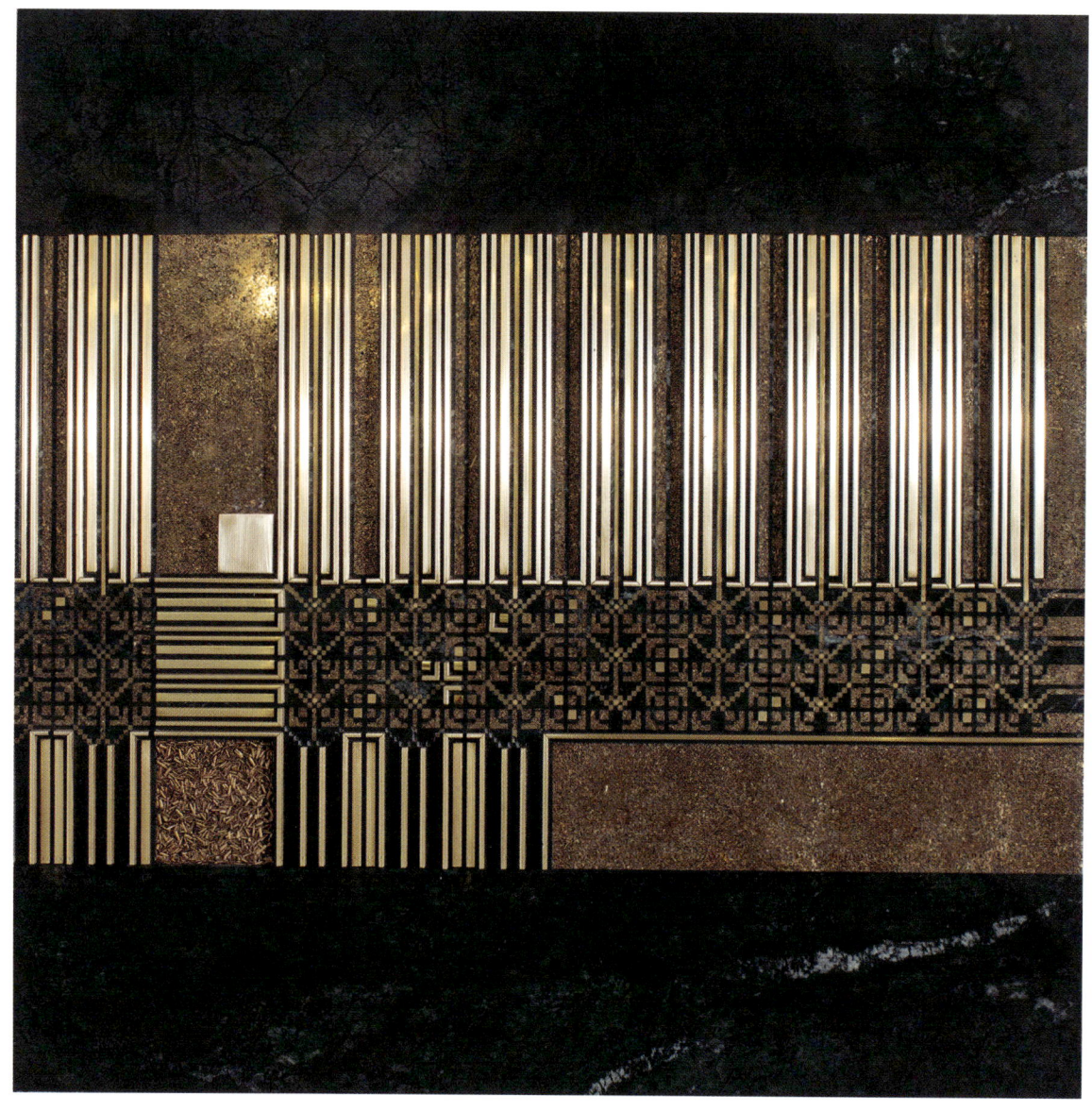

Nisreen Abudail and Nermeen Abudail of Naqsh Collective, *Full Palm Trees*, 2019. Marble and brass, 75 x 75 cm
Right: Nisreen Abudail and Nermeen Abudail of Naqsh Collective, *Yaffa Chair*, 2017. Stone and brass, 70 x 80 x 80 cm

Next spread: Nisreen Abudail and Nermeen Abudail of Naqsh Collective, *Wihdeh Wa Shatat*, 2018. Stone and brass

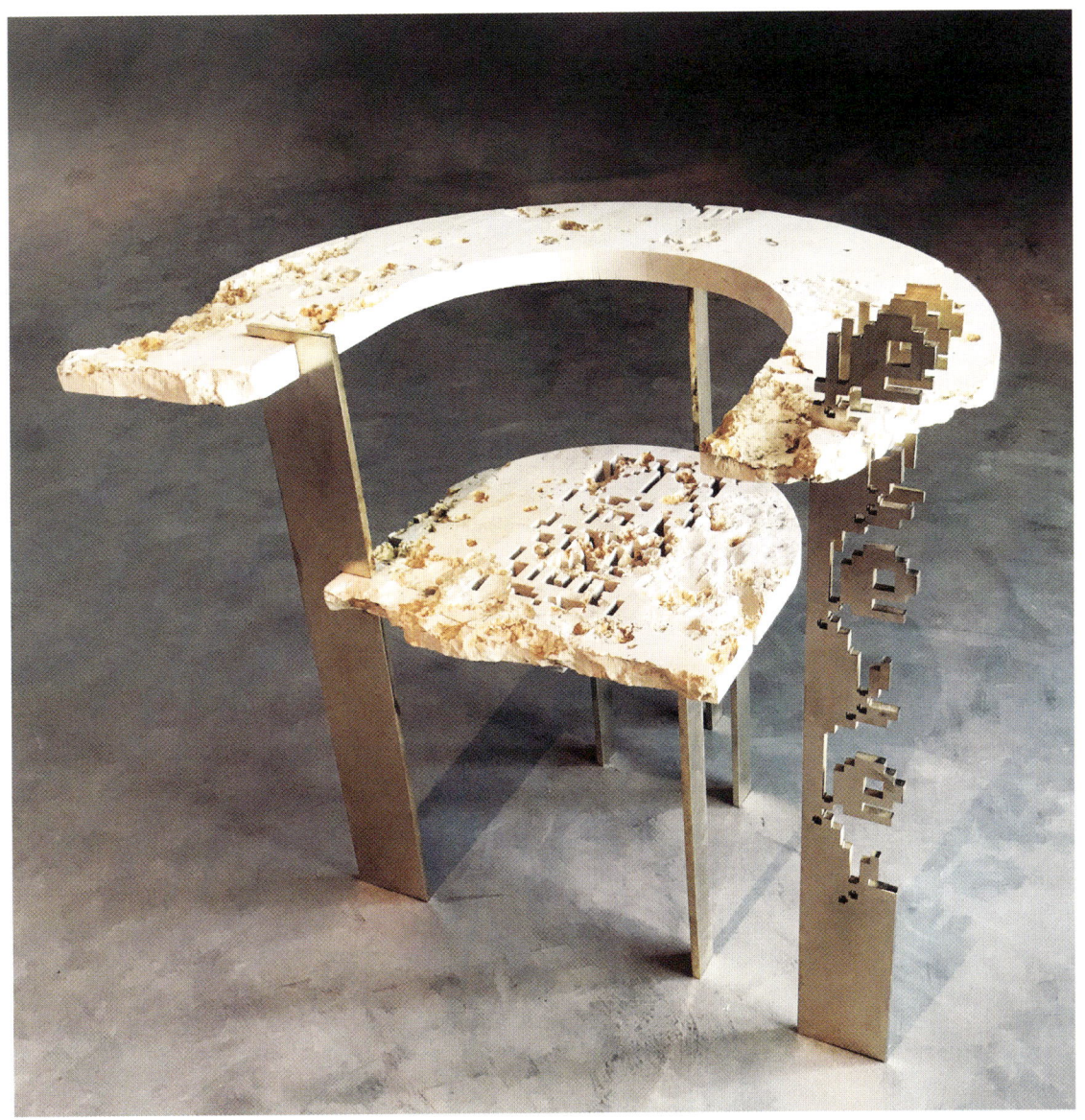

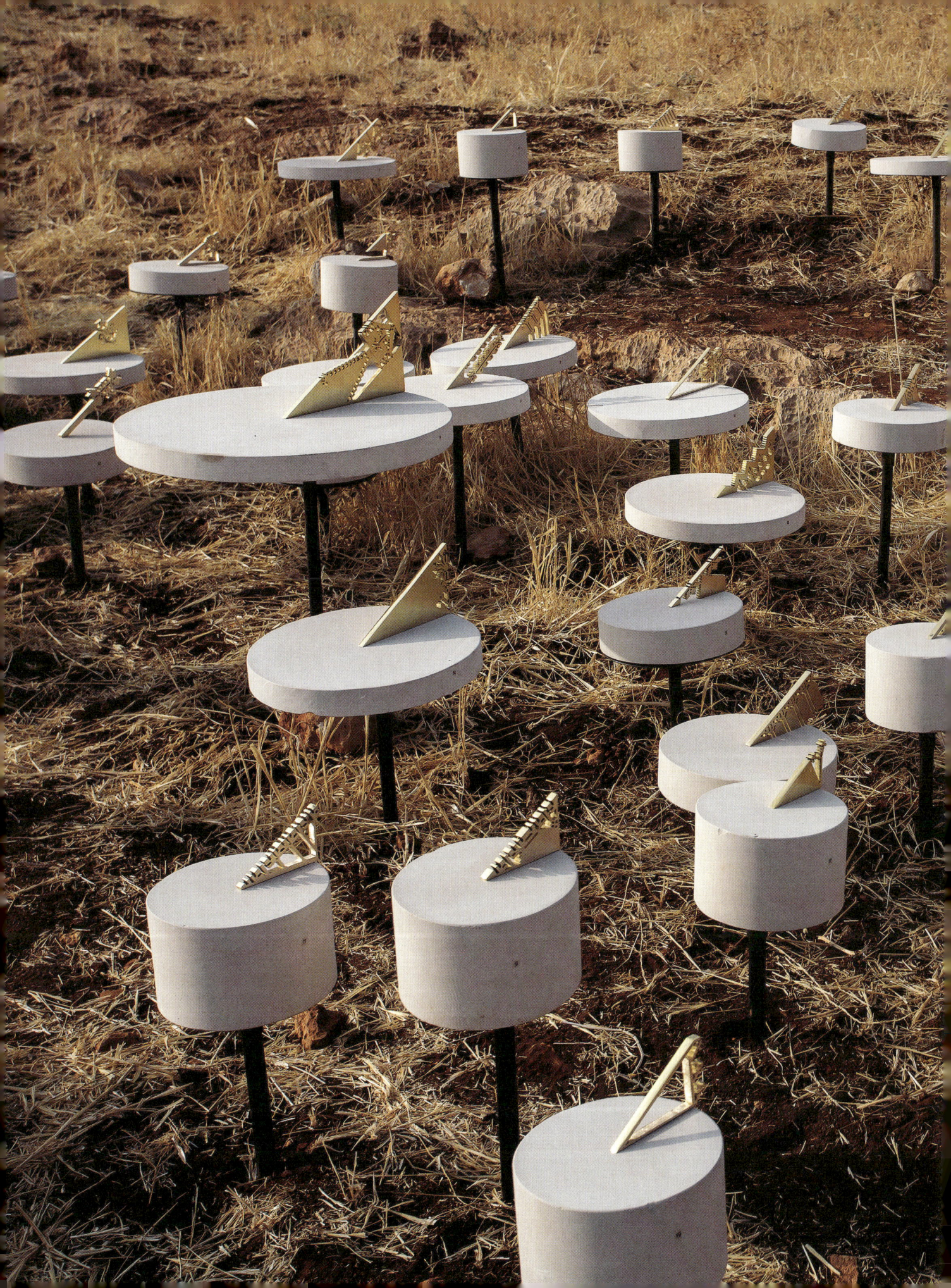